AF646157

COMPANION ENCYCLOPAEDIA OF HINDU PHILOSOPHY

Forthcoming Attraction. A Major Reference Work.......
ENCYCLOPAEDIA OF INDIAN HERITAGE, in 90 Volumes
Editor Subodh Kapoor

Forthcoming Attraction. A Pionnering Work..... The First Reference Set of its Kind
THE INDIAN ENCYCLOPAEDIA, in 25 Volumes
Biographical, Historical, Religious, Social, Ethnological, Administrative, Commercial and Scientific
Editor Subodh Kapoor

Important Books of Similar Interest Published Recently

THE BUDDHISTS.
Encyclopaedia of Buddhism, in 5 Volumes
Edited by Subodh Kapoor

THE HINDUS.
Encyclopaedia of Hinduism, in 5 Volumes
Edited by Subodh Kapoor

Encyclopaedia of Buddhist Tantra, in 5 Volumes
Sadhu Santideva

Encyclopaedia of Tantra, in 5 Volumes
Sadhu Santideva

Encyclopaedia of Indian Mysticism, in 12 Volumes
Edited by Sadhu Santideva

Encyclopaedia of Ethics and Logic, in 10 Volumes
Edited by Piet and Prasad

Encyclopaedia of Philosophy of Indian Religion, in 2 Volumes
Sadhu Santinath

Encyclopaedia of Indian Folk Literature, in 12 Volumes
Several Authors

Redescovering India
Indian Philosophy Library, in 71 Volumes
Works of Almost all Leading Indologists and Orientalists

COMPANION ENCYCLOPAEDIA OF HINDU PHILOSOPHY

AN EXPOSITION OF THE PRINCIPLE RELIGIO-PHILOSOPHICAL SYSTEMS AND AN EXAMINATION OF DIFFERENT SCHOOLS OF THOUGHT

EDITED BY
SUBODH KAPOOR

OTHER WORKS :
THE HINDUS. ENCYCLOPAEDIA OF HINDUISM
THE BUDDISTS. ENCYCLOPAEDIA OF BUDDHISM
ENCYCLOPAEDIA OF INDIAN HERITAGE, IN 90 VOLUMES

COSMO PUBLICATIONS
2002 INDIA

All rights reserved. No part of this publication may be reproduced, or stored in retrival system, or transmitted in any form or by any means without the prior permission of Cosmo Publications.

COMPANION ENCYCLOPAEDIA OF HINDU PHILOSOPHY

First Published 2002

ISBN 81-7755-203-1

Published by
MRS. RANI KAPOOR
for COSMO PUBLICATIONS Div. of
GENESIS PUBLISHING PVT. LTD.
24-B, Ansari Road,
Darya Ganj,
New Delhi-110 002, INDIA

Composed at
Cosmo Publications

Printed at
Mehra Offset Press

CONTENTS

CHAPTER I

THE ESSENTIALS OF HINDUISM

I. WHEN the invading Aryans entered India they merely sought lands on winch to settle and live. For a considerable length of time they were content with small things. But gradually there arose among them the imperial instinct, and as a result they became masters, politically and religiously, of the whole of North India, and, at a later date, of the South also.

In the course of then gradual conquest of the North the simple religion of the *Ṛigveda* was transformed into Hinduism. The thought and culture of the invaders were spontaneously advancing; the impact of the innumerable tribes of aborigines with their varied religions and modes of life necessarily brought them much fresh-material and vital quickening; while then new imperial position demanded a practical system applicable to their subjects as well as to themselves. In these circumstances a new set of beliefs arose and a new social and religious organization took form. Hinduism, the religion of India, was born. Innumerable changes have taken place since then; but they have all been within the lines of the original plan; they have all been branches of the primeval tree.

Our study of the life of the early Indo-Aryans left us with several ideas clearly defined before our minds. Their religion was a polytheistic worship of the powers of nature by means of prayer, hymn, and sacrifice, but without temples or images. We also found a few traces of a more spiritual faith and of philosophic speculation. The worship of ancestors held a large place in their minds and in their social organization. To this simple people the world was real and life was good. Men prayed to live a hundred years. Asceticism was unknown. The family was still in a healthy condition. There was no caste. There was no doctrine of transmigration. Man lived and died once, and after death was led by Yama to heaven, where he enjoyed an immortality of bliss with the 'fathers' and the gods. From this simple system was developed the elaborate theology and highly organised communities of Hinduism.

It was the doctrine of karma and rebirth that gave character and form to the new system. While on the surface it is but a theory of birth and death, it is essentially the Hindu moral theory; and as we have already seen, it enters as an element into every part of the religion.

There was another doctrine which proved of importance in the creation of the new thought, but it did not exercise such an influence as the transmigration theory did. The idea is that there exists supreme divine Being, eternal and unknowable, who is manifested in all the gods and all the religions of men. He is spiritual and real; he is in nature and in man; he is the cause of all things, the Veda and caste included; in a sense, he is all things; and yet he is free from karma, which controls all things. Since he stands apart from karma, he is actionless. Being unknowable, he cannot be worshipped; but, since he is manifested in all the gods, the worship of any god is quite legitimate. The Brāhmans thus developed a simple philosophy of religion which they used to explain matters to themselves and to all eager inquirers, as they proceeded with then work of bringing the peoples of India under their influence. They must have met with many forms of religion, some of them very strange indeed, as they extended their sway over the land; yet every form of belief and every cult could be brought under this simple formula. It is this idea of the one God behind all the gods which the Hindu villager uses to-day when any one asks him why he acknowledges many gods.

But the more clearly they envisaged the Supreme as, real, the more worthless the world became to them. Thus, ever since these ideas look form, the Hindu has held that all worldly things are vain, valueless, empty, as compared with God. The doctrine that all material things are illusion is a much later development, and is not a necessary part of essential Hinduism; but the worthlessness of the world is one of the central ideas of the religion.

But while in comparison with God the world was seen to be paltry, in the light of the doctrine of karma and rebirth, it was held to be eternal, coeval with God. It was a transitory, phenomenal system, completely controlled by karma, yet without beginning and without end. The course of the world's history is a continuous process of degeneration from the Golden down to the Iron age. Progress is impossible. But when things reach their worst, the whole world passes into invisibility and lies in peace and silence for countless ages; and, when it is re-manifested, things are once more at their best.

All souls, whether living as gods, demons, men, animals, or plants, are afloat on the stream of transmigration (*samsāra*). Their life is at once retribution for the past and opportunity for the future. But, though a man may rise by persistent good conduct, by sacrifice and austerity, to the highest position among men or even to the station of a god, release from the ever-whirling wheel of birth and death is not to be won by an ordinary life, but only by stepping out of the common course of existence into the life of world-renunciation.

The gods may be worshipped, in accordance with the old cult, by means of sacrifice, prayer, and hymn, conducted in the open air, or by means of temple and image; but, whether the old or the new method is followed, only a Brāhman is allowed to officiate as priest; and the Vedas must be acknow ledged as the one Revelation. It must he noticed, however, that the old cult is open only to the three twice-born castes, and no woman can sacrifice without her husband; while all Hindu temples are open to the four castes and to women as well as men.[1]

Caste is the Hindu form of social organization. No man can be a Hindu who his not in caste; and if a group of outsiders is admitted into the community they must organize themself as a caste.

In the times of the *Ṛigveda* there were schools for young priests. These grew in importance with the growth of the ritual and of the power of the priests. More and more literature had to be mastered by the priestly student. Only the Brāhman could teach, and only men of three highest castes were admitted to the schools. All women were excluded. During this period of reconstruction it became the custom to send every boy of the Brāhman, Kshatriya, and Vaiśya castes to school to receive the sacred education. Each boy underwent initiation before beginning his course. Nowa-days very few indeed receive the old education.

This radical system as held by the Brāhmans and taught by them, in whole or in part, according to circumstances, as they pursued their work of subjugating the races of India to their authority. The ignorant were taught only as much as was necessary to enable them to take their place in the great organization; but, when thinking men asked questions, an answer was ready for them. This system of thought and life will not be found in this cut-and-dried form, separated from all else, in any Hindu manual; yet it lies behind every form of Indian religion and philosophy which appears on the stage of history throughout the centuries. In Buddhism, Jainism, the Sāṅkhya philosophy and the great sects, one or other element has been somewhat modified; yet the forms of these systems would scarcely be comprehensible to us, did we not know the great ancestor from which they sprang.

II.The leading constituents of this system will befound to fit very well together. If we hold that the invisible God behind all things takes no part in the activity of the phenomenal universe, then we can readily believe that the whole world is destitute of worth and substance. Again, if the world is so distinctly a vain show, it is not unnatural to think that souls, once caught in its meshes, may live beclouded and dazzled for ages, finding no way back to the divine source, until their blind eyes are opened to see through the shows of Time to the one Reality. In these circumstances caste appears at once reasonable and light, as marking stages of the soul's progress towards enlightenment. The advance of the soul is of so much moment that the social system may well be made stern and unyielding, in order to conserve gains as they are made; and the spiritual advance ment which is believed to lie behind the both of every Brāhman is quite a reasonable basis for the religious authority which is demanded for him. Similarly the conception that the Veda is the eternal utterance of the divine Mind, revealed anew in divers portions to the Ṛishis at the opening of every world-era, is a reasonable ground for the practical authority claimed for it.

Perhaps the most noticeable thing about the system is the way in which it fits practically into the circumstances of the time. It is, first of all, the old system to which the people were accustomed; for it is the religion of the *Ṛigveda;* yet it is so transformed as to satisfy the intellect of the most advanced Aryans of the day. It is, on the other hand, a philosophy of religion, which enables the grossest of the pagan cults of the aborigines to be included in the same imperial system with the highest speculations of philosophy and with the elaborate sacreficial performances of the Brāhmans. Had there been no caste to bind the people together the speculative religious ideas would have been ineffectual; while, without the doctrine of transmigration, caste would have had no intellectual or moral justification and could have never laid hold of the popular conscience.

The strength and greatness of the whole group of ideas will be at once apparent. The thought of the worthlessness of the world in contrast with the glory and spirituality of Brāhman is one that lays hold of the intellect and has many interests for philosophy. The emptiness of the world is a powerful moral conception, and has been one of the chief sources of all the forms of spiritual religions which India has exhibited during the centuries. Every religion has found it necessary to persuade man to seek emancipation from the power of the sense-world. Hinduism has no need to search for reasons to support this teaching: it springs inevitably from the Hindu conception of things. Then, on the other hand, if the system deprives the world of all claim to final reality, the doctrine of transmigration and karma expresses the most powerful way possible its actuality and its grip over the human spirit. The unbending, remorseless law of karma has a cosmic grandeur and a kind of scientific completeness about it which at first sight are very captivating. driven these conceptions, the elaborate organization and the strict rules of caste appeal to the thinking mind as an orderly and reasonable system.

Here, then, we have the Hindu world-theory in all its permanent essentials: God real, the world worthless; the one God unknowable, the other gods not to he despised; the Brāhmans with their Vedas the sole religious authority; caste divine institution, serving as the chief instrument of reward and punishment; man doomed to repeated birth and death, because all action leads to rebirth; world-flight the only noble course for the awakened man and the one hope of escape from entanglements of sense and transmigration.

III. We have been accustomed to think of Hinduism as an unchanging system, the home of all the conservatism. Now, it is very true that the Hindu seeks to live in most things precisely as his ancestors lived centuries ago; yet conservatism and stagnation are not the whole story. In Hinduism there are certain large freedoms. To the European these liberties are at first sight worthless: the Hindu seems to be free where he ought to be bound and bound where he ought to be free. Yet, rightly or wrongly, there are these freedoms; and, in order to understand Hinduism and its working, it is most necessary to realize what parts of Hindu life are free and what parts are under stern regulation. In this chapter we isolate the things which are regarded by the Hindu as eternal, and therefore as allowing of no liberty.

The ordinances to which a Hindu must conform fall into three groups: the family, caste, and religion.

A. An orthodox Hindu must have been born in a Hindu family, must have undergone all the necessary ceremonies as a child and young man, and must continue to live as a member of his family, obeying all the regulations and fulfilling all the duties of a householder. These duties include the family rites mentioned in our second chapter, *viz.* the sacraments, the worship of ancestors, the worship of the family gods, and the observance of the annual feasts and seasons of worship. If he is a twice-born Hindu, he ought also to observe daily, morning and evening, the prescribed ablutions, prayers and offerings.

B. An orthodox Hindu must have been born in a Hindu caste, must have undergone initiation if he is a Brāhman Kshatriya, or Vaiśya, or some other equivalent ceremony if he belongs to a lower caste; and he must continue to observe all the rules and regulations which are traditional in his own caste, as was set forth in Chapter IV.

C. An orthodox Hindu must worship the gods either in the old Vedic fashion or in the temples. He must acknowledge the Vedas as the one revelation, and he must employ Brāhmans for all priestly duties, whether in his home or elsewhere. No one but a Brāhman can sacrifice, conduct religious ceremonies, act as a religious teacher, or proclaim the law.

All this, then, is obligatory on the Hindu. In these matters he is bound. The observance of these laws and customs is called *dharma, i.e.* right conduct. *Dharma* is explained and discussed in detail in the books known as *Dharmaśāstras,* the greatest of which is the *Mānava Dharmaśātra* or code of Manu. Here is what is laid down on this point by the highest authorities. We quote the *Gītā* first:

> Therefore, realizing the *sāstra* to be the standard for determining right and wrong, thou should'st do here the works specified in the ordinances of the *śāstra.*

Then Śaṅkara:

> The knowledge of one action being right and another wrong is based on scripture only.

The liberates of the Hindu are outside the circle of *dharma.* A man may; remain an orthodox. Hindu without believing in any god or any; theology, and without knowing or reading any sacred book. he may be a Christian,[3] a Muḥammadan, an agnostic, or an atheist in his convictions. No questions is raised so long as he conforms to usage.

---

1. See above, p.164
2. xvi. 24.
3. *S.B.E.*, xxxviii. 131.

CHAPTER II

THE MEANING AND SCOPE OF INDIAN PHILOSOPHY

Indian philosophy is not Hindu philosophy.

Indian philosophy denotes the philosophical speculations of all Indian thinkers, ancient or modern, Hindus or non Hindus, theists or atheists. 'Indian philosophy' is supposed by some to be synonymous with 'Hindu philosophy.' This would be true only if the word 'Hindu' were taken in the geographical sense of 'Indian.' But if 'Hindu' means the followers of a particular religious faith known as Hinduism, the supposition would be wrong and misleading. Even in the ancient writings of the orthodox Hindu philosophers, like the *Sarva-darśana saṅgraha* of Mādhavācārya which tries to present in one place the views of *all* (sarva) schools of philosophy, we find in the list of philosophies (darśanas) the views of atheists and materialists like the Cārvākas, and unorthodox thinkers like the Bauddhas and the Jainas, along with those of the orthodox Hindu thinkers.

The broad outlook of Indian philosophy.

Indian philosophy is marked, in this respect, by a striking breadth of outlook which only testifies to its unflinching devotion to the search for truth. Though there were many different schools and their views differed sometimes very widely, yet each school took care to learn the views of all the others and did not come to any conclusion before considering thoroughly what others had to say and how their points could be met. This spirit led to the formation of a method of philosophical discussion. A philosopher had first to state the views of his opponents before he formulated his own theory. This statement of the opponent's case came to be known as the prior view (pūrvapakṣa). Then followed the refutation (khaṇḍana) of this view. Last of all came the statement and proof of the philosopher's own position, which, therefore, was known as the subsequent view (uttarapakṣa) or the conclusion (siddhānta).

The consequent thoroughness of the Indian systems.

This catholic spirit of treating rival positions with consideration was more than rewarded by the thoroughness and perfection that each philosophical school attained. If we open a comprehensive work on the Vedānta, we will find in it the statement of the views of all other schools, Cārvāka, Bauddha, Jaina, Sāṅkhya, Yoga, Mīmāṁsā, Nyāya and Vaiśeṣika, discussed and weighed with all care; similarly, any good work on the Bauddha or Jaina philosophy discusses the other views. Each system thus became encyclopndia in its grasp of ideas. Naturally we find that many of the problems of contemporary Western philosophy are discussed in Indian systems of philosophy. Besides, we find that indigenous scholars with a thorough training exclusively in Indian philosophy are able to deal even with abstruse problems of Western philosophy with surprising skill.

If the openness of mind—the willingness to listen to what others have to say—has been one of the chief causes of the wealth and greatness of Indian philosophy in the past, it has a definite moral for the future. If Indian philosophy is once more to revive and continue its great career, it can do so only by taking into consideration the new ideas of life and reality which have been flowing into India from the West and the East, the Aryan, the Semitic and the Mongolian sources.

THE SCHOOL OF INDIAN PHILOSOPHY

Classification of the Indian schools: orthodox and heterodox:

According to a traditional principle of classification most likely adopted by orthodox H indu thinkers, the schools or systems of Indian philosophy are divided into two broad classes, namely, orthodox (āstika) and heterodox (nāstika). To the first group belong the six chief philosophical systems (popularly known an saḍ-darśana), namely, Mīmāṁsā. Vedānta, Sāṅkhya, Yoga, Nyāy and Vaiśeṣika. These are regarded as (astika) not because they believe in God, but because they accept the authority of the Vedas.[1] The Mīmāṁsā and the Sāṅkhya do not believe in God as the creator of the world, yet they are called orthodox (āstika) because they believe in authoritativeness of the Vedas. The six systems mentioned above are not the only orthodox systems; they are the chief ones, and there are some other less important orthodox schools, such as the Grammarian school, the Medical school, etc., also noticed by Mādhavācārya. Under the other class of heterodox systems, the chief three are the schools of the Materialists like the Cārvākas, the Bauddhas and the Jainas. They are called heterodox (nāstika) because they do not believe in the authority of the Vedas.

The place of the Vedas in Indian philosophy.

To understand this more clearly we should know something regarding the place of the Vedas in the evolution of Indian thought. The Vedas are the earliest available records of Indian literature, and subsequent Indian thought, specially philosophical speculation, is greatly influenced by the Vedas, either positively or negatively. Some of the philosophical systems accepted Vedic authority while others opposed it. The Mīmāṁsā and the Vedānta may be regarded as the direct continuation of the Vedic culture. The Vedic tradition had two sides, ritualistic and speculative (karma and jñāna). The Mīmāṁsā emphasised the situalistic aspect and raised a philosophy to justify and help the continuation of the Vedic rites and rituals. The Vedānta emphasised the speculative aspects of the Vedas and developed an elaborate philosophy out of Vedic speculations. As both these schools were direct continuations of Vedic culture, both are sometimes called by the common name, Mīmāṁsā; and for the sake of distinction the first is called Pūrva-Mīmāṁsā (or Karma-Mīmāṁsā) and the second Uttara-Mīmāṁsā (or Jñāna-Mīmāṁsā). But the more usual names of these two are Mīmāṁsā and Vedānta respectively, and we shall follow this common usage here. Though the Sāṅkhya, Yoga, Nyāya and Vaiśeṣika based their theories on ordinary human experience and reasoning, they did not challenge the authority of the Vedas, but tried to show that the testimony of the Vedas was quite in harmony with their rationally established theories. The Cārvāka, Bauddha and Jaina schools arose mainly by opposition to the Vedic culture and, therefore, they rejected the authority of the Vedas. These facts may be summed up in a tabular form as follows:

Indian schools of philosophy

- Schools rejecting Vedic authority (Heterodox or Nastika) (*e.g.* Cārvāka, Bauddha, Jaina)
- Schools not rejecting Vedic authority (Orthodox or Āstika)
  - Schools directly based on Vedic texts
    - School emphasising the ritualistic aspect of the Vedas (*e.g.* Mīmāṁsā)
    - School emphasising the speculative aspect of the Vedas (*e.g.* Vedānta)
  - Schools based on independent grounds (*e.g.* Sāṅkhya, Yoga, Nyāya. Vaiśeṣika)

THE PLACES OF AUTHORITY AND REASONING IN INDIAN PHILOSOPHY

The grounds of philosophy

The distinctions discussed above can be ultimately traced to distinctions in the methods of speculation, adopted by the different schools.

Should philosophy always depend on ordinary experience or should it sometimes depend on the experience of the wise few?

The two views.

Solutions of philosophical problems, like 'What is the ultimate cause of the world?', 'Does God exist?', 'What is the nature of God?', cannot be obtained by observation. The philosopher must employ his imagination and reasoning, and find out, answers consistent with truths already established by experience. Like most other branches of knowledge, philosophy proceeds, therefore, from the known to the unknown. The foundation of philosophy is experience, and the chief-tool used is reason. But the question arises here: "What experience should form the basis of philosophy?" Indian thinkers are not unanimous on this point. Some hold that philosophy should be based on ordanary normal experience, *i.e.* on truth discovered and accepted by people in general or by scientists. This is the view of most modern European thinkers. In India the Nyāya, the Vaiśeṣika, the Sāṅkhya and the Cārvāka school accept this view fully; the Bauddha and the Jaina school also accept it mostly. On the other hand, there are thinkers who hold that regarding some matters, such as God, the state of liberation etc. we cannot form any correct idea from ordinary experience philosophy must depend for these on the experience of those few saints, seers or prophets who have a direct realization (sākṣātkāra or darśana) of such things. Authority, or the testimony of reliable persons and scriptures, thus forms the basis of philosophy. The Mīmāṁsā and the Vedānta school follow this method. They base many of their theories on the Vedas and the Upaniṣads. Even the Bauddha and the Jaina school depend sometimes on the teachings of Buddha and Jinas who are regarded as perfect and omniscient. In Europe the scholastic philosophy of the middle ages was based similarly on the authority of the Christian scriptures.

Whatever be the grounds, reason is the instrument of philosochical speculation.

Reasoning is the chief instrument of speculation for philosophers of both these classes. The difference is that while by the former reasoning is made always to follow the lead of ordinary experience, by the latter reasoning is made to follow in some matters the lead of authority, as well.

The charge is often heard against Indian philosophy that its theories are not based on independent reasoning but on authority and, therefore, they are dogmatic, rather than critical. This charge is clearly not true of the majority of Indian systems which are as much based on free thinnking as any we can find in the West even in this modern age of critical speculation.

The criticism may be chiefly levelled against the two systems of the Mīmāṁsā and the Vedānta which, we have found, give an important place to authority. Though these systems start from authority, the theories they develop are supported also by such strong independent arguments that even if we withdraw the support of authority, the theories can stand well and compare favourably with any theory established elsewhere on independent reasoning alone. Man, as a rational creature, cannot of course be satisfied unless his reason is satisfied. But if arguments in favour of a philosophy are sufficient to satisfy his reason, the additional fact of its being based on the experiences of persons of clearer minds and purer hearts will rather add to its value.

HOW THE INDIAN SYSTEMS GRADUALLY DEVELOPED

The parallel growths of the Indian schools and their persistence through the lives and teachings of active followers.

In the history of European philosophy we usually find the different schools coming into existence successively. Each school predominates till another comes in and replaces it. In India, on the other hand, we find that the different schools, though not originating simultaneously, flourish together during many centuries, and pursue parallel courses of growth. The reason is to be sought, perhaps in the fact that in India philosophy was a part of life. As each system of thought came into existence it was adopted as a philosophy of life by a band of followers who formed a school of that philosophy. They *lived* the philosophy and handed it down to succeeding generations of followers who were attracted to them through their lives and thoughts. The different systems of thought thus continued to exist through unbroken chains of successive adherents for centuries. Even to-day, we find the active followers of some of the chief philosophical schools in different parts of India, though development of indigenous philosophy has all but ceased now, due to social and political vicissitudes.

Each school criticizes and influences every other school.

Indian philosophy is its own best critic

It should not be supposed, however, that the different systems developed within their respective circles of active followers, without mutually influencing one another. On the contrary, as we have pointed out previously, each philosophy regarded it as its duty to consider and satisfy all possible objections that might be used against its views. In fact it is by constant mutual criticism that the huge philosophical literature has come into existence. Due to this again, there developed a passion for clear and precise enunciation of ideas and for guarding statements against objections. Mutual criticism further makes Indian philosophy its own best critic.

How philosophical literature developed.

The sūtra works of the orthodox schools.

Bearing this fact of mutual influence in mind we may try to understand the general process by which the systems originated and developed. The Vedas, we have said, are directly or indirectly responsible for most of the philosophical speculation. In the orthodox schools, next to the Vedas and the Upaniṣads, we find the sūtra literature marking the definite beginning of systematic philosophical thinking. 'Sūtra' etymologically means 'thread,' and in this context it means a brief mnemonic statement. As philosophical discussions took place mustly orally, and as they were passed down through oral traditions handed down by teachers to students, it was perhaps felt necessary to link up or *thread* together the main thoughts in the minds of students by brief statements of problems, answers, possible objections and replies to them. A sūtra-work consists of a collection of many sūtras or aphorisms of this kind, arranged into different chapters and sections according to different topics. The *Brahma-sūtra* of Bādarāyaṇa, for example, contains the aphorisms that sum up and *systematize* the philosophical teachings of different Vedic works, chiefly the Upaniṣads, and also briefly mention and answer actual and possible objections to these views. This work is the first *systematic* treatise on Vedānta. Similarly, we have for Mīmāṁsā the sūtras of Jaimini, for Nyāya, the sūtras of Gotama, for Vaiśeṣika, the sūtras of Kaṇāda, for Yoga, the sūtras of Patañjali. According to tradition, on Sāṅkhya also there were the sūtras of Kapila, who is regarded as the founder of the system. But the sūtras now available are not-recognized by all as the original sūtras. The earliest systematic work available now is the *Sāṅkhya-kārikā* of Īśvara Kṛṣṇa.

Commentaries on the sūtras.

The sūtras were brief and, therefore, their meanings were not always clear. There arose thus the necessity of elaborate explanation and interpretation through commentaries. These chief commentaries on the respective sūtras were called the Bhāṣyas, the names and further particulars about which will be found later is the chapters on the different schools. But it should be noted that, in some cases, on the same sūtra-work different authors wrote different major commentaries (bhāṣyas) and interpreted the sūtras to justify their respective standpoints. Thus came into existence, if example, the different Bhāṣyas on the *Brahma-sūtra* by śaṅkara, Rāmānuja, Mudhva, Vallabha, Nimbārka, Baladeva and others. The followers of each interpretation formed into a school of Vedānta and there arose the many schools of Vedānta we find now.

Sub-commentaries and independent works.

As time went on, commentaries on commentaries arose and sometimes independent works also were written to supply hand books or to Justify, elaborate or criticize existing doctrines. The philosophical literature of the orthodox schools developed this way. The history of the development of the heterodox doctrines is also more or less the same. They do not start, however, from any sūtra-work of the above kind. The accounts of these will be given in the chapters dealing with those schools.

The harmony among the schools. The gradation of the schools according to the fitness of followers.

Though the different schools were opposed to one another in their teachings, a sort of harmony among them was also conceived by the Indian thinkers. They believed that all persons were not fit for all things and in religious, philosophical and social matters we should take into consideration these differences in fitness and consequent distinctions of rights (adhikāra-bheda). The different philosophical disciplines, as already pointed out, were taken India as the different ways of shaping practical lives. Consequently, it was all the more necessary to discriminate the fitness of their followers. The many systems of philosophy beginning from the materialism of the Cārvāka school and ending with the Vedānta of śaṅkara offer the different paths for philosophical thinking and living that suit persons of differing qualifications and temperaments. But even apart from this praginatic explanation, we can discover in schools, outwardly opposed, many positive points of agreement, which may be regarded as the common marks of Indian culture.

THE COMMON CHARACTERS OF THE INDIAN SYSTEMS

The unity of moral and spiritual outlook among the systems.

Its chief factors.

The philosophy of a country is the cream of its culture and civilisation. It springs from the ideas that prevail in its atmosphere and bears its unconscious stamp. Though the different schools of Indian philosophy present a diversity of views, we can discern even in them the common stamp of an Indian culture. We may briefly describe this unity as the unity of moral and spiritual outlook. To understand this let us consider its main aspects and illustrate points of agreement among the different schools.

The practical motive present in all system.

The most striking and fundamental point of agreement, which we have already discussed partly, is that all the systems regard philosophy as a practical necessity and cultivate it in order to understand how life can be best led. The aim of philosophical wisdom is not merely the satisfaction of intellectual curiosity, but mainly an enlightened life led with far-sight, foresight and insight. It became a custom, therefore, with an Indian writer to explain, at the beginning of his work, how it serves human ends (puruṣārtha).

This does not affect thier theoretical development.

But it should also be remembered that the presence of a practical motive did not narrow the scope of Indian philosophy to Ethics and Theology alone as some Western critics[2] imagine. Its scope is as wide as any philosophy springing only from theoretic motives; and even on theoretical grounds some brandies of Indian philosophy, like Metaphysics, Epistemology and Logic, can easily hold their own against any system of the West.

Philosophy springs from spiritual disquiet at the existing order of things.

The reason why the practical motive prevails in Indian philosophy lies in the fact that every system, pro-Vedic or anti-Vedic, is moved to speculation by a spiritual disquiet at the sight of the evils that cast a gloom over life in this world and it wants to understand the source of these evils and incidentally the nature of the universe and the meaning of human life, in order to find out some means for completely overcoming life's miseries.

Pressimism, in Indian philosophy, is inital not final.

The attitude of mind which looks at the dark side of things is known as pessimism. Indian philosophy has often been criticized as pessimistic and, therefore pernicious in its influence on practical life. How far this criticism is justified will be seen in the course of this book. But one general point should be noted here. Indian philosophy is pessimistic in the sense that it works under a sense of discomfort and disquiet at the existing order of things. It discovers and strongly asserts that life as it is being thoughtlessly led is a mere sport of blind impulses and unquenchable desires; it inevitably ends in and prolongs misery. But no Indian system stops with this picture of life as a tragedy. It perhaps possesses more. than a literary significance that even in ancient Indian drama rarely ends as a tragedy. If Indian philosophy points relentlessly to the miseries that we suffer through shortsightedness, it also discovers a message of hope. The essence of Buddha's enlightenment— the four noble truths—sums up and voices the real view of every Indian school in this respect; namely: There *is* suffering —There is a *cause* of suffering.—There is *cessation* of suffering —There is a *way* to attain it. Pessimism in the Indian systems is only initial and not final.[3]

The belief in an eternal moral order in the universe

The different forms of this faith.

The outlook which prevents the Indian mind from ending in despair and guarantees its final optimism is what may be described as spiritualism after William James. "Spiritualism," says James, "means the affirmation of an eternal moral order and letting loose of hope." "This need of an eternal moral order is one of the deepest needs of our breast. And those poets, like Dante and Wordsworth, who live on the conviction of such an order, owe to that fact the extraordinary tonic and consoling power of their verse."[4] The faith in 'an eternal moral order' dominates the entire history of Indian philosophy, barring the solitary exception of the Cārvāka, materialists. It is the common atmosphere of faith in which all these systems, Vedic and non-Vedic, theistic and atheistic, move and breathe. The faith in an order—a law that makes for regularity and righteousness and works in the gods, the heavenly bodies and creatures— pervades the poetic imagination of the seers of the Ṛg-veda which calls this inviolable moral order Ṛta. This idea gradually shapes itself into (*a*) the Mīmāṁsā conception of apūrva, the law that guarantees the future enjoyment of the fruits of rituals performed now, (*b*) into the Nyāya-Vaiśeṣika theory of adṛṣṭa, the unseen principle which sways even over the material atoms and brings about objects and events in accordance with moral principles, and (*c*) into the general conception of karma, which is accepted by all Indian systems. The law of karma in its different, aspects may be regarded as the law of the conservation of moral values, merits and demerits of actions. This law of conservation means that there is no loss of the effect of work done (kṛta-praṇāśa) and that there is no happening of events to a person except as the result of his own work (akṛtā-bbyupagama). The law of karma is accepted also by the Jainas and the Bauddhas.[5]

An eminent Danish philosopher, Harald Höffding, defines religion as "the belief in the conservation of values."[6] It is mainly such belief that raises Indian systems like Jainism and Buddhism to the status of religion in pite of the absence of a belief in God.

Optimism is genrated by this faith.

It is again this faith in 'an eternal moral order,' which inspires optimism and makes man the master of his own destiny. It enables the Indian thinker to take present evil as consequence of his own action, and hope for a better future by improving himself now. There is room, therefore, for free will and personal endeavour (puruṣakāra). Fatalism or determinism is, therefore, a misrepresentation of the theory of karma.

The universe as the moral stage.

Intimately connected with this outlook is the general tendency to regard the universe as the moral stage, where all living beings get the dress and the part that befit them and are to act well to deserve well in future. The body, the senses and the motor organs that an individual gets and the environment in which he finds himself are the endowments of nature or God in accordance with the inviolable law of karma.

Ignorance is the cause of bondage and knowledge is necessary for liberation.

Another common view, held by all Indian thinkers, is that ignorance of reality is the cause of our bondage and sufferings, and liberation from these cannot be achieved without knowledge of reality, *i.e.* the real nature of the world, and the self. By 'bondage' is commonly meant the process of birth and rebirth and the consequent miseries to which an individual is subject. 'Liberation' (mukti or mokṣa) means, therefore, the stoppage of this process. Liberation is the state of perfection; and according to some Indian thinkers, like the Jainas, Bauddhas, the Sāṅkhyas and the Advaita-Vedāntins, this state can be attained even in this life. Perfection and real happiness can, therefore, be realized even here, at least according to these chief Indian thinkers. The teachings of these masters need not make us wholly unworldly and other-worldly. They are meant only to correct the one-sided emphasis on 'the here' and 'the now'—the short-sightedness that worldlines involves.

But mere thoeretical knowledge is not sufficeint.

But while ignorance was regarded as the root cause of the individual's trouble and knowledge, therefore, as essential, the Indian thinkers never believed that a mere acquaintance with truth would at once remove imperfection. Two types of discipline were thought necessary for making such understanding permanent as well as effective in life, namely, continued meditation on the accepted thruths and practical life of self-control.

Continued mediatation on truths learnt is needed to remove deep-rooted false beliefs.

The necessity of concentration and meditation led to the development of an elaborate technique, fully explained in the Yoga system. But *yoga*, in the sense of concentration through self-control, is not confined to that system only. It is found in some form or other in Buddhism, Jainism, the Sāṅkhya, the Vedānta, and even in the Nyāya-Vaiśeṣika systems. The followers of these various views believed, in common, that the philosophic truths momentarily established and understood through arguments were not enough to dispel the effects of opposite beliefs which have become a part of our being. Our ordinary wrong beliefs have become deeply rooted in us by repeated use in the different daily situations of life. Our habits of thought, speech and action have been shaped and coloured by these beliefs which in turn have been more and more strengthened by those habits. To replace these beliefs by correct ones, it is necessary to meditate on the latter constantly and think over their various implications for life. In short, to instil right beliefs into our minds, we have to go through the same long and tedious process, though of a reverse kind, by which wrong beliefs were established in us. This requires a long intellectual concentration on the truths learned. Without prolonged meditation the opposite beliefs cannot be removed and the belief in these trutlis cannot be steadied and established in life.

Self-control is needed to remove passions that obstruct consentration and good conduct.

Self-control (saṁyama) also is necessary for concentration of the mind on these truths and for making these effective in life. Socrates used to say 'virtue is knowledge.' His followers pointed out that mere knowledge of what is right, does not always lead to right actions, because our actions are guided as much by reason as by blind animal impulses. Unless these impulses are controlled, action cannot fulfy follow the dictates of reason. This truth is recognized by all the Indian systems, except perhaps the Cārvāka. It is neatly expressed by an oft-quoted Sanskrit saying which means: "I know what is right, but feel no inclination to follow it; I know what is wrong but cannot desist from it."

Our speech and action cannot always follow our intellectual convictions because of the contrary impulses deeply rooted in our character due to past misconceptions about things and their values. These impulses are variously described by different Indian thinkers; but there is a sort of unanimity that the chief impulses are likes and dislikes—love and hate (rāga and dveṣa). These are the dutomatic springs of action; we move under their influence when we act habitually without forethought. Our indriyas, *i.e.* the instruments of knowledge and action (namely, the mind, the senses of sight, touch, smell, taste, sound, and the motor organs for movement, holding things, speaking, excretion and reproduction) have always been in the service of these blind impulses of love and hate and they have acquired some fixed bad habits. When the philosophic knowledge about the real nature of things makes us give up our previous wrong beliefs regarding objects, our previous likes and dislikes for those objects have also to be given up. Our indriyas have to be weaned from past habits and broken to the reign of reason. This task is as difficult as it is important. It can be performed only through long, sustained practice and formation of new good habits. All Indian thinkers lay much stress on such practice winch chiefly consists of repeated efforts in the right direction (abhyāsa).

Self-control implies the bringing of the lower self under the control of the higher.

Self-control, then, means the control of the lower self, the blind, animal tendencies—love and hate—as well as the instruments of knowledge and action (the indriyas). From what has been said above it will be clear that self-control, was not a mere negative practice, it was not simply checking the indriyas, but checking their bad tendencies and habits in order to employ them for a better purpose, and make them obey the dictates of reason.

It does not kill the natural impulses, but trains them to the yoke of reason.

Morality is not merely negative, but needs the cultivation of positive virtues.

It is a mistake, therefore, to think, as some do, that Indian ethics taught a rigorism or asceticism which consists in killing the natural impulses in man. As early as the Upaniṣads, we find Indian thinkers recognizing that though the most valuable thing in man is his spirit (ātman), his existence as a man depends on non-spiritual factors as well; that even his thinking power depends on the food he takes. This conviction never left the Indian thinkers; the lower elements, for them, were not for destruction but for reformation and subjugation to the higher. Cessation from bad activities was coupled with performance of good ones. This we find even in the most rigoristic systems, like the Yoga, where, as aids to the attainment of perfect concentration (yogāṅga), we find mentioned not simply the negative practice of the 'don'ts' (yamas), but also the positive cultivation of good habits (niyamas). The yamas consist of the five great efforts for abstinence from injury to life, falsehood, stealing, sensuous appetite and greed for wealth (ahiṁsā, satya, asteya, brahmacarya and aparigraha). These are to be cultivated along with the niyamas, namely, purity of body and mind, contentment, fortitude, study and resignation to God. Essentially similar teachings we find as much in the other orthodox schools as in Buddhism and Jaimsm which, like the Yoga, recommend, for example, the cultivation of love (maitrī) and kindness (karuṇā) along with non-violence (ahiṁsā). That the action of thd indriyas is not to be suppressed, but only to be turned to the service of the higher self, is also the teaching of the Gītā, as would appear from the following: "One who has controlled himpelf attains contentment by *enjoying objects through the indriyas which have been freed* from the influence of love and hate."[7]

Belief in the possibility of liberation is common to all systems. Liberation is regarded as the highest good.

Lastly, all Indian systems, except the Cārvāka, accept the idea of liberation as the highest end of life. The conception of liberation received, of course, slightly different meanings. All negatively agreed that the state of liberation is a total destruction of sufferings which life in this world brings about. A few went a little beyond this to hold that liberation or the state of perfection is not simply negation of pain, but is a state of positive bliss. The Mīmāṁsā, Vedānta and Jaina thinkers belong to this latter group, and even the Bauddhas, according to some.

THE SPACE-TIME BACKGROUND[8]

The idea of the vastness of the world of space and time formed the common background of Indian thought.

In addition to the unity of moral and spiritual outlook described above, we may also note the prevailing sense of the vastness of the space-time world, which formed the common bacground throught which formed the common background of Indian thought and influnced its moral and metaphysical outlook.

Modern scientific conception of Time and Space as inconceivably vast entities.

The Western belief that the world was created six thousand and odd years ago and all for the purpose of man consituted a narrowness of outlook and exaggerated the importance of man. This belief has been shaken by the biological discoveries of Darwin and others who show that the evolution of living beings has to be conceived in terms of millions of years, not thousands. The science of astronomy again, is gradually generating the belief in the vastness of the universe, the diameter of which is "at least hundreds of millions of light-years." The sun in this calculation is a mere speck in the universe, and the earth is less than one-million part of this speck. And we are reminded that each faint speck of nebula observable in the sky contains "matter enough for the creation of perhaps a thousand million suns like ours."[9]

Similar ideas in Indian literature.

Our imagination feels staggered in its attempt to grasp the vastness of the space-time universe revealed by science. A similar feeling is caused by the accounts of creation given in some of the Purāṇas, which would, but for modern discoveries, be laughed at as pure fantasy. In the Viṣṇu-Purāṇa, for example, we come across the popular Indian conception of the world (brahmāṇḍa) which contains the fourteen regions (lokas) of which the earth (bhūtala) is only one and, which are separated from one another by tens of millions (koṭis) of yojanas, and again the infinite universe is conceived as containing thousands of millions of such worlds (brahmāṇḍas).

As to the description of the vastnees of time, we find that the Indian thinker, like the modern scientist, feels unable to describe it by common human units. The unit adopted for the measurement of cosmic time is a day of the creator Brahmā. Each day of the creator is equal to 1,000 yugas or 432 million years of men. This is the duration of the period of each creation or cosmos. The night of the creator is cessation of creative activity and means destruction or chaos. Such alternating days and nights, creation and destruction (sṛṣṭi and pralaya) form a beginningless series.

It is not possible to ascertain the first beginning of creation. It would be arbitrary to think that creation began *at first* at some *particular time* and not earlier. As there are no data for fixing the *first* beginning of the universe, Indian thinkers, in general, look upon the universe as beginningless (anādi). They try to explain the beginning of the present creation by reference to previous states of dissolution and creation and think it idle and meaningless to enquire about the *first* creation. Any term of a beginningless series can only be said to he earlier or later in *relation* to others; there is nothing like an *absolute, first* term in such a series.

With this overwhelming idea of the vast universe at its background, Indian thought naturally harped on the extreme smallness of the earth, the transitoriness of earthly existence and the insignificance of earthly possessions. If the earth was a mere point in the vast space. life was a mere ripple in the ocean of time. Myriad of them come and go, and matter very little to the universe as a whole. Even the best civilization evolved through centuries is nothing very unique; there is not one golden age only in the life of the earth. In the beginningless cycles of creation and dissolution there have been numberless golden ages as well as iron ones. Prosperity and adversity, civilization and barbarity rise and fall, as the wheel of time turns and moves on.

The general influence of this outlook on metaphysics, has been to regard the present world as the outcome of a past one and explain the former partly by reference to the latter. Besides it set metaphysics on the search for the eternal. On the ethical and religious side, it helped the Indian mind to take a wider and detached view of life, prevented it from the morbid desire to cling to the fleeting as the everlasting and persuaded it always to have an eye on what was of lasting, rather than of momentary value.

REFERENCE

1. In modern Indian laguages, āstika and nāstika' general mean 'theist' and 'atheist,' respecitvely. But in Sanskrit philosophical literature, 'āstika' menas 'one who believes in the authority of the Vedas' or 'one who belives in life after death.' ('Nāstika' menas the opposite of these.) The word is used here in the first sense. In the second sense, even the jaina and Bauddha schools are 'āstika,' as the believe in life after death. The six orthodox schools are 'āstika, 'and the Cārvāka is 'nastika' in both the senses.

2. *E.g.* Thilly (*vide* his *History of Philosophy,* p. 3) Stace (*A Critical History of Greek Philosophy,* p. 14).

3. For a full discussion of this point, see Introduciton to Prof. Radhakrishnan's *Indian philsophy,* Vol. I, pp. 49-50.

4. *Pragmatism,* pp. 106-07.

5. The word *karma* means both this law and also the force generated by an action and having the potency of bearing fruit. In the second sense, three kinds of kkarma are soemtimes distinguised: (*a*) Sañcita or accumulated karma of the past which remains stored up and has not yet borne any effect, (*b*) prārabdha or current karma which also was acquired in the past but has already begun to bear fruits (such as life in the present body, and all other possessions we already have), and (*c*) sañcīyamāna or accumulating karma which is being athered in this life.

6. *Vide* Perrry, *Philosophy of the recent Past,* p. 206 f.n. Cf. Hoffding, *The Philosophy of Religion,* pp. 1-13.

7. Bhagavadgītā, 2.64.

8. Sir J.H. Jeans in *Nature,* 26-2-27. A light-year = the distance traveiled by light in a year, at the rate of 186,325 miles per sec. = 60 × 60 × 24 × 365 × 186, 325 miles = 5,875,945,200,000 miles.

9. *Ibid.*(quoted in *Everyday Science*, by L.M. Parsons, pp. 14-15)

CHAPTER III

A BRIEF SKETCH OF THE PHILOSOPHICAL SYSTEMS

THE CĀRVĀKA SYSTEM

In Indian philosophy the word 'Cārvāka' means a materialists. The Cārvāka, hold that perception is the only valid source of knowledge. They point out that all non-perceptual or indirect sources of knowledge like inference, the testimony of other persons, etc., are unreliable and often prove misleading. We should, not therefore, believe in anything except what is immediately known through perception.

Perception reveals to us only the material world, composed of the four bhūtas or elements of matter, *viz.* air, fire, water and earth, the existence of which we can directly know through the senses. All objects of this perceptible world are composed of these elements. There is no evidence that there is anything like an immaterial soul in man. Man too is made wholly of matter. We say 'I am stout,' 'I am lean,' 'I am lame.' These jugments are alleged to prove that the individual is identical with the body. There is of course consciousness in man, but consciousness is a quality of the living body which is a product of matter. It should not be thought that because the elements of matter are unconscious there can be not no consciousness in objects made of them. There are many examples in which qualities originally absent in the component parts are developed when the parts are combined together in a particular way. There are examples even of the same substance acquiring new qualities under different conditions. Betel leaf, nut and lime chewed together acquire a red tinge originally absent in any of the constituents; molasses acquires by fermentation the power of intoxication originally absent. Similarly, the elements of matter combined together in a particular way give rise to the living body having consciousness. Consciousness ceases apparently with the body. When man dies nothing is left of him to enjoy or suffer the consequences of his actions hereafter.

The survival of man in any form after death is therefore, unproved. The existence of God also is a myth. God cannot be perceived. The world is made by the automatic combination of the material elements and not by God. It is foolish, therefore, to perform any religious rite either for enjoying happiness after this life in heaven or for pleasing God. No faith should be put in the Vedas or in the cunning priests who earn their livelihood by exploiting the credulity of men.

The highest end of life, for a rational man, should, therefore, be the enjoyment of the greatest amount of pleasure here in this life, of which alone we are sure. It is foolish to forgo the pleasures of life simply because they happen to be mixed with pain. It would be as though one were to reject the kernel because of its husk or cease sowing crops for fear of cattle. We should try to get the best out of this life by enjoying it as best as we can and avoiding as far as possible the chances of pain.

THE JAINA SYSTEM

The origin of the Jaina faith lies far back in the prehistoric times. The long line of teachers through whom the faith was handed down consists of twenty-four Tīrthaṅkaras or liberated propagators of the faith, the last of whom was Vardhāmana (also styled Mahāvīra), a contemporary of Gautama Buddha.

The Jainas reject the Cārvāka view that perception is the only valid source of knowledge. They point out that if we are to reject altogether the possibility of obtaining correct, knowledge through inference and the testimony of other persons because sometimes they prove misleading, we should doubt the validity of perception also, because even perception sometimes proves illusory. In fact, the Cārvākas themselves take the help of inference when by observing *some* cases of inference to be misleading they come to hold that *all* inference is invalid, and also when they deny the existence of objects *because* they are not perceived. The Jainas admit, in addition to perception, inference and testimony as sources of valid knowledge. Inference yields valid knowledge when it obeys' the logical rules of correctness. Testimony is valid, when it is the report of a reliable authority. In fact, the Jainas hold that it on the authority of the teachings of the omniscient liberated saints (Jinas or Tīrthaṅkaras) that we can have unerring knowledge about certain spiritual matters, which our limited sense-perception and reasoning cannot reveal to us.

On the basis of these three kinds of knowledge, the Jainas form their view of the universe. Perception reveals the reality of material substances, composed of the four kinds of elements, as the Cārvākas hold. By inference they come to believe in space (ākāśa), because material substances must exist somewhere, believe in time (kāla), because changes or succession of the states of substances cannot be understood without it, and believe also in the two causes of motion and rest respectively, for without them movement and cessation of movement in things cannot be explained. These last two are called respectively dharma and adharma which should not be taken here in their ordinary moral sense, but in the technical sense of the causes of motion and rest. But the physical world, consisting of the four elements matter, space, time, dharma and adharma, is not all. Perception, as well as inference, proves the existence of souls in all living bodies. When we perceive the qualities of an orange such as its colour, shape, smell, we say we perceive the existence of the orange. On similar grounds, when we internally perceive pleasure, pain and other qualities of the soul, we should admit that the soul also is directly known through perception. Consciousness cannot be said to be the product of matter; the Cārvākas cannot point out any case where the combination of material substances is perceived to generate consciousness. The existence of the soul can also be inferred on the ground that if there had been no conscious agent to guide them, material substances could not be formed into living bodies by themselves. Without a conscious substance to regulate them the body and the senses could not do their work so systematically.

There are, then, as many souls as there are living bodies. There are souls, the Jainas hold, not only m animals, but also in plants and even in particles of (dust). The existence of very minute living beings (such as germs) in dust and other apparently non-living material things is also admitted by modern science. All souls are not equally conscious. Some, those in plants, or dust-bodies, like have only the sense of touch and have tactual consciousness alone. Some lower animals have two senses, others three, still others, four. Man and some higher animal have *five* senses through all of which they know things. But, however developed the senses may be, the soul living in the body is limited in knowledge; it is limited in power also and is subject to all kinds of miseries.

But every soul is capable of attaining infinite consciousness, power and happiness. These qualities are inherent in the very nature of the soul. They are obstructed by karmas. just as the natural light of the sun is obstructed by clouds. The karmas or the forces of passions and desires in the soul attract to it particles of matter which permeate the soul just as particles of dust permeate the light of any flame or the sun. In a word, the karmas lead to the bondage of the soul by matter. By removing karmas a soul can remove bondage and regain its natural perfections.

(The teachings and lives of the liberated saints (Tīrthaṅkaras) prove the possibility of liberation and show also the path to be followed for the purpose. Three things are necessary for the removal of bondage, *viz.* perfect faith in the teachings of the Jaina teachers, correct knowledge of the teachings, and right conduct. Right conduct consists in the practice of abstinence from all injury to life, from falsehood, from stealing from sensuality and from attachment to sense objects. By the joint culture of right faith right knowledge and right conduct the passions are controlled and the Karmas that fetter the soul to matter are removed. The obstacles being removed, the soul attains its natural perfections—infinite faith, inflnite knowledge, infinite power and infinite bliss. This is the state of liberation.

The Jainas do not believe in God. The Tīrthaṅkaras, to whom all the godly powers like omniscience and omnipotence belong, take the place of

God. They are adored as ideals of life.

Sympathy for all living beings is one of the chief features of the Jaina faiths. Coupled with this there is, in Jaina philosophy, respect for all opinions. The Jaina philosophers point out that every object has infinite aspects, judged by what it is and what it is not from different points of view. Every judgment that we ordinarily pass about a thing is, therefore, true only in relation to a particular aspect of the thing seen from a particular point of view. We should remember, therefore, the limited nature of our knowledge and judgment, and should refrain from thinking that any view is the whole truth about any thing. We should guard and qualify our own statements and also learn to appreciate the possibility of the correctness of others views.

The Jaina philosophy is kind of realism, because it asserts the reality of the extern world, and it is pluralism, because it believes in many ultimate realities. It is atheism as it rejects the existence of God.

THE BAUDDHA SYSTEM

The Bauddha system of philosophy arose out of the teachings of Gautama Buddha, the well-known founder of Buddhism. Gautama was awakened to an appreciation of sorrow by the sight of disease old_age, death and other miseries, to which man is subject. He spent years in study, penance and meditation to discover the origin of human sufferings and the means to overcome them. At last he received enlightenment, the result of which was set forth by him in the form of what has come to be known as 'the four noble truths' (catvāri ārya-satyāni). These are—the truth that there is misery, the truth that there is a cause of mistery, the truth that there is cassation of misery and the truth that there is a path leading to the cessation of misery.

The first truth about the existence of misery is admitted by all in some form or other. But Buddha with his penetrative intellect saw that misery is not simply casual; it is universally present in all forms of existence and in all kinds of experience. Even what appears as pleasant is really a source of pain at bottom.

Regarding the second truth, Buddha's conclusion is deduced from his analysis of causation. He points out that the existence of everything in the world, material and mental, is caused by some other thing. There is nothing which is unconditional and self-existent. Nothing is, therefore, permanent io the world. All things are subject to change. Our sufferings are similarly caused by some conditions. Sufferings depend on birth in this world. Birth again is caused by our desire (taṇhā or tṛṣṇā) for the worldly objects. The force of desires drags us down to the world. But our desires can be traced ultimately to our ignorance. If we had a correct knowledge o the things of the world, understood their transitory and painful nature, there would be no desire for them; birth would then cease and along with it also misery.

As sufferings, like other things, depends on some condition; it must cease when these condition are removed. This is the third truth about cessation.

The fourth truth about the path that leads to the cesstion of misery concerns the control of the conditions that cause misery. This path is known as the eight-fold noble path as it consists of the eight steps namely, right views, right determination, right speech, right conduct, right livelihood, right endeavour, right mindfulness and right concentration. These eight step's remove ignorance and desire, enlighten the mind and bring about perfect equanimity and tranquillity. Thus misery ceases completely and the chance of rebirth also is stopped The attainment of this state of perfection is nirvāṇa.

The teachings of Buddha are contained in the four noble truth described above. It will appear from this that Buddha him self was not concerned so much with the problems of philosophy as with the practical problem how human misery can be removed. He regarded it as a waste of time to discuss metaphysical problems, while man is writhing misery. But though averse to theoretical speculation he could not avoid philosophical discussions altogether. Thus we find from early literature that the following theories are attributed to him: (*a*) all things are conditional; there is nothing that exists by itself. (*b*) All things are, therefore, subject, to change, owing to the change of the conditions on which they depend; nothing is permanent, (*c*) There is, therefore, neither any soul nor God nor any other permanent substance. (*d*) There is, however, continuity of the present life which generates another life, by the law of karma, Just as a tree generates another tree through its seed, and the second continues while the first withers away.

The later followers of Buddha in India and outside developed the germs of philosophical theories contained in Buddha's teachings and many schools thus came into existence. Of these the four that became most well-known in Indian philosophy may be mentioned.

(1) *The Mādhyamika or Sūnyavādī School.*—According to this, the world is unreal (sūnya); mental and non-mental phenomena are all illusory. This view is known as nihilism (sūnyavāda).

(2) *The Yogācāra or Vijñāvāda School.*—This holds that external objects are unreal. What appears as external is really an idea in the mind. But mind must be admitted to be real. It is self-contradictory to say that the mind is unreal; for, then, the very thought that mind is unreal stands self-condemned, thought being an activity of the mind. This view is called subjective idealism (vijñānavāda).

(3) *The Sautrāntika School.*—This holds that both the mental and the non-mental are real. If every-thing that we perceive as external were unreal, then our perception of an object would not depend on anything outside the mind, but absolutely on the mind. But we find that the mind cannot perceive any object, like a tiger, at any place it likes. This proves that the idea of the tiger, when we perceive it, depends on a non-mental reality, the tiger. From the perceptual idea or representation of a tiger in the mind we can infer the existence of its cause, the tiger, outside the mind. Thus external objects can be inferred to exist outside the mind. This view may be called representationism, or theory of the inferability of external objects (bāhyānumeya-vāda).

(4) *The Vaibhāṣika School.*—This school agrees with the last on the point that both internal and external objects are real. But it differs from it regarding the way external objects are known. External objects, according to the Vaibhāṣika, are *directly perceived* and not inferred from their ideas or representations in the mind. For if no external object were ever *perceived* corresponding to any idea, it would not be possible to infer the existence of an external, object from any idea. This view may be called direct realism, because it holds that external objects are perceived directly (bāhya-pratyakṣa-vāda).

Buddhism is divided, on religious matters, into the two well-known schools, Hīnayana, flourishing now in the south, in Ceylon, Burma and Siam, and Mahayana, found now in the north, in Tibet, China and Japan. The first two of the four philosophical school? mentioned above come under the Māhayāna and the last two under the Hīnayāna. The most important religious question on which these two schools differ is: What is the object of nirvāṇa? The Hīnayāna holds that nirvāṇa should be sought in order that the individual may put an end to his own misery. The Mahāyāna thinks, on the other hand, that the object of nirvāṇa is not to put an end to one's own misery but to obtain perfect wisdom with which the liberated can try for the salvation of all beings in misery.

THE NYĀYA SYSTEM

The Nyāya system is the work of the great sage Gotama. It is a realistic philosophy based mainly on logical grounds. It admits four separate sources of true knowledge, *viz.* perception (pratyakṣa), inference (anumāna), comparison (upamāna) and testimony (śabda). Perception is the direct knowledge of objects produced by their relation to our senses. It may be external (bāhya) or internal (antara), according as the sense concerned is external, like the eye and the ear, or internal, like the mind (manas). Inference is the knowledge of object, not through perception, but through the apprehension of some mark (liṅga) which is invariably related to the inferred object (sādhya). The invariable relation between the two is called vyāpti. In inference there are at least three propositions and at most three terms, *viz.* the pakṣa or minor term about which we infer something, the sādhya or major term which is the inferred object, and the liṅga or sādhana or middle term which is invariably related to the major, and is present in the minor. To illustrate: "The hill is fiery, because it smokes; and whatever smokes is fiery." Comparison is the knowledge of the relation between a name and things so named on the basis of a given description of their similarity to some familiar object. A man is told that a *gavaya* is like a cow. Then he finds an animal in the forest, which strikingly resembles the cow, and concludes that this animal must be a *gavaya.* Such knowledge is derived from upamāna or comparison. śabda or testimony is the knowledge about unperceived objects derived from the statements of authoritative persons. A scientist tells us that water is a compound of hydrogen and oxygen in a certain proportion. Although we have not ourselves demonstrated the truth, we know it on the authority of the scientist. Here our knowledge is derived from śabda or testimony. All other sources of knowledge have been reduced by the Naiyāyikas to these four.

The objects of knowledge, according to the Nyāya, are the self, the body, the senses and their objects, cognition (buddhi), mind (manas), activity (pravṛtti), mental defects (doṣa), rebirth (pretyabhāva), the feelings of pleasure and pain (phala), suffering (duḥkha), and freedom from suffering (apavarga). The Nyāya, like many other systems of Indian philosophy, seeks to deliver the self from its bondage to the body, the senses and their objects. According to it, the self is distinct from the body and the mind. The body is only a composite substance made of matter. The mind is a subtle, indivisible and eternal substance (aṇu). It serves the soul as an instrument for the perception of psychic qualities like pleasure, pain, etc. It is, therefore, called an internal sense. The self (ātman) is another substance which is quite distinct from the mind and the body. It acquires the attribute of consciousness when it is related to any object through the senses. But consciousness is not an essential quality of the self. It is an accidental or adventitious quality which ceases to qualify the self in the state of mukti or liberation. While the mind (manas) is infinitesimal like an atom, the self is all-pervading (vibhu), indestructible and eternal. It is an agent which likes and dislikes objects and tries to obtain or avoid them and enjoys or suffers the consequences of its actions. It is ignorance of the truth (mithyā-jñāna) and the consequent faults of desire, aversion and infatuation (rāga, dveṣa and moha) that impel the self to act for good and bad ends and plunge it into the world of sin and suffering, birth and death. Liberation (apavarga) means the absolute cessation of all pain and suffering due to the right knowledge of reality (tattva-jñāna). Some people think that it is a state of happiness. But this is entirely wrong, for there is no pleasure without pain,

Just as there is no light without shade. So liberation is only release from pain and not pleasure or happiness.

The existence of God is proved by the Naiyāyikas by several arguments. God is the ultimate cause of the creation, maintenance and destruction of the world. He did not create the world out of nothing, but out of eternal atoms, space, time, ether, minds and souls. This world has been created in order that individual souls (Jīva) might enjoy pleasure or suffer pain according to the merit or demerit of their actions in other lives and in other worlds. The most popular argument for God's existence is this: "All things of the world like mountains and seas, the sun and the moon, are effects, because they are made up of parts. Therefore, they must have a maker (kartā)." The individual selves cannot be the maker or creator of the world, because they are limited in power and knowledge, and so cannot deal with such subtle and imperceptible entities as atoms, of which all physical things are composed. The creator of the world must be an intelligent spirit with unlimited power and wisdom, and capable of maintaining the moral order of the universe. God created the world not for any end of His own, but for the good of all living beings. This, however, does not mean that there must be only happiness and no misery in the world. If individual selves have any freedom of will in them, they would act for good or bad ends and thereby bring happiness or misery on themselves. But under the loving care and wise guidance of the divine being, all individuals can sooner or later attain right knowledge about themselves and the world, and thereby final release from all suffering (mukti).

THE VAIŚEṢIKA SYSTEM

The Vaiśeṣika, system was founded by the sage Kaṇāda whose real name is Uluka. It is allied to the Nyāya system and has the same end in view, namely, the liberation of the individual self. It brings all objects of knowledge, *i.e.* the whole world, under the seven categories of substance (dravya), quality (guṇa), action (karma), generality (sāmānya) particularity (viśeṣa), the relation of inherence (samavāya), and non-existence (abhāva).

A substance is the substratum of qualities and activities, but is different from both. There are nine kinds of substances, *viz.* earth, water, fire, air, ether (ākāśa), time, space, soul and mind (manas). Of these, the first five are called the physical elements (bhūta) and have respectively the specific qualities of smell, taste, colour, touch and sound. The first four are composed of the four kinds of atoms of earth, water, fire and air, which are indivisible and indestructible particles of matter. The atoms are uncreated and eternal entities which we get by breaking any material object into smaller and smaller parts till we come to such as cannot be further divided. Ākāśa, space and time are imperceptible substances, each of which is one, eternal and all-pervading. The mind (manas) is an eternal substance which is not all-pervading, but infinitely small like an atom. It is the internal sense which is directly or indirectly concerned in all psychical functions like cognition, feeling and willing. The mind being atomic we cannot have more than one experience at one instant of time. The soul is an eternal and all-pervading substance which is the substratum of the phenomena of consciousness. The individual soul is perceived internally by the mind of the individual as when one says 'I am happy.' The supreme soul or God is inferred as the creator of the world of effects.

A quality is that which exists in a substance and has itself no quality or activity. While a substance can exist by itself, a quality cannot exist unless it be in some substance. There is no activity or movement in the qualities of things. There are altogether twenty-four kinds of qualities, *viz.* colour, taste, smell, touch, sound, number, magnitude, differentia (pṛthaktva), conjunction (saṁyoga), disjunction (vibhāga). remoteness (paratva), nearness (aparatva), fluidity (dravatva), viscidity (sneha), cognition (buddhi), pleasure, pain, desire, aversion, striving (prayatna), heaviness (gurutva), faculty (saṁskāra), merit (dharma) and demerit (adharma).

An action is a movement. Like quality, it belongs only to substances. There are five kinds of action, *viz.* throwing upward (utkṣepaṇa), throwing downward (avakṣepaṇa), contraction (ākuñcana), expansion (prasāraṇa), and going (gamana).

All cows have in them a certain common nature for which they are grouped into one class and excluded from other classes. This is called 'gotva' or cowness and is the sāmānya or universal in them. Since cowness is not generated by the birth of any cow nor destroyed by the death of any, it is eternal. A universal is thus the eternal essence common to all the individuals of a class.[1]

Particularity (viśeṣa) is the ground of the ultimate differences of things. Ordinarily, we distinguish one thing from others by the differences of its parts and other qualities. But bow are we to distinguish the ultimate simple and eternal substances of the world, like two atoms of earth? There must be some ultimate difference or peculiarity in each of them, otherwise they would not be different, both having all the qualities of earth. Particularity stands for the peculiarity or individuality of the eternal entities of the world. It is the special treatment of this category of viśeṣa that explains the name 'Vaiśeṣika' given to this system of philosophy.

Inherence (samavāya) is the permanent or eternal relation by which a whole is in its parts, a quality or an action is in a substance, the universal is in the particulars. The cloth as one whole always exists in the threads, qualities like 'green,' 'sweet' and 'fragrant,' and motions of different kinds abide in some substance. This permanent relation between the whole and its parts, between the universal and its individuals, and between qualities or actions and their substances, is known as samavāya or inherence.

Non-existence (abhāva) stands for all negative facts. 'There is no snake here,' 'that rose is not red,' 'there is no smell in pure water' are propositions which express respectively the non-existence of the snake, redness and smell in certain things. All such cases of non-existence are brought under the category of abhāva. It is of four kinds, namely, prāgabhāva, dhvaṁsābhāva, atyantābhāva (these three being put together under saṁsārgabhāva or the absence of a relation between two entities), and anyonyābhāva. The first means the non-existence of a thing before (prāk) its production, *e.g.* the non-existence of a pot in clay before it is produced by the potter. The second is the non-existence of a thing after its destruction (dbvaṁsa), *e.g.* the non-existence of the pot when it is broken up. The third is the absence of a relation between two things for all time—past, present and future, *e.g.* the non-existence of colour in the air. The last kind represents the difference of one thing from another. When two things (say a jar and a cloth) differ from each other, there is the non-existence of either as the other. The jar is not the cloth, nor is the cloth the jar. This mutual non-existence of two different things is called anyonyābhāva.

With regard to the liberation of the individual soul and God, the Vaiśeṣika theory is substantially the same as that of the Nyāya.

THE SĀṄKHYA SYSTEM

The Sāṅkhya is a philosophy of daulistic realism, attributed to the sage Kapila. It admits two ultimate realities, namely, puruṣa and prakṛti, which are independent of each other in respect of their existence. The puruṣa an intelligent principle, of which consciousness (caitanya) is not an attribute, but the very essence. It is the self which is quite distinct from the body, the senses and the mind. It is beyond the whole world of objects, and is the eternal consciousness which witnesses the changes and activities going on in the world, but does not itself act and change in any way. Physical things like chairs, beds, etc., exist for the enjoyment of beings other than themselves. Therefore, there must be the puruṣa or the self which is distinct from prakṛti or matter, but it is the enjoyer (bhoktā) of the products of prakṛti. There are many different selves related to different bodies, for when some men are happy, others are unhappy, some die but others live.

Prakṛti is the ultimate cause of the world. It is an eternal unconscious principle (jaḍa) which is always changing and has no other end than the satisfaction of the selves. Sattva, rajas and tamas are three constituents of prakṛti which holds them together in a state of rest or equilibrium (sāmyāvasthā). The three are called guṇas. But they are not qualities or attributes in any sense. Rather, they are three substantial elements which constitute prakṛti like three cords making up a rope. The existence of the gunas is inferred from the qualities of pleasure, pain and indifference which we find in all things of the world. The samc sweet is liked or disliked or treated with indifference by the same man in different conditions. The same salad is tasteful to some person, distasteful to another and insipid to a third. Now the cause and the effect are essentially identical. The effect is the manifested condition of the cause, *e.g.* oil as an effect manifests what is already contained in the seeds. The things of the world are effects which have the qualities of pleasure, pain and indifference. Therefore, prakṛti or pradhāna which is their ultimate cause must have the three elements of sattva, rajas and tamas which respectively possess the natures of pleasure, pain and indifference, and cause manifestation, activity and passivity.

The evolution of the world has its starting-point in the association (saṁyoga) of the puruṣa with prakṛti which disturbs the original equilibrium of the latter aod move it to action. The course of evolution is as follows: From prakṛti arises the great germ of this vast universe which is called, therefore, the great one (mahat). The consciousness of the self is reflected on this and makes it appear as conscious. It represents the awakening of nature from her cosmic slumber and the first appearance of thought; and, therefore, it is also called the Intellect (buddhi). It is the creative thought of the world to be evolved. Ahaṅkāra, the second product arises by a further transformation of the Intellect. The function of ahaṅkāra is the feeling of 'I and mine' (abhimāna). Owing to its identification with this principle, the self considers itself to be an agent (kartā) which it really is not. From ahaṅkāra, with an excess of the element of sattva, arise the five organs of knowledge (jñānendriya), the five organs of action (karmendriya) and the mind (manas) which is at once an organ of knowledge and activity (uhbayendriya). With an increase of tamas, ahaṅkāra produces, on the other hand the five subtle elements (tanmātra) which are the essences of sound, touch, colour, taste and smell. From the five subtle elements come the five gross elements of ākāśa or ether, air, fire, water and earth in the some order. Thus we have altogether twenty-five principles in the Sāṅkhya. Of these, all but the puruṣa is comprised by prakṛti which is the cause or the ultimate source of all other physical objects Prakṛti is the uncaused cause of all objects. The seven principles of mahat, ahaṅkāra and the five ṭanmātras are causes of certain effects and themselves effects of certain causes. The eleven sense and the five gross elements are only the effects of certain causes and not themselves the causes of and thing which is substantially different from them. The puruṣa or the self is neither the cause (prakfti) nor the effect (vikṛti) of anything.

Although the self is in itself free and immortal, yet such is the influence of avidyā or ignorance that it confuses itself with the body, the senses and the mind. It is the want of discrimination (aviveka) between the self and the not-self that is responsible for all our sorrowa and sufferings. We feel injured and unhappy when our *body* is injured or indisposed, because we fail to realize the distinction between the self and the body. Similarly, pleasure and pain in the imnd seem to affect the self only because the self's distinction from the mind is not clearly perceived by us. Once we realize the distinction between the self and the not-self including the body and the senses, the mind, the intellect and the ego (viveka-jñāna), our self ceases to be affected by the joys and sorrows, the up and downs of life. It rests in itself as the dispassionate observer of the show of events in the world without being implicated of them. This is the state of liberation or freedom from suffering which has been variously described as mukti, apavarga, kaivaiya, etc. It is possible for us to attain this state while alive in this world (jivanmukti) or after this life in the other world (videhamukti). But mere knowledge or intellectual understanding of the truth will not help one to realize one's self and thereby attain final release from sin and suffering. For this we require to go through a long course of spiritual training with deep devotion to, and constant meditation on, the truth that the self is the pure eternal consciousness which is beyond the mind-body complex and above the space-time and cause-effect order of existence. It is the unborn and undying spirit, of which the essence is freedom, immortality and life eternal. The nature and methods of the spiritual training necessary for self-realization have been elaborated in the Yoga philosophy.

With regard to the problem of God, we find that the main tendency of the Sāṅkhya is to do away with the theistic belief. According to it, the existence of God cannot be proved in any way. We need not admit God to explain the world; for, prakṛti is the adequate cause of the world as a whole. God as eternal and unchanging spirit cannot be the creator of the world: for to produce an effect the cause must change and transform itself into the effect. Some Sāṅkhya commentators and writers, however, try to show that the system admits the existence of God as the supreme person who is the witness but not the creator of the world.

THE YOGA SYSTEM

The sage Patañjali is the founder of the Yoga philosophy. The Yoga is closely allied to the Sāṅkhya. It accepts the epistemology and the metaphysics of the Sāṅkhya with its twenty-five principles, but adds one more, *viz.* God. The special interest of this system is in the practice of yoga as the means to the attainment of vivekajñāna or discriminative knowledge which is held in the Sāṅkhya to be the essential condition of liberation. According to it, yoga consists in the cessation of all mental functions (cittavṛttinirodha). There are five levels of mental functions (cittabhūmi). The first is called kṣipta or the dissipated condition in which the mind first among objects. The second is mūḍha or the stupefied condition as in sleep. The third is called vikṣipta or the relatively pacified condition. Yoga is not possible in any of these conditions. The fourth and the fifth *level* are called ekāgra and niruddha. The one is a state of concentratian of the mind on some object of contemplation. The other is the cessation of even the act or function of contemplation. The last two levels of the mind (cittabhūmi) are conducive to yoga. There are two kinds of yoga or samādhi, *viz.* samprajñāta, and asaṁprajñāta. In the first, we have yoga in the form of the mind's perfect concentration on the object of contemplation, and, therefore, involving a clear apprehension of that object. In the second, there is the complete cessation of all mental modifications and, consequently, the entire absence of all, knowledge including that of the contemplated object.

There are eight steps in the practice of yoga (yogāṅga). These are: yama or restraint, niyama or ethical culture, āsana or posture, prāṇāyāma or breath-control, pratyāhāra or withdrawal of the senses, dhāraṇā or attention, dhyāna or meditation and samādhi or concentration. Yama or restraint consists in abstaining from injury to any life, from falsehood, theft, incontinence and avarice. Niyama or ethical culture is, the cultivation of good habits like purification, contentment, penance, study of the Vedas and contemplation of God. Āsana is the adoption of steady and comfortable postures. Prāṅāyāma or breath-control is regulated inhalation, exhalation and retention of breath. Pratyāhāra or sense-control consists in withdrawing the senses from their objects Dhāraṇā or attention is fixing the mind on some intra-organic or extra-organic object like the moon, etc. Dhyāna or meditation is the steady contemplation of the object without any break. Samādhi or concentration is that state in which the contemplative consciousness is lost in the contemplated object and has no awareness of itself.

The Yoga system is called the theistic (seśvara) Sāṅkhya as distinguished from the Kapila Sāṅkhya which is generally regarded as atheistic (nirīśvara). It holds that God is the highest object of contemplation for concentration and self-realization. He is the perfect Being who is eternal, all-pervading, omniscient and completely free from all defects. The Yoga argues for the existence of God on the following grounds: Whatever has degrees must have a maximum. There are degrees of knowledge; therefore, there must be such a thing as perfect knowledge or omniscience. He who has omniscience is God. The association of puruṣa with prakṛti is what initiates the evolution of the world, and the cessation of this leads to dissolution. Neither he associaiton nor the dissociation is natural to prakṛti and puruṣa. Therefore, there must be a supreme being who is able to bring about these relations betwen prakṛti and puruṣa according to the moral deserts of individual souls.

THE MĪMĀṀSĀ SYSTEM

The Mīmāṁsā (or Pūrva-Mīmāṁsā) school was founded by Jaimini. Its primary object is to be defend and justify Vedic ritualism). In course of this attempt it had to find a philosophy supporting the world-view on which ritualism depends.

As the authority of the Vedas was the basis of ritualism, the Mīmāṁsā formulates the theory that the Vedas are not the works of any person and are, therefore, free from errors that human authors commit. The Vedas are eternal and self-existing; the written or pronounced Vedas are only the temporary manifestations of these through particular seers. For establishing the validity of the Vedas, the Mīmāṁsā discusses very elaborately the theory of knowledge, the chief object of which is to show that the validity of every knowledge is perception. When there are sufficient conditions, kn owledge arises. When the senses are sound, objects are present to them and other auxiliary conditions also prevail, there is perception. When there are sufficient data, there is inference. When we read a book on geography, we have knowledge of the lands described, through authority. In each of these cases the knowledge that arises claims to be true and, we accept it without further argument. If there is any cause for doubt, then knowledge does not arise at all, because belief is absent. Similarly, by reading the Vedas we have at once knowledge and belief in what they say. The validity of Vedic knowledge is self-evident like that of every other knowledges. If any doubts arise, they are removed with the help of Mīmāṁsā arguments; and the obstacles being removed the Vedas themselves reveal their contents to the reader. The authority of the Vedas thus becomes unquestionable.

What the Vedas command one to perform is right (dharma). What they forbid is wrong. Duty consists in doing what is right and desisting from forbidden acts. Duty must be done in the spirit of duty. The ritual-enjoined by the Vedas should be performed not wilh the hope of any reward but just because they are so enjoined. The disinterested performance of the obligatory rites, which is possible only through nowledge ledge and self-control, gradually destroys the karmas and brings about liberation after death. The state of liberation is conceived in the early Mīmāṁsā as one of unalloyed bliss or heaven. But the later Mīmāṁsā conceives liberation only negatively as the cessation of birth and, therefore, of all pains).

The soul must be admitted as an immortal eternal substance, for if the soul perished on death, the Vedic injunctions that certain rites should be performed for the attainment of heaven would be meaningless. The Mīmāṁsā writers adduce independent arguments, like the Jaınas, to prove the existence of the immortal soul, and refute the materialistic view that it is nothing other than the body. But they do not admit consciousness as intrinsic tto the soul. Consciousness arises in it only when it is associated with the body and then also only when an object is presented to the organs of knowledge (the five outer sensed and the inner organ called manas). The liberated soul, which is disembodied, has no actual consciousness, though it it has the poteutiality for it.

The soul in the body has different kinds of knowledge. One school of the Mīmāṁsā founded by Prabhākara admits five different sources of knowledge (pramāṇas) namely, perception (pratyakṣa), inference (anumāna), comparison (upamāna), testimony (śabda) and postulation (arthāpatti). The first four are admitted as in the Nyāya system. There is, however, one notable difference regarding comparison According to the Mīmāṁsā, knowledge by comparison arises in a case like the following: A man who has seen a monkey goes to a forest, sees an ape and judges, 'this ape is like a monkey.' From this judgment of perception he passes to the judgment 'the monkey I saw before is like this ape. 'This last knowledge is obtained by comparison and not by perception, because the monkey is not present then. Knowledge by postulaiton arises when we have to postulate something as the only explanation of an apparent conflict. When we find that a man does not eat anything in the day, but increases in weight, we postulate that he must be eating at night. When a man is known to be alive and yet not found at home, it is known by postulation that he exists somewhere out. Another school of the Mīmāṁsā founded by Kumārila Bhaṭṭa admits another source of valid cognition, in addition to the above five. This sixth pramāṇa is called non-cognition (anupa-labdhi). It is pointed out that when on entering a room and looking round one says, 'there is no cloth in this room,' the non-existence of the cloth cannot be said to be known by perception. Perception of an object arises when our sense is stimulated by that object, and non-existence, which is the object known here, cannot he admitted to stimulate sense. Such knowledge of non-existence takes place by non-cognition. We judge the absence of the cloth not because other things are perceived but because the cloth is *not perceived.*

The Mīmāṁsā believes in the reality of the physical world on the strength of perception. It is, therefore, realistic. It believes, as we have seen, in the reality of souls, as well. But it does not believe that there is a supreme soul or God who has created the world. The world's objects are formed out of matter in accordance with the karmas of the souls. The law of karma is a spontaneous moral law that rules the world. The Mīmāṁsā also admits that when any man performs any ritual, there arises in his soul a potency (apūrva) which produces in the future the fruit of the action at an opportune moment. On account of this potency generated in the soul by rites performed here, one can enjoy their fruits hereafter.

THE VEDĀNTA SYSTEM

This system arises out of the Upaniṣads which mark the culmination of the Vedic speculation and are fittingly called the Vedānta or the end of the Vedas. As we have seen previously, it develop through the Upaniṣads in which its basic truths are first grasped, the *Brahma-sūtra* of Bādarāyaṇa which systematizes the Upaniṣadic teachings, and the commentaries written on these sūtras by many subsequent writers among whom śaṅkara and Rāmānuja are well-known. Of all the systems, the Vedānta, specially as interpreted by śaṅkara, has exerted the greatest influence on Indian life and it still persists in some form or other in different parts of India.

The idea of one Supreme Person (puruṣa), who pervades the whole universe and yet remains beyond it, is found in a hymn of the Ṛg-veda. All the objects of the universe, animate and inanimate, men and gods, are poetically conceived here as parts of that Person. In the Upaniṣads this unity of all existence is found developed into the impersonal conception of One Reality (sat), or the conception of One Soul or One Brahman, all of which are used synonymously. The world is said, to originate from this Reality, rest in it and return into it when dissolved. The reality of the many particular objects perceived in the universe is denied and their unity in the One Reality is asserted ever and again: All is God (sarvaṁ khalu idam Brahma). The soul is God (ayam Ātma, Brahma). There is no multiplicity here (neha, nānā asti kiñcana). This Soul or God is the Reality (satya). It is Infinite consciousness (jñāna) and Bliss (ānanda).

These teachings are interpreted and developed by Rāmānuja as follows: God is the only Reality. Within him there exist as parts the different unconscious (acit) material objects as well as the many conscious souls (cit). God is possessed of all supremely good qualities like omniscience, omnipotence. God creates the world of material objects out of matter (acit) which eternally exists in Him just as a spider spins the cobweb out of its own body. (The souls are conceived as infinitely small (aṇu) substances which also exist eternally. They are by their very nature conscious and self-luminous. Every soul is endowed with a material body in accordance with its karma. Bondage of the foul means its confinement to this body. Liberation is the complete dissociation of the soul from the body. The cause of bondage is karma which springs from ignorance. The soul identifies itself with the body, through ignorance of its real nature and behaves as though it were the body. It hankers after sensuous pleasures. Thus it becomes attached to the world and the force of this attachment causes its repeated rebirth. Ignorance is removed by the study of the Vedānta. Man comes to know that his soul is distinct, from the body, that it is really a part of God or Brahman, on whom his existence depends. The disinterested performance of the obligatory duties enjoined by the Vedas destroys the accumulated forces of attachment or karmas and helps the perfection of knowledge. God is known as the only object worthy of love and there is constant meditation on God and resignation to His will. God is pleased by devotion and releases the devotee from bondage. He is never born again after death. The liberated soul becomes *similar* to God, because like God it has pure consciousness free from imperfections. But it does *not* become *identical* with God as the finite can never become infinite.

According to Rāmānuja, though God is the only Reality and there is nothing outside God, yet within God there are many other realities. Creation of the world and the objects created are all as real as God. It is, therefore, not unqualified monism (advaita), but a monism of the One qualified by the presence of many parts (viśiṣṭādvaita). God *possessed* of the conscious souls and unconscious matter is the only Reality.

śaṅkara understands the Upaniṣads in a different sense. He believes that pure unqualified monism is taught there. God is the only Reality, not simply in the sense that there is nothing except God, but also in the sense that there is no multiplicity even within God. The denial of plurality, the unity of the soul and God, the assertion that when God is known, all is known, and similar views found in the Upaniṣads in fact the general tone that pervades their teachings cannot be explained consistently if we believe in the existence of many realities within God. Creation of the many things by God (Brahman) or the soul (Ātman) is, of course, related in some Upaniṣads. But in others, and even in the Vedas, creation is compared to magic or jugglery; God is spoken of as the Juggler who creates the world by the magical power called Māyā.

śaṅkara, therefore, holds that, in consistency with the emphatic teaching that there is only One Reality, we have to explain the world not as a real creation, but as an appearance which God conjures up with his inscrutable power. Māyā. To make the conception of Māyā more intelligible to ordinary experience, he interprets it in the light of ordinary illusions that we have in daily life, when a rope appears, for example, as a snake or a glittering shell appears as silver. In all such cases of illusion there is a substratum or a reality (*e.g.* rope, shell) on which something else (*e.g.* snake, silver) is imagined or superimposed due to the ignorance of the substratum, This ignorance not only conceals the underlying reality or substratum, but also makes it appear as something else. Our perception of the world's objects can be similarly explained. We perceiven the many objects in the One Brahman on account of our ignorance (avidyā or ajñāna) which conceals the real Brahman from us and makes it appear as the many objects. When the juggler produces an illusory show, makes one coin appear as many, the cause of it from *his* point of view is his magical *power*; from our mediate point of view the reason why *we* perceive the many coins, is our *ignorance* of the one real coin. Applying this analogy to the world-appearance, we can say that this appearance is due to the magical power of Māyā in God and we can also say that it is due to our ignorance. Māyā and ignorance are then the two sides of the same fact looked at from two different points of view. Hence Māyā is also said to be of the nature of Ignorance Avidyā or Ajñāna). Lest one should think that śaṅkara's position also fails to maintain pure monism, because two realities—God and Māyā—are admitted, śaṅkara points out that Māyā as a power of God is no more different from God than the power of burning is from fire. There is then no dualism but pure monism (advaita).

But is not even then God really possessed of creative power? śaṅkara replies that so long as one believes in the world-appearance, he looks at God through the world, as the creator of it. But when be realizes that the world is apparent, that nothing is really created, be ceases to think of God as a Creator. To one who is not deceived by the magician's art and sees through his trick, the magician fails to be a magician: he is not credited with any magical power. Similarly, to the few who see nothing but God in the world, God ceases to have Māyā or the power of creating appearances.

In view of this śaṅkara finds it necessary to distinguish two different points of view, the ordinary or empirical (vyāvahārika) and the transcendental or real (pāramārthika). The first is the standpoint of unenlightened persons who regard the world as real our life of practice depends on this; it is rightly called, therefore, the vyāvahārika or practical point of view. From this point of view the world appears as real; God is thought to be its omnipotent and omniscient creator, sustainer and destroyer) Thus God appears as qualified (saguṇa), by many qualities. God in this aspect is called by śaṅkara Saguṇa Brahma or Īśvara. From this point of view the self also appears as though limited by the body; it behaves like a finite ego (aham). The second or the real (pāramārthika) standpoint is that of the enlightened who have realized that the world is an appearance and that there is nothing but God. From this point of view, the world being thought unreal. God ceases to be regarded as any real creator, or as possessed of any qualities like omniscience, omnipotence. God is realized as One without any internal distinction, without any quality. God from this transcendental standpoint (pāramārthikadṛṣṭi) is indeterminate, and characterless; it is Nirguṇa Brahman. The body also is known to be apparent and there is nothing to distinguish the soul from God.

The attainment of this real standpoint is possible only by the removal of ignorance (avidyā) to which the cosmic illusion is due. And this can be effected only by the knowledge that is imparted by the Vedānta. One must control the senses and the mind, give up all attachment to objects, realizing their transitory nature, and have an earnest desire for liberation. He should then study the Vedānta under an enlightened teacher, and try to realize its truths by constant reasoning and meditation. When he is thus fit, the teacher would tell him at last: "Thou art Brahman." He would Meditete on this till he has a direct and permanent realization of truth 'I am Brahman.' This perfect wisdom or liberation from bondage. Though such a wise or liberated soul still persists in the body and in the world, these no longer fetter him, as he does not regard them as real. He is in the world, but not of the world. No attachment, no illusion can affect his wisdom. The soul then being free from As God is Bliss, so also is the liberated soul.

REFERENCE

1. 'Parvtva' stands for both remoteness in space and remoteness in time and 'aparatva' for nearness both in space and time 'Saṁskāra' really stands for three qualities, *viz.* velocity, elasticity and memory- impression.

CHAPTER IV

THE SIX SYSTEMS OF THOUGHT: GENERAL REMARKS

The spiritual aspirant, as we have read repeatedly in the course of this book, first hears the truth, second, reasons upon it, and, third, meditates upon it. The Six Systems of Hindu philosophy are concerned with the second of these three steps. They have always in view the goal of the aspirant, which is final liberation, but as a means to that goal they seek to give him a complete intellectual grasp of the Self, God, and the universe in which he lives.

The Six Systems of Hindu thought are the Vaiśeṣika of Kanāda, the Nyāya of Gotama, the Sāṁkhya of Kapila, the Yoga of Patañjali, the Mīmāṁsā (also called Pūrva Mīmāṁsā) of Jaimini, and the Vedānta (also called Uttara Mīmāṁsā) of Vyāsa. Because of certain metaphysical similarities, these six systems (independent though they were in origin) may for convenience sake be reduced to three, Vaiśeṣika and Nyāya forming one group, Sāṁkhya and Yoga a second, and Mīmāṁsā and Vedānta a third.

The exact dates of the origin of these schools of thought are not known, though it is certain that the general ideas that make up their substance existed prior to buddhism and even during the Epic Period. Nor is it known just who their founders were: Kanāda, Gotama, and the others whose names are associated with them are not their founders. The Sūtras in which the views embodied in them were systematically formulated were a series of aphorisms uttered by the sages sometime during the early Buddhistic period—roughly between 600 and 200. B.C.[1]

From a time when the art of writing was still unknown, these sūtras were preserved in memory and handed down by word of mouth from teacher to pupil. They are so extremely laconic in form as to be well-nigh unintelligible without commentaries and explanatory notes, and oral supplements of this nature were early associated with the original aphorisms and transmitted with them. More and more commentaries and notes were gradually added, and in time written down, and the custom of composing them persisted even until the sixteenth or seventeenth century of the Christian era.

The Six Systems are regarded as āstika, or orthodox, because, unlike Buddhism and Jainism, they accept the authority of the Vedas on all questions pertaining to the nature of the universe. Moreover, there is nothing unorthodox in expanding, within limits, on the original revelations. For, as has already been explained in the introductory chapter of this book, though reason is given its due part in all the philosophies of India, there is everywhere here the assumption that it will be aided be those intuitive perceptions to which the Vedas give the first recorded expression.

Actually the Six Systems of philosophy, reduced to three distinct groups, are not mutually contradictory, though in certain of their theories they would seem to be so. They really represent, not conflicting schools of thought, but a progressive development from truth to higher truth to the highest truth. Nyāya and Vaiśeṣika prepare the mind for philosophic thought and are therefore called the groundwork of philosophy; but passing beyond them through evolving ideas as pressed successively in Sāṁkhya, Yoga, and Mīmāṁsā, we at last at the flower of Indian philosophy in Vedānta. Almost without exception, critics of Indian philosophy perceive the harmony behind the apparent discord, and so could reconcile the Systems as a perception of the same truth from different angles of vision.

The individuals systems are variously looked upon. In the estimation of modern students, Vaiśeṣika is not of great importance. Nyāya for its system of logic, and Sāṁkhya for its system of cosmology and certain other metaphysical theories, are popular with scholars, but only as aids to the study of the philosophy of Vedānta. Mīmāṁsā is closely related to Hindu law and is considered useful in the elucidation of the ritual portion of the Vedas. Yoga and Vedānta are accepted as the chiet of the six schools. Yoga is concerned with the practical side of philosophical and religious life and is devotedly studied by aspirants. Vedānta, in one or the other of its various aspects, was the ancient faith of India, and all Hindus now accept it as their living faith.

In the following pages we shall briefly discuss the Vaiśeṣika, Nyāya, Sāṁkhya, and Mīmāṁsā systems, reserving the fuller treatment for Yoga and Vedānta.[2]

Before entering on this task, however, we should call the attention of Western readers to the fundamental difference between the psychology of India and the psychology of the West. This difference lies in the fact that Western psychology identities consciousness with mind, being with thought, and thought with the soul, or the Self;—whereas Indian psychology distinguishes mind from consciousness. The distinction is due to the fact that Western psychology recognizes only one plane of experience, and gives no consideration to what Hindus call the pure cit, the supreme unconditional consciousness the Being, which they regard as the real Self, or the soul, different from the rationalizing mind and realized in the superconscious, or transcendmial, state. Pure unconditional consciousness cannot be the property of the mind, they believe, for it is the source of the mind's apparent consciousness. Mind is said by the Hindu psychologist to be the 'veiling power' of the pure consciousness, the Self, and it is associated with the Self only as a necessary condition of world experience. All systems of Indian philosophy recognize a Self separate from the mind, and this poses an important problem in each of them. As we proceed with our study we shall learn their notion of the real nature of the mind as well as of the Self.

REFERENCE

1. Professor Max Müller observes: 'The sūtras or aphorisms which we possess of the six systems of philosophy, each distinct from the others, cannot possibly claim to represent the very first attempt at a systematic treatment; they are rather the last summing up of what had been growing during many generations of isolated thinkers.' (*Six Systems of Philosophy.*)

2. It should be emphatically stated that all six schools believe in the law of karma, in pre-existence, in rebirth, and in the attainment of mokṣa as the highest goal of human endeavour. All of them are concerned with the nature of the true Self, immediate experience of which makes one free.

CHAPTER V

THE CĀRVĀKA PHILOSOPHY

I. Its Origin and Scope

The meaning materialism.

Materialism is the name given to the metaphysical doctrine which holds that matter is the only reality. This doctrine tries to explain mind and consciousness as the products of matter. In general outlook materialism represents the tendency that seeks to reduce the higher to the lower or explain the higher phenomena in the light of the lower ones. In this respect it is opposed to spiritual interpretations of the universe.

No systematic work on Indian materialism is available.

Though materialism in some form or other has always been present in India, and occasional references are found in the Vedas, the Buddhistic literature, the Epics, as well as in the later philosophical works, we do not find any systematic work on materialism, nor any organized school of followers as the other philosophical schools possess. But almost every work of the other schools states, for refutation, the materialistic views. Our knowledge of Indian materialism is chiefly based on these.

'Cārvāka' is 'he word that generally stands for 'materialist.' But the original meaning of this word is shrouded in mystery. According to one view, 'Cārvāka' was originally the name of a sage who propounded materialism. The common name 'Cārvāka' is derived from this proper name and means the follower of that sage, *i.e.* a materialist. According to another view, 'Cārvāka' was even originally a common descriptive name given to a materialist, either because he preaches the doctrine of '*eat,* drink and be merry'[1] (carv— eat, chew), or because his words are pleasant and nice (cāru—nice, vāk—word). Some writers[2] again regard Bṛhaspati is the founder of materialism. This view is based on tlie facts (*a*) that some Vedic hymns ascribed by tradition to Bṛhaspati, son of Loka, are marked by a spirit of revolt and free-thinking, (*b*) that in the Mahābhārata and elsewhere materialistic views are put in the mouth of Bṛhaspati and (*c*) that about a dozen sūtras and verses are found quoted or referred to by different authors as the materialistic teachings of Bṛhaspati. Some even go a little further and say that Bṛhaspati, the teacher of the gods, propagated the materialistic views among the giants (the enemies of the gods) so that by following these attractive teachings they might come to ruin!

A materialist called Cārvāka or Lokayertika.

But whoever be the founder of Indian materialism, 'Cārvāka' has become synonymous with 'materialist.' The word used for materialism is also lokāyatamata, *i.e.* the view of common people. A materialist is accordingly called also lokāyatika.

Though the materialistic ideas are scattered here and there, they may be systematized and conveniently presented under three chief heads, namely, Epistemology, Metaphysics and Ethics.

II. The Cārvāka Epistemology

Perception is the only source of knowledge.

The entire philosophy of the Cārvākas may be said to depend logically on their epistemology or the theory of knowledge. The main problems of epistemology are: How far can we know reality? How does knowledge originate and develop? This last question involves the problem: What are the different sources of knowledge? This problem forms one of the chief topics of Indian epistemology. Knowledge of reality or valid cognition is called pramā and the source of such knowledge is called pramāna. The Cārvāka holds that perception is the only pramāṇa or dependable source of knowledge. For establishing this position he criticizes the possibility of other sources of knowledge like inference and testimony which are regarded as valid pramāṇas by many philosophers.

1. Inference is Not Certain

Inference is an uncertain leap from the known tothe unknown. For, it depends on a aniversal realtion between the middle and the major term, and no such universal relation can be ascertained.

If inference is to be regarded as a pramāṇa, it must yield knowledge about which we can have no doubt and which must be true to reality. But inference cannot fulfil these conditions, because when we infer, for example, the existence of fire in a mountain from the perception of smoke in it, we take a leap in the dark, from the perceived smoke to the unperceived fire. A logician, like the Naiyāyika, will perhaps point out that such a leap is justified by the previous knowledge of an invariable concomitance between smoke and fire and that the inference stated more fully would be... cases of smoke are cases of fire, this (mountain) is case of smoke, therefore this is a case of fire.

The Cārvāka points out that this contention would be acceptable only if the major premise, stating the invariable relation between the middle term (smoke) and the major (fire), were beyond doubt. But this invariable relation (vyāpti) can be established only if we have a knowledge of *all* cases of smoke and *all* cases of fire. This, however, is not possible, as we cannot perceive even all the cases of smoke and fire existing now in different parts of the world, to speak nothing of those which existed in the past or will exist in the future. No invariable, universal relation (vyāpti) can, therefore, be established by perception. Neither can it be said to be based on another inference, because it will involve a *petitio principii,* since the validity of that inference again has to be similarly proved. Nor can this vyāpti be based on the testimony (śābda) of reliable persons (who state that all cases of smoke are cases of fire). For, the validity of testimony itself requires to be proved by inference. Besides, if inference always depended on testimony, no one could infer anything by himself.

But it may be asked: Though it is not possible to perceive all individual cases of smoke and fire, is it not possible to perceive the constant class-characters (sāmānya) like 'smokeness' and 'fireness' which must be invariably present in all instance of smoke and fire respectively? If so, then can we not say that we at least perceive a relation between smokeness and fireness and with its help infer the presence of fire, wherever we perceive smoke? The Cārvāka replies; that even if we grant, the perception of a relation between smokeness and fireness, we cannot know therefrom any invariable relation between all *individual* case of smoke and fire. To be able to infer a *particular* fire, we must know that it is inseparably related to the *particular* smoke perceived. In fact, it is not possible even to know by perception what 'smokeness' or the class-character universally present in *all* particular instances of smoke is, because we do not perceive *all* cases of smoke. What is found to be universally present in the *perceived* cases of smoke, may not be present in the *unperceived* ones. The difficulty of passing from particulars to the universal, therefore, remains here as before.

Uniformities of experience are explained by the inherent natures of things, which also may change in future.

But it may be asked: If we do not believe in any fixed universal law underlying the phenomena of the world. How would we explain the uniformities that experienced objects possess? Why is fire always experienced to be hot and water to be cool? The Cārvāka reply is that it is due to the inherent natures (svabhāva) of things that they possess particular characters. No supernatural principle need be supposed to account for the properties of experienced objects of nature. There is neither any guarantee that uniformity perceived in the past would continue in future.

Causal relaiton is not ascertainable.

A modern student of inductive logic would be tempted to ask the Cārvāka: "But can we not base our knowledge of the invariable relation between smoke and fire on a *causal relation* between them?" The Cārvāka reply would be that a causal relation, being only a kind of invariable relation, cannot be established by perception due to the same difficulties.

The Cārvāka would further point out that a causal or any other invariable relation, cannot be established merely by repeated perception of two things occurring together. For, one must be certain that there is no other unperceived condition (upādhi) on which this relation depends. For example, if a man perceives a number of times fire accompanied by smoke and on another occasion be infer; the existence of smoke on the perception of fire, be would be liable to error, because he failed to notice a condition (upādhi), namely, wetness of fuel, on the presence of which alone fire is attended with smoke. So long as the relation between two phenomena is not proved to be unconditional, it is an uncertain ground for inference. And unconditional or absence of conditions cannot be established beyond doubt by perception, as some conditions may always remain hidden and escape notice. Inference or testimony cannot be used for proving this unconditionality without a *peiitio principii.* Because its validity also is being questioned here.

Some inferences accidentally turn out to be true.

It is true that in life we very often act unsuspectingly on inference. But that only shows that we act uncritically on the wrong belief that our inference is true. It is a fact that sometimes our inference comes true and leads to successful results. But it is also a fact that sometimes inference leads to error as well. Truth is not then an unfailing character of all inferences; it is only an accident, and a separable one, that we find only in *some* inferences.

Inference cannot be regarded, therefore, as a pramāṇa—a sure source of valid cognition.

2. Testimony is Not a Safe Source of Knowledge

Testimony relating to unperceived objectsis not reliable.

Even the Vedas are not reliable.

But can we not regard the testimony of competent persons as a valid and safe source of knowledge? Do we not very often act on knowledge received from authority? The Cārvāka replies that testimony consists of words (śabda). So far as words are heard through our ears, they are perceived. Knowledge of words is, therefore, knowledge through perception and is quite valid. But in so far as these word? suggest or mean things not within our perception, and aim at giving us knowledge of those unperceived objects, they are not free from error and doubt. Very often we are misled by so-called authority. The authority of the Vedas, for example, is regarded in high esteem by many. But in reality the? vedas are the works of some cunning priests who earned their living by duping the ignorant and the credulous. With false hopes and promisee the Vedas persuade men to perform Vedic rites, the only tangible benefit of which goes to the priests who officiate and enjoy the emoluments.

Testimony supported by inference is as uncertain as inference.

But will not our knowledge be extremely limited and practical life sometimes impossible if We do not accept the words of the experienced and do not depend on expert advice? The Cārvāka reply is that in so far as we depend on any authority, *because* we think it to be reliable, the knowledge obtained is really based on inference; because our belief is generated by a mental process like this: This authority should be accepted because it is reliable, and all reliable authority should be accepted. Being based on inference, knowledge derived from verbal, testimony or authority is as precarious as inference. And as in the case of inference, so here we often act on knowledge derived from authority on the wrong belief that it is reliable. Sometimes this belief accidentally leads to successful results, sometimes it does not. Therefore, authority or testimony cannot be regarded as a safe and valid source of knowledge.

As neither inference nor authority can be proved to be reliable, perception must be regarded as the only vlaid source of knowledge (pramāṇa).

III. Metaphysics

Matter is the only reality, because it alone is perceived.

Matter is the only reality, because it alone is perceived. Metaphysices is the theory of reality. The Cārvāka theory of reality follows from the epistemolologigcal conclusion just discussed. If perception is the only reliable source of knowledge, then we can rationally assert only the reality of perceptible objects'. God, soul, heaven, life before birth or after death and any unperceived law (like a-dṛṣṭa) cannot be believed in, because they are all beyond perception. Material objects are the only objects whose existence can be perceived and whose reality can be asserted. The Cāvākas, thus, come to establish materialism or the theory that matter is the only reality.

1. The World is Made of Four Elements

Matter is composed of four elements.

Regarding the nature of the material world most other Indian thinkers hold that it is composed of the five knids of elements (pañcabhūta), namely, ether (ākāśa), air (vāyu) fire (agni), water (ap) and earth (kṣiti). But the Cārvākas reject ether, because its existence cannot be perceived, but has to be inferred. The material world is, therefore, held to be composed of the fom perceptible elements. Not only non-living material objects but also living organisms, like plants and animal bodies, are composed of these four elements, by the combination of which they are produced and to which they are reduced on death.

2. There is No Soul

The soul is nothing but the living body, with the quality of consciousness.

But it may be asked, even if perception is the oly source of knowledge, do we not have a kind of perception, called internal, which gives an immediate knowledge of our mental states? And do we not perceive in these, consciousness which is nowhere to be perceived in the external material objects? If so, does it not compel us to believe that there is in us some non-material substance whose quality is consciousness—the substance which is called soul or spirit (ātmā)?

The Cārvākas admit that the existence of consciousness is proved by perception. But they deny that consciousness is the quality of any unperceived non-material or spiritual entity. As consciousness is perceived to exist in the perceptible living body composed of the material elements, it must be a quality of this body itself. What people mean by a soul is nothing more than this conscious living body (caitanya-viśiṣṭa-deha eva ātmā). The non-material soul is never perceived. On the contrary, we have direct evidence of the identity of the self with the body in our daily experiences and judgments like, 'I am fat,' 'I am lame,' 'I am blind,' If the 'I,' the self, were different from the body, these would be meaningless.

But the objection may be raised: We do not perceive consciousness in any of the four material elements. How can it then come to qualify their product, the body? In reply the Cārvāka point? out that qualities not present originally in any of the component factors may emerge subsequently when the factors are combined together. For example, betel leaf, lime and nut, none of which is originally red, come to acquire a reddish tinge when chewed together. Or, even the same thing placed under a different condition may develop qualities originally absent. For example, molasses (guḍa), originally non-intoxicant, becomes intoxicant when allowed to ferment. In a similar way it is possible to think that the material elements combined in a particular way give rise to the conscious living body. Consciousness is an epiphenomenon or bye-product of matter there is no evidence of its existence independent of the body.

If the existence of a soul apart from the body is not proved, then there is no possibility of proving its immortality. On the contrary, death of the body means the end of the individual. All questions about previous life, after-life, rebirth, enjoyment of the fruits of actions in heaven or hell, therefore, become meaningless.

3. There is No God

The supposition of God as creator is unnecessary. The world becomes into existence by the spontaneous combination of material elements.

God, whose existence cannot be perceived, fares no better than the soul. The material elements produce the world, and the supposition of a creator is unnecessary. The objection may be raised: Can the material element, by themselves give rise to this wonderful world? We find that even the production of an object like an earthen jar requires, in addition to clay which is its material cuase, a potter who is the efficeint cuase that shapes the material into the desired form. The four elements supply only the material cause of the world. Do we not require an efficient cause, like God, as the shaper and designer who turns the material elements into this wonderful world? In reply, the Cārvāka states that the material elements themselves have got each its fixed nature (svabbāva). It is by the natures and laws inherent in them that they combine together to form this world. There is thus no necessity for God. There is no proof that the objects of the world are the products of any design. They can be explained more reasonably as the fortuitous products of the elements. The Cārvākas, therefore, prefer atheism.

In so far as this Cārvāka theory tries to explain the world only by nature, it is sometimes called naturalism (svabhāva-vāda). It is also called mechaniam (yadṛcohā-vāda), because it denies the existence of conscious purpose behind the world and explains it as a mere mechanical or fortuitous combination of elements. The Cārvāka theory on the whole *may* also be called positivism, because it believes only in positive facts or observable phenomena.

IV. Ethics

Ethics is the science of morality. It discusses problems like: What is the highest goal or *summum banum* man can achieve? What should be the end of human conduct? What is the standard of moral judgment? The Cārvākas discuss these ethical problems in conformity with their metaphysical theories.

Heaven is a myth and cannot be the goal of life.

Some Indian philosophers like the Mimāṁsakas believe that the highest goal of human life is heaven (svarga) which is a state of unalloyed bliss that can be attained hereafter by performing here the Vedic rites. The Cārvāka rejects this view, because it is based on the unproved existence of a life after death. 'Heaven' and 'hell' are the inventions of the priests whose professional interest lies in coaxing, threatening and making people perform the rituals. Enlightened men will always refuse to be duped by them.

Liberation, as freedom fkrom all pain, is an impossible ideal.

Pleasure, though mixed with pain, is the only possible good.

Pleasure is theideal of life.

Many other philosophers regard liberation as the highest goal of human life. Liberation, again, is conceived as the total destruction of all sufferings. Some think that it can be attained only after death, when the soul is free from the body; and others believe that it can be attained even in this life. But the Cārvāka holds that none of these views stands to reason. If liberation is freedom of the soul from its bondage to physical existence, it is absurd because there is no soul. But if liberation means the attainment of a state in this life free from all pain, it is also an impossible ideal. Existence in this body is bound up with pleasure as well as pain. We can only try to minimise pain and enjoy as much pleasure as we can. Liberation in the sense of complete cessation of sufferings can only mean death.[3] Those who try to attain in life a state free from pleasure and pains by rigorously suppressing the natural appetites, thinking that all pleasures arising out of their gratification are mixed with pain, act like fools. For no wise man would reject the kernel because of its husk, nor give up eating fish because there are bones, nor cease to grow crops because there are animals to destroy them, nor stop cooking his food because beggars might ask for a share. If we remember that our existence is confined to the existence of the body and to this life, we must regard the pleasures arising in the body as the only good things we can obtain. We should not throw away the opportunities of enjoying this life, in the futile hope of enjoyment hereafter. 'Rather a pigeon to-day, than a peacock to-morrow.' 'A sure shell (courie) is better than a doubtful golden coin.' 'Who is that fool who would entrust the money in band to the custody of others?[4] The goal of human life is, therefore, to attain the maximum amount of pleasures in *this* life, avoding pain as far as possible. A good life is a life of maximum enjoyment. A good action is one which leads to a balance of pleasure and a bad action is one which brings about more pain than pleasure. This Cārvāka ethics may be called, therefore, hedonism or the theory that pleasure is the highest goal.

and neither virtue (dharma) nor liberation (mokṣa).

Wealth is good only as a means to enjoyment.

Some Indian thinkers speak of the four ends of human activity (puruṣārtha), namely, wealth (artha), enjoyment (kāma), virtue (dharma) and liberation (mokṣa). Of these four, the Cārvākas reject the last two. Liberation in the sense of destruction of all sufferings can be obtained only by death and no wise man would willingly work for that end. Virtue and vice are distinctions made by the scriptures, whose authority cannot be rationally accepted. Therefore, neither liberation nor virtue should be our end. Wealth and enjoyment are the only rational ends that a wise man can toil to achieve. But enjoyment is the ultimate end; wealth is not an end in itself, it is good only as a means to enjoyment.

Vedic rites are all useless.

Having rejected the authority of the scriptures, the notions of virtue and vice and belief in life after death, the Cārvākas are in life after death, the Cārvākas are naturally opposed to the performance of religious ceremonies with the object of either attaining heaven or avoiding hell or propitiating departed souls. They raise cheap laughter at the customary rites. If the food offered during funeral ceremony (śrāddha) for the departed soul can appease his hunger, what is the use of a traveller's taking food with him? Why should not his people make some offerings in his name at home to satisfy his hunger? Similarly, food offered on the ground-floor should satisfy a person living upstairs. If the priests really believe, as they say, that animals killed at a sacrifice (yajña) are sure to reach heaven, why do they not rather sacrifice their old parents instead of animals and make heaven sure for them?

Religion is thus reduced to morality and morality to the search of pleasure. The ethics of the Cārvāka is only the logical outcome of his materialistic metaphysics.

V. Conclusion

The contribution of the Cārvāka to Indian philosophy.

Like the Epicureans of Greece, the Cārvākas in India have been more hated than understood, 'Crāvāka' in the mind of people at large is a term of reproach. But it is useful for a student of philosophy to remember as well what Indian philosophy owes to the Cārvāka. Scepticism or agnosticism is only an expression of a free mind that refuses to accept traditional wisdom without a thorough criticism. Philosophy, as critical speculation, claims to live chiefly on free thought and the more it can satisfy the sceptic, the sounder it can hope to be. By questioning the soundness of popular notions, the sceptic sets new problems, by the solution of which philosophy becomes richer. Kant, one of the greatest philosophers of the West, recognized his debt to scepticism when he declared: "The scepticism of Hume roused me from my dogmatic slumber." And we may say that the Cārvāka similarly saved Indian philosophy from dogmatism to a great extent. As noted already, every system of Indian thought tried to meet the Cārvāka objections and made the Cārvāka a touchstone of its theories. The value of the Cārvāka philosophy, therefore, lies directly in supplying fresh philosophical problems and indirectly in compelling other thinkers to give up dogmatism, and become critical and cautious in speculation as well as in statement of views.

What has made the Cārvākas most disreputable to people is perhaps their ethics of pleasure. Pursuit of pleasure is not by itself an object of condemnation; pleasure, in some form, is recognized as desirable by other philosophers as well. It is condemned only when the nature of pleasure is coarse and the pleasure is wanted only for one's own self. It is true that some Cārvākas advocate a life of gross sensual pleasures. But a distinction found somctimes between the cunning (dhūrta) and cultured (suśikṣita) Cārvākas makes it likely that the Cārvākas were not all of the same gross, uncultured type. There is evidence that the materialists devoted themselves also to the pursuit of more refined pleasures by cultivating for example, the fine arts, the number of which is as large as sixty-four (catuḥ-ṣaṣṭi-kalāḥ), according to Vātsyāyana a recognized hedonist and author of the famous *Kāma-sūtra.* All materialists were not egoistic hedonists. Egoistic hedonism in its gross from is not compatible with social discipline. Life in society is impossible if man does not sacrifice a part of his pleasures for others. Some Cārvākas, we are told, regard the king as God. This implies their great faith in the necessity of society and its head. This view is further strengthened when we find that political philosophy and economy (daṇḍanīti and vārttā) came to be incorporated at some stage in the philosophy of the Lokāyatikas. It would appear from these facts that there were among the materialists of ancient India us cultured thinkers as we find among the positivists of modern Europe or the followers of Democritus in ancient Greece.

The best positive evidence of refined hedonism is found in the ethical philosophy propounded by Vātsyāyana in the second chapter of the *Kāma-sūtra.* It is here that we find a great hedonist himself stating and defending his own views.[5] Though Vātsyāyana believes in God and in life after death and, therefore, is not a materialist in the ordinary sense, yet he may be regarded as one, according to a wider sense of the term, namely, one who tries to explain 'higher phenomena by lower ones.[6] Vātsyāyana admits three desirable ends of human life (puruṣārtha), namely, dharma, artha and kāma (virtue, wealth and enjoyment), which should be cultivated harmoniously.[7] His materialist tendency consists in holding that dharma and artha are to be treated only as means to enjoyment, which is, therefore, the supreme end. The element of refinement in his hedonism consists in his emphasis on self-control (brahmacharya) and spiritual discipline (dharma), as well as urbanity (nāgarika-vṛtti), without which human enjoyment of pleasure is reduced to the level of beastly enjoyment. He shows that all physical enjoyment (kāma) is ultimately reducible to the gratification of the five senses. He further asserts that the satisfaction of the senses is necessary for the very existence of, the body (śarirasthiti), like the satisfaction of hunger.[8] But he also maintains that the senses must be educated, disciplined and cultured, through a training in the sixty-four fine arts. This training should be given only after a person has devoted the earlier part of his life to absolute self-continence and study of the Vedas and the other subsidiary branches of learning. He points out that without culture human enjoyment would be indistinguishable from beastly pleasures. To the impatient hedonist who would not for go present comfort and would not undergo any toil for future enjoyment in this life, Vātsyāyana points out that such attitude would be suicidal. For, this would prevent man even from the toil of cultivation and sowing seeds in the hope of the future enjoyment of a crop. In favour of regulation of the desire for enjoyment, he points out with historical examples that inordinate desire inconsistent with the principles of dharma and wealth, leads to ruin and annihilates the chances of all enjoyment. In support of scientific study of the conditions and means of enjoyment, he urges, like a modern scientific man, that some science is at the root of all successful practice; and that though all persons may not study science, they are benefited by the ideas which unconsciously and indirectly filter down to the masses, among which the few scientist live. We find, then, that Vātsyāyana represents Indian hedonism at its best. It is perhaps to thinkers of this kind that the name 'cultured hedonists' (suśikṣita-cārvāka) was applied.

Finally, it may be noted that the contribution of Cārvāka epistemology is not insignificant. The criticism of inference put in the mouth of the Cārvāka by his opponents reminds us of similar criticism made in modern times against the soundness of deductive logic. The Cārvāka view that no inference can yield certain knowledge is the view of many contemporary Western thinkers like the pragmatists and logical positivists.

REFERENCE

1. *Cf.* 'Piva, khāda ca varalocane, '*Ṣaḍ-darśana-samuccaya,* Lokāyatamatam.

2. *Ibid.* and *Sarva-darśana-saṅgraha*

3. I'Maranam eva apavargah, "*Bṛhaspati-sūtra.*

4. *Kāma-sūtra*, Chap. 2.

5. The date of Vātsyāyana, according to some, is near about the beginning of the Christian era, and Vātsyāyana tells us that be is only summarising the views of a long line of previosu writers, about a dozen in number, whose works are not available now. This shows the great antiquity of his line of thought.

6. *Vide* James, *Pragmatism,* p. 93.

7. *Parasparasya* anupaghātakam trivargaṁ severta', *Kāma-sūt,* Chap. 2.

8. Yaśodhara. the commentator on *Kāma-sūt,* explaining this, mentions that non-satisfaction of the senses might lead to deseases like inanity (unmāda).

CHAPTER VI

THE NYĀYA PHILOSOPHY

I. Introduction

Gotama was the founder of the Nyāya system

The Nyāya philosophy was founded by the great sage Gotama who was also known as Gautama and Akṣapāda. Accordingly, the Nyāya is also known as the Akṣapāda system. This philosophy is primarily concerned with the conditions of correct thinking and the means of acquiring a true knowledge of reality. It is very useful in developing the powers of logical thinking and rigorous criticism in its students. So we have such other names for the Nyāya philosophy as Nyāyavidyā, Tarkaśāstra (*i.e.* the science of reasoning), and Ānvīksikī (*i.e.* the science of critical study).

Its ulitmate endis liberation, although as main interest is a logic.

But the logical problem as to the methods and conditions of true knowledge or the canons of logical critism is not the sole or the ultimate end of the Nyāya philosophy. It ulitmate end, like that of the other systems of Indian philosophy, is liberation, which means the absolute cessation of all pain and suffering. It is only in order to attain this ultimate end of life that we require a philosophy for the knowledge of reality, and a logic for determining the conditions and methods of true knowledge. So we may say that the Nyāya, like other Indian systems, is a philosophy of life, although it is mainly interested in the problems of logic and epistemology.

Historical sketch of the system

The first work of the Nyāya philosophy is the *Nyāya-sūtra* of Gotama. It is divided into five adhyāyas or books, each containing two āhnikas or sections. The subsequent works of the Nyāya system, such as Vātsyayana's *Nyāya-bhāṣya*, Uddyotakara's. *Nyāya-vārttika*, Vācaspati's *Nyāya-vārttika-tātparyatīkā*, Udayana's *Nyāya-vārttika-tātparya-pariśuddhi* and *Kusumāñjali*, Jayanta's *Nyāyamanjarī*, etc., explain and develop the ideas contained in the *Nyāya-sūtra*, and also defend them against the attacks of hostile critics. The ancient school of the Nyāya (prācina-nyāya) is thus a development of the sūtra-philosophy of Gotama through a process of attack, counter-attack and defence among the Naiyāyikas and their hard critics. The modern school of the Nyāys (navya-nyāya) begins with the epoch-making work of Gaṅgesa, on the *Tattvacintāmaṇi.* This school flourished at first in Mithilā, but subsequently became the glory of Bengal with Navadvipa as. the main centre of its learning and teaching. The modem school lays almost exclusive emphasis on the logical aspects of the Nyāya, and develops its theory of knowledge into a formal logic of relations between concepts, terms and propositions. With the advent of the modern Nyāya, the ancient school lost some of its popularity. The syucretist school of the Nyāya is a later development of the Nyāya philosophy into the form of a synthesis or an amalgamation between the Nyāya and the Vaiśeṣika system.

The sixteen philosophcial topics of the Nyāya

The whole of the Nyāya philosophy may be conveniently divided into four parts, namely, the theory of knowledge, the thory of the physical world, the theory of the individual self and its liberation, and the theory of God. It should, however, be observed here that the Nyāya system is in itself an elaboration of sixteen philosophical topics (padārtha). These are (1) pramāṇa, the source or methods of knowledge; (2) prameya, the objects of knowledge; (3) samśaya, doubt; (4) prayojana, the end for the sake of which one acts; (5) dṛṣṭānta, an undisputed fact cited as an example; (6) siddhānta, a proved doctrine; (7) avayava, the constituent propositions of inference; (8) tarka, a hypothetical argument; (9) nirnaya, the ascertainment of truth; (10) vāda, a discussion for the attainment of truth; (11) jalpa, mere wrangling or a wordy warfare for mere victory in a debate; (12) vitaṇḍāa, a merely destructive criticism; (13) hetvābhāsa, the fallacies of inference; (14) chala, the fallacy of ambiguity or the illicit process of contradicting a statement by taking it in a sense other than the intended one; (15) jāti, a futile objection based on mere similarity or dissimilarity, without any universal principle of relation among things; (16) nigrahasthāna, the point at which one has to admit defeat.[1]

It is a systemof logical ralism

Definitions of realism an idealism

The Nyāya philosophy is a system of logical realism. In philosophy realism means the theory or doctrine that the existence of things or obejcts of the world is independent of all knowledge or relation to mind. The existence of ideas and images, feelings' of pleasure and pain, is dependent on some mind. These cannot exist unless are experienced by some mind. But the existence of tables and chairs, plants and animals, does not depend on our minds. These exist and will continue to exist, whether we know them or not. Realism is a philosophical theory which holds that the existence of all things or objects of the world is quite independent of all minds, finite or infinite, human or divine. Idealism, on the other hand, holds that things or object can exist only as they are related to some mind Just as feeling's and cognitions exist only as they are in one mind, so the objects of the world exist only as they are actually experienced or at least thought of by us or by God Now the Nyāya is a realistic philosophy in so far as it holds that the objects of the world have an independent existence of their own apart from all knowledge or experience. In the Nyāya this realistic view of the world is based, not on mere faith or feeling, intuition or scriptural testimony, but on logical grounds and critical reflections. According to it, the highest end of life, *i.e.* liberation, can be attained only through a right knowledge of reality. But a true knowledge of reality presupposes an understanding of what knowledge is, what the sources of knowledge are, how true knowledge is distinguished from wrong; knowledge, and so forth. In other word? a theory of knowledge or metaphysics presupposes a theory of knowledge or epistemology. Hence the realism of the Nyāya is based on the theory of knowledge which is the logical foundation of all philosophy. Thus we see that the Nyāya is a system of philosophy which may be justly characterized as logical realism.

II. The Nyāya theory of Knowledge

The Nyāya theory of reality is based on the Nyāya theory of knowledge. According to this, there are four distinct and separate sources of true knowledge. These are (*i*) pratyakṣa, perception; (*ii*) anumāna, inference; (*iii*) upamāna, comparison; and (*iv*) śabda, testimony. We shall explain them separately. But before we come to these pramāṇas or sources of valid knowledge, let us understand what knowledge is, what the different kinds of knowledge are, and how true knowledge is distinguished from false knowledge.

1. Definition and Classification of Knowledge

Knowledge is the manifestation of objects.

Definition of valid knowledge.

Knowledge or cognition (Jñāna or budhi) is the manifestation of objects. Just as the light of a lamp reveals or shows physical things, so knowledge manifests all objects that come before it. Knowledge is of different kinds. First we have valid knowledge (pramā or pramiti), which has been subdivided into perception, inference, comparison and testimony. Then, we have non-valid kowledge (apramā), which includes memory (smṛti), doubt (saṁśaya), error (bhrama or viparyyaya) and hypothetical argument (tarka). True or valid knowledge is a definite or certain (asandigdha), and a faithful or unerring (yathārtha) presentation (anubhava) of the object. My visual perception of the table before me is a true cognition, because in it the table is presented to me directly just as it realy is, and I am certain about the truth of my cognition. Memory is not valid knowledge, because in it the remembered object is not directly presented, since it is past but only represented or recalled by the mind.[3] Doubtful cognition cannot be called prama, because it is not certain knowledge. Error is undoubted knowledge indeed, and may also be presentative, but it is not true to the nature of its object.

Sometimes we perceive a snake in a rope is the twilight and have *then* no doubt about the reality of what we see. Still this perception is erroneous, because it is not a true cognition of the object (yathārthānubhava). Tarka is not pramā, since it does not give us any knowledge of objects. A tarka is have this: Looking out of the window of your class-room, you see a mass of smoke rising from a distant house and say that the house has caught fire. A friend contradict you and a asserts that there is no fire. Now you argue; if there is no fire, there cannot be smoke. This argument, starting with an 'if' and exposing the absurdity of your friend's position, and thereby indirectly proving your, own, is tarka. It is not pramā or valid knowledge, because to argue like this is not to know the fire, but to confirm your previous inference of fire from smoke. That there is fire, you know by inference. To argue that if there is no fire there cannot be smoke, is not to know the fire as a real fact either by way of perception or by that of inference.

How true knowledge is distinguished from false knowledge

The next question is: How is true knowledge distinguished from false knowledge? Knowledge is true when it agrees with or corresponds to the nature of its object, otherwise it becomes false. Your knowledge of the rose as red is true if the rose has really a red colour as you judge it to have (tadvati tatprakāraka). On the contrary, your perception of the an as moving is wrong, since the motion belongs really to the earth and is wrongly transferred to the in which remains relatively motionless or stationary (tadabhāvavati tatprakaraka). But then it may be laked: How do we know that the first knowledge is true and the second false? In other words: How do we test the truth or falsity of knowledge? The Naiyāyikas (also the Vaiśeṣikas, Jainas and Bauddhas) explain it in tbe following manner: Suppose you want little more sugar for your morning tea and take a spoonful of it from the cup before you and put it into your tea. Now the tea tastes sweeter than before and you know that your previous perception of sugar was true. Sometimes, however, it happens that while looking for sugar, you find some white powdered substance and put a pinch of it into your mouth under the impression that it is sugar. But to your utter surprise and disappointment, you find that it is salt and not sugar. Here then we see that the truth and falsity of knowledge consist respectively in its correspondence and non-correspondence to facts. On the other hand, the teste of the truth or falsity of knowledge is the success or failure of our practical activities in relation to its object (pravṛttisāmarthya or pravṛttivisāvāda). True knowledge leads to successful practical activity, while false knowledge ends in failure and disappointment.

2. Perception

In Western logic the problem of perception as a source of knowledge has not been properly discussed. The reason probably is this. We generally believe that what is given in perception must be true. Ordinarily, no man questions the truth of what be perceives by hit senses. So it is thought that it is unnecessary, if not ridiculous. to examine the validity of perception, or to determine the conditions of perception as a source of valid knowledge. Indian thinkers are more critical than dogmatic in tins respect, and make a thorough examination of perception in almost the same way as Western logicians discuss the problem of inference.

(a) Definition of Perception

Perception is a definite and true cognition of objects produced by sense object contact

In logic perception is to be regarded as a from of true cognition. Taking it in this sense, some Naiyāyikas define perception as a definite cognition which is produced by sense-object contact and is true or unerring.[5] The perception of the table before me is due to the contact of my eyes with the table, and I am definite that the object is a table. The perception of a distant figure as either a man or a post is a doubtful and indefinite cognition, and, therefore, not a true perception. The perception of a snake in a piece of rope is definite but false; and so it is different from valid perception.

Another definition of perception is that it is immediate cognition

The definition of perception as a cognition due to the stimulation of our sense organs by the perceived object is generally accepted by us. It is accepted also by many systems of philosophy, Indian and Western. Some Naiyāyikas, the Vedāntins and others, however, reject it on the ground that there may be perception without sense object contact. God, we are told, perceives all things, but has no senses. When I *see a,* snake in a rope, there is really no snake to come in contact with my eyes. Mental states like the feelings of pleasure and pain are directly cognised or perceived by us without the help of any sense organ. All this shows that sense-object contact is not common to, and cannot, therefore, be a defining character of, perceptions. What, however, is really common to, and distinctive of, all perceptions is a feeling of *directness* or *immediacy* of the knowledge given by them. We are said to perceive an object, if and when we know it directly, *i.e.* without taking the help of prev− vious experiences or any reasoning process (jñānākaranaka). If at midday you turn your eyes overhead, you see the sun directly, and not by means of any proces of inference or reasoning. There is neither any necessity nor any time of you to think and reason before the perception of the sun arises in your mind. So some Indian logicians propose to define perception as immediate cognition (sākṣāt pratīti) although they admit that eprceptin is in alsmost all cases conditioned by sense-object contact.[6]

(b) Classificaiton of Perception[7]

Ordinary and extraordinary perceptions

External and internal perceptions

There ar differnt ways of classifying perception. First, we have the distinciton between *laukika* or ordinary and *alukika* or extraoridnary perceptions. This distinction depends on the way in which the senses come in contact with their objects. We have *laukika* perception when there is the usual sense contact with objects present to sense. In *alaukika* perception, however, the object in such as is not ordinarily present to sense, but is conveyed to sense through an unususal medium. Ordinary perception, again is of two kinds, namely, external (bāhya) and internal (mānasa). The former is due to the external sense of sight, hearing and touch, taste and smell. The latter is brought about by the mind's contact with mental states and processes. Thus we have six kinds of *laukika* or ordinary perceptions, *viz.* the visual (cākṣuṣa), auditory (śrautra), tactual (spārśana), gustatory (rāsana), olfactory (ghyrāṇja), and the internal or mental (manassa) perception. *Alaukika* or extraordinary perception is of theree kinds, *viz.* sāmānya-lakṣaṇa, jñāna-lakṣaṇa and yogaja.

The six organs of knowledge, *viz* ***the five external senses and the internal sense, manas***

According to the Nyāya (also the Vaiśeṣkika, Mīmāṁsā, and Jaina), there are six organs of knowledge. Of these, five are external and one is internal. The five external sense are the organs of smell (ghrāṇa), taste (rasanā), sight (cakṣuḥ). touch (tvak), and hearing (śrotra). These perceive respectively the physical qualitites of smell, taste, colour, touch and sound. They are physical in nature and each of them is constituted by that very same physical element whose qualities are sensed by it. This seems to be suggested by the fact that is many cases we use the same name for both the sense organ and the physical quality sensed by it. It is probably based on the principle that only like can perceive like. Mind (manas) is the internal organ which perceives such qualities of the soul as desire (icchā), aversion (dveṣa), striving or willing (prayatna), pleasure (sukha),paia (duḥkba) and cognition. It is not made of the material elements (bhūtas) like the external senses. It is not limited to the knowledge of any particular class of things or qualities, but functions as a central co-ordinating organ in all kinds of knowledge. The Nyāya view of mind as an 'internal sense' (antarindriya) is accepted by the Vaiśeṣikas, the Sāṅkhyas the Mīmāṁsakas and others. But some Vedāntins criticse and reject the Nyāya view of mind as an 'inner sense'.

(c) Extraoridnary Perception [8]

There are three kinds of extraordinary perceptions. The first is sāmānyalakṣaṇa or the perception of classes

Alaukika or extraoridnary perception is of three kinds. The first is called sāmānyalakṣaṇa. When we say, "All men are mortal," we know that mortality; is true of all men. This means that mortality is true, not of all men who are dead and gone, but of all men who are dead and gone, but of all men in the past, present and future. In other words, it means that mortality is true of the class of men. But the question is: How do we know the whole class of men? We cannot know it by ordinary perception, since all men cannot be physically present to our senses. Yet we must somehow know *all* men. The Naiyāyika explains this knowledge of the class by extraordinary perception, in which the class *men* is presented through the class-essence or the universal "manhood." When I perceive a man *as man,* I do perceive the manhood in him; otherwise I cannot directly recognise him as man. Now this direct knowledge or perception of the universal *manhood,* is the medium through which I perceive all men so far as they classmen. To perceive manhood is to perceive all men so *in* as they are possessed of the universal "manhood." In short, to perceive manhood is to perceive all men as the individuals in which the universal "manhood" inheres. This perception of the class of men, being due to the perception of the universal (sāmānya), is called sāmānya lakṣaṇa perception and is marked off as extraordinary (alaukika) on account of its obvious difference from our ordinary perceptions.

The second is jḥānalakṣaṇa or complication.

The second kind of extraordinary perception is called jñānalakṣaṇa. We often use such expresessions as "ice looks cold," "the stone looks hard," "the grass looks soft," and so forth. This means that the coldness of ice the hardness of a stone, the softness of luxuriant grass are perceived by us with our eyes. But the question is: How can the eyes perceive touch qualities, like hardness and softness, which can ordinarily be sensed only by the sense of touch? Among Western psychologists, Wundt, Ward and Stout explain such perceptions by "complication,"[9] a process by which sensations or perceptions of different senses become so closely associated as to become integral parts of a single perception. Similarly, when on *seeing* something one says, *"I see* a piece of fragrant sandalwood," he has a perception of its fragrance by means of his eyes. How can we explain this visual perception of fragrance which can be ordinarily sensed only by the sense of smell? The Neiyāyika says that here our past of *factory* experience of fragrance as closely associated with the visual appearance of sandalwood (since every time we smelt it we saw its colour, unless that was in a dark room) brings about the present *visual* perception of fragrance simultaneously with that of its colour. This present perception of fragrance, being due to the past *knowledge* of fragrance (*śaurahha-jñāna*), has been called jñānalakṣaṇa perception, which is also extraordinary in the sense that it is brought about by sense organ which is not ordinarily capable of perceiving fragrance.

The third is yogaja or intuitive perception of yogins

The third kind of extraordinary perception is called yogaja. It is the in uitive perception of all objects—past and future, hidden and infinitesimal—by one who possesses some supernatural power generated in the mind by devout meditation (yogābbyāsa). In the case of those who have attained spiritual perfection (yukta), such intuitive knowledge of all objects is constant and spontaneous. In the case of others who are on the say to perfection (yuñjāna), it requires the help of concentration as an auxiliary condition. The reality of yogaja perception is generally accepted in Indian philosophy on the authority of the scriptures (śruti and the like). It is to he observed also that the Vedāntins[10] severely criticise and reject the Nyāya theory of sāmānyalakṣaṇa and jñānalakṣaṇa perceptions, although they do not repudiate the idea of yogipratyaksa out of respect for the scriptural texts in its favour.

(d) Three Modes of Perception[11]

There are three modes of ordinary perception.

According to another classification, ordinary perception is of two kinds, namely, nirvikalpaka or the indterminate and savikalpaka or the determinate. Here the principle of classification is the more or less developed character of perceptual knowledge. To these two we may add pratyabhijñā or recognition. Keeping in view the nature of perception, the Naiyāyikas distinguish between three modes of ordinary perception. Extraordinary perception is always determinate, since it is definite and explicit knowledge.

The first is nirvikalpaka, which is cognition of the mere existence of a thing without any explicit recognition and characterization of it.

Nirvikalpaka or indeterminate perception is the cognition of an object as just an existent thing without an explict recognition and characterization of it as this or that kind of thing. Suppose you look at an orange placed on the other side of your table. Immediately after first glance, or after the first moment of contact between your eyes and the object, you apprehend something, its coulour, shape, etc., along with a general character called orangeness. But at first sight, you do not think of its yellow or round, or as an orange. There may be a simple perception of an object and its specific and generic qualities, without any judgment of it as this or that kind of thing. Suppose on the first day of your examination you enter the bath room engrossed in thinking about the possible questions and their answers. It is not unlikely that you may finish you bath without thinking of the water used by you as water. Yet it cannot be said that you do not perceive the water: but for a very real perception of it, your act of bathing cannot be explained. This perception of water and its character, without any thought or jugement of it as *water, as liquid, as cold* etc., is the nirvikalpaka or indertminate perception of it.

The second is savikalpaka, in which the object is judged as a particular kind of thing

Savikalpaka perception is the cognition of an object *as* possessed of some character. While nirvikalpaka is the cognition of the the existence of a thing as such, savikalpaka may be said to be the recognition of its nature. Thus when, look ing at the orange, judge within myself "this is an orange," I do not only cognise the existence of the orange as such, but also explicitly recognize or mentally assert what existence it is. Here the existent fact, *this,* becomes the subject of a proposition and orangeness is related to it as a predicate. Thus we may say that nirvikalpaka is a simple apprehension and savikalpaka a predicative judgment of the same object. There cannot be any savikalpaka perception of an object without a previous nirvikalpaka perception of it. Unless we first know the existence of an object we cannot possibly know it as this or that kind of object. Unless first perceive water as something there in a pool, I cannot know it *as* water or as a substance which is qualified by certain attributes.

The third is pratyabhijñā, which is the imgnition of an object as what was cognised before

Pratyabhijñā is recognition in its literal meaning. It is a recognition of some object, *i.e.* a congnition of it as that which was cognised before. In it we know that the thing which we now cognise is the same as that which was conised before, as when one says: "This must be the same man who pusehd me down the tram-car yesterday." It should be remarked here that the distinctions of nirvikalpaka perception, savikalpaka perception, and pratyabhijñā have not been recognized, or recognized in the same way, in all the systems of Indian philosophy. While the Vaiśeṣika, the Sāṅkhya and the Mīmāṁsā system accept, on the whole, the Nyāya view *as* explained hare, the Bauddha and the Advaita Vedānta system reject it and hold very different views.

3. Inference

(a) Definition of Inference

Infernce is the process of knowlng something, not by observation, but through the medium of a mark that is invariably related to it.

After perception comes anumāna or inference. Amāna (anu—after, māna—knowledge) literally means a cognition or knowledge which follows some other knowledge. Take the following illustrations: "The hill is fiery, because it smokes, and what every smokes is fiery;" "Devdatta is mortal, because he is a man, and all men are mortal." In the first example, we pass from the perception of smoke in the hill to the knowledge of the existence of fire in it, on the ground of our previous knowledge of the universal relation between smoke and fire. In the second example, we know the mortality of Devadatta, which is not now perceived, from the presence of manhood in him. Thus we see that inference is a process of reasoning in which we pass from the apprehension of some mark (liṅga) to that of something else, by virtue of a relation of invariable concomitance (vyāpti) between the two. As Dr. B. N. Seal puts it: "Anununa (inference) is the process of ascertain in, not by perception or direct observation, but through the instrumentality or medium of a mark: that a thing possesses a certain character."[12]

(b) The Constitutents of Inference[13]

Inference has three terms and at least three propositions.

Pakṣa is the minor term, sādhya the major term, and sādhana the middle term of anumāna or inference

From the definition of inference it will appear that an inference must have as its constitutens three terms and at least three propositions. In inference we arrive at the knowledge of some character of a, thing through the knowledge of some mark and that of its universal relation to the inferred character. Thus in the above inference of fire we know the un-received fire in the bill through the perception of smoke in it and the knowledge of an invariable relation between smoke and fire. There is, first, the knowledge or apprehension of smoke as a mark in the hill. Secondly, there is a recollection of the relation of invariable concomitance between smoke and fire, as we have observed it in the past. Thirdly, we have the resulting knowledge of the existence of the un-perceived fire in the hill. Now in this inference the hill is the pakṣa (minor term), since it is the subject under consideraiton in the course of the inferential reasoning. Fire is the sādhya (major term), as that is something which we want to prove or establish in relation to the hill by means of this inference. Smoke is the liṅga (middle term), as it is the mark or sign which indicates the presence of fire. It is also called the hetu or sādhana, *i.e.* the resone or ground of inference. Thus corresponding to the minor, major and middle terms of the syllogism, inference, in Indian logic, contains three terms, namely, pakṣa, sādhya and hetu. The pakṣa is the subject with which we are concerned in any inference. The sādhya is the object which we want to know in relation to the pakṣa, or the inferable character of the pakṣa. The hetu is the reason for our relating the sādhya to the pakṣa. It is the ground of our knowledge of the sādhya as related to the pakṣa.

The three steps and propositions is an inference

In order of the events which take place when a certain thinker is inferring, the first step in inference is the apprehension of the hetu (smoke) in the pakṣa (hill), the second a recollection of the universal relation between hetu and sādhya (smoke and fire), and the last is the cognition of the sādhya (fire) as related to the pakṣa (hill). But as a matter of formal statement or verbal expression, the first step in inference is the predication of the sādhya with regard to the pakṣa, *e.g.* "The hill is fiery." The second is the affirmation of the hetu as related to the pakṣa, *e.g.* "Because the hill is smoky." The third is the affirmation of the hetu as invariably related to the sādhya, *e.g.* "Wherever there is smoke, there is fire, as in the kitchen." Thus in inference we must have at least three propositions, all of which are categorical, and may be affirmative or negative. The first proposition corresponds to the conclusion of the syllogism, the second to the minor premise, and the third to the major premise. Thus inference, in Indian logic, fire be said to be a syllogism consisting of three categorical propositions. But the order of the propositions reversed in Indian logic, in so far as it puts the conclusion of the syllogism first, and its usual premise last, in the formal statement of an inference.

Indian and Western forms of the syllogism

Indian logicians are agreed that so far as infernece is svārtha or for oneself, it requires no formal statement by way of number of propositions. It is only in the case of inference which is parārtha, *i.e.* meant to prove or demonstrate some truth, that we require to state an inference in the form of a rigorous chain of argument without any gap. This is the logical form of an inference. We may say that in Indian logic inference corresponds roughly, in respect of its form, to the categorical syllogism of Western logic. But there are certain important differences between the Indian and Western forms of the syllogism. In Western logic, the syllogism is generally stated in the form of three propositions, of which the first is the major premise, the second is the minor premise, and the last is the conclusion. According to the Naiyāyikas, however, inference, as a conclusive proof, must be stated in the form of five propositions, called its avayavas or members. These are pratijñā, hetu, udāharaṇa, upanaya, and nigamana.[14] The five-membered syllogism may be thus illustrated:

(1) Ram is mortal (pratijñā);
(2) Because he is a man (hetu);
(3) All men are mortal, *e.g.* Socrates, Kant, Hegel (udāharaṇa);
(4) Ram also is a man (upanaya);
(5) Therefore he is mortal (nigamana).

The pratijñā is the first proposition, which asserts something. The hetu is the second proposition, which rtates the reason for this assertion. The udāharaṇa it the universal proposition, showing the connection between the reason and the asserted fact, as supported by known instances. Upanaya is the application of the, universal proposition to the present case. Nigamana is the conclusion which follows from the preceding propositions.[15]

(c) The Grounds of Inference[16]

There are two conditons of an inference
Vyāpti is the logical condition of inference

Now we come to the consideration of vyāpti or invariable concomitance between the middle term and the major term, which is the logical ground of inference. In inference our knowledge of the sādhya (fire) as related to the pakṣa (hill) depends on the previous knowledge of the hetu (smoke) as related to the pakṣa, on the one hand, and universally connected with the sādhya, on the other. We infer that there is fire in the hill, because we see that there is smoke in the hill and know that smoke is always accompanied by fire. It appears, therefore, that an inference has two conditions. The first is cognition of the hetu or middle term (smoke) in the pakṣa or minor tern (the hill). The second is the relation of invariable concomitance between the middle and the major term. That there is fire in the hill is a conclusion which we can justify only if we know that there is an invariable concomitance between the hill-smoke and fire. This relation of invariable concomitance between the hetu and the sādhya, or the middle term and the major term of inference is technically called vyāpti, and is regarded as the logical ground of inference, since it guarantees the truth of the conclusion. So the questions we are to consider now, are: What is vyāpti? How is. vyāpti known by us?

There ar two kinds of vyāpati

With regard to the first question, we have to say that vyāpti literally means the state pervasion. It implies a correlation between two facts, of which one is pervaded (vyapya), and the other pervades (vyapya). A fact is said to *pervade* another when it always accompanies the other. A fact is said to be pervaded by another when it is always accompanied by the other. In this sense smoke is pervaded by fire, since it is always accompanied by fire, or, all smoky objects are fiery. But while all smoky objects are fiery, all fiery objects are not smoky, *e.g.* the red-hot iron ball. A vyāpti between terms of unequal extension, such as smoke and fire, is called asamavyāpti or viṣamavyāpti. It is a relation of non-equipollent concomitance between two terms, from one of which we may infer the other, but not *vice versa.* We may infer fire from smoke, but not smoke from fire. As distinguished from this, a vyāpti between two terms of equal extension is called samavyāpti or equipollent concomitance. Here the vyāpti holds between two terms which are co-extensive, so that we may infer either of them from the other, *e.g.* 'nameable 'and 'knowable.' What ever is nameable is knowable, and *vice versa.*

Vyāpti is an invariable and unconditional realtion of concomitsance between the middle and major terms

For any inference the minimum condition is some kind of vyāpti between the middle and the major term. This satisfies the fundamental law of syllogistic inference that one of the premises must be universal. Now the vyāpti between the middle and the major term means generally a relation of co-existence (sāhacarya) between the two, *e.g.* "wherever there is smoke, there is fire." Every case of co-existence, however, is not a case of vyāipti. In many instances fire may co-exist with smoke. Still there is no vyāpti or universal relation between fire and smoke, since there may be fire without smoke. The reason is that in such cases the relation of co-existence is dependent on certain conditions (upādhi) other than the terms related. Thus the presence of smoke in fire is conditioned by wet fuel (ārdrendhana). So we are to say that vyāpti is that relation of co-existence between the middle and the major term which is indepent of all conditions. It is an invaribale and unconditional relaiton of comncomitance (nitya anaupādhika saṁbandha) between the middle and the major term.

Different methods of ascertaining vyāpti

The Buddhist method

The second question is: How is vyāpti known? How do we get a universal proposition like 'all smoky objects are fiery," or "all men are mortal"? This is the problem of induction. For the Cārvākas, who are radical empiricists, there is no problem, because there is no inference as a source of true knowledge. All the other systems of Indian philosophy which admit, the validity of inference try to solve this problem in some way or other.

The Buddhists base the knowledge of universal propositions on the principles of causality and essential identity, which they regard as a *priori* and necessary principles of human thought and action. If two things are related as cause and effect, we know that they are universally related, for there cannot be any effect without its cause. To determine the causal relation between them, the Buddhists adopt the method of pañcakāraṇī which is as follows: (*a*) neither the cause nor the effect is perceived, (*b*) the cause is perceived, (*c*) immediately the effect is perceived, (*d*) the cause disappears, (*e*) immediately, the effect disappears. Similarly, if two things are essentially identical (*i.e.* possess a common essence), they must be universally related. All men are animals, because animality belongs to the essence of both, and men without animality will not be men.

The Vedāntin's methods

The Vedāntins hold that vyāpti or the universal proposition is the result of an induction by simple enumeration. It. is derived from the uncontradicted experience of agreement in presence between two things. When we find that two things go together or co-exist, and that there is no exception to their relation (vyabhicārādarśane sati sahacāradarśanam), we may take them as universally related.

The Nyāya mehtod which includes—

(*a*) anvaya,
(*b*) vyatireka
(*c*) vyabhicārāgraha,
(*d*) upadhinirasa,

The Naiyāyikas agree with the Vedāntins in holding that vyāpti is established by the uncontradicted experience of the relation between two things, and not on any *a priori* principle like causality or essential identity. They, however, go further than the Vedāntins and supplement uncontradicted experience of the relation between two facts by tarka or indirect proof and by sāmānyalakṣaṇa perception. The Nyāya method of induction or generalisation may be analysed into the following steps. First we observe that there is a relation of agreement in presence (anvaya) between two things, or that in all cases in which one is present, the other also is present *e.g.* wherever there is smoke, there is fire. Secondly, we see that there is uniform agreement in absence (vyatireka) between them *e.g.* wherever there is no fire, there is no smoke. These two steps taken together correspond very well to Mill's Joint method of agreement in presence and in absence. Thirdly, we do *not* observe any contrary instance in which one of them is present without the other (vyabhicārāgraha). From this we may conclude that there must be a natural relation of invariable concomitance between the two things.

Still we cannot be sure if the relation in question is unconditional or free from upadhis, which a real vyāpti must be. Hence the fourth step of the inductive method is elimination of upādhis or conditions (upādhinirāsa). I put on the switch and there is light; if I do not, there is no light. From this if anybody concludes that there is a vyāpti or invariable relation between switching on and lighting the room, then he would commit 'he mistake of ignoring the upādhi or condition, *viz.* the electric current, in the presence of which a lone there can be light. This upādhi, *viz.* electric current, must be present when there is light, but it may not be present wherever there is switching on. So an upādhi is defined as a term which is co-extensive with the major (sādbyasamavyāpti) but not with the middle term of an inference (avyāptasādhana). Taking the stock example, when one infers the existence of smoke from fire, be relies on the conditional relation of fire to smoke, since fire is attended with smoke on the condition of its being fire from "wet fuel."[17] It will be seen here that the condition "wet fuel" is always related to the major term "smoky," but not so related to the middle term "fire," as there are cases of fire without "wet fuel." Hence to eliminate the suspected conditions of an invariable relation between two things we must make repeated observation (bhūyodarśana) of their agreement in presence and in absence under varying circumstances. If in the course of this process we see that there is no material circumstance which is present or absent just when the major term is present or absent, we are to understand that its concomitance with the middle term is unconditional. In this way we can exclude as the suspected conditions of a relation of invariable concomitance between the middle and the major term and buy that it is a relation of vyāpti or invariable and unconditional concomitance.

(*e*) Taṣka.

But there is still room for a sceptical doubt about the vyāpti or universal proposition thus arrived at. It may be urged by a sceptic like Hume or the Cārvāka that so far as our past and present experience is concerned, there is no exception to the uniform relation of concomitance between smoke and fire. But there is no knowing whether this relation holds good in distant regions, like the planets, or will hold good in the remote future. To end this sceptical doubt, the Naiyāyikas try next to fortify the induction by tarka. The porposition all smoky objects are very may be indirectly proved by a tarka like this: If this proposition is not true, then its contradictory, "some smoky objects are not fiery," must be true. This mean that there may be smoke without fire. But this supposition is contradicted by the law of universal causation, for to say that there may be smoke without fire is just to say that there may be an effect without a cause (since fire is the only known cause of smoke). If any one has the obstinacy to say that sometimes there may be effect without causes, he must be silenced by reference to the practical contradictions (vyāghāta) involved in his position. If there can be an effect without a cause, why seek for *fire* to smoke cur eigar or to cook your food? This process of indirect proof of in the Nyāya may be said to correspond roughly to the method of *reductio ad absurdum* in Western logic.

(*f*) sāmānyalakṣaṇa perception

Although the Naiyāyikas take great pains to establish vyāpti or a universal proposition on the ground of the observation of particular facts, still they feel that a generalisation from particulars are mere particulars cannot give us that certainly which we claim when we lay down a general proposition like "*all* men are mortal." The proposition "all crows are black" is not so certain as the proposition "ail men are mortal." We find it less difficult to think of a crow which is not black, than to think of a man who is not mortal. Just as a cuckoo may be black or grey and spotted, so crows may be black or dark, grey or brown. We cannot, however, seriously and honestly think of ourselves as immortal, and regulate our practical activities accordingly. Why this difference in the sense of security or certainty? The answer that naturally suggests itself, and that not unreasonably, is that while there is nothing in the *nature* of a crow to prevent it from being grey or brown, there seems to be something in the *nature* of man that makes him mortal. We say that all crows are black, not because they cannot be otherwise, by because they *happen* to be so, as far as we have seen. On the other hand, we say that all man are mortal because they are men, *i.e.* because they possess some essential nature, manhood, which is related to mortality. This becomes clear when we say that "A,B,C are mortal, no because they are A, B, C, but because they are men." It follows from this that an inductive generalisation must be ultimately based on the knowledge of the essential nature of things, *i.e* the class-essence or the universal in them. Hence it is that the Naiyāyikas finally establish an induction by sāmānyalakṣaṇa perception.[18] They hold that a universal proposition like "all men are mortal," or "all smoky objects are fiery," must be due to the perception of the universal "manhood" as related to "mortality," or that of "smokeness" as related to "fireness." It is only when we perceive "manhood" as related to mortality, that we can say that *all* men are mortal, for to perceive "manhood" is to perceive all men so far as they are *man-as-such,* and not this or that man. So we may say that the essence of induction is not an *inference* of the form "some men are mortal, therefore all men are mortal." This is not a logically valid inference, because there is an obvious illicit distribution of the subject term *men.* On the other hand, induction is a process of generalisation from the particulars of experience through the knowledge of the class-essences or universals underlying such particulars.[19]

(d) The Classification of Inference

As we have seen before, inference is, in Indian logic, a combined deductive-inductive reasoning consisting of at least three categorical propositions. All inferences are thus pure syllogisms of the categorical type which are at once formally valid and materially true. Hence we have not hare a classification of inferences into deductive and inductive, immediate and mediate, syllogistic and non-syllogistic, pure and mixed type. The Naiyāyikas give us three different classification of inferences which we shall now consider.

Inference is svārtha of parārtha, according as it is meant for oneself or for others

According to the first classification, inference is of two kinds, namely, svārtha and parārtha. This is a psychological classification which has in view the use or purpose which an inference use or purpose which an inference serves. An inference may be intended either for the acquisition of some knowledge on our part or for the demonstration of a known truth to other persons. In the first case we have svārthānumāna or inference for oneself. In the second, we have parārthānumāna or inference meant for others. The first is illustrated by a man who first perceives a mass of smoke in the hill, then remembers that there is a universal relation between smoke and fire, and finally infers that there is fire in the hill. On the other hand, an inference it parārtha when in making it a man aims at proving or demonstrating the truth of the conclusion to other men, This is illustrated when a man, having inferred at known the existence of fire in a hill, tries to convince knowledge, and argues like this: "The hill must be fiery; because it smokes; and whatever is smoky is fiery, *e.g.* the kitchen; so also the hill is smoky; therefore it is fiery. [20]

It is pūrvavat or is savat, according as it passes from cause to effect, or from effect to cause

It is sāmānyatodṛṣṭa when based on certain observed points of general similairty be between objects of experience.

According to another classification, we have three kinds of inferences, namely, pūrvavat, śeṣavat and sāmānyatodṛṣṭa.[21] This classification has reference to the nature of the vyāpti or unviersal relation between the middle and major terms. While pūrvavat and śeṣavat inferences are based on causal uniformity, the last is based on non-causal uniformity. A cause is defined as the invariable and unconditional antecedent of an effect. Conversely, an effect is the invariable and unconditional consequent of a cause: Accordingly, a pūrvavat inference is that in which we infer the unperceived effect from a perceived cause, *e.g.* the inference of future rain from the appearance of dark heavy clouds in the sky. A śeṣavat inference is that in which we infer the unperceived cause from a perceived effect, *e.g.* the inference of past rain from the swift muddy current of the river. In these two kinds of inference, the vyāpti or universal relation between the middle and the major term is a uniform relation of causality between them. They are thus dependent on what is known as "scientific induction." In sāmānyatodṛṣṭa inference, however, the vyāpti or universal relation between the middle and the major term does not depend on a causal uniformity. The middle term is related to the major neither as a cause nor as an effect. We infer the one from the other, not because we know them to be causally connected, but because they are uniformly related in our experience. This is illustrated when, on seeing the different positions of the moon. It long intervals, we infer that it move-although the notion might not have been perceived by us. In the case of other things whenever we perceive change of position, we perceive motion also From this we infer motion in the moon, although the movement of the planet is not perceived. Similarly, we may infer the cloven hoof of an unknown animal simply by seeing its horns. The inferences depend not on a causal connection, but on certain observed points of general similarity between different objects of experience. Sāmānyatodṛṣṭa inference is thus similar to analogical argument.[23]

Inference is called kevalānvayi when based on a middle term which is always positively related to the major term

A third classification gives us the three kind of kevalānvayi, kevalavyatireki and anvayavyatireki inferences.[24] This classification is more logical, inasmuch as it is based on the nature of the induction by which we get the knowledge of vyāpti, on which inferences depend. An inference is called it is based on a middle term which is always positively related to the major term. Hence the knowledge of vyāpti between the middle and the major term is arrived at only through the method of agreement in presence (anvaya), since there is no negative instance of their agreement in absence. This is illustrated by the following inference:

All knowable objects are nameable;
The pot is a knowable object;
Therefore the pot is nameable.

In this inference the major premise is a universal affirmative proposition in which the predicate "nameable" is affirmed of all knowable objects. It is not really possible for us to deny the predicate with regard to the subject and say that here is a knowable object which is not nameable, because we have at least to speak of it as "unnameable." The minor premise and the conclusion of this inference are also universal affirmative propositions and cannot be otherwise. Hence, in its logical form, this inference is a syllogism of the first mood of the first figure, technically called Barbara.

It is kavalavyatireki when the middle term is only negatively related to the major

A kevalavyatireki inference is that in which the middle term is only negatively related to the major term. It depends on a vyāpti between the absence of the major term and that of the middle term. Accordingly, the knowledge of vyāpti is here arrived at only through the method of agreement in absence (vyatireka), since there is no positive instance of agreement in presence between the middle and the major term excepting the minor term. This is illustrated thus by the Naiyāyikas:

What is not-different-from-other-elements has no smell;
The earth has smell;
Therefore the earth is different-from-other-elements.[25]

In this inference the major premise is a universal negative proposition in which the predicate or the middle term "smell" is denied of the subject or the major term "what is not-different-from-other-elements." It is not possible for us to affirm the predicate "smell" of any other subject excepting the earth which is the minor term of the inference. Hence the only way in which we can relate the middle to the major is the negative way of saying that "what is not different from the other elements has no smell." Hence the major premise is a universal negative proposition arrived at only through the method of agreement in absence between the major and the middle term. The minor premise is an affirmative proposition. But although one of the premises is negative, the conclusion is affirmative, which is against the general canons of the syllogism in Formal Logic. Hence we are to say that this inference is not any of the valid moods of syllogism recognized by Formal Logic, nor should we forcibly convert the conclusion into a negative proposition. But the validity of such inferences has been admitted by Bradley as a special case of negative reasoning.[26]

It is anvayavyatireki when the middle term is both positively and negatively related to the major term

An inference is called anvayavyatireki when its middle term is both positively and negatively related to the major term. In it there is a vyāpti or universal relation between the middle and the major term in respect of both their presence and absence. So the knowledge of the vyāpti or the universal proposition is based on the Joint method of agreement in presence (anvaya) and. in absence (vyatireka). The universal proposition is affirmative when it is the result of the observation of positive instances of agreement in presence, and negative when based on the observation of negative instances of agreement in absence, between the middle and the major term. The difference between the universal affirmative and negative propositions (anvaya and vyatireka vyāpti) is that the subject of the affirmative proposition becomes predicate and the contradictory of the preoducate becomes subject in the corresponding be based on both universal affirmative and universal negative propositions. it is illustrated in the following pair of inferences:

(1) All smoky objects are fiery;
The hill is smoky;
Therefore the hill is fiery.
(2) No non-fiery object is smoky;
The hill is smoky;
Therefore the hill is fiery.

(e) The Fallacies of Inference[27]

Fallacies in Indian logic are all material fallacies

The fallacies of inference (hetvābhāsa) in Indian logic are all material fallacies. So far as the logical form of inference is concerned, it is the same all inferences. There is strictly speaking, no fallacious form of inference in logic, since all inferences must be put in one or other of the valid forms. Hence if there is any fallacy of inference, that must be due to the material conditions on which the truth of the constituent premises depends. It may be observed here that in the Aristotelian classification of fallacies into those in *dictione* and those *extra dictionem* there is no mention of the formal fallacies of inference like the undistributed middle, the illicit process of the major or minor, term, and so forth. The reason for this, as Eaton[28] rightly points out, is that "to one trained in the arts of syllogistic reasoning, they cannot sufficiently persuasive to find a place even among sham arguments." As for Aristotle's fallacies *in dictione, i.e.* those that occur through the ambiguous use of words, they are all included by the Naiyāyika among the fallacies of *chala, jāti* and *nigrahasthdna* with their numerous subdivisions.

In Indian logic, a fallacy is technically called *hetvābhāsa,* a word which literally means a hetu or reason which *appears* as, but really is not, a valid reason. The fallacies of inference being ultimately due to such fallacious reasons, the Naiyāyikas consider these only, and not such other fallacies as may infect the constituent propositions of the syllogism. According to the Naiyāyikas, there are five kinds of fallacies. These are (1) Savybhicāra, (2) Viruddha, (3) Satpratipakṣa, (4) Asiddha, (5) Badhita.[29]

The first is called savyabhicāra or the irregular middle

The first kind of fallacy is called savyabhicāra or the irregular middle. To illustrate:

All bipeds are rational;
Swan are bipeds;
Therefore swans are rational.

The conclusion of this inference is false. But why? Because the middle term 'biped' is not uniformly related to the major 'rational.' It is related to both rational and non-rational creatures. Such a middle term is called savyabhicāra or the irregular middle.

The Savyabhicara hetu or the irregular middle is found to lead to no one single conclusion, but to different opposite conclusions. This fallacy occurs when the ostensible middle term violates the general rule of inference, namely, that it must be universally related to the major term, or that the major term must be present in all cases in which the middle is present. The savyabhicāra middle, however, it not uniformly concomitant with the major term. It is related to both the existence and the non-existence of the major term, and is, therefore, also called *anaikāntika or* an inconstant concomitant of the major term. Hence from such a middle term we can infer both the existence and the non-existence of the major term. To take another illustration:

All knowable objects are fiery;

The hill is knowable;
Therefore the hill is fiery.

Here the middle 'knowable' is indifferently related to both fiery objects like the kitchen, and fireless objects like the lake. All knowables being thus not fiery, we cannot argue that a hill is fiery because it is knowable. Rather, it is as much true to say that, for the same reason, the hill is fireless.

The second is virudha or the contradictory midddle

The second kind of fallacy is called viruddha or the contradictory middle. Take this inference the middle term empty is contradictory because it disproves the heaviness of air. Thus the viruddha or the contradictory middle is one which disproves the very proposition which it is meant to prove. This happens when the ostensible middle term, instead of proving the existence of the major in the minor, which is intended by it, proves its non-existence therein. Thus, to take the Naiyāyikas' illustration, if one argues, "Sound is eternal, because it is caused," we have a fallacy of the viruddha or contradictory middle. The middle term, 'caused' does not prove the eternality of sound, but its non-eternality, because whatever is caused is non-eternal. The distinction between the savyabhicara and the viruddha is that while the former only fails to prove the conclusion, the latter disproves it or proves the contradictory proposition.

The third is satpratipakṣa or the inferentially contradicted middle

The third kind of fallacy is called Satpratipakṣa or the inferetinally contradicted middle. This fallacy arises when the ostensible middle term of an inference is validly contradicted by some other middle term which proves the non-existence of the major term of the first inference. Thus the inference "sound is eternal, because it is audible" is validly contradicted by another inference like this: "sound is *non*- eternal, because it is produced like a pot." Here the non-exiatence 'of *eternality* (which is the major term of the first inference) is proved by the second inference with its middle term 'produced,'as against the first inference with its middle 'audible.' The distinction between the viruddha and the Satpratipakṣa is that, while in the former the middle *itself* proves the contradictory of its conclusion, in the latter the contradictory of the conclusion of one middle term is proved by *another* middle term.

The fourth is asiddha or the unproved middle.

The fourth kind of fallacy is called asiddha or sādhya-sama, *i.e.* the unproved middle. The sādhyasama middle is one which is not yet *proved*, but requires *to be proved,* like the sādhya or the major term. This means that the sādhyasama middle is not a proved or an established fact, but an *asiddha* or unproved assumption. The fallacy of the asiddha occurs when the middle term is wrongly assumed in any of the premises, and so cannot be taken to prove the truth of the conclusion. Thus when one argues, "the sky-lotus is fragrant, because it has *lotusness* in it like a natural lotus," the middle has uo *locus slandi,* since the sky-lotus is nonexistent, and is, therefore, asiddha or a merely assumed but not proved fact.

The fifth is called bādhita or the non inferentially contradicted middle

The last kind of fallacy is called bādhita or the non- inferentialy contradicted middle. It is the ostensible middle term of an inference, the non-existence of whose major is ascertained by means of some other pramāṇa or source of knowledge. This is illustrated by the argument: "Fire is *cold,* because it is a substance." Here 'coldness' is the sādhya or major term, and 'substance' is the middle term. Now the non-existence of coldness, nay more, the existence of hotness is perceived in fire by our sense of touch. So we are to reject the middle 'substance' as a contradicted middle. The fallacy of satpratipakṣa, as explained before, is different from this fallacy of bādhita, because in the former one inference is contradicted by another inference, while in the latter an inference is contradicted by perception ur some other *non-inferential* source of knowledge. Another example of bādhita would be: Sugar is sour, because it produces acidity.

4. Upamāna or Comparison

Upamāna is the process of naming objects through a given description

Upamāna is the third source of valid knowledge accepted by the Nyāya. It is the source of our knowledge of the relation between a name and things so named or between a word and its denotation (sañjñasañjñisaṁbandha). We have such knowledge when we are told by some authoritative person that a word denotes a class of objects of a certain description and then, on the basis of the given description, apply the word to some object or objects which fit in with that description, although we might not have seen them before. For example, a man, who does not know what a gavaya[30] or wild cow is, may be told by a forester that it is an animal like the cow. If subsequently be happens to meet with such an animal in the forest and knows or recognises it *as a gavaya,* then his knowledge will be due to upamāna, or comparison.[31] A boy, who does not know what a jackdaw is, may be told by you that it is like a crow, but of bigger fize and glazy black colour. When next he sees a jackdaw and says, 'this must be a jackdaw,' we know that he has learnt the denotation of the word. To take another example from Dr. L. S. Stebbing, [32] suppose you do not know what "saxophone" means. You may be told by a musician: "A saxophone is a musical instrument something like a U-shaped trumpet." If, on subsequently seeing a saxophone, you are able to give its name, it will be clear that yon understand what "saxophone" means. Now, upamāna is just this way of knowing the denotation of words, or the relation between names and the objects denoted by them.

Other systems on the nature of upamāna

That upamāna or comparison, as explained by the Naiyāyikas, is a distinct source of valid knowledge, has not been recognised in the other systems of Indian philosophy. The Cārvākas.[33] contend that upamāna is not a pramāṇa at all, since it cannot give us any true knowledge about the denotation of words as maintained by the Naiyāyikas. The Buddhist logicians recognise upamāna as a from of valid knowledge,but they reduce it to perception and testimony, so that we do not require a separate source of knowledge like upamāna.[34] So also, the Vaiśeṣika[35] and the Sāṅkhya[36] system explain upamāna as a from of inference, and, therefore, neither a distinct type of knowledge nor an independent way of knowing. The jainas[37] reduce upamāna to pratyabhijñā or recognition. While recognisting upamāna as a separate source of knowledge, the Mīmāṁsākas[38] and the Vedāntins[39] explain it in a different way which will be considered under the Mīmāṁsā.[40].

5. Śabda or Testimoney

śabda consists inunderstanding the meaning of the statement of a trust worthy person.

(*a*) *The Nature and Classification of śabda*

śabda is the last pramāṇa accepted by the Nyāya. Literally śabda means verbal knowledge. It is the knowledge of objects derived from words or sentences. All verbal knowledge, however, is not valid. Hence śabda, as a pramāṇa, is defined in the Nyāya as valid verbal testimony. It consists in the assertion of a trustworthy person[41] A verbal statement is valid when it comes from a person who knows the truth and speaks the turth about anything for the guidance of other persons.[42] Bu‹ it is a matter of common observation that a sentence or statement is not by itself sufficient to give us any knowledge of things. Nor again does the mere perception of the words of a sentence lead to any knowledge about objects. It is only when one perceives the words and *understands* their meanings that he acquires any knowledge from a verbal statement. Hence while the validity of verbal knowledge depends on its being based on the statement of a trust. worthy person, its possibility depends on the understanding of the meaning of that statement. Hence śabda or testimony, as a source of valid knowledge, consists in understanding the meaning of the statement of a trustworthy person.[43]

There are two ways of classifying śabda, which give us (a) dṛṣṭārth and adṛṣṭārth;

There are two ways of classifying śabda or verbal knowledge. According to the one, there are two kinds of śabda, namely, that relating to perceptible objects (adṛṣṭārth), and that relating to imperceptible objects (adṛṣṭārth).[44] Under the the first head we are to include the trustworthy assertions of ordinary persons, the saints and the scriptures in so far as they bear on the perceptible objects of the world, *e.g.* the evidence given by witnesses in law courts, the statements of a reliable farmer about plants, the scriptural injunctions to perform certain rites to bring about rainfall, etc. The second will include all the trustworthy assertions of ordinary persons, saints, prophets and the scriptures in far as they bear on supersensible realities, *e g.* the scientists' assertions about atoms, ether, electrons, vitamins, etc., the prophets' instructions about virtue and vice, the scriptural texts on God, freedom and immortality.

laukika and vaidika śabda

According to another classification, there are two kinds of testimony, the scriptural (vaidika) and the secular (laukika).[45] In vaidika testimony we have the words of God. Vaidika or scriptural testimony is thus perfect and infallible by its very nature. But laukika or secular testimony is not all valid. It is the testimony of human beings and may, therefore, be true or false. Of lukika testimony, only that which proceed from trustworthy persons is valid, but not the rest. It will he observed here that the first classification of testimony (śabda) has reference to the nature of the objects of knowledge, the second to the nature of the source of knowledge. But the two classifications, given bv different Naiyāyikas, agree in implying that testimony must always be personal, *i.e.* based on the words of some trust worthy person, human or divine. In respect of their truth, however, there is no difference among the trustworthy statements of an ordinary person, a saint, a prophet, and the scriptures as revealed by God.[46]

(b) The Logical Structure of a Sentence

A sentence is a group of words arranged in a certain way.

śabda or testimony, we have seen, gives us knowledge about certain things through the understanding of the meaning of sentence, either spoken or written by some authoritative person. Hence the question is: What is a sentence and how does it become arranged in a certain way. A word, again, is a group of letters arranged in a fixed order.[47] The essential nature of a word lies in its meaning. A word is that which has a fixed relation to some object, so as to recall it whenever it is beard or read, *i.e.* it *means* an object. So we may say that words are significant symbols. This capacity of words to mean theif respective objects is called their *śakti* or potency, and it is said to be due to the will of God. That a word has a fixed and an unalterable relation to certain things only, or that this word always means this object and not others, is ultimately due to the Supreme Being who is the ground and reason of all the order and uniformity that we find in the world.

The four conditions of an intelligible sentence

A sentence (vākya) is a combination of words having a certain meaning. Any combination of words, however, does not make a significant sentence.The construction of an intelligible sentence must conform to four conditions. These are ākāṅkṣā, yogyatā, sannidhi and tātparya.[49]

Akāṇkṣā or the mutual need of the words of a sentence for expressing a complete sense

By ākāṅkṣā or *expectancy* is meant that quality of the words of a sentence by which they expect or imply one another. Gene rally speaking, a word cannot by itself convey a complete meaning. It must be brought into relation with other words in order to express a full judgent. When one hears the word 'bring,' he at once asks:, 'what?' The verb 'bring' has a need for some other words denoting some object or objects, *e.g.* 'the jar.' Ākāṅkṣā is this mutual need that the words of a sentence have for one another in order to express a complete sense.

Yogyatā or the mutual fitness of the words

The second condition of the combination of words in a sentence is their yogyatā or *mutual fitness.* It consists in the absence of contradiction in the relation of objects denoted by a sentence. When the meaning of a sentence is not contradicted, there is yogyatā or fitness between its constituent words. The sentence 'moisten with fire' is faulty of unfitness, because there is a contradiction between 'fire' and 'moistening.'

Sannidhi or the proximity between the words of a sentence

Sannidhi or āsatti is the third condition of verbal knowledge. It consists in the juxtaposition or proximity between the different words of a sentence. If there is to be an intelligible sentence, then its constituent words must be continuous with one another in time or space. Spoken words cannot make a sentence when separated by long intervals of time. Similarly, written words cannot construct a sentence when they are separated by long intervals of space. Thus the words 'bring—a—cow' will not make a sentence when uttered three days or written on three pages, even though they possess the first two marks of ākāṅkṣā or expectancy and yogyatā or fitness.

Tātparya or the meaning intended tobe conveyed by a sentence

Tātparya as a condition of verbal knowledge stands for the meaning *intended* to be conveyed by a sentence. A word may means differnt things indifferent cases. Whether it means this or that thing in particular case depend on the intention of the person who uses the word. To understand the meaning of a sentence, therefore, we must consider the intention of the writer or the speaker who uses it. Thus when a man is asked to bring a 'bat,' he is at a loss to understand whether be is told to bring a particular kind as animal or a wooden implement, for the word means both. This can be ascertained only if we know the intention of the speaker. Hence the understanding of a sentence depends on the understanding of its tātparya or intended meaning. In the case of ordinary sentences used by human beings, we can ascertain their tātparya from the context (prakarana) in which they are used. For the under standing of the Vedic texts we are to take the help of the logical rules of interpretation systematised by the Mīmāṁsā.

III. The Nyāya Theory of the Physical World[50]

Premeya is the world of objects of knowledge.

So far we have considered the Nyāya doctrine of pramāṇa or the meth-ods of knowledge. Now we come to the second topic of *prameya* or the objects of knowledge. According to the Naiyāyikas, the objects of knowl-edge are the self, the body, the senses and their objects, knowledge, mind (manas), pravṛtti activity, doṣa or the mental imperfections, pretybhāva or rebirth, phala or the feelings of pleasure and pain, duḥkha or suffering, apavarga or absolute freedom from suffering. There are also such objects as dravya or substance, guṇa or quality, karma or motion, sāmānya or the universal, viśeṣa or particularity, samavāya or the relation of inherence, and abhāva or non-existence.

Of these, the physical elements—time, space and ākāśa—consti-tute the physical world.

All of these prameyas or knowables are not to be found in the physical world, be found inthe physical world, because it includes only those ob-jects that are either physical (bhūta) or somehow belong to the world of physical nature. Thus the self, its attribute of knowledge and manas are not at all physical. Time and space are two substances which, although differ-ent from the physical substances, yet somehow belong to the the physical world. Ākāśa is a physical substance which is not a productive cause of anything. The physical world is constituted by the four physical substances of earth, water, fire and air. The ultimate constituents of these four sub-stances are the eternal and unchanging atoms of earth, water, fire and air.

Ākāśa or ether, kāla or time, and dik or space are eternal and infinite substances, each being one single whole. Thus the physical world is the product of the four kinds of atoms of earth, water, fire and air. It contains all the composite products of these atoms, and their qualities and relations, including organic bodies, the senses, and the sensible qualities of things. To it belong also the physical substance of ākāśa or ether, and the nonphysical substances of kāla or time and dik or space with all their various relations and apparent modification tions. The Nyāya theory of the physical world, in respect of these and other connected subjects, is the same as that of the Vaiśeṣika. The Vaiśeṣika theory, which is a more detailed account of the subject, it accepted by the Nyāya as *samānatantra* or an allied theory common to the Nyāya and the Vaiśeṣika system. So we propose to take up this subject when we come to the Vaiśeṣika philosophy.

IV. The Individual Self and its Liberation

Different conceptions of the self: materialistic, empiricist and idealistic.

The Nyāya is a philosophy of life and seeks to guide individual selves in their search for truth and freedom. With regard to the individual self (jīvātmā) we have to consider first its nature and attributes. There are four main views of the self in Indian philosophy. According to the Cārvākas, the self is the living body with the attribute of consciousness. This is the materialistic conception of the self. The Bauddhas reduce the self to a stream of thought or a series of cognitions. Like some empiricists and sensationists, they admit only the empirical self. The Advaita Vedānta takes the self as one, unchanging and self-shining intelligence (svaprakāśa caitanya) which is neither a subject nor an object, neither the 'I 'nor the 'me.' The Viśiṣṭādvaita Vedānta, however, holds that the self is not pure intelligence as such, but an intelligent subject called the ego or the 'I' (jñātā ahamartha evātmā). Both 'these views of the self may be called idealistic in a broad sense.

The realistic view of the self in the Nyāya-Vaiśeṣika system.

The Nyāya-Vaiśeṣikas adopt the realistic view of the self. According to them, the self is a unique substance to which all cognitions, feeling and conations belong as its attributes. Desire, aversion and volition, pleasure, pain and cognition are all qualities of the soul. These cannot belong to the physical substances, since they are not physical qualities perceived by the external senses. Hence we must admit that they are the peculiar properties of some substance other than and different from all physical substances. There are different selves in different bodies, because their experiences do not overlap but are kept distinct. The self is indestructible and eternal. It is infinite or ubiquitous (vibbu), since it is not limited by time and space.[51]

The self is distinct from the body, senses, manas and the setram of consciousness.

The body or the senses cannot be the self because consciousness cannot be the attribute of the mateial body or the senses. the body is, by itself, unconscious and unintelligent. The senses cannot explain functions like imagination, memory, ideation, etc., which are independent of the external senses. The manas too cannot take the place of the self. If the manas be, as the Nyāya-Vaiśeṣikas hold, an atomic and, therefore, imperceptible substance the qualities of pleasure, pain, etc., which should belong to the inanas, must be equally imperceptible. But pleasure and pain are experience ed or perceived by us. Nor can the self be identified with the series of cognitions as in Bauddba philosophy, for than memory becomes inexplicable. No member of a men, series of cognitions can, like a bead of the rosary, know what has preceded it or what will succeed it. The Advaita Vedāntin's idea of the self as eternal self shining intelligence is no more acceptable to the Naiyāyika than that of the Buddhists. There is no such thing as pure intelligence unrelated to some subject and object. Intelligence cannot subsist without certain locus. Hence the self is not intelligence as such, but a substance having intelligence as it attribute. The self is not mere consciousness or knowledge, but aknower, an ego or the 'I' (ahaṅkārāśraya), and also an enjoyer (bhoktā).[52]

Conscioness is not an essential attribute of the soul-substance.

Although knowledge or consciousness belongs to the self an attribute, yet it is not an essential and inseparable attribute of it. All cognitions or conscious states arise in the self when it is related to the manas, and the manas is related to the senses, and senses come in contact with the external objects. Otherwise, there will be no consciousness in the self. In its disembodied condition, therefore, the self will have no knowledge or consciousness. Thus the attributes of cognition, feeling and conation—in a word, conscious ness—is an accidental attribute of the self, the accident being its relation to the body.[53]

Proofs for the existence of the self.

How do we know that there is any self of the individual, which is distinct from his body, his senses and hsi mind? Some old Naiyāyikas[54] seem to thing that there cannot be a perception or direct cognition of the self. According to them, the self is known either from the testimony of spiritual authorities or by inference from the functions of desire, aversion and volition, the feelings of pleasure and pain, and the phenomenon of knowledge in us. That we have desire, aversion, etc., nobody can doubt. But these cannot be explained unless we admit permanent self. To desire an object is to strive to obtain it as something pleasurable. But before we obtain it, we cannot get any pleasure out of it. So in desiring the object we only judge it to be similar to such objects as were found to be pleasurable in the past. This means that desire supposes some permanent self which had experienced pleasure in relation to certain objects in the past and which considers a present object to be similar to any of those past objects, and so strives to get possession of it. Similarly, aversion and volition cannot be explained without a permanent self. The feelings of pleasure or pain also arise in an individual when he gets something considered to be the means of attaining a remembered pleasure, or gets into something which had previously led to a painful experience. So too knowledge as a process of reflective thinking requires a permanent self which first desires to know something, then reflects on it, and finally attains certain knowledge about it. All these phenomena of desire, etc., cannot be explained either by the body or the senses or the mind as a series of cognitions or a stream of consciousness. Just as the experience of one man cannot be remembered by another man, so the body or the senses which are really sense of different physiological states and stages, and the mind or the empirical self, which is admittedly an aggregate of different momentary psychical status and processes, cannot explain the phenomena of desire aversion and volition, pleasure, pain and cognition.[55]

Direct experience of the self in internal perception.

The later Naiyāyikas go a step further and maintain that the self is directly known through internal or mental perception (mānasapratyakṣa). Of course, when its existence is denied or doubted by any one, the self must be inferred and proved in the way explained above. The mental perception of the self may take either of two forms. It may be a perception in the form of pure self-consciousness, which is due to a contact between the mind and the pure self, and is expressed in the judgment 'I am.' According to some Naiyāyikas, however, the pure self cannot be an object of perception.The self is perceived only through some such quality of it in cognition, feeling or willing, and so the perceptual judgment is in the form, I am knowing,' 'I am happy,' and so forth. We do not perceive the self as such, but as knowing or feeling or doing something. Hence self-consciousness is a mentel perception of the self as present in some mode of consciousness. While one's own self can be perceived, other selves in other bodies can only be inferred from their intelligent bodily actions, since these cannot be explained by the unintelligent body and require a conscious self far their performance. [56]

Liberation is freedom from all pain and suffering.

In it the self ceases to have any experience painful or pleasurable, and exists as a pure substance devoid of consciousness.

The end of almost all the systems of Indian philosophy in the attainment of mukti to liberation for the individual self. This is especially true of the Nyāya system which proposes, at the very outset, to give us a knowledge of reality or realities for the realization of the highest good or the *summum bonum* of our life. The different systems, however, give us different descriptions of this consummate state of the soul's existence. For the Naiyāyikas it is a state of negation, complete and absolute, of all pain and suffering. Apavarga or liberation is absolute freedom from pain. This implies that it is a state in which the soul is released from all the bonds of its connection with the body and the senses. So long as the soul is conjoined with a body, it is impossible for it to attain the state of utter freedom from pain. The body with the sense organs being there, we cannot possibly prevent their contact with undesirable and unpleasant objects, and so must submit to the inevitable experience of painful feelings. Hence in liberation, the soul must be free from the shackles of the body and the senses. But when thus severed from the body, the soul ceases to have not only painful but also pleasurable experiences, nay more, it ceases to have any experience or consciousness. So in liberation the self exits as a pure substance free from all connection with the body, neither suffering pain, nor enjoying pleasure, nor having consciousness even. Liberation the negation of pain, not in the sense of a suspension of it for a longer or shorter period of time, as in a good sleep or a state of recovery from some disease or that of relief from some bodily or mental affliction. It is absolute freedom from pain for all time to come. It is just that supreme condition of the soul which has been variously described in the scriptures as 'freedom from fear '(abhayam), 'freedom from decog and change '(ajaram), 'freedom from death' (amṛtyupadam),' and so forth.

The way to the attainment of liberation.

To attain liberation one must first listen to the scriptural instructions about the self (śravaṇa). Then, he should firmly establish the knowledge of the self by means of reasoning (manana). Finally, he must meditate on the self in conformity with the principles of yoga (nididhyāsana). These help him to realize the true nature of the self as distinct from the body. With this realization, the wrong knowledge that 'I am the body and the mind' is destroyed, and one ceases to be moved to action by passions and impulses. When a man becomes thus free from desires and impulses, be ceases to be affected by the effects of his present actions, done with no desire for fruits.

His past karmas or deeds being exhausted by producing their effects, the individual has to undergo no more birth in this world. The cessation of birth means the end of its connection with the body and consequently, of all pain and suffering; and that is liberation.[58]

V. The Nyāya Theology

Reference to God in the Nyāya and Vaiśeṣika sūtras.

It is by no means true to say that the Nyāya and the Vaiśeṣkika sūtra make no mention of God. [59] We do find short reference to the Divine Being in both the sūtras.[60] The later Naiyāyikas give us an elaborate theory of God and connect it with the doctrine of liberation. According to these Naiyāyikas, the individual self can attain true knowledge of realities and, through it, the state of liberation only by the grace of God. Without God's grace neither the true knowledge of the categories of philosophy nor the highest end of liberation is attainable by any individual being of the world. So the questions that arise are: What is God? How do we know that God exists?

(a) The Idea of God

God is the eternal infinite self who creates, maintains and destroys the world.

God is the ultimate cause of the creation, maintenance and destruction of the world. He does not create the world out of nothing, but out of eternal atoms, space, time, ether, minds (manas) and aouls. The creation of the world means the ordering of the eternal entities, which are coexistent with God, into a moral world, in which individual selves enjoy and suffer according to the merit and demerit of their actions, and all physical objects serve as means to the moral and spiritual ends of our life. God is thus the creator of the world in the sense of being the first efficient cause of the world and not its material cause *i.e.* a sort of demiurgus or a builder of the ordered universe. He is also the preserver of the world in so far as the world is kept in existence by the will of God. So also He is the destroyer who lets loose the forces destruction when the exigencies of the moral world it require it. Then, God is one, infinite and eternal, since the world of space and time, minds and souls does not limit Him, but is related to Him as a body to the self which resides in it, He is omnipotent; although He is guided in His activities by moral considerations of the merit and demerit of human actions. He is omniscient in so far as He possesses right knowledge of all thing and events, He has eternal intelligence as a power of direct and steadfast cognition of objects. Eternal intelligence is only an inseparable *attribute* of God, and *not* His very *essence* as maintained in the Advaita Vedānta. He possesses to the full all the six perfections (saḍaiśvaryya) and majestic almighty, all-glorious, infinitely beautiful, and possessed of infinite knowledge and perfect freedom from attachment.[61]

He is also the moral governor of all living beings including ourselves.

Just as God is the efficient cause of the world, so He directive cause of the action of all living beings. No creature, not even man, is absolutely free in his actions. He is relatively free, *i.e.* his actions are done by him under the direction and guidance of the Divine Being. Just as a wise and benevolent father directs his son to do certain things, according to his gifts, capacities and previous attainments, so God directs all living beings to do such actions and feel such natural consequences thereof as are consistent with their past conduct and character. While man is the efficient instrumental cause of his actions God is their efficient directive cause (prayojaka kartā). Thus God is the moral governor of the world of living beings including ourselves, the impartial dispenser of the fruits of our actions (karmaphaladātā), and the supreme arbiter of our joys and sorrows.[62]

2. Proofs for the Existence of God

Now the more important question which naturally arises here is this: What are the proofs for the existence of God? The Nyāya-Vaiśeṣikas have to their credit an array of proofs which include almost all the arguments given in Western philosophy for God's existence. There are as many as ten proof, of which the more imporant be considered here.

(i) The Causal Argument

All composite and limited objects of the world, must have an intelligent maker who is omnipotent and omniscient, and that maker is God.

All composite objects of the world, formed by the combination of atoms (*e.g.* mountains, seas etc.) must have a cause, because they are of the nature of effects, like a pot. That all such objects of the world are effects follows first from their being made up of parts (sāvayava) and, secondly, from their possessing an intermediate magnitude (avāntaramahattva). Space, time, ether and self are not effects, because these are infinite substances, not made up of parts. Atoms of earth, water, light and air, and the mind are not the effects of and cause, because they are simple, indivisible and infinitesimal substances. All other composite objects of the world, like mountains and seas, the sun and the moon, the stars and the planets, must be the effect of some cause, since they are both made up of part sand possess medium dimensions. These object are what they are because of the concurrence of a number of material causes. Therefore, there must be an intelligent cause (kartā), for all these effect Wihtout the guidance of an intelligent cause the material causes these things cannot attain just that order, direction and co-ordination which enable then to produce these definite effects. This intelligent cause must have a direct knowledge of the material cause (the atoms) is means, a desire to attain some end, are the power of will to accomplish or realize the and (jñāna-cikirṣā-kṛti). He must also be omniscient (sarvajña) since only in omniscient being can have direct knowledge of such absolutely simple that infinitely small entities as atoms and the like. That is, He must be God and none but God.[63]

A comparison of the Naiyāyika's causal arguemnt with that of Western theologians.

The first argument of the Naiyāyikas, it will be observed, resembles the causal argument for God's exdistence as explained by some Western thinkers like paul junet,[64] Hermann Lotze[65] and James Martineau.[66] According to them, the world of finite objects requires are intelligent cause which gives order and co-ordination to their concurrent physical causes. Thus Janet lays it down as a principle that all co-ordination between divergent phenomena implies a final cause or an intelligent agent who effects the complex combination of such separate phenomena. So also, both Lotze and Martineau start from the fact of physical causation in the world and the up to the conception of an intelligent principle as its ultimate ground and reason. Indeed, the Naiyāyika view of cause as an intelligent agent strikingly anticipates Maitineau's idea of cause as will directed to the realization of ends. There is, however, some difference between these theists andthe Naiyāyikas. Western theists generally belive that God is not only the casue of the *order* and unity of things in the world, but also the creative energy that gives *existence* to the things of Nature For the Naiyāyikas, however, God is only the cause of the *order* of Nature, and not of the existence of the ultimate constituents of it.

(ii) The Argument from Adṛṣṭa

The differnces in our lot require an explanation which must be given in terms of our good or bad deed.

The second argument of theNaiyāyikas is this. The question here is: How are we to account for the differences in our lot here on earth? Some people are happy and some miserable, some wise and some ignorant. What may be the cause of all these variation in our worldly life? We cannot that they have no causes, because these are so many events in our life, and every event must have its cause. Now the causes which produce our joys and sorrows in this life are our on actions in this or some previous life. We enjoy or suffer in this life because of our good or bad actions. The law that governs the lives of individual souls in the moral law of karma which requires that every individual being must reap the fruits of its own actions, good or bad right or wrong. There is nothing strange or improbable in this. It follows logically from the law of universal causation, which means that every cause must produce its effect and every effect must be produced by its cause. That our moral actions are as good causes as our physical actions must be admitted by every one who believes in the law of causation and extends it to the moral world. Just as bodily acts produce bodily changes, and mental functions produce mental changes and dispositions, so morally good or bad actions lead to good or bad moral consequences, such as rewards or punishment, happiness or misery. Hence it is established that our joys and sorrows are due to our own actions[67].

Adṛṣṭa is the stock of merit and demerit accruing from our good and bad actions. So our lot is determined by our own actions.

But the next questions is: How do our moral actions produce their consequences which may be separated from them by long intervals of time? Many of our joy, and sorrows cannot be traced to any work done by us in this life. Even those that are due to acts done in this life, do not arise out of them immediately but after some time. A sinner in the heyday of youth may be a sufferer in the infirmity of old age. So it is maintained this. our good actions produce a certain efficiency called merit (puṇya), and bad actions produce some deficiency called demerit (pāpa) in our souls, and these persist long after our actions have ceased and disappeared. This stock of merit and demerit accruing from; good and bad actions is called adṛṣṭa. There it nothing more mysterious in the concept of adıṣṭa than in those of virtue and vice. Just as good actions have a purifying, so bad actions have a corrupting effect on our minds. And just as virtue conduces to a sense of security serenity end peace (in a word, happiness), so vice plunges the and into the ruffled waters of suspicion, distraction and uneasiness (in a word, unhappiness). In the same way, adṛṣṭa, as the sum total of merit and demerit accruing from our past actions, produces our present joys and sorrows.

But adṛṣṭa being and unintelligent principle requires to be guided by a supremely wide person, namely, God.

But how is it that adṛṣṭa manages to produce the proper consequences? It is an unintelligent principle which cannot by itself lead to just that kind and degree of joy and sorrow which are due to our past actions. So it is argued that adṛṣṭa must be guided by some intelligent agent to produce its proper consequences. Individual selves cannot be said to direct or control adṛṣṭa, for they do not know anything about their adṛṣṭa, and further, it is not infrequently that adṛṣṭa defies the control of their will. So the intelligent agent, who guides adṛṣṭa through the proper channels to produce the proper effects, is the eternal, omnipotent and omniscient Divine Being. It is God who controls our adṛṣṭa, and dispenses all the joys and sorrows of our life, in strict accordance with it. Or, as Kant would say, it is God who combines happiness with virtue and misery with vice. God gives us the fruits of our actions in the shape of enjoyments or afflictions in a way similar to that in which a wise and potent monarch rewards or punishes his subjects according to the merit or guilt attaching to their good or bad actions.[68]

(iii) ***the Argument from the Authoritativeness of the Scriptures***

The scriptures (Vedas) are valid and authoritative texts. This is due to the supreme authority of their author who must be omniscient, and so other than God.

Another argument for God's existence is based on the, authoritative character of the Vedas. The authority of the scriptures is accepted as unquestionable and infallible in all religions. Now the question, we are to consider here, is this: What is the source of the authority of the Vedas? According to the Naiyāyikas, the authority (prāmāya) of the Vedas has its, source in "the supreme authority of their" author (āptaprāmāṇya). Just as the authoritativeness of the medical science, or for the matter of that, of all sciences, is derived from the scientists who founded them, so the authoritativeness of the Vedas is derived from some person who imparted that character to them. The validity of the Vedas may be tested like that of any science, by following their injunctions about wordly objects and seeing how they produce the desired results. Of course, the truth of other Vedic tests bearing on supersensible objects cannot, like some scientific truths, be tested in this way. Still, we may accept the whole of the Vedas as valid and authoritative, in the same way in which we accept the whole of a science as true when, as a matter of fact, we can verify only some parts of it. So we must explain the authority of the Vedas by referring them to some authoritative person. Now the individual self (jīva) cannot be the author of the Vedas, since the supramundane realities and the transcendent principles related in the Vedas cannot be objects of the knowledge of any ordinary individual. Hence the author of the Vedas must be the supreme person who has a direct knowledge of all objects, past, present and future, finite, infinite and infinitesimal, sensible and supersensible. That is the Vedas, like other scriptures, are revealed by God.[69]

(iv) The Testimony of śruti

The śruti bears testimony to the existence of God.

Another proof of God's existence is this: God exits because the Vedic scripture (śruti) bears testimony to His existence. Here are some of the scriptural texts: "The highest eternal self is the Lord of all, the ruler of all, the protector of all...." "The great unborn spirit is the receiver of all offerings and the giver of ail gifts,"[70] The one God lies hidden in all, is all-pervading, is the inmost self of all and the controller and' sustainer of all.[71] "He is the ruler of all selves and the creator of the world."[72] In the *Bhagavadgītā* also, the Lord says: "I am the Father and the Mother of this world, its Foster-parent, and its eternal and immutable God." "I am the highest end of all the maintainer of all, the controller of all, the witness of all the above of all, the shelter of all, the friend of all, the creator of all the destroyer of all, the substratum of all, and the unchanging ground of the origin and destruction of all."[73]

But why should one accept the testimony of the scripture on this point?

An examination of the so-called proofs for God's existence shows that God cannot be proved in any way, for all proofs presuppose the reality of God as spirit.

It will appear from the above that the (śruti) or the scripture bears unmistakable testimony to the existence of God. But the question that may agītāte the mind of the reader, is: Why should one belive in God simply on the authority of the scriptures? A religious man may be inclined to do so, because he has not the spirit of critical enquiry in him. But a critical philosopher may say that scriptural testimony has no importance for philosophy, which is satisfied with nothing short of logically valid arguments in the attainment of true knowledge about anything, human or divine. So long as these are not forthcoming, the appeal to authority is of no avail. It may also be thought that such logical support for the belief in God is afforded by the traditional proofs of God's existence. But as Immanuel Kant [74] and after him, Hermann Lotze[75] have clearly shown, none of the so-called proofs can really prove the existence of God. To prove anything is to deduce it as a necessary conclsion from certain given premises. But God being the highest of all premises, *i.e.* the ultimate reality, there cannot be any anterior premise or premises from which we can deduce God as a conclusion. The ontological proof starts from the idea of the most perfect being and infers its existence on the ground that without existence it would not be most perfect. So, the cosmological argument starts from the sensible world as a finite and conditioned reality, and argues to the existence of an infinite, unconditioned and supersensible reality as the ground thereof. Similarly, the teleological proof lays stress and the adaptation of means to ends which we find every where in nature and infers the existence of an infinitely intelligent creator of the world. But all these proofs are vitiated by the fallacy of deducing the existence of God from the mere idea of Him. The idea of the most perfect being may involve the idea of existence, but not actual existence just as the thought of one hundred rupees in my pocket involves the image or the idea of their existence, but not their real physical existence. So, to think of the conditioned world we have to think of the unconditioned, or to explain the adaptation of things we have to think of an intelligent cause. But to think of the existence of something is not to prove its existence, since the *thought of existence* is not actual existence.

Experience is the only source of our knowledge about fact or existence.

God's existence must be known through direct experience, and not by means of reasoning.

The conclusion to bo drawn from all this is that the existence of God cannot be proved by any argument. In truth, mere reasoning or logical argument cannot prove the existence of the anything. The existence of a thing is to be known, if at all, through experience, direct or indirect. A man of normal vision may indirectly know what orange colour is, if he has seen red and yellow, but no orange as yet. But a man who is born blind can never know that colour is, however much he may argue and reason logically. If by some surgical operation, the man is blessed with the power of vision, a single glance at some coloured object shall reveal to him the world of colours. Lotze[76] told us the truth about our knowledge of God when he said: "Therefore, all proofs that God exists are pleas put forward in justification of our faith and of the particular way in which we feel that we must apprehend this highest principle." This point becomes more clear when in his criticism of Anselm's form of the ontological proof, he observes: "To him (Anselm) the assumption that it (God) does not exist seemed to conflict with that *immediate conviction* of its reality, which all our theoretic, aesthetic, and moral activities constrain our souls to entertain." "Although," he goes on to say, "weak enough as a proof, Anselm's argument expresses an *immediate fact* about our minds, namely that *impulse* which we experience towards the supersensuous, and that faith in its truth which is the starting point of all religion." It becomes abundantly clear from all this that god must be known through direct experience and not through any process of reasoning. If there is this direct experience, no proof is necessary, just as no reasoning is needed to convince you that you are now reading this book. If there is no direct experience of God, we may pile up proof after proof and yet remain as unconvinced as ever with regard to the existence of God.

Those who have no direct experience of God, must depend, for their knowledge about God, on others who have that direct experience. The śruti being the expression of such direct experience of God is a just source of our belief in God.

For the knowledge of God or of any supersensuous reality, those who have no direct experience must depend on the authority of those rare blessed souls who are pure in heart and have seen God, like the Upaniṣadic seers and the Christian saints. So, śruti or the scripture, being the embodiment of the knowledge imparted by the enlightened sages and seers of God, may be accepted as a source of right knowledge about God. Just as the great scientists and their sciences have been, for all ages, the source of our knowledge of many scientific truths, so the Vedas and Upaniṣads (śruti) constitute a just ground of our belief in one universal spiritual truth, *i.e.* God.[77]

3. Anti-theistic Arguments

The charge of arguing in a circle against the last two proofs is answered.

It may be objected here that the last two proofs given above involve us in the fallacy of reasoning in a circle. In the third proof, it is shown that God is the author of the Vedas, while in the fourth, the Vedas are exhibited as the ground of our knowledge of God. It appears, therefore, that we prove God's existence from the Vedas and that of the Vedas by the revelation of God. But that there is really no circular reasoning here becomes clear when we distinguish between the order of *knowledge* and the order of *existence*. In the order of existence, God is first and creates the the Vedas, imparting to them their authoritative character. In the order of knowledge, however, the Vedas come first, and we rise from them to a knowledge of God. But for our knowledge of the Vedas, we need not be necessarily and absolutely dependent on God, since these may be learned from an eligible and efficient teacher. All reciprocal dependence is not reasoning in a circle. It is only when there is reciprocal dependence with reference to the same order or within the same universe of discourse, that there arises the fallacy of reasoning in a circle. In the present case, however, the Vedas depend on God for their existence but not for their knowledge, while God depends on the Vedas for our knowledge of Him but not for His existence. So there is really no fallacy of reason ing in a circle.[78]

Reply to the second objection.

Another objection to the Nyāya theory of God is this: If god be the creator of the world, He must have a body, since without body no action is possible. This objection, the Naiyāyikas reply, fails because it is caugh between the two horns of a dilemma. If God's existence is proved by śruti, then the objection stands precluded for there is no point in arguing against what is already proved. On the other hand, if the very *existence* of God is not proved, there is no basis for an argument against the possibility of His *action* without a body.[79]

The third objection and the Naiyāyika's reply to it.

Still another anti-theistie argument is based on the problem of the end of creation. In creating the world God must have some end in view, for nobody acts without a desire to realize some end. But what may be the end of God's creative activity? It cannot be any end of His own, because there are no un fulfilled desires or unattained ends in the Divine Being who is perfect. Nor can it be the end or good of others He who labours only for others must not be regarded an intelligent person. It cannot be said that God was moved by compassion (karuṇā) in the act of creation. If it were really so, He should have made all his creatures perfectly happy, and not so miserable as we actually find them. Compassion is just the desire to relieve the suffer ing of other creatures without any self-interest. So it follows that the world is not created by God, the Naiyāyikas meet this objection thus: "God's action in creation is indeed caused by compassion. But we must not forget that the idea of a creation which consists only of happiness is inconsistent with the nature of things Certain eventual differences in the form of happiness on misery are bound to arise out of the good or bad actions of the beings who are to be created. It cannot be said that this will limit God's independence in so far as His compassionate creative act depends on the actions of other beings. One's own body does not hinder one. Rather, it helps one to act and achieve one's ends. In a like manner, the created world does not hinder and limit God, but serves as the means for the realization of God's moral ends and rational purposes.[80]

VI. Conclusion

The value of the Nyāya system lies especially in its methodology or theory of knowledge on which it build its philosophy. One of the charges against Indian philosophy is that it is based on religious authority and is,, therefore, dogmatic and not critical. The Nyāya philosophy is a standing repudiation of this charge. The theory of knowledge, formulated by the Nyāya, made the basis not only of the Nyāya-Vaiśeṣika, but also of other Indian systems, with slight modifications. The Nyāya applies the method of logical criticism to solve the problems of life and reality. It is by means of a sound logic that it finds out the truth and defends it against hostile criticism. But the Nyāya theory of pluralistic realism is not as satisfying as its logic. Here we have a common-sense view of the world as a system of many independent realities, like material atoms minds, individual souls and God, which are exernally related to one another in space, time and ïkāśa. It does not give us a systematic philosophy of the world as a whole in the light of one universal absolute principle. The philosophical position of the Nyāya is said to be lower than that of the Sāṅkhya or the Vedānta. This becomes manifest when we consider its theory of the individual self and God. According to it, the individual self is a substance which is not essentially conscious and intelligent, but is accidentally qualified by consciousness when associated with a body. But such a view of the self is contradicted by the evidence of our direct experience which reveals the self as a conscious subject and not as a thing with the quality of consciousness. Further, on this view, the liberated self has no consciousness and is, therefore, indistinguishable from a material substance. The Nyāya conception of God as the architect of the world, its efficient but not material cause, has an obvious reference to human relations and reduces God to the position of a human artisan who makes things out of given material. There is indeed the suggestion that the world of things and beings it related to God as one's body is to his self. But this idea is not properly developed in the direction of a full-fledged theism. Still, as a philosophy of life, the Nyāya theism is no less edifying and assuring than other forms of it.

REFERENCE

1. *Vide Tarkasaṇgraha*, pp. 32-35, 82: *Tarkabhāṣā*, p. 29; Tātparya *ibid.* 1.1.f.

2. Some Miāṁsakas exlcude memory from valid knowledge, on the ground that it doesnot give us any new knowledge. It is obly a reproduction of some past experience and not a cognition of anything not known before (anadhigata).

4. For a detailed account of the nature and forms of knowledge, and the tests of truth and error, *vide* S.C. Chatterjee, *The Nyāya Theory of Knowledge*, Chap. III, V.

5. *Nyāyta-sūtra*. 1.1.4.

6. *Vide Tarkahāṣā*, p. 5; *Siddhāntamuktāvali*, pp. 235-36; *Tattin cintāmaṇi*, pp. 539-43, 552.

7. *Vide Bhāsāpariccheda and Muktāvalī*, 52.

8. *Op. cit.*, 63-65. For a fuller account, *vide* S. C. Chatterjee, *The Nyāya Theory of Knowledge*, Ch. X.

9. Vide Stout, *Manual of Psychology*, p. 102; Wundt, *Human and animal psychology*, pp. 285-86; Ward, Article "Psycholoyg," *Encyclopṅdia Britannica*, 9th ed., vol. XX, p. 57, *Cf. Woodworth, psychology* (9th ed.) p. 115, where the perception of the smell of roses shut in a glasses and seen through the glass is cited as an example of hallucination.

10. *Vide Advaitasiddhi*, pp. 137-39; *Vedāntaparibhāṣā*, Ch 1.

11. *Vide Nyāya-bhāsya and Tātparyaṭikā*, 1.14; *Tarkabhāṣā*, p. 5; *Nyāyalīlāvatī*, p. 53. For a detailed account, *vide* S.C. Chatterjee. *The Nyāya Theory of Knowledge*, Ch. IX.

12. *The Positive Sciences of the Ancient Hindus*, p. 250.

13. *Vide Muktāvalī*, 66-67

14. *Vide Tarkabhāṣā*, pp. 48-49. for a critical discussion of the logical form of inference, *vide* S.C. Chatterjee, *The Nyāya Theory of Knwledge*, pp. 297-305.

15. The Mīmāṁsakas and the Vedāntins hold that the first three or last three propositions suffice for inference.

16. *Vide Tarkabhāṣā*, pp. 7f.; Tarkasaṅgraha, pp. 43 f.; Bhaspariccheda and Muktāvalī, pp. 137-38; *Sarvadarsan*, Ch. II; *Paribhāṣā*, Ch. II.

17. The inference is like this: "Whatever is fiery is smoky, X is fiery, therefore X is smoky." Here the conclusion is contradicted by the red-hot ball, lighting, etc. The reason is that the relaiton of the middle 'fiery" to the major "smoky" is conditional on its being fiery from "wet fuel."

18. *Vide Mutkāvali*, p. 280; *Tattvacinatāmaṇi*, ii. pp. 153-54.

19. For a somewhat similar theory of induction the reader may be unferred to R.M. Eaton, *General Logic*, part IV. *Vide the Nyāya Theory of Knowledge*, Chaps. X, XII, for a fuller account.

20. *Vide Tarkasaṅgraha*, pp. 46-49.

21. *Vide Nyāya-sūt*, and *Bhāṣya*, 1.1.5.

22. *Vide Tarkabhāṣā*, p. 2; *Tarkasaṅgraha and Tattva-dipikā*, pp. 35-36.

23. According to another interpretation, pūrvavat inference is that which is based on previous experience of the concomitance between two things, and śeṣavat is pariśeṣa or inference by elimination, *e.g.* sound in a quality because it cannot be a substance or anactivity or anything elan.

24. *Vide Tarkasaṅgraha*, pp. 51-52; *Bhāṣāpariccheda and Muktāpalī*,

25. Another example of such inference would be: The sun is different from other planets, since it is stationary, and what is not different from the other planets is not stationary.

26. Cf. Bradely, *Principles of logic*, Vol. I, pp.274-82.

27. *Vide Tarkasaṅgraha*, pp. 54-60.

28. *General Logic*, p. 334.

29. *Vide the Nyāya Theory of Knowledge*, Ch. XIV, for a detailed account of the fallacies.

30. In some parts of India, the 'gavaya' is more commonly known nigali'.

31. *Vide Tarkasaṅgraha*, pp. 62-63.

32. *Modern Introduction to Logic*. p. 13.

33. *Vide Nyāya-sūt*. and *Bhāṣya*, 21.42.

34. *Vide Nyāyavarttika*, 1.16.

35. *Vide Tarkasaṅgraha, and Dīpikā*, p. 63.

36. *Tattvakaumudī*, 5.

37. *Prameyakamalamārtaṇḍa*, pp. 97-100.

38. *Sāstradīpikā*, pp. 74-76.

39. *Vedānta-Paribhāṣā*, Ch. III.

40. *Vide The Nyāya Theory of Knowledge*, Ch. XVI, for a critical discussion of upamāna as a distinct source of knowledge.

41. *Nyāya-sūt*, 1.1.7.

42.*Tārkikarakṣā* pp. 94-95.

43. *Tarkasaṅgraha*, p. 73; *Bhāṣāpariccheda and Muktāvalī*, 81.

44. *Nyāya-sūt*, and *Bhāṣya*. 1.1.8

45. *Tarkasaṅgraha*, p. 73; *Tarkabhāṣā*, p. 14.

46. For a critical discussion of śabda as an independent source of knowledge, vide *The Nyāya Theory of Knowledge*, pp. 381-89.

47. *Tarkasaṅgraha*, pp. 63-64.

48. *Ibid.*, p. 64.

49. Ibid., p.72; *Bhāṣāpariccheda*, 82.

50. *Vide Nyāya-sūt* and *Bhāṣya*, 1.1.9.22.

51. *Nyāya-bhāṣya*,i1.10; *Padārthdharmasaṅgraha*, pp. 30f.; *Tarka saṁgraha*, pp. 18-19.

52. *Bhāṣāpariccheda* and *Mukāvali*, 48-50; *Nyāya-sūt*, and *Bhāṣya* 3.1.4.ff.

53. *Vārttika*, 1.1.22; *Nyāyamañjarī*, p. 432.

54. *Vide Nyāya-bhāṣya*, 1.1.9-10.

55. *Vide Bhāṣya*, 1.1.10.

56. *Vide Tarkabhāṣā*, p. 6; *Tarkakaumudī*, p. 8; Bhāṣāparicchedā, and Muktāvalī, 49-50.

57. *Vide Bhāṣya*, 1, 1.22.

58. *Cf. Tarkasaṅgraha and Dīpikā*, pp. 106-07.

59. *Vide* Hiriyana, *Outlines of Indian Philosophy*, p. 242.

60. *Vide Nyāya-sūt.*, 4.1.19-21; *Vaiśeṣika-sūt.*, 2. 1. 17-19.

61. *Vide Ṣaḍdarśana*, Ch. I *Kusumāñjali*, 5.

62. *Vide Nyāya-bhāṣya*, 4.1.21.

63. *Vide Kusumāṇjali*, 5; *Sarvadarśana*, Ch XI; *Tarkasaṅgraha and* Dīpikā, pp. 21-22.

64. *Vide Final Causes*, Bk. I, Ch. I.

65. *Vide Outlines of a Philosophy of Religion*, Chs. I, II.

66. *Vide A Study of Religion*, Bk. II. Ch.I.

67. If the world be created by God, who is not only omnipotent but also *morally perfect*, it is not unreasonable to think that good actions must produced good effect and bad actions must produce bad effect in our lives. If god is both the creator and moral govenor of the world it logically follows that human beings are responsible to God for their actions also that our action are judged by God as good or bad, right or wrong, accoridng as they do or do not help us to realize the end of our life, or to perform our own duties to God and man. And from this it is but natural and rational to conclude that God rewards us for our good acts and punishes us for bad ones. In other words, in a world created by God, good actions must lead to good results and evil actions must not fail to lead to evil consequences.

68. *Vide Kusumāñjali*, 1

69. *Nyāya-bhāṣya,* 2.1.68; *Kusumāñjali,* 5, p. 62.
70. *Bṛhadāranyaka Upaniṣad,* 4.4.22, 4.24.
71. *śretāśvatara Upaniṣad,* 6.11.
72. *Kauśītaki Upaniṣad,* 4.18.
73. *Bhagavadgītā,* 9. 17-18.
74. *Vide* E. Caird, *The Critical Philosophy of Kant,* Vol. II, Ch. XIII.
75. *Vide The Outlines of a Philosophy of Relgion,* Ch I.
76. *Op. cit.,* pp. 9,12. (italics ours).
77. *Cf. Kusumāñjali,* 5.
78. *Vide Sarvadarśana,* Ch. XI.
79. *Ibid.*
80. *Ibid.*

CHAPTER VII

NYĀYA-VAIŚEṢIKA[1]

Gotama is the name of the sage who systematized the philosophy of Nyāya in the form of sūtras or aphorisms. In the same way Uluka compiled the sūtras of Vaiśeṣika. Very little is known about either of these men. Tradition has it that Uluka, commonly known as Kanāda—literally, he who eats very little—was an austere soul who made his living by picking up the left-over particles of corn from the harvest, and that he attained the grace of the Lord śiva, who commanded him to systematize the philosophy of Vaiśeṣika. He flourished at some period before the birth of Buddha. Gotama came somewhat later.

The two systems systems which embodied in the sūtras composed by these two men are regarded by all authorities as constituting one school of philosophy though they differ in some details and though in their aphoristic form they were evolved independently of each Other. Chronologically Vaiśeṣika is the older of the two.

The following discussion of the twin philosophies will be divided into three parts: Part I, the first and larger part, will deal with technical in which they differ; Part III will return to the school as such. and supplement, with certain broad considerations, what was said in Part I.

I. Common Doctrine

The Seven Categories

At the very beginning of the Vaiśeṣika sūtras Kanāda asserts that the proper object of his philosophy is to expound dharma, (virtue), so that men may have abhyudaya (growth or unfoldment in life or character) and attain niśreyasa (the highest good). This niśreyasa is then explained as attainable through immediate perception of the ultimate realities of Selt and the universe. These ultimate realities—padārthas, or categories—are dravya (substance), guṇa (quality), karma (action or motion), sāmānya (genus), viśeṣa (species), and samavāya (relation). To these original six, later philosophers added another category, abhāva (negation).

No attempt is made to reduce the seven padārthas to one; on the contrary, a common-sense scientific position is sought through a perception of the universe as multiple. The padārthas, it should be added, make up the universe of external experience as well as that of the inner man.

A brief characterization of each of the seven categories follows:

(1) Dravya. substance, first and foremost of the categories, is the only one of them that has an independent existence. The remaining six depend upon it.

The substances are nine in number. They are:

The Self—the basis of consciousness and experience—though. according to a doctrine peculiar to the Nyāya-Vaiśeṣika school, its own consciousness is rather an adventitious than an essential characteristic. In reality it is unconscious; it becomes conscious only when it is joined to a mind which is itself conscious. The existence of the Self is considered a self-evident fact. The Self is eternal. Its junction with the body is known as birth, and its severance from the body is known as death.

Manas (mind)—the instrument of experience, as of happiness and misery, in the same way that the eyes are the instrument of seeing. Besides being the instrument of experience, the mind is itself an object of experience—quite as much so as the objects of sense. The Self alone is the experiencer. It wields the mind and the body as the fighter wields, according as he wills, the sword in his hand. As the Self associates itself with the mind, it becomes associated with the senses and the body and through them with the external world. This association is the primary cause of bondage and suffering. The manas accompanies the Self in death and is not dissociated from it until the attainment of mokṣa. With rebirth the body and the senses are completely renewed.

Earth, air, water, fire, ether—objective elements, since they are perceived by the external senses, though they are not perceived in their refined, causal states. In their causal states, unperceivable by the senses, conceivable only by the mind, they are called paramāṇus. They are active in the periodic process of creating the universe.

Kāla, time, and dik, space substances having objective reality.

(2) Guṇa, quality, is distinct from substance, and, like the remaining categories, dependent upon it—since it can not be known apart from the substance which it modifies. The qualities are broadly divided into general properties, such as magnitude, which are common to one or more, substances, and are perceived by one or more senses, and special qualities, such as taste, odour, colour, which specifically qualify only one substance and are perceivable by one sense only. Time and space, though substances, have no specific qualities.

(3) Karma, motion, is a distinct category, though it is dependent on earth, water, air. fire. and ether. It is of five kinds: upward, downward, con-

traction. expansion, and movement in general.

(4) Sāmānya, generality is a category independent of thought. It is also known as jāti, or the that-ness which groups together many individuals into a class, there is a higher and a lower generality. The lower generality signifies a particular quality, such as cowness, common to cows. Beingness, it may be said, characterizes the largest number of entities. This kind of generality has some resemblance to the Platonic 'idea', but it differs in that the Nyāva-Vaiśeṣika system does not recognize particulars as copies of universals.

(5) Viśeṣa, particularity, enables us to perceive that things differ from each other. It is the distinctive feature in each. (The later philosophers of the school did not admit this as an independent category.)

(6) Samavāya. necessary relation, possesses an objective reality independent of the percipient. It is that which relates a substance to its qualities, a whole to its parts, a cause to its effect. The relation concerned is inherent, as distinguished from ordinary relations, which can be brought about at will. Two or more objects, for instance, can be brought together, related to each other, and then separated; but such a relation would not be Samavāya, or necessary relation. A necessary relation is like that between the thread and the cloth made from it, or between genus and species.

(7) Abhāva, negation, is not mentioned by kahāda, who recognized but six categories. Later commentators added it in order to make the philosophy of the system realistic. They considered that the negation of false knowledge is the cause of the negation of misery and gives rise to niśreyasa, or freedom.

The Nyāya-Vaiśeṣika philosophy, to sum up the preceding analysis, postulates seven categories—the substances, their properties, and their relations. These taken together compose the universe. In their primordial form they are real and eternal. Of the seven categories, the dravya. with its nine elements, is the most important. Of the nine elements, the Self. as the substratum of consciousness, and the only experencer, is primary. The others, including mind, are objective realities, but though they possess reality they are dependent upon substance.

The Conception of God

In the Nyāya-Vaiśeṣika system, man's self is called jivātman—the individual self as distinguished from Paramātman, the Supreme Self.

The proofs of the existence of God as given by this system are neither very convincing nor very important. They bear some similarity to the argument from design as we find it in the teleological side of Christian theology. Briefly, we see in the universe a physical order and a moral order, and these imply a controller, a lawgiver, and a governor who dispenses justice. Moreover, a world which is an effect must have not only its material cause but also its efficient cause. God must therefore exist as the efficient cause. There is, finally, no way to disprove the existence of God, just as, in the words of the Sāṁkhya system, there is no way to prove his existence.

The Law of Causation

The Nyāya-Vaiśeṣika system regards cause and effect, though there must always be the relation between an invariable antecedent and consequence, as two distinguishable conditions of things. Further, its doctrine of causation has this peculiarity, that the effect is regarded as nonexistent before its actual appearance. For example, the world as an effect, which is non eternal, is a production of the eternally pre-existing substances, with their properties and relations, but is also something absolutely new. Every cycle of creation, therefore, is called ārambhavāda—that which admits of an entirely fresh creation.

II. Differences

The two systems, in so far as they differ, do so mainly in their approach to the central problems of philosophy. The Vaiśeṣika begins with the conception of being and develops its ideas from that; the Nyāya begins with knowfng. Where Vaiśeṣika has seven categories, Nyāya has sixteen, one of which contains all but one of the Vaiśeṣika seven (the exception being the Self, basis of all experience), and the remaining fifteen of which deal not with the universe, but with the means by which we understand it. The fifteen categories are proof, objects of authentic knowledge, doubt, illustration, conclusion, syllogism, argument, settlement (agreement on the truth), discussion, wrangling, idle contention, fallacy, fraud, baseless objection, and occasion for reproof. The last half-dozen of these are negative in character, calling attention to obstacles on the way to truth.

All Indian philosophy considers that ignorance bars the way liberation. Nyāya philosophy further indicates that this ignorance results from identification of the Self with the body, the senses, and the mind. Because of this identification we are slaves to raga (attachment) and dveśa (hate), and these are the cause of all our sinful acts and the principal cause of suffering and death. And death causes rebirth because of our ignorance of the true Self. When we attain to transcendental knowledge of the true Self, we have no more slavery to rāga and dveṣa, and thus the wheel of birth and death is stopped and there is an end to misery.

III. The Nyāya-Vaiśeṣika: Way to Liberation

According to the Nyāya-Vaiśeṣika system of philosophy, the ignorance which is the cause of bondage and suffering and death is not merely a lack of knowledge of the Self but a positive error, or false knowledge. This false knowledge (moha, or delusion) can be eliminated only by right knowledge, which again is not merely intellectual attainment but a transcendental insight that gives immediate perception of the truth. In order that this immediate knowledge of the transcendental Self may be acquired, we must undergo moral and spiritual disciplines.

One way of liberation, according to the school we are studying, is through understanding the different categories and realizing the true nature of the Self. And how does one realize the true nature of the Self Udavana a well-known ancient student of Nyāya philosophy, declares that one does so, with consequent liberation, through worship of God, devotion, and self-surrender. Philosophical speculation he looked upon as a mode of worship.

God, therefore, is the supreme Self, endowed with blessed attributes and devoid of evil. He is the creator and controller of all beings and all things. Individual selves are separate from God and are related to him as children to their father or as creatures to their creator. Individual souls are eternal—beginningless, and immortal—and are born into this world according to the deeds of their past. Justice and the moral order exist because of the law of karma. Man suffers or enjoys according to his own deeds. By surrender and devotion to God, and by worshipping him and meditating upon him, man, purified, becomes freed from the wheel of birth and death and realizes his true nature.

With respect to moral disciplines, this school would follow the duties of caste and of the orders of life. The rules of the conduct to followed according to one's station in life prescribe faith, non-injury, compassion, nonattachment, freedom from lusts right motive, freedom from anger, cleanliness, purity, and devotion to God.

Liberation is release from pain and suffering. Consciousness, according to this school, is an adventitious property of the Self not its inhrent nature; inevitably, therefore, the state of liberation is devoid of consciousness—a conception which seems to be identical with complete materialism or with a species of philosophic materialism. In order to avoid such a misconstruction, later philosopher of the Nyāya school describe this state, not as one of mere negation of pain, but as positive bliss.

Liberation comes after release from the body. Jivanmukti, or freedom while living, is not formally recognized by this school though it does recognize a stage corresponding to it—a stage in which a person has extricated himself from moha, or delusion, and has found enlightenment. He is not 'free', however, in the strict sense of the word. For such a soul, final liberation comes with death.

REFERENCE

1. The general reader may wish to omit this section since it is highly technical in nature—though far less elaborate and detailed than it would need to be if it fully presented its subject.

CHAPTER VIII

SĀṄKHYA-YOGA

THIS should once have been a widely influential school to judge from references to it in the Mahābhārata and kindred literature[1], but its vogue especially on the Sāṅkhya side is not very great now.[2] The surviving part of its literature also is relatively poor Modern scholars as we have already had occasion to notice are divided in their opinion as, regards its origin. All agree that references to what appear as the Sāṅkhya-Yoga doctrine are found in the Upaniṣads, especially in the later ones among them. But while some are of opinion that the system is independent origin and almost as old as the Upaniṣads, others maintain that it is an offshoot of the teaching of those ancient: treatises. There is indeed a reference in one of the Upaniṣads[3] to Kapila ṛṣi, the supposed founder of the Sāṅkha according to tradition, but both old Indian thinkers[4] and present day scholars[5] agree that it is only apparent. The expression, here means the 'red wizard,' not 'Kapila, the seer' as it may it first appear and denotes not a real person at all but Hiraṇyagarbha or some other mythical being. As the discussion of this question requires an acquaintance with the details of the doctrine, we cannot enter upon it now we shall nerely state in passing that whatever its true origin there was one stage in the history of the system when its adherents raced it to the Upaniṣads. Bādarāyaṇa, as is well known has systematized the teaching of the Upaniṣads in Ins *Vedānta-sūtra,* and one of the topics to which he recurs time and again is whether the Sāṅkhya is the teaching of the Upaniṣads.[6] His conclusion is that it is not, and his repeated reference to it cannot be satisfactorily accounted for without assuming that there were Sāṅkhya thinkers in his time who contended that was the teaching of the Upaniṣads. Even so late as the sixteenth century A.D. Vijñāna Bhikṣu, the author of the *Sāṅkhya-pravacana-bhāṣya,* which is a commentary on the *Sāṅkhya-sūtra,* maintained a similar view. This may of course be the result of later Sāṅkhya teachers trying to find support for their doctrine in the Upaniṣads, whose authority had come to prevail, but it may also indicate a desire on their part to trace it to its real source even when the modifications in it had changed its character so very much.

The relation between the Sāṅkhya and the Yoga again is difficult of settlement. It is not even clear that one of them is later than the other, for they may well have been due to differentiations in what was originally a single doctrine. In the form in which the two have come down to us, there is no doubt that the Yoga is later. If the view adopted here, viz. that the doctrine is derived from the Upaniṣads, be right, it appears probable that its starting-point should be sought in primitive Sāṅkhya-Yoga with belief in a supreme God to whom the individual selves and prakṛti, the source of the physical universe, though distinct are yet subordinate; for such a doctrine is nearer to the teaching of the Upaniṣads than the atheistic Sāṅkhya or the theistic but dualistic Yoga of classical times.[7] We have to assume that under naturalistic influence such as that of the Svabhāva-vāda, the capacity to unfold the universe was transferred completely to prakṛti, rendering the idea of God superfluous; and on test was later grafted a belief in his existence by the exponents of the Yoga[8] probably as a matter of theological expediency—'to satisfy the theists and to facilitate the propagation of the theory of the universe expounded in Sāṅkhya. This point will become clear when we trace the origin of the doctrine and point out its relation to the Vedānta.

The earliest book of authority on classical Sāṅkhya we now have is the *Sāṅkhya-kārikā,* which is a work of about the fifth century A.D. Roughly speaking, we may take its author Īśvarakṛṣṇa to have been a contemporary of Kālidāsa. It consists of seventy stanzas and is on that account sometimes designated as the *Sāṅkya-saptati.* It contains a brief but exceedingly lucid exposition of the theoretical teaching of the system and has been described as 'the pearl of the whole scholastic literature of India.' It has been commented upon by several, including Vācaspati—the well-known advaitic scholar of the ninth century A.D. This book, with a commentary whose identity is not quite certain, was translated into Chinese under the name of 'the Golden Seventy Discourse' by one Paramārtha, a Brahmin of Ujjain who went to China in A.D. 546 on the invitation of its then Emperor and spent the rest of his life there. Another work of note on the system is the *Taitva-samāsa,* which, as its name indicates, is very brief—hardly more than a table of contents, as it has been characterized. It was regarded by Max Müller as the oldest work in the subject[9] but that view is not generally accepted now.[10]A third work of importance on the system is the *Sāṅkhya-sūtra,* ascribed to Kapila himself; but the work, though much of its material may be really old, is clearly a very late production and cannot be assigned to a date earlier than the fourteenth century A.D. It is in six chapters of which four are concerned with the elucidation of the doctrine, one criticizes the rival systems and one gives the parables (ākhyāyikā) illustrating the chief points of the doctrine—rather a novel feature in a sūtra work. It has been commented upon, among others, by Vijñāna Bhikṣu, to whom reference has already been made. In this commentary the Sāṅkhya appears considerably modified, the general effect of the modification being to bring it nearer to the Vedānta. We may regard it as *later* Sāṅkhya. We shall refer to its divergences from the earlier where they are of importance. As regards the Yoga system, Patañjali's *Yoga-sūtra* is the recognized text-book. It has been aligned to about the end of the fifth century A.D.[11]; and if this date correct, the traditional identification of its author with Patañjali, the grammarian who is known to have lived in the second century B.C., must fall to the ground. It consists of four chapters which deal respectively with the nature of mental concentration (samādhi), the pathway to it (sādhana), the supernatural powers that may be acquired through it (vibhūti), and the nature of the goal of life which consists in the isolation of the sell (kaivalya). It has been commented upon by Vyāsa[12] (A.D. 500) and King Bhoja (A.D. 1000) among others. The former's commentary has a splendid gloss by Vācaspati and another by Vijñāna Bhikṣu.

I

The Sāṅkhya-Yoga like the Nyāya-Vaiśeṣika admits a plurality of selves, called puruṣas, and is likewise realistic since it regards objects as existing independently of the mind that cognizes them. But while the latter traces the physical universe to a multiplicity of sources, the former derives it from angle one, viz. prakṛti. In other words, the Sāṅkhya-Yoga, unlike the Nyāya-Vaiśeṣika, is—if we overlook for the moment the plurality of selves—dualistic, prakṛti and puruṣa or nature and spirit being the only two ultimate entities recognized. We shall now consider in some detail how each of these is. conceived—

(I) *Prakṛti*: This is the first cause of the universe—of everything excepting only spirit which is uncaused, and accounts for whatever is physical, both matter and force. Out of it, the whole variety of the universe evolves. Hence the doctrine is known as *pariṇāma-vāda* or a 'theory of change.' Even space and time are represented as aspects of prakṛti and do not therefore, exist apart from its as independent entities. This is a point which is worthy of note, for it shows that the system does not, like the generality of philosophic doctrines including much of Western thought till quite recent times, start by positing matter *in* space and time, but looks upon the primordial physical entity as including and explaining them both. The nature of prakṛti is deduced from the nature of the common things of experience by the aid of reason alone. As the material cause of these things, it should consist of what is common to all of them; for the effect, according to a fundamental postulate of the system, must be essentially the same as the material cause. By a process of analysis, the essential characteristics of the physical universe are reduced to three—named sattva, rajas and tamas; and prakṛti is conceived as constituted of them. It is thus complex in its nature, though single. These three factors are termed guṇas, whose conception is of the utmost importance in the system. The chief point about them is that they are not what their name might suggest, viz. qualities of prakṛti. That would be admitting the distinction between substance and attribute as the Nyāya-Vaiśeṣika does, but the Sāṅkhya-Yoga regards it as a pure abstraction. The guṇas are to be understood here as the components of prakṛti. They might be described as substances, if that again did not suggest the same artificial distinction. They are still termed guṇas because, it is said[13] they by intertwining make a rope (guṇa) or forge a chain for binding the self. This explanation is somewhat inconsistent with the spirit of the Sarikhya-Yoga teaching, for prakṛti not only binds but also liberates the self from bondage. Indeed puruṣa's liberation, as we shall see, is the ultimate purpose for which it evolves. There is another explanation, which again seems to run counter to the dominant thought of the doctrine. It is stated that the guṇas are so called because they form a category *subordinate* "to the puruṣa, which implies that spirit here is more important and that prakṛti is only something that ministers to it. The explanation, though supported by certain statements of old authorities[14] would destroy the avowed dualistic character of the teaching by making one ultimate entity depend upon another. As regards the nature of the guṇas: sattva represents whatever is fine or light; tamas whatever is coarse or heavy; and rajas whatever is active. It is clear from this description that the conception is arrived at as a hypothesis in accounting for the diversity of the world in its material as well as its mechanical aspects. Their triple character merely signifies that three is the minimum number of elements necessary for such an explanation[15] If only one guṇa is postulated, it would not explain variety at all; if two, they would either cancel each other's effect, thus leading to no transformation whatever, or one would dominate over the other always, thus leading to a monotonous movement in a single direction. In later Sāṅkhya is found the important development that each of the three guṇas is manifold and that the infinity of prakṛti is due to their indefinite number. In this case the triple division would be the result of grouping together like guṇas. Such a *view* undoubtedly explains better the discord and diversity of the world of experience; but at the same time it makes the doctrine more like the Vaiśeṣika[16] with its belief in an infinity of atomic reals with qualitative distinctions.

The guṇas form the substratum of change which as in Buddhism is taken to be perpetual. But change is not total here and the guṇas persist while only their modes appear and disappear. This solution of the problem of change leads to the postulating of a two-fold condition for all things—one, latent or potential and the other, potent or actual. When all the modes of prakṛti are latent, we have the' 'state of dissolution (pralaya); at other times, evolution (sarga). Even in the state of dissolution, prakṛti is supposed to maintain its dynamic character; only then, instead of producing unlike forms, it reproduces itself (sajātīya-pariṇāma) so that perpetual motion is a fundamental postulate of the system so far as the physical world is concerned .[17] The ground for the conclusion that there is perpetual movement in prakṛti is to be found in the convict of that if it ceased to be dynamic at any stage, it would be impossible to account for the reappearance of motion in it again. Here we see a realization of the truth of Newton' First Law of Motion that a body in motion or at rest con tinues to be so unless it is disturbed from outside. There is no such external agency recognized in the doctrine to interfer with its movement. No doubt the change from the state of dissolution to that of evolution is accounted for by introducing an outside influence, viz. the presence of spirit (puruṣa-saṁnidhi)[18]; but the explanation is given only in a half-hearted manner and is, as we shall see, one of the unsatisfactory features of the system, so far at least as the Sāṅkhya part of it is concerned.

There are certain special features of evolution as conceived here which deserve notice. First, it is based on a belief in the indestructibility of matter and the persistence of force. Something cannot come out of nothing; and whatever is, has always been. Production is only the manifestation (abhivyakti) of what is already in a latent form, and is not a new creation (ārambha). The so-called beginning of an object is only an event in its history; the object itself is not, and cannot be, made. Similarly, destruction means only change of form, for there can be nothing like absolute annihilation. Secondly, evolution is conceived as cyclic cr periodical. That is, there are periods of evolution and dissolution alternating so that it is not a process of continuous progress in one direction only. It would seem also that dissolution is the normal state, for there is a persistent tendency in prakṛti when in evolution, to revert to that state. Next, evolution is here regarded as teleological; but, as prakṛti is by hypothesis not sentient, we cannot take it wholly so. We may characterize it as quasi-teleological, however hard it may be to understand that term. What is meant is that the whole process serves a purpose, though it cannot be described as consciously pursued. Lastly evolution, so far as it is teleological at all, has reference to the individual and not to the species. Its object is not the elevation or improvement of the latter, even at the expense of the former, but securing worldly experience (bhoga) for the individual or bringing about his liberation (apavarga) from the ties of saṁsāra. We shall later explain the probable meaning of this double aim involved in the evolution of prakṛti.

The order of evolution of the twenty-four principles (tattvas) known to the system, if we exclude the puruṣas which stand outside the realm of change, will seen from the following scheme:—

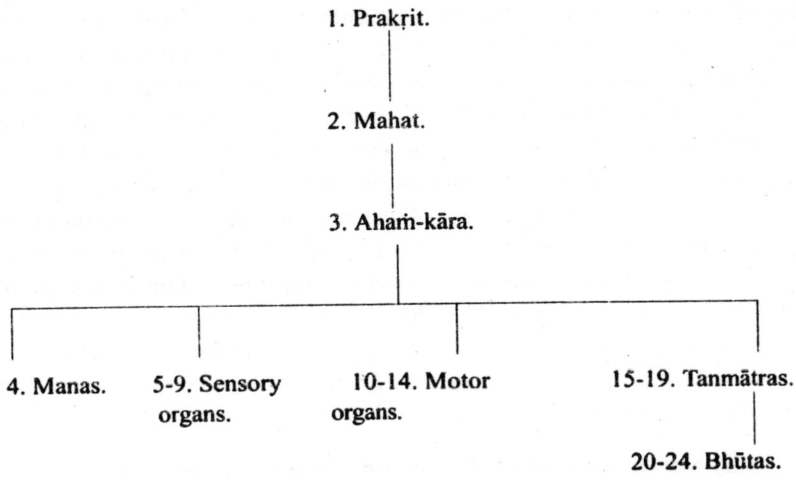

The complete significance of this scheme and of the various terms used in it will become clear as we proceed. For the present it will suffice to refer to only a few points in it:—

(i) The evolutionary series includes in addition to what are clearly physical, viz. the five subtle (tanmātras) and the five gross elements (bhūtas), certain others like the manas which appear to be psychical in character; and it may seem a contradiction to make prakṛti. which by hypothesis is non-sentient, their 'source. Really, however, there is no contradiction, for the latter are not themselves psychical, but owe that character to the influence of the self, the sole principle of consciousness acknowledged in the doctrine An illustration may make the Sāṅkhya-Yoga position clear in this respect. A mirror can reflect our features, but the surface of the wall, upon which it hangs, cannot and yet both are alike material. Similar is the case of the two, sets of entities above referred to which thought originating from the same prakṛti, behave differently towards the self—one responding to its influence readily and the other not doing so. The difference between them is therefore one of degree, not of essence. The 'psychical' factors have in fact been compared to the nervous system on its physical side.[19]

(ii) In the state of dissolution, the three guṇas of prakṛti, though perpetually active, are in perfect equilibrium. At the beginning of a period of evolution, this state ceases and is followed by one in which sattva predominates. It marks the starting-point of heterogeneous evolution and is called mahat ('the great'), or buddhi. The initial stimulus for this alteration, according to the Yoga, comes from God or Īśvara.[20] According to the Sāṅkhya on the other hand which acknowledges no such supreme Being, the change is ascribed to the 'mere presence' (sāṁnidhya-mātra),[21] as it is termed, of the puruṣa; and the possibility of its influencing prakṛti, though continuing to be passive, is illustrated by a magnet attracting iron. This is a point which is far from satisfactory. In the first place, the puruṣa is eternal and omnipresent like prakṛti so that the condition determining the evolution of the latter is ever fulfilled while its course is supposed to be interrupted at intervals by dissolution. To explain the break in the course of evolution by the past karma of beings will not do, for the puruṣa, being really untouched by good or evil, karma and its effects should be taken to characterize the buddhi and therefore as internal to prakṛti.[22] There is again the difficulty due to the admission of many selves in understanding what exactly is meant by the presence of puruṣa—whether it is of one or of all. To assume, as Vijñāna Bhikṣu does[23] that it refers to the influence of a chief Puruṣa in each kalpa or cycle of creation would virtually be to abandon the atheistic position and side with the Yoga.

(iii) Now as regards the last group in the evolution, viz. the elements: When we remember that the ultimate reals out of which the produced part of the universe is constituted according to the Nyāya-Vaiśeṣika are these elements it will be seen that the Sāṅkhya-Yoga carries its investigation farther back than that system until it arrives at a single principle. How are these elements derived and what are their characteristics? Their immediate causes are the five tanmātras and they are named after the distinguishing features of the five elements as śabda-tanmātra ('essence of sound'), sparśa-tanmātra ('essence of touch'), etc. The gross elements which spring from them show greater and greater differentiation. Their mode of origin is as follows: From śabda-tanmātra emerges ākāśa with sound as its manifest quality. From sabdatanmātra and sparśa-tanmāti combined emerges air, which therefore has the two qualities of sound and touch; from these two and rūpa-tanmātra springs fire, which has the three qualities of sound, touch and colour; from these three and rasa-tanmātra emerges water with four qualities, viz. sound, touch, colour and taste; and last, earth comes into being from all the five tanmātras and is therefore characterized by all the five qualities of sound, touch, colour, flavour and odour. The elements beginning with ākāśa are consequently more and more concrete. Each element is conceived as manifold, and consists of finite and disparate particles termed paramāṇus[24] though the expression does not signify here precisely what it does in the Nyāya-Vaiśeṣika. It is out of these atoms that the whole of the physical universe as known to us is produced.

(iv) The scheme indicates only what we may describe as primary evolution. Evolution does not stop at it. It goes further on as is shown, for example, when pṛthivī is transformed into a tree[25] or a caterpillar becomes a butterfly. This secondary evolution is in fact what we are familiar with and what takes place within any single period of evolution. When an object that has evolved in this sense breaks up, it is reduced to the form of the gross elements and the process of issolution does not extend beyond except when the of dissolution does not extend beyond except when the evolutionary period in question itself comes to an end. Example evolution is described as the differentiation into *distinct* principles (tattvāntara-pariṇāma)[26] but what constitutes distinctness is not well defined. It is clear, however, that this amounts to a recognition of grades or degrees in change.

An attempt is made in the system to deduce the being of prakṛti, not merely its nature, with the aid of reason. The deduction depends upon two principles, which the system takes as its postulates. The first of them to which we have already alluded is described as the sat-kārya-vāda. According to it, nothing new can come into being which is in clear opposition to the Nyāya-Vaiśeṣika doctrine of asat-kārya-vāda. The totality of what exists now is given from the very beginning. But what is, may be implicit or explicit—the two forms being respectively termed 'cause' and 'effect.' The jar is ever there and is so really eternal; but it is not perceivable when in a subtle or latent form. In other words, a thing always is *in itself* though it may not be *for us.*[27] It subsists always although it may exist only for a while, and existence necessarily signifies subsistence. The bearing of this postulate on the preseat question is that the physical world which is now explicit must once have been implies and it is just that implicit state which is prakṛti. That is indeed the literal meaning of the term pradhāna ('what is put before or presupposed')[28] which is ometimes used for prakṛti. The second postulate is that the finite always implies the infinite, which reminds one of the dictum of Hegel that the finite transcends itself. The notion of finitude here requires a word of explanation. Things as understood in the Sāṅkhya-Yoga cannot be said to be limited by time or space, for neither of them is recognized as a separate entity. So the word 'finite' is taken to mean 'not self-sustaining' or, as it is otherwise expressed, 'not pervasive' (avyāpi).[29] For example, ākāśa is finite in this sense because while it sustains all that is derived from it in the process of evoution, it self is sustained by its cause viz. śabda-tanmātra. This tanmātra again reveals another element more fundamental by which it sustained; and so forth backwards until we reach an entity which is all-pervasive and self-sustaining. That is prakṛti. In prakṛti itself or, what amounts to the same, in the three guṇas, we may think that there is mutual exclusion, none being caused by the others, and that they are all therefore finite. But the theory is that, though not causally related, they are absolutely dependent upon one another (anyonyā-śrava-vṛtti)[30] and that none of them is self-sustaining. In other, prakṛti is not a mere unity of aggregation, but systematic unity of parts each of which has its special place and function in the whole. This, by the way, shows the existence of limit to the investigation of the cause for the physical world; for, if we proceed farther back, we do not get anything different from prakṛti. It is therefore regarded as paramavyakta, 'the final unmanifest'[31] or the first cause whose being is unconditioned and necessary. It will be seen that the reasoning is based upon the observation of common things emerging from their respective material causes and disappearing into them again. A jar is made out of clay; and, when destroyed, it turns into clay again. Emergence and absorption thus have a terminus, viz. clay here. This process of reasoning is only extended beyond the visible material world to arrive at prakṛti or to state the same differently, primary evolution is postulated on the analogy of the secondary. Even supposing that principle which has a basis experience may be extended to what transcends experience, it may well be asked what warrant there is for assuming the very principles—mahat, ahaṁ-kāra and tanmātras—and only so many, to account forth bhūtas which alone are given in experience; and it is significant that the basis for this part of the doctrine is stated to be not inference but verbal testimony (āptāgama) or the *ipse dixit* of the Sāṅkhya-Yoga teachers.[32] That the physical world has evolved out of a certain number of elemental principles given in our experience, or perhaps from one, is a doctrine of the Svabhāva-vāda; but the further reference to mahat, etc., as intermediate stages in the evolution, which distinguishes the Sāṅkhya-Yoga, suggests that it is to be traced to a different source. We shall see in the sequel what reasons there are for concluding that source to be the Upaniṣads.

(2) *Puruṣa.*—Puruṣa is mere sentience. It is changeless, eternal and omnipresent. It is also entirely passive, all activity being restricted to prakṛti. It may accordingly be said to represent the affective or receptive side of the mind and is consequently described as an enjoyer or experient (bhoktā) without being a doer or agent (kartā). Like prakṛti, the self also is here sought to be established with the help of reason alone. Various arguments are adduced to prove why such a psychic entity should be supposed to exist.[33] First of all it is stated that the physical universe, being insentient, requires a sentient principle to experience it or that objects suggest a subject, although such an argument by recognizing a necessary relation between the two militates against the fundamental dualism of the system. Equally inconsistent with the same aspect of the doctrine is the second argument that prakṛti, which is complex, implies by contrast the existence of something which is simple, viz. the self. Again the design[34] that is found in nature, particularly in the living body, it is argued, leads to the same conclusion. A noteworthy point here is the manner in which the 'design argument' is utilized. It is explained as pointing not to the designer but to one that profits by the design. The Sāṅkhya concludes from the presence in nature of means adapted to the accomplishment of particular ends, not to God as their author, but to the self for whom it supposes them to exist. This conclusion may be taken as being on a par with the other, for any contriver

must necessarily have in view one whose need his contrivance meets. No watches for example would be made if there was none to use them. But it may be asked why it should not equally well imply God as the contriving mind whom the Sāṅkhya, as an atheistic doctrine, declines to accept. Here is a point of much importance in the doctrine especially in contrast to the Nyāya-Vaiśeṣika. In the latter, the material out of which the visible universe is made possesses no spontaneity of its own Its various parts have accordingly to be brought together and also kept together by some external factor—God or karma or both. But here there is a great advance in the conception of prakṛti in that it is of an organic entity.[35] It is able to develope of itself. Such an entity has no need for an external manipulator. This is at the bottom of the atheism of the Sāṅkhya and shows the futility of attempts like that of Vijñāna Bhikṣu to read theism into the doctrine.[36] But prakṛti, though its conception is different from that of the Nyāya-Vaiśeṣika atoms does not evolve for itself and therefore points to sentient puruṣa. It is this teleology implicit in prakṛti that the design argument here makes use of. It serves as the point of departure from the Svabhāva-vāda with which the doctrine has much common and tells us by the was the it spirit is the only true ultimate in the Sāṅkhya-Yoga. Unlike prakṛti it is not a unity of parts, nor is it non-sentient like it bo it does not in its turnrefer to anything beyond itself fourth argument is drawn from man s longing for escape from saṁsara or the spiritual instinct to be free. What strives to escape must be other than what it is to escape from, viz prakṛti. The puruṣas are conceived as many and various arguments are put forward in support of that view[37] such as the divergent histories of men and the differences in their endowment—physical, moral and intellectual. But such reasoning only shows the plurality of the empirical selves. In themselves, it is hard to see how the puruṣas can difter from one another. There is not even a semblance of explanation here as in the Nyāya-Vaiśeṣika where each self is stated to be inherently characterized by its own.

The view of causation in the system is the very reverse of that in the Nyāya-Vaiśeṣika. It is described as sat-kāryavāda, for the product according to it, is supposed to be there in the material cause always in the latent form. But sat-kāryavāda like asat-kārya-vāda, it must be remembered, refers only to the material cause. The system recognizes two other kinds of cause—the efficient and the final. The latter point to something outside the sphere of prakṛti, it being alway either worldly experience (bhoga) or release (apavarga), both of which have reference to the self. This statement, however does not seem to signify that the final aim of evolution is two fold. Apavarga or escape means, as in the Nyāya-Vaiśeṣika the restoration of the self once for all to its natural condition Prakṛti evolves for bringing about its release in this sense and it ceases to do so for a self when that particular self becomes free. When we take this along with the point already noticed, viz. that the state of pralaya or world absorption and not that of evolution is normal to prakṛti apavarga will be seen to be the only true aim. We may look upon the other aim of bhoga as its necessary antecedent. If the two aims be considered as independent or external to each other, it will not be possible to explain how blind prakṛti albeit that it is omnipotent, can exercise a choice between them and decide which is to be secured for which puruṣa and when. The introduction of karma, as already indicated, will not help the argument, for the traces which past karma leaves behind abide not the self but in the buddhi and are therefore of prakṛti. Such an interpretation saves the doctrine to some extent from the charge of self-contradiction in the conception of prakṛti, viz. that while it is stated to be non-sentient, it is supposed to be endowed with activity which implies conscious choice. The final cause is the most important of the causes and m one sense it may be said to be the only cause[38] for in its absence there would be no progressive movement at all in prakṛti. Its recognition signifies what we have already pointed out, that the conception of prakṛti is that of a systematized unity of parts or a teleological whole. The efficient cause is conceived as negative in its nature. It is useful only m removing obstacles and not in making any positive contribution towards the product, for by hypothesis whatever manifests itself is already there in the material cause. Prakṛti is characterized by universal potency, and holds in itself the possibility of all forms. It can become anything and the efficient cause is required only to determine the direction in which it is to exhibit movement by removing the obstacle in that direction. As analogous to this, we may think of water stored up in a reservoir which at every point of its sides is trying to find an outlet and flows out only where the resistance to its effort is remvoed.[39] Finally we must point out that this view of causation holds solely within the sphere of prakṛti and its transformations the self, in reality, remains untouched by it. It is neither a cause nor an effect of anything.

The most important distinction between the Sāṅkhya and the Yoga is the belief of the latter in God. Some scholars, old as well as new[46] have tried to maintain that there was no intention on the part of Kapila to deny God and that all that he meant to assert was the impossibility of rationally establishing his existence. But this seems to be contrary to the spirit of classical Sāṅkhya as already observed and it may here be added that the attempt to give a theistic colour to the doctrine appears quite late in its history. Vijñāna Bhikṣu is anxious to find a place for God in the Sāṅkhya scheme, but the support for it even in the late Sūtra *is slender.* We have already indicated how the notion of God or Īśvara as he is termed here came to be included in the Yoga; and it is therefore only loosely related to the doctrine. The very sūtras in which it is postulated in patañjali's work stand disconnected with the rest of the work.[41] As conceived here, he is a puruṣa like others, though a perfect one. He is omniscient and omnipresent; but unlike the Vedāntic Īśvara, he is external to; matter (prakṛti) as well as to the individual selves (puruṣas). In other words, he is not the Absolute and in this he resembles the Nyāya-Vaiśeṣika God, the chief difference being m the part they play in shaping the world owing to the difference in the conception the two doctrines of the material out of which it is shaped. The only argument adduced by Patañjali in support of his theistic position is the existence in our experience of a graded scale of knowledge, wisdom etc., which, he supposes points to infinite knowledge, wisdom etc., as their limit. He to whom these latter belong is God. But it may be asked how these super-excellences can belong to God if he also, being a puruṣa is bare spirit and stands aloof from prakṛiti. To ward off such an objection the doctrine views God as endowed with a sort of personality imphing actual contact with a physical adjunct which consists mainly of sattva and does not bind him. Besides affording the initial impetus for the evolution of prakṛti, he in his mercy helps his devotees in finding relea from empirical existence. But God's help is not the only means of securing it, the successful practice of yoga as shall see, being another.

Before concluding this section, we may bring together the several postulates of the Sāṅkhya-Yoga to which we had occasion to refer. They are:—

(i) Whatever is, always is; and whatever is not, never is.
(ii) Change implies something that changes.
(iii) The effect is essentially the same as it material cause.
(iv) All variety can eventually be traced to three source, which are not, however, independent but interdependent.
(v) Matter is characterizeds by perpetual motion.
(vi) Neither mind is derived from matter, nor matter from mind.

II

Here as elsewhere in Indian philosophy generally the term 'psychology' is to be understood in its etymological sense as the science of the soul. But what is the soul that can be thought of as the subject of experience in this system? We have the puruṣa, no doubt, but it really remains external to everything and cannot therefore stand for the subject of experience. There is another element that serves as an important aid in the process of knowing, viz. mahat or buddhi; but that is equally unsuited to be the subject though for quite a different reason. It is non-sentient (jaḍa) being derived from prakrit, and experience cannot therefore be ascribed to it. Thought neither by itself can serve as the defect it is stated they do so together, the buddhi contributing all the activity involved in it and the puruṣa the element of awareness (caitanya). The puruṣa illumines or is reflected in the buddhi, which though physical is fine enough to receive the reflection; and, thus illumined, it serves as the conscious subject. The buddhi may therefore be viewed as the physical medium for the manifestation of spirit. We may call their unity in this sense the empirical self to distinguish it from the puruṣa or the transcendental self. Owing to such association, each of the two elements in the empirical self appears completely transmuted—non-sentient buddhi becoming sentient, as it were, and passive puruṣa, active.[42] The illustration commonly given in this connection is the 'red-hot iron ball' where the formless glow of fire appears spherical and cold iron, hot. Every jñāna is a state of this blend. When we consider its two parts separately, the modification of the buddhi which such a state involves is called a vṛtti and the reflection of the puruṣa in it jñāna. Owing to the felt identity of the two elements, the vṛtti also is sometime designated jñāna.[43]

It will be noticed that in the evolutionary scheme are included the eleven indriyas or sense organs (including manas), ahaṁ-kāra and buddhi; but there they represent successive stages in the evolution of the universe from prakṛti. These thirteen factors have also another aspect with which are at present more particularly concerned. In this aspect they assist the individual in acquiring experience, and together constitute the psychic apparatus with which every puruṣa is endowed in the empirical state. The exact relation between these two aspects, viz. the cosmic and the individual, is a matter which shall immediately engage our attention. For the present it will suffice to recall the explanation already given of 'psychic' as applied to these factors. They are psychic in the sense that they lend themselves to be lighted up by the puruṣa unlike the other products of prakṛti, viz. the elements whether subtle or gross. It is this that distinguishes the two series, the subjective and the objective as we may call them. They are the result on the part if prakṛti to adapt itself to the requirements of the puruṣa.[44] In other words, the functions that we describe as mental are really mechanical processes of physical organs, which assume a psychical character only when illumined by spirit. The senses are here derived from the ahaṁ-kāra, and not from the elements (bhūtas) as in the Nyāya-Vaiśeṣika (p. 48). Though traceable to one and the same source, each sense functions differently—the eye apprehending colour; the ear, sound; and so forth—owing to the difference in the collocation of the guṇas in them.

The Sāṅkhya-Yoga, like the Sautrāntika but unlike the Nyāya-Vaiśeṣika, believes that perception is effected by means of a psychic sign, viz. an image or idea (ākāra) of the object in question. The image is not transferred to the buddhi and found in it as may be supposed, but the buddhi itself assumes the form of the object, when a suitable stimulus is received from outside. The modification of the evolvent buddhi, viz. vṛtti, is a characteristic not only of perception but also of all forms of consciousness, and when it is inspired by spirit, experience results. The psychic apparatus as a whole mediates between the puruṣa and the outside world thereby securing for the former the experiences of life (bhoga) or, if the time for it is ripe, final freedom (apavarga) through right knowledge (viveka). The details of the process of knowing are as follows: The object first impresses one or other of the senses, and the jñāna that arises then is quite vague and general. It is 'bare awareness' (ālocana-mātra) and marks the nirvikalpaka stage. The first stage in perception does not accordingly refer, as in the Nyāya-Vaiśeṣika (p. 251), to the isolated and discriminate particular. It becomes properly explicated later when interpreted by the manas, and is therefore termed 'determinate' or savikalpaka. Pratyakṣa does not accordingly start here from detached elements and synthesize them, but from an indistinguishable whole into which it introduces order afterwards.[45] This completes the process from the objective standpoint; but there follow two other stages before perception is psychologically fully explained. The first is the appropriation of the experience by the ahaṁ-kāra or the reference of the self in question. If now the perception upon what action the buddhi intervenes and decides upon what action has to follow and issues instructions, so to say, to the proper motor organ (karmendriya), the result being either some action or desistence from it. The buddhi thus corresponds to the will-aspect ot conscious life. If we use a single term—antaḥ karaṇa—for the last three elements of the psychic apparatus, we see how the internal organ in one or other of its phases is engaged, when once the senses have been stimulated in reacting to the stimulus. The order in which the psychic organs function, it will be seen, is the reverse of that in which they appear in the evolutionary scheme given above. In internal perception such as that of pain or pleasure, as also in mediate knowledge, the process is exactly the same: only the co-operation of the external senses (jñānendriya) is not required and they do not therefore function then. This analysis of the psychic process, which takes perception as an increasing differentiation in a presented whole, is very much sounder than that 'if the Nayāy-Vaiśeṣika but owing to the denial in the doctrine of direct interaction between the buddhi and spirit their is even here a difficulty in understanding how experience emerges all at once out of a purely physical or physiological process. The illustration of a glowing iron ball is not apt, for the iron ball and tire are actually in relation there unlike the' buddhi and the puruṣa here.

Now as regards the double sense in which the principles from mahat onwards, excluding the elements in this two fold form, are to be understood in the system. It is not difficult to understand their significance from the standpoint of individual experience. The process of perception, as just set forth, makes it quite clear. But the same cannot be said of their cosmic aspect, and it is impossible from the premises of the system to discover why these psychical terms should be applied to the ontological entities in question. The only Puruṣa and regard the whole process of evolution as an *ideal* presentation to him. That will give us at once a rendering psychical terms of these ontological principles. If we identic the mahat—as cosmic buddhi illumined by spirit—with this Puruṣa, the next stage in evolution, viz. the ahaṁ-kāra will stand for the sense of self-hood which arises in him, position on the one hand what we have described as the objects series or not-self; and on the other the subjective series, more strictly, the apparatus of thought adapted to cognize it.[46] Since in the case of such a cosmic subject the order of psychological presentation coincides with that of actual evolution[47] the above assumption also accounts for the order in which the several principles occur in the evolutionary scheme which, as observed already, is the reverse of that which they function in individual mental life. When we remember that this is exactly the position of the Upaniṣad and that they mention more or less the same stages describing the creation of the world by the personal Brahman (mahān ātmā), it will be clear that the inclusion by the Sāṅkhya of these principles in its scheme is to be traced ti the teaching of those treatises. But in its reaction agains Absolutism, the doctrine has discarded the idea of a universa—soul and by sundering it into two—prakṛti and puruṣa—has reduced each to a mere abstraction. For the activity of prakṛti is meaningless with puruṣa; and puruṣa, were it no for its association with prakṛti; would be hardly distinguishable from nothing. The result is that while the system professes to be dualistic, its implication is quite the reverses.[49]

III

The view that knowledge arises through a psychic medium (buddhi-vṛtti) may easily lead to subjective idealism as it does in the Yogācāra school; but the Sāṅkhya-Yoga lays down a postulate at the very outset that all knowledge necessarily points to some object outside it. Belief in the plurality of selves which is an essential part of the doctrine furnishes a support for the postulate, since the agreement between what different people experience may be taken to vouch for the existence of a common or trans-subjective basis for it all.[50] The psychic medium accordingly is here but a connecting link between the knower and the known and does not displace the latter. A natural corollary to this view is the correspondence theory of truth. That knowledge is true in which the form assumed by the buddhi rightly represents the object perceived. This is the Nyāya-Vaiśeṣika view as well; only the theory of representative ideas (vṛttis) is not accepted there. A more important difference between the two is that whereas in the Nyāya-Vaiśeṣika which makes the manas merely the pathway of knowledge, knowledge is supposed ordinarily to show objects *as they are,* there is here no garantee that it does so. The buddhi which so far as our present purpose is concerned may be taken as the equivalent of the manas of the Nyāya-Vaiśeṣika[51] is conceived here not as passive but as endowed' with self-activity and as the abode of numberless impressions acquired through experience during a beginningless past. Owing to this circumstance, every buddhi has its own special bent and different persons may therefore be impressed in the same manner by the same object. Though one, the object becomes 'severalized,' as it were, in the act of being apprehended on account of the bias of individual percipients. These two factors, viz. the objects and the particular bent of the percipient, co-operatc in all knowledge and the resulting image may not, and generally is not, an exact copy of the former. It is in this power of meddling with the object which the buddhi possesses that we have to seek for the source of error. But the power only emphasizes one aspect rather than another of what is given and does not add any new feature to it. In other words, the activity which the buddhi exercises is selective, the theory being that only so much of the nature of object is known as is in kinship with the perceiver's mood at the time. Like only appeals to like.[52] This alters very much the complexion of the resulting error. It is one of omission and not of commission as in the Nyāya-Vaiśeṣika. It is right so far as it goes; only it does not go sufficiently far. To get at the true nature of the object, we have accordingly to supplement our personal view by taking into consideration all other possible views of it. The doctrine admits, like Jainism, that such comprehensive knowledge[53] is possible, but it can be attained only when the buddhi is purified by continuous self-discipline, so that generally speaking what we perceive is only partially true. Incompleteness is a common deficiency, of our knowledge, and much of the evil in life is to be traced to viewing it as complete. Two people may disagree about an object though both may be right in part, because each is obsessed by the idea that he is in possession of the whole truth about it. There is also another deficiency characterizing all knowledge excepting only that of a 'freed man' of jīvan-mukta. As neither the buddhi by itself, nor the self by itself can, according to the system, be the conscious subject, we have to seek for it, as has already been pointed out, in the two together; and no experience is possible until we mistake them for one, or to be more correct, we fail to notice that there are two factors constituting it. This failure, termed aviveka or non-discrimination[54] which again is an error only in a negative sense, is a pre-condition of all experience. It leads to a fatal confusion between the puruṣa and the buddhi in which the characteristics of each are ascribed to the other and we talk of the buddhi as knowing and of the puruṣa as acting. It is the removal of this error, we may by the way, through discrimination (viveka) between the two factors constituting the empirical self that the doctrine holds to be the chief aim of life.

Error may thus be of two kinds: (i) where only one object is involved, it is mistaking a part for the whole; and (ii) where two objects are involved, it is overlooking the distinction between them and so virtually identifying them with each other. The two kinds can be reduced to the same form, for the second may be looked upon as a particular case of the first. Not knowing the puruṣa or the buddhi completely we confound the one with the other; and when complete knowledge of them is attained the mistake will of itself disappear so that it also, like the first, may be said to result from incomplete knowledge. The two instances of incorrect knowledge given above may together be described as 'metaphysical error.' They are what vitiate all experience, and there is no escape from it until jīvan-mukti is achieved. But apart from this basic error of which man is not commonly aware, there is another with which he is quite familiar. Thus a white crystal appears red when it is placed by the side of a red flower; and we sometimes think we see silver when closer scrutiny discovers it to be only shell. Their explanation is similar: In the case of the first, the red flower is well as the white crystal is given, and it is because we lose sight of the fact that they are two that we mistake the: colour of the crystal. It is non-discrimination (aviveka) as in the case of the puruṣa and the buddhi, the confusion between which is the cause of empirical life. The moment we realize that there is the flower *in addition to* the crystal, the error vanishes, In the case of the second, only one object, viz. shell, is presented and our error is owing to our stopping short at grasping its features which it has in common with silver for which it is mistaken. That is, it is incomplete knowledge that gives rise to error here, as in the case of the other variety of what we have termed 'metaphysical error.' Though thus the two forms of common illusion correspond to the two forms of the other, there is an important difference between them from the practical standpoint. To dispel the latter, *complete* knowledge is necessary; but in the case of the former it will suffice if we acquire such knowledge as does not leave out the feature which is *relevant* in the given context to distinguish the objects confounded with each other. To take the second of the two illusions we are considering, such a feature is the lightness of the shell as compared with the heaviness of silver. Because we overlook the fact that the object before us is too light to be silver, we fall into the error; and the moment we discover it, the error disappears.

Though the explanations of the several kinds of error may differ in matters of detail, their underlying principle is the same. Error is lack of sufficient knowledge (akhyāti)[55] not wrong knowledge (anyathā-khyāti) as in the Nyāya-Vaiśeṣika; and the way to avoid it is to acquire more, if not complete, knowledge. The most important point in this explanation is that when the error is discovered, nothing of what was cognized before is sublated (bādhita). What is given in knowledge is always and necessarily a fact;

only it may not be the whole of the fact. In other words, there is no subjective element in error. Truth does not supplant, but only supplements what is given in the so-called error. This view is what is generally found expressed in earls Sāṅkhya-Yoga works.[56] But the *Sāṅkhya-Sūtra* modifies it in a fundamental manner by admitting an ideal element in explaining error.[57] Thus it describes the illusion of the red-crystal as involving a positive relaiton between the two objects—the crystal and redness, whichis not given, but is fanceid so that, though the relata as such are real, the the realtion between them is not so. That is, error shows what is gtiven as well as what is not (sadasat-khyāi)[58]—an explanation which seems to be inconsistent with the fundamental postulates of the doctrine.[59] This later Sāṅkhya view of error, we shall see, is very much like the explanation given by Kumārla (viparīta-khyāti), while the earlier one resembles that given by Prabhākara (akhyāti).

The pramāṇas accepted here are only three: perception, inference and verbal testimony. The system, being derivative, has not developed these details separately and seems to have borrowed them from the Nyāya-Vaiśeṣika, so far as they are, not inconsistent with its metaphysical view-point.[60] In perception alone is there any difference which is worth mentioning: and that difference is mainly due to the view taken of the process of knowing as already explained. In the case of inference and verbal testimony, the agreement with the Nyāya-Vaiśeṣika is almost complete. As regards validity (prāmāṇya), the Sāṅkhya-Yoga represents a position which is the exact opposite of the Nyāya Vaiśeṣika. Validity and invalidity are both stated to be normal aspects of jñāna,[3] since according to the sat-kārya-vāda the potential alone can become the actual, and whatever manifests it self at any time should be regarded as already there. Both are therefore regarded as inherent in jñāna; and which of them shows itself at any time is determined by the circumstances that explain the genesis or apprehension of the jñāna in question. This is a statement which seems self-contradictory; but it is not out of keeping with the Sāṅkhya-Yoga principle that the phase of reality which reveals itself to us is always relative to our standpoint.

IV

The Sāṅkhya-Yoga, like the other systems, believes in karma and transmigration What transmigrates, however, is not the self, which because it is all-pervading does not admit of change of place, but the subtie body (liṅga-śarīra) consisting of the eleven organs of sense together with buddhi, ahaṁkāra and the five rudimentary elements (tanmātras). This is a permanent annexe, so to speak, to each self which leaves it only at release. Death and birth mean only the change of the gross body and not of the subtle. In the latter are stored up all traces of past thought and action; and the acquisition of right knowledge depends upon the cleansing of this empirical outfit or more strictly of the buddhi which forms its pre-eminent element. Dharma and adhanna are here conceived not as qualities of the self as in the Nyāya-Vaiśeṣika, but only as modes of the buddhi which, owing to the congenital confusion between it and the puruṣa, are mistaken to belong to the latter.[61] It means that, like experience, morality also has significance only on the empirical plane. Intrinsically, neither the puruṣa nor tne buddhi can be. described as moral. In the Nyāya-Vaiśeṣika likewise is the ethical life confined to the empirical sphere; but while it constitutes there an actual, though only a temporary, phase in the history of the self, here good and evil do not so much as touch the puruṣa. To remain always absolutely untainted is, infact, the essence of spirit as conceived here. The *Karika*[62] says: 'No puruṣa is bound or liberated; nor does any migrate. It is prakṛti in its manifold form that is bound, is liberated and migrates.'

The ideal is kaivalya or aloofness from prakṛti and all its transformations, which is quite in consonance with the pessimistic attitude of the doctrine. It is also termed apavarga, for the self in that state *escapes* from the realm of suffering. But no positive bliss is associated with it. The self not only has no pain or pleasure in that condition; it is also without knowledge, for it has not the means, viz. the buddhi and its accessories, wherewith to know. This reminds us of the Nyāya-Vaiśeṣika ideal; but sentience being conceived here as the very substance of the self, the charge of insentience cannot be brought against it as in the other system. The immediate cause of such aloofness is viveka or discriminating knowledge, which removes the cause of bondage. But the knowledge should be more than a mere belief that nature is different flam spirit. It should be an immediate experience and the truth should become known by the practical, we might say, as distinct from the theoretical reason. Thus in this doctrine also ignorance or ajñāna is the cause of suffering. It is not wrong knowledge as in the Nyāya-Vaiśeṣika; but, according to the view of error set forth in the previous section, incomplete knowledge.

The Sāṅkhya, as it has been handed down to us, is almost silent regarding the method of acquiring the intuitive experience that results in release; the Yoga, on the other hand, is mainly concerned with its elaboration. The only reference to the disciplinary means. found in the basic work of the Sāṅkhya, viz. the *Kārikā,* is meditation upon the truth that prakṛti and puruṣa are distinct[63]; and the rest of it has to be gathered from the sister system. As in so many other doctrines, the path to salvation here also lies through, detachment (vairāgya) and meditation (yoga). Detachment[64] in the beginning can only be provisional (apara-vairāgya), for in its mature form (para-vairāgya) it presupposes complete knowledge. The provisional detachment which results from an awakening to the ills of life as it is commonly led, will gradually lead to the higher form of it, if meanwhile the disciple engages himself in learning and meditating upon the ultimate truth—a view which shows that the means of achieving the ideal is as much intellectual as it is moral. The discipline laid down by Patañjali is what is familiarly known as yoga. We cannot enter into the details of this training, which are somewhat technical, but can mention only its broad features:

(1) The preliminary moral training is incuded under the first two heads which we had occasion to mention already of yama and niyama of the eight-fold means (aṣṭāṅga) of yoga[65] Yama is mostly negative—consisting of on-injury (ahiṁsā), truth-speaking (satya), abstention from stealing or misappropriation of others' property (asteya), celibacy (brahma-carya) and disowning of possessions (aparigraha).[66] Niyama, which signifies the cultivation of positive virtues, comprises purity (śauca), contentment (saṁtoṣa), fortitude (tapas), study (svādhyāya) and devotion to God (Īśvara-praṇidhāna)[67] These are so to speak the ten commandments of the Yoga, and their general tendency is ascetic. Of the first group, non-injury is the most important and is stated to be the end and beginning of yama.[68] The remaining four virtues must not only be rooted in it, but also help to perfect it so that it may finally come to be practised irrespective of time, place and circumstance.

(2) After this ascetic preparation begins the yogic training proper. This is a form of discipline which is very old in India and was known both to the orthodox and heterodox circles. It finds a prominent place in the Upaniṣads as well as in doctrines like Buddhism. The references to it in the Mahābhārata also indicate its great vogue. But there were important differences in the way in which it was understood in the various schools. It was for instance practised by some with a view to acquire occult or supernatural powers and by others for the attainment of mokṣa. Among the latter, some took it as the means of becoming one with the Absolute: others, like the followers of the present doctrine, as that of merely shaking off the yoke of matter. Yoga as treated of by Patañjali, is very much rationalized; and, though he refers to the acquisition of certain supernatural powers, he dismisses them as really hindrances[69] to self-realization. This yogic training may be divided into two stages—the first comprising the next three of the eight-fold help—āsana ('posture'), prāṇāyāma ('control of breath') and pratyāhāra ('withdrawal of senses from their objects')—which aim at restraining the mind from the physical side; and the second comprising the remaining three of dhāraṇā, dhyāna and samādhi, which are different forms of concentration and aim directly at controlling the same. The principle underlying the whole discipline is that man's faculties are by long habit adjusted to the preservation of the empirical self and that they must be readjusted[70] so as to secure the totally opposite aim of restoring the puruṣa-element in it to its true condition. Of these several stages in reaching yogic perfection, it is necessary to add a few words of explanation only on the last, viz. samādhi, which

directly leads to kaivalya. It is divided into a lower and a higher form known respectively as saṁprajñāta and asaṁprajñāta samādhi. The latter is the goal[71] the former serving but as a stepping-stone to it. In both alike there is need for the highest power of concentration. The first is a state in which the buddhi continues to function though it is wholly absorbed in the contemplation of a particular object, everything else being excluded—even the fact that one is having a vision of it. It is accordingly described as 'conscious samādhi.' All sources of distraction are eradicated here and the buddhi shines forth with its sattva element in the ascendant. In asaṁprajñāta-samādhi, the consciousness of the object also disappears, and it is therefore described as 'superconscious.' The buddhi ceases to function then or its vṛttis, as it is expressed, become latent or get lost in their source.[72] In that condition not only are the inferior vṛttis arising from the deninance of rajas and tamas overcome, but also those arising from sattva. When in the final form of asaṁprajñāta-samādhi the buddhi is thus concentrated on the self, it vanishes once for all, leaving the puruṣa apart and alone. If we compare our common mental state to the ruffled surface of water in a lake which reflects an object like a tree on the bank as a distorted image, the saṁprajñāta condition may be likened to the calm surface containing steady and faithful image of it and the asaṁprajñāta to the condition where the tree is by itself and there is no image at all for the lake has dried up. There are thus altogether three levels of life that may be distinguished: the first in which rajas or tamas is the chief governing factor, the second in which sattva predominates and the third which transcends sattva also. The lower samādhi is quite intelligible psychologically; but the higher, because it presupposes the suppression of the mind, takes us beyond normal psychical life. We pass in it to the realm of mysticism.

A person that has reached this stage, when his lease of life runs out, attains kaivalya once for all and there is no return thence. But that is the goal of life in the eschatological sense (videha-mukti). There is another that can be reached in this life, viz. jīvan-mukti, which the doctrine explicitly admits.[73] In this condition the puruṣa continues to be related to the buddhi, but it is the buddhi which has been purged of its defects and is fully enlightened. The attitude of the jīvan-mukta towards the world is very much like that of the perfected man according to the Nyāya-Vaiśeṣika ideal. He participates in its life, but is detached from it. Though in the world, he is not of it.

REFERENCE

1. See SS. p. 227
2. ERE xi p. 189.
3. *śvet Up.* v. 2.
4. Cf. śaṁkara on VS. II. i. 1.
5. See PU p. 200; Prof. Keith; *The Sāṁkhya System,* pp. 8, 40-1.
6. Cf. śaṁkara on VS. I. i. 5-11. i. i-3. This refutationis different from the one in VS. II. ii. 1-10, where the Sāṅkhya is criticized on rationalistic grounds.
7. Cf. dr. Belvalkar: *Bhandarkar Commemoration Volume,* pp. 183-44.
8. Vācaspati in his *Bhāmatī* (II. i. 3.) seems to give support to two such stages in the history of the doctrine on its Yoga side.
9. SS. p. 242.
10. Prof. Keith: *op. cit.*, p. 89. But see *Journal of Oriental Research* (Madras) for April 1928, pp. 145-7.
11. Prof. Jacobi: *Dates of Philosophical sūtras.* JAOS (1911).
12. It is diffiult to say who this Vyāsa was. Tradition identifies him with the well-known author of that name.
13. SPB, i. 61.
14. YS. ii. 23; YSP i. 4.
15. The idea of guṇas here, if not derived from the medical theory of the three dhātus, has at least a parallel in it. Cf. STK st. 13.
16. SPB. i. 127-8. As regards the antiquity of the guṇa-doctrine, see OST. vol. v. p. 377. The conception occurs as early as AV., and the Mbh. is full of references to it.
17. Pratikṣaṇa-pariṇāmino hi sarva eva bhāvā ṛte citi-śakteḥ: STK.
18. SP. i. 96.
19. ERE. xi. p. 190.
20. See *Bhoja-vṛtti* onYS. i 24.
21. SPB i. 96.
22. SP i. 16
23. SRR i. 96.
24. Cf. YSB. i. 40, 45; iii. 44, 52.
25. As in the Nyāya-Vaiśeṣika, no distinction is made here between mechanical and organic products. See p. 239 ante.
26 STK st. 3.
27. Cf. YS iii. 13.
28. SPB. i. 125.
29. STK. st. 15-16.
30. STK st. 12:YB ii. 15. Such a view of course, is open to criticism with refering to spirit which neither pervades nor is pervaded by the guṇas leading to the conclusion that both prakṛti and puruṣa are finite. See *Bhamati* II. ii. 1.
31. STK. st. 15-16.
32. STK. st. 6.
33. SK. st. 17.
34. This argument is foreshadowed already in the Upaniṣads. See p. 66 *ante.*
35. Sk. st. 57.
36. SPB. i. 92-8.
37. SK. st. 18.
38. Cf. Sk. st. 31: Purusārtha eva betuh
39. YS. iv. 3.
40. See SPB. i. 92-8; v. 2-12; SS. pp. 302-4.
41. YS. i. 23-9. Cf. ERE. vol. xii. p. 831.

42. SK. st. 20.
43. YSB. ii. 20: iv. 20.

44. Instead to saying, as we ordinarily do, that we adjust ourselves to our environment, we should here say that prakṛti adjusts itself to our needs.

45. SK st. 27, 28 and 30 Vijñāna Bhikṣu somewhat modifies this view which is based upon STK. See SPB. ii. 32.

46. According to YSB. ii. 19, it would seem the tanmātras are derived from mahat and not from aham-kāra. Such a view would give us the notion of the not-self at the same level at which the notion of self is given. But see YSB. i. 45.

47. See IP. vol. ii, p. 277; Prof. Keith: *Religion and Philosphy of the Veda*, pp. 535ff.

48. Cf. *Kaṭha Up*. I. III.10-13, II. III. 7-100; *Praśna Up* iv. 8; *Bṛ. Up*. I. iv.i.

49. In connection with early history of śānkhya, reference may be made to Prof. Dasgupta's *History of Indian Philosophy*, vol. i. pp. 213-22.

50. This is the significance of the word viṣaya and sāmānya used in SK. st ii. Cf. also YS. iv. 15.

51. Strictly it is the antaḥ-karaṇa, of which the buddhiis only one means of Nyāya-Vaiśeṣika

52. Compare the illustration of one and the same damsel appearing differently to different persons, given in STK. st. 13.

53. See STK. st. 4, where such knowedge is described as ārṣam jñanam. Cf. YS. i. 48.

54. For the use of this term or its equivalents see STK. st. 2, 21, 66, etc.

55. This may also be described at sat-khyāti as nothing but the given is apprehended.

56. See references givenin footnote 3 on p. 289 as well as YS. ii. 26; *Bhaja-vṛtti* on YS. iv. 33.

57. Sp iv. 6.
58. SPB v. 26 and 56.

59 See for a further discussion of this point *Indian Philosophical Quarterly* (1929), pp. 99-105.

60. SK-st. 4. YS i 7. See also STK st. 5. 3 SD p 20, SDS p 129.

61. See SP. v. 20-5.
62. St. 62.

63. St. 64.
64. YS. i. 12-16.

65. YS. ii. 29ff.

63. The resemblance of this part of the training to the 'five vows' of Jainism may be noted. See p. 166 *ante*.

67. This is explained as cultivating a spirit of absolute self-surrender to God in whatever one does suggesting the influence of the Gītā ideal of disinterested action. Here it appears as part of the preliminary discipline; but in YS. i. 23 such devotion to God is represented as a means, alternative to yogic practice, of attaining samādhi and, through it, kaivalya. For a possible explanation of this contradiction. see Prof. Dasgupta: *The Study of Patañjali* (Calcutta Uni. Pr.), pp.

68. YSB. ii. 30-1.
69. iii. 27.

70. YSB. ii. 33.

71. YS. i. 3 and 4.

72. YS i.2.

73. SK. st. 67-8.

CHAPTER IX

THE YOGA SYSTEM OF PATAÑJALI

Introduction

Truth is of two kinds: (1) that which is perceived by the five ordinary senses or inferred from the data they provide, and (2) that which is perceived by the subtle, supersensuous power of yoga.

The first kind of truth is called scientific, or empirical, knowledge; the second kind is milled transcendental, or yogic, knowledge.

The person in whom supersensuous power is manifested is called a ṛṣi, a seer, a yogi who has achieved union with God.

To develop supersensuous power is to practise genuine religion. So long as a spiritual aspirant does not develop tills power, so long is religion a mere empty word to him. He has not yet taken the first step towards his goal.

So we must strive for supersensuous perception, and there exist methods or processes which we may use if we will. These require as a prerequisite, if the are to be effective, a life of lofty ethical attainment, but they are in themselves definite spiritual disciplines. They are known to the Hindus as yogas. The primary meaning of the word yoga, which is related to the English word yoke, is union, and what is referred to is union with the true Self, or God; in its secondary meaning it is a method for achicving that union. Patañjali employs it to signify a striving towards the realization of Puruṣa or the Divine. Self—'an effort to separate Puruṣa from prakṛti'. From the earliest times aspirants have followed the practices of yoga. All the earliest Hindu scriptures and all the subsequent systems of philosophy not only express their conception of spiritual truth-but also offer practical methods for realizing the divine consciousness. These methods, however, receive but casual mention in the Vedas, the Upaniṣads, and other early works, and whatever references there are to them deal with the specific and detailed processes of Self-realization handed down orally, generation after generation, from teacher to disciple. The same process have been followed even to the present day. All aspirants after spiritual things must practise them if they would acquire personal experience of the truth the are seeking.

Patañiali, the author of the Yoga system of philosophy can therefore scarcely be called the founder or originator of yoga, but he was the first to gather together the spiritual practices known to the yogis and build them into a system.

It is impossible to assign a definite period to the life of this great yogi. One Patañjali, a grammarian, lived in the middle of the second century BC, but it is uncertain whether he and the author of the *Yoga Aphorisms* are one and the same.

Conception of God in Yoga Philosophy

The Yoga system as formulated by Patañjali is a systematized religious discipline providing a means of attaining the highest consciousness, which in turn leads to final release. All spiritual aspirants in India, whatever may be their individual religious preference, accept the discipline of yoga, though, strictly speaking, Yoga philosophy in its metaphysical aspects is closely allied to Sāṁkhya, with one important difference—its acceptance of God Sāṁkhya, as we have seen, leaves no room for God, either in its system of metaphysics, or in its scheme of salvation. While Sāṁkhya a asserts that there can be no proof of the existence of God, Patañjali advances certain proofs, and in his plan of salvation declares that worship of God and meditation upon him are only if the means of attaining supreme knowledge and liberation. He does admit, however, that it is not absolutely necessary to believe in God in order to experience the truth of religion, holding that truth will make itself felt in spite of belief or disbelief provided one follow the practices of yoga. He only says that it is easier to gain the end of spiritual enlightenment through faith in God and through worshipping him and meditating upon him.

For those, however, who cannot believe in a personal deity, other methods are provided that will bring them the same enlightenment. Indeed, religious truths, as we have already pointed out over and over in our account of Indian philosophy and religion, are not mere dogmas, adapted on faith, but facts made visible by an inner light. Belief or no belief, it is Patañjali's claim that if we follow any of the yoga practices faithfully, we shall be led directly to the spiritual goal.

Devotion to God is one of the means, declared Patañjali, to attain liberation and the truth of the spirit In Sanskrit, God is called Īśwara, interpreted by Bhoja, the well-known commentator, to mean the 'One who by his mere wish has the power to give liberation to all who seek him.'

Patañjali himself has defined Īśwara as a 'special-kind of Being'—distinct from man, inasmuch as 'he is untouched ignorance and the products of ignorance. He is 'not subject to karmas or saṁskāras; or the results of action.[1] Unlike man—in other words—he is no bound by the law of karma; he has neither birth nor death; he is eternal unborn, undying and unchangeable. And he is free from desires.[2]

But Īśwara, as the yogis look upon him, is not the creator of the universe. Its evolution had been explained by Sāṁkhya without admitting the existence of a creator. Yoga arrives at a proof of God's existence in a peculiar fashion of its own. Patañjali says:. 'In God knowledge is infinite; in others it is only a germ.[3] From this aphorism the commentators have derived their proof of the existence of God. The Puruṣas, they declare, are all endowed with knowledge, some with more and some with less, and the fact of limited knowledge proves the existence of unlimited knowledge. There must therefore exist a Being possessed of infinite knowledge. This argument should be compared with the remark of Kant that the concept of the finite involves the the existence of the infinite.

Patañjali also says of Īśwara: 'He was the teacher even of the earliest teachers, since he is not limited by time.[4] The deduction from this aphorism is that no knowledge can come without a teacher—and that God is the teacher of all teachers. Swami Vivekananda remarks:

It is true, as the modern philosophers say, that there is something in man which evolves out of him; all knowledge is in man, but certain environments are necessary to call it out. We cannot find any knowledge without teachers. If there are men teachers, god teachers, or angel teachers—they are all limited; . . . who was the teacher before them? We are forced to admit, as a last conclusion, (the existence of) one Teacher, who is not limited by time; and that one Teacher infinite knowledge, without beginning or end, is called God.

How may one express devotion to God, how worship him and meditate upon him? In spite of all definitions "and all descriptions, God remains to the human mind but an abstraction. Patañjali, realizing this fact, offers a definite, concrete way of understanding. God which the mind may meditate upon. He says: The word which expresses his is Om. This word must be repeated with meditation upon its meaning. Hence come knowledge of the Puruṣa and restruction of the obstacles to that knowledge[6]

In the Upaniṣads, as we have already noted, the word Om was held sacred by sages and seers, being regarded as a symbol of Brahman from Vedic times until the present day it has been so understood, and it has been employed as an aid in meditation by all aspirants after God. It is accepted both as one with Brahman and as the medium, the Logos, connecting man and God. It is Cod, and by its aid pnan may realize God. The entire history of the syllable is in the revelations of the Vedas and the Upaniṣads, and this history in the hands of the later philosophers developed into what became known as sphoṭa-vāda, or philosophy of the Word. The similar doctirne of the Logos, later also than the Vedas and the Upaniṣads, we discover among Greek meta-physicains—a doctrine which influenced the writer of the Fourth Gospel.

As indicated, the sphoṭa-vāda is not precisely the Logos of the Greek philosophers. The Greeks first conceived of the Logos as, a bridge over the gulf that separates man and God, the known and the unknown. The earliest Greek conception was a crude one. The Logos was identified with one or another of the physical elements, according as one or another was thought to be the ultimate substance of the universe. Heraclitus, who lived in the sixth century BC, was the first who tried to break away from a purely physical conception of creation substituting for the material first cause of his predecessors a principle which he called intelligence. This principle of intelligence was the Logos, The advance Heraclitus made, however, was rendered some what equivocal by his identification of the Logos with the physical element fire.

In the hands of Plato the theory of the Logos underwent a complete transformation. He regarded the Logos as the cosmic purpose, the highest idea, the supreme Good, under which all lesser ideas—ie. eternal archetypes of things, relations, qualities and values—are subsumed. According to him, these ideas are arranged in a logical order, and are governed by the Logos: thus the universe is a unity in diversity, a rational, organic whole.

The Stoics denied the validity of Plato's supersensual archetypes, accepting rather the essential theory of Heraclitus: like Heraclitus, they posited a principle of reason immanent and active in the universe. To them the Logos was this eternal reason, 'made concrete in the endless variety of the physical world'. The fact that this rational principle was regarded by the Stoics as the essence of human nature is of special significance, as far as their ethical teachings are concerned. A man is tree, they believed, insofar as he lives in conformity with his reason, and hence, in harmony with the rational nature of the universe.

The Stoic conception of the Logos as an active principle pervading the universe and determining it was adopted by the Hellenzied Jewish philosopher. Philo of Alexandria, a contemporary of Jesus of Nazareth. But whereas the Stoics, by conceiving of the Logos as the principle of reason inherent in all things, endeavoured to escape from there cognition of a divine Creator, Philo was committed from the beginning to the Jewish belief in a supreme, self-existent Deity to who there as on of the world must be made subservient. Philo also accepted Plato's idea of the logos as the transcendent Good in which all individual ideas are comprehended, but he made this conception of the Logos as the immantent and active reason. All of these theories of Philo regardinghtelogos stem ultimately from his view of God as a transcendent Being of whom no thing can be predicated, and from the transcendent Being of whom nothing can be predicated, and from the necessity of explaining how such a pure and perfect Being could have any contact with the finite world.

Philo's descriptions of the logos as mediator between God and the world reflect the two sources from which he drew—Greek philosophy and Jewish religion. He speaks of an infinite variety of Divine Forces, through which an active relation between God and the world is effected.

'Sometimes he describes these powers as properties of God, as ideas or thoughts of God, as parts of the universal power or reason, sometimes as messengers or servants of God, as souls, angels, or demons—thinking not in terms of Greek philosophy, now in terms of the Jewish religion. All such powers he combines into one, the Logos, the Divine Reason or Wisdom. . . . The Logos is the container or place of all ideas, the power of all powers, the highest of the angels, he first-born son-of God, the image of God, the second God, the God-man.[7]

Philo's system contains an unresolved conflict between the Greek and Hebraic conceptions: sometimes, in accord with the Greeks, he represents the Logos as an independent and personal Being, a 'second God,' and sometimes, in accord with the Jews, he conceives of it as distinct and subordinate thing, a mere aspect of the divine activity.

The author of the Fourth Gospel used Philo's Logos theory as the 'basis for his interpretation of the life of Christ, but gave it new expression to serve the theological needs of Christianity.[8] The Logos, that is, which is identical with God, and through which the universe was created, was 'made flesh' in Jesus Christ. Thus Jesus, one with the Logos, became the 'only begotten son of God' and identical with him. 'In the beginning was the Word,' says St John, 'and the Word was with God, and the Word was God.' The verse is almost identical with one in the Vedas: 'Prajāpatir vai idam agre āsit—In the beginning was Prajāpati (Brahman); Tasya vāg dvītiya āsit—with whom was the Word; Vāg vai Paramaṁ Brahma—and the word was verily Brahman '

In adapting Philo's doctrine of the Logos to his account of a historical person, St. John altered it in several respects. In addition to the change we have already described, that of attributing a real personality to the Logos, he emphasized, not its creative aspect but its redemptive function, its communication of spiritual power men. Also, he stressed more than Philo did the Old Testament conception of the Logos as word, as distinguished from the Greek view of the Logos as Reason; that is, he interpreted it as an expression of the divine will, an outpouring of God's goodness and power, light and love.

The Philonic and Johannean conceptions of the Logos may conceivably owe no debt to Indian thought, for the truth is no monopoly of any race or nation, and with spiritual growth the same truth is often realized by different peoples independently of one another. Yet it is also possible that both Greek philosophers and Christian theologians were in some degree under obligation to India for their initial ideas, since it is a well-known fact that Hindu thought exercised a strong influence upon the minds of early Western thinkers.

Not only however, are there general points of similarity between the Eastern conception of the Logos and that which took root in the West; there are differences that are quite as great. To a Hindu mind, the expressed sensible universe is the form behind which stands the eternal Sphoṭa, the inexpressible, the Logos or Word. This eternal Sphoṭa, the essential material of all ideas or names, is the power through which God creates all things[9] Īśwara, Brahman conditioned by māyā, first manifests himself as the Sphoṭa, the inexpressible Word, out of which he then evolves as the concrete, sensible world. The Christian Logos, on the other hand, is not regarded as the material cause of the universe, for God, according to Christianity, is only an efficient cause.

The Christian Logos, as we read in the Fourth Compel, 'was made flesh, and dwelt among us (and we beheld his glory, the glory as of the only begotten of the Father), full of grace and truth'. There is 'here a second interesting difference between the Christian and the' Hindu Logos. The Christian Logos was incarnate once, in the person of Jesus, whereas the Sphoṭa of the Hindus was and is and will be incarnate in all persons—and not in persons only but in all other beings, throughout the universe—each of whom may directly realize God through his power, the power of the Sphoṭa. Says Swami Vivekananda:

'This Sphoṭa has one word as its only possible symbol and this is 'Om. And as by no possible means of analysis can we separate the word 'from the idea, this Om and the eternal Sphoṭa are inseparable; and therefore it is out of the holiest of all holy words, the mother of all names and forms, the eternal Om, that me whole universe may be supposed to have been created. But it may be said that, although thought and word are inseparable, yet as there may be various word-symbols for the same thought it is not necessary that this particular word Om should be the word representative of the thought out of which the universe has become manifested. To this objection we reply that this Om is the only possible symbol which covers the whole ground. The Sphoṭa is the material of all words, yet it is not any definite word in its fully formed state. That is to say, if all the particularities which distinguish one word from another be removed, then what remains will be the Sphoṭa; therefore this Sphoṭa is called the Nada-Brahman, the Sound-Brahman.

'Now, as every word-symbol intended to express the inexpressible Sphoṭa will so particularize it that it will no longer be the Sphoṭa, that symbol which particularizes it the least and at the same time most approximately expresses its nature, will be the Om, and the Om only; because these three letters A, U, M, pronounced in combination as Om, may well be the generalized symbol of all possible sounds. The letter A is the least differentiated of all sounds. Again, all articulate sounds are produced in the space within the mouth beginning with the root of the tongue and ending in the lips—the throat sound is A. and M is the last lip sound; and the U exactly represents the rolling forward of the impulse which begins at the root of the tongue and continues till it ends in the lips. If properly pronounced, this Om will represent the whole phenomenon of sound production, and no other word can do this; and this, therefore, is the fittest symbol of the Sphotak which is the real meaning of the Om. And as the symbol can never be separated from the thing singnified, the Om and the Sphoṭa are one. And as the Sphoṭa, being the finer side of the manifested universe, is rarest to God, and is indeed the first manifestation of Divine Wisdom, this Om is truly symbolic of God.'[10]

More than this, the yogis say that through meditation one may hear this word Om vibrating through the universe.

According to Patañjali, worship of God can be effected by repeating 'Om and meditating upon its meaning.

What Yoga Is

Patañjali, the father of Indian Yoga philosophy, has defined yoga as 'the control of thought-waves in the mind'. The mind (citta), according to Patañjali, is made up of three 'domponents, manas, buddhi, and ahaṁkāra. Manas is the recording faculty, which receives impressions gathered by the senses from the outside world. Buddhi is the discriminative faculty, which classifies these impressions and reacts to them. Ahaṁkāra is the ego-sense, which claims these, impressions for its own and stores them up as individual knowledge. The mind seems to be intelligent and conscious. Yoga philosophy teaches that it is not. It has only a borrowed intelligence. Puruṣa is intelligence itself, is pure consciousness. The mind reflects that consciousne ss and so appears to be conscious. Knowledge, or perception, according to Patañjali, is a vṛtti, a thought have in the mind. All knowledge is therefore objective. Even what Western psychologists call introspection or self-knowledge is objective knowledge according to Patañjali, since the mind is not the seer, but only an instrument of knowledge, an object of perception like the outside world. The Puruṣa, the real seer, remains unkown.

Every perception arouses the ego-sense, which says: 'I know this.' But this is the ego speaking, not the Puruṣa, the real Self. The ego-sense is caused by the identification of Puruṣa with the products of prakṛti—the mind, the senses, etc.

When an event or object in the external world impinges on the senses, a thought-wave is raised in the mind. The ego-sense identities itself with this wave. If the thought-wave is pleasant, the ego-sense feels, 'I am happy'; if unpleasant, it feels, 'I am unhappy'. This false identification is the cause of all our misery; even the ego's temporary sensation of happiness brings anxiety, a fear that the object of pleasure will be, taken away—unhappiness in itself and a preparation for possible more acute unhappiness to come. The Puruṣa, in contrast, remains forever outside the power of thought-waves; eternally pure, enlightened, and free, it experiences the only true, unchanging happiness. It follows, therefore, that man can never know his real Self as long as Puruṣa is identified with the products of prakṛti In order to become enlightened we must bring the thought waves under control, so that this false identification may cease.

To clarify this matter the commentators employ a simple image. If the surface of a lake they say, is lashed into waves, or if the water is muddy, the bottom cannot be seen. The lake represents the mind, and the bottom of the lake the Puruṣa, the Self.

Whenever the mind is made tranquil knowledge of the Self is revealed.

Subduing the thought waves that would possess the mind is not a simple act nor ore to be quickly accomplished, for it completely transforms the mind. It is an act, however, made possible by vogic discipline. Doubtless St Paul had reference to a discipline of this kind when he said, 'Be ye transformed by the renewing of your mind.

In order to achieve this renewal of the mind Yoga psychology considers not only the actual states of the mind but also the latent states called the the saṁskāras, or potentialities. Before we can hope to restrain the thought-waves successfully, we must endeavour to eradicate the potentialities, the root impressions which control the actual states. For when one mental state passes into which mother, it is n of altogether lost, but leaves behind it an impression—latent state or saṁskāra—which in turn tends to give rise to actual states similar to itself. Thus the actual states causes the saṁskāras, and the saṁskāras cause the actual states. The saṁskāras are deep roots in the soil of the mind from which grows the plants, the actual states, the thought-waves. To destroy the weeds, we must eradicate the roots, and to do this it is not enough to restrain the actual states, it is necessary also, through yoga discipline to overcome, weaken, and destroy the saṁskāras, the potentialities of the actual states.

Modern Western psychology, particularly Freudian, takes into consideration these potentialities. Freud postulates three 'areas', or states of mind the unconscious the preconscious, and the conscious. The unconscious is the receptacle of such of our past experiences as have been definitely forgotten and cannot be recalled by the ordinary method of recollection. The preconscious is that part of the mind in which are are stored experiences which, though apparently forgotten can be recalled by an effort of the will. Modern Western psychologists diner in their explanation of the unconscious mind, some holding that it is the receptacle of our individual past experiences and of these alone, while other would include with them the common experiences of the race.

Yoga psychology agrees with the Western view that the unconsious is a depository of certain individual past experiences, but as to the extent of our individual past it differs radically. To Patañjali, our individual past is not limited to the present like, all Western psycholegists would assume, but continues indefinitely backward through a succession of incarnations. According to the law of karma, our birth is the result of our past lives, in each of which, and in the present life, we possess the same mind. In the unconscious mind, if we may adopt the Freudian term, are stored the impressions and the tendencies which have been formed in our previous existences and in our present existence up to this moment and with taken together, have made us what we are.

The saṁskāras or potentialities represent therefore the root impressions received from all our past experiences, including those of our former lives, and they have moulded our characters so that, even though largely forgotten, they still indirectly control or influence our every act and thought. They may also take on fresh life and potency without our conscious effort or will. Now Yoga philosophy—and this is the very core of its doctrine—proposes a discipline whereby these root impressions may first be overcome, and then destroyed, and whereby in consequence a complete transformation of character may in the end be effected Yoga psychology agrees with Freud that the conscious is controlled and guided by the unconscious, but it insists that there is a power inherent in the mind through which the mind restraining itself, can overcome the unconscious and all its tendencies, and achieve by so doing a complete renewal. Thus is its original purity restored—a purity that reflects the supreme purity and infinite knowledge of the Puruṣa Thus at last does the Puruṣa learn his true nature—his utter separateness from prakṛti—and attain to freedom.

Any thought-wave arising in the mind, or any perception apprehended by the mind, is. a vṛtti—or what we have called an actual state. The objects at perception and of thought are innumerable: innumerable, therefore, are the vṛttis. These Patañjali has roughly classified into two main divisions kliṣṭa, painful, and akilṣṭa, not painful. A painful wave, according to Patañjali's use of the term, is not necessarily a wave which *seems* painful when it first arises in the mind, it is a wave which brings with it an increased degree of ignorance, addiction, and bondage Similarly, a wave which seems painful at first may actual belong to the category of the not painful, provided that it impels the mind toward greater freedom and knowledge. For example Patañjali would describe a lustful thought wave as painful because lust, even when pleasantly satisfied, causes addiction, jealousy and bondage to all person desired. A wave of pity, on the other hand he would describe as not painful, because pity is an un selfish emotion which loosens the bonds of our egotism. We may suffer deeply when we see others suffering, but our pity will teach us understanding—and hence freedom.

This distinction between the two kinds of thought-wave is very important in the practice of yoga discipline. For the thought-waves cannot all be controlled at once. First, we have to overcome the painful thought-waves by raising waves which are not painful. To our thoughts of anger, desire, and delusion, we must oppose thoughts of love, generosity, and truth. Only much later, when the painful thought-waves have been completely stilled, can we proceed to the second stage of discipline: the stilling of the not painful waves which we have deliberately created.

The idea that we should ultimately have to overcame even those thought-waves which are good, pure, and truthful may at first seem shocking to a student who has been trained in the Western approach to morality. But a little reflection will show him that this must be so. The external world, even in its most beautiful appearances and noblest manifestations, is still superficial and transient. It is not the basic reality, we must look the rough it, not at it, in order to see the Puruṣa. Certainly, it is better to love than to hate, better to share than to hoard, better to tell the truth thus to lie. But the thought-waves which motivate the practice of virtue are nevertheless disturbances in the mind. We all know instances of admirable, earnest men who become so deeply invited in the cares of great reform movement or social relief project that they cannot think of anything beyond the practical problems of their daily work. Their minds are not calm. They are full of anxiety and restlessness. The mind of the truly illumined man is calm—not because he is selfishly indifferent to the needs of others, but because he perceives the peace of the Puruṣa within all things, even within the appearance of misery, disease, strife, and want.[11]

Now it is a characteristic of the citta, the mind that it tends both towards good and towards evil. Vyāsa, an ancient commentator, compares it to a river that should flow at the same time in opposite directions. Though, again, the citta plays this dual role, its tendency towards good, the will to freedom inherent in every man, is the greater of the opposed forces. Having noted this superior strength of the will to freedom, Professor Das Gupta observes, in substance:

'This point is rather remarkable. It affirms that there is within us, at bottom, a greater desire for liberation than for what as ordinary human beings we count as pleasure or happiness.'

Could it be, one wonders, that the will to freedom described in Yoga philosophy is the force which Freild wrongly interprets as the 'death-instinct'? Freud finds within us two innate tendencies: the life-instinct and the death-instinct. But the death-instinct is not, he thinks, to be found in its pure form, but is inextricably mixed with its opposite, the life-instinct—a theory that would explain the strange phenomena of sadism and masochism and the feeling of alternate love and hate towards the same object. We are not concerned, however, with the truth or falsity of Freud's explanation of the phenomena we have just mentioned, but rather with the fact that by his characterization of the two instincts as antithetical he almost arrived at the position taken by Yoga psychology—and yet somehow' failed to do so. Yoga mention the two opposed instincts: the will to live and the will to freedom. The will to liberation exists, according to Yoga, side by side with the will to live (the will to desire), though in some men it is dormant and in others expressed.'It is the principal purpose of Yoga psychology to show how the will to freedom, the higher will, may be strengthened and the will to live overcome.

As the will to freedom gains in strength, the will to live, what Freud calls the life-instinct, grows weaker. Evidence of this fact may be seen in the lives of all who check impulse and desire. And, strange though it may seem, impulse and desire can be completely overcome, though the will to freedom cannot.

The concrete means by which spiritual control is exercised Patañjali analyses in considerable detail. Control comes, he says, 'from practice and nonattachment'.

By 'practice' is meant, he tells us, the exercise of the ethical and spiritual disciplines. These are yama, cultivating of moral virtues, such as truthfulness, noninjury, continence; niyama, acquiring regular habits of study and worship; āsana, sitting quietly in order to achieve tranquillity; prāṇāyāma, taking breathing exercises in order to, gain control of the mind; pratyāhāra, freeing the mind from the thralldom of the senses; dhāraṇā, concentrating; dhyāna, meditating; and samādhi, rising to the superconscious state.[12]

The eight disciplines we are to practise, and along with the practice, says the yogi, we must sow the seed of nonattachment in our hearts. In fact, practice and nonattachment must go together. Nonattachment, in Patañjali's words, is 'that effect which comes to those who have given up their thirst after objects either seen or heard'.

There are stages of nonattachment through which we pass, the commentators point out, as we practise the yoga disciplines and as we strive to attain to complete renunciation. There are four such stages. The first is yatamāna, during which there arises aninner struggle from our not permitting the mind to seek gratification of the senses. The second is syatireka, during which, through self-analysis, we realize the measure of our own achievement in the field of self-control. We realize what desires we can control and what we as yet cannot. Then with vigour and enthusiasm we must continue to attack all desires that still remain in the way of illumination. The third is ekendriya, during which greater self-control is achieved, and the heart no longer desires the objects of enjoyment, knowing their ephemeral and shadowy naturc, vct thcrc may still remain in it a longing curiosity. When this longing also has been overcome, we attain the fourth and highest stage of renunciation. This is known as vaśīkāra.

This, the supreme goal in, is achieved only by him who has attained complete enlightenment when, through knowledge of the Puruṣa, one ceases to desire any manifestation of prakṛit then one experiences the highest kind of non attachment,[13] says Patañjali. And the Gītā says:

The abstinent run away from what they desire
But carry theirdesires with them:
When a man enters Reality,
He leaves his desires behind him.[14]

Again the Gītā summing up the whole truth of yoga:

'When men have thrown off their ignorance, they are free from pride and delusion. They have conquered the evil of worldly attachment. They live in constant union with the Ātman. All craving has left them. They are no longer at the mercy of opposing sense reactions. Thus they reach that state which is he' end all change [15].

How to Become a Yogi

Bhoja, the commentator, indicates how rare are the souls who at birth are endowed with minds having an aptitude of yoga. Most men, he says, have to mature slowly as they gradully equip themselves with minds fit for practising it. And the learned commentator proceeds to discover in minds five types.

The first three of these may be grouped together, he first is the scattered mind, which is filled with rajas and impelled by its power to be ever in search excitement in the external world; never at rest, but ever tossed up and down the waves that bring to it the manifold experince of pleasure and pain. The second is the dull mind, its perceptions veiled by the power of tamas; such a mind revolts from undertaking even the obligatory duties of life and is a slave to low passions. The third is the cuddling or average mind, restless at times and again momentarily calm and serene. Those possessed of minds represented by one or another of these three types are not suited to higher yoga practices. They must first undergo the preliminary disciplines of habitual ethical conduct.

Bhoja fourth and fifth types, unlike the others, are one-pointed, concentrated. Whenver sattwa predominates in it the mind is characterized by a natural purity, it is tranquil, never agitated by the rise of passions from below, but possesing the power of control over them, and it rises continually towards higher and higher planes of being. Such is the one-pointed mind. The concentrated mind not only is pure and tranquil, but also is absorbed inthe contemplation of Puruṣa, the Self, or God, forgetful of the body.

Attaining the state of absorption, and advancing beyond it to samādhi and illumination, can come only graually, step by step, and only by following the prescribed rules of conduct and the other practices of yoga. In a general way the necessary discipline has been defined by Patañjali in the following aphorism: 'The concentration of the true spiritual aspirant is attained through faith, strenuousness, recollectedness, absorption and illumination.[16]

The primary requirement is faith. The word faith, however, must not be understood in its generally accepted meaning of belief in something that reason cannot penetrate. At the very beginning there must be understanding, a conviction in the mind; then comes the effort to have faith—which means response in the heart. Most people, in an abstract sort of way, believe in the existence of God. But as to *realizing* God—few do anything about that. When one has faith, one will *act on* that faith. Bhoja, the commentator, explains the Sanskrit word śraddhā, translated faith, as signifying a condition in which the heart 'pleasantly inclined towards attaining yoga'.

There must, moreover, be spiritual strenuousness. Buddha pointed out that if there is any sin it is laziness. Strenuousness grows by strenuous acts. As faith increases and strenuousness grows, the mind takes a direction. It becomes *recollected,* in the basic meaning of this word. Our thoughts have been scattered all over the mental field. Now we begin to gather them together and direct them toward a definite goal—knowledge of the Puruṣa. As we do this, we find ourselves becoming increasingly absorbed in the thought of God. And so, at length, absorption merges in illumination, and the knowledge is ours.

Success in yoga depends upon the amount of energy we put forth in our struggles for its attainment. Patañjali says: 'Success in yoga comes quickly to those who are intensely energetic': and to the same purpose 'Sucess varies accoridng to the strength of the effort expended to attian it—mild, moderate, or intense'.[17]

Again, in order that we may put forth energy for success in yoga, we must remote certain physical and mental obstacles that stand in the way 'Sickness, mental laziness, doubt, lack of enthusiasm, sloth, craving for sense-pleasure, false perception, despair caused by failure to concentrate and unsteadiness in concentration these'distractions are the obstacles to knowledge. These distractions are accompanied by grief, despondency, trembling of the body, and irregular breathing. They can be-pamoved by the practice of con-centration upon a single truth'.[18]

In order to achieve this concentration, we must calm and purify our minds Patañjali tells us have to do this.

'Undisturbed calmness of mind is attained by cultivating friendliness toward the happy, compassion for the unhappu, delight in the virtuous, and indifference toward the wicked.[19]

Hatred, jealous, fear—in short, the restless, distracted states of mind—are the root causes of most of our physical and mental ills. Every reaction in the form of hatred, or jealousy, or anger, is so much loss to body and mind, and each time we restrain ourselves from such reactions, good energy is stored up in our favour for conversion into higher powers. In order, again, that we may restrain ourselves from the evil reactions to the end that we may establish our minds in tranquillity, Patañjali advises that we assume a mental attitude that will purity our hearts and bring peace of mind. He teaches that we must learn to be happy in the happiness of others, that we must be merciful towards those who are in pain. Let us be glad when others do good deeds and be indifferent to the wicked. By raising opposite waves in the mind, the waves of love and friendliness and mere, we may overcome offensive mental of jealousy, hatred, and anger. By arousing tranquillity in the heart through such transforming practices, we also free ourselves from physical and mental ills.

This consideration of how to gain control over the mind leads us to think of the preliminary disciplines that work towards yoga. In the words of St. Paul, which we have already quoted, the spiritual life requires a renewing of the mind', and this is achieved by a gradual entire readjustment of outlook and habits, for the impurities of the mind are nothing else than habits of life and thought, and to overcome one set of habits one must form another and contrary set of habits This process consists in the practice of kriyā yoga, the accessory disciplines of yoga: 'austerity, study, and the dedication of the fruits of one's work to God[20]

Austerity is the practice of conseriing energy and directing it towards the goal of yoga, towards realizing the true nature of the Puruṣa. Obviously, in order to engage in this, we must exercise self-discipline, we must control our physical appetites and passions. In the Gītā, the three kinds of true austerity are defined: 'Reverence for the devas, the seers, the teachers, and the sages; straightforwardness, harmlessness, physical cleanliness, and sexual purity'—these are the virtues whose practice is called austerity of the body. To speaks without ever causing pain to another, to be truthful, to say always what is kind and beneficial, and to study the scriptures regularly—this practice is called austerity of speech. The practice of serenity, sympathy, meditation upon the Ātman, withdrawal of the mind from sense-rects, and integrity of motive, is called austerity of the mind.[21]

The practice of austenty, as described by commentators on the *Yoga Aphorisms*, may also include the regular performance of ritualistic worship. The observance of ritualism is an excellent training for the wandering mind of the beginner. Each successive act recalls his mind to the thought behind the act. He is too busy to think of anything else. Thought and action, action and thought, form a continuous chain; and it is amazing to find what a comparatively high degree of concentration he can achieve, even from the very first.

'It is of vital importance', said Swami Brahmananda, my master, 'that a man begin his spiritual journey from where he is. If an average man is instructed to meditate on his union with the absolute Brahman, he will not understand. He will neither grasp the truth that lies behind the instructions nor be able to follow them. . . . However,. .. if that same man is asked to worship God with flowers, incense, and other accessories of the ritualistic worship, his mind will gradually become concentrated on God, and he will find joy in his worships.[22]

'Study' in tne context of the *Aphorisms*—it should be noted—means study of the scriptures and of other books which deal with the spiritual life. It also refers to the practice of japa, the repetition of the sacred name of

God.

To dedicate the fruits of one's work to God is towork with non-attachment, to practise karma yoga.

'All the great religions yield ash primary article of their faith that the Self is innately pure and divine God made man in his own image'. All of them hold further that original purity and that divinity have somehow been lost. Christianity attributes the fall of man from his pristine state of announce to the fall of the first man, Adam, and believes that now we art 'born in sin and iniquity' through having inherited his weakness and that we can be saved only through the grace of a merciful heaveniy rather as repealed in the sacrifice of his Son, jesus Christ. The truth in this doctrine would appear to be that man in his original nature is innocent and pure, a perfect image of God, but that it as an effect of some inexpkicable cause he has lost his pristine attributes. The sin which the story of the Fall of Adam informs us we have. inherited cannot however, be real and permanent cannot really have altered our original nature Christianity itself offers us the goal of conquest over sin and the attainment of liberation and a rented perfection we are to become perfect—even as the 'Father which is in heaven is perfect'. This goal would be meaningless, because it could never be attained, had we been born in sin. For it is not possible to change the innate character of a substance without destroying the substance itself. One cannot change the nature of fire, which be that very nature must radiate heat, except by destroying fire itselt. Nevertheless its inborn nature, its heat, may be smothered a covering of ash. Remove the ash, fan the fire, and you will again have both fire and heat. The same thing is true of the Self—its innate purity and divinity may be covered by ignorance but not lost Indian philosophy proclaims: 'You are forever free and divine Your apparent imperfection is due to ignorance, realize what you are, and be free. The same truth appears m Christian teachings, although it may not be recognized as such by all theologians, for does not the Bible say: 'The light shineth in darkness and the darkness comprehended it not'.

We are pure, free, and divine, Suffering, sin, limitations, and all imperfections are due to avidyā, ignorance, which veils the true nature of the Self, causing us to identify ourselves with the non-Self.

Patañjali says:

'The obstacles to enlightenment—the causes of man's sufferings—are ignorance, egoism attachment aversion, and the desire to cling to life.

And again:

'To regard the non-eternal as eternal, the impure as pure, the painful as pleasant and the non-Self as the Puruṣa—this is ignorance.[23]

The ignorance is of course universal, and is the basis of our ordinary, finite lives, the cause of all conditioned experience.

Ignorance, says Patañjali, leads to egoism, attachment, aversion, and the desire to cling to life—the immediate causes of suffering and confusion.

To identify consciousness with that which merely reflects consciousness—this is egoism.[23]

The central act of ignorance is the identification of the Puruṣa, which is consciousness itselt, with the mind-body—'that which merely reflects consciousness.' This is what Patañjali defines as egoism.[24]

'At whose behest does the mind think?' asks the Kena Upaniṣad 'Who bids the body live? Who makes the tongue speak? Who is that effulgent Being that directs the eye to term and colour and the ear to sound? The Ātman is the ear of the ear mind of the mind, speech of the speech. He is also breath of the breath and eye of the eye. Having given up the false identification of the Ātman with the senses and the mind, and knowing the Ātman to be Brahman, the wise become immortal. [25]

Western philosophy has produced two schools of thought with regard to the problem of consciousness—the materialist and the idealist. The materialists believe that consciousness is the product of a process that it arises when certain conditions are fulfilled and is lost when these conditions do not exist. Thus, according to the materialist philosophers, consciousness is not the property of any single substance. The idealists, on the other hand, believe that consciousness is the property of the mind, and are therefore faced with the conclusion that it must cease whenever the mind becomes unconscious.

Modern scientists would seem inclined to reject both these hypotheses, and to believe that consciousness is always present everywhere in the universe, even though its presence cannot always be detected by scientific methods. In this they approach the viewpoint of Vedānta. And indeed there are some distinguished scientists and scientific writers whose thinking has brought them to a study of Hindu philosophy. For example, Erwin Schrödinger in his book *What is Life* ? writes as follows:

'Consciousness is never experienced in the plural, only in the singular... How does the idea of plurality (so emphatically opposed by the Upaniṣhad writers) arise at all? Consciousness finds itself intimately connected with, and dependent on, the physical state of a limited region of matter, the body.... Now, there is a great plurality of similar bodies. Hence the puralization of consciousness or minds seems a very suggestive hypothesis. Probably all simple ingenuous people, as well as the great majority of Western philosophers, have accepted it. ... The only possible alternative is simply to keep to the immediate experience that consciousness is a singular of which the plural is unknown; that there *is* only one thing and that, what seems to be a plurality, is merely a series of different aspects of this one thing, produced by a deception (the Indian Māyā); the same illusion is produced in a gallery of mirrors, and in the same way Gaurisankar and Mount Everest turned out to be the same peak seen from different valleys. . . .

'Yet each of us has the undisputable impression that the sum total of his own experience and memory forms a unit, quite distinct from that of any other person. He refers to it as "I". *What is this* "I"?'

'If you analyse it closely you will, I think, find that it is just a little bit more than a collection of single data (experiences and memories), namely the canvas *upon which* they are collected. And you will, on close introspection, find that, what you really mean by "I", is that ground-stuff upon which they are collected. You may come to a distant country, lose sight of all your friends, may all but forget them; you acquire new friends. You share life with them as intensely as you ever did with your old ones. Less and less important will become that fact that, while living your new life, you still recollect the old one. "The youth that was I", you may come to speak of him in the third person, indeed the protagonist of the novel you are reading is probably nearer to your heart, certainly more intensely alive and better known to you. Yet there has been no intermediate break, no death. And even if a skilled hypnotist succeeded in blotting out entirely all your earlier reminiscences, you would not find that he had killed *you*. In no case is there a loss of personal existence to deplore. Nor will there ever be.'[26]

The mind merely retlects consciousness and is the instrument of perception and experience; the identification of the Puruṣa, who is consciousness itself, with the instrument, the mind, is, as we have seen, egoism. We say 'I am happy' or 'I am suffering', but happiness or suffering is but waves of thought arising in the mind. Through egoism the Self, becoming identified with the mind, identifies, itself with the waves or thoughts in the mind, and either enjoys or suffers.

Through egoism there arises the desire for pleasurable sense experiences, and there grows attachment to them. Desire for sensational and emotional experiences and attachment to them cause suffering. Therefore attachment to those experiences and a desire for them must be avoided if we are to obtain tranquillity of mind and heart. Opposed to attachment is aversion, which is also a cause of suffering, and to be avoided. Śrī Kṛṣṇa says in the Gītā,

When he has no lust, no hatred,
A man walks safely among the things of lust and hatred.
To obey the Ātman
Is his peaceful joy:
Sorrow melts
Into that clear peace:
His quiet mind
Is soon established in peace.[27]

Not a complete withdrawal of the senses from the world, nor a denial of the normal experiences of life, is required for tranquillity of mind, but a freeing of the mind from both attraction and aversion.

The last of the 'pain-bearing obstructions', according to Patañjali, is the desire to cling to life, a feeling which may perhaps be correlated with Freud's life-instinct. Commentators have explained it as fear of death, which exists instinctively in all living beings. This fear of death is another cause of unhappiness.

These five causes of suffering are the chief obstacles in the path of yoga; of them all, ignorance is the root cause. They exist universally in all beings, though in different states and degrees in different people. Patañjali says, 'They may exist either in a potential or a vestigial form, or they may have been temporarily overcome or fully developed.'[28]

In most people these obstacles exist fully developed, in some in a repressed or overpowered condition. Through the practices of yoga and self-discipline, they may be attenuated and finally destroyed.

The goal of yoga is to eradicate these obstacles completely and thus to remove the causes of suffering. The root cause, as we have seen, is ignorance, which is the 'productive field' for all other obstacles; and its removal is possible by means of its opposite, vidyā, or knowledge. Patañjali says, 'Ignorance is destroyed by awakening to knowledge of the Puruṣa, until no trace of illusion remains.'[29] This knowledge that removes the ignorance is not knowledge such as is associated with the intellect, but rather an immediate, direct illumination in one's own soul. 'The experiencer gains this knowledge,' says Patañjali, 'in seven stages, advancing toward the highest.[30]

The seven stages are as follows:

(a) The realization that the source of all spiritual wisdom is inside ourselves, that the kingdom of heaven is within us. As Swami Vivekananda says:

'After long searches here and there, in temples and churches, in earths and in heavens, at it last you come back, completing the circle from where you stated to,your own soul and find that He, for whom you have been seeking, all over the wild for whom you have been weeping and prying, in churches and temples, on horn you were looking as the mystery of all mysteries shrouded in the clouds, is nearest of the near is your own Self, the reality of your life, body and soul'.[31]

These are stirring words, to which our hearts can immediately respond, but a firm realization of their truth is not so easily achieved. It is not enough to accept it as an intellectual proposition. It is not enough to glimpse it in moments of religious emotion or temporary insight. We cannot claim to have reached the first stage until we are, continuously aware of the presence of the Ātman, or Puruṣa[32] within us. When we are aware of this, we know also, without any doubt, that union with the Ātman in is possible, since no external obstacles can arise to prevent it.

(b) The cessation of pain Pain, as we have seen, is caused by our attachment or aversion to the phenomena of the external universe. As the mind turns inward towards knowledge of the Ātman, this attachment or aversion loses its power. We have already quoted the (Gītā phrase 'Yoga is the breaking of contact with pain'.[33]

(c) Samādhi—complete realization or, and union with, the Ātman. The objective universe disappears. The Ātman is experienced as total existence consciousness and joy In this experience all sense of individual separate ness and differentiation is lost.

(d) The state of consciousness following samādhi. When a man comes out of samādhi returns to consciousness of the objective universe but this consciousness differs from the kind which we all experience. To one who has achieved samādhi, the external world is known to be merely an appearance. In Sāṁkara s phrase, 'it is and is not'. The man of illumination no longer identifies the external world with the Ātman. He sees that it is only a reflection of the Ātman—not, indeed utterly unreal since it is projected by the Reality; yet lacking substance and independent existence like an image in a mirror.

In this stage, a man knows that he is no longer bound by any worldly duty or obligation. This does not mean, of course, that a man who has achieved samādhi will thenceforward do nothing at all. On the contrary, most of the great saints have been very active, particularly in teaching others. 'They are like big steamships,' said Śrī Ramakṛṣṇa, 'which not only cross the ocean themselves but carry many passengers to the other shore.' But the actions of the saint differ from the actions of ordinary men, because they are not motivated by any attachment or selfish desire. They are, in the most literal sense of the word, voluntary actions. Action, for the rest of us, is only partially voluntary; it always contains anlement of compulsion due to our past karmas and present involvements in the life of the senses this reason, the behaviour of a saint is often very hard for us to understand; it seems strange, arbitrary, or capricious, precisely by iuse it is not subject to our familiar compulsions. A great teacher was once asked to explain one of the most seemingly mysterious actions recorded in the Gospels, Christ's cursing of the barren fig tree. 'Become a Christ,' he replied smilingly, 'and then you will know why he did that.'

(e) Freedom from need of the mind and the objective world—the realization that the mind and the objective world have both ended their services. The mind has been the instrument, and the world the object of the experience whereby the experience has come to know the Ātman, his real nature. The mind has been used to transcend the mind—just as we use a ladder to transcend a ladder once we have reached the sill of the window against which it rested, the ladder can be kicked away; we do not need it any more.

(f) Freedom from 'impressions and guṇas. Now the stored-up impressions within the mind, and the guṇas themselves, fall away forever, like rocks, to quote one of the classic commentators, 'fallen from the top of the mountain peak, never to return'.

(g) Union with the Ātman. And so the final stage is reached—the state of eternal existence in union with the Ātman. Now there is no more returning from samādhi to partial sense-consciousness, no more identification of the Ātman with the mind We realize, in the words of Vivekananda,

'. . . that we have been alone throughout all time, neither body nor mind was ever related, much less joined, to us. They were working their own way and we, through ignorance, joined ourselves to them. But we have been alone, omnipotent omnipresent, ever blessed, our own Ātman was so pure and perfect that we required nothing else.. . . Throughout the universe there can be nothing that will not become effulgent before our, knowledge. This will be the last state, and the yogi wll become peaceful and calm, never to feel any more pain, never to be again deluded, never to be touched by misery. He will know that he is ever blessed, ever perfect, almighty.[34]

The Limbs of Yoga

Two of the yoga aphorisms provide the text for this section:

'As soon as all impurities have been removed by the practice of spiritual disciplines—the "limbs" of yoga—a man's spirit opens to the light-giving knowledge of the Puruṣa.

'The eight limbs of yoga are: the various forms of abstention from evil-doing (yama), the various observances (niyama), pasture (āsana), control of the prāṇa (prāṇāyāma), withdrawal of the mind from sense objects (pratyāhāra), concentration (dhāraṇā)—meditation (dhyāna) and absorption in the Puruṣa (samādhi).[35]

Yoga has been aptly compared to a tree bearing luscious fruit. The seed of the yoga-tree is nourished by yama and niyama; as it begins to germinate it is further fed by posture and prāṇāyāma; and as it matures and becomes a full-grown tree it bears flowers in the practice of pratyāhāra, and abundant fruits in concentration, meditation, and samādhi.

So important are the eight limbs that each will be accorded special comment.

Yama, the first, has been analysed in the two following aphorisms:

'Yama is the abstention from harming others, from falsehood, from theft, from incontinence, and from greed.

'These forms of abstention are basic rules of conduct. They must be practiced without and reservations as to time, place, purpose, or caste rules'.[36]

It will be noticed that yama, thus understood, embraces the ethical principles universally taught in all the great religions.

Abstention from harming others is living and acting in such a way as never to cause and pain to a living soul by one's thought, word, or deed. It is said to be the greatest of the virtues. In its positive, aspect the injunction is to do good to all and to learn to live in love and harmony with all.

'When a man becomes steadfast in his abstention from harming—others, then all creatures will cease to feel enmity in his presence.[37]

> When a man has truly and entirely renounced violence in his own thoughts, and in his dealings with others, he begins to create an atmosphere around himself within which violence and enmity must cease to exist, because they find no reciprocation. Animals too are sensitive to such an atmosphere. There is a saying that the tiger and the lamb will play together before a true yogi. 'The test of ahiṁsā (harmlessness) is absence of jealousy, . . .' said Swami Vivekananda. 'The so-called great men of the world may all be seen to become jealous of each other for a small name, for a little fame, and for a few bits of gold. So long as this jealousy exists in a heart, it is far away from the perfection of ahiṁsā.[38]

Abstention from falsehood is truthfulness in thought, word, and deed. In the Gītā we are admonished 'to speak without ever causing pain to another, to be truthful, and to say always what is kind and beneficial'. And thus Patañjali:

'When a man becomes steadfast in his abstention from falsehood he gets the power of obtaining for himself and others the fruits of good deeds, without having to perform the deeds themselves'.[39]

Such a man cannot think or even dream a lie; everything he says is or becomes true. Facts, as it were, follow his words. If he blesses someone, that person becomes blessed.

Abstention from theft has a deeper significance than what the phrase literally means. We must realize that nothing belongs to us; consequently, we may not harbour the idea of possession or own attachment to things of this world. 'When a man becomes steadfast in his abstention from theft, all wealth comes to him'.[40] Swami Vivekananda, commenting upon this aphorism, remarks, 'The more 'you fly from nature, the more she follows you, and. if you do not care for her at all, she becomes your slave'.[41]

Abstention from incontinence is chastity in thought, word, and deed. 'When a man becomes steadfast in his abstention from incontinence, he acquires spiritual energy[42] Such energy is indispensable to a religious teacher. With it comes tremendous force and gigantic will to turn humanity into the path of good.

Abstention from greed is freedom from covetousness.
The foregoing are the virtues included under yama.

The second limb of yoga is niyama Patañjali has defined it thus:

'The niyamas [observances] are purity, contentment, mortification, study, and devotion to God'.[43]

Purity is cleanliness both physical and mental just as a regular habit of bathing is formed for physical cleanliness, in the same way a regular habit is to be formed of bathing our inner organ, the mind, by feeling within it the living presence of God. From the practice of cleanliness physical and mental, 'one achieves purification of the heart, cheerfulness of mind, the power of concentration, control of the passions, and fitness for the vision of the Puruṣa'.[44]

Commenting on this aphorism Swami Vivekananda remarks:

'The first sign of your becoming religious is that you are becoming cheerful. When a man is gloomy, his condition may be dyspepsia, but it is not religion. To the yogi everything is bliss, every human face that he sees brings cheerfulness to him. This is the sign of a virtuous man'.[45]

Contentment is the practice of quiet acceptance of whatever comes in the course of our lives and the maintenance of an inner poise.

The remaining three regular habits have already been discussed in our explanation of kriyā, that is, the preliminary practices for achieving growth towards yoga. We may note, however, that study, which has been interpreted as the chanting of sacred words and prayers, is of three kinds: verbal, semi-verbal, and mental. The first is audible chanting, the second is the moving of the lips from which no sound issues as one repeats the sacred word; and the third is the repetition of the sabred word in the mind. In all these cases repetition must be accompanied by meditation upon the meaning ot the word or prayer.

For the effective practice of the virtues mentioned above, Patañjali suggests: To be free from thoughts that distract one from yoga, thoughts of an opposite kind must be cultivated.[46] When a wave of anger, for example has entered the mind, let it be controlled by raising an opposite wave of love.

Yama and niyama are the first two limbs of yoga; āsana, posture, is the third. A series of exercises, for the most part mental, is to be followed each day until certain of the higher states of consciousness are reached. It is necessary that we should learn to be seated in a firm position, Patañjali advising that the easiest and most natural one should be chosen. 'Proper posture requires that one be seated in a position which is firm but relaxed'.[47] 'The Gītā says, 'His posture must be motionless, with the body, head and neck held erect...'[48] Swami Vivekananda suggests, 'Let the whole weight of the body be supported by the ribs, and then you have an easy, natural posture, with the spine straight'.[49] In one of the Sāṁkhya Sūtras we read: 'Any posture which is easy and steady is an āsana: there is no other rule'.[50]

With regard to posture Patañjali gives this advice:

'Posture becomes firm and relaxed through control of the natural tendencies of the body, and through meditation on the Infinite.[51]

The purpose of āsana is to calm the mind, and calm is achieved if when seated we meditate on the all-pervading presence of God, or fix our minds upon some thought concerning astness or infinitude. 'Thereafter, one is no longer troubled by the dualities of sense experience.[52] After a period during which we observe our bodies in a certain posture, we gain in control over them, and then the dualities, heat and cold and the other pairs ot opposites in our empirical lives, cease to disturb the equilibrium of our minds.

In this connection it may be interesting to learn what Vedānta philosophy has to say with respect to posture. The following are 'aphorisms from Vyāsa:

'Worship is possible in a sitting posture, because this encourages meditation. The meditating person is compared to the immovable earth. There is no law of place; wherever the mind is concentrated, there worship should be performed.[53]

The fourth limb of yoga is prāṇāyāma. This word means control of vital energy, or of the life-principle. Just what the life-principle really is, no one can tell, but we do recognize its expression. If is the energy that enables us to act, to think, to breathe. Prāṇāyāma is control of this energy, and the word lias come to be associated with breathing, exercises based on a principle somewhat analogous to that propounded by William lames to the Western world. The principle may, be stated thus: The mind and the body are closely related, and act and react upon each other; emotions cause characteristic changes in the body, and changes in the body evoke corresponding emotions in the mind. On this principle of experimental psychology, discovered in the West in recent years, but known to the yogis of India from almost a beginningless past, there is taught control of the breath to bring calmness and concentration to the mind. The state of the mind, whether it be lethargic or restless or calm, is first observed in the breathing, for the rise of passions brings about characteristic changes in the way we breathe. If, then, breathing can be made rhythmic, calm is the inevitable result. If, moreover, the mind is in process of concentration, we scarcely breathe, and when the mind is in a state of complete concentration, we do not breathe at all. Prāṇāyāma needs therefore to be practiced first in order to win control over the body and mind, and finally to control the very life energy itself. In the words of Swami Vivekananda:

'In this body of ours, the breath motion is the "silken thread"; by laying hold of and learning to control it we grasp the pack thread of 'the nerve currents, and from these the stout twine of our thoughts and lastly the rope of prāṅa, controlling which we reach freedom.[54]

According to Patañjali, the prāṇāyāma consists of three parts: inhalation, exhalation, and pause. This pause may be either internal, when the breath is held in the lungs, or external, when it is prevented from entering them. A fourth kind of prāṇāyāma exist when in the process of meditation the yogi enters the stage of kumbhaka, or natural cessation of breathe.[55]

The fifth in order of the limbs of yoga is pratyāhāra, the practice undertaken to gain detachment of the mind from objects of sense by not permitting the mind to join itself to the centres of perception or the organs of sense. In the words of the Gītā:

The tortoise can draw in its legs:
The seer can draw in his senses.

I call him illumined.[56]

That is pratyahara. Swami Vivekananda remarks:

'He who has succeeded in attaching his mind to the centres of perception at will, or in detaching it from them, has succeeded in pratyahara, which means "gathering towards", checking the outgoing powers of the mind, freeing it from the thraldom of the senses. When we can do this we shall really possess character; then alone we shall have taken a long step towards freedom.[57]

How difficult it is to gain control over the mind, which has been aptly compared to a maddened monkey drunk with wine and stung by a scorpion! Like that monkey, the human mind is restless, drunk with the wine of desires and stung hy the passions. Control over this restless mind is not an easy task, but through the discipline of yoga it can be attained. In the beginning, the yogi would let the mind run its full course while he learned to become a witness to its action. Let us listen again to Swami Vivekananda, who has the comparison to a maddened monkey in mind:

'The first lesson is to sit for some time and let the mind run on. The mind is bubbling up all the time. It is like that monkey jumping about. Let the monkey jump as much as he can; you simply wait and watch. Knowledge is power, says the proverb, and that is true. Until you know what the mind is doing, you cannot control it. Give it the rein; many hideous thoughts may come into it; you will be astonished that it was possible for you to think such thoughts. But you will find that each day the mind's vagaries are becoming fewer and less violent, that each day it is becoming calmer. In the first few months you will find that the mind will have a great many thoughts, later you will find that they have somewhat decreased, and in a few more months you will find that they are fewer and fewer, until at last the mind will be under perfect control—but we must patiently practice every day.[58]

Concentration, the sixth limb of yoga, has been defined by Patañjali as 'holding the mind within a centre of spiritual consciousness in the body, or fixing it on some divine form, either within the body or outside it'.[59] We again repeat that the kingdom of heaven is within; that is to say, Puruṣa, or the Divine Self, is within the sanctuary of the body. Thus all the forms of worship or of concentration and meditation taught to aspirants alter spiritual life are directed towards the search for this kingdom of heaven within one's own self. The Upaniṣads teach that the self is to be meditated upon within the cavity of the heart. There are within the body, declare the Indian yogis, different spiritual centres within when one may turn one's mind upon the light of God. Patañjali, in detimng concentration, has reference to the turning of the mind intently towards these centres of spiritual consciousness.

But this practice must be undertaken only under the instruction of an adept. Men vary both in capacity and in temperament. A single form of concentration may not suit all men in their search for spiritual realization. Patañjali suggests a few simple forms, however, which everyone may practice. The first two of these are contained in the following aphorisms.

'This word (Om) must be repeater with meditation upon its meaning'.[60]

'Concentration may also be attained by fixing the mind upon the Inner Light, which is beyond sorrow'.[61]

This inner light deserves comment. The ancient yogis believed that there was an actual centre of spiritual consciousness, called 'the lotus of the heart', situated between the abdomen and the thorax, which could be revealed to the aspirant in deep meditation. They said that it had the form of a lotus and that it shone with an inner light. It was said to be beyond sorrow', since those who saw it were filled with an extraordinary sense of peace and joy.

From the very earliest times, the masters of yoga emphasized the importance of meditating upon this lotus. According to the Kaivalya Upaniṣad:

'The supreme heaven shines in the lotus of the heart. Those who struggle and aspire may enter there. . . . Retire into solitude. Seat yourself on a clean spot in an erect posture, with the head and neck in a straight line. Control all sense organs. How down in devotion to your teacher. Then enter the lotus of the heart and meditate there on the presence of Brahman—the pure, the infinite, the blissful.[62]

And in the Chāndogya Upaniṣad we read:

'Within the city of Brahman, which is the body, there is the heart, and within the heart there is a little house. This house has the shape of a lotus, and within it dwells that which is to be sought after, inquired about, and realized.

'What, then, is that which dwells within this little house, this lotus of the hearth What is it that must be sought after, inquired about, and realized?

'Even so large as the universe outside is the universe within the lotus of the heart. Within it are heaven and earth, the sun, the moon, the lightning, and all the stars. Whatever is in the macrocosm is in this microcosm also'.

'All things that exist, all beings and all desires, are in the city of Brahman; what, then, becomes of them when old age approaches and the body dissolves in death'?

'Though old age comes to the body, the lotus of the heart does not grow old. It does not die with the death of the body. The lotus of the heart, where Brahman resides in all his glory—that, and not the body is the true city of Brahman. Brahman, dwelling therein, is untouched by any deed, ageless, deathless, free from grief, free from hunger and from thirst. His desires are right desires, and his desires are fulfilled.[63]

And in the Muṇḍaka Upaniṣad:

'Within the lotus of the heart he dwells, where the nerves meet like the spokes of a wheel. Meditate upon him as Om, and you may easily cross the ocean of darkness.[64] In the effulgent lotus of the heart dwells Brahman, passionless and indivisible. He is pure. He is the light of all lights. The knowers of Brahman attain him'.[65]

Meditation in the heart centre is helpful because it localizes our image of the spiritual consciousness towards which we are struggling. If the body is thought of as a busy and noisy city, then we can imagine that in the middle of this city there is a little shrine, and that within this shrine the Ātman, our real nature, is present. No matter what is going on in the streets outside, we can always enter that shrine and worship. It is always open.

Or again—a third form—one may meditate 'upon the heart of an illumined soul, that is free from passion'. In the Upaniṣads we read, 'A knower of Brahman has become Brahman'. By worshipping such a knower, we actually worship God. And such a knower is any one of the God-men—for example, Kṛṣṇa, Buddha, or Christ.

Or—a fourth form—one may substitute 'a dream experience, or the experience of deep sleep'.[67] By 'a dream experience' Patañjali means a dream about a holy personality or a divine symbol. Such a dream can properly be called an experience, because it brings a sense of joy and revelation which remains with us after we have awakened. In the literature of Indian spirituality we find many instances of devotees who dreamed that they received a mantra from some great teacher. Such a dream-mantra is regarded as being just as sacred as one received in the waking state, and the devotee who is blessed by it will continue to use it and meditate upon it throughout the rest of his life.

Or, finally, one may substitute 'any divine form or symbol that appeals to one as good'.[68] One of the most attractive characteristics of Patañjali's philosophy is its breadth of vision, its universality. There is no attempt here to impose any particular cult upon the spiritual aspirant. God is within us, and it is by the light of his presence—no matter how dimly it shines through the layers of our ignorance—that we fashion our own pictures and symbols of goodness and project them upon the outside world. Every such picture, symbol, or idea is holy if it is conceived in sincerity, it may be crude and childish, it may not appeal to others; that is unimportant. All-important is our attitude towards it. Whatever we truly and purely worship, we make sacred.

As concentration deepens, we arrive at the next, the seventh limb of yoga, called meditation. 'Meditation (dhyāna) is an unbroken flow of thought toward the object of concentration'.[69]

In other words, meditation is prolonged concentration. The process of meditation is often compared to the pouring of oil from one vessel to another in a steady, unbroken stream. We have seen that Patañjali defines thought as a wave (vṛtti)[70] in the mind. Ordinarily a thought wave arises, retains in the mind for a moment, and then subsides, to be succeeded by another. In the practice of meditation a succession of identical waves is raised in the mind; and this is done so quickly that no one wave is allowed to subside before another rises to take its place. The effect is therefore one of perfect continuity. If you shoot a hundred feet of film without moving your camera or your object, and then project the result on a screen, the spectator might just as well be looking at a single still photograph. The many identical images are fused into one.

It will be seen that Patañjali's dhyāna does not exactly correspond to our usual understanding of meditation. We commonly mean by it a more or less discursive operation of the mind around a central idea. If, for example, we say that we have been meditating on Christ, we are apt to mean that we have not only tried to fix our minds on Christ's ideal form but have also been thinking about his teachings, his miracles, his disciples, his crucifixion, and so on. All this is very good, but it is a mere preliminary to what may properly be called dhāraṇā and dhyāna.

The final stage of meditation is samādhi, absorption. This is the last, the eighth limb of yoga. This absorption is not precisely samādhi in the sense of transcendental consciousness, which will be explained later; it is rather the door to its attainment. It is the state we achieve when meditation deepens and the mind takes cn the form of the object of meditation. Then is the mind entirely freed from any other thought, then there is complete forgetfulness of everything but the object of meditation, and the sense of time is annihilated. 'The mind becomes one-pointed when similar thought-waves arise in succession without any gaps between them'.[71]

Patañjali declares that these three—concentration, meditation, and absorption—are more direct and to spiritual experience than the five limbs previously described'.[72] They represent the three stages of the process ot contemplation, of which the third is the culmination and together the are known as saṁyama, which in turn is to be followed by the lower stage of samādhi, transcendental consciousness. The other five limbs of yoga are preparatory to the practice of contemplation.

When one has passed through saṁyama—that is, when one has attained perfection in meditation—illumination arises in the mind. 'By the practice or saṁyama comes the light of knowledge'.[73] Before, however, we discuss this last victory that rewards the aspirant's efforts, we ought briefly to consider the psychic experiences and occult powers which now may be in his possession.

Yoga and Occult Powers

While engaged ir an explanation ot concentration and meditation, Patañjali refers to the way in which the mind, while becoming deeply absorbed in and particular object or thought, acquires bibhutis, or occult powers and psychic phenomena occur. Different powers are acquired as a result ot concentrating upon different objects. If one, for instance should exercise saṁvama on the peculiar signs or features in another s hod, one gains knowledge of his mind. Or, 'if one exercises samyama on the form of one's own body, obstructing its perceptibility and separating its power of manifestation from the eyes of the beholder then one's body becomes invisible'.[75] A yogi, for example, though he may not actually depart from the room in which he is seated, may disappear from the sight of everyone present. He has realm attained to that power of concentration wherein form and the thing termed have become separated. As he exercises samyama on his own form the power to perceive forms by other is is so obstructed that he become invisible.

Patañjali describes exercising saṁvama on various objects and concepts and claims there from the acquisition of various occult powers and the appearance of various psychic phenomena have read in the Bible how Christ pertormed many miracles—for example, walking on the water, turning water into wine, feeding a multitude with five loaves and two fishes, healing the sick, and raising the dead. According to Indian logic claims, such miracles are not exceptions, rather can they be performed by every man provided he follows certain practices and the principal apparatus or testing the validity of these claims is the mind cultivated by the practices of concentration and meditation. If it is asked whether these powers and phenomena are capable of scientific demonstration, the answer is yes and no. They are demonstrable in the senseithat the yogi can exhibit his powers before anybody, but not in the sense that he can explain to just anybody how he does so. To comprehend his demonstration, one must oneself in some degree be a yogi—just as to understand a demonstration in physics or chemistry one must be already, in some degree, a scientist. The educated man will understand the demonstration, but will a boor, or a moron?

The law ot cause and effect, as we know it in the world of science, does not apply to the process of meditation upon a particular object or concept and to the development to a particular result therefrom. But that there is here an invariable sequence can be proved through continued experiment. Certain powers are easily attainable, while others are the result of long and strenuous practice. Such powers as clairvoyance, clairaudience, thought-reading, telepathy, are child's play compared with some other yogic powers, such as the power of becoming invisible, of levitation, of walking on water, and the like. All these occult or psychic powers may be developed by an exact application of Patan all's special instructions, or they may suddenly come to a yogi is not seeking to acquire them but whose mind is concerned with spiritual illumination through a simple following of yoga practices.

However, the yogi who is true to his ideal of spiritual lite pays no heed to the occult powers he may discover in himselt, nor does he exercise them Patañjali proves that these powers are not abnormal phenomena nor magic—that they live within all men and can be developed by all, but he shows at the same time that they have nothing at all to do with spiritual life. On the contrary, they are veritable obstacles, stumbling blocks on the road to spiritual attamment. 'They are powers in the worldly state, but they are obstacles to samādhi[75]. The greatest power, is contended by al! yogis, is the power to control these other powers when they are present. Just as there are physical obstacles and lusts of the flesh which must be overcome, so there are psychic phenomena—the subtler lusts of the mind, the temptations of power—which one must wholly overcome if one would approach the door to God.

We read in the life o Śrī Ramakṛṣṇa how when he received occult powers he discarded them as heaps of rubbish. The following simple story that he used to tell illustrates how futile and vain they are.

'There were two brothers. One of them withdrew from the world in his search for truth. After twelve years, years of struggle and self denial, he returned to his brother, who then asked him, "What have you gained in these years of austerity?" "Come and I will show you," answered the first brother. They came to a river bank, and the yogi-brother crossed the river by walking on the water. The lay brother called for a boat, paid the boĀtman a copper, and was ferried across. Then he said, Brother, is this all you have gained in twelve long years of struggle—to be able to do something that can be had for the price of a copper piece?" '[76]

Samādhi or Transcendental Consciousness

'The knowledge which is gained from inference and the study of scriptures is knowledge of one kind. But the knowledge which is gained from samādhi is of a much higher order. It goes beyond inference and Scriptures'.[77]

Here Patañjali describes the two kinds of knowledge: knowledge obtained through the mediation ot the reason, and knowledge obtained by direct, superconscious experience. Ordinary knowledge comes to us by was of sense perception, and the interpretation of this by our reason. Ordinary knowledge is therefore necessarily limited to ordinary objects; that is to say, to those objects which are within the grasp ot our senses. When ordinary knowledge attempts to deal with what is *extraordinary*, its impotence is immediately revealed.

For example, we have the various scriptures and writings which tell us about the existence of God. We may read these and accept their teachings—up to a certain point. But we cannot claim to know God because we have and them. All that we can say we know is that these scriptures were written by men who claimed to know God. Why should we believe them?' True, our reason-may suggest to us that the authors of the scriptures were probably honest and reliable, not self-deluded or insane, and that therefore we should believe what the tell us. But such belief can only be partial and provisional. It is very unsatisfactory. It is certainly not knowledge.

So now we have two alternates. Either we must decide that there is only one kind of knowledge, limited to the objects of sense-contact, and thereby resign ourselves to a permanent agnosticism concerning the teachings of the scriptures. Or we must admit the possibility of another, a higher kind ot knowledge which is supersensory and therefore capable ot confirming the truth of these teachings through direct experience. Such is the knowledge which is obtained through samādhi. And each one of us has to find it for himself. Said Swami Vivekananda:

'Realization is real religion; all the rest is only preparation. Hearing lectures, or reading books, or reasoning, is merely preparing the ground, it is not religion. Intellectual assent and intellectual dissent are not religions'.[78]

Religion is, in fact, a severely practical kind of research. You take nothing on trust. You accept nothing but your own experience. You go forward alone, step by step, like an explorer in a virgin jungle, to see what you'will find. All that Patañjali, or anybody else, can do for you is to urge you to attempt the exploration and to offer certain general hints and warnings which may be of help to you on your way.

Patañjali tells us that in the state of nirvicāra samādhi the mind becomes 'pure' and 'filled with truth'. The mind is said to be pure because, in this state, all the minor thought-waves have been swallowed up by one great wave of concentration upon a single object. It is true that 'seeds' of attachment still exist within this wave, but only in a state ot suspended animation. For the moment, at least, they can do no harm, and it is very improbable that they will ever become ferttle again, because, the devotee having progressed thus far, it is comparatively easy for him to take the final step, which will cause their annihilation.

The mind, in nirvicāra samādhi, is said to be filled with truth because it now experiences direct supersensory knowledge. Those who have meditated on some Chosen Ideal or spiritual personality experience direct contact with the object of meditation, no longer something subjectively inagined, but something objectively known. If you have been meditating on Kṛṣṇa, or on Christ, and trying to picture either of them to yourself in your imagination, you will find that your picture dissolves into the reality of a living presence; and, in knowing that presence, you will see that your picture of it was imperfect and unlike the original. Those who have had this experience liken it to the action of a magnet. In the preliminary stages of meditation, the effort seems to come entirely from oneself; one keeps forcing one's mind to remain pointed at its object. But later one becomes aware of an outside force, a magnetic power, which draws one's mind in the desired direction, so that the effort is no longer one's own. This is what is known as grace.

How can we be sure that the revelations obtained through samādhi are genuine revelations, and not some form of self-delusion or autohypnosis? Common sense suggests several tests. For instance, it is obvious that the knowledge so obtained must not contradict the knowledge which has already been obtained in the same way by others; there are man knowers but there is only one truth. Again, it is clear that this knowledge must be something which is not knowable by other means—not knowable, that is to say, by means of our ordinary sense experience. And, finally, this knowledge must bring with it a complete renewal of the mind and transformation of character. The right relation between prayer and conduct', wrote Archbishop Temple, 'is not that conduct is supremely important and prayer may help it, but that prayer is supremely important and conduct tests it? If this is found true in the preliminary phases of spiritual life, it should be even more strikingly demonstrated in the final, unitive state of samādhi. In achieving that, a man becomes a saint. For, as Patañjali says: 'The impression which is made upon the mind by samādhi wipes out all other impression'.[79] And now he goes on to tell us how to take the ultimate step into complete union with Brahman:

'When the impression made by the samādhi is also wiped that, so that there are no more thought-waves at all in the mind, then one enters the samādhi which is called "seedless'."[80]

It has already been explained that samādhi is achieved by raising one object, one great wave of concentration in the mind by which all other thought-waves, all saṁskāras, or past impressions, are swallowed up. But now even this one wave has to be stilled. When it has subsided, we enter the highest samādhi of all, which is called nirvikalpa in the Vedānta system ot philosophy. Nirvikalpa samādhi is said to be seedless because it is nothing but pure, undifferentiated consciousness; it contains no phenomenal impressions whatever, no seeds of desire and attachment. In nirvikalpa samādhi one is no longer oneself, one is literally one with Brahman; ine enters into the real nature of the apparent universe and all its forms and creatures.

It is hard to follow Patañjali to such heights, even theoretically; and perhaps it will be well, before concluding this chapter, to go back to its beginning and try to recapitulate in a simple and nontechnical manner what he has taught us.

We have to start, we are told by training the mind to concentrate, but Patañjali has warned us that this practice of concentration must be accompanied by nonattachment; otherwise we shall find ourselves in trouble. If we try to concentrate while remaining attached to the things ot his world, we shall either fail altogether or our newly acquired powers will bring us into great danger, because we shall inevitably use them for selfish, unspiritual ends.

What is the simplest way to acquire nonattachment? We must begin by cultivating attachment to the highest object we can conceive of, to God himself. We can do this, first of all, on the lowest level, the level of gross phenomena. Take some great spiritual teacher, a Buddha or a Christ, or any other major saint of any country or religion. This man actually lived on this earth in human form. You can read about his life. You can approach him as a human being. It is easy to grow to love him, to want to be like him, to try to serve him and spread his message by modelling your life upon his. Through this service and this love, nonattachment to other, lesser loves and objectives comes naturally. It is not that we become indifferent to other people or to our own work and duties. But our love for others is included in our love for our Ideal—it ceases to be exclusive and possessive; and our work, because it is now done as service to that Ideal, takes on a new meaning, and we feel more enthusiasm for it than ever before.

Through devotion to our Ideal and meditation upon his life, we shall come gradually to an understanding of the spirit within the man; and so we pass from the level of gross phenomena to the subtle or spiritual level. We shall no longer admire a Buddha or a Christ as a human being within time, but we shall worship him as an eternal spiritual being. We shall know him in his divine aspect. That is ther second stage.

There is, however, a third stage, a third level of consciousness. For behind Buddha, behind Christ, behind any conception of a personal God, there is Brahman, the central reality of which these figures are only partial, individual projections. When we become united with Brahman, we are united with that which was manifested in Christ and hidden within our unregenerate selves, but which is eternally present in all of us. And this union is the state of nirvikalpa samādhi.

The lower stages of samādhi all contain a vestige of the sense of duality; it is still 'I' who am meditating upon 'my' Ideal; there is a separation between our Ideal and ourselves. And it is natural that even the great saint finds it painful to surrender his intense personal love for his Ideal in order to achieve final, impersonal union. In describing how he first reached nirvikalpa samādhi, Śrī Ramakṛṣṇa said:

'Every time I gathered my mind together, I came face to face with the blissful form of Divine Mother. However much I tried to free my mind from consciousness of Mother, I didn't have the will to go beyond. But at last, collecting all the strength of my will, I cut Mother's form to pieces with the sword of discrimination, and at once my mind became "seedless", and I reached nirvikalpa. It was beyond all expression.[81]

Nirvikalpa samādhi has been described by śaṁkara as follows:

There is a continuous consciousness of the unity of Ātman and Brahman. There is no longer any identification of the Ātman with its coverings. All sense of duality is obliterated. There is pure, unified consciousness. The man who is well established in this consciousness is said to be illumined.

'A man is said to be tree even in this life when he is established in illumination. His bliss unending. He almost forgets, this world of appearances.

'Even though his mind is dissolved in Brahman, he is fully awake, but free from the ignorance of waking life. He is fully conscious, but free from any craving. Such a man is said to be free even in this life.

'For him, the sorrows of this world are over. Though he possesses a finite body, he remains united with the infinite. His heart-knows no anxiety. Such a man is said to be free even in this life'.[82]

While in nirvikalpa Śrī Ramakṛṣṇa experienced union with the impersonal Brahman. But, on returning to normal consciousness, he would speak of God in the aspect of the Divine Mother, his Chosen Ideal. The Divine Mother did not lose her reality for him because he had known Brahman. It is important to remember this, for, in our ordinary speech, the word real is used vaguely and loosely, and is apt to lead to confusion. When *we* say that Brahman alone is real, we do not mean that every thing else is illusion, but rather that Brahman alone is fundamental. The several aspects of God, the divine incarnations, have their own relative order of reality. The materialists—those who describe themselves as being 'down" to earth'—are the ones who are living in an unreal world, because they limit themselves to the level of gross sense perception. The perception of the illumined saint ranges over the whole scale, from gross to subtle and from subtle to absolute; and it is only he who knows what the nature of this universe actually is.

REFERENCE

1. Man is subjcct to unhappiness becasue of his false identification of himself with the buddhi through ignorance. God has not this ignorance; hence he is free from suffering and unhappiness.

2. Man identifies himself with the buddhi through ignorance and is therefore controlled by desires arsing from impressions of past deeds and thoughts. God is free from identification of himself with the buddhi and has therefore no stored impressions of past deeds or thoughts.

3. *Yoga Aphorisms* I. 25.

4. *Ibid.*, I. 26.

5. *Complete Works of Vivekandanda,* vol. I, p. 217.

6. *Complete Works of Vivekandanda,* vol. I, p. 217.

6. *Yoga Aphorisms,* I. 27-9.

7. Frank Thilly, A History of Philosophy, p. 148

8. Cf. J. Reville; *La Doctrine du Logos dans le quatrieme Evangile et dans les Oeuvres de Philon.*

9. Patañjali, however, did not agree with this last statement, for the universe was to him a product of prakṛti. The Vedānta accepts the Sāṁkhya-Patañjali view and then reduces its dualism to nondualism by regarding prakṛti as māyā, or the power of God the power to create, preserve, and dissolve the universe.

10. *Complete Works of Vivekanand*, vol III, pp. 57-8.

11. A holy man is freed from all saṁskāras, but the thought-wave of compassion stayswith him to the last moment of his life,—Śrī Ramakṛṣṇa.

12. These 'limbs of yoga', as they are called, are later explained more fully.

13. *Yoga Aphorisms,* 1.16

14. II. 59.

15. XV. 5.

16. *Yoga Aphorisms,* I. 20.

17. *Yoga Aphorisms,* I. 21-2.

18. *Ibid.*, I 30-2. 19. *Ibid.*, 1.33
20. *Yoga Aphorisms*, II. 1. 21. XVII. 14-16.
22. Swami prabhavananda, *The Eternal Companion*, p. 115.
23. *Yoga Aphorism,s* II. 3,5. 24. *Ibid.*, II. 6.
25. I. 1-2
26. (New Yor: Cambridge Unviersity Press, 1955), pp. 90ff.
27. II. 64. 28. *Yoga Aphorism*, II. 4.
29. *Ibdi.*, II. 26. 30. *Ibid.*, II. 27.
31. *Complee Works of Vivekananda*, vol. II, pp. 81-2.
32. Ātman and Puruṣa are interchangeable terms.
33. VI. 23.
34. *Compelte Works of Vivekananda*, vol. I, pp. 258-9.
35. *Yoga Aphorism'* II, 28, 29. 36. *Ibid.*, II. 30, 31.
37. *Yoga Aphorisms'* II. 35.
38. *Complete Works of Vivekananda*, volo. III, pp. 67-8.
39. *Yoga Aphorisms*, II. 36. 40. *Ibid.*, Ii. 37.
41. *Complete Worksof Vivekananda*, vol. I, p. 263.
42. *Yoga Aphorisms*, II. 38. 43. *Yoga Aphorisms*, II. 32.
44. *Ibid.*, II. 41.
45. *Complete Works of Vivekananda*, vol. I, p. 264.
46. *Yoga Aphorisms*, II. 33. 47. *Yoga Aphorisms*, II. 46.
48. VI. 13.
49. *Complete Works of Vivekananda*, vol. I, p. 138.

50. The posture as taught by Patañjali has nothing to do with the postures and practices mistakenly associated with the word yoga. The West, ignorantly, has connected the word yoga with acrobatic feats, sword swallowing, lying on spikes, crystal-gazing, and so on. The so-called yogis who are to be met with in the busy streets of Banaras or in the places of pilgrimage are never regarded by the Hindus as genuine yogis. They make a practice of showing their feats, or lie in the public gaze, proclaiming the mortification of their flesh in order to obtain a few cents from the credulous and the ignorant. They are misguided in the same way as are the American pole-sitters and marathon dancers, and their number is correspondingly small Unfortunately, however, the pictures of these fakirs are printed and reprinted in American newspapers and magazines as pictures of the genuine yogis of India.

In hatha yoga, which is radically different trom Patañjali's system, greats importance is attached to the practice of āsanas, or postures Hatha yoga is system of physical exerciscs and can hardly be correlated with systems the purpose of which is the attainment of spiritual freedom. Physical health is its principal objective of the exercises in posture are not similar to the practices recommended by Delsarte and other Western teachers. The hatha-yoga exercises no doubt have definite therapeutic value.

51. *Yoga Aphorisms*. II. 47.

52. *Ibid.*, II. 48.

53. Vedānta, Sūtras, IV. i. 7-9, 11.

54. *Complete Works of Vivekananda*, vol. I, pp. 143-4

55. I have purposely refrained from giving the breathing exercises known to the yogis, for they should never be practised without previous instruction from an adept teacher. Many books published in America on the subject of yoga describe

breathing exercises which are not the prāṇāyāma as taught by Patañjali, but rather that belonging to the school of hatha yoga. I am certain that those who write indiscriminately of yoga breathing exercises do much unintentional harm. For these exercises are dangerous to the beginner without the proper personal guidance. Furthermore, it is my opinion that the many varieties of breathing exercises taught by hatha yogis are dangerous even when practised under the supervision of teachers skilled in hatha yoga. They may sometimes aid in building the physical body, but they just as often injure the brain. There are instances in India, to my personal knowledge, of men who have become mentally unbalanced by such practices. Unfortunately an interest in breathing exercises that go by the name of yoga has been created in America by irresponsible authors and teachers.

I do not wish, however, to entirely disappoint readers who may wish some healthful exercises for their individual practise. Preliminary to prāṇāyāma there is a breathing exercise which is very easy to practice and quite harmless. As great an authority as śāṁkara, one of the greatest of all yogis and Vedāntists, recommends it. He says, 'The mind whose dross has been cleared away by prāṇāyāma becomes fixed in Brahman; therefore prāṇāyāma is taught. First, the nerves are to be purified; then comes the power to practise prāṇāyāma. Stopping the right nostril with the thumb, through the left nostril breathe in air, according to capacity; then, without any interval, expel the air through the right nostril, closing the left one. Again, inhaling through the right nostril, expel the air through the left, according to capacity. By practising this three or five times at four periods of the day, before dawn, during midday, in the evening, and at midnight, in fifteen days or a month one may attain purity of the nerves.'

56. II. 58.
57. *Complete Works of vivekananda,* vol. I, pp. 173-4.
58. *Complete Works of Vivekananda,* vol. I, pp. 174-5.
59. *Yoga Aphorisms,* III. 1.
60. *Yoga Aphorisms,* I. 28.
61. *Ibid.,* I. 136.
62. 3, 4,5
63. VIII. i. 1-5.
64. II. ii. 6.
65. *Ibid.,* 9.
66. *Yoga Aphorisms* I .37.
67. *Ibid.,* I. 38.
68. *Ibid.,* I.39.
69. *Yoga Aphorisms,* III. 2.
70. *Ibid.,* I.2.
71. *Ibid.,* III. 12.
72. *Yoga Aphorims* III. 7.
73. *Ibid.,* III. 5.
74. *Ibid.,* III. 21.
75. *Yoga Aphorisms,* III. 38.
76. Swami Brahmananda, *Śrī Ramakṛṣṇa Upadeśa,* p. 78.
77. *Yoga Aphorisms,* I. 49.
79. *Yoga Aphorisms* I. 50.
78. *Complte Works of Vivekanda,* vol. I, p. 232.
79. *Yoga Aphorisms* I. 50
80. *Ibid.,* I. 51.
81. *Līlāprasaṅga,* Sādhak bhāv, pp. 319-20.
82. *Vivekacūḍmaṇi,* vss. 427-30.

CHAPTER X

THE SUMMIT OF INDIAN THOUGHT

If a cultured Hindu were asked to select the loftiest aspect of his religion, there can be little doubt that he would name the Vedānta philosophy. To that, therefore, this chapter will be given. In order to understand it, we shall have to trace its history in outline.

I

There are a number ol philosophic hymns in the *Ṛigveda* and also in the *Atharvaveda*, and some of the ideas suggested in them reappear in later philosophy; but, for the purpose we have in view here, it will suffice if we begin our survey with the conceptions expressed in the Bruhmanas. Amid the innumerable speculation and guesses scattered through these priestly works two are worthy of all attention.

The first conception is Brahman, which by derivation is connected with the idea of sacred utterances, whether hymn or prayer, but which in the Brahmanas is thought of as the one source of the visible universe. Brahman was called the source of all things, the Creator and the Ruler of the universe.

The other concept is Ātman, which means self. At first the word was used in various senses; but gradually it came to stand more distinctly for the conscious thinking power,whether in man or in the universe. There was no sharp distinction between the self in man and the Self of the universe. The idea seems to have been that of an all-pervading consciousness, which appears in each man as a speck of light, the thought-power within him, while remaining the Self of the universe. This concept, like Brahman, the reality of the universe, was to used explain the world. The Ātman was spoken or as the Creator and the Controller of the world.

There were thus two outstanding conceptions, Brahman and the Ātman each of which had been declared the source of all things. Brahman, however, had been reached objectively, by the considering the world as a system of nature subject to religious influenes, while it was the inner psychical world which had given birth to the conception of the universal Ātman.

Next came the moment when some thinker combined them, saying, 'Brahman is the Ātman.' The source of all thing thus came to be definitely recognized as intelligent, psychical. The 'Brahman-Ātman was regarded as the secret of the universe, and as present in every man. The identification of the two would greatly stimulate thought; and the consciousness, unity, universality, and divine character of Brahman-Ātman would gradually rise in men's minds and receive clearer definition.

The Ātman was further defined in contrast with the gods. These early thinkers, watched the religious life around them and saw that each god was conceived as eager to receive the homage and the sacrifices of men, and in order to receive them was ready to give men gifts in return. Each god was thus an indivudal spirit, having his own selfish interests, and was subject to motive similar to those that rule men. Hence the Ātman was conceived as free from desire, and, therefore, not 'liable to be tempted by the sacrifices of men. He was desireless actionless, at peace.

There is no doubt that these thinkers had lighted on a most difficult problem. Turn to the religions of Egypt, Babylonia, Greece, of Rome, and you will and that the above description is true of their gods. They listen to praise and prayer, and are responsive to human need, but they quarrel about the things of earth, intrigue to gel the support of men, and show the vilest passions. This is true even of the mighty Zeus of Greek poetry, who is conceived as the Supreme and so named.

The formation of the developed conception of the spiritual. Reality behind the world necessarily modified thought in other directions. The world began to appear changeful and ordinary in the light of the thought of the spiritual, invisible, unchangeable Ātman. The gods also took a subordinate position when contracted with this omnipresent, omnipotent, omniscient Divinity. Necessarily, a desire arose to attain-union with the Ātman; and there are certain passages in the Brahmanas which teach that men may rise to him by knowledge and find immortality and release from desire and action[1] Once or twice we receive intimations of the coming of the great doctrine of the identity of the human soul and Brahman;[2] but as yet the idea is not seriously taken up.

Up to this point Indian thought contained innumerable speculations, some of them barren, others full of promise. But we must draw broad line between these early flashes of speculative genius and the rise of the earliest Indian philosophy. It was the coming of a new element into Hindu-belief and thought that finally led to the production of something like a speculative system. It was the rise of the doctrine of transmigration and karma that proved the occasion at least, if not the cause, of that splendid excitement of the Indian mind which created Hind philosophy. This fact must never be lost sight of in our study of the evolution of Hindu thought. Clearly, belief in transmigration and karma was taken very seriously by the men of those days. The soul, as they conceived it, was a prisoner fast bound in the system of rebirth, inevitably preforming actions which would in turn bind it as fast in another life.

The doctrine of karma fitted in very well with the conception of Brahman-Ātman also. He had been conceived as unborn, immortal, ever free, and also is desireless and action-less. Hence, when the theory of karma and rebirth appeared, he was the only being in the universe that was nut under the away of karma. Being desirelass and actionless karma could not lay hold of him. Had the been conceived is acting, he would necessarily have been thought of as hound by karma and liable to birth.

From this time, then, forward we recognize three strands of thought in in the idea of the Supreme. As Brahman, he is most closely connected with the material world; as the Ātman, he is intelligent, self-conscious spirit; as free from desire and karma, he is actionless.

As a result of the appearance of the doctrine of rebirth and karma we also note a deepening of the contrast between the Ātman and the world. The whole universe is subject to karma but the Ātman is free. The world is full of sorrow and everywhere in bonds: no spirit is exempt; every man and every animal suffering or enjoying the inevitable requital of former deeds. Plants also are regarded as under transmigration. The whole creation is held in the hard grip of this remorseless force. Even the gods are recognized as being temporary brings, enjoying for a time in heaven the glorious reward of noble conduct in other lives, hut destined each in turn to rebirth and possibly to a return to a far lowlier condition. They belong to the phenomenal universe as truly as man and the animals. Men could not fail to realize much more clearly than before the pitiful contrast between the world, on the one hand, with its pain and sorrow, its trouble and strife, it petty gods and sacrifices, its transmigration and karma, and the Ātman, on the other, in all its spirituality, power, and freedom. The Ātman was altogether free from the world. It had no share in its action, no relation to its religion or its morality, was undistrubed by its sorrow, unchained by its karma.

Thus thoughtful men began to feel most keenly their position in the world, subject to karma and rebirth, to suffering and repeated death. They were filled with a great loathing for these repeated births and deaths. It seemed to them a miserable thing to be whirled round for ever on this wheel of existence. They longed for something imperishable.[3] They could not acquiesce in continuous reincarnation. Was there no possibility of finding release from this galling necessity? Philosophy sprang into existence in response to that urgent question.

It was with the Ātman that the process began. At first the Ātman or Self seems to have been thought of as a sort of conscious essence diffused throughout the universe, present in all things, only showing itself most distinctly in man's conscious life, the human self. But as thinkers brooded over these ideas, the truth about spirit as such became clearer to their minds. They thought of the self as pervading all things and appearing everywhere, yet beyond both space and time, and in, above, and beneath all things, yet truly one. In this way it became impossible to think of the Self as a subtle *physical* essence diffused throughout the universe: that idea was too materialistic and mathematical. Nor could they think of the self as appearing *part* in each man; for that was to divide the unity of the divine Spirit. Yet they found within themselves the basis of all their thought about the Self. In their own souls they found the unity, the intelligence, the unlimited thought which they predicated of the Divine. Hence some one was bold enough to say, 'The self in man is not merely the divine Self showing itself at one point; the human self the divine Self, the divine Self whole and complete,' '1 am Brahman.' It was but a natural inference from foregoing thought, yet it was the boldest, the greatest venture ever made by the Indian mind.

Now, note carefully the inevitable result. When this mighty thought came home to a man as true, when he realized that he was the eternal Brahman, he felt instantly transported from his old worldly life to the changeless freedom of Brahman. Being the eternal Ātman, he was *not* bound by transmigration and karma. In his new knowledge he stood emancipated for ever. Brahman is altogether free: I am Brahman; therefore I am free.

By this experience the man was completely transformed. He had hitherto regarded himself as an individual living being in the multitudinous kingdom of nature, not so very different from the animals, dependent altogether on the things of time and of the senses, hopelessly entangled in karma and rebirth. He now realizes that that is all a dream; that he is a spiritual being to whom all nature is but an empty show;[4] an immortal being to whom fear, sorrow, and death are meaningless;[5] an eternal being for whom the changes of time are less than nothing; [6] a self-sufficing spirit, requiring nothing and therefore desiring nothing; a universal being to whom individuality is but a speck; a free spirit, far beyond the reach of the fetter of karma, whether of past or of future actions. The experience has brought him such a joyous elevation of spirit that he can never fall to the old levels again. He knows himself the eternal God, present in all the universe, the sum and substance of all reality. He stands immortal, fearless, desireless, beyond the reach of pain, or sorrow, or doubt, his experience all ended his soul filled with the blessedness of a great peace.

The necessary result of this condition of mind was that the man at once gave up all his connexion with the world. He did not belong to the fleeting world, but to the world of Brahman. What had the eternal Brahman to do with worship, children, comfort, pleasure, business, property, or government? Brahman had nothing to do with action, 'that evil thing.[7] Now that the man had realized his own true being, he could never return to his old life of vanity, folly, and sorrow. For Brahman alone is peace; 'all else is full of sorrow'.[8] What shall we do with offspring, we who have this Self and this world?[9] Those worlds are in truth joyless,[10] 'Sunless are those worlds, covered with binding darkness.[11] How could the man who, through his enlightenment, 'overcomes hunger, and thirst, sorrow, passion, old age and death',[12] return to the life that is filled full of all these evils ?

So the result of the transforming experience was that the man abandoned home, marriage, family, property, business, caste, his sacred thread, the worship of the gods, the worship of ancestors, and wandered about homeless, seeking solitude, sleeping at the foot of a tree or in a cave, and getting his food by begging. He was therefore called a Renouncer, *sannyasi* a Wanderer, *parivrājaka,* a Beggar, *bhikshu.* The word *sannyāsi,* Renouncer, is the most significant. The idea is that the man surrenders the world. They gave up all amusements, laid aside all jewellery and ornaments, shaved their heads, and wore only a minimum of clothing, or even went stark naked. Each carried a rod and a bowl in which he received the food he begged. It is most remarkble that these men not only gave up everything that makes life comfortable and attractive, but gave up caste also, thus stepping outside Hindu society altogether.[13] The thoroughness of the process is explainable only by reference to the conception of Brahman, who, conceived as the Absolute, was believed to be altogether untouched by any of the activities of phenomenal existence.

II

The deep sincerity and seriousness of the movement stand out perfectly plain in the extraordinary features of the life which we have just described. No thinking man can forbear to admire with the utmost heartiness the boldness of the thought and the supreme strenuousness of the discipline to which these men submitted themselves. We do not wonder that they made a tremendous impression upon the people of their time and gained influence by their life.

All scholars recognize at once the great insight revealed and the essential truth attained in the conceptions of Brahman as the spiritual Self of the universe and of the identity of Brahman and the individual self. These ideas form the fountain-head of all the greatest thinking that has been done in India.

The conception of the Ātman is clearly and vividly spiritual. While conceived as immanent in all things and transcending all things, as truly omnipresent and universal, yet the Self is described as invisible, impalpable, timeless, spaceless, a perfect unity. Consciousness and omniscience are the very nature and being of the Self; and the perfect unity of tile eternal mind is beyond the reach of sorrow, change, or death. So far as it is positive, the conception of the infinite Spirit is true and rational.

The doctrine of the identity of man with God suggests great many valuable thoughts. No modern thinker is likely to accept the dogma as it stands; but all will agree that it comes so near to being the right expression of a group of priceless truths that it is no wonder that early India hailed it as a revelation. Every one will recognize how close the relationship is between the doctrine and the following ideas: man's dignity and spiritual grandeur; the immensity of his intellectual faculty; the boundlessness of his desires; his passion for immortality; his nearness, likeness, and kinship to God; the immediacy of the intercourse which he may have with God; God's actual presence in every human heart and conscience; and lastly, the spontaneous desire of the soul for union with God. The doctrine is thus of very great value as a testimony to the divine side of human nature.

But we may go one step farther. These men had not merely thought out a conception of God and of man. Their new belief touched them in the depths of their spiritual nature, and overflowed in religious experience. The exalted language of the best passages[14] of the earliest literature is sufficient to attest the reality of their intercourse with God. In these passages several distinct elements of their experience are frequently described, which further strengthen our inference.

(a) ***The Ātman has become inexpressibly dear to them:***

Were a man to offer this earth surrounded by water and filled with wealth, yet is this more than that, more than that.[15]

He who sees, perceives and understands this loves the Self, delights in the Self, revels in the Self, rejoices in the Self.[16]

This which is nearer to us than anything this Self, is dearer than a son dearer than wealth, dearer than all else[17]

(b) ***The world has lost all its power over them:***

Wishing for that world only, mendicants leave their homes. Knowing this the people of old did not wish for off-pring.' What shall we do with offspring, they said, 'we who have this Self and this world?' and they, having risen above the desire for sons, wealth and new worlds, wander about as mendicants.[18]

They're simpletons who follows outward pelasrues!
They fall into the snare of widespread Death.

But wise men, understanding immortality.
Seek not the Unchangeable mid things that change.[19]

He who beholds that Loftiest and Deepest,
For him the fetters of the heart break as under.[20]

(c) ***In their rconscious knowledge of God they feel they have reached immortality:***

On whom the fivefold host of living beings.
Together with space depend,
Him know I as my soul,
Immortal the Immortal?[22]

All this existing universe.
Moves in the Life from which is sprang.
A mighty terror 'tis, a thunderbolt upraised:'
The men who know It, they become immortal.[23]

When man forgoes all those desires
That lie within his heart,
The mortal then becomes immortal
And here an now gains Brahman[24].

III

The relation of the Ātman to the universe is of so much importance that we must attempt to make the connecting ideas as clear as possible. The human soul was held to be identical with God, as we have seem. We have now to realize that the world also was in with identified with God. The great phrase in which this idea was expressed is *Ekam eva aditiyam,* 'One there is, without a second.' frequently the world is simply said to he God. This idea corner clearly, from the original conception of Brahman as the invisible *sarce* and support of all that is. In the earliest literature the phrases are still fluid and living, not carefully, defined. Hence thinkers developed the idea in different directions, One would construe the one Existence as physical, absolutely identifying Brahman with the universe, losing the spiritual in the material. Another would strain towards an idealistic interpretation, making the spiritual Brahman the sole existence and almost depriving the physical world of reality. A third would think the monistic thought fully satisfied if he spoke of the world as a product of Brahman and everywhere interpenetrated by him. This last comes nearest the original idea; and, in whatever direction thinkers may have leaned, they never forgot that God was all-pervading.

But, as we have seen, the Ātman, being completely free from desire, was actionless. Thus God pervades the universe in every part, but he does not upon upon it. The idea is rather difficult to hold, but it must be grasped if we are to understand the system. God is imminent in the universe, all-pervasive yet he does not act. To conceive the Ātman as acting would be to subject him to karma and therefore to birth, sorrow, and death. Hence these thinkers declared that he was altogether untouched by what happens in the world. Here is one of the passages where this conviction is vigorously expressed:

> He, however, the Ātman, is not so, of so (*neti, neti*). He is incomprehensible, for he is not comprehended; indestructible, for he is not destroyed; unaffected, for nothing affects him he is not fettered, he is not disturbed, he suffers no harm.[25]

Śaṅkara constantly empliasizes the actionlessness of Brahman.[26] From this absolute severance of the all-pervading Ātman from the work and experience of the world several results of the utmost importance followed.

A. The first result of declaring Brahman to be apart from all action is that he is conceived as being above morality. He is quite apart from the petty distinctions of right and wrog Moral rules belong to human life, not to the transcendent life of the Source of the universe. Brahman is declared to be reality, consciousness, bliss, but he is never said to be righteousness. He is fully recognized as the intelligence behind the universe, but he is never spoken of as having a character, or as being the source and centre of the moral order. Indeed, we are carefully taught that, as the Absolute, he is separate from all action, whether good or bad, just as lie is above time and change:

> The Self is a bank, a boundary so that these worlds may not be confounded. Day and night do not pass that bank, nor old age, death and grief; neighter good nor evil deeds.[27]

> Distinct from right, distinct from worng,
> Distinct from causes and effects,
> Distinct from past and future too,—
> What seems tothee like that, declare[28]

Hence emancipation is not conceived as being dependent on morality in any way. It arisen altogether from knowledge. Realization of one's unity with Brahman is itself release from rebirth and from the world. This clear and comprehensible doctrine is taught without any ambiguity in the early literature and is expounded and defended by the greatest authorities[29]. Brahman not being conceived as the source of morality, the method whereby a man realizes his identity with Brahman is not a moral process. Only enlightenment could give the end aimed at, namely complete emancipation from transmigration and karma.

Even when a man has found emancipation, he does not necessarily become moral. Even if he be guilty of vicious actions, his actions do not stain him. Indeed, for the man who has realized his identity with Brahman, all moral distinctions have lost their meaning. Morality is only one ment of the phenomenal life, and the difference between fright and wrong disappears like all other differences in the blaze of the light of the Absolute. Morality belongs to the unreal world, which the released man sloughs off in completeness on finding release. It belongs to the sphere of 'change' and 'becomking' with which he has nothing more to do. Hence the life of the monk was originally under no moral law:

Then (i.e when he has realized his identity with the Ātman) he is unaffected by good, unaffected by evil.[30]

He is not exalted by good, works he is not degraded by evil works[31].

He who has found it is no longer sullied by any evil deed[32]

As water does not cling to a lotus leaf, so no evil deed clings to one who knows it. [33]

He does not distress himself with the thought, 'What good have left undone, what evil done.[34]

As the water-bird is not defiled by moving in the water, so a liberated yogi is not polluted by merit or by demerit.[36]

Evil adheres not to an enlightened man any more than water clings to a leaft; but much sin sticks to the unenlightened man, just as lac to woods.[36]

Abandoning truth and falsehood, pleasure, and pain, the Vedas, this world and the next, he shall seek the Ātman.[37]

And no sin can such them, though they behave and conduct themselves in any way that pleases them.[38]

Even the Gītā contains this doctrine:

He who neither loveth nor hateth, nor grieveth, nor desireth, re-nouncing good and evil, full of devotion, he is dear to me.[39]

Thus, in the earliest days, the search for the Ātman; was not conditioned by morality. But soon many men they did not know Brahman but were eager to come to a realization of their identity with him became monks. Thus the monastic life came to be thought of as a discipline leading to knowledge of Brahman. Consequently, three forms of discipline from the life of the hermit (which we deal with in our next chapter)[40] were adopted. First, the practice of austerities, *tapas,* was accepted by many monks as a means of complete conquest over their own souls. The systematic exercises for the regulation of breathing and the control of the intellectual processes called *yoga* were also adopted by many sannyasis. Lastly,, the law of *ahimsā,* harmlessness, was imposed on all, that is, the law against killing any animal or breaking a twig from any living plant. The conception of Brahman as unaffected by any passion gave the rule for their conduct to unaffected viz., *Indifference* [41] "love and hate," gratitude and resentment envy and pride are to be all crushed. Hence also, complete chastity, truthfulness and honesty were demanded. As time went on, the moral side of monastic life produced a beautiful ideal of the passive virtues.

B. The second result of depriving Brahman of action was that men tended to conceive him as impersonal. He was self-conscious thought, but not will. Hence it did not seem, natural to credit him with personality. The earliest texts are by no means consistent in this matter, for many passages are distinctly theistic in tone; [42] but there can be no doubt that the farther rejection went the stronger became the drift towards an impersonal Supreme.

C. The third result was this, that Brahman was necessarily conceived as not communicating with man. One of the great statements which they made about him is that he is 'beyond the reach of thought and voice'. This phrase is repeated thousands of times in the later literature. Hence, though Brahman pervades the whole universe, and is close by us all the time, it is quite impossible to worship him, or even to utter prayer to him. He can neither hear prayer nor receive worship. We have already seen that sannyasis gave up ordinary Hindu worship. We now see that Brahman could not be worshipped. The monk worshipped no one. His time was spent in realizing his identity with Brahman.

D. The fourth result was that he could not he thought of as creating the universe. Such an act would have involved him in karma. In the earliest literature phrases may be found which come very near representing him as Creator, but the more careful thinkers avoid such statements; and the farther down the stream we go the more clearly do we find the point realized.

These four points will come up again later[43]

IV

The relation of these thinkers to popular Hinduism must also be made clear. We have already seen that they gave up completely the worship of the Hindu gods. We must now note that in the earliest texts we find these gods, the priests who worship them, their sacrifices, their liturgy, and the books in which these are enshrined all spoken of most contemptuously[44], as worthless to the man who knows Brahman. They seem to have shaken themselves free from popular religion as completely as from ordinary society. The Vedas and the Vedic School were now useless. What need had they to sacrifice to the gods? They no long desired those things which Hindus expected to receive from the gods in return for their sacrifices.

But, although it is perfectly plain that they stood apart supreme contempt from the whole Hindu system at first yet they raised no protest against either the religion, or the life, or the literature. They were simply altogether indiffernt to it. Another thing which strikes one as very strange is this, that they did not declare all the old gods notions of the imagination. We should be inclined to think that any mind virile enough to think its way through so many obstacles to the splendid conception of the one God, spiritual, absolute supreme, would have had vigour and sense enough to see that the whole mythology of Hinduism was a web of baseless imaginations. But that was not so. All the philosophers up and down the centuries, even the founder of Buddhism himself, believed in the existence of all the Hindu gods. They regarded themselves as superior to these gods, and neither worshipped nor honoured them any longer; but there was not in their thought sufficient real insight to expel the vast noxious growth of the pantheon and the mythology from their beliefs. The gods are transmigrating souls, just like men, only through their conduct in past lives they have risen to the position of divine beings. When their merit is consumed, they will be born again, and mav possibly be in very lowpositions. It is of the utmost consequence that we should remember this in all our study of Indian philosophy; for without it the course of the history is unintelligible.

The discussions where created this system of philosophy did not take place in the Brahmanic schools, but in the streets, in the forest and .'it sacrifices; and men of any caste, and women also, took part in them. It was at first a most democratic movement. Yet, though the movement was powerful enough to send many men out into the forests as monies, it might soon have withered arid have produced no very pennanent result.

But in this matter the genius of the Brahman showed its masterly power once more. Though the new thought was revolutionary as to drive men away from ordinary Hindu worship and to make them despise the Veda, yet the Brāhman saw how it could he tained. They introduced it into their schools and taught it as the last and highest subject of the course. Students studied the sacrificial system first, and then the philosophy. They called it the Vedānta, i.e. Veda + end, the final aim of the Veda. Gradually the oral instruction, in which the philosophy was taught, took definite shape and was handed down from teacher to pupil in fixed language, each school having its own sacied deposit. Thus were formed those wonderful treatises which we know as the Upanishads. To this period belong only the *Bṛihadāranyāka, Chhāndogya, Taittirīya, Aitareya, Kaushītaki, and Kena* Upanishads. They are in simple discursive prose, and show clearly the process of transition from the old sacrificial teaching of the Brāhmanas to philosophy. We must remember that only boys of the three highest castes were admitted to the Brāhmanical shcools, that no gives admitted, and that only Brāhmans were allowed to teach. Hence, from this time onward, the Vedānta was taught only to men of the three highest castes, and only Brāhmans were allowed to teach it.

Note how it was possible to introduce the new philosophy into the school. It could not have happened if the new-thought had led the monks to a serious protest against the whole practice on Hinduism as dishonouring to God; but as their attitude to the gods was a good-humored if superior contempt, there was no inseparable barrier between them and the old religion; and thus the philosophy could be drawn into the schools and shut up under the stern caste rules of the Brāhmans.

V

We now pass on to the second period of the history of .Indian philosophy The chronology here becomes a little clearer. We may date this period as beginning about 550 BC or soon after. The chief mark of the new period is this, that there are now many competing systems of philosophy. The almost complete monopoly enjoyed at first by the thinkers of the Upanishads has passed away. Everywhere one meets a philosopher with a system of his own and with his following of monks. It would he impossible, even if it were advisable, to give anything like a complete catalogue of the extraordinary variety of belief professed in North India at this time. Three things, however, are well worth notice. The first of these is this, that the one aim of all the systems is to win release from transmigration. Each is a philosophy of emancipation. The second point is this, that all these philosophers practised the monastic life, giving up the world and wandering about in beggary. Though their theories of the world varied very greatly, they all agreed that in the ordinary life of man it was impossible, or next to impossible, to win release. The third point is the most interesting of all. Of the many varied schools of thought then existing only three found their way to fame and survived, and these three have one great characteristic in common: they all deny the existence of Brahmāns, the Absolute. It is surely a matter of the very deepest interest that this, the foundation of a philosophy so striking and so profound, should have already been so seriously discredited that the greatest of the new thinkers of the time should have turned away from it altogether. But the reason is not far to seek. The Brahman of the Upanishads is so exceedingly abstract and tenuous that for the ordinary man it is very hard to grasp the conception and feel its utility. This clearly had become evident to many; so that the acutest thinkers of the period actually formed their systems without using God. It is of the utmost importance to realize that, though these system-builders denied the existence of a supreme Spirit, they, like the rest, continued to believe in the existence of the Hindu gods.

The three schools which have survived are the Jains, the Sāṅkhyas, and the Buddhists. The three seem to form a sort of progressive series, when taken in the order in which we have named them; and tradition suggests that this is also the order of their appearance.

Jannism in its ideas of the world stands very near essential Hinduism. The world and souls and the gods are all real. It does not accept the doctrine of the supreme Ātman. In this matter we may either regard it as representing the old unconscious thought of the people before the emergence of the belief in Brahman, or as maintaining a sceptical attitude to that philosophic conception. The former is probably the best way to look at the matter; for early Jainism is more closely connected with animism than with philosophy. There is very little speculation in it. Indeed, we shall understand the system best if we think of it as merely a specialisation and intensification of the old hermit[45] discipline under the influence of an extreme reverence for life and of a dogmatic belief that not only men, animals, and plants, but the smallest particles of earth, fire, water, and wind are endowed with living souls. Consequently, a very large part of the Jain monk's attention was directed to using the extreme care not to injure any living thing.[46] So eager were the Jains to part with the world to the uttermost that many of their monks wore not a scrap of clothing. Twelve years of most severe isceticism were necessary for emancipation. After that, if monk did not with to live longer, he was recommended to starve himself to death.

The Sāṅkhya system also holds that the world and souls and the gods are real, but a large sceptical element comes in; for Sāṅkhyas say that the soul is not the organ of the intellectual or volitional life of man.

Philosophically, the system is a dualism. It denies the existence of the supreme, and teaches the existence of *prakṛiti* an eternal fundamental substance from which all phenomenal nature arises, and of innumerable individual souls, existing as gods, demons, men, animals, and plants. Every soul is an eternal self-conscious spirit, but without desire, or object, or power to act. It is light, but no more than light. The soul is eternally free, but, through its association with matter, the man believes himself to be bound. Every man who will accept the Sāṅkhya philosophy and lead a life of world-renunciation as a sannyasi will in time awake to the knowledge of the true relation between the soul and matter, and will thus reach emancipation. His soul will be set free from matter, and there after will live for ever in that isolation. *(Kaivalya)* which is its native right and joy.

It is most striking that the individual soul is conceived in this system precisely as Brahman is conceived in the Upanishads. Intelligence, self-consciousness, freedom from desire, from action, from karma, and from suffering, and isolation from phenomenal existence, are the marks of spirit and the spiritual life to early Indian thinkers.

The Sāṅkhya has not had any great influence as a religious system. But the character of its principles compelled those who held it to think out the way in which the things of the universe come into existence and also the relation of the soul to matter. The metaphysical and psychological doctrines which they reached in this process were found to be acceptable in the main to Indian thinkers, and they were therefore adopted at a later date, with or without modification by all the schools. It would take far too long to expound these ideas fully, but it is important that we should grasp the two most salient features of this part of the system.

We take first the process whereby the things of nature come to be. During a pralaya, or period between the dissolution and the reappearance of the world, matter is in its quiescent, invisible, impalpable state: it is *prakṛiti.* When the moment for a new creation comes, there is evolved from this primordial stuff a subtle cosmic substance called *bunddhi* (intelligence). From *buddhi* is evolved a second subtle cosmic substance called *ahamkāra* (egoism). Front *ahamkāra* are evolved five subtle cosmic elements, earth, air, water, fire, ether. Finally, from these five subtle elements are evolved the actual constituents of matter, earth, air, water, fire, ether. This series of emanations from beginning to end is material.

Next comes the psychological problem. The two subtle cosmic substances, *buddhi* (intelligence) and *ahamkāra* (egoism), reappear in the individual. Here *ahamkāra* evolves another subtle substance called *manas* (mind), and with it the five senses, each corresponding to one of the constituents of matter, and with them the five organs of action. Once more the whole series of emanations is purely physical. Now, the significant point to he grasped is that the whole of our inner life intellectual and volitional, is held by Sāṅkhyas to be conducted by these physical substances. Man has no real personal life: the belief that we think and will is a pure hallucination. All that happens within us is the work of these physical powers. The senses, straining outward, obtain impressions of physical things, because they correspond them. The *manas* receives these impressions from the sense and conveys them to *ahamkāra* and *buddhi.* This latter power discriminates the impressions of the senses and acts upon them. Thus all our inner life is physical and there is no personal activity in it.

What, then, does the soul do ? The self-conscious soul, enmeshed in the body, sheds the light of its self-consciousness upon these inner organs; and the man, confusing this self-conscious light with the automatic physical work of the inner organs, forms the foolish fancy, 'I personally do all this,'stamps each sense impression as it passes through *ahamkāra* as mine,' and calls the discrimination and determination of the *buddhi* 'mine' also. The soul has thus nothing to do with intellectual or moral life: that is all carried on outside the soul. The process may he graphically represented thus:

Gautama, the Buddha, like the Jain and the Sāṅkhya leaders, denied the existence of the Supreme; but he went still further. The Sāṅkhyas had deprived the soul of all real share in life. Buddha took the next step: he denied the existence of the soul altogether.

In contrast with Jainism, Buddhism recommended a mild asceticism, but condemned self-torture, and sought emancipation,by *knowledge'* and *right living.* Hence the Buddhist monk pressed on beyond the Hindu monk in the matter of morality, and Buddhist ethics exercised a precious influence later on in Hinduism. The knowledge which Buddha taught was summed up in three propositions, known as 'the three characteristics of being', namely,

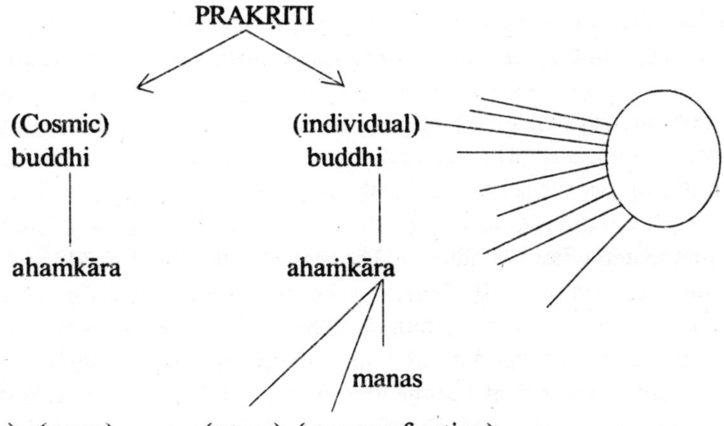

(Subtle)	(gross)	(sense)	(organs of action)
either →	either:	hearing :	speech
air →	air:	touch :	grasp
fire →	fire:	sight :	gait
water →	water:	taste :	evacustion
earth →	earth:	smell :	procreation.

All its constituents are transitory;

All its constituents are misery;
All its constituents are lacking in an ego.

This last proposition is the most important. If nothing has an ego, then the world has no God, man has no soul, and all things are phenomenal. Man consists of five groups of phenomenal elements. Desire is the power that leads to the formation and the preservation of the individual. Buddha's method of life[49] leads to the elimination of desire, and hence to the dissolution of the individual. This insistence on desire produced large results later on.

The Buddhist word for emancipation *nirvana*, the etymological meaning of which is extinction, i. e. of a light. It is used in two senses. A man who lives faithfully as a Buddhist monk will experience the *nirva* of lust, hatred, and ignorance. At death he will pass into final *nirvana:* he will not be born again. No one knows whether Buddha believed final *nirvana* to he annihilation or not. He refused to discuss that question. But what is absolutely clear is that the characteristics of final *nirvana* are identical with the negative characteristics of the philosophic Brahman and of the individual soul in the Sāṅkhya system, viz. isolation from phenomenal life, from desire and from action, freedom from transmigration and karma, from pain and from suffering. Nirvana in Jainism is conceived in precisely the same way.

The Sāṅkhya, Buddhist, and Jain systems had one point in common with the Vedānta; the monks of all four systems practised no worship. The three had also one point of order in common which distinguished them from the Vedānta: only men of the three twice-born classes could study the Upanishads and the system of the Vedānta; while the monastic orders of the other three systems were open to all men. Buddhists and Jains had each an order of nuns also. The Sāṅkhyas remained in Hinduism, while the other two philosophies went out and finally became distinct religions. The reason for this breach did not lie in their doctrines. These could have easily been accommodated within Hinduism. The reason is that they would not submit to being included in the Brahmanic schools and brought under the authority of Brahmans, while the Sāṅkhyas agree !. Hence the Sāṅkhya system is to this day acknowledged to the one of the orthodox philosophic systems of the country. Their denial of the existence of God did not stand in the way at all. From this point, then, Buddhism and Jainism drop out of Hinduism, though they continue to influence the religion of the country very seriously for more than fifteen hundred years.

VI

We know very little about what happened in the school of the Vedānta during the five centuries preceding our era. Doubtless an unending succession of twice-born students learned the Upanishads from the lips of their gurus; and at some time during those centuries the first attempt to systematize the doctrines of the Vedānta in a set of *sūtras* occurred. These are aphorisms of the briefest and most pregnant description, requiring a commentary to make their meaning clear. But of all this we have no record. The one thing that stands out in full certainty is that towards the Christian era the school rose to extraordinary influence among thinking men; for, as we shall see, its leading doctrines won their way in whole or in part into all the leading sects.

But, though we cannot trace the history of the school during those centuries, a little of its literature has survived. The best part of it is the little group of verse Upanishads the *Kāthaka Iśā, Svetāsvatara, Mundaka and Mahānārāyana.* The pithy aphoristic character of these poems shows that they were written to be committed to memory. In the main they teach what was taught in the earliest Upanishads, but there are also several new points to notice. There is first the appearance, especially in the *Kāthaka,* of a number of Sāṅkhya ideas and phrases, which show that the two schools were drawing nearer to one another. Along with these are a number of references to Yoga methods; but, as yoga exercises were probably introduced among the monks at a very early period, these need occasion no surprise. The most noteworthy fact, however, is that a new theistic strain of thought makes its appearance in these poems, especially in the first three. It is very slight in the *Kāthaka,* more marked in the *Iśa,* but very prominent indeed in the *Svetāśvatara,* Clearly there was a group of men in the school of the Vadanta who believed that Brahman was personal. In the *Svetāśvatara* he is identified with the ancient Vedic god Rudra. The grace of God is here spoken of in connexion with Brahman, and the or *bhakti,* or loving faith of the devotee of a personal god, is once referred to.

After the Christian era we get a little more light on the history of the Vedānta. By this time the six orthodox schools of philosophy were will in existence, and each was taught by means of a sūtra-manual elucidated with a commentary. From time to time a new set of Sūtras, or an amended edition of an old set, might force its way to the front and become the recognized manual of a school. In other cases a sūtra-work might remain the standard work for centuries. That is what happened in the school of the Vedānta. For many centuries. Bādarāyana's *Vedāntha-sūtras* have stood supreme. At quite an early date it was recognised as inspired; and ever since has been a part of the canon of the Vedānta. No one know when it was written. Various dates from the Christian era down to the fourth century have been suggested for it. The tendency at present is towards an early date. It is quite clear that it is, founded on earlier manuals.

The theistic tendencies of the verse Upanishads culminate in the

Bhagavadgitā, a remarkable poem which occurs as an episode in the *Mahābhārata*, and which is one of the fundamental scripture of the Vishnuite sect. Scholars are not all agreed as to how the *Gitā* cane to be what it is, but probably all would acknowledge that, in its present form at least, it is post-Christian. We deal it at greater length in Chapter IX. Here we merely want to ralize its relationship to the school of the Vedānta. The following the *Prasthānatraya* or triple canon of the school:

(a) The *Upanishads*.
(b) The *Bhagavadgitā*.
(c) The *Vedānta-sūtras*.

How a sectarian work such as the *Gītā* is ever came to occupy this position is a most difficult question. It teaches that Brahman is personally that he is identical with Vishṇu, and that he became incarnate in Kṛishṇa. This is all very strange in the school which sprang from the teaching of the *Bṛihadārānyaka* and *Chhāndogya Upanishads* and which accepts Badarayana's *Vedānta-Sūtras* as an inspired expression of its teaching. Badarayan's work does not acknowledge the doctrine of incarnations and in no sense sectarian. Some scholars suppose there was a long-continued struggle between the Vishnuite Church and the Vedānta school and that the *Gītā* marks a stage of compromise in that war. To the present writer it seems more likely that from the very beginning there were Vedantists who tended to think of Brahman as personal, that they leaned on the theistic expressions of the earliest Upanishads for support, that the theistic elements of the verse Upanishilds are evidence of their presence in the school, and that the *Gītā* marks rather the moment when the leaders of the Vishnuite sect, feeling the need of the support of the Vedānta, joined forces with the theists within the school. The discussion in Chapter IX will make this theory much more comprehensible.[49]

VII

Were this a work on the philosophy of the Vedānta, it would be necessary to discuss the work of śaṅkara at considerable length; but, as our purpose is to understand Hindusism as a religion, we need only draw out the significant points in his historical position. He is said to have been born in South India in the year 788 AD, and scholars believe he lived until about 850 AD. He was a sannyāsī of the school of the; Vedānta; and his fame rests on his commentaries on the Upanishads, the *Bhagavadgitā* and the *Vedānta-sutas* his greatest work being his *blasliya* on the *Vedānta-sūtras* .

He was a man of great learning and of high philosophic ability. He worked out the Vedānta philosophy so as to make it a more self-consistent system than it ever was before. Necessarily, in the process certain points became elaborated which give form and character to his interpretation. Of these the most important are the emphatic declaration that Brahman is impersonal, the equally express declaration that the world is not only worthless as compared with Brahman but is in very truth illusion, *maya,* and the positing of an illusory personal god, the lower Brahman, Brahma, as the ruler of the world of maya and the object of theistic worship.

For our purpose the points that are most significant are those we discussed above[50] in seeking to understand what is meant by the doctrine that Brahman is actionless.

A. Since Brahman is actionless, he is non-moral.[51] We saw how clearly this is recognized in the early literature. We saw also that, according to the Vedānta, nothing but knowledge can obtain emancipation, and nothing else is needed Morality is without significance in this matter. This point is dealt with by śaṅkara at the beginning of his great commentary, and is most clearly set forth.

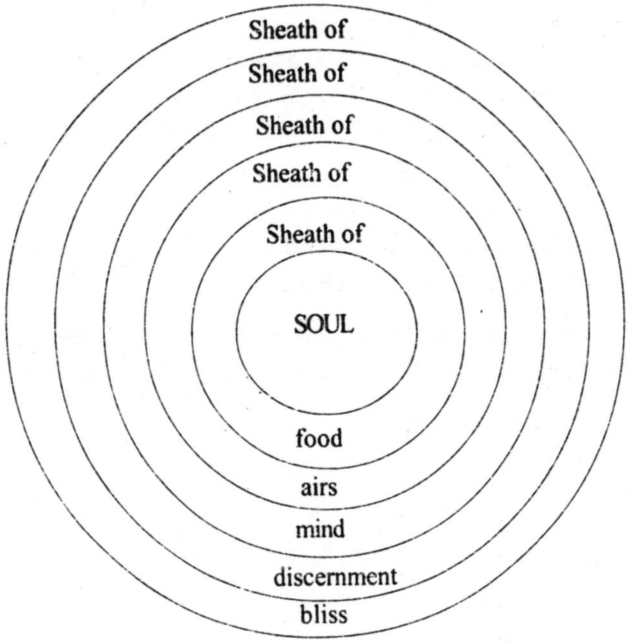

VEDANTA	SANKHYA
mind, manas	= *manas*
discernment, vijnana	= *buddhi*
bliss, ananda, ahamkara	= *ahamkara.*

B. Since Brahman was conceived as actionless, the early thinkers tended towards an impersonal theology. śaṅkara's systematic thinking led him to the definite result that Brahman is impersonal. Here theistic thinkers differed seriously from him, as we shall see. But śaṅkara in the severe consistency of his thought made the human spirit impersonal also. In the full Vedāntic account of man as given by him the soul is encased in several physical sheaths, and in these physical she athsore all the personal and moral faculties. Thus śaṅkara frankly makes the divine-human spirit impersonal and unmoral. This doctrine of sheaths is clearly deferred seriously from mainly, from the well-known passage in the anandavalli of the *Taittiriya Upanishad;* but it seems to have a rise under the influence of the Sāṅkhya doctrine set forth above[52], as the diagram suggests.

C. Since Brahman is cut of from all communication with man, he cannot be worshipped. The early sannyasis, in consequence, worshipped no one. But in Sankara we have some thing very different. The early thinkers acknowledged the existence of all the gods; but they disdained toworship these temporary, transmigrating beings. śaṅkara on the other hand, worshipped them and taught their worship. He says they do not eat the sacricfices, but he acknowledges that they enjoy them, and he explains how a god can be present at a number of different places at the same moment to receive and enjoy the secrecies. Further, he recognized these of idols and is himself represented by idols and worshipped as a divinity in many temples to-day.

D. Since Brahman is actionless, he cannot be conceived as the Creator. This thought is very explicit in śaṅkara. Brahman is the source of the world, but there is no action involved in .ts production. All that brahman does is mere sport, *lila,*[53] and thus involvslno karma.

The full significance of the development of the Vedānta philosophy will be considered when we have before us the history of the sects which worship Vishnu and śiva.

REFERENCE

1. *Taittiriya B.*, III. 12.9,8; *Satapatha* B., x. 5.4. 15; x. 6. 3; Deussen, p. 343.
2. *Satapatha B.*, x. 6 3.2.
3. Aśvaghosha, *Buddhacharita*, v. 26.
4. *Kaṭhaka U., iv. 2; Mandukya Karika*, i. 16.
5. *Brihadaranyaka U.* iv. 4, 15; *Chhandogya U.*, vii. 26, 2.
6. *Kaivalya U.*, 19.
7. *Taittiriya B.*, III. xii. 9, 8 Deussen, 343, 361.
8. *Brihadaranvaka U.*, iii. 4, 2.
9. *Brihadaranyaka U.*, iv. 4, 22.
10. Ib., iv. 4, 11.
11. *isa U.*, 3.
12. *Brihadaranyaka, U.*, iii. 5, 1.
13. For further details see below, pp. 254, 262-263.
14. *Chhandogya U.*, vii. ii; viii. 4; *Brihadaranyaka U.*, i. 4, 8 ii. 4, 5; iv. 4, 12 25; *Kaṭhaka U.*, vi. 9-15; vi. 2-3, 9. 14-15.
15. *Sankhayana A.*, xiii.
16. *Chhandogya U.*, vii. 25, 2.
17. *Brihadaranyaka U.*, i, 4,8,
18. Ib., iv. 4. 22.
19. *Kaṭhaka U.*, iv. 2.
20. *Mundaka U.*, ii. 2,8.
21. *Mandukya Karika*, i. 16.
22. *Brihadavanyaka U.*, iv. 17.
23. *Kaṭhaka U vi. 2.*
24. *Kaṭhaka, U.*, vi. 14.
25. *Brihadaranyaka, U.*, iv 2, 4; Deussen, 147.
26. *S.B.E.*, xxxiv. 33, 62; xxx viii. 355.
27. *Chhandogya U.*, viii. 4, i; *S.B.E.* i. 130.
28. *Kaṭhaka* U., *ii. 14. Cf. Brihadaranyaka U.*, iv. 4, 5.
29. For Sankara, see S.B.E. xxiv, 29, 63, &c.; for Ramanuja, S.B.E. xiviii. 9, &c.
30. *Brihadaranyaka Umiv, 3, 22.*
31. Ib., iv. 4, 22.
32. Ib., iv. 4, 23.
33. *Chhandogya U.*, iv. 4, 3.
34. *Taittiriya U.*, ii. 9.
35. *Mahabharata*, xii. 247, 17.
36. Ib. xii. 299,7.
37. *Apastamba*, ii. 9, 21.'13.
38. *Maahan·rvana, T.*, viii. 268.
39. xii. 17.
40. p. 249 f.
41. Gītā, v. 19; ix. 29.
42. Deassen, 175ff.; see also p. 352, below

43. See below, pp. 244-246, 392-407.

44. See below, pp. 260-261.

45. See below pp. 249-253.

46. See below, p.258.

47. See below pp. 258-259.

48. These fall into three pairs, the *Karma Mimāmsa* and the *Vedānta*, the *Sāṅkhya* and the *Yoga, the Vaiseshika* and the *Nvaya.*

49. The question is often asked whether the *Gītā* or the *Vedānta-sūtras* is the earliest work. The truth probably is that each work is the result of growth and progressive diting, and that they were thus parallel rather than successive in origin. If this is so, we can believe that the *Vedānta-sūtras* refers to the *Gītā*, as allearly commentators say, and that the *Gītā* refers to the *Vednata-sūtras* in the phrase *Brahma-sutra-padais*, xii. 4.

50. See above, pp. 283-232.

51. In śaṅkara he is ever pure, but he nas no character, and no moral act is attributed to him.

52. pp. 237-239.

53. See below IX. 403-407

CHAPTER XI

THE VEDĀNTA PHILOSOPHY

1. Introduction

(a) Origin and Development of the Vedānta

The Vedānta may be regarded as the end of the Vedas in different senses:

(1) ***as the last literary products of the Vedic period,***
(2) ***as studied after the other Vedic literature,***
(3) ***as the culmination of the Vedic culture.***

'Vedānta 'literally means 'the end of the Vedas.' Primarily the word stood for the Upaniṣads though afterwards its denotation widened to include all thoughts developed out of, the Upaniṣads. The Upaniṣads may be regarded as the end of the Vedas in different senses. (1) First, the Upaniṣads were the last literary product of the Vedic period. Three kinds of literature of this period can be broadly distinguished; the earliest being the Vedic hymns or mantras compiled in the different Samhitās *(viz.* Ṛk, Yajus, Sāma), the next being the Brāhmaṇas which are treatises guiding and encouraging the Vedic rituals and the last, the Upaniṣads which discuss philosophical problems. All these three were treated as revealed texts (śrutis) and sometimes also called the Vedas, in the wider sense of this term. (2) Secondly, in respect of study also, the Upaniṣads came last. As a rule, a man studied the Samhitās first; the Brāhmaṇas were required next for guiding him when he entered life and had to perform the rituals enjoined on a householder; and last of all the Upaniṣads (some of which are also known as āraṇyaka or forest-treatises) were needed to help him when he retired from the world, led a secluded life in forests and tried to understand the meaning of life and contemplate the mystery of the Universe. (3) Thirdly, the Upaniṣads may be regarded as the end of the Vedas also in the sense that they mark the culmination of the Vedic speculation. In the Upaniṣads themselves we are told that even after the study of the Vedas with other branches of learning a man's education is not complete till he receives instructions in the Upaniṣads.

The literature of the Vedānta.

The schools of the Vedānta.

The practical followers of the Vedānta.

The word 'Upaniṣad 'means either 'that which gets man near to God,' or 'tha' which gets man near to the teacher (upa-ni-ṣad).[2] The last meaning tallies with the fact that the Upaniṣadic doctrine were esoteric, *i.e.,* they were very secretly taught only to the select pupils seated close to (upāsaṇa)[3] the teacher. The Upaniṣads were regarded as the inner or secret meanings (rahasya) of the Vedas, hence their teachings were sometimes called Vedopaniṣad[4] or the mystery of the Vedas. The Upaniṣads were many[5] in number and developed in the different Vedic schools (śakhās) at different times and places. The problems discussed and solutions offered presented differences inspite of a unity of general outlook. The need was felt, therefore, in course of time for systematizing the different teachings so as to bring out the hermony underlying them. Bādarāyaṇa's *Brahma-sūtra* (also known variously as *Vedānta-sūtra, śārīraka-sūtra* or *śārīraka-mīmāmsa, Uttara-Mīmāṁsā)* undertakes this task. Bādarāyaṇa attempted to set forth the unanimous teachings of the Upaniṣads, and defend them against possible and actual objections. His sūtras, being brief, were liable to different interpretations. Various commentaries thus came to be written to elaborate the doctrines of the Vedānta in their own light. Each tried to justify its position as the only one consistent with the revealed texts (śrutis) and the sūtras. The author of each of these chief commentaries (bhāṣya) became the founder of a particular school of the Vedānta. Thus we have the schools of śaṅkara, Rāmānuja, Madhva, Vallabha, Nimbārka and many others. Each school of the Vedānta consists not simply of the philosophers who theoretically accept its views but also of large number of lay followers who try to mould their lives accordingly. It is in this way that the Vedānta in its different forms still persists in the lives of millions. After the chief commentaries, the literature of the Vedānta developed through the innumerable subcommentaries, glosses and independent treatises written by the leading intellects of each school to support its views and refute those of the other schools. The total output of Vedānta literature thus became very large, though only a .small fraction of it has been printed as yet.

The Chief problem on which the schools of the Vedānta differ.

The most common question on which the schools of the vedānta are divided is: What is the nature of the relation between the self (jīva) and God (Brahman)? Some, like Madhva, hold that the self and God are two totally different entities; their view is called dualism (dvaita). Some others, like śaṅkara, hold that the two are absolutely identical; this view is known as monism (advaita). Some others, like Rāmānuja, again hold that the two are identical on in some special sense; this view may be called qualified monism (viśiṣṭādvaita). There were many other views, each specifying a particular type of identity (abheda), difference (bheda) or identity-in-difference (bhedābheda) between the self and God, too many to be mentioned here. But the best known among the Vedānta schools are those of śaṅkara and Rāmānuja which will be discussed here.

The three periods of the Vedānta

Three stages in the development of the Vedānta may be distinguished in the light of what has been said above: (1) The creative stage represented the revealed texts (śrutis) or the Vedic literature, chiefly consisting of the Upaniṣads. The fundamental ideas of the Vedānta take shape here mostly in the poetic visions and mystic intuitions of the enlightened seers. (2) The stage of systematization represented by the Brahma-sūtras which gather, arrange and justify the ideas of the previous stage. (3) The stage' of elaboration represented by all works beginning from the chief commentaries downwards in which the ideas and arguments are cast into the proper philosophical forms, appeal being made not simply to earlier authority but also to independent reasoning. Though it is possible to consider separately the philosophical speculations of each of these periods, in consideration of space we shall discuss them together. Orthodox Indian writers themselves generally look upon the entire current of thought, spread over the successive stages, as one flow, inseparable at source, but developing and ramifying in its onward course.' Let us have a bird's eye view of the development of the Vedānta through the Vedas and Upaniṣads.

2. How did the Vedānta Develop through the Vedas and the Upaniṣads?

The belief in the moral nature of the universe.

Of the three Vedas, Ṛk, Yajus and Sāma, the first is the basic work, the second two contain Ṛk hymns (mantras) in different arrangements to suit their application to sacrifices. The hymns of the Ṛg-veda mostly consist of praises of the different deities—Agni, Mitra, Varuṇa, Indra, and so on. They describe the mighty and noble deeds of the various deities, and pray for their help and favour. Sacrifices offered to the gods consisted in pouring oblations of clarified butter and other things into the sacrificial fire along with which the hymns in their praise were recited and sung. These deities were conceived as the realities underlying and governing the different phenomena of nature, such as fire, sun, wind, rain and others, on which life, agriculture and prosperity depended. Nature, though peopled with different gods, was conceived as subject to some basic law (called Ṛta) by which the whole world, objects of nature as well as living beings, was regulated. Its function was not only the preservation of order and regularity in planets and other objects, but also the regulation of justice.

The Vedic faith in gods. Is it polytheism?

Belief in many gods is called polytheism. The Vedas are, therefore, often said to be polytheistic. But there is a peculiarity in Vedic thought that makes this view doubtful. Each god, when praised, is extolled by the hymn as the supreme God, the Creator of the universe and the Lord of all gods. Max Müller thinks, therefore, that polytheism is not an appropriate name for such a belief, and he coins a new word 'henotheism 'to signify this. But whether the Vedic faith is really polytheism or henotheism, depends largely on the explanation of this phenomenon. It is polytheism, if the raising of each god to the supreme position be not the indication of a real belief in the supremacy, but only a wilful exaggeration, a poetic hyperbole. But if the Vedic poets really believed what they said, henotheism would be a better name. The latter view is rendered more than probable by the fact that in the Ṛg-veda we come across passages where it is explicitly stated that the different gods are only manifestations of one underlying reality. "The one reality is called by the wise in different ways: Agni, Yama, Matariśvā" (Ekam sad viprā babudhā vadanti ....). Such a clear statement leaves little doubt as to the existence of a real belief in the unity underlying all gods.

Is henotheism a transition phenomenon?

The persistent feature of Indian monotheism.

According to many writers, there is a development noticeable in Vedic thought and they believe that the idea of God gradually developed from polytheism through henotheism ultimately to monotheism, *i.e.* belief in one God. This hypothesis may be true. But let us not forget, in our eagerness to satisfy critics, that even in its most developed form, Indian monotheism retains the belief that though God is 'one', He has various manifestations in the many gods, any one of which may be worshipped as a form of the Supreme Deity. Even to day we have in India the divergent cults—śaivism, Vaiṣṇavism and the like—flourishing side by side and almost every one of them is at botton based on a philosophy of one Supreme God—perhaps even one all-inclusive reality. Indian monotheism in its living forms, from the Vedic age till now, has believed *rather in the unity of the gods in God, than the denial of gods for God.* Hence Indian monotheism has a peculiarity which distinguishes it from the Christian or the Mahomedan. This is a persistent feature of orthodox Indian faith throughout, not a mere passing phase of the Vedic times.

The unity of all existence

Illustrated in the Hymn of Man.

Belief in the unity of all gods which we find in the Ṛg-veda is only a part of a greater thought which also we find there in a clear form, namely, the unity of all existence. In the famous *puruṣa sūkta* which is even now daily recited by every devout Brahmin, the Vedic seer visualizes, perhaps for the first time in human history; the organic unity of the whole universe. Some stanzas are quoted below:

The Man had a thousand heads, a thousand eyes, a thousand feet: he covered the earth on all sides and stretched ten fingers' length beyond it.

The Man was all that is and all that will be-ruling over immortality, he was all that grows by food.

Such was his greatness; and the Man was greater still: this whole world is a fourth of him, three fourths of him are immortal in the sky.

For with three-fourths the Man went on high but a fourth of him remained here, and then spread on all sides, over the living and the lifeless world.[6]

The transcendence and immanence of God.

All existence—earth, heavens, planets, gods, living and non-living objects—is conceived here as the parts of one great person (Puruṣa), who pervades the world, but also remains beyond it. In Him all that is has been and will be, are united. We have in this hymn the poetic insight not only into the universe as one organic whole, but also into the Supreme Ideality which is both immanent and transcendent; God pervades the world, yet He is not exhausted thereby; He remains also beyond it[7] In terms of Western theology, this conception is panentheism (pan—all, en—in, theos—God), not pantheism; all is not equal to God, but all is *in* God, who is greater than all. One flash of the seer's imagination we have in the above hymn, reveals to us a variety of ideas that inspired the Vedic mind, monism, panentheism and organic conception of the world.

The Imprsonal Absolute

In another hymn (commonly known as the nāsadīyasūkta), we are introduced further to the Vedic conception of the Impersonal Absolute. There reality underlying all existence—the primal one from which everything originates—cannot be described, it says, either as existent or as non-existent (ua sat, na asat). Here we have perhaps the first flash of a conception of the Indeterminate Absolute, which is the reality underlying all things, but in itself indescribable.

The hymn thus begins:

There was then neither what is, nor what is not,
there was no sky, nor the heaven which is
beyond.

It concludes:

He from whom this creation arose, whether he made it or did not make it; the highest seer in the highest heaven, he forsooth knows, or does even be not know ?[8]

The relation between the personal and the impersonal ideas of God.

As for the relation between the conception of ultimate reality as a Person and the conception of its as an Indeterminate Absolute, we may note that the clue to the latter is to be found in the former. For even in the description of Reality as Person, there is a mention of its transcendent aspect, which is, therefore, not describable in terms of the objects of the world and, therefore, indeterminate.

Philosophy based on arguments in absent in the Vedas.

It is found first in the Upaniṣads in a rudimentary form.

Though many of the important elements of the Vedānta are to be found thus in the Ṛg-veda, they are presented in a poetic way. The method by which the sages arrive at these views is not mentioned, neither the arguments which support them. Philosophy proper must be based on explicit reasoning and argument chiefly. There is, therefore, no regular philosophy, strictly speaking, in the Vedas. The first attempt at philosophical speculation is to be found in the Upaniṣads, where problems about self, God and the world are clearly put and discussed. But even here the philosophical method of arriving at conclusions rigorously supported by arguments is only partly in evidence. Some of the Upaniṣads are written in verses and they contain, like the Ṛg-veda, inspired utterances on philosophical matters. So also are some other Upaniṣads, though written in prose. The only approach to philosophical method is to be found in the few Upaniṣads, where, through dialogues—questions and answers—attempt is made to lead the sceptical pupil step by step to some conclusion. But inspite of the lack of strict argumentative form, the Upaniṣads have a profound charm and appeal. This is due to the joint effect of the loftiness of ideas, the depth of insight, the mysterious appeal to all that is good and sublime in man and the irresistible force with which the views are asserted as though they are born of a direct vision of truth. A famous German philosopher, Schopenhauer, impressed by the Upaniṣads, declared: *"In the whole world there is no study so beneficial and so elevating as that of the Upaniṣads. It has been the solace of my life, it will be the solace of my death."*

The problems of the Upaniṣads

The problems of the Upaniṣads, to mention only some of the more frequent ones, are: What is the Reality from which all things originate, by which all live and into which all dissolve when destroyed ? What is that by knowing which everything can be known ? What is that by knowing which the unknown becomes known ? What is that by knowing which one can attain immortality ? What is Brahman ? What is Ātman ? As the very nature of these questions implies, the Upaniṣadic mind was already steeped in the belief that there is an all-pervasive reality underlying all things which arise from, exist in and return into it, that there is some reality by *knowing* which *immortality can be attained.*

The belief in an all pervasive reality called Brahman or Ātman.

"The name given to this Reality is sometime Brahman (God), sometimes Ātman (self), sometimes simply Sat (Being). 'At first there was the Ātman alone,' say the *Aitareya* (1.1.1.) and the *Bṛhadāraṇyaka* (1. 4.1.). 'All this is Ātman,' says the *Chāndogya* (7.-25.2.). Ātman being known . . . everything is known," says the Bṛhadāraṇyaka again *(*4 5.6.). Similarly we find . "There was only Being (Sat) at the beginning, it was one without a second" *(*Chānd 6.2.1.). Again, "All this Brahman" *(Muṇḍuka,* 2.2,11. and *Chānd.* 3.14.1.). Brahman and Ātman are used synonymously in these different contexts. We are also told explicitly in some places that "This self is the Brahman" *(Bṛhad.* 2.5.19.), "I am Brahman" *(Ibid.,* 1.4.10.)

Interest is shifted from gods to the Self.

The real self behind the outer sheaths.

The Upaniṣads shift the centre of interest from the Vedic gods to the Self of man. They analyze the Self, distinguish between its outer husk and its inner reality. The body, the senses, the manas, the intellect and pleasures arising out of them are all sifted and found to be passing, changeful modes, not the permanent essence of the Self. These are merely the sheaths (kośas), the outer covers, so to say, which conceal an inner, permanent reality, which cannot be identified with any of these, though all of these are grounded in it and are its manifestations. This Real Self is pure consciousness, every particular consciousness of objects being its limited manifestation. Not being limited by any object, this pure consciousness is also infinite. The Real Self is called Ātman. As infinite, conscious reality (satya n, jñānam, anantam) the self of man is identical with the Self of all beings (sarva-bhūtātmā) and, therefore, with God or Brahman. In the *Kaṭha* we are told: "This Self is concealed in all things, and does not, therefore, appear to be there. But it is perceived by the keen-sighted with the help of a sharp, penetrating intellect" (3.12).

Self-realization is the highest knowledge.

All attempt is made to help man discover this his Real Self. Realization of the Self (ātma-vidyā or ātma-jñāna) is regarded as the highest of all knowledge (parā-vidyā), all other knowledge and learning being inferior to it (aparā-vidyā). The method of self-realization lies through the control of the lower self, its deep-rooted interests and impulses, and through study, reasoning and repeated meditation (śravaṇa, manana, nididhyāsana), till the forces of past habits and thoughts are completely overcome by a firm belief in the truths learnt. It is a difficult path which can be followed only if one is strong and wise enough to reject what is pleasant (preyas) for what is good (śreyas).

Rituals are inadequate.

Knowledge of the Self or God is the means of attaining the highest good.

The Vedic belief in sacrifices is shaken by the Upaniṣads which declare that with these one cannot achieve the highest goal of immortality. The Muṇḍaka says that these sacrifices are like leaky rafts *(i.e.* they are unable to take one across the sea of worldly misery) and those fools that take these as the superior means, suffer again the pangs of old age and death. A ritual in at best secure a temporary place in Heaven, and when the merit (punya) earned by it is exhausted there is again birth into this world. A deeper significance is attached to sacrifice, when the worshipping self and the gods worshipped are realized to be the same. The ceremonies of offering oblations to gods thus come to be looked upon as mere external affairs fit for the ignorant who do not understand the mystery of the universe. Sacrifice to the Self or Brahman is regarded as superior to sacrifice to gods. It is only through the realization of the Self or Brahman that rebirth can be stopped and along with it all misery. One who truly realizes his unity with the Immortal Brahman, realizes immortality.

Brahman is the ultimate source of all joy.

The Upaniṣads conceive Brahman not only as the pure ground of all reality and consciousness, but also as the ultimate source of all joy. Worldly pleasures are only the distorted fragments of that joy, just as worldly objects are limited manifestations of that Reality.[11] One who can dive into the deepest recess of his Self, not only realizes his identity with Brahman but gets to the heart of Infinite Joy. The proof that the Self is the source of all joy (says Yājñavalkya to his wife Maitreyī) is that it is the dearest thing to man.

All is dear because of the Self

One loves another person or thing because he identifies himself with that person or thing, regards him or it as his own Self. Nothing is dear for its own sake, says Yajnavalkya. The wife is not dear because she is wife, the husband is not dear because of being a husband, the son is *not* dear because of being a son, wealth is not dear for its own sake. All is dear because of the Self.[12]. That the Self in itself is bliss is shown also by pointing out that when a man falls into dreamless sleep, forgets his relation with the body, the senses, mind and external objects and thus retires into his own intrinsic state, be is at peace, he is untouched by pleasure and pain.

Desire to live is due to the joy that lies in life.

Self-realization is the greatest joy.

Modern biology tells us that self-preservation is a basic instinct in all living beings. But why is self or life so dear? The answer is given by the Upaniṣads. Life is so dear because life is joy. Who would like to live if life was not joy ?[13] The joy that we have in daily life, however disturbed and meagre it might be, sustains our desire to live. Greater joy is not obtained by running further away from the Self, after worldly objects. Desires for objects are the fetters that bind us to the world, to the painful vicious circle—birth, death and rebirth. The forces of desires take us away from the Self and condition our existence in the way we banker after. The more we give up our hankerings for objects and try to realize our identity with the true Self (Ātman) or God (Brahman), the more do we realize true happiness. To feel at one with the Self is to be one with the Infinite God, the Immortal and the Infinite Joy. Nothing then remains unattained, nothing left to be desired. The *Kaṭha* declares, therefore, that a mortal attains immortality and unity with Brahman even here, in this very life, when his heart is free from all desire.[14]

Creation of the world out of Brahman or Ātman.

If Brahman or Ātman is the Reality underlying the whole universe, then the question may arise as to the exact relation between Brahman and the world. The accounts of creation given in the different Upaniṣads do not exactly tally. But all appear to be unanimous in holding that Ātman (or Brahman or Self is both the creator and the material cause of the world. And in most of these accounts the starting-point of creation is described somewhat like this: At first there was the soul. It thought, 'I am one, I will be many,' 'I will create the worlds.' Description of the subsequent steps by which things are created varies, some stating that out of Ātman first arises the subtlest element 'Ākāśa,' thence gradually all: the grosser ones: others give different accounts.

The denial of multiplicity.

From these statements creation would appear to be' real and God *(i.e.,* The Absolute Soul) a real creator. But in many places we are told that there is no multiplicity here ('neha nānā asti kiñcana')[15] that one who sees the many here is doomed to death ('mṛtyoḥ sa mrtyum āpnoti ya iba nāneva paśyati')[16] Its explanation of the unity of all things, which appear to be many, examples like these are cited: Just as different articles made of gold are all really one, gold is the only real substance in them and the different names' and forms (nāma-rūpa) which make them appear as many, are merely matters of verbal distinctions, similarly in all objects there is the same Reality, and their differences are merely verbal.[17] The objects of the world are denied separate, individual existences. Brahman (or Ātman) is also described in many passages not as Creator, but as a reality which is indescribable, being not only unspeakable, but even unthinkable. Brahman cannot be an object of worship even. Thus the *Kena* declares: "That (Brahman) is other than what is known and beyond the unknown. What is not expressed by speech and by which speech itself is expressed, know that to be Brahman, and not what one worships as Brahman."[18]

Is creation then real?

These two different kinds of statements about the world and God naturally present a puzzle. Is God really the creator of the world and the world also real therefore ? Or, is there really no creation and, is the world of objects a mere appearance? Is God a determinate knowable reality which can be described by suitable attributes or is God an indeterminate, unknowable something? What is the real view of the Upaniṣads ? Subsequent Vedānta treatises take up these problem for solution. The *Brahma-sūtra* of Bādarāyaṇa attempts to systematize and ascertain the real views of the revealed texts. But its brief statements themselves admit of different meanings. Subsequent writers who commented on the Brahma-sūtra give their own interpretations to the Upaniṣads and sūtraṣ very clearly and elaborately. Of the different rival schools that came into existence in tins way, tnat of saṅkarācārya is the best known. In fact what ordinarily passes now-a-days as the Vedānta, and sometimes even as Indian philosophy to outsider?, is really the Advaita Vedānta of the śaṅkara school. Next comes, in point of popularity, the Viśiṣṭādvaita school of Rāmānujācārya. We shall discuss the philosophy of the Vedānta as developed in these two schools under three heads: The world. God and the Self.

II. The Śaṅkara and Rāmānuja Schools of the Vedānta

1. The World

(a) The Unanimous Views

The unanimous Vedānta conception of the world.

śaṅkara and Rāmānuja are both monists.

Both śaṅkara and Rāmānuja reject theories which explain the world (1) either as the product of material elements which by themselves combine together to form objects, (2) or as the transformation of an unconscious nature that spontaneously evolves all object (3) or as the product of two kinds of independent reality, such, as matter and God, one of which is the material, the other the efficient cause which creates the world out of the first. Both agree that an unconscious cause cannot produce the world, and both hold that even the dualistic conception of two ultimately independent realities, one conscious and another unconcious, producing the world by interaction, is unsatisfactory. Both take their stand on the Upaniṣadic view that 'All is Brahman' (sarvam khalu idam Brahma), and matter and mind are not independent realities but grounded in the same Brahman. Both are, therefore, monists or believers in one ultimate Reality in which the world of multiple objects is rooted.

Both follow Bādarāyaṇa and reject other views.

Bādarāyaṇa, whom both Sāṅkara and Rāmānuja follow, discusses at length the unsatisfactory nature of other alternative theories of the world. Refutation of other views is based both on independent reasoning and the testimony of earlier scriptures. We may briefly sum up here the independent arguments by which the chief theories are refuted.[19]

Refutation of the Sāṅkhya view of creation.

The evolution an ordered world is not possible without conscious guidance

The Sāṅkhya theory that unconscious primal matter (prakṛti), composed of the three guṇas (sattva, rajas and tamas), gives rise to the world without the guidance of any conscious agent, is not satisfactory. Because the world is a harmonious system of nicely adjusted objects which cannot be believed to be the accidental product of any unconscious cause . As the Sāṅkhya itself admits, this world, consisting of bodies, senses, motor organs and other objects, is made just to fit the diverse souls born into it in accordance with their past deeds. But how can an unconscious nature carry out such a complicated plan ? In admitting that there is a purpose in admitting that there is a purpose in the world, but denying at the same time the existence of a conscious creator, the Sāṅkhya commits itself to an absurd position. Unconscious teleology is unintelligible. Adaptation of means to ends is not possible without conscious guidance. The spontaneous flow of milk from the cow for the sake of a calf is cited by the Sāṅkhya as an example of unconscious but purposive act. But it is forgotten that the cow is a living, conscious being and milk flows impelled by her love for the calf. No undisputed example of an unconscious object performing a complicated purposeful act can be cited. The souls (puruṣa) that the Sāṅkhya admits; are said to be inactive and, therefore, they also cannot help the evolution of the world.

The refutation of the Vaiśeṣika view.

Unconscious atoms cannot produce this world.

The Vaiśeṣka theory that the world is caused by the combination of atoms is similarly untenable because these unconsicous atoms cannot produce this wonderfully adjusted world. For the regulation of the atoms in the formation of the world the moral law of adṛṣṭa is, of course, admitted by the Vaiśeṣika But this law is also unconscious and the difficulty is not removed. Besides, how atoms at first begin to move in order to create the world is not explicable. If movement were the inherent nature of the atoms, they would never cease to move and the dissolution (pralaya) of objects, as the Vaiśeṣika admits, would never occur. Souls are of course admitted, but they are not admitted to have any intrinsic consciousness. Consciousness arises after the souls are associated with bodies and the organs of knowledge; and these do not exist *before* creation. Hence atoms cannot receive any conscious guidance even from souls.

Refutation of the Bauddha view.

Against those Bauddha thinkers who explain the objects of the world as aggregates of different momentary elements, it is pointed out that momentary things cannot possess any causality. Because to produce an effect the cause must first arise and then act and, therefore, stay for more than one moment, which is against the doctrine of momentariness. Even if the separate momentary elements be somehow produced, no aggregate can be caused, for no substances are admitted (by these Bauddhas) which can bring together the elements and produce the desired objects. As consciousness itself is admitted to be the effect of the aggregation of the different elements, it cannot exist before aggregation, and the difficulty of unconscious cause, seen before, arises here also.

Bauddha idealism which denies the external world, is untenable.

Bauddha nihilism is therefore, untenable too.

Against those Bauddhas who hold the view of subjective idealism (vijñānavāda) and declare that the world, like a dream, is only an illusory product of the imagination, the following important objections are pressed by śaṅkara. (a) The existence of external objects cannot be denied because they are perceived to exist by all persons. To deny the existence of pot, cloth or pillar while it is being perceived, is like denying the flavour of the food while it is being eaten it is a falsification of immediate experience by sheer force. (b) If immediate experience is Disbelieved, then even the reality of mental states cannot be believed in. (c) To say that ideas of the mind illusorily appears *external objects* is meaningless unless at least something external is admitted to be real. Other wise, it would be as good as to say that a certain man looks *like* the child of a barren woman. (d) Unless different perceived objects like put and cloth are admitted, the idea of a pot cannot be distinguished from that of a cloth, since, as consciousness, they are identical. (e) There is a vital difference between dream-objects and perceived objects: the former are contra-dicted by waking experience, while the latter are not. External objects perceived during waking experience cannot be said to be unreal so long as they are not felt to be contradicted. So subjective idealism, and along with it also nihilism (śūnyavāda), fail to explain the world satisfactorily.

Deistic theories of creation are not tenable.

Even a deistic theory (held by the Saivas, Pāśupatas, Kāpālikas and Kālāmukhas) which holds that God is the efficient cause and matter is the material cause of the world is not accepted. The chief objection raised is that as such a view is based not on the Vedas, but on independent reasoning and ordinary human experience, it should tally with what we observe in life; but it does not do so. So far as our experience goes, a spirit can act upon matter only through a body, consisting of organs of perception and movement. Again his activity is caused by some motive, such as attainment of pleasure and removal of pain. But God is said to be devoid of body as well as passions and desires. In the light of empirical experience we fail, therefore, to understand the manner as well as the motive of God's creation of the world.

(b) Rāmānuja's Conception of the World

Rāmānuja accepts the Upaniṣadic account of the creation literally.

The world is created by God from matter which exists in Him.

Three subtile elements are first created and then mixed up together to form the gross elements.

But inspite of their agreement in the above respects, śaṅkara and Rāmānuja differ as to the exact way the world arises out of the one Reality, Brahman. Rāmānuja takes the Upaniṣadic accounts of creation, stated previously, in a literal sense. He holds that the Omnipotent God creates the manifold world out of Himself by a gracious act of will. Within the All-inclusive God (Brahman) there are both unconscious matter (acit) and the finite spịrits the first is the source of the material objects and as such called prakṛti (*i.e.* root or origin) after the śvetaśvatara upaniṣad; the Purāṇas and smṛtis, whose authority Rāmānuja highly values. This parakrit is admitted, as in the Sāṇkhya, to be an uncreated (aja), eternal reality. But unlike the Sāṅkhya, Rāmānuja believes that it is a part of God and controlled by God just as the human body is controlled from within by the human soul. During the state of dissolution (pralaya) this primal unconscious nature or prakṛit remains in a latent, subtle (sūkṣma) and undifferentiated (avibhakta) form. God creates out of this the world of diverse objects in accordance with the deeds of the souls in the world prior to the last dissolution. Impelled by the omnipotent will of God the undifferentiated subtle matter gradually becomes transformed into three kind of subtle elements—fire, water and earth. These differentiated elements manifest also the three kinds of qualities known as sattva, rajas and tamas. Gradually the three subtle elements become mixed up together and give rise to all gross objects which we perceive in the material world.[22] In every object in the world there is a mixture of three elements. This process of triplication is known as trivṛtkaraṇa

Creation is a real act of God.

Rāmānuja holds, therefore, that creation is a fact and the created world is as real as Brahman. Regarding the Upaniṣadic texts which deny multiplicity of objects and assert the unity of all things, Rāmānuja holds that these texts do not mean to deny the reality of the many objects, but only teach that in all of them there is the same Brāhman, on which all are dependent for existence, Just as all gold articles are dependent on gold. What the Upaniṣads deny is the independence of objects, but not their dependent existence.

Māyā means the wonderful power of real creation that is in God.

It is true, Rāmānuja admits, that God has been described (in the *śvetāśvatara)* as welder of a magical power (māyā), but this only means that the inscrutable power by which God creates the world is as wonderful as that of a magician. The word 'māyā' stands for God's power of creating wonderful objects (vicitrārtha-sargakāri śakti). It also stands sometimes for prakṛti to signify her wonderful creativity.[23]

Rāmānuja holds that all knowledge is true.

Rāmānuja denies, therefore, that creation and the created world are illusory. To strengthen this position he further holds that all knowledge is true (yathārtham sarva-vijñānam) and that there is no illusory object anywhere. Even in the case of the so-called illusory snake in the rope, he points out that the three elements (fire, water, earth) by the mixture of which a snake is made, are also the elements by the mixture of which a rope is made, to that even in a rope there is something of a snake and this common element *really existing* in the rope is perceived when we take it for a snake. No unreal object is perceived then. The constituent elements of every object being in every other thing, every so-called illusion can be similarly explained away. This theory of Rāmānuja resembles in essential respects the view of some modern realists like Boodin, who hold that all immediate experience of objects is true on the strength of the quantum theory of Schrödinger, according to which each of the electrons, which compose material objects, pervades the whole world, so that "Everything is immanent in everything else."[24]

(c) śaṅkara's Conception of the World.

śaṅkara finds it difficult to reconcile the Upaniṣadic statements of creation, taken in the literal sense, with those denying the world of multiplicity. Considered in the light of the general trend and spirit running throughout the Upaniṣads, the stories of cration seem to him, to be out of joint. Description of Brahman as really devoid of all assignable marks becomes unintelligible if His creatorship is real. The teachings about the disappearance of all multiplicity on there realization of Brahman cannot also be understood. If the world were real how could it disappear? The dawn of the knowledge of Reality can dispel only the unreal appearing as real, not what is rally real. This idea furnishes śaṅkara with the clue to the mystery of the world. If the world is a mere appearance, as our dream objects are or as objects appearing in illusion are, then the present appearance of the world and its disappearance on the knowledge of Reality become intelligible. This reconciliation is suggested by the Upaniṣads themselves. Even in the Rgveda[25] the one Indra (God) is said to appcar in many forms through powers of creating illusion (māyā). The *Bṛhadārańyaka* also accepts this. The *śvetāśvatra* clearly states that the origin (prakṛit) of the world lies in the magical power (māyā) of God.[27]

Māyā, the magical power of creation, is indistinguishable from God.

Māyā as a power of God is indistinguishable from Him, Just as the burning power of fire is from the fire itself. It is by this that God, the Great Magtician, conjures up the world-show with all its wonderful objects. The appearance of this world is taken as real by the ignorant, but the wise who can see through it finds nothing but God, the one Reality behind this illusory show.

Creation understood in the light of an ordinary illusion.
Ignorance, with its double function of concealment and distortion.

If we try to understand the process by which ordinary illusions in life take place, we find that an illusion, say, of snake in a rope, is due to our ignorance of what really is there behind the appearance, *i.e.* ignorance of the substratum or ground (adhiṣṭhāna), in this case, the rope. If we could know the rope as the rope, there would be no illusion about it. But mere ignorance of the rope cannot give rise to the illusion. For, otherwise, even a person who has never known what a rope is would always see serpents in things. The ignorance creating an illusion does not simply conceal from our view the real nature of the ground, the rope, but positively distorts it, *i.e.*

makes it appear as something else. Concealment (avarana) of reality and distortion (vikṣepa) of it into something else in our mind are then the two functions of an illusion-producing ignorance (avidyā, or ajñāna).

The magician's show deceives only the ignorant, but not himself.

When an illusion is produced in us by some one else, for example, when a magician makes one coin appear as many to us, it is an illusion for us, the perceivers, and not for the conjurer. From our standpoint, then, illusion is the product of our ignorance, which prevents us from seeing the real nature of the thing and which makes us see something else in its place. If any spectator can persist to see the one coin as it is, the magician's wand will create no illusion for him. For the magician, the illusion is only a conjuring will, by which his spectators are deceived, and not himself.

The conception of māyā as a magic power and producer of the world-show.

In the light of such cases, māyā, the cause of the world-appearance, may also be under-stood from two standpoints. For God, maya is only the will to crate the appearance. It does not affect God, does not deceive Him. For ignorant people like us, who are deceived by it and see the many objects here instead of one Brahman or God, māyā is an illusion-producing ignorance. In this aspect maya is also called, therefore, 'ajñāna' or 'avidyā (synonyms for 'ignorance') and is conceived as having the double function of concealing the real nature of Brahman, the ground of the world, and making Him appear *as* something else, namely, the world. In so far as māyā positively produces some illusory appearance it is called positive ignorance (bhāva-rūpam ajñānam); and in so far as no beginning can be assigned to the world, māyā is also said to be beginningless (anādi). But, for those wise few who are not deceived by the world-show, but who perceive in it nothing but God, there is no illusion nor, therefore, illusion-producing māyā. God to them is not, therefore, the wielder of maya at all.

śaṅkara's interpretation of māyā differs from Rāmānuja's.

We have seen previously that Rāmānuja, following the *Svetāśvatara,* speaks also of māyā, but he means thereby either God's wonderful power of real creation or the eternal, unconscious primal matter which is in Brahman and which is really transformed into the world. śaṅkara also speaks of māyā as the power of God; but this creative power, according to him, is not a permanent character of God, as Rāmānuja thinks, but only a free will which can, therefore, be given up at will. The wise who are not deceived by the world-appearance need not conceive God at all as the bearer of this illusion-producing power. Besides, even when conceived as a power, maya is not a distinct entity in Brahman, but inseparable and indistinguishable from it as the burning power is from fire, or will is from the mind that wills. Even when śaṅkara identifies māyā with prakṛti, he means nothing more by it than that this creative power is the source or origin (prakṛti) of world-appearance, to those who perceive this appearance. The difference between Rāmānjua and śaṅkara, then, is that while, according to Rāmānuja the matter which exists in God (and, therefore, also God[28]) really undergoes modification. śaṅkara holds that God does not undergo any real change; Change is only apparent, not real.

Rāmānuja behaves in real change, but śaṅkara does not.
Pariṇāma-vada and Vivarta-vāda are the two forms of Satkaryavāda.

Illusory modification of any substance, as of the rope into the snake, is called rirarta, and real modification, as of milk into curd, is called *parinama, śaṅkara's* theory of creation, as described above, is, therefore, known as vivarta-vāda *and is* distinguished from the Sāṅkhya theory of evolution (by the real modification of prakṛti) which is called *pariṇāma-vāda*, because he admits that the unconscious element in God really changes it to the world. Vivārta-vāda and pariṇāma-vāda both agree, however, in holding that the effect is already contained somehow in its cause and, therefore, both come under satkarya-vāda or the theory that the effect (kārya) is existent (sat) in the cause, and is not a new thing. The process of the imaginary attribution of something to where it does not exist is called *adhyāsa*. In modern psychological terminology a process of this kind is called projection. In all illustion there is such projection adhyāsa). the serpent is projected (adhyasta) by imagination on the rope, and the world on Brahman.

Māyā is sometimes called prakṛti.

The Upaniṣadic accounts of creation, then are to be understood in the sense of the evolution of the world out of Brahman through its power of māyā. this māyā, śaṅkara admits is in some scriptures called also avyakta or even prakṛti having the three elements of sattva, rajas and tamas. But this should not be mistaken to be the same as the Sāṅkhya doctrine in which prakṛti is an independent reality.[29] It is absolutely dependent on God.

In addition to the advantages of consistent interpretation of scriptures, the theory of pretation of scriptures, the theory of vivarta, śaṅkara points out, gives also a more rational explanation of creation. If God is the creator of the world and creates the world out of any other substance like matter, then in addition to God, another reality is to be admitted and God ceases to be the all-inclusive only reality; His infinity is lost. But if that matter be conceived as something real and *within* God, and the world be conceived as a real transformation of it, we have to face a dilemma.[30] Either matter is a part of God, or identical with the whole of God. If the first alternative is accepted (as Rāmānuja does), then we are landed into the absurdity that God, a spiritual substance, is composed of parts like material substances, and is consequently also liable to destruction, like such objects, if the second alternative (namely that primal matter is the whole of God) be accepted, then, by the transformation of matter, God is wholly reduced to the world and there is no God left after creation. Whether God changed partly or wholly, if change be real, then God is not a permanent, unchanging reality. He then ceases to be God. These difficulties are avoided by vivarta-vāda according to which change is apparent.

How Rāmanuja explains the difficulties of creation

These difficulties are felt also by Rāmānuja. But he thinks that the mystery of creation is beyond human intellect, and we are to accept the account so of creation given in the scriptures. As for difficulties, once we admit that God is omnipotent omniscient and has wonderful powers, nothing should be thought impossible for him. Though śaṅkara also believes that without the help of the revealed scripture the mystery cannot be solved simply by the unaided humar; reasoning (kevalena tarkeṅa),[32] he points out that the scriptures themselves have told us holy the many can illusorily appear not of the one. Following the light shed by the scripture we can employ our reasoning and understand, even in the likeness of our ordinary experiences of illusion, the mystery of creation so far as it is humanly possible.

(d) In what sense śaṅkara calls the World Unreal?

The world is not a dream

Dreams are contradicted by waking experience

But while speaking of śaṅkara's theory of creation it is necessary to warn the reader against a very common misunderstanding of his theory, for which some of his latter-day followers also are partly responsible. śaṅkara wants us to understand that the world is like a dream or illusion but is not identical with it. If he believed that the objects we perceive normally in waking experience are of the *same* status as dream or illusory objects, then he would accept subjective idealism. But we find that he rejects such idealism of the vijñānavādins and asserts in that connection that the objects of ordinary perception do not possess the same status as dream-objects, because the latter are, contradicted by waking experience, while the former are not. contradiction (bādha) is the test of error, whereas non-contradiction (abadhi-tatva) is the test of truth. The world is unreal in the sense that it is contradicted by the experience of one who realizes that Brahman is the only reality. Till the world-appearance is so contradicted by that superior experience, it enjoys uncontradicted reality.

The three levels of experience and threefold existence corresponding to them,

This position of śaṅkara has been developed later into the well-known theory of three- fold existence (sattā-traividhya) corresponding to three levels of experience. Dream-experience and ordinary experience of illusion (of the snake-rope kind) stand lowest and the objects of such experience enjoy the lowest kind of existence. Such existence is named prātibhāsika-sattā, because objects possessing it exist only so long as they appear to some mind. The reality of such experience and its objects is disproved when normal waking experience contradicts them. The objects of normal experience enjoy, therefore, an existence superior to that of dreams and illusions. Normal waking experience is known as practical or empirical experience (vyāvahārika), because our practical life is based on this. The existence of the objects of such experience is called practical or empirical existence (vyāvahrika-sattā). But even such experience, with its objects, is contradicted by the supreme experience, namely, the realization of Brahman (Brahma-jñāna). As such knowledge is nothing other than the immediate intuition (aparokṣānubhūti) of the Self itself. There is no distinction here between experience and object: both are one. This supreme experience, which is another name for Ātman or Brahman, has absolute existence (pāramārthika-sattā), because there is nothing to contradict it. The reality of these three kinds of existence—merely apparent (or subjective), empirical and absolute—is contrasted with utter falsity (alikatva or tucchatva), as of the child of a barren woman. The latter does not even appear as an object of any experience, and there is no question of its being contradicted, whereas even an illusory serpent at least appears to exist in some experience, however short-lived it may be.

The objects of ordinary empirical experience (vyāva-hārika,) stand midway between illusory or dream object (pratibhāsika and Brahman or the Absolute Reality (paramārthika-sattā). They are real for our sense experience, but not ultimately real, or, as Kant would say they are empirically real and transcendentally ideal.

(c) Rāmānuja's Criticism of the Advaita Theory of Illusion

The difficulties of the Advaita theory of Ignorance.

Rāmānuja who lived long after śaṅkara had the opportunity of criticizing severely the views of śaṅkara as well as of his followers in the course of his commentary on the Brama-sūtra. We are indebted to him for exposing many of the obscure points (of the Advaita school. Though the charges raised by Rāmānuja have been replied to by the advaitins, they have great value for understanding more clearly both Rāmānuja and śaṅkara. We shall mention here Rāmānuja's chief objections against the Advaita theory of māyā or ajñāna and also show briefly how they can be met.

(i) ***Where does Ignorance exist ?***

Where does the Ignorance (ajñāna), that is said to produce the world, exist? It cannot be said to exist in an. individual self (jīva), by Ignorance and the cause cannot depend on its effect. Neither can Ignorance be said to be in Brahman, because then it ceases to be omniscient.

These difficulties are based on some misconceptions.

The reply to this, in defence of śaṅkara, would be that even if Ignorance be said to be in the individual self, the difficulty arises only if we regard the one as preceding the other. But if we regard Ignorance and individuality as but the two interdependent aspects is of the same fact, as a circle and its circumference, or a triangle and its side; or fatherhood and sonship, the difficulty does not arise. But if, on the other band, Brahman be regarded as the locus of ignorance, even then the difficulty can be removed by removing a misunderstanding on which it is based. Māyā in Brahman is ignorance only in the sense of the power of producing ignorance and illusion in individuals; it does not affect Brahman any more than the magician's power of creating an illusion affects his own knowledge.

(ii) ***If Ignorance conceals Brahman, then its self-revealing nature is destroyed.***

It is said that māyā or ajñāna conceals the real nature of Brahman. But Brahman is admitted to be essential self-revealing. if māyā conceals Brahman it means that. His self-revealing nature is destroyed by it and Brahman ceases to be.

The reply to this is that Ignorance conceals Brahmin in the sense of preventing the ignorant individual from realizing His realnature, just as a patch of cloud conceals the sun by preventing a person from perceiving the sun. So ignorance does no more destroy the nature of Brahman than the cloud destroys the self-manifesting nature of the sun. Self-manifestation means manifestation of itself in the absence of obstacles—and not inspite of obstacles The sun does not cease to be self-revealing because the blind cannot see it.

(iii) ***Ignorance is said to be neither real nor unreal, but in de scribable***

What is the nature of the Ignorance? Sometime the Advaitins say that māyā is indescribable (anirvacanīya), it is neither real nor unreal. This is absurd. Because our experience shows that tings are other real or unreal. How can there be a third category besides these two contraditories?

The real meaning of indescribable' (anirvacnīya)

The reply to this is that māyā, as well as every illusory object, is said to be indescribable owing of a genuine difficulty. In so far as it *appears to be* something, an illlusion or illusory object canot be said to be unreal like a square-circle or the son of a barren woman, which never even appears to exist. Again in so far as it is sublated or contradicted afterwards by some experience, it cannot be said to be absolutely real like Ātman or Brahman whose reality is never contradicted. Māyā and every illusory object have this nature and compel us to recognize this nature as something unique and indescribable in terms of ordinary reality or unreality. To say that maya is indescribable is only to describe a fact, namely our *inability* to bring it under any ordinary category, and it does not mean any violation of the law of contradiction. In fact as 'real' means here the 'absoluterly real' and 'unreal' the absolutely 'unreal,' they do not constitute a pair of contradictories any more than two words like 'extremely cold' and 'extremely hot' do.

(iv) *How can Ignorance be positive?*

Again sometimes māyā or adidyā is said by the Advaitins to be positive ignorance (bhāva-rūpam adjñāam). This is also meaningless. Ignorance means want of knowledge and how can it be positive then?

The reply in defence would be that as the illustion producing ignorance is not merely an abasine of the knowledge of the ground of illusion, but positively makes this ground appear as some other object, it is properly described as positive, in this sense.

(v) *How can positive Ignorance be destroyed?*

Granting that maya is something positive, how can it be destroyed by the knowledge of Brahman? Nothing that positively exists canbe removed from existence by knowledge.

The reply is that if the word 'positive 'be understood *in* the sense given above, this misunderstanding would not arise. In our daily experience of illusory objects, like the serpent in a rope, we find that the object positively appears to be there and yet it vanishes when we have a clear knowledge of the ground of the illusion, *viz.* the rope.

(vi) *The Advaita Theory of Error*

We have already noticed that Rāmānuja makes an attempt to deny the possibility of illusion altogether, on the ground that every apprehension is true. If his contention be true, then the Advaita position breaks down altogether. The Advaitins, therefore, take great care to discuss the nature of error, and their literature on the theory of error is so vast that we can mention here only a few salient points, relevant to our discussion.

Rāmānuja's explanation of error is not satisfactory.

All illusroy object appears to be immediately present.

Such an object is a creation of ignorance.

Rāmānuja holds that as the constituents of every object are present in every other object (all objects being made out of the mixture of three elements), there can be no illusion. But even if some common characters be granted to exist in two objects like snake and rope, we should not ignore that there are also differences between them, otherwise all things would appear alike. Distinctions of appearances inspite of the commonness of component substances must then be admıtted. Illusion concerns this appearance. When a rope appears as rope, the knowledge is veridical. If it appears as a snake it is false. The Advaitins lay stress on the point that in our experience of illusion the illusory object immediately appears to be present before us. So it is an object of immediate apprehension like 'This is a snake, and not merely an object of wrong inference. The illusory object, whose nature, as we have seen, cannot be described as utterly unreal or absolutely real is called an indescribable creation (anirvacanīya sṛṣṭi) something. The appearance of the illusory object is, therefore, said to be the product of an indescribable creation (anirvacanīya sṛṣṭi). Just as the world is the creation of a long-enduring ignorance, which is termed the root-ignorance (mūlāvidyā), enjoy objectivity, though of two different grades; both are creations of ignorance. This Advaitn theory of error known as anirvacanīya-khyāti-vāda *(i.e.* the view that the indescribable object appears in illusion), whereas Rāmā-nuja's theory of non-illusion is sometimes called sat-khyta vāda (*i.e.* the view that the real appears in so-called illusion).

A comparative estimate of the views of śaṅkara and Rāmānuja regarding the world.

To sum up the Vedānta theory of the world: According to the Vedānta, the world is grounded in God. While Rámānuja holds that God is the ground of the world as nay organic whole of its parts, śaṅkara believes that God is the ground of the world as the rope is of the serpent or the mind is of any dream. Rāmānuja believes, therefore, that the world is absolutely real like God, being a part of God. But śaṅkara believes that the world is only practically real, real for all practical purposes and till one realizes Brahman, its ground. The reality of the world is then not on a par with that of dream-object, but superior to it; neither is it on a par with the reality of God, but inferior to it. śaṅkara's theory. thus should be called not nihilism but phenomenalism. Though the world is, in a certain sense, illusion according to him. it is not a groundless illusion but is to borrow Leibniz's phrase, a well-grounded phenomenon *(phenomena bene fundata).* What is falsified of the world by the knowledge of Brāhman is the diversity of particular phenomena, but not the pure existence on which it is grounded. In this aspect of pure existence, the world is in every sense identical with God and is eternally real like God, as śaṅkara clearly declares.[34] There are two aspects of the teachings of the Upaniṣads, as well as of śaṅkara's views, the negative and the positive. On the negative side, the world is an appearance, on the positive, the world is God. Unfortunately, the negative doctrine had been unduly stressed by some of his followers and it had its baneful effect on Indian life. But there is no reason why we should not emphasize the positive aspect which inspired the Upaniṣadic sages with the sense of a living presence of God in the world and made their life so Joyous. It is thus that the Vedānta can redeem life from the sloth that its misunderstanding has caused and spiritualize the daily life in its practical sphere.

2. God

According to the Vedas, Upaniṣads and the Vedānta, God is both immanent and transcendent.

We have seen that God was conceived even as early as the Vedas in two aspects: God pervades the world, but He is not exhausted in the world; He is also beyond it. God is both immanent and transcendent. These two aspects of god persist throughout the Upaniṣads and the later Vedānta, though the meanings of transcendence and immanence are not the same in all thinkers. It is usual to call the theory of the presence of God in all things 'pantheism' and Vedānta is commonly described by this name. Pantheism etymologically means all-God-theory. But if all is God, the question remains open whether God is the mere totality of all objects of the world, or the totality of things and something more. When such distinction is made, the word 'pantheism 'is generally confined to the first view, whereas 'panentheism '(a word coined by a German philosopher, Krause) is used for the second. To avoid the ambiguity of the word 'pantheism,' and to remind ourselves of the fact that God in Vedānta is not simply immanent, but also transcendent, we should call the Vedānta theory of God panentheism, rather than pantheism.

Belief in God starts from an acceptance of scriptural testimony.
No independent argument can prove God.
Testimony of Kant, Lotze and others on this.
Reason is necessary to justify faith already present.

Another point of agreement among Vedāntins is that all of them believe that the knowledge of the existence of God is, at the first instance, obtained not by reasoning but from the testimony of the revealed scriptures. It is admitted, of course. that on the perfection of religious life the presence of God can be realized by the devout souls. But to start with, we have to depend an indirect knowledge of God through the undoubted testimony of the scriptures. Scarcely any attempt is made, therefore, in the Vedānta, as in the Nyāya and other theistic systems, to aduce purely logical proofs for the existence of God. Arguments are confined generally to showing the inadequacy of all theories of God, not based on scriptures, and to the justification of the scriptural views. This attitude of the Vedānta appears to be dogmatic and is sometimes made the object of criticism. It should be noted, however, that even many Western philosophers (like Kant, Lotze and others) have ever and again rejected such proofs as inadequate. Lotze makes it clear that unless we start with some faith in god, the rational proofs are of little avail. As he puts it: "Therefore, all proofs that God exists are pleas put forward in justification of our faith." This faith according to him springs from "the obscure impulse which drives us to pass in our thought—as we cannot help passing—from the world given in sense to a world not given in sense, but above and behind sense".[35] According to the Vedānta also an initial faith is necessary for religious life and thought. This faith, though starting from a personal feeling of inadequacy and disquiet and a longing for something higher, remains mere blind groping in the dark till it is enlightened the teachings of the scriptures that show the way to the real zation of God. Reasoning is necessary for the understanding of the teachings, for removing doubts, and realizing their cogency. By itself reasoning is an empty form or method of thinking which can work only when materials are supplied. The scriptures supply to reason the matter for speculation, argumentation and meditation. This kind of dependence of reason on matter supplied from a non-rational source is nothing peculiar to theology. Even the greatest discoveries in science can be traced back to some non-rational origin like intuitive, flashes of truth in imagination which reasoning afterwards attempts to justify, by further observation, experiment proof and elaboration. "Dialectic," says Bergson.[36] is necessary to put intuition to the proof." Though all Vedāntins primarily depend on the scriptures for belief in God, they make full use of reasoning in the justification and elaboration of that belief. They learn from the Upaniṣads that God is the Infinite, Conscious, All-inclusive Reality, the Creator of the universe as well us its Preserver: and Destroyer. Each one tries in his own way to develop what he thinks to be the most consistent theory of God.

(i) *Rāmānuja's Conception of God*

God is the Absolute Reality, possessed of matter and finite souls.

God, according to Rāmānuja, is the Absolute Reality possessed of two integral parts, matter and the finite spirits. Brahman is said by him to be the only Reality in the universe in the sense that outside or independent of God there is no other reality. But God contain within Himself the material objects as well as the finite souls which are real. The Absolute One contains the many. This monism of Rāmānuja is known, therefore, as Vśiṣṭādvaita" which mean the Unity (advaita) of Brahman possessed (viśiṣṭa) of real parts (the concious and the unconscious). It is not a distinctionless unity. Three types of distinction (bheda) are generaly distinguished by the Vedāntins The distinction that anything—say, a cow—has from things of other classes, such as horses, asses, is called a heterogeneous distinction (vijātīya-bheda). The distinction that one cow has from another cow *(i.e.* an object of the same class) is called a homogeneous distinction (sajātīya-bheda). In addition to these two kinds of external distinctions, there is a third kind, *i.e,* internal distinction (svagata-bheda), which exists within an object, between its different parts, such as between the tail and the legs of the same cow. Judged in the light of this threefold classification of distinctions, Rāmānuja's Brahman is said to be devoid of the two kinds of external distinctions (vijātīya and sajātīya). because there nothing besides God, either similar or dissimilar to Him. But God is possessed of internal distinctions (svagata-bheda), as there are within Him different conscious and unconscious substances which can be mutually distinguished.

God has all good qualities.
God as the unmnaifested cause.
God as the manifested effect.

God is possessed of an infinite number of infinitely good qualities such as omnipotence, omni science, benevolence. Therefore, God is not characterless (nirguṇa), or indeterminate, but possessed of qualities (saguṇa), When the Upaniṣads deny qualities of Brahman, the, really mean that God is free from all bad qualities o imperfections. God really creates the world, sustains it and withdrawn it. When the world is withdrawn and its objects are destroyed, even then there remains in God matter in an undifferentiated, homogeneous state, as well as the souls, because both are eternal objects made by the modification of matter undergo change, growth and decay, but matter out of which they are created always remains there. Similarly the spirits always remain, though their bodies may change or perish. In the state of dissolution, when objects are absent. Brahman remains with pure matter and bodiless souls in an unmanifested form (avyakta). This may be called the casual state of Brahman (kāraṇa-brahma). When again objects are created, God becomes manifested as the world of objects and embodied souls. This second manifested form of God may be called its effect-state (kārya-brahma). Those texts of the Upaniṣads which deny the existence of objects and describe God negatively as being beyond thought, speech, etc. really indicate the unmanifested state of Brahman.[37]

Rāmānuja's difficulties regarding the relation of God to matter and spirits.

If matter and spirits are parts of God, as Rāmānuja repeatedly asserts, then does not God really undergo modification with the change of matter?

Does He not become also subject to the miseries from which the spirits suffer? Are not then all the imperfections and defects which we find in the world really in God ? In the face of these difficulties Rāmānuja seems to give up sometimes the imagery of parts and whole and employ other similies. Sometimes he takes recourse to the analogy of the body and the soul. God is the soul of which the material objects and spirits compose the body. Just as the soul controls the body from within so God controls matter and spirits. He is thus conceived as the Antaryāmin or regulator of the universe from within. With the help of this analogy, Rāmānuja tries to explain away the charge of God's being subject to misery and imperfection. The soul, he says, is not affected by the bodily changes and imperfections; similarly God is not affected by the changes in the universe; He remains beyond them or *transcends* them. Sometimes, again Rāmānuja tries to save Gods immunity by the analogy of the king and his subjects. The ruler, inspite of having a, body, is not affected by the pleasures and pains suffered by the subjects due to the obeying or disobeying the ruler's laws.[38] These explanations of Rāmānuja show that he is not very sure in his mind as to the' exact nature of the relation between god and the universe. The relation between the soul and the body is surely very much different from that between this king and his subjects; and none of these two again contains the relation of whole and parts. Besides, when Rāmānuja also speaks of the universe as a qualifying character (viśeṣaṇa) and God as the substantive (viśeṣya), it is difficult to understand have God remains unaffected by the imperfections of the universe. Rāmānuja himself is aware of the unsatisfactory character of his explanation and in one place he makes an important confession which is not quite in harmony with his general position. The essence (svarūpa) if God, he says there, remains unchanged by, changes in the Universe, and, therefore, God is unaffected [39] If this admission is to be logically followed, then, Rāmānuja has to admit further that matter which is subject to change is not essential and internal to God, but externally related to Him. Then his central theory that matter and spirits form real parts of God and God is really qualified by them becomes considerably weakened. To conceive matter and spirits as really existing within God and as really undergoing change, and to hold at the same time that God is not affected by these changes, is to hold a very precarious position.

Rāmānuja's view of God is theism.

Rāmānuja's conception of God is a kind of theism. Theism, in this narrow sense, means belief in God who is both immanent and transcendent,[40] and is also a Person, *i.e.*, a self-conscious being possessed of will. We have seen that all these characters are present in Rāmānuja's conception of God.

God is the object of worship and the goal of our religious aspiration. It is by pleasing God through prayer that we obtain salvation through His mercy.

(ii) *śaṅkara's Conception of God*

From the empirical standpoint God is the omniscient and omnipotent creator, possessed of qualities.

God, according to śaṅkara, can be conceived from two different points of view. If we look at God from the ordinary practical standpoint (vyāvahārika dṛṣṭi) from which the world is believed to be real, God may be considered as the Cause, the Creator, the Sustainer, the Destroyer of the world and, therefore, also as an Omnipotent and Omniscient Being. He then appears as possessed of all these qualities (saguna). God in this aspect is called Saguna Brahma or Īśvara in śaṅkara's philosophy. He is the object of worship.

But this view of God does not reveal His essence.

But the world, as we have seen, is conceived by śaṅkara as an appearance which rests on our ignorance. description of God as the Creator of the world is true only from the practical point of view, so long as the world-appearance is regarded as real. Creatorship of the world is not God's essence (svarūpa-lakṣaṇa); it is the description of what is merely accidental (taṭastha-laksaṇa) and does not touch His essence.

Let us try to understand with the help of an ordinary example the distinction that śaṅkara wants to make here. A shepherd appears on the stage in the role of a king, wages war, conquers a country and rules it. Now, the description of the actor as a shepherd gives what he is from the real point of view. It is *essential* the description of him (svarūpa-lakṣaṇa). But the description of him as a king, ruler and conqueror, is applied to him only from the point of view of the stage and his rōle there; it is merely a description of what is accidental to the person (taṭastha-Iakṣaṇa) and does not touch his essence.

From the transcendental standpoint God is consciousness, real and infinite.

Similarly, the description of God as conscious, real, infinite (satyam, jñānam anantam Brahma)[41] is an attempt to describe His essence (svarūpa), whearas the description of him as Creator Sustainer and Destroyer of the world, or by any other characteristic connected with the world, is a mere accidental description and it holds good only from the point of view of the world. (vyāvahārika-drṣṭi). As we can regard the actor on the stage from a point of view other than that of the stage, so we can look at God also from a non-worldly point of view (pārāmārthika-drṣṭi) and try to dissociate Him from the point of view of the world. God in this aspect of what He really is, without any reference to the world, is called by śaṅkara Parambrahma or the Supreme God.

The analogy of the magician.

For understanding this higher aspect of God as He is really in Himself (without relation to the world) along with the lower aspect, śaṅkara constantly draws on the analogy of the magician (māyāvī) as suggested in the *śvetāśvatara*. The magician is a Juggler only to those who are deceived by his trick and who fancy that they perceive the objects conjured up. But to the discerning few who see through the trick and have no illusion, the juggler fails to be a juggler. Similarly, those who believe in the world-show think of God through this show and call Him its Creator, etc. But for those wise few who know that the world is a mere show, there is neither any real world nor any real Creator.

śaṅkara tries to reconcile the immanence and the transcendence of God

This is the only way, thinks śaṅkara, in which we can understand in the light of common experience how God can be both in the world and yet beyond it—understand, that is to say, the immanence and the transcendence of God, which are taught by the Upaniṣads. The world, so long as it appears, is in God, the only Reality, just as the snake conjured out of the rope is nowhere else except in the rope. But God is not really touched by the imperfections of the world just as the rope is not affected by any illusory characters of the snake, or even as the actor is not affected by the loss and gain of kingdom on the stage.

This reconciliation is difficult for Rāmānuja.

Rāmānuja, we have seen, finds difficulty in in reconciling the immanence of God with His transcendence. He vacillates in his explanation of how God can be said to be in the world and yet to remain unaffected by the world's imperfections. This difficulty, however, is not peculiar to Rāmānuja alone. It is present in most Western forms of theism also, which, like Rāmānuja's, look upon creation as real.

God is an object of worship only when viewed from the lower standpoint.

God as the object of worship is based essentially on a belief in the distinction between the worshiping self and the god worshipped. The reality of the limited self like that of a worldly limited self like that of a worldly object is based on ignorance—on the failure to realize that God is the only Reality. Besides, God is worshipped because God is thought, of as the creator and controller of the world. So worship and the God worshipped are bound up with our lower standpoint (vyāvahārika-dṛṣṭi) from which the world appears as real and God appears as endowed with the many qualities in relation to the world. It is this Saguṇa Brahma or Īśvara who can be regarded as an object of worship.

God from thetranscendental standpoint is devoid of all qualities and distinctions

Brahman from the higher or transcendental point of view (pāramārthika-dṛṣṭi) cannot be described by qualities which relate to the world or to the ego. Brahman in this aspect is devoid of all distinctions, external as well as internal (sajātīya, vijātīya and svagata bhedas). Here, therefore, śaṅkara differs from Rāmānuja who believes that God is possessed of at least internal distinction (svagata bheda), because within Him there are the really distinct conscious and unconscious realities. Brahman, in this absolutely transcendent aspect, says śaṅkara, cannot be described at all and it is, therefore, called indeterminate or characterless or nirguna. The description of Brahman even as infinite, real, consciousness, though more accurate than accidental descriptions, cannot directly convey the idea of Brahman. It only serves to direct the mind towards Brahman by denying of it finiteness, unreality and unconsciousness.[42]

To predicate a quality is to limit God.

God, from the real standpoint, is indeterminate.

Every quality predicated of any subject is a sort of limitation imposed on it. This follows from thelogical principle of obversion. If S is P, then it is not non-P and therefore, non-P is excluded from S, which becomes then limited to that extent. *A great* Western philosopher, Spinoza, recognizes this and lays down the dictum, 'Every determination is negation.' He also, therefore, thinks that God, the ultimate substance, is indeterminate and cannot be described by any positive qualification. The Upaniṣads recognize this principle and deny of God ail predicates, even worshipability.[43] This conception is developed by śaṅkara who calls Brahman this transcendent aspect, nirguṇa.

Māyā is attributable to god only from the lower standpoint, not from the higher.

We have said previously that the world-appearance is due to māyā. God regarded as the Creator of the world is, therefore, described as the wielder of māyā. Ignorant people like us believe that the world is real and that, therefore, God is really qualified by māyā, *i.e.* possessed of the power of creating the world (māyā-viśiṣṭa). But really creativity is not an essential character of God, it is only an apparent, accidental predicate (upādhi that we illusorily ascribe to God. God is only apparently associated with creativity (māyopahita). God as immanent (saguṇa) and God as transcendent reality (nirguna) are not two, any more than the man on the stage and that man outside the stage are two The first is only the apparent aspect of the second. The first is relative to the world, the second is irrelative or absolute.

The distinction of points of view is made in daily life

Distinction between standpoints is always made by us in life and is nothing new or queer in Advaita philosophy as it may appear to some. In daily life, we say that a currency note is really paper, but conventionally it is money; a photograph is really paper but appears as a man; the image in a mirror *appears* as a real object, but is not really so; and so on. This ordinary kind of distinction between the apparent and the real is; philosophically utilized by Vedānta for explaining the relation of God to the world. Thus the vyāvahrika and the pāramārthika—the empirical (conventional or practical) and the transcendental (absolute or irrelative which the Vedānta' distinguishes are neither uncommon nor unintelligible. It is only the extension of a common distinction.

The view of God as immanent leads to that of God as transcendent.

Gradual revelation of Truth.

Though God as creator is only apparent, yet His importance and value should not be ignored. It is only through the lower stand point that we can gradually mount up to the higher. Advaita Vedānta, like the immanent lead that we can gradually mount up to the higher. Advaita Vedānta, like the Upaniṣads, believes in the gradual revelation of truth in stages through which spiritual progress takes place. The unreflecting man who regards the world as a self sufficient reality feels no urge to look beyond it and search for its cause or ground. When be comes to realize somehow the insufficiency of the world and looks for something which sustains the world from behind, he comes to discover God as the Creator and Sustainer of the world. He feels admiration and reverence and begins to pray to the Creator. God thus becomes the object of worship. With the further advancement of thought, so the Advaita thinks, the man may discover that God, whom be reached through the world is really the only reality, the world is only an appearance. Thus at the first level, the world alone is real; at the second, both the world and God; at the last, only God. The first is atheism. The second represents theism as we find in Rāmānuja and others. The last is the Absolute monism of śaṅkara. śaṅkara recognizes that the last level has to be reached only gradually through the second. He, therefore, believes in the utility of worshipping God (as Saguna Brahma). For, this purifies the heart and prepares one for gradually reaching the highest view, and without it no God, immanent or transcendent, would ever be found. śaṅkara gives a place even to the worship of the many deities, because it redeems the spiritually backward at least from utter atheism, and it serves as a stage on the way to the highest truth.

3. The Self

Man's position is central in Vedānta.

The sūtras of Bādrāyaṇa have for their subject-matter God and are, therefore, named *Brahma-sūtra*. But they are written for man, the embodied soul, and, therefore, called also *śārīraka-sūtra*. Man, therefore occupies a central place in the Vedānta. It is for his enlightenment and his salvation that the Vedānta undertakes philosophical discussion. But what is the real nature of man ? The Upaniṣads teach us that man is not different from God. But what is the sense in which this teaching should be understood ?

(i) Rāmānuja's Conception of the Self, Bondage and Liberation

Between self and God there is identity as well as difference.

The meaning of 'that thou art'.

Qualified monism.

Rāmānuja holds that the identity between God and man taught by the Upaniṣads is not really an unqualified one. It is unthinkable that man who is finite can be identical with God in every respect. Man is not different from God in the sense that God pervades and controls man as well as every other thing in the universe. Just as the existence of a part is inseparable from the whole, that of a mode or quality from the soul which controls its life from within, similarly the existence of man is inseparable from God. Identity cannot be asserted, it is true, between two altogether different terms; but it is also meaningless to assert any identity between exactly identical terms; because it would be a needles tautology. Identity can be asserted between two terms which are in some respects different and yet the same at bottom (*e.g.* between the first son of 'Daśaratha' and 'the husband of Sītā'). The Upaniṣadic dictum 'That thou art' (Tat tvam asi) should, therefore be taken in this last sense. 'That should, therefore, be taken in this last sense. 'That, stands for God, the omniscient, omnipotent creator of the universe. 'Thou, stands for God existing in the form of man, the embodied soul (acid-viśiṣṭa-jīva-śarīrakam). The identity asserted here is, therefore, between God with certain qualification and God with certain other qualification—an identity of the two differently qualified terms which are the same at bottom (viśiṣayoraikyam). In view of this Rāmānuja's philosophy is called Viśiṣṭādvaita or the identity of the qualified.[44]

The human body and soul are both finite.
The soul is eternal but infintely small.
Consciusness is the essential quality of the soul.

Man, according to Rāmānuja, has a real body and a soul. The body is made of matter which is a part of God. It is obviously finite. The soul is, of course, not made, it is eternally existing. It is also a part of God, and cannot, therefore, be infinite, The all-pervasive nature of the soul which the Upaniṣads describe cannot, therefore, be taken, in the literal sense. The real sense of the pervasiveness of the soul is that the soul is so subtle (sūkṣma) that it can penetrate into every unconscious "material substance."[45] Having denied that the soul is infinite, Rāmānuja has to hold, like the Jainas, that it is infinitely small (aṇu). For if the soul has neither of these two extreme dimensions, it must be admitted to these two medium one, which things composed by the combination of parts (such as tables and chairs) have; and then like such objects the soul also would be liable to destruction. The consciousness of the soul is not accidental to it; it is not dependent on its connection with the body. Consciousness is an intrinsic quality of the soul and it remains under all conditions. In dreamless sleep and even in the state of liberation, when the soul is altogether disembodied, the soul remains conscious of itself as 'I am.' The soul is, therefore, identified by Rāmānuja with what we mean by the word 'I' or the 'ego '(aham.)[46]

The bondage of the soul is due to karma.

The bondage of the soul to the body is due to its karma. As the effect of its karma, the soul is associated with the particular kind of body it deserves. Being embodied, its consciousness is limited by the conditions of the organs of knowledge, and the body it possesses. Though the soul is infinitely small, it illumines or renders? conscious every part of the body in which it is, just as a small light illumines the entire room in which it is. It identifies itself with the body and regards it as itself. Egoism (ahaṅkāra) is a name for this identification of the self with the not-pelt' Avidyā or ignorance consists in this base propensity[47] Karma also is sometimes identified by Rāmānuja with this ignorance.

The liberation of the soul is sought through work and knowledge.

The necessity of performing rituals for destroying karmas.

The necessity of the knowledge of Vedānta.

The attainment of liberation must be sought through work and knowledge, because they pave the way for devotion. By work (karma) Rāmānuja means here the different obligatory rituals enjoined by the Vedas on persons according to their respective castes and stations in life (varṇāśrama). These should be performed life-long, as bounden duties without any desire for reward, like heaven. Disinterested performance of such duties destroys the accumulated effects of the past deeds which stand in the way of knowledge. For the correct performance of these rituals it is necessary to study the Mimāṁsa philosophy. Rāmānuja regards, therefore, the study of the Mimāṁsa as a necessary pre-requisite to the study of the Vedānta. By the study of the Mīmāṁsā and performance of the duties in its light, one comes to realize also that the sacrificial rites cannot lead to any permanent good and cannot help man to attain salvation. This persuades him to study the Vedānta. The Vedānta reveals to him the real nature of the universe. He come to know that God is the creator, sustainer and controller of all beings, and that his soul is not identical with the body, but is really part of God who controls it from within. He further learns that liberation can be attained not by 'study and reasoning,' but only if God is pleased to choose him for liberation.

The knowledge of God matures into constant remembrance or devotion.

This study of the Vedānta produces only book-learning and does not bring about liberation. It is true, as the Upaniṣads say, that liberation is brought about by knowledge. But that real knowledge is not a verbal knowledge of scriptures; for then everyone who reads them would be liberate at once. Real knowledge is a steady, constant remembrance of God (dhruvā smṛti). This is variously described as meditation (dhyāna), prayer (upāsana) devotion (bhakti).[48] Constant meditation oh God, as the dearest object of love, should be practised continuously along with the performance of the obligatory rituals which remove the obstacles to knowledge. Intense remembrance of God, or devotion thus practised, ultimately matures into an immediate knowledge (darśana or sākṣātrara) of God. This is, therefore, the final means to liberation. This brings about the destruction of all ignorance and karmas by which the body is caused. Therefore, the soul that realizes God is liberated from the body for ever, without any chance of rebirth. We should remember, however, that liberation cannot be attained simply by human efforts. God, pleased by devotion, helps the devotee to attain perfect knowledge by removing obstacles. God lifts from bondage and misery the man who flings himself at the mercy of God and constantly remembers Him as the only object of love.

The liberated soul is like God, not* identical *with God

Liberation is not the soul's becoming identical this God. The liberated soul having pure consciousness, untainted by any imperfection, becomes, in this respect, similar to God (brahma-prakāra). This similarity of nature is what is meant by the Upaniṣads which say that the liberated soul attains unity with God.[49]

(ii) śaṅkara's Conception of the Self, Bondage and Liberation

The self is absolutely identical with Brahman.

We have found already that śaṅkara believes in unqualified monism. All distinctions between objects and objects, the subject and the object the self and God are the illusory creation of māyā. He holds fast to the conception of identity without any real difference and tries to follow it out logically in every respect. He accepts, therefore, without any reservation, the identity of the Soul and God, that is repeatedly taught in the Upaniṣads.

The body is not real.

The meaning of 'That thou art.'

Identity jugmentis neither tautological nor impossible

Man is apparently composed of the body and the soul. But the body which we perceive is, like every other material object, merely an illusory appearance. When this is realized, the Utility that remains is the soul which is nothing other than God. The saying, 'That thou art,' means that there is an unqualified identity between the soul, that underlies the apparently finite man, and God. It is true that if we take the word 'thou 'in the sense of the empirical individual limited and conditioned by its body, there cannot be an identity between the 'thou 'and 'that,' the supreme Brahman. We have to understand, therefore, the word 'thou 'to stand for what is real in man, namely, the soul. Between this soul and God complete identity exists- and is taught by the Vedānta. An identity judgment like 'This is that Devadatta '(which we pass on seeing Devadatta for a second time) makes the above point clear. The conditions which the man had the previous day cannot be exactly identical with those he has the second day. Therefore, there cannot be any identity between the man qualified by one set of conditions with the man qualified by another set. What we mean, therefore, must be that the man, viewed apart from the different conditions, is the same. similar is the case with the identity taught between the Self and God. The Self, viewed apart from the conditions, *i.e.* the reality underlying the conditioned individual, is identical with God. Such identity jugment is not autological and superfluous, because it serves the purpose of pointing out that what are illusorily taken as different are really one. The identity that is taught between man and God a real identity between terms which appear as different. Being identical with God, the soul is in reality what God is It is the supreme Brahman—the self-luminous, infinite, consciousness. This soul appears as the limited, finite self because of its association with the body which is a product of ignorance.

The gross body and the subtle body are the products of māyā.

The body is not composed simply of what we perceive through the senses. In addition to this gross perceptible body, there is also a subtle one, composed of the senses, the motor organs (these two groups together being called indriyās), vital elements (prāṇas), and the internal mechanism of knowledge (antaḥkaraṇa). While the gross body perishes on death, the subtle body does not and it migrates with the soul to the next gross body. Both of these are the products of māyā.

The evolution of the material elements out of Brahman.

The subtle elements and the gross ones.

Vedānta works, like the Upaniṣads, are not always unanimous regarding the exact process by which and the order in which the product arise out of Brahman through māyā. The number and nature of the constituents of the subtle body are not also .the same according to all writers. According to a well-known account, at first there arise out of Ātman or Brahman the five subtle elements, in the order—ākāśa (ether), vāyu (air), agni (fire), ap (water), kṣiti (earth). These five are again mixed up together in five different ways to give rise to the five gross elements of those names. Gross ākāśa is produced by the combination of the five subtle elements in the proportion, ½ ākāśa + 1/8 fire + aire + 1/8 water + 1/8 earth. Similarly each of the other five gross elements is produced by the combination of the subtle elements, in the proportion of half of that element and one-eighth of each of the other four. This process is known as combination of the five (pañcīkarana). The subtle body is made of the unmixed subtle elements, and the gross body as well as all gross objects of nature is produced out of the gross elements which arise by the mixture of the five subtle ones.

Bondage is the soul's association with the body through ignorance.

The ego (aham) is not the self (ātman).

Due to ignorance the beginning of which cannot be assigned, the soul erroneously associates itself with the body, gross and subtle. This is called bondage. In this state it forgets that it is really Brahman. It behaves like a finite, limited, miserable being which runs after temporal worldly objects and is pleased to get them, sorry to miss them. It identifies itself with the finite body and mind (antahkarana) and thinks 'I am stout,' I am lame,' 'I am ignorant.' Thus arises the conception of the self as the 'Ego 'or 'I.' This limited ego opposes itself to the rest of existence, which is thought to be different from it. The ego is not, therefore, the real self, but is only an apparent limitation of it.

The consciousness of the self is bondage is limited.

Consciousness of the self also becomes limited by the condition of the body. the senses and antaḥkaraṇa (the internal organ of knowledge) become the instruments through which limited consciousness of objects takes place. Such empirical, finite knowledge is of two kinds, immediate and mediate. Immediate knowledge of external objects arises when, through any sense, the antahkarana. flows out to the object and is modified into the form of the object. In addition to immediate knowledge (pratyakṣa), the Advaitins admit five different kinds of mediate knowledge, namely, inference (anumāna), testimony (śabda), comparison (upamāna), postulation (arthāpatti) and non-cognition (anupalabdhi). The Advaitins agree. in the main, with the Bhāṭṭa school of Mīmāṁsā regarding these sources of knowledge. As the Bhāṭṭa views have been already stated we need not repeat them here.[50]

Waking experience, dream and dreamless sleep—the three levels of ordinary consciousness.

When a man is awake, he thinks himself identified with the gross body, as well as with the internal and external organs. When he falls asleep and dreams, he is still conscious of objects that arise from memory-impressions, and therefore, the feeling of his limitation as a subject or knower opposed to objects still persists there. When he has deep, dreamless sleep, he ceases to have any ideas of objects. In the absence of objects, he ceases to be a knower as well. The polarity of subject and object, the opposition between the knower and the known, vanishes altogether. He no longer feels that he is confined to and limited by the body. But yet consciousness does not cease in dreamless sleep; for otherwise how could we remember at all on awaking from sleep that we had such a state ? How could we report 'I had a peaceful sleep, had no dreams,' if we were unconscious then ?

The study of dreamless sleep gives as a glimpse of what the self really is when dissociated from its feeling of identity with the body. The soul in its intrinsic state is not a finite, miserable being. It does not separate itself from the rest of existence and does not limit itself by a feeling of the 'I' '(aham)' opposed to a 'thou' 'or' 'this' 'or' 'that.' I also free from all worries that arise from hankerings after objects, then is an unlimited consciousness and bliss.

The attempt of śaṅkara and his followers is to show how this intrinsic, pure condition of the self can be regained. The fact that the blissful state of dreamless sleep is not permanent and man once more returns to his finite, limited, embodied consciousness on waking up, shows that there remain even in dreameless sleep, in a latent form, the forces of karma or avidyā which draw man into the world. Unless these forces, accumulated from the past, can be completely stopped, there is no hope of liberation from the miserable existence which the self has in this world.

Vedānta helps man to destroy ignorance completely.
Preparation, necessrly for the study of Vedanta, is not the study of any ritualistic work.

The study of the Vedānta helps man to conquer these deep-rooted effects of longstanding ignorance. But the study of the truths taught by the Vedānta would have no effect unless the mind is previously prepared. This initial preparation, according to śaṅkara, is not the study of the Mīmāṁsā sūtras, as Rāmānuja thinks. The Mīmāṁsā, which teaches the performance of sacrifices to the various gods, rests on the wrong conception of a distinction between the worshipper and the worshipped. its spirits is, therefore, antagonistic to the absolute monism taught by the Vedānta. Far from preparing the mind for the reception of the monistic truth, it only helps to perpetuate the illusion of distinctions and plurality from which suffers already.

But the fourfold culture of the mind alone makes one a fit studnet of Vedānta.

The preparation necessary for undertaking the study of the Vedānta is fourfold, according to śaṅkara.[51] One should first, be able to discriminate between what is eternal and what is not eternal (nityānitya-vastu-viveka). He should, secondly, be able to give up all desires for enjoyment on objects here and hereafter (ihāmutrārtha-bhoga-virāga). Thirdly, he should control his mind and his senses and develop qualities like detachment, patience, power of concentration (śamadamādi-sādhana-sampat). Lastly, he should have an ardent desire for liberation (mumukṣutva).

Study, reasoning and contemplation are necessary forthe realization of truth.

With such preparation of the intellect, emotion and will one should begin to study the Vedānta with a teacher who has himself realized Brahman. This study consists of the three fold process: listening to the teacher's instructions (śravaṇa), understanding the instructions through reasoning until all doubts are removed and conviction is generated (manana), and repeated meditation on the truths thus accepted (nididbyāsana).

Realization of the identity between the self and Brahman is liberation from bondage.

The forces of deep-rooted beliefs of the past do not disappear so soon as the truths of the Vedānta are learned. Only repeated meditation on the truths and life led accordingly can gradually root them out. When wrong beliefs thus become removed and belief in the truths of the Vedānta becomes permanent, the seeker after liberation is told by the teacher 'Thou art

Brahman.' He beigns then to contemplate this truth steadfastly till at last he has an immediate realization of the truth in the form 'I am Brahman.' Thus the illusory distinction between the self and Brahman at last disappears and bondage, too, along with it Liberation (mukti) is thus attained.

Liberation is possible even while the soul is associated with the body.

Even on the attainment of liberation the body may continue because it is the product of karmas which had already borne their effects (prārabdha-karma). But the liberated soul does never again identify itself with the body. The world still appears before him, but he is not deceived by it. He does not feel any desire for the world's objects. He is, therefore, not affected by the world's misery. He is in the world and yet out of it. This conception of śaṅkara has become well-known in later Vedānta as Jīvan-mukti.[52] (The liberation of one while he is alive). It is the state of perfection attained here. Like Buddha, the śaṅkara, the Jaina and some other Indian thinkers, śaṅkara believes that perfection can be reached even here in this life. It is not a mere extra-mundane prospect, like heaven, to be attained hereafter in an unperceived future. It is true that the seeker after liberation is asked to begin with some faith in the testimony of the scriptures regarding the utility of the spiritual discipline he is required to follow. But his faith is fully Justified and more than repaid by the end it secures in this very life.

Three kinds of karma can be distinguished. Karmas gathered in past lives admit of two divisions, those that have borne their effects (prārabdha-karma) and those that still lie accumulated (sañcita-karma). In addition to these two kinds, there are karmas which are being gathered here in this life (sañcāyamīna). Knowledge of reality destroys the second kind and prevents the third and thus makes rebirth impossible. But the first kind which has already borne effects cannot be prevented. Hence the present body, the effect of such karma, runs its natural course and ceases when the force of the karma causing it becomes automatically exhausted, just as the wheel of a potter which has been already turned comes to a stop only when the momentum imparted to it becomes exhausted. When the body, gross and subtle, perishes, the jīvan-mukta is said to attain the disembodied state of liberation (videba-mukti).

It is not a new product.

Liberation is not the production of anything new, nor is it the purification of any old state; it is the realization of what is always there even in the stage of bondage, though not known then. For, liberation is nothing but the identity of the self and Brahman, which is always real, though not always recognized. The attainment of liberation is, therefore, compared by the Advaitins to the finding of the necklace on the neck by one who forgot its existence there and searched for it hither and thither As bondage is due to an illusion, liberation is only the removal of this illusion.

Liberation is positive bliss.

Liberation is not merely the absence of all misery that arises from the illusory sense of distinction between the self and God. it is conceived by the Advaitin after the Upaniṣads, as a state of positive bliss (ānanda), because Brahman is bliss and liberation is identity with Brahman.

It is not incompatiable with work without attachment.

The value of disinterested work for both the wise and the ignorant.

Though the liberated soul, being perfect, has no end to achieve, it can work still without any fear of further bondage. śaṅkara, following the Gītā, holds that work fetters a man only when it is performed with attachment. But one who has obtained perfect knowledge and perfect satisfaction, is free from attachment. He can work without any hope of gain and is not, therefore, affected by success or failure śaṅkara attaches great importance to disinterested work. For one who has not yet obtained perfect knowledge, such work is necessary for self purification (ātma-śuddhi), because it is not through inactivity but through the performance of selfless action that one can gradually free oneself from the yoke of the ego and its petty interests. Even for one who has obtained perfect knowledge or liberation, selfless activity is necessary for the good of those who are still in bondage.[53]

The life of the liberated should be a worthy ideal of society.

The liberated man is the ideal of society and his life should be worthy of imitation by the people at large. Inactivity or activity that would mislead them should, therefore, be avoided by the perfect.[53] Social service is not, therefore thought by śaṅkara to be incompatible with the perfect life but rather desirable. In his own life of intense social service śaṅkara follows this ideal. This ideal is also advocated by some eminent modern Vedāntists like Svāmī Vivekānanda[54] and Lokamānya B.G. Tilak.[55]

Does the Vedānta disregard the distinction between right and wrong?

The critics of Advaita Vedānta have often urged that if Brahman be the only reality and all distinctions are false, the distinction between right and wrong also would be false. Such a philosophy is, therefore, fruitful of dangerous consequences for society. This objection is due to the confusion of the lower and the higher standpoint. From the empirical standpoint, the distinction between right and wrong, like other distinctions, is quite valid. For one who has not yet attained liberation, any action which directly or indirectly leads him towards the realization of his unity with Brahman, is good and that which hampers Buch realization, directly or indirectly, is bad. Truthfulness, charity, benevolence, self-control and the like would be found to fall under the first category even according to this criterion, whereas falsehood, selfishness, injury to others would come under the second. One who has attained perfect knowledge and liberation would look back upon these moral distinctions as being relative to the lower standpoint and, therefore, not absolutely valid. But neither would he perform a bad action in so far as the motive of every bad action is based on the ignorant identification of the self with the body, the senses and the like, in a word, on the lack of *the* of unity between the Self and Brahman.[56]

Conclusion

In conclusion, we should observe that the Vedānta of śaṅkara, in its different aspects, is an attempt to follow to the Upaniṣadic idea of the unity of all existence to its logical conclusion. With all its defects and excellence, it stands in the history of human thought as the most consistent system of monism. As William James puts it (in appreciation of śaṅkara's Vedānta as presented by Svāmī Vivekānanda in America): "The paragon of all monistic sterns is the Vedānta philosophy of Hindustan.[57] It is true that such a system fails to appeal to those who turn to philosophy for the justification of their imperfect ideas of worldly distinctions and worldly values, or to those who turn faint-hearted to religion for help and mercy. The philosophy of Rāmānuja would be more satisfying to them. Like the teachings of early Buddhism and Jainism, the monistic philosophy of śaṅkara is only for the strong-hearted who can follow logic dauntlessly and face conclusions however subversive of ordinary ideas of reality and value. But, for those few who have the heart for it, Advaita monism is not without recompense and is not even without emotional satisfaction. As James puts it: "An *Absolute One, and I that One,*—surely we have here a religion which, emotionally considered, has a high pragmatic value: it imparts a perfect sumptusosity of security".[58] "We all have some ear for this monistic music: it elevates and reassures."[59] Reagarding śaṅkara, the greatest advocate of this philosophy, we may conclude with the words of Radhakrishnan: "Supreme as a philosopher and a dialectician, great as a man of calm judgment and wide toleration, śaṅkara taught us to love truth, respect reason and realise the purpose of life. Twelve centuries have passed, and yet his influence is visible... Even those who do not agree with his general attitude to life will not be reluctant to allow him a place among the immortals".[60]

REFERENCES

1. *Vide Chāndogya,* Chaps. 6 and 7.

2. *Vide* śaṅkara's Introduction to *Kaṭha, Taittirīya, Bṛhdāraṇyaba.*

3. The verb 'upaniṣad' ('go near') is repeatedly used in the Upaniṣads to describe the pupil's approaching the teacher for instruction.

4. *Vide Taittirīya,* I.11.

5. *Vide* Dasgupta, *History of Indian Philosophy,* p. 28, for a list of 112 Upaniṣads.

6. *Rg-veda,10.90 (Peterson's trans.).*

7. Sa bhūmim viśva to vṛtvā atyatiṭṣṭhad daśāṅgulam, pādo'sya viśvā bhūtāni, tripādasya amṛtaṁ divi" *Ibid.*

8. *Ṛg-veda* 10.129 Max Müller's trans.).

9. The texts translated here are respecitvely: 'Om ātmā vā idam eka eva agre āsīt.' 'Atmā eva idam agre āsīt.' 'atma eva idam sarvam.' 'Ātmani khalu are drste śrute mate vijñāte idaṁ sarvaṁ viditam,' 'Sad eva saumya idam agre āsīt, ekam eva aditiyam,' 'Sarvaṁ khalu idam brahma' (*Chānd.).* Brahma eva idam viśvam' (*Muṇḍ).* 'Ayam ātma brahma' 'aham brahma asmi.'

10. *Muṇḍaka,* 1.2.7

11. *Bṛhadāraṇyaka,* 4, 3. 32.

12. *Ibid.*, 4, 5, 6.

13. *Tait.*, 2.7.

14. *Kaṭha,* 2. 6.14.

15. *Kaṭha,* 2.4.11; *Brhad.*, 4.419..

16. *Ibid.*,

17. *Chānd., 6. 1.*

18. Kena, 1. 3-4.

19. *vide* Sec. 2, Chap. II of the *Brahma-sūtra,* and the *Bhāṣya* of śaṅkara and Rāmānuja thereon.

20. for this four classification of non-Vedic deistic schools Rāmānuja's *Bhāṣya* on 2.2.35, which quotes *śaivāgama.*

21. *Sret.*, 4.5 (ajām ekām lohita-śutra-kṛṣṇām, etc.) and 4.10 (māyām tu prakṛtim vidyāt, māyinam tu Meheśvaram; tasya avayavabhūtaistu vyaptam sarvam idam jagat). Also *vide Brahma-sut* 1.4.8 and Rāmānuja's *Bhāṣya* thereon.

22. *Vide Śrībhāṣya, Vedāntasāra and Vedāntadipa* on 1.4.8.10, 1.1.1 and 2.1.15 (note that the gunas are conceived here, after the Gītā as qualities, and as *produced* by Prakṛti, not as the essence thereof.)

23. *Śrībhāṣya,* 1.1.1.

24. *Vide* J.E. Boodin's paper on 'Functional realism,' *The Philosophical Review,* March, 1934.

23. Rg., 6.47.18.

25. Indro māyābhiḥ puru-rūpa iyate' *Vide Bṛhad.*, 2.5.19 and śaṅkara thereon.

27. Māyām tu prakṛtim vidyāt māyinam tu Mahesvaram.' *Vide Svet.*, 4.10. and śaṅkara thereon.

28. Rāmānuja himself tries, of course, to avoid this deduction partly by saying that the essence (svarūpa) of God does not change. How far this is consistent we shall consider hereafter.

29. *Vide*

29. *Vide* śaṅkara on *Brahma-sūt*, 1.4.4 and on *śvetāśvatara*, 4.5 and 4.11

30. *Brahma-sūt.*, 2.1.26-28.

31. *Vide śrībhāṣya* on 2.1. 26-28 and 1.1.3.

32. *Vide śaṅkara on Brahma-sut*, 2.1.27.

33. *Vide Brahma-sūt.*, 2.2.28.

34. *Vide Bhāṣya on Brahma-sūt.*, 2.1.16 "Yathā kāranam Brahma triṣu kāleṣu sattvam na vyabhicarati, tethā kāryam api jagat triṣu kāleṣu sattvam na vyabhica rati,".

35. Lotze, *Outlines of a Philosophy of Religion*, pp. 8-10.

36. *Creatire Evolution*, p. 251, Eng. Tr. by a. Mitchell.

37. *Vide śrībhāṣya*, 1.1.1., 1.1.2, 2.1.15.

38. *Vide śrībhāṣya*, 2.1.14.

39. *Ibid.*,

40. *Vide* Ward, *Realm of Ends*, p. 234.

41. *Tait*, 2.1.

42. *Vide* śaṅkara's com. on Tait., 2.1.

43. *Vide Kena*, 1.5.

44. *vide śrībhāṣya*, 1.1.1

45. *Ibid.*, vyapi, ati-sukṣmatayā sarvāceta nantah-praveśana-sva bhavah"

46. "Svarupena eva ahamarthaḥ atma;" "muktau api ahamarthal prakasate," *Ibid.*,

47. śarīragocarā ca ahambudhir avidyāiva"; "anĀtmani deht ahambhāva-karaṅa-hetutvena ahankāraḥ," *Ibid.*,

48. Ato..dhyānopāsanādi-śabda-vācyam jnapam"; "vedanam upasanam syāt"; "upāsana-paryāyatvat bhakti-śabdasya," *Ibid.*,

49. Jñāaikākārataya Brahma-prakāratā ucyate," *śrībhāṣya*, p. 71 (R.v. & Co. end.)

50. For a critical discussion of the Advaita theory of knowledge, *vide* D.M. Datta, *The Six Ways of Knowing.*

51. *Vide* śaṅkara's Bhāṣya on Sūtra I.1.1.

52. *Vide* śaṅkara's *Bhāṣya on sut.* I.1.4; "siddham jīvato'pi vidnṣaḥ asarīrtvam."

53. *Vide* śaṅkara's *Bhāṣya on the Bhagavadgītā*, 4.14, 3.20-26 and *passim.*

54. *vide* his *Practical Vedānta.*

55. *Vide his Gītārahsya* (a Marathi treatise on the Gītā) on the above verses and Introduction sec. 12.

56. For a fuller discussion, *vide* Radhakrishan, *Ind. Phil.*, vol II. pp. 612-34, and speeches of vivekānanda quoted by James in *Pragmatism*, pp. 152 f.

57. *Vide* James, *Pragmatism*, p. 151.

58. *Loc. cit.*, p. 153.

59. *Ibid.*, p. 154.

60. *Ind. Phil.*, vol. II, p. 658.

CHAPTER XII

PŪRVA-MĪMĀṀSĀ

The distinguishing feature of this system, as compared with the others so far considered, is its adherence to the Veda as in itself an infallible authority. We have seen systems like Jainism refusing altogether to recognize its authority and others like the Nyāya attempting to subordinate it to some other. The Mīmāṁsā differs from them all in that it places the Veda or śruti on a footing peculiarly its own. As to the exact place it assigns to reason, we have to refer the reader to what was stated in an earlier chapter. It will suffice now to observe that though thus authoritative in its own right, revealed truth comes to us through the medium of words whose interpretation is by no means easy. Hence the need for Mīmāṁsā or the investigation of the principles according to which the texts enshrining that truth are to be interpreted.[1] It is only when thus assisted by reason that the Veda will disclose its true import. The primary aim of the Mīmāṁsā as a branch of learning may, therefore, be described as getting back from the expression to the idea behind it, the solving of the important problem of the relation of speech and thought Since the view taken of language here is that it is independent of the individual using it,[2] the system involves a great deal of discussion relating to social or folk psychology. This psychological inquiry contains much that is valuable for the modern science of Semantics or the branch of knowledge dealing with meaning in relation to linguistic forms. The Mīmāṁsā in this respect serves as a necessary complement to Vyākaraṇa or Grammar, whose treatment of words is mainly formal. The indirect advantage thus resulting to psychology and philology, forms one of the most important features of the study of Mīmāṁsā. The laws of interpretation formulated by Jaimini and his successors are quite general, and they are applicable as much to works outside the Veda as to that ancient text. They have, in fact, become widely current and are utilized for arriving at a right interpretation of all old texts, particularly legal treatises (dharma-śāstra).

Speaking generally, we may say that the Mīmāṁsā attaches greater importance to the Brāhmaṇas than to the Mantras, which means that it looks upon the Veda as essentially a book of ritual. It not only subordinates the earlier Mantras, but also the later Upaniṣads. Its designation as Pūrva-Mīmāṁsā has reference to this latter phase, viz. its being concerned with the teaching of those portions of the Veda that come before the Upaniṣads, the darśana dealing with the latter being termed Uttara-Mīmāṁsā. The sacrificial inquiry which forms the main subject-matter of the Mīmāṁsā is, no doubt, very old. It is the chief purpose of the Srouta-sūtras and is found even in the Brāhmaṇas. Doubts and discussions regarding ritual are but natural, especially when once the stage of its inception is passed. The Mīmīmsā only extends the scope of the inquiry and makes it more systematic. We must not understand from this that it deals with sacrifices precisely as taught in the Brāhmaṇas. Separated as it must have been in its origin from the Brāhmaṇas by several generations, the Mīmāṁsā marks both growth and decay in its conception of ritual. It does, a matter of fact, reinterpret and in reinterpretng considerably modify the old system of rites. The doctrine as known to us also exhibits a far more important change, viz. the subordination of the idea of sacrifice itself to that of the attainment of mokṣa. The aim of life as originally conceived was, to state it in general terms, the attainment of heaven (svarga). The replacement of this aim by the ideal of mokṣa points to a radical transformation of the doctrine. By it, the Mīmāṁsā ceases to be a mere commentary on Vedic ritual and becomes a darsana. It is therefore in its present form vastly different from what its other name, Karma-mīmāmā, may suggest. The emphasis that it lays on the performance of rites, so far that emphasis is still has now in effect become quite secondary. This important change should have been brought about by a desire on the part of the later exponents of the Mīmāṁsā to bring it into line with the other systems of thought and not allow it to remain a mere liturgical discussion blaring upon rites which probably had by that time become more or less defunct The change has not taken place in the Kalpa sūtras if we leave out the few references to self realization (ātma-lābha) in them[1]; but it is clearly seen in Upavarṣa and Sabarasvāmin, early commentators on the *Sūtra* of Jaimini, and is very common in their successors The darsana aspect of it is, therefore, comparatively late The speculative spirit underlying it is not new to the Veda as a whole for it is found in the Upaniṣads and in the allegorical interpretations of rites sometimes given in the Brāhmaṇas themselves But the special type of philosophic theory which it now represents follows quite other lines It is not derived from the philosophy of the Mantras, neither does it continue Upaniṣadic speculation It is traceable to sources other than the Veda and is therefore neither a religion of nature nor a philosophy of the Absolute Some of its minor tenets may be allied to what is found in the philosophic prisons of the Veda but strange as it may seem, the larger part of them and the more important among them have as we shall see been borrowed from the Nyāya-Vaiśeṣika. The spirit of the Brāhmaṇas was to supersede the simple nature-worship of the Maṅtras the spirit of the fully developed Mīmāṁsā is to supersede ritualism as taught in the Brāhmaṇas and later systematized in the Srouta Sūtras But the supersession in neither stage is complete, so that the Mīmāṁsā as now known is an admixture of the rational and the dogmatic, the natural and the supernatural and the orthodox and the heterodox It is with the darsana aspect of the system that we shall deal here and not with its ritualistic theories or its exegetical principles.

The main source of authority in regard to this system is Jaimini is *Mīmāṁsā sūtra* Its date, as in the case of the other philosophical sūtras is quite indefinite, but it is commonly beloved now to have been the earliest of them all and assigned to about 200 AD. The system of thought itself, however, is much older, references to it being found in such early works as the Dharma-sūtras[3] and possibly also in the *Mahābhāṣya* of Patañjali (150 B.C.).[4] The sūtras are considerable over 2,500 in number and are divided into twelve chapters with sixty sub-sections in all There are nearly a thousand topics discussed so that the work is by far the biggest of the philosophical sūtras Like the others of its class the work when read by itself is for the most part unintelligible, and the aid of a commentary which preserves the traditional interpretation is indispensable for understanding it Such an idea we have in the bhāṣya of Sabarasvāmin, who wrote it probably about 400 A.D. Tradition fondly associates Sahara with King Vikramāditya, who is supposed to have lived in the first century B.C., but there seems to be no truth in it There was at least one earlier commentary on the work by Upavarṣa (A.D. 350), but nothing of it is known to us, except a possible extract from it in Sabara's bhāṣya 3 The bhāṣya has been explained in two ways by Prabhākara (A.D. 650) and Kumārila Bhaṭṭa (A .D. 700), who differ from each other in certain essential respects Prabhākara's 'great commentary' known as the *Brhatī* is yet in manuscript, except for a small fragment which has been published, and the same is the case with the *Rju-vimala,* commentary upon it by Salikanatha, believed to have been a pupil of Prabhākara The views of the school have therefore to be gathered from the *Prakarana-pancika* of the latter, which also has unfortunately not been recovered completely Bhavanatha was another influential writer of the school with his yet unpublished *Naya-viveka* As regards the second school, which for a long time has practically superseded the first, we have adequate material for reference. Kumārila s own huge and important work is fully printed and consists of a general or philosophical part called the *Sloka-vartika* and two others—*Tantra-vartika* and *Tup-tika* The first of these has been commented upon in a most lucid manner by Parthasarathi Misra in his Nyāya-*ratankara* Mandana Misra, probably a pupil of Kumārila, was a famous thinker who has to his credit many works on the Mimamsa like the *Vidhi-viveka* and the *Bhāvanā-viveka.* Several other works of this school are also known, amongst which we may note Parthasarathi's *Sāstra dipikā,* Mādhava's *Nyāya-mala-vistara* (A.D. 1350) and Khaṇḍadeva's *Bhāṭṭa-dīpikā* (A.D 1650). These follow in their explanation the order of the sūtras of Jaimini. Several independent treatises also are known which serve as useful manuals on the ritualistic or the interpretative side of the system. Such is the *Mimamsa-nyāya-prakāsā* of Āpadeva (A.D 1650) and a digest—or, according to some, the chief basis[5] of it—by Laugāksi Bhāskara, the *Artha-saṁgraha.* Another work which deals with the philosophic teaching of the school of Rumania or the Bhāṭṭa school, as it is termed, is the *Māna-meyodaya*. It has come to light only latterly and is the composition of two writers who lived about the sixteenth century A.D. Our treatment of the system will be general; but wherever there are important divergences between the two schools from the philosophical view-point, we shall notice them. The chronological relation of these schools is yet a matter of dispute; but, speaking on the whole, the Prābhākara school seems to be the older and to preserve better the distinctive lineaments of the original Mimamsa or at least to be nearer in spirit to it than the other.[6]

I

The conception of ātman is somewhat different in the two schools, but both agree regarding its plurality. To consider first the school of Kumārila: The view is very much like the Nyāva-Vaiśeṣika one and ātman is conceived as both an agent (kartā) and an enjoyer (bhoktā). But while the Nyāya-Vaiśeṣika admits no action in the self—neither change of place (spanda), nor change of form (par-mama)—here thought the former is denied, the latter is admitted.[7] That is the system recognizes the possibility of modal change in the self. Though undergoing modifications it is regarded as eternal, for Kumārila rejects the view that even internal change militates against permanence. Experience acquaints us daily with many things that change almost constantly, but yet maintain their identity. Jñāna or knowledge is a mode of the self. It is described as an act (kriyā) or process (vyāpāra)8 and is naturally spoken of as supersensible, since it is found in so ethereal a 'substance' as the self. Till change or disturbance which takes place in the ātman brings about a certain relation with the object know.- The self, being by hypothesis omnipresent, is necessarily in relation with all existent objects; but that relation is not the same as the one we are now considering. If it were, Jñāna would arise in respect of all objects as long as they existed. The relation resulting from Jñāna is unique and is described as 'comprehension' (vyāptr-vyāpyatva). The act or process of Jñāna is viewed as transitive so that its result (phala) has to be sought in something other than where it manifests itself. The act of cooking, for example, is seen in the agent, but its result—'softness' (vikleda)—is found in the material cooked, viz. the rice-grain. The former is the subject; and the latter, the object. When Jñāna arises in the self relating it to an object, the latter is affected in a particular way so that experience is not wholly a subjective modification, but has also an objective modification corresponding to it. The object becomes 'illumined' (prakāsa-visiṣta) thereby; and its being thus illumined or made known (prākaṭya or jñātatā) serves as the means for our concluding that Jñāna must have arisen in the self previously. The arising of Jñāna is thus only to be inferred. While it can reveal other objects, it has no power to manifest itself. Though knowable, Jñāna is conceived here as known indirectly through inference and not directly through introspection as in the Isyaya-Vaiśeṣika (p. 251). The new feature of being illumined which characterizes the object, as a consequence of Jñāna arising in respect of it, may mean that it is known mediately or immediately. According to this double nature of the result, Jñāna is either mediate (paroksa) or immediate (pratyakṣa).

The proximate cause of perception which leads to direct knowledge (visadāvabhāsa) is the contact of the senses with their respective objects. The knowledge that we so get is in the first instance quite vague and indefinite and is named ālocana as in the Sāṅkhya-Yoga (p. 285). It gains clarity and definiteness only afterwards. The earlier stage in this process is described as 'indeterminate' (nirvikalpaka); and the later, 'determinate' (śavikalpaka)[9]. The conception of the two stages here is therefore different from that in the Nyāva-Vaiśeṣika. Another important divergence from the Nyāva-Vaiśeṣika is that the nirvikalpaka here is not merely theoretical supposition which, beyond explaining the savikalpaka, serves no practical purpose (p. 251). It is quite useful and the Mimāmsaka admits that activity may be, and Actually is based upon it. Children and animals whose mental growth is incomplete or imperfect act only under the promptings, of this primitive stage of perception and even elderly people do the same when in a flurry[10] That is, the nirvikalpaka is not here a mere hypothesis formulated to account for some known phase of experience, but is a part of normal experience itself. Like the Nyāya-Vaiśeṣika, the Mimamsa also recognizes manas as a sense (indriya) in addition to the five admitted by all and its co-operation is laid down as indispensable for all Jñāna. Regarding the structural character of the senses also, there is a general agreement—the first four senses of sight, flavour, odour and touch being taken as derived from the elements whose distinctive qualities are their respective objects. In the case of the manas, the view is that it may or may not be derived from the elements (bhūtas). As regards the remaining sense, viz that of sound, the school, relying on the Vedic statement that 'the organ of hearing proceeds from dik,[11] makes it "delimited space" (dik)[12] and does not connect it with ākāśa. The senses including the manas, with or without contact with objects according as the knowledge is immediate or mediate, furnish the external conditions which induce change in the self constituting knowledge; and it is the dissociation once for all from them in mokṣa that will set the self free as in the Nyāya-Vaiśeṣika.

So far we have taken into consideration the waking state. More or less the same description applies to dream also; only the co-operation of the five external organs of sense is there withdrawn. In regard to sleep (suṣupti), Kumārila holds a somewhat peculiar view. He admits of course that the self endures in it as other Indian thinkers generally do; but in consonance with his view of knowledge, he regards the self as characterized then by the potency to know (Jñāna-śakti). In this, he differs from the Nyāya--Vaiśeṣika, which denies Jñāna in every form to the self in sleep. He also dissents from the Upaniṣads because he recognizes no happiness then. The !ater reminiscence of happiness to which the Vedantin pointedly draws our attention (p. 72), Kumārila explains negatively—as due to the absence at the time of all consciousness of pain. If the self were really in the enjoyment of the highest bliss then, it would be impossible, he says, to explain the feeling of regret which a person feels; afterwards if he comes to know that by going to sleep he has missed some common pleasure.[13]

There is one other point to which we must allude before we leave this part of the subject and it is the way in which, according to Kumārila, we become aware of our own self. It is known directly through the aham̐-pratyaya or the 'notion' as we may render it.[14] This forms an important point in the teaching and requires explanation. Kumārila understands 'self-consciousness' literally and holds that the self can at once be both subject and object—the knower as well as the known (jada-bodhātmaka) and adduces as evidence therefor the common saying: 'I know myself.'[15] a Ascribing such an apparently contradictory character to the self is quite in harmony with the ruling principle of his thought, which, as we shall see, is that the nature of things cannot be rigidly determined as such and such (bhed-bheda-vāda).[16] In a sample of knowledge like 'I know the jar 'there are two elements—one comprehending the self (aham̐-vṛtti) and the other comprehending the object in question (e.g. ghata-vṛtti). That is, self-awareness is constant and accompanies all states of consciousness, being absent only in deep sleep where no object is known. When we say that the self is thus known in all experience, we must not take it to mean that it is known as the subject in the act of knowing. The fact of knowing is itself not known at the time and has, as already pointed out, to be inferred later. We cannot, therefore, know the self then as characterized by or as own such knowledge, which is what is meant by the term 'subject.' But yet the self cannot be unknown, for that would go against the felt personal identity in all one's experience. It is therefore explained as being known then as the object of the 'I-notion.' If we take tins along with the view that the self to be known at all must at the time become aware of some object or other, we see that self-consciousness, according to Kumārila, implies not only an internal difference—a self which is opposed to itself as its object, but also an external difference—a self which is distinguished from the not-self.

Prabhākara dısagrees with Kumrila in two important respects in his view of the self, and in both the sides with the Nyāya-Vaiśeṣika[17]. Not believing in parināma, he does not admit that the self suffers change. Again he objects to the description of the self as 'knowable,' and avers that agent and object can never be the same in any act. It is only objects that are knowable. The self, on the other hand, is a subject and is revealed as such in all jāna. If it were not so revealed simultaneously with the object, one's jānana would be indistinguishable from another's from this, it .should not be thought that the ātman is self-luminous. It is wholly non-sentient (jaṇa), and therefore requires for its revelation the presence of some knowledge to which the character of self--luminousness is assigned.[18] Though thus dependent upon and aid the self, to be realized, does not require a separate mental act, it being manifest equally whenever any object is known. The word which the Prābhākara's use for knowledge or experience is samvit which, being self-luminous (sva-prakāṣa), needs nothing else to make it manifest. Though ultimate in this sense, it is not eternal. It appears and disappears; and, as it does so, reveals both the object and the self simultaneously with itself. This triple revelation is what is described as tripuṭī-jñāna. So far as other psychological details are concerned, it will suffice to remark that there is a still closer approximation here to the Nyāya-Vaiśeṣika than in the previous school.

II

The main object of the Mīmāmsaka is to establish the authority of the Veda; but he does not like to do so solely on dogmatic considerations and therefore tries to seek rational grounds for it. He contends that his system does not consist merely in delivering settled judgments (upadesa-sāstra), but is a reasoned inquiry (parīkṣā-sāstra).[19] The very classification by him of revelation along with perception and inference under pramāṇa shows it. The testimony of the Veda is but a particular means of knowing the truth; and whatever value there is in it, the Mīmāmsaka holds, is due to its being a pramāṇa like perception or inference. It is thus that he enters the arena of logic; and, though he may not be a rationalist in the full sense of the term, he cannot at the same time be described as a mere dogmatizer.

The system starts by postulating what is called the svatah-pramāṇya or the self-validity of knowledge (p. 260) both in respect of its origin (utpattau) and assertainment (jnaptau).[20] If *a, be,* ...and *c* (say) account for the genesis of knowledge, those causes themselves explain its validity also. Similarly the validity of knowledge is known when the knowledge itself is known; and no additional means are required therefor. All knowledge is presumably valid and an explanation is called for only where any particular knowledge fails to be so. We proceed to act always on the supposition that the knowledge we get is true; but if any part of it is discovered to be not so, we seek for the cause of its invalidity in extraneous circumstances that must have interfered with the free functioning of this means. The cause of invalidity is some defect in the means or source of knowledge (karaṇa-doṣa). Thus a person may think that he sees a particular thing, silver, while it is only shell because his eyesight is defective. This is how wrong knowledge arises. It is found out by its incompatibility with subsequent experience (bādhaka-pratyaya). When the person, who fancies that he sees a serpent, at a distance, approaches it and discovers it to be a rope, he concludes that his previous knowledge was erroneous. While thus the Mīmāṁsā agrees with the Nyāya-Vaiśeṣika in its view of the invalidity of knowledge (aprāmāṇya), it disagrees with it in respect of the view it takes of its validity (prāmānya). The chief reason for the disagreement is the disaccord between the nature of truth as defined in the Nyāya-Vaiśeṣika and the manner in which it proposes to verify it. Truth is stated to be correspondence with reality, but the test does not, indeed cannot, ascertain that correspondence. So the doctrine proposes an indirect test—fruitful activity (samvādi-pravṛtti). What serves as the test is thus really another experience—that of thirst being quenched, to cite the example already given. Now this second experience cannot validate the first without itself being similarly validated; and netting about verifying it would only mean going on *ad infinitum*. Even supposing that this second experience needs no verification, it cannot vouch for the presence of a corresponding reality outside knowledge. A person may dream of water and also of quenching his thirst by drinking it. There is fruitful activity here, but no objective counterpart. What the test actually finds out is only whether two experiences cohere, and to accept such a test as adequate is virtually to give up the realistic position because the supposed correspondence with reality is left wholly unverified. Thus we see that though the Nyāya-Vaiśeṣika starts as realism, it fails to maintain its position in the solution of what is one of the crucial problems of philosophy—that of truth and error. The fact is that a realistic doctrine cannot adhere to the view that validity is determined *ab extra* (parataḥ-prāmānya). That is why the Mīmāṁsā, which likewise upholds realism, advocates the opposite view of svatah-pramāṇya and, by presuming all knowledge to be valid, normally dispenses with the need for testing it.

We may now point out the bearing of such a view of prāmāna upon the authority of the Veda which is of paramount importance to the Mīmāmsaka. Neither the circumstance that renders knowledge invalid nor that which leads to its discovery exists in the case of the Veda. There can be no flaw at the source (karaṇa-doṣa); for the source in the case of verbal testimony is the speaker or writer, the Veda, according to the Mīmāmsaka, is self-existent and has had no author at all (apauruseya). Nor is there the possibility of its coming into conflict with perceptual or other form of common experience, for what it teaches refers, by hypothesis, only to matters beyond this life and is therefore empirically unverifiable (p. 180). We may think that though not contradicting common experience, the Veda may be discrepant with itself by teaching one thing here and another there. But no such discrepancy will be found, it is maintained, if we properly understand the Veda. It is in determining what a proper understanding of it is that the rules of interpretation, to which we referred above, are laid down. This view, which is peculiar to the Mīmāṁsā, requires further elucidation.

The Veda here stands for a form of uttered words and it is in this sense that the Mīmāmsaka holds it to be self-existent. He bases his view mainly upon the following considerations:

(1) The relation between a word and its meaning is natural and therefore necessary and eternal. We ought not to think that things were there already before they were named. The word and the thing it names go together and it is impossible to think of either as having had a beginning in time.[21] But we must carefully note what in this view is meant by the terms 'word' and 'thing.' In order to know the character of the former, it is necessary to distinguish first between varṇa and dhvani. A varṇa is an articulate sound. It is conceived as integral (niravayava) and omnipresent (sarva-gata) and therefore also eternal (nitya). That a varṇa can be uttered several times or in several ways does not mean that there are many particular cases of it with a universal running through them. What thus diversify it are its accidental features, and, however much they may change, a varṇa remains the same. One of the important arguments adduced in support of its permanence is the ready recognition we have when the same varṇa is uttered more than once, which implies that all those utterances refer but to an identical thing. We say for example that the a sound is uttered ten times and not that ten sounds are uttered. If they did not refer to the same the recognition would have to be explained—without adequate reason for doing so—as an illusion, no identity being possible between the fleeting utterances themselves. The latter, viz. dhvani, is viewed as the means of manifesting the vama which has all along been there; and it may be compared to the written symbol, the chief difference being that, when there are several varṇas, we have a temporal series of utterances in the one case, but a spatial series of written signs in the other. The variety of ways in which a varṇa may be uttered, as *e.g.* with different stresses, is explained as due to differences in this means of utterance. The nature of dhvani is explained in alternative ways, but we need not enter here into a discussion of such details. It is enough for our purpose to regard it as 'tone' which, as the means of revealing varṇas, must be different from them. It is also transient and limited to the place where it is heard. A word' (sabda) is two or more of these varṇas, and is regarded as merely an aggregate (sam udāya) and not' as a whole (avayavin) distinguishable from each of its constituent parts and from all of them. But yet the necessity is recognized in the case of every word for the varṇas in it occurring in a specific order: for otherwise words like dīna ('pitiful') and nadi ('river'), which consist of the same varṇas but placed in

a different order, would not differ in their connotation. and not to the varṇas themselves which are, by hypothesis. present everywhere and at all times. Their gradual or progressive utterance does not interfere with the unity of the word as the perceptual process, for instance, which also is gradual, does not affect the unity of an object like a tree when it is seen. As regards the 'things' signified by words, we are not to understand the particular facts of experience which come into being and disappear, but the corresponding universals which are eternal and of which the passing individuals are nothing more than signs. That is, the significance of the word is general[22] though, when associated with other words to form a sentence, it may come to denote a particular word and the meaning being both eternal, the relation between them also is necessarily so. It does not -follow from this that the Mīmāmsakā rejects the conventional clement in language. He only assigns a subordinate place (sahakari) to it though a necessary one, the purpose it serves being illustrated by that of light in seeing.[23] If the conventional element were not admitted, tuition or instruction regarding the meanings of words by one who is already familiar with them, which is known to be necessary for learning a language, would become superfluous. The problem discussed here is a philological one and the solution reached is that language is not a creation of the human or even of the divine mind—the former being the view held in modem and the latter, in ancient Nyays[24]—but a natural phenomenon.[25] In holding such a view, the Mīmāṁsā resembles the older school of modem philolologists, which maintained that philology was a natural science.

(2) The permanence of the relation between a word and its meaning, even though it be granted, does not establish the eternity of the Veda. It merely serves as a negative aid to it by precluding the conclusion which one may draw at once that whatever is verbal in form must necessarily have had an origin in time. The Veda consists of words, and so far it is like any other literary work. If the permanence of the word and meaning constituted the criterion of eternity, all literary works, in fact all uttered statements, would alike be eternal. If the Veda alone is so and not other works also; it should be traced to some unique feature it possesses; and such a feature, it is said, is the *particular order* (ānupūrvī) in which the several words occur in it. When the Mīmāmsaka states that the Veda is eternal, is this permanence of the text that he means. He views the Veda as produced by no author—human or divine; and he maintains that it has been preserved intact during a beginningless period by being handed down from teacher to pupil with scrupulous care. This belief is based on the circumstance that tradition, though going back to a far-distant antiquity, has throughout been silent in regard to the authorship of the Veda, while in the case of even very ancient works—like those of Buddha or the Mahābhārata—mention is made

of some author or the other. While the order of the words in those works was determined by their authors, it is self-determined in the Veda. This argument again, granting that tradition is really silent on the authorship of the Veda, is negative and can lead to nothing that is decisive.

Thus the Mīmāmsakā doctrine of the fixity of the Vedic text rests upon a certain view of language it takes and upon the supposed absence of all references in long-standing tradition to its having been composed by one or more authors. In neither case, it is clear, is the premise adequate to support the important conclusion that is drawn from it. The belief in its present form is therefore nothing more than a dogma. This 'idolatry of scripture' appears comparatively late and seems to have been arrived at by extending to the form of the Veda what was once taken to hold good of its content. The truth concealed under this purely scholastic view, therefore, is that the Veda embodies eternal verities. In the case of smṛtis, as distinguished from the śruti it is even now held that this content constitutes the truth revealed, though an attempt is made, under the influence of views similar to the one we are now considering, to trace it (p. 91) eventually to some śruti which is no longer extant. In this connection it is instructive to cite the opinion of the grammarian Patañjali of the second century B.C., that while the sense of the Veda is eternal the order of the words in it is not so. 'Is it not said that the Vedas were not composed—but are eternal Quite so; but it is their sense that is so, not the order of the syllables in them.[26]

Coming now to the Mīmāmsakā theory of knowledge, we have to note that it is realistic, both according to Kumārila and Prabhākara; and there is no knowledge which does not point to a corresponding object outside it.[27] But all knowledge is here presumed to be true, according to the theory of self-validity and verification becomes necessary only when any doubt is cast upon its validity[28]. The one kind of knowledge that does not come under this description is memory. According to the Bhāṭṭas, recollection is not valid for novelty is a necessary condition of validity.Truth should not only be not contradicted by subsequent knowledge (abādhita); it should also point to something not hitherto known (anadhi-gata). Prabhākara does not accept this condition, for all experience (anubhuti)—whether the object be already known or not—is valid for him. Even the so-called error, as we shall immediately see, satisfies this requirement. But he also differentiates recollection from anubhuti, for it is not experience in the primary sense of the term, being dependent upon a former one (sapeksa)[29].If all experience by its very nature is valid, it may be asked how error arises at all. Kumārila and Prabhākara differ considerably in their answers to this question and their explanations are known respectively as viparita-khyati and akhyati. It would be better to begin with a description of the latter and then contrast the former with it.

1. The term Akhyāti, which is literally equivalent to 'no knowledge,' is applied to Prabhākara's theory to indicate that error, according to it, is not a unit of knowledge, but a composite of two jñānas[30]. When shell is mistaken for silver and we say to ourselves, 'This is silver,' the 'this' is actually perceived as also certain features of the shell which it possesses in common with silver. The knowledge of those features revives in our mind the impression of a former experience and we recollect silver. The so-called error here really consists of these two jñānas—perception immediately followed by memory. Of these the first is true so far as it goes, though it may not go sufficiently far. Its object 'this' is not subiated afterwards since, even when the error is discovered, we feel '*This* is shell' The same, no doubt, cannot be said of the second jñāna because its object, silver is not found in the given context. But in this it only exhibits its normal character; for it is memory—although we are at the time lose sight of that fact (smṛti-pramosa)[31]—and does not as such signify that the object is present then. That is, the former knowledge claims to be valid and the claim is justified; the latter does not put forward any such claim at all. Indeed, Prabhākara does not admit that knowledge can ever play false to its logical nature; and there is consequently no error, according to him, in the common acceptance of the term. In what passes for error, we overlook the fact that there are two jñānas[32] and, as a natural consequence, we also fail to notice the separateness of their respective objects. This failure to know, however, cannot by itself account for the 'error'; because, if it did, errors would occur in dreamless sleepy[33] which also is characterized by absence of knowledge. The negative factor of failure is therefore viewed as operating in giving rise to error with a positive one to which we have already referred, viz. the perception of the 'this' as characterized by the features that are common to shell and silver. We may therefore describe what is commonly supposed to be error as partial or incomplete knowledge; only in so doing we must be careful to remember that there is no single unit of knowledge to which that term is applicable. To take another instance: A white crystal placed by the side of a red flower may be wrongly regarded as a red crystal. There also we have two jñānas, viz. the perception of the crystal minus its true colour and the sensation of the redness alone of the flower. Each of these jñānas is quite valid so far as it goes; only here both the jñānas are derived through the senses. As before they convey a partial knowledge of the objects, viz. the crystal and the flower; but the basis of error here lies in the contiguity of the objects, not in their similarity as in the previous example. Further, there are two objects bodily given here instead of one and the features comprehended are what characterize them singly and not their common ones. But the distinction between the two jñānas as well as that between their objects is not as before grasped and we are therefore said to fall into error. Here also the akhyāti view lays down two conditions—one positive and the

other negative for error becoming possible at all—a partial knowledge of the things presented, and a failure to note the distinction between them[34]

(2) Viparita-khyati.[35]—maintains that knowledge always points to an object beyond itself. In shell-silver, for instance, there is something directly given, viz. the 'this'; but the silver is not so given. Yet it should not on that account be taken as ideal or non-existent, for its notion, being due to the suggestion of a former experience, goes back eventually to an objective counterpart. This view, like the previous one, splits up the object of erroneous knowledge into two parts—the 'this' (visaya) and the 'what' (parakāra)—and explains them separately. The first of them as before is not sublated when the mistake is rectified; and the explanation of the second element also is practically the same as before. Though not given here and now, the silver must have been experienced before; for otherwise it could not at all have been fancied in the shell. The difference between the two views is that while, according to akhyāti, error is due to a losing sight of the fact that the presentative and the representative factors stand apart unrelated (asamsargāgraha), here in viparita-khyāti it is ascribed to a wrong synthesis of them (samsarga-graha). In the former case error, so far as that term is applicable at all, is due to omission because it only fails to grasp some relevant part of what is given. Hence its disovery, when it takes place, does not mean the discarding of any feature previously cognized. In the latter, the error becomes one of commission, for it includes as its content more than there is warrant for in the reality that is presented. In other words, illusion is here explained as unitary knowledge instead of as two jñānas. The subject and predicate elements consequently seem related in it, while they are not so in reality. Similarly in the case of the red crystal, the two relate, viz. the crystal and the redness, are actually given; but while they are not unified in fact, they appear so in error. As a consequence the redness of the flower, instead of standing apart, shows itself in the crystal and makes it appear differently (viparita) from what it is. This view is no doubt more in accord than the previous one with experience which points to the object of illusion as a synthetic whole, but epistemologically it presents a difficulty, viz. the inclusion of an ideal element within the content of knowledge. However unconvincing the akhyāti view may be, it is true to its realistic postulate in admitting no subjective element whatsoever. Knowledge may not be adequate to the given reality, but it never goes

'This, by the way, accounts for, the name viparita-khyāti, which literally means 'appears as other.' See SV. p. 245, st. 117 and p. 312, st. 160 (corn.). The Bhatta view is commonly identified with the Nyāya-Vaiśeṣika one. There is no doubt much that is common between the two, but there are differences in matters of detail. The Bhattas do not, for example, recognize what is known as alaukika-pratyaksa which is essential to the Nyāyā-Vaiśeṣika explanation of beyond it. Here, on the other hand, it overshoots the mark[36]. That is, error is partial misrepresentation; and to admit that knowledge can misrepresent its object, even though it be only in part, is to abandon to that extent the realistic principle on which the doctrine claims itself to be based.

These views of error imply a fundamental contrast between the two schools of Mīmāṁsā in their conception of knowledge. Kumarila recognizes error as such, and it can therefore be easily distinguished from truth. According to Prabhākara, on the other hand, there being truly no error at all the distinction disappears. The distinction, however, being universally recognized must have some basis; and if Prabhākara would explain it, he cannot like Kumarila do so from the purely logical point of view, but has to seek another. The new standpoint he finds in the view he takes of knowledge—that it is essentially a means to an end and that its sole function is to guide action or subserve vyavahāra, as it is said. All knowledge, according to him, prompts activity[37] and, judged by this fresh criterion of practical utility, truth becomes quite distinguishable from error. Knowledge, no doubt, can never deceive on its logical side; but it may be such as does or does not 'work.' In the one case, we have truth; in the other, error. The latter has cognitive value as much as the former, but it lacks practical worth; and when we describe it as error, we only mean this—that it is decognitive in respect of the claim it puts forward to be serviceable.[38]Accordingly when after rectification error yields place to truth, what happens is not any modification of its logical meaning but only the abandonment of the activity that has been prompted by it.[39] In other words, the effect of the discovery of error is seen on the reactive side of consciousness—not on its receptive side. In viparitā-khyāti also its discovery arrests activity; but that is locked upon as only a further result, the immediate one being a readjustment of our cognitive attitude towards the object. Any effect this readjustment may have on our volition is only subsequent to it. Rumania's attitude towards knowledge is thus prima rily detached and scientific; that of Prabhākara, pragmatic,

The Mīmāmsakās of the Bhāṭṭa school recognize these pramānas, while those of the other accept only five of them:—

(i) *Perception* (pratyakṣa), which has already been con sidered.

(2) *Inference* (anumāna).—There is a general resemblance herewith the Nyāya-Vaiśeṣika, as, for example, in the view taken of inductive generalization (vyapti). But there are differences also. It will take us too far away from our purpose here to dwell upon them or upon the features distinguishing the views of the two Mīmāmsa schools-in their conception of this pramāna.

(3) *Verbal Testimony* (sabda)[40]—The place of this pramāna in Mīmāmsa

logic has been indicated already and it now remains to point out one or two of the more important differences between the two schools: The Prabhakaras, unlike the Bhattas, adhere to what appears to have been the earliest view of sabda as a pramāna (p. 178) and equate it with the Veda, explaining other forms of verbal testimony as mere inference (p. 257.[41] Again a verbal statement, according to Rumania, may point to an existent something (siddha) or to something that is yet to be accomplished (sadhya). For example. the sentence 'There are fruits in the next room' refers to a fact, while 'Fetch a cow' refers to a task. Though thus admitting the two-fold character of the import of propositions, he restricts it to the sadhya or what is yet to be done, when he comes to speak of the Veda.[42] Prabhakara declines to admit that verbal statements, whether Vedic or not, can ever point merely to existent things and limits their scope to the sadhya, in keeping with the pragmatic view he takes of all knowledge. All utterance should be relevant to some context in practical life and therefore point to an action as its ultimate meaning. Whatever be the difference between the two thinkers in this respect, we see that they agree in holding that action is the final import of the Veda. Assertive propositions found in it, they explain, as fully significant oni when construed with an appropriate injunction or prohibition found in the particular context. On this view depends the well-known division of the Veda broadly into two parts, viz. vidhi or 'injunction' and artha-vada or 'explanatory passage.' The latter, consisting of statements describing things as they are or were, have accordingly no independent logical status and are to be understood as complementary to what is taught in the other portion, viz. vidhi. As complements of injunctions they commend what is prescribed; as complements of prohibitions, they condemn what is forbidden.[43] The bearing of this view of scripture on Upaniṣadic statements like Tat tvam asi, which are not injunctive, is that they also are to be construed with reference to some action taught in the Veda—a point to which we shall recur when treating of the Vedānta.

(4) *Comparison* (upamāna).[44]—The Mīmamsākā like the Naiyayıka disagrees with the view that this is not an independent pramāna and can be brought wholly or partly under one or other of the other pramānas. But he conceives it altogether differently from the latter. According to the Nyāya, it may be remembered, this pramāna has for its sole object the relation between a word and its meaning learnt under certain conditions (p. 259). Here it is reciprocal similarity that is known through it. When a person who is familiar with the cow (say) casually comes across a gavaya, an animal of the same species, and notices the resemblance of the latter to the former, he discovers that the cow is also similar to the gavaya. It is this second resemblance or, to be more exact, the recollected cow characterized by it that is known through upamāna. This view, no doubt, renders the pramāna liable

to be classed under inference. But the Mīmāṁsākā defends his position by pointing out that the basis for inference, viz. a knowledge of inductive relation (vyapti) is not needed here. The relevant major premise here would signify that if one thing, say B, is similar to another, say A, that other is similar to the first. As giving expression to a general truth, it implies the simultaneous observation of both A and B. But the conditions of upamāna do not require it, as even a person who has never seen two similar things together but meets with a cow and thereafter a gavaya in the manner described above is able to arrive at the conclusion in question. A matter of metaphysical importance here is that 'similarity' (sadrsya) is conceived as dual, the similarity of A to B being distinct from that of B to A.

(5) *Presumption* (arthāpatti).—This is postulating something to account for what apparently clashes with experience and is therefore in the nature of a hypothesis. We may otherwise state it as rendering explicit what is already implicit in two truths both of which have been properly tested, but which appear mutually incompatible. Thus if we know that Devadatta is alive and do not find him in his house, we conclude that he should be somewhere else. Another example commonly given in this connection is that of a person who, though not eating by day, continues to be healthy and strong, which leads to the conclusion that he should be eating by night. That this is a valid form of discovering the unknown from the known is clear, but it may appear to be only inference. Some like the Naiyayika therefore class it under anumāna, and do not regard it as a distinct pramāna. The argument in support of the opposite view is as follows: The result here cannot be represented as reached through inference inasmuch as there is no middle term at all to serve as its means. To take the first of the above examples, 'being alive' *by itself* cannot serve that purpose, for that does not necessarily lead to the conclusion in question viz. that Devadatta is outside his house. He may then as well remain in his house as elsewhere. Nor can 'not being in his house' by itself take that place, since that reason may equally properly lead to the conclusion that Devadatta is no longer alive. So we are forced to view the middle term as formed by combining both these—'being alive' and 'not being at home.' But in this combined form it involves a reference to what is to be established through the inference viz. that Devadatta is somewhere outside his houses.[45] That is. the conclusion is already included in the middle term which is never the case in inference. We might add another reason: while in inference the ground ('the fact of smoke') is explained by the conclusion ('fire'), here the ground ('being alive and not being found in the house') explains the conclusion ('being elsewhere[46]. The truth is that arthapatti is disjunctive reasoning and is not syllogistic in the ordinary sense of the expression. If we reduce it to the syllogistic form, the major premise will be a negative universal refer-

ring to things beyond the universe of discourse; and it therefore ceases to be significant. In this connection it may be stated that, unlike the Naiyayikas, the Mīmāṁsākās of both the schools reject the negative universal as the major premise in a syllogism. They consider that it can generally be expressed in a positive form. The scope for arthapatti is just where it cannot be so expressed.

(6) *Non-apprehension* (anupalabdhi)[47] is the specific pramāna by which negation, not nothing, is known, *e.g.* the absence of a jar or of atoms somewhere. Like the Māyā (p. 237), the Bhafa school of Mīmāmsa admits negative facts (abhava); but, unlike it (p. 249), it formulates a separate pramāna for knowing them. The word anupalabdhi means the 'absence of apprehension,' *i.e.* the absence of knowledge derived through any of the five foregoing pramānās. This means that, as knowledge got through any of the pramānās points to the existence (bhava) of objects, the absence of such knowledge indicates, other conditions remaining the same, their non-existence (abhava). Only it should he remembered that the absence, to serve as the index of non-existence, must be aided by the mental presentation of the relevant object. There may be several objects not found in a particular place; but wc think of the absence of that alone among them all, which some other circumstance has made us think of. The Naiyayika divides 'negations' into two classes according as their correlate (pratiyogin) is perceivable or not. The means of knowing the former kind, he holds, is perception; that of the latter, inference. Here in the Mīmāṁsā, this sixth pramāna is postulated as the common means of knowing both varieties of negation. The knowledge of no negation, it is contended, is perceptual. For, in the first place, no sense-contact which is necessary for such knowledge is conceivable in the case of negation.[48] Secondly, there are instances where a knowledge of the negation of perceivable objects arises even when no organ of sense is functioning. Thus a person who did not think of an elephant at all in the morning on a particular day, may later come to realize, owing to some circumstance or other, that he did not see it then. The knowledge, because it refers to the past, cannot be connected with the functioning of the senses at the time of realizing the negation. Nor can it be ascribed to their functioning in the morning, since the correlate (pratiyogin), viz. the elephant, was by hypothesis not thought of then for its negation to be apprehended. Again the pramāna by which negation is known cannot be brought under inference; for, if it is, the major premise of the syllogism will be 'Wherever there is absence of knowledge of a thing, there is—other circumstances being the same—absence of the corresponding object.' This premise relates two negations and, as an inductive generalization should eventually be based upon perception, it assumes that their knowledge is perceptual which is against the present contention that it is inference. The Prabhakaras do not

admit this pramāna, for they do not recognize negation which is its sole object. They explain abhava in terms of the positive factors involved in it, as we shall see in the next section.[49]

III

The Mīmāsāka is a realist, and his realism has some features of its own. Unlike the Sautrantika and the Vaibhasika, for example, he believes in the existence of permanent dravyas which are the substrata of qualities and are not merely aggregates of fleeting sense-data. So far, the doctrine agrees with the Nyāya-Vaiśeṣika. But it differs from that doctrine also—to confine our attention first to the Bhāṭṭa school—in not admitting that a dravya can be produced anew, and recognizing the principle of change instead. Every dravya is eternal, and endures however much its forms or attributes may change. The clay that we see before us may at one time be made into a jar, at another time into a saucer; it may be brown now, and red hereafter. But in all these transformations the same material persists. The dravya endures; its modes alone appear and disappear.[50] In other words, Kumarila dismisses the notion that things are self-identical units which ever remain the same, excluding all difference.[51] This view of reality exhibits kinship with the Sāṅkhya-Yoga in general. It is parinama-vada, and the relation between the material cause and the effect is, as in the other system, one of identity in difference (bhedabheda). One important difference between the two doctrines is that here the changing dravyas are ultimately many and not only one. Another difference, by the way, is in that the Mīmāmsa extends the notion of modal transformation to the Ātman also which is absolutely static and passive according to the other doctrine. The change that characterizes the physical reality is ever in progress. It. never began and is never going to end, the Mīmamsāka recognizing no creation (srsti) or dissolution (pralaya) of the universe as a whole.[52] There was never a time,' he says, 'when the world was otherwise than now': *Na kadacit anidrsam jagat.* Individual things, no doubt, come and go; but that is accounted for by the self-evolvent character of reality. Whatever stimulus is required for such change to take place comes from the past karma of the selves that are on life's pilgrimage at the time. This means the abolition of the idea of God[53] from the system, which is indeed a strange tenet to be held by a school claiming to be orthodox *par excellence.* To characterize the whole view in one word, it is pure empiricism[54] only in one point, viz. the recognition of a supernatural sphere of being and of a revealed authority through which a knowledge of it can be attained. As regards the other sphere—that of common experience—it beats every naturalistic school of thought known to history. Intact, a standing charge against the Mīmāmsa, at least in one stage of its growth was that it was thoroughly materialistic in its outlook.[55]

The Mīmaṁsaka is also a pluralist and believes that variety is at the root of the physical universe.[56] The school of Kumarila accepts all the nine dravyas known to the Nyāya-Vaiśeṣika and its conception of them is more or less the same. It adds two more to them, viz. tamas 'darkness' and sabda or 'sound',[57] Time is perceivable[58] the view being that all perceptual experience, no matter through what sense it is acquired, includes a reference to this element. It cannot, however, be apprehended by itself, but only along with some other object. Other dravyas also are regarded as perceivable excepting only the manas which is known mediately.[59] It is curious that ....irkness should be regarded as a positive dravya in preference to the Nyāya-Vaiśeṣika view, which is also Prabhakara's[60] of equating it with the absence of light. The reason assigned, viz. that it is characterized by colour and movement which can only be found in dravyas, is too naive to appeal to anyone. Salikanatha describes it as 'crude.' The statement that it cannot be negation (abhava), since its suppose correlate (pratiyogin), 'light,' is not thought of wherever darkness is seen is equally unconvincing. Of these dravyas, the first four as well as darkness are stated to be of atomic structure and the remaining ones, including soul, are described as infinite and ultimate. By 'atom' in this system should not be understood the infinitesimal paramanu of the Vaiśeṣika. but the smallest particle which experience acquaints us with, viz. the mote in the sunbeam which corresponds to the tryanuka of the other doctrine. The Vaiśeṣika conception of atom is described as purely speculative, but it does not seem to be altogether rejected.[61] From all the atomic substances, objects of different magnitudes may, as in the Nyāya-Vaiśeṣika, be derived; only the relation between the material cause and the effect is here viewed as bhedabheda or tadatmya ('identity in difference'), instead of samavaya (p. 239), in accordance with the Bhaa belief in sat-karya-vada. These dravyas form only the support, as it were, of the universe. There are also other features of it which are divisible' into three classes—guna, karma and samanya or jati, which together with dravya form the four positive categories of Kumarila's system. But it must be remembered that they are not conceived as entirely distinct from the dravyas to which they belong. The relation between them is one of id^ntity in differenced,[62] so that the significance of 'category' here is not the same as in the Nyāya-Vaiśeṣika. Kumarila's list also includes negation (abhava), and we therefore have five categories in all.[63] The first of them has already been described and it is sufficient for our purpose to state that the notion of the others is for the most part like that in the Nyāya-Vaiśeṣika.

The Prābhakaras accept four more positive categories of which we need refer here only to one, viz. samavaya. Its recognition means the entire rejection of the relation of identity in difference (bhedabhava) admitted by the Bhāṭṭas.[64] As a consequence substance and attribute, universal and particular, material cause and effect come to be conceived as altogether distinct, and the doctrine does not subscribe to the sat-karya-vada. This signifies a vast difference between 'the two schools in their conception of reality. While siding with the Nyāya-Vaiśeṣika in this respect, the Prabhakaras differ from it in discarding abhava as an independent category, their view being that it can always be represented as a positive something. Thus the absence of a jar in a room is the mere empty room; its prior negation, the clay; and so forth.[65] Amongst the eight positive categories recognized, the dravyas are nine as in the Nyāya-Vaiśeṣika, and their conception also is generally the same.

IV

The admixture of the rational with the dogmatic which we noticed in connection with the theoretical teaching of the Mīmāmsa is equally striking on its practical side. So far as ordinary morality goes, the doctrine adopts a point of view which is severely secular and explains virtue as a conscious or semi-conscious adjustment of conduct to interest. Sahara says that charitable acts like providing water-huts (prapa), though for the benefit of others and therefore good, are not yet dharma.[66] That is, the Mīmāmsa judges conduct by a utilitarian standard; but it is not egoistic and, as is indicated by the very example given by Śabara, is based upon the realization of the social nature of man. A scheme of morality founded upon such a principle is not without parallels in the history of ethics. But what is peculiar about the Mīmāmsa is that it refuses such morality the highest place in life's ideal. As in metaphysics, here also it conceives of another sphere of activity whose significance is extra-empirical and confines the title of dharma to it alone. Common morality, according to the Munamsaka, is purely an empirical affair which none but the short-sighted fail to understand. True spirituality consists in fixing one's attention on dharma or such acts of duty as lead to success in the life beyond. It may appear that such a shifting of the attention from the present life to the coming one will throw morality into the shade and thus tend to reduce its value in the eyes of man. It does nothing of the kind. For, as conceived in the Mīmāṁsā, ceremonial life does not exclude common morality; it is, on the other hand, founded in it. 'The Vedas cleanse not the unrighteous.[67] Though not viewed as the highest, ethical purity is regarded as a pre-condition as well as a necessary accompaniment of religious or spiritual life. The few occasions on which the dictates of common morality seem to be neglected, as for example in the immolation of an animal in a rite are explained as only the exceptions that prove the rule. However unconvincing the explanation given in justification of these acts, it should be admitted that generally the Veda supports conclusions that are ethically quite unexceptionable. In the present case, for instance, it explicitly forbids injury to living beings: Na himsyat sarva bhutani.

When dharma is understood in this unique sense, it naturally requires an equally unique pramāna to make it known (p. 109). That pramāna is the Veday.[68] While the standard of judgment for common morality is human, that for dharma is superhuman. 'We should distinguish,' Kumarila says, 'between what relates to dharma and mokṣa which is known from the Veda and what relates to artha and kama which is learnt by worldly intercourse.[69] It is not merely common human experience that is of no avail in knowing dharma and adharma, but also the higher faculty of yogic perception recognized for the purpose in doctrines like the Nyāya Vaiśeṣika (p. 262). The single name of apurva[70] (literally meaning 'never before') which Prabhakara gives to dharma and adharma emphasizes their inaccessibility to the other pramānas (manantarapurva). It is conceived by him as the result of sacrificial and such other acts—not those acts themselves as in the Nyāya-Vaiśeṣika—and corresponds to the punya and papa of the other doctrine. But it abides like the latter in the self (atma-samavayi), so that apurva is a sub jective feature to be distinguished from the objective act leading to it. According to Kumarila these forms of activity are themselves dharma and adharma[71]—the former standing for permitted or obligatory deeds like a sacrifice, the latter for prohibited deeds like drinking or killing an animal: and it is to know what is prescribed or prohibited that we have to seek the aid of the Veda. That is, though there is nothing transcendental about the acts themselves described as dharma and adharma, the fact of their being the means of a supernatural good is not humanly ascertainable. It is from this standpoint that they are represented here as known through revelation and revelation alone.

The Veda reveals dharma, according to both the schools, as the subject of a mandate (vidhi or niyoga)—as something to be accomplished, in accordance with the Mīmāmsa conclusion that action is the final import of the Veda. But they differ considerably in their view of the motive for obeying that mandate. In fact, this question of the motive has split the Mīmāmsakas into several camps.[72] It is not necessary to refer to them all.[73] We shall only note the commonly recognized distinction between the two schools. According to the Bhattas, the Veda not only acquaints us with dharma and adharma, but also specifies the desirable results to be obtained by following the one and abstaining from the other, viz. the attainment of some pleasure or the avoidince of some pain. In the usual example of the jyotistoma sacrifice, it is heaven (svarga) that is held out as the end; in the case of destroying life, it is hell (naraka) against which one is warned. Thus the Bhāṭṭa school, like the Nyāya-Vaiśeṣika (p. 263), believes that pleasure and pain are the only ultimate motives. 'Not even the stupid act,' Kumārila remarks in a parallel context, 'without some good in view.[74] But we should not conclude from this that the end is included in the behest and that it commands us either to seek pleasure or to shun pain.[75] The desire for good is already there in man, and the Veda merely admits it as a psychological fact w ithout pronouncing any judgment on the value of pleasure or on the lack of it in pain. In other words, we have here what is described as psychological hedonism and not ethical hedonism. But it should be acknowledged that the injunction, in this view, utilizes subjective desire by appealing to it as the incentive to make itself operative. The Prabhakaras demur to the admission of a hedonistic aim as necessary for the Vedic imperative to operate. The Veda, they say,[76] is not so helpless as to need an extraneous, aid in enforcing its mandatory power. It neither coaxes nor threatens anyone; anri the only motive it presupposes is reverence for the mandate itself. But Vedic injunctions like 'one should sacrifice' (yajeta) do no apply to all. They are addressed only to some, and expressions like 'he that desires heaven' (svarga-kama) found in them do not point to any benefit to be derived by obeying them, as the Bhaftas assume, but only limit the sphere of its applicability by specifying the persons (niyojya) whose duty those injunctions set forth.[77] In the case of any particular injunction, only those will respond who answer to the description contained m it. What prompts them to act is this consciousness that it is their duty to do so (karyata-jñāna), and never the prospect of satisfying any desire that they may have (ista-sadhanata-jñāna).[78] The good or evil that may result therefrom is accordingly looked upon as a consequence rather than as an end directly aimed at. There is no doubt that the idea of the fruit resulting from ritualistic activity is pushed farther into the background here than in the other school; but for all practical purposes the two views are the same, because both alike admit that an end is attained—no matter what name they give it.[79] The specially important point to note here is the concern which both the schools exhibit to maintain that it is not of the essence of a command to contain either a promise or a threat and the consequent exclusion from Vedic teaching proper of the idea of recompense, which doubtless constituted originally the sole motive of sacrifices.

We have thus far considered what are termed kāmya and pratisiddha karmas or optional and forbidden deeds (p. 108), which constitute the sphere of the hypothetical imperative, and seen that there is practically no difference between the Bhattas and the Prabhakaras in their attitude towards them. There is, however, an important distinction between the two views and it comes out clearly in the case of the third variety of 'unconditional duties' (nitya-karma) like the regular offering of twilight prayers (sandhyā), which after all constitute, as we shall see, the essential part of the discipline of the Mīmāṁsā regarded as a darsana. In accordance with the hedonistic basis of conduct accepted in the Bharta school, these duties also are conceived as serving an end, viz. overcoming past sin (durita-ksaya). Further, by adherence to s them, one keeps off the sin (pratyavaya) that is sure to result from their neglect.[80] In neither case does their performance bring any positive gain, but they are not without an aim. According to the other school, such deeds have no consequence whatsoever and are to be performed for their own sake. They are not a means to an end, but are themselves the end[81] While according to the Bhattas dharma even in its form of nitya-karmas is only of instrumental value, this school pursues it as the supreme good, regarding it as definitely above artha and kama or empirical motives taken in their totality. Here we have a conception of duty for duty's sake, and that in a sense far more rigorous than in the Gītā, since even motives so pure as 'cleansing the heart' and 'subserving the purposes of God' (p. 125) are excluded and the doing of duty is placed on a basis of absolute disinterestedness. The law governing dharma here may therefore be said to correspond to the 'categorical imperative' of Kant. But what, it may be asked, is the penalty, according to the Prabhakaras, if one should disobey such mandates ? The reply to this question, we shall state in the words of the *Tantra*[82] *rahasya/one* of the few published works of the school:—

> 'The personal ending such as that of the potential mood (lin), you say, teaches apurva as a duty to be accomplished. In that case one may not set about it, although it is known as a duty, because it serves ho end.'
>
> 'Even in respect of optional deeds, which are known to have an end, one may not act. What is to be done? The function of a pramāna ceases with the mere revealing of its object.'
>
> 'Well, in the case of the optional deeds, the failure to perform them means missing their fruit and that is the penalty. What is the penalty in the case of unconditional duties?'
>
> 'The Vedic mandate will not then have been carried out.
>
> 'What of that?'
>
> 'That itself is the punishment, for obeying the Vedic mandate itself is of ultimate value (puruṣartha). It is on the analogy of these karmas that we say that carrying out the mandate is the true end even in the case of optional deeds and that the attainment of the so-called phala is incidental.'
>
> 'How can their non-accornplishmcut be itself the punishment?'
>
> 'The good, who praise those that obey the Vedic behest and blame those that do not, will answer that question. Or one's own conscience, which feels guilty of having proved faithless to it, will do so.'

The appeal here, it will be seen, is first to the judgment of the better mind of the community and then to the verdict of our own conscience.[83] But it is conscience not in the sense that it is an independent guide in discriminating right from wrong, but in the sense that it constrains us to follow dharma when it is once known. The communication of what is right or wrong is still left to an external code. The appeal in its double form, we may add, implies that man is conceived here not merely as a spiritual being himself, but also as a member of a society of spiritual beings.

In one important respect the aim of the Mīmāṁsā, it is clear, should differ from that of the other systems. It should pursue not the ideal of mokṣa but dharma, whether as a means to an end or as an end in itself. Such seems to have been its aim till a certain stage was reached m the history of the system In that early period in the growth of the Mīmāṁsā, only dharma, artha and kama (tri-varga) were accepted (p. 100) as human values and not the fourth one of mokṣa. also.[84] To speak generally, dharma is still the highest ideal in the Kalpa-sūtras; but the doctrine in its preset form has practically thrown it overboard, and replaced it by the ideal of mokṣa. The transformation means the virtual abandonment of many of the rites taught in the Veda.[85] But the changer is of a far more subversive kind in the case of the Prabhakara school than in that of Kumarila. The latter conceive of dharma as a means to an end and the introduction of the mokṣa ideal means only the substitution of one end for another. If the old aim was svarga, the attainment of some positive good, the new one is apavarga, the negative one of escape from saṁsāra. But in the case of the former, which pursued dharma as its own end, the acceptance of the new ideal means deserting its cherished principle of doing duty for its own sake, and going over completely to the side of the Bhattas; for its idea of mokṣa, to judge from Sālikanātha's description, is also the seeking of an-end, viz. escape from the trials and travails of saṁsāra.[86]

We shall now briefly touch upon the nature of this new ideal and the discipline laid down for its attainment. *Om* knowledge of the Nyāya-Vaiśeṣika conception of bondage and release will be of much use here, for the two doctrines resemble each other in this respect so very much. We may add that almost the same criticism applies to the one ideal as to the other. The self is conceived in the Mīmāmsa as eternal and omnipresent; but, as a matter of fact, it is conditioned by various adjuncts which are not at all indispensable to it. Its empirical encumbrance is three-fold[87]: To begin with, there is the physical body as limited by which alone it enjoys pain or pleasure; secondly, there are the organs of sense which are the sole means relating it to the outside world; and lastly, there is that world itself so far as it forms the object of the individual's experience. It is this connection with things other than itself that constitutes bondage, and release means separation from them once for all. The Mīmāmsaka refutes the Vedāntic view that the physical world is sublated or transcended in mokṣa. Nor does he admit that the relation between the world and the individual self is unreal as the

Sāṅkhya-Yoga does. According to him the world is real and endures in exactly the same form even when a self becomes free; and mokṣa means only the realization that the relation of the self to it though real is not necessary. Tins state is described negatively as excluding all pain and along with it all pleasure also.[88] There seem, however, to have been one or more interpreters of Kumarila who maintained that it is a state of bliss or ananda.[89] It is controverted by Parthasarathis[90] and a consideration of Kumarila's remarks[91] in that connection seems to support him. No such difference of opinion seems to have existed in the case of the other school. In this condition, all the specific characteristics of the self such as jñāna, pain and pleasure disappear. The self is not conscious then even of itself, for the manas has ceased to operate. But unlike the Nyāya-Vaiśeṣika, the Mīmāṁsā of the Bhāṭṭa school maintains that the capacity for manifesting such features persists. The only advantage gained by this deviation from the Nyāya-Vaiśeṣika is the maintenance of consistency in regard to the parinama-vada which the school advocates; for the latent capacity to know, to feel or to will which is supposed to persist in itself then is never manifested again. Distinctions like these, moreover, affect only the state attained after death. So far as mokṣa may be taken . to represent the condition of the enlightened in this life, there is entire agreement with the Nyāya-Vaiśeṣika.

As in the other doctrines, detachment from worldly concerns and faith in the teaching are needed here also as preliminary requirements. Without them, no serious effort is possible towards securing final freedom. The direct means of release is deduced from the general Indian belief which the Mīmāmsaka shares that karma is the cause of bondage. When the cause is removed, the effect must necessarily cease to be; and abstention from karma, the Mīmāmsaka thinks, should automatically result in restoring the self to its original state. The karmas to be abstained from, however, are not all but only those of the optional (kāmya) and the prohibited (pratisiddha) types. The performance of the one gives rise to some merit; that of the other, to some demerit. They are thus a means of renewing bondage and have to be eschewed by a person that is seeking freedom. The third or the nitya variety of karma, even the oeeker after mokṣa should perform; for otherwise he will be disobeying the Vedically law enjoying them.[92] That would be equivalent to indulging in prohibited deeds, the only difference being that while the first counts as a sin of omission, the second does as one of commission. It is to avoid becoming entangled again in the miseries of samsāra as a consequence of such sin, that of should carry on the nitya-karmas. Thus the course discipline laid down here is two-fold: (1) abstention from the optional and forbidden deeds, and (2) adherence to tl obligatory ones. In neither case, it should .be added, is the anything positive effected, the conception of mokṣa beil negative in the system, viz. the restoration of the self to normal condition. As regards the exact part which a knowledge of the self, according to Kumarila, plays in securii freedom, there is some doubt owing to a discrepancy between the *Sloka-vartika* and the *Tantra-vdrtika* in that respect.[93] Without entering into the polemics of this question we state, following Parthasarathi's interpretation, that a knowledge of the self or more strictly the insight bom of meditati upon its true nature, is a contributory aid to freedom, so th the doctrine is what is technically described as jñāna-kanr samuccaya-vada. The followers of Prabhakara agree in tl respect; only they do not admit any purpose in the perfor ance of nitya-karmas beyond obeying the call of duty. The acceptance of the need for jñāna as a means of release, alo with the performance of unconditional duties, is qu explicitly stated.[94]

REFERENCES

1. See e.g. PP p. 104. Mīmāṁsā is viewed as aform of tarka, since it assists a pramāṇa cf. Note I and I. 182.

2. Compare SD. Sabda-sadhutve hi prayoga-paravaśā vayam na svayam īśmahe (p. 122). Yathā-lokam ca śabdārthāvadhāraṇam na.

3. See Notes 1 on p. 93.

4. See Prof. Keith: *Karma-mīmāṁsā*, p. 2.

5. Cf. IV. i. 14.

6. I. i. 5.

7. Prof. Edgerton: *Mimamsa-nyāya-prakāśa* (Yale Uni. Pr.), pp. 22-3.

8. SD. pp. 56-7.

9. SD .pp. 36 and 40.

10. SD p. 40 (cm,). The reference to the behaviour of animals and children is noteworthy.

11. *Muṇḍaka Up.* II. i. 4.

12. See SD p. 36.

13. SD. p. 124.

14. *Ibid.*, p. 122.

15. This saying is to be viewed as only partially representing experience as it actually occurs, for it necessarily includes a reference to an object (say a 'jar') other than the self which is left out here.

16. Sd p. 101.

17. See PP. chap viii, espeically pp. 152 ff.

18. PP. p. 51.

19. See SD, p. 18 and cf. *Jaimini-sūtra*. I. i. 3.

20. SD . pp. 19-23 and 48-50; PP ch. iv.

21. SD pp. 99-7 and 116-17. See also p. 44 com.

22. The meaning of proper names is regarded as due to mere convention (See PP. pp. 135-6 and SV. p. 674, st. 120). But even here the connotationis general e.g. 'Devadatta' means not the person so named in any particular stage of life but the individual who, in spite of minor changes, endures throughout life. cf. mammata's *Kāvyaprakāśa*, ii. 8.

23. SD. p. 91.

24. SM. p. 361.

25. It is social also in so far as it involves a conventional element. the diversity of existing languages is explained as the result of corruption in on original ideal

speech. that is to put the cart before the horse.

26. (I) *Akhyāti*—The word khyāti means 'knolwedge' and IV iii. 101.

27. See e.g. SV p. 217 st. 3; PP. iv. 66.

28. SD. p. 45;; SV. p. 431 st. 104-6.

29. PP. pp. 42-3, 127.

30. Strictly this should be 'samvit.' But to secure uniformity of terminology. inconsidering this topic of truth and error in the two schools, we use 'jñāna.

31. Dreams according to prabhakara, are memory without the consciousness at the time that they are so. See NM p. 179.

32. Recognition likewise partakes of the character of both perception and memory, but one is aware at the time of there collective element there. It is therefore different fromthe instance we are considering ..

33. PP. iv. st. 5.

34. Compare the earlier Sāṇkhya view of error, set forth in the previous chapter.

35. SV. pp. 242-6; SD. 58 9.

36. Compare the later Sāṅkhya view of error as stated on p. 291 *ante*.

37. Compare the view of sabda-pramāṇa as stated in PP. pp 91-94.

38. PP. iv. st. 37 ff.

39. In cases where error has led to suspension of activity, its discovery will prompt it.

40. SD pp. 72-3; PP. pp. 87 ff.

41. See PP. p.94.

42. *Laimini-sūtra* I ii 1-18.

43. To give the stock illustration: There is in the Yajurveda (II i.

44. an injunction 'One should sacrifice a white animal to Vayu,' and in the same context is seen the assertive proposition 'Vāyu verily is the swiftest deity the latter is a glorification of Vayu and is, according to the principle stated above, to be construed with the former. When so construed, it signifies that it is good to offer this sacrifice; for the reward will be speedy.

45. SV p. 455, st. 19ff.

46 MN.p. 44.

47. SD. pp. 83-7.

48. SV p. 479, st. 18.

49. PP. pp. 118-25.

50. SV. pp. 443, st. 32-3.

51. Cf. SV. p. 476, st. 12.

52. SV. p. 673, st. 113.

53. The Gods of Indian mythology also are repudiated, and sacrifical offerings, it is explained are made as if there were Gods. See p. 36 ante.

54. Cf. Yatha samdrsyate tatha: SV. p. 552, st. 29.

55. SV p. 4, st. 10.

56. Cf. Vilaksana-svabhavatvat bhāvānām. SD. p. 102.

57. *Māna-meyodaya*, p. 66.

58. SD. pp. 45-6.

59.*Māna-meyodaya*, p. 66.

60. PP. pp. 144 ff.; *Māna-meyodaya*, p. 68.

61. SV. p. 404, st. 183-4.

62. *Mana-meyodaya*, p. 6.

63. *Id.* p. 65.

64. PP. p. 27.

65. Cf. SD. pp. 83 ff.

66. I. iii. 2.

67. Acara-hinam na punanti Vedāh: Quoted by śaṁkara in his com. on VS. iii. i. 10.

68. *jaimini-sūtra*, I. i. 2.

69. *Tantra-vārtika*, I. iii.2.

70. See PP. pp. 187, 195.

71. Yāgādireva dharmah: SD. pp. 25-6. The term yaga strictly stands for a

certain resolve which is the prelude to the performance of a sacricice andis explained as tyaga, or, the spirit of renunication involved in giving away what belongs to oneself. (Cf. the formula 'no more mine'—na mama—uttered at the time of the offer.) Devatām uddisya dravya-tyago vāgah (*Nyāya-mālā-vistara,* IV. ii. 27-8). In this sense, dharma would of course be a characteristic of the subject.

72. See *Tantra-rahasya,* ch. iv.

73. For a fuller discussion of this and allied topics, reference may be made to *Ethic of the Hindus,* by Dr. S. K. Maitra (Calcutta Uni..

74. Prayojanam anuddisya na mandopi pravartate: SV. p. 653, st. 55.

75. SV. p. 125, st. 266.

76. NM. p. 350

77. PP. p. 191.

78. Ibid., pp. 177 and 180.

79. It is termed here not phalla but niyojya-viśeṣaṇa: PP. p. 191.

80. SD. p. 130.

81. Apurva, in general is described as svayam-prayojana-bhuta. See....

82. P. 66.

83. The former ofthese two explanations seems to be more in keeping with the Prābhākara ideal; the latter is hardly different fromt he Gītā teaching of sattva-śuddhi.

84. Compare NM. pp. 514 ff; VS. III. iv. 18.

85. In this connection we may draw attention to the view of some later exponents ofthe doctrine who, following the teaching of the Gītā, replace the divergent phalas of the several karmas by the single one of 'plesing God' by their performance (*Mīmāṁsā-nyāyaprakāśa,* p. 273.) This change is quite against the atheistic spirit of the Mīmāṁsā and shows how completely the Gītā ideal influenced

86. PP. pp.56-7. This glaring discrepancy can be explanined only by supposing that the stress laid upon dharma as the ultimate purusārtha, or the disinclination to bring duty and pleasure into relation with each other, was a characteristic of an earlier phase of the Prābhākara doctrine andthat it remains as but a relic in śālikanāth'a exposition of it. For evidence in support of the existence of such a phase, see *Jounral or Oriental Research* (Madras) pp. 99-108.

87. SD pp. 125.

88. SD. pp. 136-7

89. Māna-mevodaya, *pp. 87-9.*

90. *SD. pp. 127-8,*

91. *SV* p.670, st. 107.

92. The influence ofthe Gītā is again clear in this restriction of activity.

93. Cf. SV. pp. 669ff.; and *Tantra-vartika,* I. iii. 25.

94. PP. p.57.

CHAPTER XIII

THE UTTARA-MĪMĀṀSA OR THE VEDĀNTA SŪTRAS

The word Sūtras means literally, the end of the Vedas, with specific reference to the Upaniṣads, the fast portion of hte essential part of each of the four Vedas. The Upaniṣads, as we have already noted, make on attempt to order their contents but merely record the extraordinary experiences of the seers. There accordingly arose the necessity of interpreting them in terms of human reason and organizing them into a systematic philosophy, Bādarāyaṇa is the author of the Vedānta Sūtras in which the systematizing attempt is made. From hi we learn of other sages who preceded him in the same attempt but whose have not been preserved.

About Bādarāyaṇa little is known, though Indian tradition identifies him with Vyāsa, author of the Mahābhārata, who flourished sometime between 500 and 200 BC.

The Vedānta Sūtras are also known as Brahman Sūtras because they expound the philosophy of Brahman, and as śariīraka Sūtras because they deal with the nature of hte unconditioned Self embodied in human form. Though the Sūtras undertake to interpret and organize the Upaniṣads, they are themselves quite unintelligible without commentaries. The commentaries, moreover, are so diverse and often so conflicting that it is well-night impossible to arrive at the precise views held by Bādarāyaṇa. The Vedānta Sūtras are unquestionably of great authority, however, for every important philosopher has written commentaries upon them. They are indeed one of the three great works upon which all the theologies of Indian rest. The others are the Upaniṣads, of course, and the Gītā.

The understand the place of the three works in modern Indian philosophy, we recall to mind once again the three steps in attaining Self-knowledge prescribed by the Upaniṣads. We must hear of the truth of hte Self, we must reason upon this truth, and we must meditate upon the Self.[1] The Upaniṣads speak to us of the truth of the Self. The Vedānta Sūtras aid us to reason and understand. Finally, the Gītā affords us practical ways and means of living and prescribes details of conduct and methods of meditation. Of the many philosophers who have commented upon these fundamental scriptures, the chief are śaṁkara, Bhāskare, Yādava Prākas, Rāmānuja, Nimbārka, Keśava, Nīlakaṇṭha, Mādhwa, Baladeva, Vallabha, and Vijñānabhikṣu. Five of these have had a large following. śaṁkara, the exponent of mondualism: Rāmānuja, the exponent of qualified monism; Nimbārka, the exponent of the philosophy of unity in difference Mādhwa, the exponent of dualism; and

Vallabha, the exponent of the philosophy of devotion. Of these śaṁkara and Rāmānuja are the most famous.

It is difficult to state with any definiteness which of these philosophers presents the correct view of the original Vedānta Sūtras of Bādarāyaṇa, for opinions differ, and each school of thought believes that it represents the true tradition. Dr G. Thibaut is of the opinion that Rāmānuja is the truest interpreter. My brother monk Swami Vireswarananda, in the learned introduction to his translation of the Vedānta Sūtras, has argued that śaṁkara's interpretation closely follows Bādarāyaṇa. A brief summary of the Vedānta Sūtras and of the points of agreement regarding them may help to clarify what really is most obscure and complex problem.

The Sūtras contain four chapters in all. The first deals with Brahman, his relation to the world and to the soul of man. An attempt is made to reconcile metaphysically the various Vedic passages on the subject, the recorded experiences of Brahman on the part of the early ṛṣis, or seers. The second chapter meets the objections to the view of Brahman, the soul, and the world expounded in the first, and reveal the fallacious nature of all rival theories on the subject. The third chapter is mainly concerned with methods by which an individual can attain knowledge of Brahman, but incidentally discusses the question of rebirth for those who fail to attain logical topics. The fast chapter takes up the fruits of the knowledge of Brahman—these differing in relation to the differing experiences of aspirants and knowers, the deeper the experience, the greater the fruits. It also discusses at length mokṣa and the two paths possible after death—return (rebirth) and nonreturn (gradual liberation).

According to Bādarāyaṇa, perception and inference are the two sources of all knowledge. On the spiritual plane, he indefinite perception, direct divine insight, with śruti, or the revealed scriptures, particularly the Upaniṣads; and inference with Smṛti, the auxiliary scriptures—the Gītā the Bādarāyaṇa, and the Laws of Manu. Perception in relation to knowledge of Brahman (pratyakṣa upalabdhi) is not sense perception, for nobody sees God with physical eyes—it is supersensuous perception; spiritual inference depends on revelations, for logic independent of revelation is blind and leads nowhere.

Brahman is regarded by Bādarāyaṇa as the material as well as the efficient cause of the universe, its origin and support, himself uncreated and eternal. It is difficult to state with any definiteness, however, what Bādarāyaṇa actually believed concerning the universe, whether that it is a transformation of Brahman or that it is only somethings superimposed upon him. Nor is it clear how the individual soul is related to Brahman, whether as a part of him or as a mere reflection of him. Because of these obscurities or uncertainties, the various schools of thought have flourished. But all are agreed that the ultimate goal to Vedānta is certainly the knowledge of Brahman and that it can be attained in this life. The knowledge, once attained, burns away all the seeds of karma and gives the promised liberation.

The other various metaphysical, ethical, and psychological aspects of the Vedānta Sūtras will be fully explained when we discuss the philosophers who commented upon them.

REFERENCES

1. Bṛhadāraṇyaka, II. iv. 5.

CHAPTER XIV

ADVAITA PHILOSOPHY

The particular type of monism taught by śaṁkara is very old, though in its final form it owes a great deal to his contribution. Its most distinguishing feature. on the theoretical side is its conception of nirguna Brahman as the ultimate reality with the implied belief in the May a doctrine, the identity of the jīva and Brahman and the conception of mokṣa as the merging of the former in the latter; on the practical side, it is the advocacy of karma-samnyāsa or complete renunciation with its implication that jñāna and jñāna alone is the means of release. The earliest extant formulation of this doctrine is found in Gauḍapāda's *Karikā* which purports to summarize the teaching of the *Māṇḍūkya Upaniṣad,* but really accomplishes much more by giving an admirable summary of advaitic teaching. The main points of śaṁkara's philosophy—its basic principles such as the inapplicability of the notion causality to the ultimate reality—are already there. The most important of śaṁkara's works is the bhāṣya on the *Vedānta-sūtra,* which is as remarkable for the charm of its style as for the logical consistency of its arguments. We have already mentioned that he therein maintains the vivarta-vada or the doctrine that the world is a phenomenal appearance of Brahman. According to him, the belief to be refuted before the Advaita is established is not so much the Sāṅkhya or Prakṛti-parinama-vada as Brahma-pariṇāma-vāda. On account of the fact that the treatise on which he comments alludes so frequently to the Sāṅkhya, Sarhkara also considers it at length and shows how far removed it is from the Upaniṣadic doctrine; but his real objective is to establish the vivarta-vada or Māyā-vāda as against the pariṇāma-vāda of certain commentators on the *Vedānta-sūtra,* especially Bhartr-prapanca that preceded him. śaṁkara has also another aim in his bhāṣya: Owing to the resemblance, though only seeming, of his doctrine of nirguna brahman to that of the sunya or 'void' of the Madhyamika form of Buddhistic idealism[2] one might identify the two and regard the Advaita as alien to the Upaniṣads So he emphasize now and again the fact that his teaching is not negative or nihilistic How far this contention can be maintained we shall see later He does not expressly mention this phase of Buddhism except in one placed and there lie dismisses it summarily, but there is no doubt that he throughout tries to steer clear of these two doctrines opposed to his own, but yet so similar to it, viz the Brahma-parināma-vāda of some Vedāntins and the sūnya of the Mādhyamikas.

Besides the bhāṣya on the *Vedānta sūtra,* śaṁkara wrote commentaries on the principal Upaniṣads and the *Bhagavad-gitā* Those. especially on the *Bṛhadāraṅyaka* and *Chāndogya* treat of several points that are not dealt with in detail in the *Sūtra-bhāṣya* and are of immense value in the comprehension and appreciation of the doctrine of Advaita In addition to them, we have his *sdhaśrī,* which, though somewhat terse, gives splendid account of his Mews śaṁkaras doctrine was defended and amplified in matters of detail by various thinkers after him, and this has given use to some diversity of opinion among his followers I Two of the schools resulting from such divergences of view are in particular well known—the Vivarana school which goes back to the fragment of a commentary on śaṁkara's by his own pupil Padmapāda and the slightly later Bhāmatī school represented by Vācaspati (A.D. 841) The Pañca-pādikā was commented upon by Prakāśātman (A.D. 1000) in his *Vivarana,* from which the first school takes its name The Vivarana has a gloss known as *Tattva-dipana* by Akhaṇḍānanda, and it thing has also been most lucidly lucidly summarized by (A.D 1350) in his has been explained by Amalananda (A.D. 1250) in his *Kalpa taru* winch in its turn has been annotated by (A.D. 1600) in the Parimala. There are also various other commentaries of greater or less value on the Sūtra-bhāṣya such as the Brahmavidyābharana of Advaitananda (A.D. 1450). Of the numerous hand-books written to explain the Advaita system, we may mention here the *Nmskarntya-siddhi* of Suresvara, who was at first probably a Mimamsaka, and the *Samkfepa-sdrtraka* by hisi pupil, SarvajnĀtman Another work of particular value, especially in regard to the Maya doctrine, is the *Ifta-siddhi* of Vimuk-tĀtman (A.D. 1050). Later still are the *Nydya-makaranda* of Ananda (A.D. 1050) and the *Pafica-dasi* of Vidaranya, a popular treatise. The *Siddhanta-lesa-sathgraha* of Appaya Dikita descnbes the divergences of view, already mentioned, which arose within the doctrine as a result of its wide expansion in the centuries following mkara. The *eddnta-paribhdd* of Dharmaraja Adhvarindra puts it as a technical and systematic exposition of the doctrine, especially on its logical and epistemological side; and the *cddnia-si'ird* of Sadanand (A.D. 1550) is an easy introduction to Advaita philosophy. Among the exclusively polemical work written on the system should be mentioned the *Khandana-khanda-khddya* of riharsa the poet of the *aisadfiiyii-cania* and the *Advaita-siddht* of Madhusudana Sarasvati (A.D. 1650) with its commentary, the *Laghu-candnka* by Brahmananda, whose study is now regarded along the pundits as quite essential to true advaitic scholarship.

I

The Advaita resembles the Sāṅkhya-yoga in regard to its conception ol the psychic appaiatus, and it also behaves, like the othci in the theory of representati\e knowledge The only difference that may be noticed is that while, according to the Sāṅkhya-Yoga, the ten senses arc traced to ahaṁkara, here they are supposed to be derived from the elements much are in the Nyāya-Vaiśeṣika.[2] The internal organ (aṅtah-karana) also is liere conceived as bhautika and as constituted of all the elements through it consists ot the five elements, tejas, predominates, which accounts for its being sometimes described as taijasa ('made out of tejas'). It accordingly partakes more of the character of that element than of any other and is unstable—always liable to alter its form either where it is or where it readies by 'streaming out,' as it is said, through a sense. That is, the aṅtah-karana is always active, except only in states like suṣupti, where it becomes latent. Each of the forms it assumes by exercising this activity is known as a vṛtti as in the Sāṅkhya-Yoga. The explaination that all these organs are bhautika is important on account of the recognition it implies of the indispensableness of physical aids for the manifestation of consciousness. Though indispensable, their distinction from the psychical element is not in the least ignored. It is in fact the constant association of these two incompatibles as implied in common experience that forms, as we shall see the crux of the philosophic problem according to Samskara.

As regards the nature of the conscious element also, the explaination is almost the same as in the Sāṅkhya-Yoga. It is conceived as extraneous to the apparatus, which yet in some way helps its manifestation. It is not, however, ultimately different from the apparatus here as in the other system; for according to the Advaita the apparatus goes back eventually to the same source, viz. Brahman or spirit, the sole reality acknowledged. For this reason, the interaction between the two—the physical apparatus and the psychical principle—is more satisfactorily explained here than in the other doctrine. But, whatever the metaphysical difference, it does not affect the explanation with which we are concerned in this section. Accordingly we may assume for our present purpose that the two are distinct as in the Sāṅkhya-Yoga. The psychical element is viewed as wholly inactive. The activity it manifests only seemingly belongs to it and is in reality to be traced to its physical accompaniment, viz. the internal organ. The element of consciousness is known as saksin[3] and corresponds to the puruṣa. of the Sāṅkhya-Yoga—the passive, observer of the states of the internal organ as they unfold themselves. It appears never by itself, but always in association with the internal organ in its latent or manifest form. The reverse also is true and no internal organ is conceivable without involving a reference to some saksin or other. Thus it is only the unity of the passive saksin and the active aṅtah-karana that is real for all practical purposes. That is what knows, feels and will? In this complex form it is known as the jīva or the empirical self. Such a conception satisfactorily accounts for what would otherwise be wholly unintelligible viz. the double character of subject and object which one and the same jīva exhibits in so-called self-consciousness. But for the presence within it of the objective complement of the aṅtah-karana one could not, it is said, speak of knowing oneself, since what knows can never be the same as what is known—a view which is entirely opposed to that of Rumania who regards the ego to be simple and yet ascribes this double character to it (p. 305). This complex entity is believed to endure in one form or other till the time of release. Who at last it breaks up. the internal organ is absorbed by or loses its identity in its source, Maya, which for the moment we may take to be the same as the prakṛti of the Sāṅkhya-Yoga, and the saksin losing its sākṣi-hood, as will become clear later. becomes Brahman indeed. The saksin and the jīva are thus not identical, though at the same time they are not quite different either. While the jīva may become the object of self-consciousness on account of the objective element it includes, it is wrong to speak of the saksin as knowable, for it is the pure element of awareness in all knowing; and to assume that it is knowable would be to imply another knowing element—a process which leads to the fallacy of infinite regress. But the saksin does not therefore remain unrealized, for being self-luminous, by its very nature, it does not require to be made known at all. Its presence is necessarily equivalent to its revelation and it is therefore never missed. 'That is self-luminousness,' says the *Pañca-daśī*. 'which is revelation without any aid.[4] In other words, the jīva is spirit as immanent in the aṅtaḥ-karana, while the sākṣin is spirit as transcendent.[5]

By jāana or knowledge in general we must understand in the system neither a vṛtti of the internal organ nor the sākṣin by itself, but a blend of both -the vṛtti as inspired by the sākṣin. In jāana thus understood, the vṛtti element is contingent; the other, viz. the element of consciousness, is eternal, being intrinsically Brahman itself which, owing to its association with the vṛtti that appear and disappear, only seems to be characterized by change, but is really untouched by it. It is sometimes termed saksi-jāana to distinguish it from vṛtti-jāana or empirical knowledge which is a result of the interaction of subject and object. It is present always and it is impossible to think it away. It is 'the light of all our seeing' and does not cease to be even in deep sleep. The aṅtaḥ-karana may have modal transformations (pariṇārna) other than vṛtti-jāana, such as pain and pleasure. In fact, all internal states are viewed as its modes. But the system does not in theory regard those other states as states of consciousness so that they have to be known through a vṛtti-jāana. This distinction does not mean that pain and pleasure, for instance, may exist and yet be not experienced; for as states or modes of the internal organ they are necessarily 'Hummed' by the sākṣin and are therefore known as they arise just: is jāana itself is[6] only shows that the doctrine differentiates the cognitive from the other phases of the mind. If we take this explanation with what we have already stated, viz. that except in states like sleep the internal organ .will be ceaselessly operating we see that the jīva is never without some jāana or other.

Knowledge may be mediate or immediate, the distinction between the two being that while in the former only the 'that' of an object is known, in the latter, the 'what' also is revealed.[7] Both kinds of knowledge are alike vṛttis of the internal organ in which the sākṣin is immanent. Knowledge which gives the object directly is not here equated with sensory perception, and there may be immediate knowledge not involving sense-perception. The empirical sell for instance is immediately known, but it cannot be said to be *presented.* to any sense. Hence the word pratyaksa, which literally means 'presented to a sense,' is here usually replaced by the wider term aparoksa or 'not mediate.' If the following conditions are satisfied, knowledge will be immediate, no matter whether it comes through a sense or not. First, the object must be such as can be directly known (yogya). For example, a table can be so known but not virtue. This is not so much a condition of immediacy as an indication that not all things are perceivable. Secondly, the object must be existent at the time; otherwise even a perceivable object will not be immediately known. Our recollection of a table that no longer exists cannot for the—reason be immediate. Lastly, there should be established a certain intimate relation between the subject and the object in question. The means of such relation is the vṛtti which flows out[8] in the case of external objects, but remains within where it originates in the case of internal ones like pain or pleasure. It will be convenient to take the former variety of immediate knowledge for finding out the meaning of this condition. The subject and object are here by hypothesis removed from each other and occupy different positions in space; and the vṛtti which relates them brings about for the time being what may be described as an identity of ground for the two. The exact manner in which this takes place is stated as follows: When an organ of sense is brought into contact with an object, the antah-karana, like a searchlight as it were, goes out towards it and gets itself determined by it or assumes the 'form' of that object. The existence of the object previous to the appearance of knowledge is thus necessary so that psychologically the theory is realistic. When the vṛtti coincides with the object, perceptual knowledge arises. The coincidence of these two, since the vṛtti is a mode of the internal organ, is really the coincidence of the jīva and the object. They thus come to have the same ground; or the being of the object, as it is stated, ceases then to be different from the being of the subject.[9] It is their identification in this manner that constitutes the third and the last of the conditions for an object being known immediately. Perception conceived here is accordingly the result of a communion between the knower and the known and it would therefore be more appropriate to describe the object as 'felt' then rather than known.[10] In the case of internal perception, when the first two conditions are satisfied, *i.e.* when the object is perceivable and is actually present at the time, the last condition is invariably fulfilled, for internal states like pain or pleasure are not, as already explained, different in fact from the vṛtti through which they are supposed to be experienced. So if those states admit of being directly perceived at all (yogya)[11] they do become immediately known whenever they exist. If knowledge occurs when one or more of these conditions are lacking, it will be mediate. The table beyond the wall can be known only mediately, for the vṛtti cannot flow out to it to bring about the. needed relation, contact with one or other sensory organ being a necessary condition for the starting out of the antah-karana towards the object. But even here, we should remember, a vṛtti is recognized though it remains internal.

The above view of knowledge implies a classification of objects into those that can be directly known and the that cannot be known. They may belong to the external world or may be states or modes of the internal organ. External objects may be perceivable and may also be present at the time; yet they may or may not be directly known. Internal states, on the other hand, when they satisfy those two conditions are necessarily known immediately. To these two kinds of objects must be added a third which is not only necessarily known immediately but is always so known. That is the empirical ego—the jīva or aham padārtha as the same sometimes designated. It is no doubt the object side that is commonly attended to in knowledge; but it does not mean that the subject remains unrevealed in it, although it may not always show itself quite explicitly. As in the Prābhākara school, all knowledge alike involves a reference to it; and since the jīva, according to the Advaita is never without some jñāna or other, the consciousness of self becomes a constant feature of all experience. It is this sense of self that explains how one person is able to distinguish ..is experience from that of others. It is absent only in states like suṣupti or fainting.

So far we have treated of knowledge during the waking state. But there is dream experience as well and even sleep is not quite bereft of experience. We have now to consider these states specifically. As already stated in the chapter on the Upaniṣads, the essential distinction between dreams and waking is that the senses co-operate in the latter, but not in the former. Further, unlike waking, dreaming is not marked by an association with the gross body. Yet there is in it the feeling that the senses are co-operating and that a gross body—not necessarily similar to that of the waking state—is also present. We may dream of an elephant and we may feel that we are riding on it. The consequence is that we experience objects as existent at the time. This peculiarity precludes the explanation of the state as due to a mere revival of past impressions. Dreams are really more than revived impressions; they are new creations. A revival of the impressions left by previous experience is of course necessary for them, but it does not furnish their whole explanation. Dreams, so far as they are direct experience, should be placed on a par with waking; and it is accordingly assumed that objects are present then, apart from their knowledge. In memory on the other hand that is not the case, the reference in; to things as past being quite clear. The character of dream-objects, however, is held to be different from that of the objects of wakeful experience; but the explanation of this point we have to postpone till we reach the next section.

If the internal organ functions by itself in dreams unaided by the senses, that also becomes latent in sleep. Of the two elements that make up the jīva, one, viz. the aṅtah-karana, is lost in its cause Māyā or, to state it more definitely, in that part or aspect of it called avidyā which constitutes the adjunct of individual jīvas[12] What endures them is the sākṣin *plus* avidyā which is known as the karana-sarira or the radical adjunct of the self as distinguished from its subtle body (linga-sarira).[13] Consequently there is in sleep no subject at all as such and no states of consciousness as in dreams or waking. This makes the 'experience' of dreamless sleep quite unique, though occurring normally and almost universally. What we have in that condition is the sākṣin—not the jīva—associated with its own avidyā, in which the internal organ has provisionally merged. In this state also, we must remember, individuality persists; but the individuality then is due to the union of the sākṣin with avidyā and not with the internal organ. The avidyā operates in sleep only partially. It obscures the true character of reality, but does not split it up into a variety of 'names' and 'forms' as in dreams or in waking, since the discontinuous and mutually excluding vṛttis of the internal organ are absent there. The experience of sleep involves a reference to both these elements—continuance of personality and absence of all variety—as is shown by the later reminiscence[14] that one was asleep and did not know anything. Over and above these there is felt in sleep bliss which, according to a fundamental postulate of the system, is the very nature of the self'and which, owing to the absence of all distractions then, becomes manifest. This unalloyed happiness survives even after waking, as shown by the state of repose that continues for a while; but it disappears is man lapses back into the vortex of common life—a belief which is Wordsworthian in its character.[15] 'All beings visit that Brahma-world day after day, but not one realizes it.[16] None of these features of sleep, it must be noted, is 'known' at the time, for no knowledge, whether mediate or immediate, is possible in the absence of the internal organ. But they are nevertheless realized then as shown by the fact of their being recalled afterwards.

II

There seem to be strictly but two views in regard to the implication of knowledge—either to deny, like the Yogācāra school of Buddhism, that it ever points to an object outside or to admit that it does so always. To postulate the object where knowledge is true while denying it either directly or indirectly where knowledge is erroneous is self-contradictory. To śaṁkara, all knowledge in the common acceptance of the term points to an object as it does to a subject, and there is no knowledge which does not involve this double implication. Where there is no object, there can be no knowledge.[17] The 'round square' and the 'barren woman's son' are unreal (asat) and there can consequently be no knowledge of them beyond a merely verbal one. But it may be asked how, if all knowledge alike points to an object, illusions occur. In answering the question it will be necessary to refer to the example given in the previous chapter to illustrate the pramāṇa known as arthapatti which the Advaitin also recognizes. If Devadatta continues to be strong and healthy, though not eating by day, we do not at once modify or give up our belief about the need of food for living beings, but try to reconcile the observed fact with it, and in so doing we assume that he must be eating by night. That is, when we are face to face with a fact which contradicts a well-tested view, we do not all at once revise that view, but endeavour to harmonize the new fact with it by means of a suitable hypothesis. In the present case, since it is inconceivable that knowledge should arise without an objective counterpart to it, the Advaitin assumes that there is an object even in-the so-called illusion; and, in order to distinguish illusion from non-illusory knowledge, postulates a difference between the *types* of objects cognized in them. The distinction between illusion and ordinary knowledge is not accordingly due to the absence and presence respectively of an object outside corresponding to its content, but to the difference in the character of the object that is pointed to in either. Objects of illusion are not common to several or general, their presence not being vouched for by collective experience. The serpent (say) which a person sees in the dark where there is only a rope is special to him and may not be seen by others. It may therefore be described as 'private' or personal to him, while objects of common knowledge such as a real serpent are public, for they are cognized by others as well. A second difference between the two types of objects is that while an object of illusion lasts only as long as its knowledge lasts—neither for a longer nor for a shorter period—that of ordinary knowledge is more enduring. The latter is already there before it comes to be apprehended and, generally speaking,[18] continues to be after its apprehension ceases, as is shown for instance by our recognition of it later[19]; the former on the other hand comes to exist *as* we apprehend it and ceases to be when our apprehension of it ceases. The one is described as vyāvahārika or empirical; the other as prātibhāsika or apparent; Dream objects, to whose difference from those of the waking state we have already referred, are of the second type.

The objects which we have described as private, it is necessary to remember, are not mere ideas or purely subjective. If they were, the advaitic theory of knowledge would be the same as the Yogācāra one which śaṁkara unreservedly criticizes,[20] viz. that there is no object apart from its knowledge and that the commonly recognized distinction between them is a fiction. No private object can indeed be conceived except as dependent upon a particular individual; the point to be noted is that it is not mental, but an object of mind. This is brought out clearly in the explanation given of the origin and nature of prātibhāsika things to which we shall soon refer. For the present we merely note that the foregoing account shows how mistaken is the common belief that śaṁkara views the objects of everyday experience to be false or unreal. So far from doing this, he claims some kind of reality even for objects of illusion. To be perceived is for him *to be,* and his theory may therefore be described as an inversion of the one associated in western;, philosophy with the name of Berkeley. This explanation has one great merit. It accounts for illusion as it occurs. What we experience in it is that we *see* the serpent or silver; and this fact of knowing an object as present then and there is not explained, but is rather explained away in other theories of illusion.

In the light of this distinction among the objects of knowledge, we may explain error as arising when different types of things are related in a judgment.[21] In the example 'This is silver,' the 'this' (*i.e.* shell) is empirically real and 'silver' which is superposed upon it is only apparently so. In other words, error is 'illegitimate transference' or adhyasa as śaṁkara puts it in his celebrated Introduction to the *Vedānta-sūtra.* Though the empirical and the apparent spheres are both objective, we, for the reasons assigned above, take that which is superposed as less real than that on which it is. The falsity of such knowledge is not realized until we become conscious of the disparity between the objects related in it. When a person is seeing silver where there is only shell, he certainly does not know it to be false. On the other hand, he then feels convinced that it is quite as valid as any other knowledge. But when he approaches the object, picks it up and discovers that it is too light to be silver, he at once realizes that he was in error. What leads to the discovery is therefore this other knowledge[22] whose object, because it is of the empirical kind, is not similarly sublated.[23] Now as regards the relation between the two terms involved in error: It cannot be identity, for things belonging to different levels of being cannot be identified. Nor can it be difference, for then the terms would not appear as subject and predicate in the same judgment as 'This is silver.' We cannot take it as identity-indifference either, for that conception, as we shall see in the next section, is self-discrepant. The relation is therefore regarded as unique and is called tādātmya.[24] It is not real, because it obtains between terms that belong to two different orders of being. The water that is quaffed in a dream will not quench actual thirst. At the same time the relation is not unreal, for it is experienced. It is therefore like the lower of the two objects it relates, apparent, not empirical. We may further remark that the relation is such that negating the higher of the two relate necessarily negates the lower. But the reverse is not true. If the shell is denied, the silver is not; but the negation of the silver is quite conceivable with the affirmation of the shell.[25] This what constitutes appearance. We accordingly describe the shell as the ground[26] of which the silver is an appearance.

It is necessary to eludicate further the idea of adhyāsa. From the fact that wherever there is adhyasa, there is a confusion between two orders of being, we deduce that it presupposes ignorance. It is because we are obvious of the shell that we see silver in its place. There are other causes also, such as the previous experience of silver, defective eye-sight, etc., to account for the mistake; but it will suffice for our purpose to confine our attention to the most important of them, viz. ignorance or avidyā. Now avidyā, which is only another word for ajñāna, implies, like jñāna, some person to whom it belongs (asraya) and some object to which it refers (visaya) The notion of 'knowledge' is not complete until we mention the subject that knows and the object that is known. Similarly, in the case of avidyā, there must be someone whom it characterizes and an object which is misapprehended in it. In the present case, the person that mistakes the shell for silver is its asraya, and the shell is its visaya.[27] It is avidyā thus determined that is described as the cause of silvery[28]; and it operates in a double manner. It conceals the fact of shell and shows up silver in its place. To see silver where there is only shell, a necessary condition is the concealment of the shell. Suppression precedes substitution. These two aspects of it are respectively termed avarana or 'veiling' and viksepa—or 'revealing.' As the avidyā does not put the shell entirely out the sight, it is not lack of apprehension—a mere gap in thought—but misapprehension and is therefore described as positive (bhāva-rūpa). It is the contrary of vidyā, not its contradictory: and the condition for the resulting error to disappear is the removal of avidyā which happens when vidyā arises in the self-same person in regard to the self-same object. It is the reference to a particular individual and to a specific object which this avidyā involves that explains the 'uniqueness of the silver of which it is described as the source. Because it has a specific external object as its basis, the silver to which it gives rise appears out there—spatially determined—and is not a mere idea; and, because it has a particular person for its asraya, the illusion which it occasions is special to him. It is this personal character that distinguishes private objects from the empirical ones which, as we shall see later, spring into being directly from Māyā and are 'public' or verifiable by others also. Though the objects we are now considering form an order by themselves, they are not altogether sundered from the other, for avidyā which occasions private objects is dependent upon the same source to which the common order of nature is due, viz. Māyā,[29] and is therefore described sometimes as tūlāvidyā or auxiliary avidyā.[30] It is owing to this sameness of the source that when Māyā is overcome in mokṣa both realms of objective being disappear alike. Otherwise though the common order of nature may cease to be then, the other might persist.

There is one important instance of adhyāsa which we must specially consider now—the ego or ahaṁ-padartha. Systems like the Nyāya-Vaiśeṣika and the Mīmāṁsā regard it as a simple and ultimate entity. It is in fact synonymous with the self (ātman) in those doctrines. But the Advaitin denies the integrity of the self in this sense and take it, we know, to be a complex of the sākṣin and the internal organ. His reasons in favour of this position are chiefly two: One is the fact of self-consciousness which by showing in the same self the contrary features of subject and object indicates its mixed character. The other is the uniqueness of sleep experience.If the ego or jīva were simple and endured throughout, all experience would alike involve a reference to it. But that is not the case, for sleep as interpret' 'here is without such reference. We are therefore compelled to explain it as consisting of two elements one of which, viz. the sākṣin alone, endures through the three states. The other, viz. the internal organ, is common only to waking and dream; and to it accordingly should be ascribed all the specific features of those states. 'Love, desire, pleasure, pain and so forth are experienced when the internal organ functions, but not in sleep; . hence they must be of the internal organ.[31] Now the Nyāya-Vaiśeṣika and the Mīmāṁsā, which hold that the ego is not analysable, maintain that it is distinct from the body, senses, etc. But there is ordinarily an implied identification of these distinct entities, as for instance when one says 'I am stout,' 'I am blind,' where 'stoutness' and 'blindness' which are respectively the characteristics of the body and the sense of sight are predicated of the self. These systems explain the identification as more or less consciously made, as for example when we describe a man as a 'giant' and as therefore having only a secondary or rhetorical significance (gauna)—supporting' their position by reference to the equally familiar experience finding expression as 'my body,' etc., where the distinction appears explicitly. The Advaitin does not accept this explanation. He contends that the characteristic of gauna or secondary usage, viz. the consciousness at the time of the distinction between the objects identified, is lacking here and ascribes the identification to an unconious confusion between the entities involved, viz. body, senses, etc., on the one hand, and the sākṣin on the other. It accordingly involves, in his view, ignorance of the true character of those entities and is a case of error or adhyasa. There are indeed occasions, he admits, when we do distinguish between the two, as when we speak of 'our body,' but he explains them as only flashes of the truth which are soon veiled from us. This argument is applicable to the aṅtah-karana also and when a person feels pain, for example, and says 'I am suffering,' he is illegitimately transferring to the, true ātman what according to the previous reasoning belongs to the antah-karana.[32] If the ego is complex and is an instance of adhyasa, the entities constituting it must belong to different orders of being. We get a hint here of a third kind of reality: for the internal organ, one of the two involved in it, is an empirical reality being an effect of Māyā and as such stands higher than appearances having avidyā for their source. The higher reality is the saksin or more strictly[33] sākṣi-svarūpa which is Brahman itself. It is designated true or pāramārthika reality.[34]

If error signifies that the objects related in it belong to different orders of being, truth by implication should consist in relating objects of the same order; but, for reasons to be explained presently, we shall take this definition as holding good only within the sphere of empirical things and not in the case of appearances which are contradicted when we judge them in relation to that sphere. A dream-judgment like 'This is an elephant' is not true although its two terms alike stand for realities of the pratibhasika type, because both are set aside so soon as one awakes[35] Pramāṇa we accordingly define as that which leads to knowledge whose content is not sublated (abādhita) as the result of later experience.[36] The silver seen where there is only a shell disappears the moment we scrutinize it, but the shell does not vanish in the same manner. The knowledge of the silver is therefore bhrama and that of the shell, prama. True, even the latter may prove a delusion from a higher standpoint; but such a consideration may be excluded when we are con trailing empirical things with appearances. What is meant when we say that the knowledge of the shell is prama „ is that, unlike that of the silver, it justifies its claim for truth throughout empirical life[37]—not that it is ultimately real. As regards the question whether novelty (anadhigatatva) should be regarded as a necessary element in truth, the Advaitin is indifferent; but with his partiality for the Bhāṭṭa view, he would prefer to include it among the conditions of validity. In accordance with the orthodox view of revelation (p.180), this condition is necessary in the case of śruti.[38]

The Advaita recognizes all the six pramāṇas mentioned in connection with the Kumarila school of Mimamsa and generally agrees with it in matters of detail also.[39] Of the—points of difference between the two, it will suffice to touch upon only the following here, all of them having reference to verbal testimony:—

(i) The Mimamsa rejects the view that the Veda was ever composed by anybody (p. 312), and the Nyāya-Vaiśeṣika ascribes its authorship to Īśvara

(p. 258). The position of śaṁkara in regard to this point, like that of the other Vedantins, is midway between the two. Like the Mimamsaka, but unlike the Nyāya-Vaiśeṣika, he admits that the Veda is apauruseya; but he re-defines that word so as to make it signify not that the Veda has no author and is eternal, but that it is produced or, more properly, resuscitated at the beginning of each kalpa by one that cannot interfere either with its content or with the order of its words. In the case of works like the *Raghuvamśa,* the author composes it just as he likes. Here, on the other hand, the first promulgator of the Veda in every cycle who is God repeats it anew, but precisely as it was in earlier cycles. That is, the Veda is self-existent in this view also; only it is not the self-same Veda that always is, but a series of what may be described as re-issues of an eternal edition which goes back to beginning-less time. This, it will be seen, is not in substance different from the Mīmāmsa view, excepting that it finds a place for God in the doctrine.

(ii) Śaṁkara, following Kumarila, admits sabda to be a pramāṇa outside the Veda also; but he does not restrict its independent logical validity, within the Veda, to injunctive statements (p. 318). Assertive propositions found there may be equally valid, so that there is nothing in the nature of the Veda as verbal testimony to preclude it from treating directly of matters of fact (bhūta-vastu) like Brahman or the highest reality. Statements like Tat tvam asi which occur in the Upaniṣads, thereby acquire independent logical value here; and there is no need to subordinate them in one way or the other to ritualistic commands as in the Mīmāmsa.

(iii) The truth revealed by the scriptures, contrary to what the Mimamsaka thinks, is here the fundamental unity of Being. We shall see later in what sense this unity is to be understood in the Advaita, and may now consider the place m the scheme of pramāṇas of perception which seems to vouch for the truth of diversity and thus to come into conflict with the teaching of revelation that all is one. The primary aim of perception, like that of the other pramāṇas, is, according to śaṁkara, to serve empirical purposes. It gives, no guarantee for metaphysical validity[40] so that what we commonly hold real may not be truly so. 'Common knowledge is true,' he says[41] 'so long only as the identity of oneself with Brahman is not realized, as dreams are until one does not awake.' In other words, the transcendental ideality of the world does not exclude its empirical reality.[42] Such a view considerably-modifies the notion of inherent validity (svatah-prāmāṇya) which the Advaitin, like the Mimamsaka (p. 307), accepts. That knowledge is true requires, according to the Advaita also, no explanation, for by its very nature it is so. This self-validity, however, for the reason just mentioned, is to be understood here as relative and not absolute as in the Mīmāmsa. Even the validity of the Veda, generally speaking, is only such. When it teaches that svarga can be attained through the performance of a certain sacrifice, it is of course true; but the Veda does not thereby vouch for the *ultimate* reality of either the svarga or anything connected with it. The fact is that the Advaita recognizes a lumber, viz the absolute standpoint from which all pramāṇas alike, inclusive of the Veda, lose their relative validity. An exception is made only in the case of Upaniṣadic statements that teach the unity of all being. These statements are pramāṇa in the absolute sense, for the knowledge which they convey is never shown to be wrong. But it does not secure for the pramāṇa itself ultimate reality, for in mokṣa where nothing but Brahman remains, even that pramāṇa as such must disappear. It signifies that a false means may lead to a true end—a position which may appear untenable; but there are many instances in life where this happens. The image of a person as reflected in a mirror is not real, but it does not therefore fail to serve as the means of showing to him so many facts about his appearance. The roaring of a lion in a dream is not real, but it may wake the dreamer to actual life. It is necessary, however, to remember in thus admitting the utility of error that nothing here is absolutely unreal so that even a false means is not without a nucleus of truth.[43]

So much about vṛtti-jñāna or knowledge as it is commonly known to us. But according to the advaitic analysis of it. empirical knowledge is a complex consisting of a physical factor and a psychical one, neither of which by itself is adequate to explain experience as we are familiar with it. We have now to point out the full implication of this analysis on its psychical side. The sākṣin which is the psychical element is always present like an ever-luminous lamp, the enduring and changeless element in experience which does not cease to be even in deep sleep. It is individual and determinate, being denned by reference to the particular internal organ with which for the time being it seems associated. It is accordingly termed jīva-saksin. What comes within the range of one saksin—through the medium of its own antah-karana in the waking and dream states and through avidyā in deep sleep—is not necessarily within the experience of other sākṣin. But existent objects as a whole can be understood only as presented to some sākṣin, for consistently with the eventually idealistic position of the Advaita there can be no reality outside what either knows or is known. This line of reasoning leads to the postulating of a cosmic sākṣin if absolute consciousness (Īśvara-saksin) which sustains everything that is.[44] it is, in reality, the ground of the whole universe and is, as we shall see more fully in the next section, the Brahman of the Advaita. It is designated svarupa-jñāna or pure consciousness., The vṛtti-jñāna draws its breath and substance from it, and the whole complex of empirical or finite knowledge would be nowhere without the light of this absolute or infinite consciousness.

To sum up: Our analysis of experience has led us, on the one hand, to an infinite consciousness or absolute spirit (anubhuti or caitanya); and, on the other, to two realms of objects which, however, have no being apart from that spirit. We may deduce this principle from the nature of the sākṣin as we have just done or from the nature of those realms of being. We may argue that just as the pratibhasika reality points to a vyavaharika one, the vyavaharika in its turn does, to a paramarthika reality. If an appearance lasts only as long as its jñāna lasts and the empirical persists ever afterwards, this higher reality is timeless. Thus we have altogether three orders of being of which two alone are related to time. The third, which is the same as the svarupa-jñāna referred to above, is the Brahman of the Vedānta. The recognition of this higher reality reveals a new form of error. The one we have drawn attention to thus far is that in which a pratibhasika object is superposed upon a vyavaharika one. It is error as is familiarly known. But if error is illegitimate transference, true superposition of an empirical 'what' on the highest Being also should be erroneous. This is not, however, error which occurs *within* the world of experience like the other, but lies at the root of it. It is involved in the very notion of the ego or the knowing subject (pramata) because in it two incompatibles are, as we have seen, confounded with each other. It therefore vitiates all our knowledge at its source. The whole of the universe in the form in which it is experienced by us is due to this metaphysical error wtn-rein the empirical is mistaken for the real, and is an abstraction apart from its ground, viz. Brahman.[45] That is, there is a higher standpoint from which even empirical things are only appearances. It is in this sense that the Advaita maintains that the world is not real (mithya) and that Brahman is the sole truth. The conception of truth and error in the system thus becomes relative, and it is essentially wrong to speak of any knowledge as true or false without mentioning at the same time the sphere with reference to which it is adjudged. It was for this reason that we defined truth above relatively to a particular level of being, viz. the empirical. really, however, even tills 'truth' is an error. Only we should not forget that, according to the Advaita, all error is but partially so, for it contains a core of truth—the shell for instance in the case of silver and in the case of the shell itself when we regard it as not real, the higher reality of which it is an appearance.

III

The ontological position of the Advaita has already been indicated generally in dealing witli its view of knowledge. We shall now restate the same, adding some details. Of the three types of being mentioned, we need treat only of two here, viz. the empirical and the true or the metaphysical. The former, we have already stated, is common to all and exists independently of individual consciousness. It also, as experienced by different individuals, is no doubt partly divergent, for each cognizes only so much of the world as is within the reach of his limited faculties and is in kinship with his particular temperament. To give the illustration of the *Pañca-dasī*[46] a father may think that his son who has gone away from home to a distant place is alive while as a matter of fact he is no more. One and the same object again may occasion different and even opposite feelings in different persons. But these worlds as given in the experience of individuals are not entirely separate. They have, as indeed we ordinarily take for granted, a common basis unlike the dream-worlds, for instance, of two or more persons. That is the world as it is; and it is termed Īśvara-srsta ('God-created'), while the same as it exists in the medium of one's individual consciousness is described as jīva-srsta[47] ('jīva-created'). Such a view implies that we accept many selves. There is of course nothing preventing us from criticizing this position as a begging of the question, but the only alternative to it is solipsism, which, though as a theory it may be irrefutable, is repugnant to thought and really stultifies all efforts at philosophizing. We shall accordingly take for granted the plurality of selves so far as our present discussion goes. These selves or jīvas differ from the common objects of experience in being coeval with time and not in it like them—a belief which the Advaitin shares with the followers of the other orthodox systems. Thus each of the indefinite number of selves we have assumed has been there from the beginning of time or is anadi. The empirical world which is vouched for by collective experience presents both unity and diversity, there being a common and enduring element along with different and changing ones in it. It may be described as a systematic whole, for it exhibits a causal order. It also involves a purpose inasmuch as its creation, as explained in the chapter on the Upaniṣads, rests upon a moral necessity. Such indications of physical and moral order in it, no doubt, are not altogether conclusive; but there is the significant fact that they become more numerous and clearer with the advance of knowledge and the growth of human institutions. When once the cosmic character of the world is admitted, we trace it back to a source which, though simple, accounts for all aspects of it. This source or the first cause is Māyā which symbolizes to us the unitary character of the physical world. Diversity is only implicit in it, while in the objective world that develops from it, it is quite explicit. There is, however, one important difference between Māyā and its products. The latter, as their very description as 'products' testifies, have all a beginning in time; but the former being the first cause can obviously have no such beginning. It also is therefore anadi like the jīvas alluded to above. Jīvas and Māyā thus form a new type of entities and differ from common objects which are all in time; but they are not, it should be added, altogether unrelated to time like Brahman or the ultimate reality.

It has been stated that the sphere of empirical objects is independent of individual consciousness. On the principle, however, to which we have already referred that whatever is, if not itself mind, must be for mind, it should depend upon some consciousness; for otherwise the statement that it would be meaningless. Granting such an all-sustaining consciousness, it is easy to see what conditions it must satisfy. It should last as long as the world in its causal or effect form lasts. That is, it must be anadi. It cannot be any finite consciousness in the sense in which a jīva is, for it must know the contents of the entire universe. Not only this, whatever is known must also be correctly and directly known by it, for error and mediate knowledge which imply limitation of one kind or the other are, by our hypothesis, excluded in the case of that consciousness. That is, its experience must be direct, complete and correct. This cosmic subject, as we may term it, to whom the whole of existence is related as an object, is the Īśvara of Advaita and it is the third of the entities coetemal with time along with Māyā and the jīvas. Here we find the triple factor forming the subject-matter of all philosophy and religion. To them we may add a fourth viz. time itself to which we have all along been alluding but which cannot be brought under any of the other three heads.

We shall now briefly state the nature of these four entities which, though they are not distinct from the empirical universe, stand on a footing of their own:—

(1) *Jīva*—This is the empirical self, the true nature of which has already been considered. It is manifold, each jīva having its own peculiar features, although agreeing with the rest of its class in many respects. It represents the spiritual element in the universe; but it is the spiritual element appearing not by itself, but invariably in association with physical adjuncts such as the aṅtah-karana. Its essential associate, however, is avidyā, the individual's share of May a which is the adjunct of Īśvara. Just as the whole universe is the effect of Māyā, the portions of the universe which constitute the gross and subtle bodies of an individual self are conceived as the effects of that particular self's avıdyā. In fact, the relation of Īśvara to the world is exactly parallel to that of the jīva to its own organism. Considered apart from these individual and cosmic accompaniments, the jīva and Īśvara are one or, more strictly, are not different. That is the significance of Tat tvam asi. The jīvas which we have assumed to be many are in consequence only empirically so; and the individuality characterizing each is due to its adjuncts such as the body and the senses. Intrinsically they are but one, for each is alike the supreme reality.

(2) *Māyā.*—This is the first cause of the physical universe and consequently corresponds to the prakṛti of the Sāṇkhya-Yoga; but there are important differences and metaphysically the two are poles asunder. From it spring into being not only organic bodies that house jīvas but also all inorganic nature. The things arising from Māyā we commonly regard as

real; but truly they cannot be described as either sat or asat. They are known (drsya) and to that extent at any rate cannot be unreal, for the absolutely unreal, like 'the hare's horn,' is only words. Nor can they be regarded as real in their own right, for they are objective (jaḍa) and hence depend entirely upon spirit for their being. This characteristic of not being finally classificable as either real or unreal (sadasadvilakṣaṇa) constitutes the uniqueness of the things of experience aim—should naturally be found also in their cause. Māyā. They are neither something nor nothing, and are therefore termed mithya. They arc not unreal as commonly assumed by the critics of the doctrine; only they are not ultimate. Or. in other words, their reality is relative and they may be regarded as appearances when contrasted with the higher reality of Brahman. In giving rise to such things, Māyā resembles avidyā, the source of common illusions, and is therefore described as the principle of cosmic illusion. In this it differs from the prakṛti of the Sāṇkhya-Yoga which is real in the full sense of the term.

(3) *Īśvara.*—We described Māyā as the source of the physical universe. But this source, for reasons already assigned, being altogether dependent upon the cosmic saksil. cannot act by itself. In strictness, therefore, the two elements should together be reckoned as giving rise to the world. Here we find another point of difference from the Sāṇkhya-Yoga where prakṛti is supposed to be endowed with the spontaneity required for manifesting of itself the whole of the physical world. It is the cause of the world in this complex form or spirit together with Māyā that is the Īśvara of Advaita. Or as it is somewhat differently expressed, Māyā is the potency (śakti) inherent in Īśvara through which he manifests the objective world with all its diversity of names and forms.[48] But he at the same time sees rough the diversity, so that he never misses its underlying unity as we do. Though the universe as emerging from Īśvara is not around but within him, the exercise of this potency gives rise to a sense of 'the other'; and Māyā may therefore be regarded as the principle of self-consciousness or self-determination. It interpolates a distinction where really there is none. In this sense, Māyā cannot be the source of the universe, but is a mere accessory to Īśvara in bringing it into existence out of himself. For reasons similar to those adduced in explaining the parallel conception of avidyā—the source of ordinary illusions, Māyā or the principle of cosmic illusion is conceived as more than a negation of jñāna. The very fact that it serves as the cause of the visible universe shows that it should be so far positive. It is again, on the analogy of avidyā, described as having two powers—āvaraṇa and vikṣepa. In its vikṣepa phase it projects the aggregate of names and forms constituting the world. The function of āvaraṇa is to obscure the unity of Being; but since that unity is never concealed from Īśvara, Māyā in its āvaraṇa aspect is stated to be powerless over him. Nature does not veil

spirit from him. This sets a vast golf between the jīva and Īśvara. It, in fact, accounts for the bondage of the one and the freedom of the other. Owing to the power which the āvaraṇa phase of May a or avidyā wields over it, the jīva believes in the ultimacy of mere variety, and to this belief, as also to its fragmentary view of the world already mentioned, should be traced all the evil to which it is subject. It ordinarily identifies itself with the organism with which it is bound up and looks upon the rest of reality as wholly external. It develops likes and dislikes for a small part of it, and assumes an attitude of indifference towards the rest. In the case of Īśvara, on the contrary, such preferences and exclusions are impossible according to our hypothesis. He identifies himself with the whole world and the identification is not, as in the case of the jīva and its organism, due to any confusion (adhyāsa) between the self and the not-self, but is the outcome of a continual realization of the true nature of both. The ideal of morality as conceived in the Advaita, we may state in passing, is gradually to replace the narrow view held by the jīva by one like that of the cosmic self, whose interests coincide with those of the universe.[49] 'Considerations of "mine" and "thine" weigh only with the little-minded; to the large-hearted, on the other hand, the whole world is like a single household.[50]

Such a conception naturally lends itself to a two-fold presentation, and that is why it is described not only as Īśvara or 'the Lord' but also as the saguṇa Brahman. The former being personal may be taken as the ideal of advaitic religion—standing for an all-knowing almighty God, the creator, preserver and destroyer of the world; the latter, not being so, as that of advaitic philosophy—standing for the Absolute which explains the world-system as it is. When we consider the universe in reference to this supreme subject, there is only one type of reality in place of the two found in the case of the jīva; and that is of the phenomenal or prātibhāsika type. For by hypothesis whatever is, known to Īśvara and no part of it lasts longer than the time during which it is experienced. In this sense, Īśvara may be described as an eternal dreamer. But we must not think that he is deluded. That would be so if he did not realize the identity of the objective world with himself, or if any aspect of the truth about it remained unrevealed to him. What is meant by Scribing Īśvara's world as prātibhāsika is that its unity with himself being always realized, .all variety *as such* is known to him to be a mere abstraction. It is just this distinction between the relation of the world to Īśvara on the one hand and to the jīva on the other that critics overlook when they say that according to śaṁkara the objective world is unreal. It is no doubt an appearance to Īśvara, but not to us who have not realized its unity with ourselves. Till we are able to do so and make our life .1 mirror of our new convictions, we must view it as real whatever its ultimate nature may be.

(4) *Time.*—We have so far assumed an entity like time and taken it as lying outside the remaining three. It really represents the relation between spirit and Māyā.[51] Of these, the former alone is completely real and not Māyā also. Hence the relation between them, like that between the shell and silver, cannot be fully real. That is, time is phenomenal. In this connection it is necessary to point out the advaitic view of space. It is regarded as an offshoot of Māyā and the first object to be created,[52] so that the Advaitin does not place time and space on the same footing. Its conception presupposes the principle of causation already at work, but not so the conception of time. While all things born, excepting space,, are in time and space, space is in time only jīva, Īśvara and Māyā are neither in time nor in space.

These are the fundamental atities of the Advaita considered from the empirical standpoint. It is not necessary to enter here into cosmological details, for they are practically the same as those mentioned in the chapter on the Upaniṣads. These entities, it should be clear from their description given above, are not disparate. They are interrelated and together constitute a system which, as time is included in it, may be taken to be dynamic in its character. The question now to consider is to whether such a conception is satisfactory enough to remain final. The conclusion of the Advaita is that it is not, whether we judge it from the standpoint of practical religion or from that of speculative philosophy:—

(i) Thus to view it as representing a theistic ideal: There is the well-known difficulty—to mention only one—of reconciling God's assumed goodness and power with the presence of physical and moral evil in the world.[53] Even supposing that evil exists only from our standpoint and not from that of God or Īśvara as denned above, the theistic position does not become fully comprehensible. We cannot, for instance, understand why God should have created the world. To ascribe a motive to him would be to admit that he has ends to attain; and that would be to question his perfection or all-sufficiency (paritrptatvam). To deny a motive and ascribe the work of creation to his intrinsic nature or to some sudden impulse in him would be to reduce God to an automaton or attribute caprice to him; and either way his supposed omniscience is compromised.[54] There are solutions of such difficulties suggested in the Advaita as in theistic doctrines generally; and these attempts at justifying the ways of God to man are not without their appeal to the religious mind. But, as śaṁkara observes, they are not final because they have reference to the world of names and forms founded upon avidyā.[55] In other words, such solutions, like the problems they solve, keep us tied to the realm of relativity and. as the essence of the relative is to point beyond itself for its complete explanation, the theistic conception cannot be regarded as ultimate.

(2) The same conclusion is reached when we regard it as the philosophic Absolute. The relation for instance which appears to constitute its several elements into a system will on examination be seen to be not really intelligible. Let us consider first the place of the jīvas in it: Since, according to the doctrine, the jīvas do not originate and are anadi like the saguna Brahman itself, the relation between the two should be anādi. So much is certain. But what is the nature of this relation ? It is not identity, for the saguna Brahman cannot be the same as any of the jīvas with its fragmentary experience. Nor can it be regarded as a collection of all of them, for that would give us only a collection of individual experiences and not, as required, an integral one which alone can serve as the ground and explanation of the whole universe. That is, we cannot identify the saguna Brahman with either any of the jīvas or with the totality of them. Equally impossible is it to think of it as altogether different from or outside them, for in that case there would not be that intimate connection between the two which is implied in the description of the whole as a system. A similar reasoning applies to the relation between the saguna Brahman and the physical universe emerging from it; only as the latter unlike the jīvas has a beginning, being produced, the relation is not anādi.[56] It cannot be identity, for an effect as such is not the same as its cause, nor is it difference, for then the two cannot be represented as cause and effect.

But it may appear to us that the relation in question is one of identity-in-difference. Such a conception itself, according to the Advaitin, is self-discrepant. This is a point which is discussed at great length in advaitic works.[57] It is not possible to enter here into all the details of the discussion; so we shall content ourselves with drawing attention to its main features[58] Let M and N be two entities between which the relation in question is supposed to exist. Now neither of them can as *such* be both identical with and different from the other. It would mean that M is both N and not-N and that N similarly is both M and not-M, which is a violation of the law of contradiction. When two things are distinct in fact, they cannot be the same. We cannot accept both sides of a contradiction to be true. But it may be said that this deficiency, if it be one, is vouched for by experience and that, since experience is our only guide, we must acquiesce in it. Such an argument seems to the Advaitin like a refusal to think. He admits that we finally depend upon experience for determining the truth about things, but he does not therefore relinquish the right to re-examine the meaning of experience when it results in a palpable self-contradiction and seek for a new explanation of it. if possible. The data of experience, merely because they are such, put us under no constraint to accept them under all circumstances as logical varities. Further, it may be granted for the sake of argument that there is no valid ground or doubting the reality of the content of experience as it ordinarily occurs, when there is agreement among thinkers about it. But the point in question is not one about which we find any such agreement. Even the realist Naiyāyika, we know, postulates the new-fangled relation of samavāya in such cases with a view to avoid the necessity for admitting the real to be self-contradictory. Whatever view, therefore, we may hold about the verdict of experience in general, the present case at any rate is *not* one where it can be accepted without scrutiny. If M and N do not constitute an identity in difference directly, 'it may be thought that they do so mediately through features or elements in them—some of which are identical and others different Thus we may say that M and N possess one or more 'common features which may be represented by *a* and, at the same time, exhibit differences represented by x and y respectively. According to this explanation, what is identical is quite distinct from what is different; yet the entities, viz. M and N, by virtue of such features, it may be said, are identical with and, at the same time, different from each but the solution is only apparent, for it merely shifts the difficulty to another set of things. It assumes that M and N are characterized by *a x* and *a y* respectively, and the assumption leaves us where we were, for we cannot satisfactorily explain the relation between a thing and its so-called characteristics. Now the relation between M and *a x*, to take only one of the entities, cannot be identity, for then the distinction between *a* and *x* would vanish, both being identical with the same M; and with it also the relation of identity-in-difference between M and N. Nor can *a* and *x* be different from M, for then their character, whatever it may be, will cease to affect M and therefore also its relation to N. So we are driven to think of identity-in-difference as the only possible relation between these. That is, in explaining the relation in question between M and N, we presuppose the same relation within each of them; and pursuing the inquiry further will only lead to an infinite process.[59]

For such reasons the Advaitin views the relation between the saguṇa Brahman and its constitutive elements as unique or as tādātmya in the sense explained in the previous section—not to be characterized as identity or difference or identity-in-difference. Hence the conception of saguṇa Brahman involves adhyāsa, and like that of Īśvara cannot be regarded as ultimate. Or to state it differently, the saguṇa Brahman includes not merely reality but also appearance, which is something less than the real. The element of reality in it is the ultimate of Advaita. It should be carefully noted that this reality is not the mere unity underlying the diversity of the universe, for unity and diversity are relative to each other, and it is impossible to retain the one as real while rejecting the other as an appearance. Both of them are alike appearances and the advaitic Ultimate is what is beyond them—their non-phenomenal ground (nirviśeṣa-vastu). It is for this reason that, śaṁkara describes his doctrine as advaita or 'non-duality,' and not as aikya or 'unity.' By discarding the notion of bhedābheda or, more specifically, by refusing to accept a changing Brahman as ultimate, śaṁkara differentiates his doctrine from Brahma pariṇāma-vāda advocated by other Vedāntins according to whom both the physical universe and the jīvas actually emerge from Brahman.[60] Brahman according to him does not evolve in this sense, but only gives rise to appearances which, though entirely depending upon it, affect it no more than the silver does the shell in which it appears. He thus enunciates a new view of causation which is different from both the pariṇāma-vāda and the ārambha-vāda with which we are familiar. According to it, the cause produces the effect without itself undergoing any change whatsoever. It is vivarta-vāda or the doctrine of *phenomenal* development. Viewed in the light of this theory, Brahman only appears as the world. It is the original of which the world, as it has been said[61] may be regarded as 'a translation at the plane of space-time'; and Brahman depends as little for its being on the world as an original work does on it in translation. This is what is otherwise known as the Māyā doctrine.[62] Though the doctrine as it appears here naturally shows considerable development in matters of detail, it has, as we have pointed out, a definite basis in the Upaniṣads. The charge that it is alien to the Vedānta is therefore really without foundation. Again, by postulating a Reality behind the self-discrepant world of experience, śaṁkara differentiates his doctrine from the sunya-vāda of the Mādhyamika. The discrepancy characterizing the saguṇa Brahman or its relativity only degrades it to the level of appearance; it does not dismiss it altogether. If according to the Mādhyamika it is impossible for thought to rest in the relative, it is equally impossible for it, according to śaṁkara, to rest in absolute nothing. To use the terminology of the Upaniṣads, the Advaita denies only 'names'and 'forms' but not that which appears under their guise. Or, as an old writer has observed, while the Advaitin negates only distinction (bheda), the Mādhyamika negates it as well as the distincts (bhidyamāna).[63] That there is a Reality at the back of all empirical things again is not a mere assertion, for it is maintained here, as we know, that the thinking subject in us is not different from it so that its being becomes an immediate certainty. If we denied it, the very fact of denial would affirm it.[64] We may not know what it exactly is; but its presence itself, owing to the basic identity of ourselves with it, can never be doubted.

What is the nature of this Reality? As indicated in an earlier section, it may be represented on the one hand as the infinite Consciousness implied by empirical knowledge or as the infinite Being presupposed in all finite existence. But it is neither empirical knowledge nor phenomenal being, for each of them has appearance superadded to the real and so far fails to represent the latter in its purity. Such knowledge and being, though revealing the ultimate, do not represent it truly and the same is the case with all empirical things. While they are not apart from it, they cannot either singly or in combination stand for it. That is why Brahman as the ultimate is termed nirguna or 'indeterminate,' which does not amount to saying, as it is ordinarily assumed, that it is nothing, but only means that nothing which the mind can think of can actually belong to it. Whatever we think of it for that very reason objective (drsya) and it cannot therefore be an element in that which is never presented as an object (drk). The familiar categories of thought therefore are all inapplicable to it. Hence no direct description of it is possible. But we can indirectly point to it utilizing the appearances as aids; for an appearance, which can never be independent, necessarily signifies a reality beyond itself. In this sense every percept and every concept can be made to indicate the Absolute. The Upaniṣads prefer to direct our attention to it through terms like tvam or aham denoting the subject, for unlike other terms they, besides dispelling all doubt about its being, afford a better clue to its nature.[65] When such terms are combined with another like tat or Brahman in an assertive proposition like Tat tvam asi or Aham Brahma asmi, the reference to Reality becomes ensured. For the attributes which they respectively connote of the individual and of the cosmic subject—such as the bondage of the one and the freedom of the other—being mutually incompatible[66] our mind abandons the explicit sense of the terms, and travels beyond those attributes to that in which they are grounded (nirviseṣa-vastu) as constituting the true import of the proposition. The dropping of these attributes, we should add, signifies little because they are but illusive barriers erected by Māyā between the jīva and Īśvara. It should also be pointed out that we do not here identify the ground of one set of attributes with that of the other, for such identification would be meaningless without some difference equally real between them. To avoid this implication we merely deny the distinction between the two, so that what the proposition in strictness means is that the jīva is *not other* than Brahman.

The advaitic Absolute is not merely indefinable; we cannot know it either, for the moment it is made the object of thought it becomes related to a subject and therefore determinate. That is another important reason why the idea of Īśvara or saguṇa Brahman is rejected as inadequate to be the true goal of philosophy which the Advaita, like the other Indian doctrines, views as not merely arriving at a speculative notion or a conceptual formula of the ultimate reality, but to realize what it is in itself. The ideal of the determinate Brahman has been elaborated in thought and it therefore remains a reality for thought. It is Brahman in 'an empiric dress'—the Absolute as it appears to us, and not as it is in itself. Its internal self-discrepancy to which we have drawn attention is in fact the result of its relation to thought. It is, as it is expressed, jneya Brahman or Brahman that can be known. In itself, it excludes all relations (asamsrsta), including that between subject and object, and is therefore unknowable. But though it cannot be known it can, as we shall point out presently, be realized.

One should therefore be careful in understanding what exactly is meant when the Upaniṣads describe Brahman as nirguna and therefore as indefinable and unknowable. It is not in every sense beyond the reach of words. To suppose that it is so would be to deprive the Upaniṣads of the whole of their purpose. Even granting that the negative definition is the only possible one, it does not follow that the nirguna Brahman is a blank.[67] For all propositions directly or indirectly refer to reality and negation necessarily has its own positive implication. As a matter of fact, however, the Advaitins assign Upaniṣadic statements like neti neti—'Not this, nor that'—a secondary place while the primary place is given to those like Tat tvam asi, which point to the reality in us as the ultimate. That is, the negative statement is not to be understood in isolation, but along with positive ones like Tat tvam asi. Negation is only a preliminary to affirmation.[68] It means that the Absolute is not conceived here objectively—as merely inferred from outer phenomena; but as revealing itself within us.[69] This alters totally the significance of the negative description, for we are thereby constrained to nature. It is not thus a bare or contentless being for which the Absolute stands here. Nor should the statement that Brahman is unknowable lead us to regard the doctrine as agnostic. It, no doubt, rules out all discursive thought as inapplicable to Reality; but it does not represent it as extra-empirical—as something wholly outside the world of experience. The nirguna Brahman is not the negation or the antithesis of the saguṇa, but is its very truth and is immanent in everything that goes to constitute it. Hence every aspect of experience, whether on the subject or object side, reveals it. Indeed irrepressibility (svayam-prakāśatva) is its very essence and, like the sun behind a cloud, it shows itself in a sense even in being hidden. We seem to miss it ordinarily on account of the bewildering mass of appearances. But that is like not seeing the ocean for the waves. It is true that it cannot be grasped as an object of knowledge. But there may be other ways of 'experiencing' it; and the whole tenor of the advaitic theory of perception as well as its scheme of practical discipline, to which we shall refer in the next section, shows that there is such a form of experience and that we can 'know' Brahman by being it. This higher type of experience is not altogether unfamiliar to us. There are moments, though all too rare, when we transcend ourselves and when even the experience that is being lived through is not cognized. We pass in it not only beyond common consciousness in which the thought of self is implicit, but also beyond explicit self-consciousness to where thought merges in experience. It may be taken as a distant analogue of the attitude of the sage who, having through long discipline learnt to feel his identity with all that exists, at last succeeds in passing beyond even that state, and losing sight of the objective world and of himself as such, is straight away installed within Reality. That constitutes the consummation of Advaitic teaching.

Though the ideal of the saguṇa Brahman is thus inadequate to be the ultimate of philosophy, it must not be regarded as useless. We have already seen how it furnishes an ethical ideal by following which the disciple can rise above his congenital limitations and acquire that moral fitness which is indispensable for success in achieving the advaitic goal. Even from the purely theoretic standpoint, it is not without its own value, as is shown for instance by the method followed in the Advaita. This method, we know, starts with the more or less diverse worlds as given in individual experience and discovers as their basis a common one. Systematizing the variety that is manifest in it, it then arrives at unity. And it is only afterwards, since this world of unity in diversity is itself an appearance on the reasoning adopted above, that the doctrine concludes to the spirit which lies beyond it as the sole reality. The contradictions and anomalies of ordinary experience have at first to be resolved at least in the seeming orderliness signified by the ideal of the saguṇa Brahman, if we are to reach the advaitic ultimate unerringly. Without the synthesis effected in it or, to express the same thing differently, without the jīva's avidyā being universalized as Māyā, we would land ourselves in subjectivism reducing the world to a mere private show, for there would then be no reason for postulating anything beyond what is present to individual consciousness. The Advaitin's criticism of the saguṇa Brahman should accordingly be understood as showing only the inadequacy of that conception to serve as the goal of philosophy and not as signifying that it is valueless.[70] But its value is restricted to the empirical sphere—a view which is entirely in consonance with the general advaitic position that practical utility need not rest on metaphysical validity. It is this distinction that has given rise to what are familiarly known as the 'two grades' of teaching in the Advaita -the higher one of the nirguna Brahman (para-vidyā) and the lower one of the saguna (apara-vidyā).

IV

Since mokṣa, according to śaṁkara, is not a state to be newly attained, but is the very nature of the self, we can hardly speak of a means in its ordinary sense for achieving it. It is realizing what has always been one's own innate character but happens for the time being to be forgotten. The Upaniṣadic statement is 'That thou art,' not 'That thou becomest.' The common illustration given here is that of a prince, brought up as a hunter from infancy, discovering afterwards that he is of royal blood. It involves no becoming, for he has always been a prince and all that he has to do is to feel or realize that he is one. We might illustrate the point equally well by referring to the distinction between a solar and a lunar eclipse. In the latter, the light of the sun is actually cut off from the moon by the earth coming between it and the sun, so that the passing off of the eclipse signifies real change in the condition of the moon, viz. the part that was enveloped in darkness becoming it. In a solar eclipse, on the other hand, the luminary continues to be during the eclipse exactly as it was before or will be afterwards. It only appears to be eclipsed because the intervening moon prevents it from being seen as it really is. The re-emergence of the bright sun accordingly means no change whatsoever in it, but only a moving farther away of the moon or the removal of the obstacle preventing the sun from showing itself as it is. Similarly in the case of advaitic mokṣa, all that is needed is a removal of the obstacle that keeps the truth concealed from us and the discipline that is prescribed is solely with a view to bring about this result. It is therefore only in a negative or indirect sense that we can talk of attaining mokṣa here. Empirical life being entirely the consequence of an adhyāsa, the obstacle is ajñāna and it is removed through its contrary jñāna. The jñāna that is capable of effecting it should be, for the reasons mentioned more than once before, direct or intuitive (sākṣāt-kāra); and it should refer to one's own identity with Brahman, for it is the forgetting of this identity that constitutes samsāra. Such knowledge is the sole means of liberation. Neither moral perfection nor religious acts are required as direct aids to it. The cultivation of the will and the purification of the affections are of course necessary, but they are only aids to jñāna[71] not to mokṣa. It means that the morally impure will not seriously set about acquiring the saving knowledge. When once jñāna arises, it does of itself dispel a jñāna and the simultaneous revelation of spirit in all its innate splendour is mokṣa. To state the same in another way, ethical improvement and religious discipline are necessary for mokṣa but not enough. That is what is meant by karma-samnyāsa as advocated by śaṁkara. The conception of jīvan-mukti is the logical result of such a view of the world and of escape from it. If knowledge is the sole means of release from bondage, freedom should result the moment it is gained; and there is nothing in the psychical or other equipment of the human being which renders its acquisition impossible here and now.[72]

The discipline is to be undergone in two stages—one, preliminary which qualifies for entering upon the serious study of the Advaita; and the other, Vedāntic training proper which directly aims at self-realization. Of these, the former is identical with karma-yoga as explained in the chapter on the Gītā and its aim is the cultivation of detachment. The latter consists of sravana, manana and nididhyaṣana. These have been already explained in the chapter on the Upaniṣads, but it is necessary to restate the position calling attention to what is peculiar to the Advaita. (1) *Sravaṇa.* This is study and discussion ol the Upaniṣads with the assistance of a *guru* that has realized the truth they teach. The implication of this requirement is two-fold: First, it signifies that the ultimate philosophic truth is to be learnt through a study of the revealed texts. Secondly, it emphasizes the need for personal intercourse with a competent teacher, if the study is to be fruiful and shows that mere book-learning is not of much avail. (2) *Manana.* This is arguing within oneself, after knowing definitely what the Upaniṣads teach, how and why that teaching alone is true. The main object of this process is not to discover the final truth, for that has been learnt already through sravana, but to remove the doubt (asambha-vana.) that it may not after all be right. It is intended to transform what has been received on trust into one's own true conviction and brings out well the place assigned to reason in the Advaita. The recognition of the value of analytical reflection, we may note by the way, is rather a unique feature in a doctrine which finally aims at mystic experience. (3) *Niddidhyāsana.* Manana secures intellectual conviction. But there may still be obstacles in the way of self-realization. For despite such conviction, there may be now and again an unconscious reassertion of old habits of thought (viparīta-bhavana) incompatible with what has since been learnt. Nididhyāsana is meant to overcome this kind of obstacle. It is meditation upon the identity between the individual self and Brahman—the central point of Vedāntic teaching. It should be continued till the desired intuitive knowledge arises and that identity becomes immediate (aparokṣa)[73] When it does, one becomes a jīvan-mukta. The ultimate philosophic fact is no doubt to be known through the testimony of the Upaniṣads; but if the knowler'qe conveyed by it is to bring real freedom, one should verify it by one's own living experience in the form 'I am Brahman' or Aham Brahma asmi.[74] It is this immediate experience or direct intuition of the Absolute, which is described as vidvadanubhava to distinguish it from lay experience, that accordingly becomes the final criterion of Truth. here.[75]

The jīvan-mukta's life has two phases: It is either samādhi or mystic trance when he turns inwards and loses himself in Brahman, or the condition known as vyutthana or reversion to common life when the spectacle of the world returns but does not delude him since he has once for all realized its metaphysical falsity. Diversity continues to appear then as the sun, we may say, continues to appear as moving ever after we are convinced that it is stationary. A jīvan-mukta experiences pain and pleasure, but neither really matters to him. He does not necessarily give up all activity as is abundantly illustrated by the strenuous life which śaṁkara himself led,[76] but it does not proceed from any selfish impulse or even from a sense of obligation to others. Blind love for the narrow self which ordinarily characterizes man and the consequent clinging to the mere particular are in his case replaced by enlightened and therefore equal love for all. The basis for this universal love is furnished by the Upaniṣadic teaching 'That thou art.' We should do unto others as we do to ourselves, because they are ourselves—a view which places the golden rule of morality on the surest of foundations. 'Who sees all beings in himself and himself in all beings—he will dislike none,' as the Upaniṣad[77] says; or as the Gītā puts it, 'He harms not self by self.[78] The common laws of social morality and ritual which are significant only in reference to one that is striving for perfection are meaningless for him.[79] The jīvan-mukta, having transcended the stage of strife, is spontaneously virtuous. Impulse and desire become one in him. He is not then realizing virtue but is revealing it. 'In one that has awakened to a knowledge of the self, virtues like kindness imply no conscious effort whatsoever. They are second nature with him.[80] When at last he is dissociated from the physical accompaniments, he is not reborn, but remains as Brahman. That is videha mukti.

REFERENCE

1. Cf. yt śūnya-vādinaḥ śūnyam tadeva Brahma māyihah Madhva *Anbhāṣya* on VS II. ii. 29.

2. It may be noted that the Nyāya-Vaiśeṣika does not recognize karmendriyas, and explains their functions as those of prāṇa or vital air.

3. The word means 'witness' or a disinterested looker-on. the conception is thus relative; and the sākṣin as such is not therefore ..

4. xi. 32.

5. This is expressed as follows in Sanskrit: Antaḥ-viśṣṭo jīvaḥ; antaḥ-karṇopahitaḥ sāksī: VP. p. 102.

6. VP. pp. 79-82.

7. Mediate knoweldge removes only the ignorance concerning the existence of an object (asattvāpādakājḥāna); immediate knowledge, that regarding its exact nature also (abhānāpādakājñāna). See SLS. pp. 94 and 147; *Pañca-daśī*, vi. 16.

8. The metaphor is drawn from water in a tank flowing through the sluice to a field to be irrigated and assuming its shape. VP. p. 57.

9. VP. p. 77.

10. The theory of perception adopted by the Advaita Vedānta is rather crude onthe scientific sidethough its metaphysical insight is valuable.' IP. volii. pp. 4923.

11. For example, religious merit (puṇya) and demerit (pāpa), which also are regarded as modes of the antaḥ-karaṇa, are notperceivable alos are regarded as modes of the antaḥ-karauṇa, ar not perceivable because they lack this condition of yogyatva or fitness. They are only.

12. There is some divergence in the use ofthese terms—Māyā and avidyā. We confine them here respectively to Māyā in its cosmic character and in its indicence.' so to speak, onthe individual.

13. In place of the two adjuncts of the self as conceived in the Sāṇkhya-Yoga, we thus have three here: (i) kāraṇa-śarīra, (2) linṅga-śarīra and (3) sthūla-śarīra.

14. The recollection by the jīva of what was experienced by the sākṣin ... see SLS. pp. 155-6.

15. *Pañca-daśī,* xi pp 75-65.

16. *Ch.* Up. VIII, iii. p. 2.

17. See e.g. com. on VS. II ii. p. 28.

18. See *Gaudapāda-kārika,* ii. 14. An object may of course disappear and cease to be as we are apprehending it.

19. It is possible to say that this feature characterizes illusion also, and that so far the distinction of the objects of ordinary knowledge from those of illusion vanishes. For example, the 'rope-serpent,' once seen, may be recognized after some time, if in the meanwhile the mistake has not been rectified. Such a position cannot be proved to be false; and there have been Advaitins whom maintained it (Cf. SLS

20. VS II. ii. 28-32.

21. Cf. VP. p. 153. Satya-mithyāvastu-tādātmyāvagāhitvena bhramatva-svīkārāt.

22. Parataḥ eva apraāmāṇyam: VP. 338.

23. It sould be noted in this connection that pain, pleasure and other modes of the antaḥ-karaṇa, though 'private,' are not thus sublated and are therefore not prātibhāsika. The same remark applies to the antaḥ-karaṇa also.

24. Literally the word means 'identity' and is used in the Nyāya-Vaiśeṣika in the sense of the abstract identity of a term with itself. It is also used in the sence of 'identity-indifference' by some like Kumārila. Here it has neither of these senses.

25.For this reason the silver is described as ananya with reference to the shell which Sāṁkara explains as 'not existing apart from.' Ananyatavam vyatirekena abhavah. See com. on VS. II. i. 14.

26. That is, the proximate ground. The altimate ground is always spirit or caitanya.

27. This avaidyā should not be confounded with the one described above as the radical adjunct of the jīva. That is constitutive of the jīva: this is only a passing characteristic of it. The one continues till mokṣa is attained: the other disappears with the error it has occasioned.

28. Avidyā is directly the cause of the illusion, but all knowledge has by hypothesis an object and that object, viz. 'silver,' here is ascribed to the same avidyā, not being tracable to any other source. See VP. p. 137.

29.

30. VP p. 168 Māya is then termed mūlāvidyā.

31. Rāgecchā-sukh-duḥkhādi buddhan satyām pravartate:

Suṣuptau nāsti tannāśā tasmāt buddhestu nātmanaḥ.

These are all vṛttis as inspired by the sākṣin and it is their vṛrtti aspect alone that belongs to the antaḥ-karaṇa. The resemblance to the as Sāṅkhya-Yoga here is clear.

32. The notion of hte sākṣin, as already pointed out, is relative to an antah-karana and cannot therefore be regarded as ultimate Sākṣi-svarupa means the essence of hte saksin.

33. Some recognize only one kind of being. See VP. pp. 221-3. Some again the not make any distinction between vyāvahārika nad prātibhāsika being. According to the latter, the reality on the waking state does not stand higher than that of the dream state—what is true according to either being sublated in the other. See Note 2 on p. 350.

34. The ground of the adhyāsa here is taken to be spirit or caitanya, as indeed it is in the case of 'shell-silver' also eventually (VP. pp. 162-3). The only difference is that in the latter the illusion is mediated by an empirical object, viz. the shell, while in the former it is direct.

35. VP. pp. 19 ff.

36. VP. pp. 36-8.

37. VP. p. 298.

38. Compare the saying: Vyavahāre Bhāṭṭa-nayaḥ.

39. Cf. *Naiṣkarmya-siddhi.* ii. 5; ii. 44 and 8306.

40. VS. II. i. 14.

41. See Deussen: *System of the Vedānta,* p. 55. Cf. stanzas cited by śaṁkara at end of his com. on VS. I. i. 4.

42. See śaṁkara on VS II. i. 14: *Naiṣkarmya-siddhi,* ii. 108-9.

43. VP. pp. 102 ff.

44. Contrast the Sāṅkhya-Yoga view where the elements constituting the empirical ego are independently real.

45. iv. 20-35.

46. It is the world as it exists for an individual that is the source of bondage to him, not the world as it is.See *Pañca-daśī,* iv. 32.

47. Cf. śaṁkara on Vs. II. iii. 16 and 17.

48. See śaṁkara on VS. I. iv. 3.

49. See śaṁkara on *Ch. Up.* III. xiv. i and on VS. I ii.p. 1-8.

50. Ayam nihaḥ paro veti gaṇaā laghu-cetasam:

51. See *Vana mālā* on śaṁkara's com. on *Tait. Up.*, p. 131 (śrīrangam Edn.).

52. *Tair. Up.* ii. i.

53. VS. II. i. pp. 34-6.

54. Ibid., 32-3.

55. Sūtra 33 and finem., cf. *Bhāmalī* on sūtra 34.

56. If we take instead of the visible universe, its source Māyā, the relation is anādi.

57. See e.g. BUV. IV ii. st. 1637-1787; *Bhāmalī,* I. 1. 4.

58. Cf. *Ista-sddhi (*Grekwad's Oriental Series), pp. 18-22.

59. It doe snot alter the matter if M andN, instead of being two objects are two moments in the history of one and the same object, say P. The arugment would still be applicable tothem, the only difference being that what are described as identicalfeatures are truly so in the latter, but are only similar and remain separate in..

60. Some like Bhāskara take the unvierse alone as the pariṇāma, of Brāhman and no the jīvas also.

61. IP. vol. ii. 570.

62. If the advaita in sometimes uses term simplying belief in pariṇāma, he should be understood as speaking from the empirical standpoint.

63. See SAS. iv. p. 20.

64. Ya eva hi nirākartā tadeva tasya svarūpam: śaṁkara on VS. II. iii. 3.

65. Cf. *Naiskarmya-siddhi,* iii. 100-3. all objects like reveal being (sat) of some type or other. The subject which cognizes them reveals not only being but also thought (cit). Thus we may say that the Advaita recognizes kinds as well as degrees of reality.

66. As other examples of distinction between the two, we may mention the folloiwing: The jīva's knowledge hasmany limitations,while God is all-knowing; God is mediatelyknown, while thejīva is..

67. Being the Absolute in the true sense of the term, it may appear as 'nothing' to the dull-witted (manda-buddhi) as śaṁkara says (see com. on *Ch. Up.* VIII. i.) Compare: 'I still insist that for thought what is not relative is nothing'— Bradley: *Appearance and Reality,* p. 30.

68. See *Samksepa-śārīraka,* i. p. 250-6.

69. If an objective reality be negatively described ans all knowable features are abstracted from it,we may conclude that there is nothing of it left behind. The observation that 'pure being is pure nothing' may accordinly apply to nother form of Advaita which is named Sattādvaita, in cntradistinction to the Ātmādvaita of śaṁkara, and takes mere Being (sattā-sāmānya) to be the Absolute. See *Naiṣkarmya-siddhi,* iii. 101.

70. See Śaṁkara on *Ch. Up.* viii i. 1 and *Kalp-taru,* i. i. 20.

71. VS. III. iv. 26.

72. The only othe rlevel of existence where theself can be realized according tothe Upansiads is Brahma-loka or the world of Brahma (*Kaṭha Up.* II. iii. 5) themokṣa thus achieved being designated (*Kaṭha Up.* II. iii. 5), the mokṣa thus achievedbeing designated karma-mukti as stated inthe chapter onthe Upansiads (p. 74). It results, according tothe Advaita, from the combination (samuccaya) of Vedic karma with meditation upon the saguna Brahman regarding it as the highest reality, either because the disciple doe snot know it as the highest reality, either because the disciple does not know it as the highest reality, either becausethe disciple does not know there is a higher one or because,knowing it, he feels himself unequal to the task of realizing it.

73. VS. IV i. 1.2.

74. Cf. Kim tu śrutyādayo anubhavādaśca yathā-sambhavam iha pramāṇam anubhavāvasānatvāt bhūta-vastu-viṣayatvācca brahma-jñānasya: Com. on VS, I. i. 2 See Dr. Belvalkar: *op. cit.,* p. 14.

75. Apart from the question of direct recvelation, theUpaniṣads also should inthelast resort be regarded as recording onlysuch intuitional knowledge of ancient sages. See Note 4 on p. 182.

76. Cf. *Pañca-saī,* vi. 270-8. It is interesting in this connection to refer to śaṁkara's statement at theendofhiscom. on VS. IV i. 15, which tradition views as an allusion to his own direct experience of the ultimate truth.

77. Īśa *Up.* 6.

78. xiii. 27.

79. Śaṁkara on VS. II iii. 48.

80. *Naiṣkarmya-siddhi,* iv. 69.

CHAPTER XV

VIŚIṢṬĀDVAITA

THIS is the system which is associated with the name of Rāmānuja. Its most striking feature is the attempt which it makes to unite personal theism with the philosophy of the Absolute. Two lines of thought, both of which can be traced far back into antiquity, meet here and in this lies the explanation of a great part of its appeal to the cultured as well as the common people. It resembles in this respect the teaching of the Gītā, though it naturally shows greater systematization both on the religious and on the philosophical side. Historically speaking, the elements of thought combined here are distinct. The first of them, viz. theism, is of the Bhāgavata type, inculcating belief in a personal and transcendent God who saves, out of mercy, such as arc whole-heartedly devoted to him and are for that reason described as ekāntins ('single-minded'). The second element in the teaching is still older, being based upon the Upaniṣads. Of the two Upaniṣadic views to which we have alluded (p. 62), neither in its entirety proved acceptable to Rāmānuja, but his teaching is more like what is described as Brahma-pariṇāma-vada[1] than Brahma-vivarta-vāda. The ideas of the unity of ultimate reality and of its immanence in the universe, as also the doctrine that jñāna[2] is the means of salvation, are derived from this source. As to the success with which the two teachings are synthesized here, we shall say a few words later; for the present, it will suffice to mention that the synthesis was not initiated by Rāmānuja, though that should not be understood as minimizing the value of his contribution to the final shaping of the doctrine. The attempt to bring together theism and the philosophy of the Absolute is very old and may be traced even in parts of Vedic literature itself. We know that a similar synthesis is found in the Gītā where, as in the Viśiṣṭādvaita, it appears with the added feature that the theism is of the Bhāgavata type, not directly traceable to the Veda. The same also is found in one or other of its various phases of growth in the Mahābhārata, especi ally in the section known as the *Nārāyaṇiya* (p. 100) and in the Purāṇas such as the *Viṣṇu-purāṇa*. Only, in the time of: Rāmānuja there was a fresh circumstance, viz. the reaction against the purely absolutist philosophy of Śaṁkara and it-seeming negations calling for a new formulation of this old synthesis. There was, for instance, the advaitic identification of the jīva and Brahman which explains the Vśiṣṭādvait; assertion of the reality of the individual or its attempt to give the Hindus their souls back[3] as Max Müller has put it. It was as a protest against views like these that the doctrine was: given out in the South about 1000 A.D., and systematized somewhat later by Rāmānuja.

The sources of authority for the doctrine are two-fold, for which reason it is described as Ubhaya-vedānta; one, the Veda including the Upaniṣads and works like the Purāṇas which are for the most part based upon it; the other, the literature of the South found in Tamil which, though largely indebted to Vedic teaching, undoubtedly contains elements of non-Vedic thought. Of the immediate predecessors of Rāmānuja in this work of synthesis we may mention Nāthamuni (A.D. 1000), none of whose writings, however, has yet been discovered, and his grandson Ālavandār or Yāmunācārya (A.D. 1050), whose several works form splendid manuals of the essentials of the Vśiṣṭādvaita as they were understood before Rāmānuja took up the work of systematization. They are *Āgama-prāmāṇya, Mahāpuruṣa-nirṇaya* which is designed to show the supremacy of Viṣṇu as against śiva, *Gītārtha-saṁgraha, Siddhi-traya* and two hymns—*śrī-stuti* and *Viṣṇu-sluti.* Rāmānuja or the 'prince of ascetics' (yati-rāja), as he is described, is reputed to have been his pupil's pupil and his commentary on the *Vedānta-sūtra,* known as the *śrī-bhāṣya,* that on the *Bhagavadgītā*[2] and his *Vedārthasaṁgraha* which gives an independent exposition of the creed, form the chief scriptures of the system. His other works are *Vedānta-sāra, Vedānta-dīpa, Nitya-grantha,* dealing with forms of worship, and *Gadya-traya.* Of those who came after him, we may note Sudarśana Sūri (A.D. 1300), the author of commentaries on the *śrī-bhāṣya* and on the *Vedārtha-saṁgrah.* Then came Veṅkaṭanātha, better known as Vedānta Deśika (A.D. 1350), whose many-sided scholarship and long labours contributed much to establish the doctrine of Rāmānuja on a firm basis. First, he formulated even better than his predecessors had done the objections to the Advaita, taking into consideration the defence put up by its exponents since Rāmānuja's time. Not only did he thus render the doctrine stronger on its critical side; he also undertook the task of internal systematization and set aside once for all whatever departures from strict tradition had taken place by his time.[5] His is the second great figure in the history of Vśiṣṭādvaita and the early promise he gave of his future eminence is well indicated by the following blessing which Varadaguru, a famous teacher of the time, is said to have bestowed upon the boy when five years old: 'May you establish the Vedānta on a firm basis, vanquishing heterodox views; may you become the respected of the orthodox and the abode of abundant auspiciousness.[6] His works are too numerous to mention here. Some of the chief among them are his *Tattva-tīkā* an incomplete commentary on the *śrī-bhāṣya, Tātparya-candrikā,* gloss on Rāmānuja's *Gītā bhāṣya, Nyāya-siddhāñjana, Tattva-muktā-kalāpa* with his own commentary upon it called the *Sarvārtha-siddhi* and the *Satadușaṇī* which is a vigorous attack on the Advaita. The *Yatindra-mata-dīpikā* of Śrīnivāsācārya (A.D. 1700) is a short manual useful for beginners.

I

While Rāmānuja. holds in common with many others that knowledge implies both a subject and an object, he differs essentially from them in certain other respects. The most important of these is that discrimination is essential to all knowledge and that it is impossible for the mind to apprehend an undifferentiated object. What is known is necessarily known as characterized in some way, its generic feature being in any case apprehended along with it. The importance of this view we shall appreciate by comparing it for instance with the Nyāya-Vaiśeṣika one of nirvikalpaka according to which isolated reals are all that are apprehended at first (p. 250). According to Rāmānuja, such a stage in perception is a psychological myth and the savikalpaka of the Nyāya-Vaiśeṣika is itself primal. Any analysis of it into simpler elements is the result only of reflection and has nothing corresponding to it in the mental process as it actually takes place. This should not be taken to mean that Rāmānuja does not admit the distinction of savikalpaka and nirvikalpaka; only to him, the two alike involve a complex content. Perceptual experience is termed nirvikalpaka when the object is cognized for the first time. It is primary presentation that does not call up any previous impression of the same. A child sees a cow, let us say, for the first time; even then it sees the object as qualified in some way. When it sees a cow again, the sight of it is accompanied by a revival of the former impression and it is this second or subsequent apprehension[7]—the cognizing of the new in the light of the old—that is described as savikalpaka by Rāmānuja. While 'This is a cow' represents the form of perceptual experience at the Savikalpaka level. 'This also is a cow' does the same at the savikalpaka. Accordingly the psychological development implied by 'determinate' perception is not from the simple to the complex as in the Nyāya-Vaiśeṣika; rather the complex itself, hitherto new, ceases to be so and becomes familiar through it. To put the same in another way, while according to the Nyāya-Vaiśeṣika only the savikalpaka involves judgment, the nirvikalpaka merely furnishing the material for it, according to the Viśiṣṭādvaita all perceptual experience alike involves it. The savikalpaka does not thereby become the same as recognition (pratyabhijñā): 'This is that Devadatta,' for the latter refers to one and the same object as perceived twice whereas the former arises when different objects of the same type are cognized. In both alike, no doubt, a present object is associated with the revival of a past impression: but while in the savikalpaka it is only the impression of the attributive element that revives, in recognition that of the particular individual (vyakti) also does. Further, though all perception equally entails judgment, recognition includes a specific reference to the distinctions of time and place in which the object is cognized on the two occasions. It is not only at the primal stage of perception that the unqualified object (nirviśeṣa-vastu) is not known; all jñāna, including that of the ultimate reality, is necessarily of an object as complex (saguṇa).[8] This constitutes a radical difference from śaṁkara, who represents the Upaniṣadic ultimate as nirguṇa (P. 373). 'If the Upaniṣads describe Brahman as without qualities,' Rāmānuja says, 'all that the description can mean is that *some* qualities are denied while there are still others characterizing it.'[9]

To know the nature of jñāna, according to Rāmānuja, it is necessary to understand the classification of ultimate objects which is peculiar to his doctrine. To the well-known distinction between spirit and matter which are respectively termed cetana and jaḍa in Sanskrit, he adds another which is neither. Jñāna is of this intermediate type. It is unlike material entities in that it can unaided manifest itself and other objects neither of which is possible for them. But what it thus manifests is never *for itself* but always for another. That is, it can only show but cannot know. In this latter respect it is unlike spirit, which knows though it is unable, according to the doctrine, to show anything but itself. To take an example from the physical sphere, jñāna is like light, which can reveal the presence of a jar (say) as well as of its own, but cannot itself know either, its revelation of things being always for another. It exists not for itself but for someone else. Its teleology takes us beyond it. The classification of things here is accordingly not into jaḍa and cetana, but jaḍa ('matter') and ajaḍa[10] ('the immaterial'), where the second term stands for cetana and what is unlike it but is yet distinct from jaḍa. Jñāna pertains to one or other of the two kinds of spiritual entities recognized in the system, viz. jīvas and Īśvara. It is consequently described as dharma- bhūta-jñāna—literally 'subsidiary or attributive jñāna[11]—which implies that there is substantive jñāna also. The various jīvas and Īśvara are jñāna in this higher sense. They are compared to the flame of a lamp to which belongs and from which proceeds their dhanna-bhūta-jñāna like rays. This jñāna is supposed to be eternally associated with a subject—whether jīva or Īśvara—and constitutes its unique adjunct. When it 'flows out,' as it is expressed, from the subject to which it belongs and comes into contact with an object, it is able to manifest that object to it. Throughout mundane existence, it functions in a more or less restricted manner but it ever endures. Even in deep sleep it is; but it does not function then and does not therefore show itself, the theory being that jñāana is known only along with some object or not at all.[12] Then the jīva remains self-conscious along with the unrevealed presence of its dharma-bhūta-jñāna. In dreams, as will be seen in the next section, the actual presence is postulated of the objects dreamt of. Hence jñāna also is then known; but its action being much more impeded than during waking, the knowledge of dream-objects is dim and hazy. In mokṣa, on the other hand, entirely free action is restored to it. It becomes all-pervasive, with the result that there is nothing then which falls outside its range. The liberated soul consequently knows everything. The analogy of the lamp and the rays may suggest that the dharma-bhūta-jñāna is of the same stuff as the jīva or Īśvara, but only appearing in an attenuated form. That, however, is not the view of Rāmānuja, who takes it as a distinct entity,[13] though always associated with and dependent upon another. It is, however, difficult to see the reason for postulating two kinds of jñāna, except it be the desire to make spirit in itself changeless and thus harmonize the doctrine with the teaching of the Upaniṣads whose whole weight, as śaṁkara is never tired of insisting, is in favour of its constancy (avikriyatva).[14]

Jñāna operates through the manas alone or the manas as assisted by some organ of sense through which it streams out towards its objects which are supposed to be already there. Rāmānuja describes the process of knowing as starting from the soul, then reaching the manas and then, emerging through the senses, meeting the outside objects. When thus it comes into contact with an object, it is stated to assume the 'form' (ākāra) of that object and somehow reveal it to the subject in question. It is clear that the conception of dharma-bhūta-jñāna corresponds to that of the antaḥ-karaṇa in the Advaita, which also is supposed to go out similarly towards objects and assume their form before giving rise to knowledge (p. 345). But while the antaḥ-karaṇa in that doctrine is physical (jaḍa) and requires an extraneous aid, viz. the śākṣin, to transform it into jñāna, this is jñāna in itself. The aids it requires, like the manas and the indriyas, are only for determining its appearance in particular ways as knowledge of colour, of sound, etc. It is not only knowledge that is regarded as a modification of dharma-bhūta-jñāna; internal states like desire and anger are also its transformations, so that they are forms of knowing at the same time.

II

To turn now to the logical implication of knowledge.[15] We have just drawn attention in noticing Rāmānuja 's description of the process of knowing to the fact that objects are viewed as existing before they are known. They are therefore to be reckoned as real; and, since they depend in no way upon the self or the knowledge which brings them into relation with it, their reality is not merely relative but absolute. Rāmānuja traces this realistic view to the old teaching of the Veda, using terms in doing so which are reminiscent of the description of knowledge given in the Prābhākara school.[16] In particular, his view is described as sat-khyāti which means that what exists (sat) is alone cognized and that knowledge in the absence of a real object corresponding to its content (yathārtha) is inconceivable. It is not enough for securing the correspondence here meant, if something or other exists outside to serve as a presentative basis. Consistently with Rāmānuja's view that a bare identity is a metaphysical fiction and cannot be known, the character of the object also should be as it is given in knowledge. In other words, the agreement implied in knowledge extends from the *that* (prakārin) to the *what* (prakāra) also of the object presented. While it is easy to understand this position so far as normal perception is concerned, the question will arise as to how it can be maintained in the case of illusions where we seem to have knowledge without corresponding things. Rāmānuja's explanation of them is two-fold:—

(1) In some cases the realistic position is maintained by him on the basis of the Vedāntic doctrine of quintuplication (pañcī-karaṇa) according to which objects of the visible world, winch are all compounds, contain all the five bhūtas or elements though in varying proportions (p. 65). Thus in the case of the mirage, what is being looked at is a heated sandy waste which contains not only pṛthivī, the preponderating part of it, but also ap and the other elements however slight; and the apprehension of water there, we have to understand, is therefore only of what is actually presented to the eye. But such an explanation may do only in cases where the object of illusion, as in the example given, is one or other of the five bhūtas. Illusions, however, are by no means confined to such rare cases. We may mistake shell for silver where neither is itself a bhūta. To explain such cases, Rāmānuja resorts to an extension of the principle underlying pañci-karaṇa. The illusion of shell-silver is due, among other causes, to the similarity between the two things, viz. their peculiar lustre. This similarity means to Rāmānuja the presence in the shell, though only to an extremely limited extent, of the very substance which constitutes silver. . Likeness is to him another term for partial identity of material[17] and so what is perceived even here is what is actually presented. That is, Rāmānuja justifies his view of sat-khyāti in such cases by pointing to what is a fundamental tenet of his system, viz. the unity of the physical world and the structural affinity that is discoverable among the things that belong to it.

(2) In other cases like the white conch seen yellow by a person with a jaundiced eye a different explanation becomes necessary, for as the yellowness is admitted by all to be there outside the knowing self, viz. in the eye-ball, the point requiring elucidation is not whether it is real but how it comes to be seen as characterizing the conch. The explanation of Rāmānuja, which is based upon the theory of vision current at the time, assumes that the yellowness found in the diseased eye-ball is actually transmitted from there to the conch along with the 'rays' of the organ of sight (nāyana-raśmi) as they travel to it in the process of seeing and that the new colour thus imposed upon the conch obscures the whiteness natural to it. The conch is accordingly supposed to become actually yellow, though only for the time being. Here also then knowledge is of what is given in respect not only of the relata but also of the relation between them. To the objection that if the conch becomes actually yellow others also should find it so, the answer is given that the yellowness here is of too subtle a kind to be perceived by anyone who, unlike the person in question, has not followed it

throughout its course of transmission.[18] The explanation is no doubt arbitrary and unconvincing; but what our present purpose requires us to note is the spirit of persistent realism that underlies it, not its scientific correctness. The question will readily occur as to how dreams are to be accounted for. There at least we seem to have experience without corresponding objects existing at the time. The explanation once again is arbitrary and it is stated, now on the authority of the Upaniṣads[19] that objects like the elephant seen in a dream are not subjective but are present there at the time. 'They are created by the supreme Person (parama-puruṣa),' says Rāmānuja[20] and adds that the reason for creating such unique things is the same as in the case of objects of the waking state, viz. the providing of *suitable* means for the individual to experience pain or pleasure according to his past karma. He creates these objects, which are special to each jīva and last only as long as they are experienced, in order that it may reap the fruits appropriate to the extremely minor deeds of virtue and vice it has done.'[21]

It is instructive to find out the significance of this twofold explanation. The yellow-conch and the dream-elephant are objects solely of individual experience; and though not unreal they last only as long as the illusion lasts and can, in the nature of the case, be testified to only by the person that sees them. The illusion of the mirage or the shell-silver also in a sense has reference to particular individuals; but the water and the silver perceived there by one, because they by hypothesis persist even after the illusion is over as actual parts of what is presented, are verifiable by all. This shows that Rāmānuja distinguishes two classes of objects—one which is cognized by all or many and may therefore be called 'public,' and the other, special to single persons and may therefore be termed 'private.' But it must be distinctly understood that such a classification does not mean that he admits different types of reality—an admission which would place his doctrine epistemologically on the same footing as śaṁkara's Advaita (p. 350). In fact, it is in denying that there is such a distinction that he formulates the doctrine of sat-khyāti. In point of reality, private and public objects differ in no way. Both alike are outside and independent of knowledge, and both are absolutely real. A thing's being private does not take away from its reality. Our pains and pleasures are personal to each one of us, but they are not the less real on that account.

However diverse the explanation in the two cases and whatever we may think of its scientific value, it is clear that the aim of sat-khyāti is to show that jñāna, including the so-called illusion, never deviates from reality and that even in the case of objects whose existence can be vouched for only by individuals, there is no ideal or purely subjective element. If all knowledge be equally valid, it may be asked how the distinction between truth (pramā) and error (bhrama), which is universally recognized, is to be explained. It may appear to us from the examples cited above that error here is incomplete knowing. Thus in the case of the yellow conch, it is caused by our failure to comprehend its whiteness or, more strictly by our overlooking the fact that it is obscured. The omission and the consequent error are clearer still in the case of another example given[22]—the, 'firebrand-circle' (alāta-cakra) where a point of light, owing to its rapid movement, is mistaken for its locus, because while the fact that it occupies every point on the circumference is apprehended, the other fact that the occupation takes place successively and not simultaneously is altogether lost sight of. But we must remember that there may be elements of omission, according to the doctrine, even in truth. When for instance we perceive shell as shell, there is by hypothesis present in it silver, but it is ignored quite as much as the shell aspect is when the same object is mistaken for silver.

Similarly in the case of the desert when we cognize it as such, our mind lets slip the element of ap supposed to be contained in it. The fact is that while sat-khyāti postulates that only what is given is known, it does not admit that all that is given is known. Knowledge, no doubt, is always of the given and of nothing but the given; but it need not be of the *whole* of what is given.[23] It would not, therefore, be right to conclude that error in general is incomplete knowing. Since completeness like validity fails to differentiate truth from error, Rāmānuja enunciates a new principle, viz. that for knowledge to be true in its commonly accepted sense it should, in addition to agreeing with outside reality, be serviceable in life. When the mirage and the shell-silver are described as false, what we have to understand is not that water and silver are not present there, for in that case we could not have become conscious of them at all, but that they are not such as can be put to practical use. The distinction between truth and error comes thus to be significant only from the practical standpoint; from the theoretical one, it does not exist. All knowledge without exception is valid and necessarily so, but such validity need not guarantee that what is known is adequate to satisfy a practical need. A geologist . may correctly adjudge a piece of ore as golden; but it does not mean that bracelet (say) can be made out of the metal in it. This is the significance of including in the definition of truth not only yathārtha or 'agreeing with outside reality.' but also vyavahārānuguṇa or 'adapted to the practical interests of life.[24] If knowledge should conform to vyavahāra, it should satisfy two conditions. It must, in the first place, refer to objects of common or collective experience. It is deficiency in this respect that makes the yellow-conch and the dream-elephant false. Because their being private to a particular individual is overlooked at the time, they are confounded with the corresponding objects of the waking state; and this deficiency when discovered exposes their falsity. In the second place, it should comprehend the preponderating element in the object presented.

The object we call shell may contain silver, but the shell part predominates in it; and it is this predominance that explains its being put to use as the one and not as the other. The silver, though certainly present, does not count practically on account of its slightness (alpatva); and this feature when discovered reveals the erroneous character of the knowledge in question. Pramā not only apprehends rightly so far as it goes, but also goes far enough to be of service in life. Brhama also is right so far as it goes; but it does not go far enough and therefore fails to help us in the manner in which we expect it to do. So when erroneous knowledge disappears and truth comes to be known, as Rāmānuja's commentator says, the object (artha) is not negated but only activity (pravṛtti) is arrested.[25] The discovery of error, as we said in connection with Prābhākara's view (p. 317), affects the reactive side of consciousness, not its receptive side.

Two important corollaries follow from such a view. The practical activities of life do not require a complete knowledge of our surroundings. It is enough if we know them approximately fully. In other words, purposive thought is selective, not exhaustive; and partial or imperfect knowledge is not necessarily a hindrance to the attainment of the common ends of life. The doctrine also recognizes a social or inter-subjective side to knowledge. So far as theoretic certainty is concerned, there is no need to appeal from the individual to common consciousness; for, as we have more than once remarked, it is in the very nature of knowledge without reference to its being peculiar to one or common to many to point to reality; but its serviceability depends upon the general though tacit testimony of society—upon the 'common' sense of mankind. These observations are sure to suggest a likeness between the doctrine of sat-khyāti and what is now known as Pragmatism. Both recognize the instrumental character of knowledge and adopt practical utility as the criterion of truth. But there is one important difference. Rāmānuja admits the cognitive value of knowledge apart from the practical, whereas Pragmatism in its familiar form makes no such distinction. Even in error, there is some revelation of reality so that in adopting the pragmatic attitude he does not relinquish the logical. In fact, knowledge according to him has not one but two functions to perform—to reveal reality and to serve the purposes of practical life. Both are equally important; and if either is to be emphasized more than the other, it would undoubtedly be the former. In other words, Rāmānuja, unlike the pragmatist,.is interested in truth for its own sake and values knowledge 'more for the light it brings than for the fruits it bears.'

The theory which we have so far sketched very much alters the nature of the epistemological problem. The question to be decided about knowledge is not whether it is logically valid or not—for by deficiency in this respect knowledge would lose its very title to that name—but whether it has or has not a bearing upon practical life. In other words, it is not quality that varies in knowledge but relevancy. If we take this along with what was stated above, viz. that even truth commonly reveals reality only incompletely, we see that the sat-khyāti doctrine contains the suggestion of an ideal form of knowledge which is not only valid and has practical value but is also complete or all-comprehensive. This ideal of perfect knowledge, which we may deduce from the premises of sat-khyāti, is actually recognized by Rāmānuja as characterizing the jīva in mokṣa. Throughout saṁsāra, jñāna operates under limitations for defects of one kind or another interfere with its free activity. Consequently common knowledge, including pramā or truth, only half reveals reality. Its full revelation is possible only in mokṣa when all deficiencies are overcome and all possibility of 'error' is removed. Man's vision then becomes extended to the maximum. 'It blossoms to the full,' enabling the liberated to know everything fully and as it is.[1]

As regards pramāṇas, Rāmānuja recognizes only three: perception, inference and verbal testimony. His conception of the first from the psychological as well as the logical standpoint has already been explained, and there is nothing of importance to be noted about the second. In regard to verbal testimony, Rāmānuja follows the Mīmāṁsākas in general and holds that its subject-matter is special to it—what never falls within the range of the other two pramāṇas. In agreement with the other Vedāntins he also maintains logical validity for assertive equally with injunctive propositions Though resembling śaṁkara in his views so far, he differs from him in other respects. It will suffice to refer to two of them here. The Veda, we know, is in two sections, which seem to contradict each other in what they teach; and, since both alike are looked upon as revealed, it becomes necessary for every school of Vedānta to explain their mutual relation in some manner. According to śaṁkara, the two are really antithetical, and he gets over the antithesis between them by assuming that they are addressed to different classes of persons (adhikārin). The karma-kāṇḍa is intended for one who is still under the spell of avidyā and the jñāna-kāṇḍa, for one that has seen the hollowness of the activities it commends and is striving to transcend them. What is desirable and true from a lower standpoint is thus undesirable and not altogether true from the higher. Such a gradation of the teaching is permissible according to the Advaita with its belief in the relativity of pramāṇya (p. 359). Rāmānuja does not admit any such antithesis, and maintains that the two portions of the Veda together form but a single teaching intended for the same class of persons. They are complementary to each other in the sense that the uttara-kāṇḍa dwells upon the nature of God and the pūrva-kāṇḍa upon the modes of worshipping him.[26] But such a co-ordination of the two sections, it must be added, presupposes that the pūrva-kāṇḍa is to be understood in the spirit of the Gītā teaching and that the various karmas taught in it are to be performed not for obtaining their respective fruits but for securing God's grace.[27] In thus attaching equal logical value to the two sections of the Veda, he differs not only from śaṁkara but also from the Mīmāṁsaka who subordinates (p. 299) the Upaniṣads to the Brāhmaṇa portions (karma-kāṇḍa) of the Veda. The exact bearing of this view on the practical discipline prescribed in the Viśiṣṭādvaita for the attainment of mokṣa, we shall consider later. The second point of difference is that Rāmānuja reckons not only the Veda as revealed but also the Pāñcarātrāgama[28] regarding the whole of it, unlike śaṁkara, as eventually going back to a Vedic or some equally untainted[29] source. The āgamas deal, generally speaking, with the worship of idols, particularly in temples; and the Pāñcarātrāgama, as distinguished from the śaivāgama, is devoted to establishing the supremacy of Viṣṇu.[30]

III

Rāmānuja recognizes as ultimate and real the three factors (tattva-traya) of matter (acit), soul (cit) and God (Īśvara). Though equally ultimate, the first two are absolutely dependent upon the last, the dependence being conceived as that of the body upon the soul. Whatever is, is thus the body of God . and he is the soul not only of inorganic nature but also of souls or jīvas.[31] It is in this connection that Rāmānuja formulates the relation[32] so important in his system, of apṛthak-siddhi or 'inseparability' which obtains between substance and attribute and may be found between one substance and another. It may be described as the pivot on which his whole philosophy turns. It is parallel to, but not identical with, the Nyāya-Vaiśeṣika samavāya. The two agree in so far as the relata which they bring together are regarded as quite distinct and real; but while samavāya (p. 235) is an external relation, the conception of aprthak-siddhi is that of an internal one. The example given in illustration of it, viz. the relation between body and soul, brings out clearly its intimate character. The body is defined by Rāmānuja as that which a soul controls, supports and utilizes for its own ends.[33] Matter and souls, being the body of God, are to be regarded as directed and sustained by him and as existing entirely for him. The inseparable unity of matter, souls and God—the first two being entirely subject to the restraint of the third in all their forms—is the Brahman or Absolute of Rāmānuja. Since Rāmānuja identifies the relation here involved with that between the body and the soul, his conception of the Absolute may be described as that of an organic unity in which, as in a living organism, one element predominates over and controls the rest. The subordinate elements are termed viśeṣaṇas and the predominant one, viśeṣya. Because the viśeṣaṇas cannot by hypothesis exist by themselves or separately, the complex whole (viśiṣṭa)[34] in which they are included is described as a unity. Hence the name 'Viśiṣṭādvaita.'

This conception of unity may be illustrated by taking a common example like a 'blue lotus.' Here the blueness is quite distinct from the lotus, for a quality cannot be the same as a substance. But at the same time the blueness as a quality depends for its very being upon a substance—the lotus here, and cannot therefore be regarded as external to it. The complex whole of the flower in question is, in this sense of *necessarily* including within itself the quality of blueness, spoken of as a unity. It will help us to understand this view well if we contrast it with those of some other schools. Rāmānuja recognizes real distinction between the quality of blueness and the substance of lotus. Hence his view differs from the Advaita for which all distinctions are alike only apparent. It differs likewise from the Nyāya-Vaiśeṣika though maintaining a real distinction between the two entities, because it regards that they are not external to each other. But this should not lead us to think that Rāmānuja, like Kumārila (p. 323), advocates the bhedābheda view for he does not admit identity of any kind whatsoever between the entities supposed to be distinct, the unity, affirmed being only of the complex whole.[35] The term 'Viśiṣṭādvaita' is more usually explained in a somewhat different manner—especially in interpreting verbal statements affirming unity like Tat tvam asi. But the idea underlying it is the same. If we take the proposition 'The lotus is blue,' the quality of 'blueness' according to this explanation, because of its attributive character, points necessarily to some substance to which it belongs. This blue substance is a complex whole. The lotus also may similarly be looked upon as a complex whole, comprising the attributive element of 'lotus-ness' and a substance which it characterizes. The identity that is expressed by the proposition is of these two, complexes,[36] Or, in other words, the two terms—'blue' and 'lotus'—have distinct meanings but refer to the same substance (prakāryadvaita). What is signified is not therefore a bare identity which excludes the viśeṣaṇas. It includes them and it is their difference that calls for an affirmation of identity in the above sense. Otherwise we may be misled into thinking that the two complexes are distinct. In the example that we have taken, there is only one viśeṣaṇa. There may be several, which again may be co-existent or may appear in the visesya successively. When for instance we think of a youth whom we knew as a child, the two viśeṣaṇas due to distinction of age appear one after the other; but they do not lie outside the unity of the individual in question. Such identity is found not only in the case of substance and its attributes as the above examples may suggest but also in that of substance and its modes, *e.g.* clay and jar. In fact, it obtains wherever we have inseparable correlatives. Of two such entities, the major member is designated prakārin; and the minor, prakāra.

The central point of the teaching of the Upaniṣads, according to Rāmānuja, is the unity of Brahman in this sense; and he, like śaṁkara, cites in support of his view the two kinds of co-ordinate propositions that occur in them—one, affirming the identity of the soul and Brahman, and the other, that of Brahman and the material world. But he differs totally from him in their interpretation. Before stating his explanation of them, we must briefly refer to another aspect of the doctrine. According to Rāmānuja all things that are, are eventually forms or modes (prakara) of God. Similarly all names are his names[37] so that every word becomes a symbol of God and finally points to him. This deeper significance of words, described as vedānta-vyutpatti, is what only the enlightened comprehend. According to it no word ceases to signify after denoting its usual meaning, but extends its function till it reaches the Supreme[38] In fact, it is only the latter that is conceived as the essential significance of a word. Now let us select for illustrating Rāmānuja's interpretation the well 'known Upaniṣadic maxim—Tat tvam asi. The term tvam in it which commonly stands for the jīva really points to God who is the jīva's inner self (antaryamin) and of whom the jīva and, through it, its physical body are alike modes. What the term tat means in it is also the same, but viewed in a different aspect, viz. God as the cause of the universe, as shown by the context in which it occurs in the *Chāndogya Upaniṣad.* The identity meant by Tat tvam asi, according to the explanation of the term Váiṣṭādvaita given above, is of the- two complexes—God as the indweller of the jīva and God as the source of the world. The final import of the statement is that though the world and the individual souls are real and distinct, the Absolute in which they are included is one.[39] 'They are eternal with God but are not external to him. In the advaitic intercretation of the same, the distinction due to the viseṣaṇa elements is rejected as but an appearance though, as we have tried to show, no identity as such is taken to be implied by it (p. 374). Here the distinction is not denied; and, at the same time, the organic unity of the whole is affirmed.

This is only a general account of the Viśiṣṭādvaita view of Reality. To state the same now more in detail: Rāmānuja recognises: is it is clear by now, the distinction between substance and attribute; but me attributes are not further distinguished. as in the Nyāya-Vaiśeṣika, into guṇa, karma, jāti, etc[40] and are comprehensively termed adravya or 'what is other than substance.' There are thus only two main categories of which the second, adravya, is always and necessarily dependent upon the first, dravya, although neither, in consequence of the unique relation that obtains between them, can be or be thought of apart from the other.[41] The adravyas are reckoned as ten. Five of them are the qualities of the five bhūtas—sound, etc.—and the next three are the gunas in the special sense of sattva, rajas and tamas, which are the characteristics of matter (acit) or prakṛti. Three of the adravyas are thus general; and five, specific. Of the remaining two, śakti or 'potency' is that property of a causal substance by virtue of which it produces the effect, e.g. plasticity in clay, attractive power in a magnet, burning capacity in fire. The tenth adravya is samyoga, by which is meant as in the Nyāya-Vaiśeṣika an external relation like that between the floor and a jar.

Not only is adravya distinct from dravya in this system; rhe dravyas themselves are to be distinguished from one another. But what is a dravya?[42] According to the Visisttādvaita conception, whatever serves as the substratum of change is a dravya It means that Rāmānuja accepts the parinama-vāda or sat-karya-vada. But it is the attributive elements (viśeṣaṇa) alone that change, for which reason the complex whole (viśiṣṭa) is also spoken of as undergoing modifications. The substantive element (viśeṣya) in itself is changeless. God viewed as the viseṣya is changeless and the soul also is so[43] but the dharma-bhūta-jñāna which belongs to them changes. Matter, which is entirely a viśeṣaṇa, itself changes.[44] The relation between it and its transformations," say, clay and jar is, as already pointed out, aprthak-siddhi. But if we consider a lump of clay (piṇḍa) which, and not mere clay (mrt), is regarded here as the material cause of the jar, the relation between them is stated to be identity (ananyatva, literally, 'non-difference'). Whatever difference there is between the two is explained away as the material is the' very same, though the disposition of its constituent parts in them may differ.[45] There are six dravyas answering to this description; and they are divided into two classes-jaḍa and ajaḍa, as already explained. The jaḍa includes prakṛti and time (kala); and the ajaḍa—dharma-bhūta-jñana, nitya-vibhūti or suddha-sattva, jīva and Īśvara. We shall now add a few words of explanation regarding each of these:—

(i) *Prakṛti.*—This is the dwelling-place of the soul and, through it, of God himself. Nature is thus alive with God. 'Earth's crammed with heaven, and every common bush afire with God.' We shall best understand its character aconceived in this system by contrasting it with the Sāṅkhya view of it with which it has much in common. The chief differences are: (i) The three gunas—sattva rajas and tamas—are supposed in the Sāṅkhya to be its constituent factors, and prakṛti is merely the complex of them all. Here, on the other hand, the guṇas are conceived as characterizing tt so that they are distinct although inseparable from it. (ii) That-prakṛti of the Sāṅkhya is infinite, but here it is taken to be limited in one direction, viz. above, by the nitya-vibhūti of which we shall speak presently, (iii) in the Sāṅkhya, prakṛti is theoretically independent of the puruṣa, but here it is entirely under the control of spirit, *i.e.* jīva or Īśvara. The relation between them is aprthak-siddhi so that neither admits of separation from the other. Owing to this difference, Rāmānuja's conception of prakṛti is much superior to the Sāṅkhya one. The entities evolved out of prakṛti and the order of their evolution are exactly as stated under the Sāṅkhya.

(2) *Kāla.*—Time is viewed here as real; but it is not outside the sole reality recognized, viz. Brahman or the Absolute, though it does not merge in it. So it does not subsist by itself, as it does according to the Nyāya-Vaiśeṣika (p. 229). Nor is it but a phase of prakṛti as in the Sāṅkhya-Yoga (p. 270). Time also, like prakṛti of which it is the companion, so to speak, admits of change or undergoes pariṇāma, and moments, days, etc, are represented as its e volutes. Unlike time, space is derived from prakṛti and is included only through it in the highest reality. Of prakṛti and time, neither can be said to be prior to the other; but the same cannot be said of space, for prakṛti is prior to it.

(3) *Dharma-bhūta-jñāna.*—As we have already dealt with this, only a few words need be added now. It c hracterizes Jīvas or Īśvara and is always, as its name indicates, secondary to them, the relation between them being inseparable. It is conceived as both a dravya and a guṇa[46]—a dravya inasmuch as it, through contraction and expansion[47] is the substrate of change; a guṇa inasmuch as it is necessarily dependent upon a dravya, viz. jīva or Īśvara and cannot be by itself and not through another jñāna (p. 251), for it is self-luminous and shows itself though it cannot become self-conscious.

(4) *Nitya-vibhūti.*—We have seen that prakṛti is characterized by the three guṇas. If of these we leave out rajas and tamas and conceive of it as characterized only by sattva, we get an idea of nitya-vibhūti and see why it is called śuddha or unalloyed sattva. On account of this peculiar character, it ceases to be material (jaḍa) and becomes 'immaterial' (ajaḍa) in the sense already explained. It is sublimated prakṛti, a sort of super-nature. Since, however, the three gunas are represented here as constant attributes or qualities prakṛti and not as its constituent factors as in the Sāṅkhya, it becomes hard to imagine how any *one* of them can alone conceived of as a characteristic when the contrast of the otherr two is removed. Further, according to the explanation given, prakṛti and nitya-vibhūti possess a common feature, viz. sattva, and therefore prakṛti also to that extent should ^ non-material. In that case its entire separation from the ajaḍa category would not be quite accurate. These discrepancies are in all probability to be explained is. due to the system being eclectic in its details, and have led the later Viśiṣṭādvaitin to differentiate between the two sattvas and declare that they are altogether distinct (vilaksana).[48] Except in this important respect, nitya-vibhūti is similar to prakṛti. Briefly it is the material out of which the things of the ideal world, and the bodies of God and of the liberated souls are made. It is 'matter without its mutability' and has been described as a fit means to the fulfilment of divine experience.[49] The domain of nitya-vibhūti is limited below by prakṛti but is infinite above. Vakuṇṭha, the city of God, is supposed to occupy a part of it. Though a sharp demarcation is made between prakṛti and nitya-vibhūti, the latter, it is stated, is found within the

region of the former as for instance in the holy idols worshipped in sacred places like śrīrangam, those idols being viewed as permeated through and through by the material. The reverse cannot happen and prakṛti does not encroach upon the region of nitya-vibhūti.

(5) *Jīva.*—In dealing with dharma-bhūta-Jñāna, we have already referred to the nature of the jīva. It is of the essence of spirit and has dharma-bhuta-Jñāna always associated with it. In these respects consists its essential affinity with God. The Jīva is not here, as in the Advaita, merely the assumed unity of individual experience, but an eternal reality. In its natural condition of mokṣa, its Jñāna expands to the maximum, reaching the ends of space, and there is nothing then which it fails to comprehend. In saṁsāra as a whole the Jñāna is more or less contracted, but never absent, not even in deep sleep where it only ceases to function and does not therefore reveal objects. The jīva itself, apart from its jñāna, is viewed as of atomic size—a mere point of spiritual light, and its functioning in places where it is not, as for example in seeing distant things, is rendered possible by the expansion and contraction of its dharma-bhūta-jñāna. 'Though monadic in substance it is infinite in intelligence.[50] The jīva is not merely sentience; it is also of the essence of bliss. This aspect of the jīva's nature again will remain more or less obscured in saṁsāra, becoming fully manifest only when liberation is achieved. The diminution in its capacity to know or to enjoy is temporary; when released, it is restored to its omniscience and eternal happiness. The jīva with its physical body derived from prakṛti and with God for its indweller is the meeting-point, so to speak, of the material and the divine which explains the gulf which often separates man's ideal aspirations from his actual life. The jīvas are infinite in number, and in addition to those that are on their trial here (baddha) or have already achieved their salvation (mukta), the doctrine recognizes what are described as nitya which have never been in bondage. They are beings like Viṣvaksena who have from all time been attending upon God. Each jiva is in reality both a kartā and a bhokta, *i.e.* an active and purposeful being. It is also free and God, who is its 'inner ruler immortal,' must be supposed to control it without interfering with the freedom that belongs to it.[51]

(6) *Īśvara.*—The conception of God also in the system has by this time become clear, rendering it unnecessary to say much about it now. Īśvara too is of the nature of spirit or intelligence and is of the essence of unsurpassed bliss.[52] Like the jīva, he also possesses dharma-bhūta-jñāna whose transformations constitute his several psychical states. Owing however, to his omnipresence, there is really no need for such an aid in his case; and its postulation is intended solely to secure constancy to spirit in itself. The term Īśvara is used in a double sense. First, it stands for the entire universe with all its spiritual and material elements included in it. In this sense, Īśvara

may be thought of in two stages—as cause and as effect. In dissolution (pralaya) he subsists as the cause with the whole of the universe latent in him; in creation (sṛṣṭi), what is latent becomes manifest. Subtle matter becomes gross; and souls, expanding their dharma-bhūta-jñāna, enter into relations with physical bodies appropriate to their past karma. The causal form includes within itself everything that is required for the development signified by creation, so that Īśvara is the whole and sole cause of it. In other words. God is self-determining and the universe develops from within unassisted by any external agency (p. 82). It is because he *grows* into this cosmic variety that he is called 'Brahman' (p. 54). That would ascribe change to God which is against the prevalent teaching of the Upaniṣads; but Rāmānuja tries to explain the difficulty away by holding that the change is only to be secondarily understood—as sa-dvāraka. God does not suffer change in himself, but only through the entities comprehended in the whole of which he is the inspiring principle. But it is not easy to see how he can be said to remain changeless when his inseparable attributes are changing. This Īśvara in himself, regarded as the unchanging centre of the changing universe, is the other meaning of the term. Such an Īśvara of course does not exist isolated by himself, but it is still legitimate to make the distinction because the viśeṣya element in the Absolute, like the viśeṣaṇas, is real and ultimate. In the former sense, Īśvara is the Absolute of Rāmānuja; in the latter, he is the antar-yāmin and dwells within whatever is—whether soul or matter.

This absolutist view which is chiefly based upon the Upaniṣads is intertwined in the system with the details of a theistic creed which, historically speaking, goes back to a different source. In that phase. God is conceived as completely personal. He is looked upon as having pity for erring man and as actuated by a desire to show mercy to him. Benevolence, indeed, is one of his essential features. He is known as Nārāyaṇa or Vāsudeva, and the latter designation is a sign nf the presence in the doctrine of elements drawn from the Bhāgavata religion. He is also known as Para or the Supreme. In this form he dwells in his own citadel Vaikuṇṭha which, as we said, occupies a corner in the domain of nitya-vibhūti. He manifests himself in various ways to help his devotees: One of the most important is known as vyūha. It is fourfold: Vāsudeva—a differentiation within Para Vāsudeva and therefore to be distinguished from him—Samkarṣaṇa, Pradyumna and Aniruddha. They are all incomplete manifestations, and God appears in them in different garbs. Another way in which the Supreme manifests himself is as avatārs (p. 98) which are well known. They are classed together as vibhava. Still another manifestation is known as the antaryāmin whose presence within is common to all the jīvas and who guides them like a friend. It is God (incorporate—possessing a rupa—and should be distinguished from the one referred to above which bears the same name and which, as taught in the *Bṛhadāraṇyaka Upaniṣad*[54], is the essence (svarūpa) of God.[55] The last of the manifestations called arcāvatāra, is as holy idols worshipped in sacred places like Srīraṅgam.

Now as regards the success with which the two teachings have been assimilated here: The attempt, so far as it aims at identifying the ultimate of philosophy with the ultimate of religion, has its undoubted excellences. But it is one thing to think of the two as the same and quite another to try combining a particular philosophic doctrine with a particular religious creed. The theistic creed that finds place in the present synthesis had, as the result of its long history, developed a host of concrete details, not all of which for lack of adequate rational support could fuse with philosophy. The philosophic doctrine included in it was, on the other hand, the result of one of the most daring speculations in the whole field of thought; and its conception of Reality was the least personal. Hence there are some discrepancies in the doctrine resulting from the synthesis, such as those we had occasion to mention in speaking of the notions of antaryāmin and nitya-vibhūti. Another instance of the same disaccord is found in what we shall point out in the next section, viz. the retention in the doctrine of the 'esoteric restriction' of the saving knowledge of bhakti by the side of the popular pathway to release of prapatti. The fact is that the Vaiṣṇava religion was there in all its completeness in the time of Rāmānuja. As a practical creed, it had indeed served human needs in an excellent manner and given rise within its fold to more than one saint of pre-eminent mystical power. But it lacked support from the Upaniṣads and this lack of support should have become the more conspicuous after śaṁkara had expounded them in a specific manner. The attempt made in the Viśiṣṭadvaita was to secure for Vaiṣṇavism the needed support. It was thus practical exigency rather than any organic connection between the two teachings that led to their synthesis. We may illustrate best the resulting discrepancy by reference to the conception of the Absolute in the system. Rāmānuja admits several ultimate entities, but holds at the same time that there is only one Being—that of the viśeṣya, all the attributive, elements deriving their being from it.[56] If all these entities are existentially one, it is difficult to see how the distinction between them can be ultimate. It is just this lack of independent being that the Advaitin means when he denies reality to elements of diversity in the Absolute.[57] If to avoid the above difficulty we assume that each viśeṣana has its own *separate* being, the absoluteness of the Absolute vanishes and it will be hard to think of it as a unity except in a secondary or figurative sense. The only other alternative is to define the relation between the several entities constituting the Absolute as bhedābheda, thus predicating both identity and difference of them. But such an explanation, even supposing it is logically sound, is, as already pointed out, totally unacceptable to Rāmānuja.

The notion of aprthak-siddhi on which the conception is based is as imperfect as that of the Nyāya-Vaiśeṣika samavāya which it is intended to replace. The only difference is that while samavāya tries to unite what are supposed to be distinct, apṛthak-siddhi tries to separate what is supposed to be one. Both alike represent efforts to seek what it is not possible to have, viz. a half-way house between inclusion and exclusion. The system, so far as it is based en Vaīśṇavism, endeavours to secure ultimate reality for the souls as well as matter; but loyalty to the Upaniṣads drives it to modify it, thus rendering the result logically unsatisfactory.

IV

As in the Advaita, the practical discipline here also begins with karma-yoga in the Gītā sense, which purifies the heart and fits a person for knowing the truth; but it is quite different in what follows. The training that is distinctive of Viśiṣṭādvaita is two-fold:—

(1) *Jñāna-yoga.*—This means meditation upon the jīva after knowing its true character through śravaṇa or study of the scriptures under a proper *guru.* Those only that have achieved success in karma-yoga can enter upon it. Its object is to realize how the self is different from its several accompaniments like the body, senses and so forth with which man usually identifies it and how attachment to them impeded spiritual progress. When this yoga is carried to fruition, the discipline does not terminate, for according to Rāmānuja, the jīva though an ultimate fact is not the Ultimate. The disciple may have succeeded in realizing his nature in relation to the physical environment; but there yet remains the task of discovering the same in relation to God, the highest fact of the universe. Man cannot, according to Rāmānuja, know himself truly until he knows God. The means prescribed for such knowledge is termed bhakti-yoga.

(2) *Bhakti-yoga.*—This marks the culminating stage of the discipline. It presupposes a reasoned conviction regarding the nature of God as taught in the Viśiṣṭādvaita, and those alone that have successfully pursued jñāna-yoga in the sense just explained can begin it. Bhakti here is equated with dhyāna and may therefore be taken as upāsana or meditation implies also love. It is not a mere austere concentration of the mind on Reality, but a loving contemplation of a personal God.[58] There is also another implication in it which is equally the result of the conception of the jīva characteristic of the doctrine, viz. the feeling of one's absolute dependence (śeṣatva) upon God as the -sole power in the universe. Bhakti-yoga also thus consists in meditation like jñāna-yoga; but it is. meditation that is suffused with feelings of love and dependence. Success in this part of the discipline results in the attainment of what may be described as divine vision, actual mokṣa

resulting when the soul is severed from the probation of flesh. This is in accordance with the ancient ideal of finding release in a life hereafter, and no jīvan-mukti as such (p. 19) is recognized here as in śaṁkara's Advaita.

Another important difference from the Advaita is that the obligation to perform karma is not a feature of the preparatory stage only. It continues even when one enters upon bhakti-yoga, so that the ideal of karma-samnyasa as known to the Advaita (p. 339) is rejected here. Man should never abandon karma of the nitya variety or unconditional duties, for he will then become sinful and miss salvation on account of neglecting what is enjoined in the Veda. So far Rāmānuja agrees with Kumārila. But there is here the positive purpose that bhakti, which has been described as 'salvation in becoming,'[59] might grow through karma and ripen into intuition. Adherence to karma in this stage is not therefore for subjective purification as in the earlier one, but for advancing further and further in the life of the spirit. And karma, with its purpose thus transformed, will continue till the very end, for the immediate experience of God is not believed to arise until the moment before departing this life. The discipline for mokṣa thus consists of both jñāna and karma; yet it is the former alone that is regarded as the *direct* cause of release, the latter being taken to be only an accessory and not a co-ordinate aid. Hence, though insisting upon the performance of karma throughout life, the Visiṣṭādvaita like the Advaita (p. 379) does not advocate what is known as samuccaya-vāda.[60] Before we close this topic we must draw attention to the widening in its scope which karma undergoes in the system. It includes not only whatever is prescribed in the Veda but also prayer and devotional worship as understood in Vaiṣṇavism (kriyā-yoga).[61]

As in the other Indian systems, mokṣa is conceived here also as freedom from mundane existence. But over and above this is the idea here of reaching a supra-mundane sphere and there enjoying in the presence of God the highest bliss. The imperfect prākṛtic body of the jīva is then replaced by a perfect one, so that release does not mean here a disembodied state as it does in many another doctrine. It is this ideal world—'the Highlands of the blest'—that is constituted out of śuddha-sattva. Picturesque descriptions are given of the place. There God is seated on his white throne and is served by his consort Lakṣmī—interceding on behalf of man—and by all the souls of the nitya and mukta variety. It is a place of absolute peace and perfection, and the joy of all there lies in following the will of the Supreme. When a bound soul is liberated, it is led to this region and, welcomed by all there, it is at last received by God as his very own. An account of the triumphal progress of the spiritual pilgrim till he arrives at the throne of the Lord is given in the first chapter of the *Kauṣītakī Upaniṣad.*

This is the normal or regular means to release. But a person, to follow it, must belong to one or another of the three higher castes of Hindu society; for it is only such that are qualified to receive instruction in the Veda and the Upaniṣads. So the course described heretofore becomes considerably narrowed in its usefulness. The Viśiṣṭādvaita therefore recognizes along with it another pathway to God which any one, irrespective of caste or rank, may follow. That is known as prapatti.[62] The word is derived from *pra-pad,* meaning 'to take refuge with' or 'to piously resign,' and points to a belief that salvation is obtained through free grace. It is described as saranagati or flinging oneself on God's compassion. It consists in absolute self-surrender, and signifies a resolve 'to follow the will of God, not to cross his purposes, to believe that he will save, to seek help from him and him alone and to yield upone's spirit to him in 'all meekness.[63] In one of its forms described as 'resignation in extreme distress' (ārta-prapatti), it Is believed to bring deliverance immediately. A single moment of seriousness and sincerity is considered enough; and this also testifies, in the eyes of the Vśiṣṭādvaitin, to its superiority over bhakti which means a long and laborious process of training. The inclusion by Rāmānuja in his doctrine of a means to salvation which is accessible to all, explains the wide popularity it has always commanded; and the social uplift of the lower classes to which it has led is of great value in the history of India. But it is outside our purpose to dwell upon that aspect of the Viśiṣṭādvaita at any length. Rāmānuja attaches so much importance to prapatti that he makes it essential to bhakti also in its final stages.[64] He maintains that it represents a form of knowledge and is not therefore in conflict with the Upaniṣadic view that jñāna alone is the means of release—an explanation rendered necessary by prapatti being the distinctive characteristic of Vaiṣṇavism rather than of the Vedānta. The prominent place given to it in the teaching shows the need for absolute self-suppression whatever course of discipline a person may follow. Though zealously upholding the persistence of personality, Rāmānuja commends the cultivation of an attitude which makes one feel and act as if that personality did not exist. He means thereby that it is not belief in a permanent self but selfishness which is the enemy of true life.

REFERENCE

1. See e.g. SB I. iv. 27.

2. This as we shall see is termed bhakti by Rāmānuja.

3. SS. p.189.

4. The Upansiad were not explained by him separately and that

5. *Cf. Adhikarana-sārāvalī.* Introductory stanza, 25. Pratiṣṭhāpita-vedāntaḥ pratikṣipta-bahirmataḥ: Bhūyāḥ traividyā-mānyaḥ tvam bhūri-kalyāṇa-bājanam.

7. I t is pointed out that if at the second apprehension the former impression is not revived, the knowledge will be only nirvikalpaka and that it will continue to be so till such revival takes place. See VAS p. 51. (com.).

8. SB. pp. 70-5. 9. SB. p. 71

10 *Yatīndra-mata-dīpikā* (Ānandāśrama Series), p. 51.

11. Jñāna, though attributive to jīva or Īśvara,is in itself regarded as a substance as will become clear later.

12. In the case of Īśvara the dharma-bhuta-jñāna, being all-pervasive, does not contract or expand; but yet it undergoes transformations. The consequent changes of form are what are meant by divine.

13. According to the Nyāya-Vaiśeṣika, the flame comes into being first and the particles of tejas which constitute its rays are supposed to radiate from it afterwards. Cf. SV. pp. 842 f.

14. That such is the aim will become clear when we consider the case of Īśvara, who by hypothesis is everywhere unlike the atomic jīva and therefore does not stand in need of any such aid. 15. SB. pp. 183-8.

16. Yathārtham sarva-vijñānam iti veda-vidām matam. Cf. PP. p. 32.

17. Tadeva sadrsam tasya yat taddravyaika-desa-bhāk: SB. p. 184.

18. The analogy is here adduced of a small bird soaring in the sky which he, that has followed its course from the moment it began to fly, is able to spot easily but not others.

19. *Br. Up.* IV. iii. 10. 20. SB III ii. 3.

21. SB III ii. 5. 22. SB p. 187.

23. The peculiar view upheld in sat-khyāti, however, makes one thing certain. There can be no errors of commission. Here is a point of agreement between Rāmānuja's sat-khyāti and Prabhākara's akhyāti. The two not, however, identical. Compare Vedānta Deśika's description of the former as akhyāti-samvalita-yathārtha...

24. *Vatindra-mata-dipikā.* p.3.

25. Jñāna-phala-bhūta pravṛtti-bādhyatvam: SB. (com.) p. 185.

26. Compare the kevala-jñāa of Jainism (p. 159).

27. *Yatindra-mata-dīpihā*, p. 27.

28. To all appearance, Bādarāyaṇa is against āgama. Compare śaṁkara on VS. II. ii. 42-5.

29. This is known as the Ekāyana-śākhā. See SB (com.) p. 559 (Madras Edn.).

30. The Vaikhānasāgama, which also upholds the supremacy of viṣṇu seems to exhibit closer kniship with the Veda.

31. Since according to Rāmānuja inorganic matter also is ensouled, god is its self only mediately through the jīva (see VAS. pp. 30-1). Yet he is sometimes spoken of as being so directly. Cf. *Rahasya-trayasara,* iii. pp. 121-2 (bangalore

Edn.).

32. The Nyāya-Vaiśeṣika postulates the relation of samavāya between things that are inseparable. The Vśiṣṭādvaita discards this relation as superfluous and views inseparability itself, which it regards as the nature (svarūpa) of the two relata, as aprthak-siddhi. Strictly it is not therefore a relation (see SB II. ii. 12); but it is still sometimes.

33. SB. II i. 9. This intimacy of relation is expressed thus—niyamena ādheyatvam niyamena, vidheyatvam, niyamena śeṣatvam.

34. Cf. SB p. 122 (com): Viśistāntarbhāva ev aikyam.

35. Cf. SB. pp. 75, 204-5; VAS. pp. 50, 97-8.

36. SB. p.132. 37. Some exceptions are made . See SB pp. 205-7.

38. Aparyavasāna-vrttiḥ śabda-vyāpāraḥ Cf. VAS p. 36.

39. SB. pp. 198-9.

40. Karma or action is explained as mere disjunction and conjunction and therefore as expressible in terms of saṁyoga and its opposite, vibhaga. jāti as in Jainism or in the Sāṅkhya-Yoga is only a certain disposition of the several parts constituting the thing. Abhāva is conceived positively as in the Prābhākara school.

41. Prthak-pratipatti—sthivanarha: SB p. 205.

42. SAS. p. 590.

43. Not all viśeṣaṇas therefore change, though whatever changes is necessarily a viśasana. 44. SB III. ii.p. 31.

45. SB II. i.p. 15.

46. The term guṇa here means 'secondary' and does not bear the significance which it does in the Nyāya-Vaiśeṣika.

47. SB p. 82. 48. See Vedānta Deśika: *Rahasya-traya-sāra*.

49. Prof. P. N. śrīnivasachari. *Rāmānuja's Idea of the Finite Self* (Longmans) p. 62. 50. Prof. P. N. śrīnivasachari: *op. cit.*, p. 26.

51. VAS pp. 120-12. 52. VAS p.240.

53. *Yatīndra-mata-dīpikā*, p. 88. 54. II. vii.

55. See *Rahasya-traya-sāra*, v. pp. 283-4.

56. Cf. SB. II. ii. 31. See also the discussion of this point by Raṅgarāmānuja in his com. on *Muṇḍaka Up.* I. i. 3.

57. See Note I on p. 353.

58. Sneha-pūrvam anudhyānam bhaktiḥ. Quoted in SB. p. 35 (com.)

59. IP. vol. ii. p. 705 60. SB. III. iv. 26.

61. Cf. VAS. p. 5. 62. See *Gadya-traya*, iii.

63. Ānukūlyasya saṁkalpaḥ prātikūlyasya varjanam: Rakṣiṣyatīti viśvāsḥ goptṛtva-varaṇam tathā: Ātman-nikṣepa-kārpaṇye ṣaḍvidhā śaraṇāgatiḥ

64. See com. on BG. xviii. 66.

CHAPTER XVI

THE VEDAS: GENERAL ASPECTS

The oldest scriptures of india, and the most important are the Vedas. Orthodox Hindus, who include all schools of indian thought past and present except Buddhists and Jains, recognize in them the origin of their faith and its highest written authority. Buddhists and Jains reject them, though in varying degree: the Buddhists renouncing them altogether, the Jains acknowledging their spiritual validty but denying that they are in any peculiar sense sacred. Of Jains there are in India today about a million and a quarter; of Buddhists, in India proper, there are virtually none. For the vast majority of modern Hindus, therefore, amongst all their sacred writings, the Vedas are supreme.

This does not, however, suggest the whole story. For the term Vedas, as used by the orthodox, not only names a large body of texts composed in times indefinitely remote, and handed down by generation after generation to our own day, but in another sense stands for nothing less than Divine Truth itself, the inexpressible truth of which the Vedic texsts are of necessity but a pale reflextion. Regarded in this second aspect, the Vedas are infinite and eternal. They are that perfect knowledge which is God.

Even more than the other scriptures of the world the Vedas make a special claim to be divine in their orign. The Bible, the Koran, and other revelation of the word of God one their authoirty to delivery of the sacred message through an angel, or prophet, or other special messenger from God to certain chosen persons. And these revelations must be accepted on faith. No question is raised as to whether any human being today can verify these releations in his own experience. The Vedas, on the other hand, are said to be apauruṣeya, which mean divine in origin. In fact, in the word of Sāyanācārya, the learned commentator on the Vedas, Yo vedabhvaḥ akhilam jagat nirmame—God created the whole universe out of the knoweldge of the Vedas. That is to say, Vedic knowledge existed even before the creation of mankind. The authority of the Vedas does not depend upon anything eternal . They themselves arc authority, being the knowledge of God And, as we shall see later, their truth is verifiable by any spiritual aspirant in transcendental consciousness

But it is the Vedas in the concrete sense of scriptures with which alone we are henceforth concerned. As such, they are divided into four major parts, and each of these, in turn, is further divided and subdivided—as may be conveniently seen in the following table:

Veda	Division	Texts
Rk[1]	Work Knowledge (Upanisads)	Samhitas Brahmans Aranyakas
Sama	Work Knowledge (Upanisads)	Samhitas Brahmans Aranyakas
Yajur	Work Knowledge (Upanisads)	Samhitas Brahmans Aranyakas
Atharava	Work Knowledge (Upanisads)	Samhitas Brahmans Aranyakas

Many questions suggested by this classification we shall pass by for the moment while we inquire how in the view of orthodox Hindus, this body of sacred texts came into being. The answer involves certain Hindu beliefs with which, if only in preliminary fashion, we should now become acquainted. To the Hindu, creation is beginning-less and endless That it is beginning less he proves simple process of logic. If creation had a beginning, then must the creator also have had a beginning since until there is a creation there can be no creator, but to admit that the creator had a beginning would be to admit that God had a beginning, since God is not God until he creates—and to think of God as having had a beginning would, to the Hindu, be a manifest absurdity God, who contains within himself the seed, the material cause, of the universe, first brings forth the universe out of his own being, and then in due time takes it back again to himself. This process of creation and dissolution goes on for ever and ever, for it is as endless as it is beginningless. Eternity is witness, not of one universe only—that, for example, of which we are now a part—but *of* an infinite succession of universes. The birth, life, and destruction of a universe constitutes a cycle. To say that there was never a first cycle, and will never be a last, is only a was of affirming that the creative function of God is, like himself eternal

Further beliefs concern the stuff of which the successive universes are composed. This stuff is simply an immense multitude of beings, some animate, some inanimate. Plants, animals, and men are animate; rocks and stones are inanimate. But all are alike beings. These, by their nature, are involved in a process the final goal of which is their complete absorption into God—in his quiescent, or noncreative aspect. When an individual being is thus absorbed he is free forever from the cycles of finite existence; but the process leading to this blessed state may be a long one. Not only may a being be born, live, and die, and then be born again, live, and die, indefinitely, within the bounds of a single universe, but he may also be born again and again into an indefinite series of universes The history of a particular individual, the number of times he experiences rebirth, or reincarnation as it is called, depends entirely upon the quality of his will, upon the moral effort he puts forth. As he rises in moral and spiritual stature he is born into an ever higher plane of existence until at last he returns to the world as man. Birth as a human being is extolled as a sacred birth, not because to be born as man necessarily leads to immediate liberation—far from it—but because the achievement of liberation possible to man alone

Against the background of these conceptions the orthodox view of the origin of the Vedas may be quickly sketched. At the very beginning of each cycle, holy seers are born into the world, men who in previous universes have ascended towards the supreme goal and are therefore especially capable of perceiving divine truth. These blessed saints—rsis, the Hindus call them—meditate on God, and while so meditating discern the everlasting laws of the spirit, and it is the concrete record of these laws so discerned, that constitutes, in each cycle, the most authoritative or sacred writings. The record of the meditations of the rsis born at the beginning of our own cycle is, then, what we know as the Vedas

Thus far the account is, to orthodox eves, literal truth. However, around the origin and early development of the Vedas are clustered many myths and symbols. Some of these we may now glance at—though in so doing we should realize that gods of the Hindu, or devas as he calls them, must always be sharply distinguished from God. God is the one supreme being, the uncreated, while the gods, though supernatural, belong (together with many ot her orders of supernatural beings) among the creatures. Like the Christian angels, they are much nearer to man than to God.

'As smoke and sparks arise from a lighted fire kindled with damp fuel'—runs one account—'even so, Maitreyi, have breathed forth from the Eternal all knowledge and all wisdom—what we know as; the Rg-Veda[2] the Yajur Veda, and the rest. They are the breath of the Eternal.[3] And another, more circumstantial: 'The gods performed a sacrificial rite, meditating on the transcendental being as the sacrifice itself. From out that sacrifice came Rk, Sāma, and Yajur[4]. (The Atharva—see the Table, above—which was probably later than the others, and of minor importance, is not here mentioned.) And another relates, with still more circumstance, how the god Brahma was once meditating on his creator when there was manifested within the shrine of his heart the eternal word Om—the seed of all knowledge and of all thought. One by one were also manifested the sounds of all the letters, and through these letters there became known unto Brahmā the wisdom of the Vedas. Then in order to spread this knowledge through the world he taught it to his disciples—to Marīci, Atri, Aṅgiras, and others—and these in turn to the world around them. In this fashion did the Vedas become known to all mankind.

By way of accounting for certain subdivisions of the Yajur a story is told[5] which has about it, like so many of the ancient scriptural narratives, a quaint, childlike humour. On a certain occasion the ṛṣis, it seems, planned a conference. 'Whoever fails to attend', they announced, 'will commit a great sin—equal to that of killing a brāhmin.[6] Now Vaiśampāyana failed to attend, and, as a consequence, the curse of all the other ṛṣis fell upon him. In order to expiate his offence he requested his disciples to practise austerities. One disciple, however, Yājñavalkya by name, remonstrated thus 'Master, how can you expiate your sins by austerities of these the worthless disciples': I am the *one* amongst them who alone can bring good unto these practices.' At this Vaiśampāyana grew angry, and said: 'How dare you speak thus? I want no such hot-headed, egotistical disciple as you! Give back what you have learned from me, and be off!'

So the egotist Yājñavalkya spewed from his mouth all that he had learned, and departed. His fellow disciples, unable to endure this insult to their knowledge, assumed the form of tittiri birds and gathered up the lore that had been ejected and taught it to their pupils. Thus it was that the branch of the Yajur called the Black Yajur, or, with reference to the birds, the Taittirīya, came into being.

Now Yājñavalkya, having cast away his knowledge of the Vedas, felt how empty he was, and realized what a very beast a man becomes who is destitute of this wisdom. But where might be find a teacher . Then it occurred to him that the sun-god never separates himself, from the Vedas; for in the morning he is adorned with the Ṛg-Veda, at noon with the Yajur Veda, and in the evening" with the Sāma Veda. And so, accepting the sun-god as his raster, Yājñavalkya prayed to him for knowledge. The sun-god, pleased with the ardour of his new votary, did according to his desire, and the portion of the Vedas which he taught him was henceforth known as the White Yajur. Yājñavalkya then, in his turn, taught this to his disciples.

For the study of the Vedas, according to long tradition, and even according to the Vedas themselves, one must have—as Yājñavalkya had—a master, or guru: 'Approach a teacher', we read in the Ṛk, 'with humility and with a desire to serve'; and in the Upaniṣads: 'To many' is not given to hear of the Self. Many, though they hear of it, do not understand it. Wonderful is he who speaks of it; intelligent is he who learns, of it. Blessed is he who, taught by a good teacher, is able to understand it.[7]

The function of the 'good teacher', as Hinduism conceives it, is two-fold. He of course explains the scriptures, the spirit as well as the letter; but, what is more important still, he teaches by his life—by his little daily acts, by his most casual words, sometimes even by his silence. Only to be near him, only to serve and obey him in humility and reverence, is to become quickened in spirit; and the purpose of the study of the Vedas is not merely or primarily to inform the intellect, but to purify and enrich the soul:

> Pleasant indeed are the study and teaching of the Vedas!
> He who engages in these things attains to concentration of
> mind,
> And is no longer a slave to his passions;
> Devout, self-controlled, cultivated in spirit,
> He rises to fame and is a blessing to mankind.[8]

We have said that the orthodox Hindu regards the Vedas as his highest written authority Any subsequent scripture, if he is to regard it as valid, must be in agreement with them it may expand them, it may develop them, and still be recognized, but it must not contradict them. They are to him, as nearly as any human document can be, the expression of divine truth. At the same time it would be a mistake to suppose that his allegiance to their authority is, in the final analysis, blind and automatic. If he considers them the word of God, it is because he believes their truth to be verifiable, immediately, at any moment, in his own personal experience. If he found on due examination that it was not so verifiable, he would reject it. If he found that any part ot it was not so verifiable, he would reject that. In short, he conceives that his faith in the Vedas is as well founded, and on grounds exactly as critical as is the natural scientist's belief in any physical law. And in this position these very scriptures themselves, he will tell you, uphold him The real study, they say, is—not study of themselves—but study of that 'by which we realize the unchangeable'. In other words, the real study, in religion, is first-hand experience of God.

The Vedas teach the knowledge of God, and lay down work as a means to that knowledge—the word work here signifying both sacrificial rites and unselfish performance of secular duty. When through we our hearts are purified, we are ripe for divine knowledge, Work and knowledge—these two are the subjects of the Vedas and name the parts into which (as a Table has already indicated) Ṛk, Sāma, Yajur and Atharva are each divided

The two following, chapters will deal, respectively, with the work portion ot the Vedas and with the knowledge portion—the latter and much the more important being universally known as the Upaniṣads.

CHAPTER XVII

SAMHITĀS, BRĀHMAṆAS, ĀRAṆYAKAS

The work portion of the Vedas, immensely important though it has been to the concrete practice of religion in India, has less interest for us today than the knowledge portion. Still, we must not fail to obtain some further idea of it, and especially of the first of its three divisions—the Samhitās.

Samhitās

The Samhitās are collections of mantras, or hymns, most of which sing the praises of one or another personal god. Sometimes the god is conceived as little more than a magnified man. In one hymn for example, Indra, the god of rain, has a body clad in golden armour, is very strong, and descends to earth, where he lives and eats with his votaries, fights and overcomes their enemies the demons, and establishes his dominion. Similarly Varuṇa, in another hymn, is described as a mere nature god, presiding in anthropomorphic form over air and water. But, again, the god—even at times the same god that was just now so much a man—becomes nothing less than the Supreme Being, omniscient, omnipresent, omnipotent—and that within which the visible world is contained. Thus Varuṇa:

Wherever two together plot, and deem they are alone,
King Varuṇa is there, a third, and all their schemes are known.
This earth is his, to him belong these last and boundless skies;
Both seas within him rest, and yet in that small pool he lies.
Whoever far beyond the sky should think his way to wing,
He could not there elude the grasp of Varuṇa the king.
His spies descending from the skies glide all this world around,
Their thousand eyes all-scanning sweep to earth's remotest bound
Whate'er exists in heaven and earth, whate'er beyond the skies,
Before the eyes of Varuṇa, the king, unfolded lies.
The ceaseless winkings all he counts of every mortal's eyes:
He wields this universal frame, as gamester throws his dice.[9]

In Varuṇa in his more exalted manifestation, dwells Ṛta—conceived as the principle of universal law and order, physical and spiritual. Existing forever in Varuṇa, in complete perfection, this principle is but palely reflected in the created world Yet it is because of it that there exists a moral order, because of it that the sun, moon, and stars, morning and evening, day and night, keep their appointed times 'The dawn follows the path of Ṛta, the right path—as if knowing it before. Never does she lose her way. The sun follows the path of Ṛta.[10]

Perhaps highest in conception of the gods with concrete names is Hiraṇyagarbha

'Before the universe appeared, there first appeared Hiraṇyagarbha. He, being manifest, became the one lord of the manifested universe. Out of himself came the invisible world, out of himself came the sky and this earth Unto him whose being is unknown and unknowable, whose desire it as that this universe be created, who is the source of happiness—unto him we offer our sacrifice! Unto him who is the purifier of our hearts, who is the giver of strength, whose command all beings, together with the gods, obey, whose shadow is immortality as well as mortality, whose being is unknown and unknowable, whose desire it was that this universe be created, who is the source of happiness—unto him we offer our sacrifice![11]

In the following; famous hymn, the Puruṣa Sūkta, the Supreme Being, or God is represented as at once concrete ('infinite heads', 'unnumbered eyes') and in the highest degree abstract—beyond all predicates: He both is and is not the created universe, for while the created universe is a part of his being it is not the whole of it.

'The Universal Being has infinite heads, unnumbered eyes, and unnumbered feet. Enveloping the universe on every side, he exists transcending it. All this is he—what has been and what shall be. He is the lord of immortality. Though he has become all this, in reality he is not all this. For verily is he transcendental. The whole series of universes—past. present, and future—express his glory and power; but he transcends his own glory. All beings of the universe form as it were, a fraction of his being; the rest of it is self-luminous, and universe. That part of him which is the relative universe appears as sentient and insentient beings. From a part of him was born the body of the universe and out of this body were born the gods, the earth, and men.[12]

In the passage, it may be observed in passing, there is a definite rejection of pantheism: 'Though he has become all this, in reality he is not all this: 'The words are characteristic of all Indian thought, and will be echoed and re-echoed in later pages of this book. There is, properly speaking, whatever appearances may sometimes suggest to the contrary, no pantheism in India. The Hindu sees God as the ultimate energy in and behind all creation, but never, either in ancient or in modern times, as identical with it.

It is a far cry from the rain-god Indra, with his golden armour, to a Universal Being who envelops and transcends the world; but a step still remained to be taken, and this also the Saṁhitās took. Indra and the Universal Being had one thing in common: they were both personal gods. It is true that the Universal Being was said to be 'beyond all predicates', it also, in almost the same breath, he was said to possess heads, and eyes, and feet, and to transcend, his own glory'.

'Who has seen the first-born when he that had no bones bore him that has bones? Where is the life, the blood, the self of the universe? Who went to ask of any who knew?[13] Thus from the conception of God as a personal being the Vedic seers passed on to almost their final conception of him as utterly impersonal, so remote indeed from resemblance to anything human that no longer will they refer to him as 'he' or 'him', but only as TAD EKAM—in English, THAT. It is under this designation that he appears in the hymn of creation, called the Nāsadīya hymn:

Existence was not, nor its opposite,
Nor earth, nor heaven's blue vault, nor aught beyond.
The subtle elements that are the veil
Of this so insubstantial world, where then
Might they find out a place? by whom be known?
The deep abyss of waters—where was that?
Death was not yet, nor deathlessness, the day
Was night, night day, for neither day nor night
Had come to birth. Then THAT, the primal font
Of life—breathless—to its own maya joined—
Brooded eternally. Itself beside,
In the wide universe there nothing was.
In the beginning gloom—gloom hidden in gloom!
From its cause undistinguished stood the world:
But lo, thereafter, from its darkling state—
Yet undistinguished from its cause—it rose,
By the pure will of THAT made manifest
Whence came this will? From out a seed it came
Asleep within the heart of THAT—the seed
Of vanished worlds that have in order wheeled
Their silent courses from eternity:
The manifest in the unmanifest they found—
The sages, searching deep within themselves . . . .
Ah, what are words, and what all mortal thought!
Who is there truly knows, and who can say,
Whence this unfathomed world, and from what cause?
Nay, even the gods were not! Who, then, can know?
The source from which this universe hath sprung,
That source, and that alone, which bears it up—
None else: THAT, THAT alone, lord of the worlds,
In its own self contained, immaculate
As are the heavens, above, THAT alone knows

The truth of what itself hath made—none else.[14]

This famous hymn has provided the basis for a great deal of philosophic speculation. For in it God is represented (it may be observed) as both the material and the efficient cause of the universe—both that out of which it has made, and that by which it was made. In it also is that extraordinary conception of the universe, alluded to in the preceding chapter, as continually alternating between the phase of expression and the phase of potentiality; birth, existence, destruction—then a state of quiescence—then again birth, existence, destruction; and so on forever.

The preceding brief survey of the varying conceptions of God in the Samhitās quite naturally raises two questions. The first is this: Why is it that now one god, now another, is lifted to the loftiest position and celebrated as the supreme divinity? Professor Max Muller has observed this phenomenon, and named it henotheism, but has done little to fathom its mystery. Its true explanation is to be found in the hymn themselves; 'and it is a grand explanation,' declares. Swami Vivekananda 'one that has given the theme to all subsequent thought in India and one that will be the theme of the whole world of religions: ekaṁ sat viprāḥ bahudhā vadanti[15]—"That which exists in One: sages call it by various names."[16]

The subject is worth pausing with, for in the quoted words lies the secret not only of an aspect of the Vedic hymns but also—as Swami Vivekananda suggest—if an aspect of the religious life of India throughout her long history. Casual visitors to this ancient land carry away with them the impression of an elaborate polytheism. True it is that India has always had many Gods—but in appearance only. In reality she has had but one God, though with prodigal inventiveness she has called him 'by various names'. Indra, Varuṇa, Hiraṇyagarbha—Rāma, Kṛṣṇa, Śiva: What does it matter? Whichever of these or of many others the Hindu chooses for his adoration, that one becomes for him God himself, in whom exist all things, including, for the time being, all other Gods. It is because India has been so permeated with the spirit of Ekaṁ sat viprāḥ bahudhā vadanti that she has known relatively little of religious fanaticism, of religious persecution, of religious wars. Characteristically she has sought the truth in every faith—even in faiths not her own.

But there was a second question: Why is it that in the, Vedic hymns we find elementary ideas of God as well as the most advanced. To the Western scholar there is here no mystery; for he is accustomed to think of all things in terms of evolution, as he conceive evolution, and in the simpler anthropomorphic notions he sees the first stages of a growth which slowly ripens to abstraction. But not so the orthodox Hindu. What he sees in the graduated scale of Vedic conceptions is a beneficent correspondence to varied stages of religious attainment, Some men are but barbarians in spiritual things; others are seers and sages. The Vedas (and this, say the orthodox, was a clear purpose of the exalted rsis) minister to all according to their needs. Some they teach to fly; some they must first teach to walk. To those at a low sage they offer polytheism, even at times materialism; to those at a higher stage monotheism; and to those at the top of the scale a notion of God so utterly impersonal, so devoid of anything describable in human terms, as to be suited only to the greatest saints, and to these only in their most strenuous moments.

For it would appear, in general, that even the greatest of Hindu saints have found the, conception of God as abstract reality too rarefied for constant use. Occasionally they rise to it, but not for long. Like more ordinary mortals they too have yearned for a notion of divinity close to their minds and hearts, something they could readily and meditate upon, and worship.

In the contrasting spiritual levels of the Vedic hymns, as interpreted by the orthodox, we touch on a general aspect of Indian thought to which we must often return: its variety and flexibility, despite its extraordinary central oneness—its remarkable genius for adaptation.

Brāhmaṇas

The Brāhmaṇas, in comparison with the Saṁhitās, are concerned with practical, everyday things—with the details of sacrificial rites and with specific duties and rules of conduct.

Brāhmaṇāḥ vividiṣanti yajñena dānena—The Brāhmāṇi desire to know, with the sacrifices and charity as the means. That is, when the heart becomes purified by the performance of sacrifices and charity, there arises the knowledge of Brahman. Thus is acknowledged the need for the performance of sacrifices and for the ceremonials and rites of religion. But it is true that at times undue importance was laid on these things, as well as on the mere chanting of the words of the Vedas, so much so that the sacrifices themselves often took the place of a living religion—a circumstance that occurs in the development of all religious institutions.

Under such conditions, prayer and supplication before the object of worship becomes unnecessary; for by the performance of elaborate and fixed sacrifices the Gods may be forced to grant one's desires. Professor Das Gupta believes that in these sacrificial rites is to be found the germ of the law of karma (which Manu later systematized philosophically): 'Thou canst not gathet-what thou dost not sow. As thou dost sow, so wilt thou reap.[17]

This hardening of the institutional part of religion exalted in time the power of the priests; and it was in opposition to the externalizing and crystallizing of what should .have remained living symbols of truths behind appearances, and also in opposition to the tyranny of a rising priesthood, that Buddha rose in revolt. The Bhagavad-Gītā had already condemned the tendency to attribute undue importance to ritualistic sacrifices.

The duties and rules of conduct prescribed by the Brāhmaṇas are largely those common to all religious creeds. Self-control is emphasized, and love, and kindness; theft, murder, and adultery are forbidden. We are all deep in debt, declare the Brāhmaṇas, the most important of our obligations being those to the Gods to the seers, to the spirits of the dead, to living men and to animals. Our debt to the gods we must pay with sacrifices; to the seers with feelings of admiration and devotion; to departed spirits with prayers in their behalf; to living men with love and kindness; to animals with food and drink—and to all of these, whenever we partake of nourishment, we must render a portion to the accompaniment of fitting prayers.

By the due discharge of these our moral debts we achieve no merit but if we neglect them we become unworthy of our priviledge status as human being. Our duties must be performed, moreover with no thought of self for selfish ends, but simply because they are or a righteous man, duties—and because they purify the heart.

Āraṇyakas

The Āraṇyakas, or forest treatises, need detain us but a moment. They may most simply be regarded as a supplement to the Brāhmaṇas—and corrective. Like the Brāhmaṇas, they deal much in rites and ceremonies, but unlike the Brāhmaṇas they do not rest in them. They are vividly aware that not in rites and ceremonies, but in the truths they stand for, lies their real importance; and so from the fruit or flesh of the sacrifice they pass to its spiritual interpretation.

In so doing, in so occupying themselves less with the outward symbol than with the inner reality, they come close to the chief and central glory of all the Vedas—the universally admired Upaniṣads.

Before we come to deal with the Upaniṣads, a few remarks regarding the division of each of the Vedās seem pertinent. Professor Paul Deussen has rightly declared that this division into Saṁhitās, Brāhmaṇas, Āraṇyakas, and lastly Upaniṣads is based on the principle of dividing life into āśramas, or stages. According to Vedic teachings, man's life is divided into four stages. First is the brāhmachrya, or student life, when a boy lives with his teacher and receives both religious and secular instruction. The youth is trained in self-control and acquires such duties as chastity, truthfulness, faith, and self surrender. The next stage is gārhasthya, or married life. The chief injunction for this stage is to practise the ritualistic sacrifices as explained in the Brāhmaṇas. At the stage of vanaprastha, or retirement, a man is no longer required to adhere to ritualism, but is instructed to follow the Āraṇyakas and engage in symbolic meditation. Finally, he enters upon the life of renunciation, in which he is bound neither by work nor by desire, but is dedicated wholly to acquiring knowledge of Brāhmaṇa.

Thus the general plan of life as taught in the Vedas is, successively, student life, married life, the life of retirement, and the life of renunciation. Each of these periods of a man's mortal existence has its special duties and observances, though it is also true that through a special Vedic declaration a person may enter immediately into the life of renunciation, and not pass through the intermediate stages of probation.

Through the institution of monasticism a man may begin early the life of renunciation. When one enters a monastery, one passes through a Vedic ritual, meanwhile meditating upon the truths of the Upaniṣads. According to Vedic teachings, monastic life is the highest stage a man may attain. Modern India retains this idea, and there are not wanting today men highly trained in Western science and literature who are willing to assume monastic vows. Thus the influence of the Vedās has been perpetuated through the ages.

Parenthetically it may be said that the daily life and conduct of the people of India even today are guided by the injunctions of the Vedās. This is particularly true of the ceremonies connected with birth, marriage and death. In the words of Professor S. N. Das Gupta, 'The laws which regulate the social, legal, domestic and religious customs and rites of the Hindus even to the present day are said to be but mere systematized memories of old Vedic teachings, and are held to be obligatory on their authority.' Every brāhmaṇa repeats daily the Vedic prayer called the Gāyatrī mantra, which is a verse from the Ṛg-Veda: It runs as follows:

Om bhur bhuvaṇ swaḥ tat savitur vareṇyam, bhargo devasya dhīmahi, dhiyo yo naḥ pracodayāt, Om. (May) meditate on the effulgent Light [or power] of him who is worshipful, and who has given birth to all worlds. May he direct the rays of our intelligence towards the path of good.)

REFERENCE

1.Ṛk, when joined with Veda, becomes Ṛg, by a regular change of consonant.

2. Ṛk, when joined with Veda, becomes Ṛg, by a regular change of conosnant.

3. Bṛhadāraṇyaka Upaniṣad, II. iv. 10.

4. Ṛg-Veda, x. 90: Puruṣa Sūkta, 9,

5. From the Sanskrit quoted in the Introduction to Durgacharan Sāṁkhya-Vedānta Tirtha's Benglai translation ofthe Īśa Upaniṣad with śaṁkara's commtary (Calcutta: Kshirode Chandra Majumdar).

6. A member, that is, of the Brāhmin, or priestly, caste.

7. Kaṭha, I. ii. 7.

8. Satapatha Brāhmaṇa, Mādhyandini śākhā, XI v.p 7, Swādhyā praśaṇsā.

9. John Muir (trans,); Atharva Veda, iv. 16.p. 1-5.

10. Ṛg. Veda, i. 24.

11. *Ibid.*, x. 12. 1-2.

12 *Ibid.*, x. 90 1-5.

13. Ṛg-Veda, i. 4. 164. Qutoed by s. Radhakrishnan, *Indian Philosophy,* vol. I, p. 93 (London, Allen & Unwin, 1929).

14. Ṛg-Veda, x. 129. 1-7 Swami Prabhavanda and Frederick Manchester (trans.) *Voice of India,* vol. III. no. 1.

15. *Ibid.*, i. p.164.

16. *Complete Work of Swami Vivekananda,* vol. I, p. 347

17. Cf. 'Whatsoever a man soweth,that shall he also reap' (Gal. vi. 7.)

CHAPTER XVIII

THE SMṚTIS, THE PURĀṆAS, THE TANTRAS

The Smṛtis

The Smṛtis embody the laws formulated by saints and sages—Manu, Yājñavalkya, and others.

No date can be definitely assigned to these scriptures, since Oriental scholars differ by as much as several centuries in their estimates. The Code of Manu, for instance, is assigned by Sir William Jones to 1250 B.C., and by Sir Monier Williams to as late as 500 B.C. We can be safe in asserting that the Smṛtis are post-Vedic, in as much as the code of laws found in them is traditionally supposed to be based on the Vedas.

Since to the Hindu mind only the Vedas are wholly sacrosanct, it follows that the Smṛtis at best possess but a secondary authority. They record civil laws, social obligations, and ceremonies performed it the birth of a child, during initiation into Vedic mantra, at marriage, and at the moment of death. They comprise, in short, the daily duties, usages, and customs to be observed by the several castes and by people in different stages of life; and their avowed purpose is to aid all men to attain the highest spiritual development.

The extraordinary thing about these ceremonies, usages, and customs, for daily observance and for special occasions, as practised every in part of India, is their infinite variety and yet their substantial underlying unity. The variety is accounted for by the fact that they were given many different forms, each developing independently of the rest in a particular part of the country; their unity by their common source in the Vedic religion.

For centuries the authority of the Smṛtis has held sway over the minds of the people of India, who have rigidly followed the social laws of these codes. At the present time, however, there is discercible certain laxity in their observance, due to the revolutionary changes that have everywhere occurred. Orthodox Hindus do not feel unduly alarmed at this, for they have always regarded the Smṛtis as of secondary importance. Swami-Vivekananda once remarked to a disciple that a new Smṛti ought to be written for the guidance of modern India. It has already been observed that a distinction is made between Smṛtis, or traditions, and śruti, or revelations. The śrutis are direct, immediate experience of Reality; the Smṛtis are man-made laws. The latter embody, to be sure, certain eternal truths, but they are truths capable of adaptation to changing times.

Of all the Smṛtis, the Code of Manu possesses the highest authority. Manu, according to the orthodox view, was the first man.[1] Tradition declares that Brahmā gave him a code of laws in one hundred thousand verses, which for practical purposes he reduced to four thousand.

Among the duties and disciplines prescribed by the Laws of Manu are conquest of the senses, freedom from lust and greed, study of the sacred scriptures, and detachment from the world. One must speak only when necessary, honour old age, respect one's parents, and injure no one, whether in thought, word, or deed. In the twelve books of Manu there is an account of creation, and there are teachings regarding education, marriage, domestic life, laws of the state, punishments, reincarnation, and ultimate freedom. The main-purpose of the code was to preserve a fixed society, and it has actually maintained during many centuries the racial integrity of the Indian people.

Fundamentally, the code insists upon the intelligent exercise of the will in conformity to the will of God. The principles involved, not necessarily the laws as crystallized by long and formal application, are universal in their truth and in their acceptability. Self-control, for example, receives great stress. A man must subdue his lust, and even while he is a student he must not consciously lapse from strict continence. All this is in preparation for marriage and for the ultimate state of sannyas, or renunciation.

The Purāṇas[2]

The word purāṇa literally means ancient, the name being applied to certain scriptures to mean 'that which lives from of old' or 'that which is ever new though old'. The Purāṇas were written mainly to popularize the abstract ethical and spiritual truths of the Vedas and the Upaniṣads by means of concrete illustrations from the lives of avatārs, saints, sages, kings, and devotees, whether historical or legendary. K. S. Ramaswami, the Indian scholar, has thus described them:

'. . . the Purāṇas are a vital portion of the scriptures of the Hindus. They are primarily an extension, amplification and illustration of the spiritual truths declared in the Vedas. Outsiders may call them legends like the works of fiction current today. Some insiders too may regard them as mere illustrative fictions or allegories, or as relating to yogic realities unconnected with the external material world. But the bulk of the Hindus and the main body of traditional opinion attribute to the Purāṇas a double character, viz. illustrative value and impressive actuality. They have largely moulded public life. belief and conduct in our land for thousands of years, and they must be fully utilized by us if we are to realize the truths of the Vedas.

Herein lies their permanent and supreme value to us.[3]

Altogether there are eighteen Purāṇas, six devoted to Viṣṇu, six to Brahmā, and six to śiva. All of them are written in verse, and all are usually attributed to Vyāsa, the reputed author of the Mahābhārata and editor of the Vedas. Their date may safely be assigned to the somewhat uncertain Epic Period.

At this time the Vedic gods, such as Indra, Mitra, Varuṇa, and Skanda, were transformed into the three divinities Brahmā, Viṣṇu, and śiva; and these in turn were conceived as but manifestations of, the one primeval Spirit, the Lord adored by all, the one undecaying Brahman.[4] Brahmā, Viṣṇu, and śiva (the last of these being also called Rudra, Mahādeva, and Maheśwara) are known as the Trimūrti, or Trinity, of the Hindus. In the words of the Viṣṇu Purāṇa: 'The Lord Cod, though one without a second, assumes the three forms respectively of Brahmā, Viṣṇu, and Śiva for creation, preservation and dissolution of the world.' And in the Padma Purāṇa we read: 'Brahmā, Viṣṇu, and Śiva, though three in form, are one entity. No difference between the three exists except with respect to attributes.' Moreover, the votaries of this Trimūrti make no distinction between them, as they identify one with another. Viṣṇu, for example, is described as Śiva's arrow, and Śiva as Kṛṣṇa's flute. Kṛṣṇa, again, is regarded as the incarnation of Viṣṇu.

The Purāṇas, then, popularize the abstract teachings of the Upaniṣads by means of stories concerning saints, sages, and kings. Some of these legends and tales are common to all the Purāṇas, though in details and in method of presentation they differ widely. The principal beauty of the Purāṇas lies in the fact that they reconcile knowledge and devotion. Śrī Ramakṛṣṇa, speaking of the Bhāgavata Purāṇa, quaintly but suggestively remarks, 'It is fried in the butter of knowledge and steeped in the honey of love.'

The Bhāgavatam is not only the most popular of all the Purānas but is regarded by the Vaiṣṇavas as one of the genuinely authoritative scriptures. For these reasons we shall choose it for special attention.

Vyāsa, according to legend, wrote the Bhāgavatam and taught it to śuka his son, who in turn made it public.

As an introduction to the Bhāgavatam, the narrator tells an interesting story concerning this śuka, who is regarded by all Hindus as one of the greatest saints of all the Ages.

'Suka, the son of Vyāsa, was indeed a great yogi, a knower of Brahman, who realized unity in the midst of diversity. His mind and consciousness were always united with God. We have heard about him, and how, after beginning the life of renunciation, having no consciousness of his body, he would walk about naked. One day, while thus walking in the wood, he passed by a lake in which some nymphs were bathing. They watched him pass, feeling no shyness in his presence; but as Vyāsa, who was following his son, approached, they hastily got out of the water and clothed themselves. This surprised the great sage, and he asked the nymphs, "Why do you act so strangely, my children? You did not shrink from the young śuka, who was naked, yet you feel shy before me, an old man, fully clothed." To this the nymphs replied: "Revered sir, in you there lingers a trace of the consciousness of sex, but in your son Suka there is none."[6]

Following is śuka's prayer to the Lord as recorded in the Bhāgavatam. It is typical of the Hindu mind.

O thou Lord supreme, I bow down to thee!
For thy sole pleasure and play midst thou bring forth this universe.
Thou art the highest in the highest! Who can sing thine infinite glory?
Thou art the innermost ruler of every heart;
Thy paths are mysterious;
Thy ways are blessed.

Thou dost wipe away all the tears of thy devotees;
Thou dost destroy the wickedness of the wicked.
Thy form is purity itself, and thou dost give purity and Self-knowledge to those who seek thee.
Salutations to thee again and again, O Lord of hosts!

I praise thee, O Lord!
Thou art the strength and support of all thy worshipers;
Thou art manifest in the hearts of all true yogis;
The evildoer findeth thee not.
Thou art one without a second.
Thou dost shine in thine own glory, in thy resplendent, blissful Self.

What sweetness is in thy name,
What joy is in thy remembrance!
Those who chant thy holy name, and meditate on thee, become forever free from all evils;
The wise, worshiping thy feet, conquer all fears of life and death:
Thus do they realize thee, thou supreme goal of all true seekers.

Before thee there is no barrier of caste, or race, or creed:
All thy children attain purity through thy holy name.
Calm souls worship thee, knowing that they are one with thee.
Thou art the Lord supreme,

Thou art indeed the Vedas,
Thou art the Truth,
Thou art the goal of all discipline;
Thy lovers meditate on thy blissful form, and become lost in the joy thereof.

Shower thy grace upon me, O Lord, and in thy mercy look upon me!
Thou art the Lord of wealth,
Thou art the Lord of all creation,
The Lord of all thy lovers and devotees.
Look upon all beings with thy mercy!
Blessed are they that meditate on thy Lotus Feet,
For they shall be purified;
Blessed are they that are purified,
For they shall attain Self-knowledge.
The wise call thee the impersonal, without attributes;
They also call thee the personal God with divine attributes;
Thou art both, and thou dost manifest thyself as the one or the other,
According to our understanding.
O Lord, forever look in mercy upon me![7]

Cosmology has a definite place in all of the Purāṇas. The following is a resume of the story of creation as we find it recounted in the Bhāgavatam.

'Creation has no absolute beginning. The present universe is but one of a series of worlds that are past and of worlds that are to be. The cosmic energy alternates between periods of potentiality and of expression. The phase of potentiality is known as dissolution; the phase of expression is known as creation.

'Created things are of different kinds. The avyakta, or cosmic energy, consists of three gunas. When the equilibrium of the gunas 'is disturbed, .there are manifested universal intelligence, universal ego, the mind the senses and the organs of sense, the subtle principle of the elements, and the elements themselves. As these combine and recombine in various ways, all beings attain to existence.

'Among them there are sthavara, or stationary beings, such as herbs, shrubs, creepers, and plants. They have unmanifested consciousness. In them the sense of touch alone has evolved.

'Then there are the brute species, the animals in which the sense of smell is highly developed.

'Next comes man.

Lastly, there are the devas, the pitris, the gandharvas, and Kinnaras. These are gods, demigods, angels, and spirits.

'All things whatsoever were created by Brahma.
'Thus it was that Creation came to pass:

'While the world was yet submerged beneath the ocean, God lay brooding on Naga, king of the serpents, as Naga floated upon the waters. God was resting with eyes closed, but his consciousness was fully awake. He was completely merged in the bliss of his own Self.

'As the time of creation drew nigh. God felt a stir within his being, and there issued forth from the centre of his person a full-blown Lotus. Its light was dazzling, and the whole ocean was illumined by its splendour.

'Within this Lotus were all ıe materials for creation.

'Immediately Brahma came forth from the Lotus, and, seating himself upon it, turned his head in all directions to see whether any other beings were present. Hence he is called the four-faced Brahma.

'Brahma did not recognize himself, and had no recollection of his previous creations. After a time he became restless and felt a desire for knowledge. Looking about him and seeing in the external world no hope for the fulfilment of this desire, he sought in meditation for the knowledge which he realized must be within himself, and at last he found the Truth, and God himself, within his own heart. He then saw God everywhere, and felt blest indeed.

Then God spoke to him, saying:

"Oh Brahma, I command thee again create the world, as thou hast often done in times past. To create is to thee not new. Whatsoever is to be created is already within me, as 'thou well knowest. Creation is only the projection into form of that which already exists.'"

'While God was yet speaking, a strong wind arose and lashed the water into a fury. With the knowledge and power which he had acquired through the practice of tapas, Brahma withdrew into himself the wind and all the waters of the sea; and then finding himself floating on the water, still seated on the Lotus, he re-entered the heart of the Lotus, and dividing it into three sections created the 'three spheres—heaven, earth, and sky.

'Brahma also gave to the world the four Vedas: the Rig, the Sama, the Yajur, and the Atharva.'

'Brahma is the personification of what the philosophers call the Sphota, the word Om. He is called the first-born of God.

'Brahma's first human creations were saints, who, immediately upon being created, fell into deep meditation, finding no interest in the things of the world. Thus, through them, Brahma saw no possibility of propagation of their species. While he was meditating upon what course he should pursue, his own form divided itself; one half became man and the other half became woman.'

'The man was called Manu, and the woman Shatarupa; and from them have sprung all mankind.'[8]

As we have already seen, neither the Purāṇas nor the other scriptures of the Hindus, nor the philosophers of India at any time, declare in favour of an absolute beginning or an absolute end of creation. Rather, they believe that the cosmic universe passes through phases of potentiality and manifestation. The Purāṇas assert, moreover, that the universe moves in cycles. They describe the historic evolution of life by a division of these into four, called the four yugas—satya, tretā, dwāpara, and kali. The duration of kali yuga, which is the present age, is 432,000 years. That of satya, tretā, and dwāpara is respectively, four times, three times, and twice the duration of kali yuga. All four yugas combined form a mahāyuga, or great cycle.

The peculiar characteristics of each of the four are named in the Purāṇas. In satya yuga, for example, virtue is in the ascendant, and it grows progressively less through the cycles until in kali yuga it is practised least. After kali yuga; however, satya yuga again appears, and so on through eternity.

According to the orthodox view, Rāma, the hero of the Rāmāyaṇa, lived in tretā yuga, and Kṛṣṇa lived near the end of dwāpara yuga. At Kṛṣṇa's passing, kali yuga came into existence, and about 400,000 years of this cycle have already elapsed. The final impression left on the mind by this vast procession of numbers is that this world of ours is very, very old. Many a civilization has appeared and in time disappeared, and still human life continues.

Of the twelve books into which the Bhāgavatam is divided, the tenth and the eleventh are the most important. The tenth tells the life story of Kṛṣṇa, and the eleventh contains the instructions he gave to his disciple and friend Uddhava.

The chief part of Śrī Kṛṣṇa's story is the rasa-līlā, his play with the shepherdesses; and this part is most glaringly misrepresented by Western scholars, who have failed to understand the—meaning of the original. A brief summary of the episode will help us to interpret correctly the significance of Śrī Kṛṣṇa to the Hindu mind.

He embodies the quality of love. Love is divine, and love finds expression in many forms. To Yaśodā, God was her own baby Kṛṣṇa. To the shepherd boys he was Kṛṣṇa, their beloved friend and playmate, and to the shepherd girls he was Kṛṣṇa, their beloved friend, lover, and companion.

When Kṛṣṇa played on his flute, the shepherdesses forgot everything, even their own bodies, and ran to him for the sake of his great, compelling love. Once Kṛṣṇa, to test their love for him, said to them, 'Oh, ye pure ones, your duties must first be to your husbands and children. You do not need to come to me, for if you only meditate on me you will gain salvation.' The shepherdesses replied, 'Oh, thou cruel lover, we aspire to serve only thee. Thou knowest the scriptural truths, and thou dost advise us to serve our husbands and our children. Yes, we will abide by thy teachings. But thou art in all, and thou art all. By serving thee we serve all.'

Kṛṣṇa, who gives delight to all and is blissful in his own being, divided himself into as many Kṛṣṇas as there were gopīs, or shepherdesses, and danced and played with them. Each gopi felt the divine presence and the divine love of Śrī Kṛṣṇa. Each one felt herself most blessed, and each one's love for him was so absorbing that she felt herself one with him—each one even realized that she was Kṛṣṇa.

Truly has it been said that those who meditate on the divine love of Śrī Kṛṣṇa, and upon this sweet relationship with the gopīs, become free from lust and sensuality.

Swami Vivekananda has made some pertinent remarks upon the ideal of the shepherdesses in the life of Kṛṣṇa:

'Ah, that most marvellous passage of his life, the most difficult to understand, and which none ought to attempt to understand until he has become perfectly chaste and pure, that most marvellous expansion of love, allegorized and expressed in that beautiful play in Brindaban, which none can understand but he who has become mad with, and drunk deep of, the cup of love. Who can understand the throes of the love of the gopīs—the very ideal of love, love that wants nothing, love that does not care even for heaven, love that does not care for anything in this world or the world to come?

"The historian who records this marvellous love of the gopīs is one who was born pure, the eternally pure śuka, the son of Vyāsa. So long as there is selfishness in the heart, so long is love of God impossible; it is nothing but shopkeeping."[9]

'Aye, forget first the love for gold, and name and fame, and for 'this little trumpery world of ours. Then, only then, you will understand the love of the gopīs, too holy to be attempted without giving up everything, too sacred to be understood until the soul has become perfectly pure...

'That is the very essence of the Krishna incarnation. Even the Gītā, the great philosophy itself, does not compare with that madness, for in the Gītā the disciple is taught slowly how to walk towards the goal, but here is the madness of enjoyment, the drunkenness of love, where disciples and teachers and teachings and books, all these things, have become one, even the ideas of fear and God and heaven! Everything has been thrown away. What remains is the madness of love. It is forgetfulness of everything, and the lover sees nothing in the world except that Krishna, and Krishna alone—the face of everything becomes a Krishna, his own face looks like Krishna, his own soul has become tinged with the Krishna colour. That was the great Krishna.'

The eleventh book contains the teachings of Kṛṣṇa regarding love, knowledge, service, and meditation. They are essentially the teachings of the Upaniṣads and the Gītā. Perhaps they are best summarized in the following words of Kṛṣṇa, addressed to Uddhava, from the eleventh book:

'The first requisites for spiritual life are these: doing no injury; being truthful, honest, non-attached, modest; abstaining from wealth; maintaining faith in an after-life; practicing continence, silence, patience, forgiveness, fearlessness, physical and mental purity, austerity, self-reliance, hospitality; chanting the name of the Lord; performing sacrifices; surrendering the self to me; making pilgrimages; working for the good of others; and serving the teacher. These are known in yoga as the practices of yama and niyama. These, my friend, if rightly followed, bring great spiritual unfoldnent.

Calmness is a steady flow of the mind toward God.
Self-restraint is control of the organs of sense.
Patience is bearing the burden of life cheerfully.
Steadiness is overcoming the palate and the impulse of sex.
The highest charity is refraining from violence.
Austerity is the giving up of desire.
Valour is the conquest of one's own self.
To know the truth is to see the oneness of the Self with God.
Truthfulness is true and agreeable speech as exemplified by the sages.
Purity is nonattachment to work.
Renunciation is overcoming the world.
'Virtue is the treasure which men covet.
I, the supreme Lord, am the sacrifice.
The greatest gift is the gift of knowledge.
The greatest strength is the control of prāṇa.
Fortunate is he who meditates on my divine powers.

The highest profit is in devotion to me.
Wisdom is removing false ideas of multiplicity and realizing the unity of the Self.
Modesty is abhorrence of evil deeds.
Excellence of character arises from disregard of worldly considerations.
Happiness is the transcending of both pleasure and pain.
Misery is hankering after pleasures of sense.
Learned is he who discriminates between bondage and freedom.
Ignorant is he who identifies himself with the body.
The right path is that which leads to me.
The wrong path is that which causes restlessness of the mind.
Heaven is the domination of sattwa in the mind.
Hell is the predominance of tamas.
The teacher who has realized his oneness with me is the true friend.
He indeed is rich who is rich in virtues.
Poor is he who is discontented.
Mean is he who is, not master of his senses.
Godly is he who is not attached to objects of sense.
Divine is he who has overcome both good and evil.[10]

The Tantras

The Tantras are the scriptures by means of which knowledge is spread in order to save humanity from ignorance. They are also known as Āgamas—revelations, in conformity, that is, with the revelations of the Vedas. Their authorship is unknown, though there is a tradition that śiva uttered them to his divine consort śakti (the Divine Mother), and that through her they reached mankind. Their date is uncertain, but since Buddha was familiar with them they are obviously pre-Buddhistic. Buddhistic Tantras exist, however, belonging to the Tibetan school of Buddhism.

The original Tantras are divided into three main groups according as the deity chosen for worship is Viṣṇu, Śiva, or Śakti. Thus there are Vaiṣṇava Āgamas (or Pañcarātra), the śaiva Āgamas, and the śākta Āgamas, besides the later Buddhistic Āgamas composed in Tibet. The śākta group is the most popular, so much so that the word Tantra has come to mean, generally though mistakenly, only the śākta Āgamas. It is to these that we shall give our attention.

The Tantras are all broadly divided into three parts: sādhanā, which includes spiritual practices and disciplines and ritualistic forms of worship; siddhi, or attainments from such practices; and philosophy. Let us examine the last of these first.

The philosophy of the Tantras is based on the Upaniṣads. It is nondualistic, upholding the identity of the individual soul with Śiva-Śakti—that is, in the language of the Upaniṣads and of śaṁkara, the identity of the individual self with Brāhman, or the Universal Self. śaṁkara calls the creative power of the universe māyā, or illusion, the universe for him possessing in itself no absolute reality, whereas the Tantras call this creative power Śakti, or God the Mother, and regard the universe as her play when she has become mind and matter. Here, in their interpretation of reality, the Tantras apparently approach the philosophy of Rāmānuja, who looked upon the universe of mind and matter as a transformation of Brahman—as, in effect, the body of God.

This Śakti, or God the Mother, is not distinct from Śiva, or Brahman, the Absolute of the Upaniṣads, but is the power of the Absolute. In the transcendental plane, which is static, where there is but one undivided, absolute existence, and where there is no universe, the truth is known as Śiva, or the Absolute Existence-Knowledge-Bliss; but in the active, immanent plane, that is, the plane in which the universe is known, there is experienced by the seer the play of Śakti, of God the Mother. Śrī Rāmākṛṣṇa was wont to say that just as fire and its burning power are inseparable, so inseparable are Brahman and Śakti. 'When I meditate upon Reality as at rest,' he once remarked, 'that is, without the activities of creation, preservation. and dissolution, I call it Brāhman. When I meditate upon Reality as creative, I call it Śakti. In either case I am concerned with one and the same truth, the difference being only in name and aspect.[12]

According to the Tantras, God the Mother has within herself the seeds of creation. At the end of a cycle she gives birth to a new world and lives within it. In the Upaniṣads a figure is given of the female spider and her web. The spider weaves her thread out of herself and then lives upon it. God the Mother is both the container and the contained.

'It is the desire for the life of form [writes Sir John Woodroffe, in explaining the philosophy of the Tantras] which produces, the universe. This desire exists in the collective Vāsanās [thirst or desires], held like all else in inchoate state in the Mother-Power, which passing from its own (Svarūpa) formless state gives effect to them. Upon the expiration of the vast length of time which constitutes a day of Brahma the whole universe is withdrawn into the great Causal Womb (Yoni) which produced it. The limited selves are withdrawn into it, and again, when the creative throes are felt, are put forth from it, each appearing in that form and state which 'its previous Karma had made for it. Those who do good Karma but with desire and self-regard (Sakāṁa) go, on death, to Heaven and thereafter reap their reward in good future birth on earth—for Heaven is also a transitory state. The bad are punished by evil births on earth and suffering in the Hells which are also transitory. Those, however, who have rid themselves of all self-regarding desire and work selflessly (Niṣkāma Karma), realize the Brahman nature which is Sacchidā-nanda. Such are liberated, that is never appear again in the World of Form, which is the world of suffering, and enter into the infinite ocean of Bliss Itself. This is Mokṣa or Mukti or Liberation. As it is freedom from the universe of form, it can only be attained through detachment from the world and desirelessness. For those who desire the world of form cannot be freed of it. Life, therefore, is a field in which man, who has gradually ascended through lower forms of mineral, vegetable and animal life, is given the opportunity of heaven-life and Liberation. The universe has a moral purpose, namely the affording to all existence of a field wherein it may reap the fruits of its actions. The forms of life are therefore the stairs (Sopāna) on which man mounts to the state of infinite, eternal, and formless Bliss. This then is the origin and the end of man. He has made for himself his own past and present conditions and will make his future one. His essential nature is free. If wise, he adopts the means (sādhanā) which lead to lasting happiness, for that of the world is not to be had by all, and even when attained is perishable and mixed with suffering.[13]

This quotation adequately summarizes the attitude not merely of the Tantras but of the whole body of the Hindu scriptures toward the origin and end of man.

The teachings of the Tantras are never at variance with those of the Upaniṣads. Even the worship of God the Mother is not new in the Tantras. In the Kena Upaniṣad we find, for example, when the gods grew arrogant because of their victory over the demons, that it was Umā, God the Mother, who brought them to their senses and offered them the supreme knowledge. (Correspondingly, the Tantras hold that by worship of God in the aspect of Mother supreme knowledge and liberation can be achieved. 'She brings to light and freedom those with whom she is well pleased.') Further, there is a hymn in the Rg-Veda in honour of God the Mother, which reads: 'I spread the heavens over the earth. I am the energy in Brahman, I am the mother of all. It is for me that Brahman resides in all intellects, and it is he who have penetrated all the worlds with my power and am holding them in their places . . . Again, apart from the heavens and apart from this earth, I remain always the all-intelligent primal energy, as well as the one intelligent being, perfect and untouched by my magic creation.[14]

Sādhanā and Siddhi

The Tantras are primarily and fundamentally practical scriptures on sādhanā. The word sādhanā means a striving or discipline for the attainment of a certain prescribed goal. And that goal, or Siddhi (attainment), as may be guessed, is Mokṣa, liberation from the bondage of ignorance, and from the chain of recurring birth and death, through knowledge of the true Self as one with Śiva, or Brahman. The attainment of this knowledge, though possible only through effort, must be direct and immediate. According to the Tantras and all the other Hindu scriptures, infinite knowledge, power, and bliss are latent in every man. The object of sādhanā is just to unfold this knowledge and power and to realize this bliss.

The authority of the scriptures does not depend upon mere belief in them as revelations, but upon the fact that their truths can be revealed in one's own soul. In other words, the test of their validity is primarily a positive one. They contend, moreover, that the spiritual practices they inculcate will bring the promised results in all who follow them. Briefly, they insist that one must act in order to experience the truth of God.

The sādhānas, or spiritual disciplines, however, should be undertaken only with the help of a guru, or spiritual teacher. All Hindu schools of thought, in fact, maintain that submission to the direction of a competent teacher is essential if one is to attain to knowledge of God, for religion is a practical science to which neither books nor scriptures can be a complete guide. The aspirant must therefore associate himself with one who is competent and holy, who has demonstrated the truths of religion in his own life, and who can therefore initiate the disciple into the secrets of spiritual unfoldment. The Tantras define two kinds of dīkṣa, or initiation: śāmbhavi (or śakti) and mantri. śāmbhavi occurs when the disciple immediately experiences divine vision, attaining the supreme knowledge by the mere wish or touch of the guru. Though to us this sudden transformation may seem fantastic, we may see it substantiated in the lives of Kṛṣṇa, Christ, and Rāmakṛṣṇa. Christ said to his disciple, 'Be thou whole [perfect]', and the disciple instantly attained perfection; Kṛṣṇa by a word gave divine sight to Arjuna, and the realization of God; and within living memory Rāmakṛṣṇa by a touch gave illumination to his disciples.[15]

But this form of initiation is possible only through supreme teachers. Lesser teachers must have recourse to the other form of initiation, namely, mantri, in this the guru initiates the disciple by presenting him with a mantra, or sacred word or formula. In the Tantras the philosophy involved in the mantras is given detailed explanation, the underlying principle being that words and thoughts are inseparable, and that a person may effect a complete change in his character by meditating upon a thought with the help of a word and by repeating the word. The root of initiation, declare these scriptures, is the mantra; the mantra is the body of God; and God is the root of; śiddhi, or attainment of knowledge and perfection.

Men vary in capacity, temperament, and level of growth in the intellectual, moral, and spiritual spheres. Accordingly, the Tantras classify humanity into three general categories: divya, or divine; vīra, or heroic; and paśu, or animal. The paśus, in whom animal passions predominate, must avoid all objects of temptation and regularly observe the ritualistic forms of worship and meditation. The vīras, in whom there is a greater love for spiritual than for material things, may abide in the midst of the objects of temptation, while they learn to maintain their equanimity and self-control by devoting their thoughts more and more to God. And the divyas, who have become established in self-control, whose minds are absorbed in the thought of God, and in whom is to be found an expression of all divine qualities, such as love, kindness, and truthfulness—like the emanation of fragrance from a flower—these are beyond all needs of Spiritual discipline.

Four forms of worship and meditation are prescribed in the Tantras. The highest is Brahma-sadbhava—meditating on the identity of the inner Self of man with Brahman as he exists in all and all exist in him. The second in this scale is constant meditation on the chosen ideal of God within one's own heart. The third is japa, repetition of the mantra (the word corresponding to the chosen ideal of God) and prayer. And the last and lowest is external worship of an image or a symbol.

Those who are advanced enough to meditate on the identity of the inner Self with God do not need the aid of external symbols or rituals, but for others symbols and rituals are always very helpful and in most cases are needed. Says Sir John Woodroffe:

"Brāhmanism thus sagely resolves the Western dispute as to the necessity or advisability of ritual. It affirms it for those who have not attained the end of all ritual. It lessens and refines ritual as spiritual progress is made upwards; it dispenses with it altogether when there is no longer need for it. But until a man is a real "Knower", some sādhanā is necessary if he would become one. . . . What may be suitable for the unlettered peasant may not be same for those more intellectually and spiritually advanced. It is however a fine general principle of Tāntric worship that capacity, and not social distinction-such as caste, determines competency for any particular worship.[16]

The Tantras developed elaborate rituals and symbols for those who needed them, and supplied most of the temple rituals in India. In the worship of something outside the Inner Self—for examine, a Chosen Deity—an external symbol, such as an image, a picture, an emblem, or a geometrical design called yantra, may be used. In practising ritualism worshippers must also practise inward meditation and adoration. Those who follow the ritualist path are falsely accused by the ignorant of being idolaters, for if one will only learn their form of worship, one may perceive for oneself what disciplines are involved. As a matter of fact, in this process of external Worship there is a wonderful harmony and blending of jñāna (knowledge), bhakti (love), karma, and raja yoga. Sir John Woodroffe has correctly explained the matter:

According to Hindu views, primary importance is attached to mental states, for as the Divine Thought made the world, man makes his character therein by what he thinks. If he is always thinking on material things and has desires therefore [*sic*] he himself becomes material and is given over to lust and other passions. If, on the contrary, he has always his mind on God, and associates everything with the thought of Him, his mind becomes pure and divine.[17]

As we have already noted, the Sakta Tantra teaches the Motherhood of God—God as śakti, or the power which creates and preserves the universe and dissolves it into herself. The concept Mother, indeed, takes many forms, has many aspects, and what is experienced as terror and death and destruction is included in her play. These three—terror, death, and destruction—are but the obverse of bliss, life, and creation. The tender Mother shows her benign aspect to those who are her votaries, in whatever form or aspect they may worship her. And she is to be seen and realized everywhere in the universe. A beautiful prayer occurs in the Caṇḍī, a prayer book of the Śakta Tantras:

'O Mother, thou art the embodiment of all knowledge. Wherever there are intelligence, and learning, there art thou manifest. All women are thy forms. Thou hast thy being in the universe, filling and permeating all things.'

Thou spiritual aspirants are taught to look upon all women as the embodiment of Śakti, or Mother.[18]

A most important portion of the Tantras is that which deals with what is technically known as kuṇḍalinī yoga. The word kuṇḍalinī literally means the coiled up. According to the scriptures, the divine energy remains unmanifested within us, and to the yogi's eye it has a form like that of a coiled serpent. The object of spiritual practices is to awaken this sleeping power in man. There are, assert the Tantras, seven centres of consciousness, the seventh of which is located in the brain. These centres, resembling lotuses, are technically known as cakras. Through certain prescribed exercises the kuṇḍalinī, or Divine Energy, rises through the centres until it reaches the seventh, and in this seventh occurs a mystic union with the Supreme Lord, who there resides. Then it is that one attains transcendental consciousness.

This kuṇḍalinī and these seven cakras or lotuses are not physical but subtle and vital, and the mystic with his divine sight opened sees them. He also experiences various psychic and spiritual visions as his sleeping energy awakens to full life.

Once Śrī Rāmākṛṣṇa spoke of the centres of energy in this way:

'In the scriptures mention is made of the seven centres of consciousness. When the mind is attached to worldliness, consciousness dwells in the three lower centres, the plexus sacro-coccygeal, sacral, and solar. Then there are in it no high ideals or pure thoughts. It remains immersed in lust and greed. The fourth centre of consciousness is the region of the heart. Spiritual awakening comes when the mind rises to this centre. At this stage man has a spiritual vision of the Divine Light and is struck with wonder at its beauty and glory. His mind then no longer runs after worldly pleasures. The region of the throat is the filth centre of consciousness. When the mind rises to this centre, man becomes free from nescience and ignorance. He then talks only on subjects relating to God and grows impatient if any worldly topic is discussed. He avoids hearing about worldly subjects. The sixth centre is between the eyebrows. When the mind rises to this centre, man becomes merged in divine consciousness. There is still left in him, however, the consciousness of a separate ego. Seeing the beatific vision of God he becomes mad with joy and longs to come closer to him and be united with him. But he cannot, for there is still the ego which stands between them. One may compare God to the light in a lantern. You seem to feel its warmth; yet though you wish to do you cannot touch it, on account of the glass intervening. The centre in the brain is the seventh centre, when one rises to this plane, there is samādhi. That is the transcendental consciousness, in which one realizes his oneness with God.[19]

SELECTED PASSAGES FROM THE MAHĀNIRVĀṆA TANTRA

The Lord of this universe becomes pleased with him who is engaged in doing good to the world, since the Lord is its soul and refuge.

He is one. He ever is. He is the Truth, one without a second. He is the supreme Being. He is self-effulgent, ever shining. He, is eternal consciousness and bliss.[20]

He is unchangeable, self-existent, and serene, and he is beyond all predicates. He is the witness of all, the Self of all, pervading everything; he is the omnipresent.

He, the eternal, dwells concealed in the heart of all beings. Though himself devoid of senses, he is the illuminator of all the senses, the source of their powers.[21]

He knows all, but none knows him.[22] The world of-forms appears real because he, the ground of all existence, is real.[23]

Through fear of him the wind blows, the sun gives heat, the clouds shower rain, and the trees in the forest flower.[24]

All Gods and Goddess—nay, the whole universe from Brahma to a blade of grass—are his forms.[25] If he be pleased, the universe is pleased.[26]

Just as the pouring of water at its root nourishes the branches and leaves of a tree so by worshipping him all the gods and goddesses attain bliss.[27]

As all rivers must go to the ocean, so all acts of worship reach him as the ultimate goal.[28]

For the attainment of liberation with ease and delight, there is no way but to worship him to meditate upon him, and to pray to him.[29]

REFERENCE

1. See the story of creation in the next section.

2. 'A Purāṇa or sacred poetical work, supposed to be compiled or composed by the poet Vyāsa; and comprising the whole body of Hindu theology; each Purāṇa should treat of five topics especially: the creation, the destruction and renovation of worlds; the genealogy of gods and the heroes; the reigns of the Manus, and the transaction of their descendants; but great variety prevails in this respect and few contain historical or genealogical matter. There are eighteen acknowledged Purāṇas.' (*Shabda-Sagara [Sanskrit-English Dictionary]* by Pandit-Kulapati Jīvananda Vidyāsagara (Calcutta: Bhattacharyya, 1900].)

3. *Cultural Heritage of India,* vol. I, pp. 181. f.

4. Brahman (neuter) denotes the impersonal God, and Brahmā (masculine) is the personal Creator, one of the Trimūrti.

5. Vaiṣṇavism, which teaches the idea of love for God and complete self-surrender to him, is sometimes called the Bhāgavata reiligion.

6. I. iv. 1-5.

7. II. iv. 11-24.

8. See *The Wisdom of God,* Bk. III, chap. 2, pp. 42-5.

9. *Complete Work of Vivekananda,* vol. III. p.257.

10. Bhāgavatam, XI. xix. 32-45.

11. Of all Indian scriptures, the Tantras are most often misunderstood by Western scholars, and even native scholars are not altogether free from error in

dealing with them. But must declar. But I must declare in this connection that in recent years one Western Student of Eastern philosophy, Sir John Woodroffe, an Englishman and at one time Chief Justice of the High Court of Calcutta, has, through a lifetime devoted to the study of Tāntric literature, done yeoman service in the cause of a proper understanding of these difficult scriptures, both through translations of original manuscripts and through correct interpretations of their spirit. 'Tantra Shastra [scriptures],' he says, '—('is') generally spoken of as a jumble of "black magic", and "erotic mysticism"cemented together by a ritual which is "meaningless mummery". A large number of persons who talk in this strain have never had a Tantra in their hands, and such Orientals as have read some portions of these scriptures have not generally understood them, otherwise they would not have found them to be so "meaningless". They may be bad, or they may be good, but they have a meaning. Mer are not such fools as to believe in what is meaningless.'

12. *Kathāmṛta,* vol. I, p. 49.

13. *śakti and Sākta,* pp. 11f.

14. Ṛg-Veda, x. 125. 3,7.

15. I myself had the blessed fortune to live in the society of many of Śrī Rāmakṛṣṇa's disciples, each one of whom testified to the fact that he had attained samādhi through the master's touch. The effects of that touch one could perceive in their lives and their characters.

16. *śakti and śākta*, p. 514.

17. *śakti and śākta,* pp. 530. f.

18. It should be noted that there evolved a school of thought amongst the Sāktas known as vamacara. Its ritual of wine and women, apparently a pure sensualism, gained some notoriety. If, however, we penetrate a little into the meaning of the accessories used we shall find no ground for condemnation. The symbols of wine and women were employed in order to teach freedom from lustful passions by trying to see everywhere the Divine Mother. In course of time, it is true, the original spirit of the ritual was forgotten, and degeneration of the whole form of worship ensued. The idea involved was an admirable one, but in its application it became dangerous and actually evil.

19. *Kathāmrta,* vol. I, pp. 72-3.

20. II. 33-4.

21. *Ibid.*, 35-6.

22. *Ibid.*, 37.

23. *Ibid.*, 38.

24. *Ibid.*, 44.

25. *Ibid.*, 46.

26. *Ibid.*, 47.

27. *Ibid.*, 48.

28. *Ibid.*, 50.

29. *Ibid.*, 52.

CHAPTER XIX

THE UPANIṢADS

Now take up the study of the Upaniṣads which stand by aselves although tradition associates them closely with Brāhmaṇas. Primarily they represent a spirit rent from and even hostile to ritual and embody a try of the universe quite distinct from the one that under—the sacrificial teaching of the Brahmans. All the earlier niṣads in some form or the other indicate this antagonism in a few it becomes quite explicit.[1] Thus in the *Muṇḍaka Upaniṣad*[2] we have one of the clearest onslaughts against the ficial ceremonial, in the course of which it is stated that soever hopes for real good to accrue from these rites is a and is sure to be overtaken again and again by death and epitude. This opposition more often appears indirectly in substitution of an allegorical for a literal interpretation he rites.[3] An illustration will show how this is done The medha is a well-known sacrifice whose celebration .fies overlordship of the world. It is to be performed by a ttriya and the chief animal to be sacrificed in it is a The *Bṛhadāraṇyaka Upaniṣad*[4] gives a subjective turn his sacrifice, and transforms it into a meditative act in the contemplative is to offer up the whole universe in of the horse and by thus renouncing everything attain ue autonomy—a result analogous to the overlordship related with the performance of the regular aśva-medha. antagonism between the two teachings gradually pears or at least is considerably softened, indicating that as the Upaniṣadic doctrine more and more triumphed, an attempt was made to reconcile them. The reconciliation is clearly traceable in the later Upaniṣads. The *Svetāśvalara Upaniṣad* for example alludes approvingly to Agni and Soma, the chief sacrificial deities, and commends a return to the old ritualistic worship.[5]

The divergence between the two views as embodied in the Brāhmaṇas and the Upaniṣads respectively is now explained by some scholars as due to the divergence in ideals between the Brahmins and the Kshattriyas—the priests and princes of ancient India. There is indeed some ground for such a view, because the Upaniṣads ascribe more than one of their characteristic doctrines to royal personages and represent Brahmins as seeking instruction of them in respect of those doctrines. But it does not afford, as some modern scholars themselves recognize, sufficient warrant for connecting this difference in ideals with a social distinction. The prominence given to the Kshattriyas in the Upaniṣads may after all mean nothing more than that kings were patrons of Brahmins and that the doctrines, though originating among the latter, were first welcomed by the former rather than by the ritual-ridden section of the Brāhmins themselves.[6] It also implies that Brahma-knowledge (Brahma-vidyā) was not confined to the priests as the knowledge of the sacrifice, for the most part, was. But we need not further consider this question for, being a purely historical one, it does not directly concern us.

The word 'upaniṣad' has been variously explained by old Indian commentators, but their explanations cannot be regarded as historically or philologically accurate, for what the commentators have done is merely to read into the word the meaning which, as the result of long use, it had come to possess, by their time. Moreover, the same commentator often derives the word in alternative ways showing thereby that he was speaking not of a certainty, but only of what he considered a mere possibility.[7] While thus the commentators give us no help, we fortunately find the word used in the Upaniṣads themselves., and there it generally appears as synonymous with rahasya or secret. That should accordingly have been it original meaning. Etymologically the word is equivalent to sitting (sad) near by (upa) devotedly (ni),' and in course of time it came to signify the secret instruction imparted at such private sitting.[8] That the teaching of these works was regarded as a mystery and that much care and anxiety were bestowed upon keeping it from the unworthy lest it should be misunderstood or misapplied, come out clearly in several Upaniṣads. According to the *Praśna Upaniṣad,* for example, six pupils go to a great teacher seeking instruction of him in respect of the highest reality; but he asks them to live with him for a year before instructing hem, obviously with the purpose of watching them and satisfying himself of their fitness to be taught by him. Again, when Naciketas, according to the *Kaṭha Upaniṣad,* desires to now whether or not the soul survives after death, Yama does not reply until has tested the sincerity and strength of mind of the young inquirer The reluctance to impart the highest truth to every one without discrimination, we may observe in passing, was not peculiar to India, but was common to all ancient peoples Heraclitus in early Greece, for example, is reported to have stated, 'If men care for gold; hey must dig for it otherwise they must be content with traw.'

The origin of Upaniṣadic literature as it has been handed own to us is somewhat hard to trace. Hindu tradition places on the same footing as the other species of Vedic literature the Mantra and the Brahmanas—regarding them all like as śruti or 'revelation,' *i.e.* as works not ascribable to human authors. In the absence of any help from this source, are left to mere conjecture. In the Upaniṣads we now and when come across short and pithy statements which bear he impress of set formulas, and the literary material in which they are found imbedded seems merely to amplify and ilustrate the truth enshrined in them. Further, these sayings are not infrequently styled there as 'upaniṣad.' From this it has been concluded, with much probability, that the term was in the beginning applied only to these formulas which contain in a nutshell some important truths of Upaniṣad philosophy. As an example of them we may instance' *Tat tvam asi,* 'That thou art,' which teaches the ultimate identity of the individual and the cosmic souls. It was these philosophic formulas alone that were once communicated by teacher to pupil, the communication being preceded or followed by expository discourses. The discourses, it is surmised, assumed in course of time a definite shape though not committed to writing yet, giving rise to the Upaniṣad as we now have them. To judge from the way in which these texts have grown, they contain not the thoughts of a single teacher, but of a series of teachers, and thus represent growth in which new ideas have mingled with the old. Such a view explains the heterogeneity sometimes seen in the teaching of even one and the same Upaniṣad. At a later time when all the ancient lore of the Hindus was brought together and arranged, the Upaniṣads in this form were appended to the Brāhmaṇas. The significance of such close association of the Upaniṣads with the Brāhmaṇas is that when this; grouping was effected the two were regarded as equally old—so old that neither of them could be referred to any specific authors. Standing thus at the end of the Veda, the Upaniṣads came to be known as 'Vedānta' or 'end of the Veda'—much as the Metaphysics of Aristotle owed its designation to its being placed after Physics in his writings. A word which at first only indicated the position of the Upaniṣads in the collection developed later the significance of the aim or fulfilment of Vedic teaching, it being permissible to use *anta* in Sanskrit, like its equivalent 'end' in English, in both these senses.

The number of Upaniṣads that have come down to us is very large—over two hundred being reckoned, but all are not equally old. The great majority of them in fact belong to comparatively recent times and hardly more than a dozen are of the period we are now considering. Even among these classical Upaniṣads, chronological differences are traceable; but generally speaking they all exhibit a family likeness both in their thoughts and in their language in which those thoughts are clothed. Hence all of them may be referred to practically the same stage in the evolution of Indian thought. we shall take into account here only the older or canonical Upaniṣads. Their date cannot be exactly determined, but they may all be regarded as pre-Buddhistic. They represent the earliest efforts of man at giving a philosophic explanation of the world, and are as such invaluable in the history of human thought. They are the admitted basis of at least one of the most important systems of Indian philosophy, viz. the Vedānta, 'which controls at the present time nearly the higher thought of Brāhminical India. Their importance is much more than historical, for their unique spiritual power and the elements of universal appeal which they contain may exercise a considerable influence on the re-construction of thought and realignment of life in the future.

A word may now be added as regards the manner of these works. They are generally in the .form of dialogues, especially the larger ones among them. Their method is more poetic than philosophic They have been described as philosophical poems and indicate truths generally through metaphor and allegory. The language, although never bereft of the charm peculiar to the Upaniṣads, is sometimes symbolic. The style is highly elliptical and shows that the works were intended to be expounded orally by one that could readily supply whatever was lacking in their presentation of the subject. These peculiarities render the interpretation of many passages not a little difficult and account for the varied explanations given of them in the past as well as in the present. But the indefiniteness is only in regard to details, the general tenor of the teaching being quite unmistakable. Among the work-, comprising Vedic literature, the Upaniṣads were the first to attract the attention of foreigners Several of these works were translated into Persian in Moghul times and were thence rendered into Latin about the beginning of the last century. It was through this Latin translation that thev came to be known for the first time in Europe. and it was through it that Schopenhauer, for instance, learnt admire them [9] In recent times, numerous translations them, direct from the Sanskrit, have appeared in Wester languages. The subject-matter of Upaniṣadic teaching also.' has repeatedly engaged the attention of foreign scholar; and, among the many works published, should be mentione Deussen's masterly work on the philosophy of the Upaniṣadi particularly for the wealth of information it contains an for the care and thoroughness of its analysis.

I

The first point that has to be considered is whether all the Upaniṣads—even the genuine ones—teach the same doctrine or not. Indian commentators have all along held the view that they do[10]; and it is inconceivable that they should have thought otherwise, for they believed that these works were revealed in the literal sense of that word. The agreement of the commentators, however, does not extend beyond the general recognition of the unity of Upaniṣadic teaching. As to what the exact nature of that teaching is, they differ widely from one another. This diversity of opinion should be a long-standing one, for we have references to it even in the earliest extant work systematizing the teaching of the Upaniṣads, viz. the *Vedānta- sūtra* of Bādarāyaṇa.[11] Such wide divergence in interpretation naturally suggests a doubt that, in spite of the traditional insistence to the contrary, the Upaniṣads do not embody a single doctrine; and the doubt is confirmed by an independent study of these ancient works. A modern student, not committed beforehand to follow any particular school of Vedāntic thought, will be forced to think that there are not two or three discordant views in the Upaniṣads, but several. Nor is there anything surprising in this, for the problem dealt with in them lends itself to such a variety of solutions and these works were moulded into their present form in a more or less casual way. All the doctrines presented in them do not, however, stand out equally prominent. Some are merely flashes of thought, others are only slightly developed and still others are but survivals from the older period The most prominent and the best developed teaching may, if we overlook for the moment minor details, be described as monistic 'and idealistic. Statements like 'There is no variety here,' 'All this is Brahman,' which insist on the unity of everything that exists, are neither few nor far between in the Upaniṣads. This monistic view may be described as idealistic for. according to an equally striking number of Upaniṣadic sayings, there is nothing in the universe which, if it is not itself mental, does not presuppose mind. 'No there the sun shines, nor the moon or the stars, not these lightnings either. Where then could this fire be? Everything shines only after the shining spirit; through its light all this shines.[12]

Before giving an account of this doctrine we should explain the Upaniṣadic terms for the ultimate reality. These terms are two—'Brahman' and 'ātman,' which have been described as 'the two pillars on which rests nearly the whole edifice of Indian philosophy.' Their origin is somewhat obscure. The word 'Brahman' seems at first to have meant 'prayer,' being derived from a root *(bṛh)* meaning 'to grow' or 'to burst forth.' Brahman as prayer is what manifests itself in audible speech. From this should have been derived later the philosophic significance which it bears in the Upaniṣads, viz. the primary cause of the universe—what *bursts* forth spontaneously in the form of nature as a whole and not as mere speech only.[13] The explanation of the other word is more uncertain. In all probability 'ātman' originally meant 'breath' and then came to be applied to whatever constitutes the essential part of anything, more particularly of man, *i.e.* his self or soul.[14] Thus each of these terms has its own independent significance: the distinctive meaning of 'Brahman' is the ultimate source of the outer world while that of 'ātman' is the inner self of man. What is remarkable about these terms is that, though entirely different in their original connotation and though occasionally bearing it still in Upaniṣadic passages, they come to be prevailingly used as synonymous—each signifying alike the eternal source of the universe including nature as well as man. The development of the same significance by these two distinct terms means that the Indian, in the course of his speculation, identified the outer reality with the inner; and by such a happy identification at last reached the goal of his long quest after unity—a goal which left all mythology far behind and was truly philosophical.

It is necessary to dwell at some length on how this identification was brought about and what its full significance is. We have stated that the word ātman developed in course of time the meaning of soul or self. That was the result of a search for the central essence of the individual as distinguished from the physical frame with which he is associated. The method here was subjective and the result was arrived at through introspection. In place of the body, breath, etc., which may easily be mistaken for the individual, we find here a deeper principle, which is psychical, finally regarded as the essence of man. Now there was from the time of the later Mantras and Brāhmaṇas the habit of seeking for a correspondence between the individual and the world and trying to discover for every important feature of the one, an appropriate counterpart in the other. It represented an effort to express the world in terms of the individual. Such an attempt at rising from the known particular to a knowledge of the unknown universal is clearly seen in the Puruṣa-sūkta for example, where parts of the universe are described as parts of Puruṣa or a giant man (p. 45). It is equally clear from one of the funeral hymns[15] which, addressing the departed, says: 'Let thine eye go to the sun; thy breath, to the wind, etc.' And we have it again when prāṇa, which as vital breath stands for an important aspect of the individual, is universalized and, as cosmic Prāṇa, is represented as the life of the world (p. 41). This notion of parallelism between the individual and the world runs throughout the literature of the later Vedic period and is found in the Upaniṣads as well.[16] The practice of viewing the whole world as a cosmic individual naturally had its influence on the conception of ātman and transformed what was but a psychical principle into a 'world-principle. Ātman, which as the soul or self is the inmost truth of man, became as the cosmic soul or self the inmost truth of the world. When the universe came once to be conceived in this manner, itsself became the only self, the other selves being regarded as in some way identical with it.

Though this process secures the unity of the self, it does not take us as far as the unity of all Being. For the self in the case of the individual is distinguishable from the not-self such as the body; and the world-self similarly has to be distinguished from its physical embodiment, viz. the material universe. Now there was all along another movement of thought just complementary to the one we have so far sketched. It traced the visible universe to a single source named Brahman. The method there was objective, for it proceeded by analysing the outer world and not by looking inward as in the line of speculation of which ātman was the goal. In accordance with the general spirit of Indian speculation, several conceptions were evolved here also[17]—each more satisfying than the previous one to account for the universe, and Brahman was the last of the series of solutions. At some stage in the evolution of thought, this primal source of the universe, *viz.* Brahman, was identified with its inmost essence, *viz.* ātman. Thus two independent currents of thought—*i.e* resulting from the desire to understand the true nature of man and the other, that of the objective world—became blended and the blending led at once to the discovery of the unity for which there had been such a prolonged search. The physical world, which according to the ātman doctrine is only the not-self, now becomes reducible to the self. The fusing of two such outwardly different but inwardly similar conceptions into one is the chief point of Upaniṣadic teaching and is expressed in the 'great-sayings' (mahāvākya) like 'That thou art,' 'I am Brahman' or by the equation Brāhman = ātman. The individual as well as the world is the manifestation of the same Reality and both are therefore at bottom one. There is, in other words, no break between nature and man or between either of them and God.

Such a synthesis, besides showing that Reality is one, carries with it an important implication. The conception of Brahman, being objective, can at best stand only for a hypothetical something—carrying no certainty necessarily with it. It is also likely for that very reason to be taken as non-spiritual in its nature. The conception of ātman on the other hand has neither of these defects; but in the sense in which we commonly understand it, it is finite and cannot represent the whole of Reality. Even as the cosmic self, it is set over against the physical world and is therefore limited by it. When, however, the two conceptions of Brahman and ātman are combined, then by a process of dialectic a third is reached which is without the flaws of either taken by itself. Like ātman it is spiritual and at the same time it is infinite unlike it. It is also indubitable, since it is conceived as fundamentally one with our own immediate self. So long as we look upon the ultimate as something not ourselves—as mere Brahman—it remains more or less an assumption and a dogma; but the moment we recognize it as one with our own self, it becomes transformed into a positive certainty, we being under an intuitive obligation to admit the reality of our own existence, however much we may be in the dark in regard to its precise nature. It is this higher reality that is described for instance as satyam jñānam anantam,[18] where satyam points to its immeuiate certainty, jñānam to its spiritual nature and anantam to its all-inclusive or infinite character. That is the Upaniṣadic Absolute—neither Brahman nor ātman in one sense, but both in another. It manifests itself better in the human self—though not fully even there—than in the outer world which inhibits still more of its nature, because it appears there as mere insentient matter.[19] The enunciation of this doctrine marked the most—important advance in the whole history of India's thought. It introduced almost a revolution in the point of view from which speculation had proceeded till then. The following illustration may perhaps be of use in comprehending the nature of this change. Let us suppose that some people know Venus as only appearing in the East, and others know it as appearing only in the West—each set of people regarding the planet they observe as distinct from what the others do. If then the discovery is made by some one that the two are but the same and that the Eastern star is the Western star, the resulting transformation in the view of Venus would correspond to the change in the present case. The true conception of unity was reached in India only at this stage.[20]

All this is very beautifully brought out in a celebrated section of the *Chāndogya Upaniṣad*.[21] It is in the form of a dialogue between a father and, his son. The name of the father is Uddālaka and that of his son, śvetaketu. śvetaketu has been to a *guru* and has just returned home after completing his education in the conventional sense. The father, who notices a lack of humility in śvetaketu, fears that he might not after all have learnt from his teacher the true meaning of life. Inquiry only confirms him in this view; and he himself therefore undertakes to instruct his son. The teaching that is imparted, as is clear from these preliminaries, should be of the highest value. Uddālaka begins by postulating an ultimate entity which is to be regarded as mental or spiritual because it is stated to have *thought* (aikṣata) and which he terms Sat or Being. He then proceeds to describe how the whole universe is a manifestation of it. In the beginning Sat alone was, without a second. It thought "May I be many." 'Its diversification—first into the three elements, viz. tejas or 'fire,' ap or 'water' and pṛthivī or 'earth' and then into others until organic bodies, including those of human beings, have emerged—is afterwards explained. What is made out by this is that the spiritual entity postulated in the beginning is all-comprehensive and that whatever is, has sprung from it. Then 'suddenly and with dramatic swiftness' the original Sat is identified with the self of śvetaketu: Tat tvam asi, Svetaketo. The purpose of the identification is obviously to bring home to the mind of śvetaketu the undoubted reality of the postulated source of the universe. However splendid the account of Sat and its transformations which `Uddālaka gives at first, it objective and therefore lacks a most essential feature, viz. certitude. It is merely to be taken for granted. `Uddālaka puts it forward as a hypothesis and, though convincing to `Uddālaka himself because he has realized the truth, it can be nothing more than a probability for śvetaketu. But this probable source of the universe becomes a positive certainty to him the moment he realizes that it is identical with his own self, which he knows to be real even without being taught. This teaching of course does not leave śvetaketu's view of his own self unchanged, for it is not his individual self that he can regard as the source of the world, but rather the universal self that is immanent in it. It is true that the world has emerged from the one and that that one is śvetaketu's self; yet it is not his private self that can explain the universe, but his self only in so far as it is one with Sat or the universal self. 'I live; yet not I, but God liveth in me.'

When we come to consider in detail this doctrine of idealistic monism, we find it appear in two forms between which there is rather an important difference. In some passages the Absolute is presented as cosmic or all-comprehensive in its nature (saprapañca); in some others again, as acosmic or all-exclusive (nisprapanca). There are many Passages and even whole sections in the Upaniṣads treating of either. To illustrate their character, we shall refer here to one of each type:—

(1) *Cosmic Ideal.*—One of the best-known descriptions of this ideal is found in a section of the *Chāndogya Upaniṣad*[22] designated Sāṇḍilya-vidyā. After defining Brahman cryptically as tajjalān—as that (tat) which gives rise (ja) to the world, reabsorbs (li) it and supports (an) it—the section proceeds to describe it as 'comprehending all activities, all desires, all odours, all tastes, reaching all, and so self-complete as ever to be speechless and calm.' Then follows its identification with the individual self: 'This is my self within the heart, smaller than rice, or barley corn, or mustard seed or grain of millet or the kernel of a grain of millet; this is my self within the heart, greater than the earth, greater than the mid-region, greater than heaven, greater than all these worlds. This is Brahman. May I become it when I depart hence.

(2) *Acosmic Ideal.*—For this we shall select a passage from another Upaniṣad[2]: Here a learned lady, Gārgī by name, asks Yājñavalkya, the greatest thinker of the age and probably the first idealist of the world, to tell her what the basis of the universe is. Yājñavalkya, tracing it to its penultimate source, answers that it is space (ākāsa) Further asked to explain what constitutes the basis of space itself, Yājñavalkya mentions a principle which he describes only in a negative way, implying thereby that the ultimate reality is beyond the grasp of human experience. The negative description given is as follows: 'This is the imperishable, O Gārgī, which wise people adore—not gross, not subtle, not short, not long, not red, not adhesive, without shadow, without darkness; without air, without space; unattached, without taste, without smell, without sight, without ears, without speech, without mind, without light, without breath, without mouth, without form, and without either inside or outside. Not that does anything eat; nor that does eat anything.' Lest the description should be taken to mean 'pure nothing,' Yājñavalkya adds immediately after it that whatever is, owes its being to this transcendental reality, suggesting that if the Ultimate a sheer blank or non-entity, it could not have given to the world of appearance.

It is not difficult to discover the basis for this two-teaching in pre-Upaniṣadic tradition. The first or saprapa ideal resembles the doctrine underlying the 'Song of Creat (p. 42). Only the First Principle here, unlike Tad Ek there, is not conceived objectively, but as Brahman—ātr in the sense explained at the beginning of this section. regards the second or niṣprapañca ideal, we have already. drawn attention (p. 41) to the prevalence of the pantheis tendency in the later Mantras and the Brahmaṇas described it as somewhat inconsistent, since it aims at us and yet clings to the double notion of God and nature. arrive at true unity, one only of these two should be retain If it is the notion of nature that is retained, there will be God apart from the world. This outcome of the pantheis' tendency, viz. viewing the unity of the world as itself Absolute, does not figure very much in the Upaniṣad probably because it tends towards naturalism, which though not wholly unfamiliar to them, is widely removed from their prevailing spirit.[23] If, on the other hand, it is notion of God that is selected for retention in preference that of nature, the world of common experience with all variety will cease to exist apart from God. That is precise the acosmic conception; only the theistic term is replaced by the philosophic one of Brahman.

The determination of the relative position and important of these two conceptions is one of the most difficult problem connected with the Upaniṣads and has occupied the attention of thinkers for a very long time. According to śaṁkara, problem is discussed by Badarayana in the *Vedānta-sūtra*[24] and it is not improbable that at one stage it engaged attention of the Upaniṣadic sages themselves.[25] The views as they appear here have been explained by Saṁka as really the same, and the apparent distinction between them as due to a difference in the standpoint from which the Absolute is looked at—cosmic from the empirical standpoint, but acosmic from the transcendental. This view is supported by, the juxtaposition sometimes of the two conceptions in one and the same passage, as for example in the *Muṇḍaka Upaniṣad*[26] where we have 'What is invisible, intangible, colourless, nameless, eyeless and earless, devoid of hands and of feet—that is what is coeval with time and space, is all-pervading, subtle and changeless, which the wise know to be the source of beings.' The saprapañca conception must in that case be understood negatively as signifying that the world is not outside Brahman and the niṣprapañca conception positively as signifying that Brahman is more than the world. There is no world apart from Brahman, but it is not therefore unreal for it has its basis in Brahman. Brahman again is not nothing for it furnishes the explanation of the world, though it is not identical with it or exhausted in it. The former view would emphasize the immanence of Brahman and the latter, its transcendence, the Upaniṣadic view being that it is both immanent and transcendent. Or probably we have here two different views as the result of a difference in interpreting the result of the synthesis of the conceptions of Brahman and ātman alluded to above. The Upaniṣadic Absolute which represents this result is not, as we have seen, something objective; nor is it the subject as such, though neither is unrelated to it. Such an Absolute may be understood as being both. That would be saprapañca Brāhman. In this view, the manifold things of experience have a real place in the Absolute. They actually emerge from it and are re-absorbed into it. It is Brahma-pariṇama-vāda or the doctrine which maintains that Brahman evolves into the world. Or the Absolute may he regarded as the mere ground of both the subject and object, in which case we would have the niṣprapañca ideal. The things of common experience are then to be regarded as only phenomena. Brahman being the noumenon. That would be Brahma-vivarta-vāda[27] or the doctrine which maintains that Brahman does not change into, but merely appears as, the world. Whatever the truth may be, the distinction has given rise to a good deal of controversy. We shall have to consider this question when treating of the Vedānta system. Meanwhile we shall proceed on the basis that, though idealistic monism is the prevalent teaching of the Upaniṣads, that doctrine is presented in them in two somewhat distinct forms.

The second of these forms necessarily involves the notion of Māyā, it being understood as the principle which shows the niṣprapañca Brāhman as saprapañca. It is not, therefore, right to maintain, as some have tried to do, that the doctrine of Māyā is unknown to the Upaniṣads. It is already there, but naturally it does not yet exhibit all the various features which, as the result of later elaboration and development, are associated with it in śaṁkara's Advaita. The word 'māyā' again, it is true, occurs only rarely in the earlier Upaniṣads; but it is found in literature still older though its meaning there may not always be clearly determinable, and also in the Upaniṣads which are not very late.[28] Even in the earliest Upaniṣads where we do not find 'Māyā,' we have its equivalent 'avidyā.[29] There are also statements in them like the following: 'Where there is duality *as it were* (iva) one sees another[30] which, as recognized by scholars like Deussen[31] clearly point to the existence in the Upaniṣads of the idea that the world is an appearance.

In whichever of these two forms they may present Brahman, the Upaniṣads distinguish from it the common things constituting the universe as known to us by pointing out that they are merely nāma and rūpa. By rūpa is here meant the specific form or nature of a thing; and by nāma, the name or word that serves as its sign. By the two terms together we have to understand, in the case of any object, its particularity or determinate character; and the emergence of the world from Brāhman is conceived as the differentiation of names and forms. Whether we regard these particular things as actual modes or as only appearances of Brahman, they are not real apart from it, which according to the monism of the Upaniṣads is the sole reality. It is not easy to discover the necessity for nāma in this characterization, as rūpa by itself seems sufficient for particularization. It probably has reference to a belief, current at the time, in the existence of a speech-world answering to the world of things and to the need there generally is for names as much as for things in practical life.[32] Sometimes the description of emphical objects is made more complete by introducing a third term, karma or 'movement,[33] and thus explicitly referring to the dynamic factor, an important aspect of the world of experience.

As regards the details of the things derived from Brahman which are characterized by nāma and rūpa, there is to be made at the outset a distinction between the inorganic and the organic. While the latter are the abode of transmigrating souls or jīvas, the former are not. They serve only as 'the stage erected by Brahman on which the souls have to play their part.' In the inorganic realm, the Upaniṣads recognize five fundamental elements (bhūtas) termed pṛthivī (earth), ap (water), tejas (fire), vāyu (air) and ākāsa (ether). All the five were not known from the beginning. 'Water' seems to have been the sole element thought of at first (p. 44). The next stage of advance is marked by the recognition of three elements, earth, water and fire, as in the *Chāndogya Upaniṣad,* which are stated to emerge from Brahman in the reverse order. They correspond roughly to the solid, fluid and gaseous phases of the material universe. The last stage in the evolution of this thought, which was final and was accepted by practically all the later philosophers of India, was reached when the number of the so-called elements was raised to five by the addition of air and ether.[34] It is clear that in this its last form the classification is connected with the five-fold character of the sensory organs, whose distinctive objects, viz. odour, flavour, colour, temperature and sound, are respectively the distinctive features of earth, water, fire, air and ether. But these elements, it should be remembered, are subtle or rudimentary (sūkṣma-bhūta). Out of these are made the gross ones (sthula-bhūta), each of which contains an admixture of the other four, but gets its name as a compound from the element predominating in it.[35] The gross elements are what we find in nature; and strictly it is they that are to be understood by the terms pṛthivī, ap, etc., the corresponding subtle elements being known as pṛthvī-mātra, āpo-mātra, etc.[36] The organic bodies are divided into three classes 'born from the egg' (aṇḍa-ja), 'born from the germ' (jīva-ja) and 'bursting through the soil' (udbhijja).[37] To these is afterwards added[38] a fourth variety 'bom from sweat' (śveda-ja), thus making four classes altogether. When organic bodies disintegrate, they are reduced to the form of the five gross elements out of which other similar bodies may be built up. Their dissolution into their constituent subtle elements does not take place until the whole universe breaks up. Regarding the time when such breaking up takes place, there is some vagueness. As in the earlier .literature (p. 44), the theory of kalpa or the eternal recurrence of creation and dissolution is not explicit in the Upaniṣads. We have not, however, to wait long for its appearance. The *śvetāśvatara Upaniṣad,* which, though one of the classical Upaniṣads, is among the latest of them and is so rich in suggestions helpful in tracing the history of early Indian thought, points to it in more than one place. Thus the Highest is there stated to have 'got angry at the end of time and retracted all the worlds' and to repeat that act many a time.[39] The theory is closely connected with the doctrine of karma to which we shall refer in a subsequent section.

II

When the word 'psychology' is used in Indian philosophy, it should be understood in its original sense as the science or doctrine of the soul ('psyche'), for its teaching, except in one or two cases, is based upon the supposition that the soul exists. This study in India never branched off from philosophy and every system has therefore its own psychology. The various psychologies have, of course, a common body of doctrine; but each has its own special features as well, which are adapted to the particular school of thought to which it is affiliated. To the Upaniṣadic seers the existence of the soul is a necessary presupposition of all experience. It is the basis of all proof and itself therefore stands in need of none. 'By which, one knows all this—whereby could one know that ? Lo, by what means could the knower be known' ?[40] Although for this reason the Upaniṣads do not attempt to adduce any direct proof of the existence of the soul, they contain various suggestions touching the point. For example, the soul or jīva is often described as puruṣa, which is explained as puri-śaya or 'what lies in the citadel of the body.' It means that the existence of the physical body, with its diverse but co-operating parts, implies the existence of something whose end it serves. That something, apart from which the mechanism of the body would be meaningless[41] is the soul. Another suggestion, which is based upon the karma theory, is sometimes found. In the narrow span of a single life, we cannot possibly reap the fruits of all that we do. Nor can we, so long as we confine our attention to this life alone, fully account for all the good or evil that may come to us. A single birth being thus inadequate to render intelligible all the observed facts of life, we must, if the common belief in moral requital be well founded, admit a transmigrating soul to whose actions in past lives we must look for an explanation of whatever is inexplicable in its present condition and in whose continuance after death we must find redress of any seeming injustice in this life.[42]

The relation of the soul to the ultimate reality or of the jīva to Brāhman is somewhat differently conceived in the two views of the Absolute found in the Upaniṣads. According to the cosmic view it is an actual, though only a provisional, transformation of Brāhman and is as such both identical with and different from it. According to the acosmic view, it is Brāhman itself appearing as the jīva and therefore not at all different from it. Whether the jīva is an actual transformation or not, its jīva-hood consists in the forgetting of its essential identity with Brāhman. Though ordinarily believing that it is finite and therefore distinct from the Absolute, the soul sometimes—whenever, for any reason, desire is absent—rises above such belief and ceases to be conscious of its individuality. Such self-transcendence suggests, according to the Upaniṣads, that the jīva is not in reality the limited entity it generally takes itself to be. The question is dealt with in what is known as 'the doctrine of koṣas' in the *Taittirīya Upaniṣad.*[43] The unique experience characterizing this self-transcendent state is represented there as higher than the experience of the conscious (manomaya) and the self-conscious (vijñānamaya) levels of life, because the conflicts and confusions typical of them are overcome in it; and it is described as ānandamaya[44] to indicate that its essential mark is peace. Yet it is not identifiable with mokṣa[45] for it is only a passing phase and those who rise to it quickly fall away from it. The peace and self-forgetfulness that distinguish it show that the attitude induced by the contemplation of Art is its best illustration.[46] It stands midway between common experience and Mokṣa, where the soul's true nature is fully revealed; and if it points in one direction to the empirical self with its many struggles and imperfections, it does so equally definitely in the other to its oneness with Brahman, which is beyond all strife and contradiction.

The word 'jīva' is derived from the root *jīv,* which means 'to continue breathing.' The name gives prominence to one of the two aspects of life's activity, viz. the biological or unconscious such as breathing, which goes on even when the mind is quiescent as in deep sleep. The Upaniṣads use two other terms for the soul, viz. bhoktā, 'experient' and kartā[47] 'agent,' which together emphasize the other, viz. the psychological or conscious aspect of the activity. The principle of unconscious activity is termed prāṇa; and that of conscious activity, manas. Every soul is conditioned by these two principles throughout its empirical existence. To these comparatively permanent adjuncts of it should be added the material body, which alone is replaced at every birth. These three together—the body, prāṇa and manas[48] form a sort of 'empirical home' for the soul. The conscious side of the soul's activity is carried on by manas with the aid of the ten indriyas—five of knowledge, viz. cakṣus, śrotra, tvak, ghrāṇa and rasanā, which are respectively the organs of sight, hearing, touch, smell and flavour; and five of action—vāk, pāṇi, pāda, pāyu and upastha, which are respectively the organs of speech, holding, moving, excretion and generation. Various faculties of manas like vijñāna and ahaṁ-kāra are mentioned; but the Upaniṣads, at the same time, are careful to emphasize its unity. The *Bṛhadāraṇyaka Upaniṣad,* after giving a list of several such faculties, avers 'All these are manas only.' As the central organ of consciousness, it is one, however widely its functions may differ. It controls both the sensory and motor organs. It co-ordinates the impressions received from outside through the former and also resolves, when necessary, upon acting with the aid of one or other of the five organs of action. The relation of manas to these two sets of organs has been compared[49] to the relation of brain to the sensory and motor nerves.

The theory of cognition according to the Upaniṣads is not easy to find out. Yet there are a few hints which we may put together here: The usual Upaniṣadic expression for the things of experience, we know, is nāma-rūpa, which signifies that whatever is thought of or spoken about is the particular. The mind and the organs of sense function only within the realm of names and forms. That is, empirical knowledge is inevitably of the finite. But this does not mean that Brāhman the infinite, is unknowable. The very purpose of the Upaniṣads is to make it known. So Brahman also is knowable; only its knowledge is of a higher type than empirical knowledge. The *Muṇḍaka Upaniṣad*[50] classifies all knowledge into two—the higher (para vidyā) and the lower (aparā vidyā), which are respectively the knowledge of Brahman and of empirical things. The higher knowledge may not enlighten us about the details concerning particular things, but it gives us an insight into the principle of their being, as the knowledge of a lump of clay for example may be said to do in regard to everything made of clay.[51] In this sense it may be descrted as complete knowledge, and, as such, different from the lower knowledge, which even at its best is fragmentary. But there is no conflict between them. That is, however, only according to the cosmic conception of Brāhman. There is another view equally prominent in the Upaniṣads, which harmonises with the acosmic conception. Brāhman, according to it, transcends the very conditions of knowledge and consequently cannot be known. 'Speech and thought recoil from it, failing to find it.[52] The Upaniṣads bring out this unknowability of Brahman in itself in various ways. The *Īśa Upaniṣad,* for example, does so by predicating contradictory features of Brahman: 'It moves;—it moves not. It is far; it is near. It is within all this and also without all this.[53] 'But the best instance of it seems to have been found in an Upaniṣad no longer extant, to which śaṁkara refers in his commentary on the *Vedānta-sūtra*[54] Bādhva, asked by Bāṣkah to expound the nature of Brāhman, did so, it is stated, by keeping silent. He prayed: 'Teach me. Sir.' The other was silent, and, when addressed a second and a third time, he replied: 'I am teaching, but you do not follow. The self is silence: Upaśantoyam ātmā.' This view denies the name of vidyā to empirical knowledge, which, from the ultimate standpoint, is not knowledge at all, but only a sort of ignorance or avidyā. It may be asked whether such a view, by denying the possibility of knowing Brahman, does not make the teaching agnostic. The answer is that though we cannot *know* Brahman, we can *be* it. 'He who "knows" Brahman will be Brāhman.[55] It is to the means leading to such a consummation that the name vidyā is confined here. Even before this result is reached we may realize *that* Brāhman is though not *what* it is, for Brahman being fundamentally the same as our self, its existence, as already pointed out, is an immediate certainty. We cannot think of the Absolute, but all the same we are always in immediate contact with it in our own selves. Indeed we can never miss it.

We have so far had in view only the waking state. The Upaniṣads take a wider view of life and study the self under three other heads, viz. dream, dreamless sleep and what is termed the turīya state. Of these, dreaming like waking falls under psychology proper, for in it the mind functions; but the other two are supra-mental and are considered with a view to discover the real nature of the soul. It is noteworthy that at so early a period Indian thinkers should have thought of studying phenomena under varying conditions, which by eliminating or introducing one or more factors aid the discovery of their true character. Out of these four states only two seem to have been known at first, viz. waking and dream.[46] Later, not only is a distinction made between dream and dreamless sleep, but a *fourth* or the turīya state is added whose very name implies a precedent stage when only three states were recognized. We shall now briefly characterize these three states:

(1) *Dreams*.—The references to dreams in the Upaniṣads are frequent, implying that they attracted a good deal of attention at the time. The dream-state is intermediate between waking and deep sleep. Its physical condition is that the organs of sense should become wholly quiescent; and the senses then are stated to unite with the manas. The essential difference therefore between waking and dreams is that while the manas in the former receives from outside impressions which it builds up into ideas, in the latter it fashions a world of forms unaided and by itself. For this purpose it uses the material of waking hours—generally visual and auditory. Although the stuff of which dreams are made is thus revived impressions, the experience of a dream is quite unlike reminiscence. It is felt as real for the time being—as real as perceptual experience, for as everybody knows the things dreamt of are apprehended as present and not as belonging to the past. For this reason, dreams have been described as 'perception without sensation.'

(2) *Dreamless sleep*.—In this state, described as suṣupti, the manas as well as the senses is quiescent and there is consequently a cessation of normal or empirical consciousness. There is no longer any contrasting of one object with another or even of the subject with the object, and the embodied self is then said to attain a temporary union with the Absolute. As however suṣupti is not identified with the state of release, this statement has to be understood negatively—as only signifying that the consciousness of individuality is absent at the time though the individual himself continues to be, as shown by the sense of personal identity connecting the states before and after sleep. It is not a state of consciousness in the

ordinary sense; but it is not a state of blank or absolute unconsciousness either, for some sort of awareness is associated with it. It is not, however, the 'objectless knowing subject' that endures in it, as it is sometimes stated[56]; for along with the object, the subject also as such disappears then. It is rather a state of non-reflective awareness, if we may so term it. This state is above all desire and is therefore described as one of unalloyed bliss. 'Sleep makes us all *pashus.*' In a dream-state the interests of the waking state may be absent, but it can by no means be called disinterested. It has its own pains and pleasures and lacks that complete calm which characterizes deep sleep. The perfect peace or happiness of sleep we even recollect after waking, for then our feeling is not merely that we have slept but that we have slept soundly.

(3) *Turīya state.*—This is a state which, as its improvised name suggests, is not within the experience of ordinary man. It may therefore be regarded as lying outside the strict limits of any empirical investigation. It is brought about voluntarily by the elimination of discursive thought, and resembles dreamless sleep in all respects but one. There is in it the same withdrawal of normal consciousness, the same absence of desires and the manifestation of almost the same bliss. But while the self fully reveals itself in the fourth state, the experience of dreamless sleep is extremely dim. The turīya is a mystic state to be testified to only by the person that is gifted with yugic power. But the truth he vouches for is not wholly beyond us. For we have on the one hand the negative evidence of suṣupti and on the other the positive one of the ānandamaya phase of experience, which together enable us to get a 'conjectural insight' into the nature of the knower's experience. The attainment of this state is regarded as the culmination of spiritual training.

III

The diversity of views noticed in connection with the theoretical teaching of the Upaniṣads has its reflex in their practical teaching—both in regard to the ideal to be achieved and the means of achieving it. To take the latter as an example: We find one Upaniṣad[57] mentioning three such different means for the attainment of immortality—devotion to truth, penance and Vedic study—and ascribing them to three specific teachers. There is sometimes also an attempt made to reconcile two opposing views current at the time, each of which was probably pursued independently. The *Īśa Upaniṣad,* whose main feature seems to be this spirit of synthesis, tries to harmonize two such views in regard to attaining salvation. In the first of its eighteen verses it inculcates renunciation, but in the next verse qualifies it by adding that incessant exertion also is necessary. The Upaniṣad means thereby that one should not renounce activity and withdraw from the world, but give up only all thought of reaping any personal benefit from it—thus anticipating the well-known teaching of the Bhagavadgītā. We cannot consider all this diversity of views here, but shall refer only to the more prevalent among them.

The basis of Upaniṣadic ethics is to be found in the conception of evil, not as offending against the will of the gods or swerving from sacrificial rectitude as in the earlier period, but as the result of a metaphysical error which sees variety alone where there is also the unity of Brāhman.[58] Empirical thought, failing to grasp the ultimate reality, distorts it or cuts it up into parts and presents them as distinct from one another. Evil is due on the practical side to this mistaken view of Reality as finiteness is on the theoretical side. It is thus contingent and has no place in the Absolute rightly understood. This misleading presentation of Reality is seen in the case not only of the objective world, but also of the self. It is because each of us regards himself as distinct from others that he strives to guard or aggrandize himself. 'When unity is realized and every being becomes our very self—how can there be any delusion or sorrow then?[59] In other words, all evil is traceable to ahaṁ-kāra, the affirmation of the finite self, and the consequent tendency to live not in harmony with the rest of the world, but in opposition or at best in indifference to it. The impulse behind this ahaṁkara is not in itself bad and does not need to be wholly suppressed. The instinct to live or to strive to be, which is what ahaṁ-kāra signifies, is a common feature of animate existence and is only a manifestation of the desire for self-realization. But, being really a desire transcend finite being, it will remain unsatisfied until it is rationalized through a knowledge of the ultimate truth and e wider self is averred in place of the narrower one. That is the meaning of Aham Brāhma asmi[60] which represents the realization of Brahman in one's own self as the highest ideal of life.

There are two well-defined descriptions of the ideal in the Upaniṣads. What is sought after in the Mantras and the Brāhmaṇas is the continuance after death of individual existence in some exalted form. This ideal of reaching's goal after death survives in the Upaniṣads; and Brahma-realization is represented as taking place after dissociation om the physical body, as for instance in the passage quoted in a previous section to illustrate the cosmic ideal.[61] This eschatological ideal, however, appears here very much modified for, in accordance with the prevalent view of the upaniṣads, what is to be reached is represented not as other than but as identical with what reaches it. 'This is Brahman. May I become it when I depart hence.' The significance of such a view is that mokṣa is a state of eternal bliss (āṇanda), for it transcends duality which is the source of all strife.[62] Along with this is found another ideal [63] wnich regards mokṣa as a condition, not to be attained after death, but to be realized here and now, if one so wills. A person that has reached this state continues to see variety, but he is not deluded by it because he has realized in his own experience the unity of all. We have already drawn attention (p. 19) to he significance of this ideal in the history of Indian thought. What is most noteworthy about it is its recognition of the adequacy of the present life to perfect oneself. Unlike the former, it signifies that Mokṣa or release does not consist in a *becoming* something. It only means the discovery of what has always been a fact, and is compared to the discovery of a treasure which was all along lying hidden under the floor of one's, house, but which one had so far failed to find, though passing to and from over it constantly.[64] It is the view that accords with the acosmic conception of Brahman with its implication of the phenomenality of the universe.

The practical teaching of the Upaniṣads is devised to bring about Brahma-realization in the above sense. It aims, as all such teaching should do, at the rectification of our thoughts and of our deeds. Broadly speaking, the course of discipline prescribed comprises two states:—

(1) *Cultivation of detachment (vairāgya).*—The prime object of Upaniṣadic discipline is the removal of ahaṁ-kāra, which is the basis of all evil; and vairāgya is the name given to that attitude towards the world which results from the successful eradication of the narrow selfish impulses for which it stands. Its accomplishment necessarily presupposes a long course of training through the three āśramas or disciplinary stages—those of the religious student (brahma-carya), the householder (gārhasthya) and the anchorite (vānaprastha)—so far as they were understood at the time. As the very word asrama ('toil') means, they are stages of strife when selfishness is slowly but steadily rooted out. 'The good is one thing, the pleasant, another; and he that wishes to, live the life of the spirit must leave the sensual life far 'behind.'[65] This training leads to saṁnyāsa; but we should remember that the term does not yet bear in the Upaniṣads its present significance of a formal stage in the spiritual ascent of man. It there means only the transcending of the triple mode of asrama life, and is regarded as a consequence of Brahma-knowledge rather than a means of attaining it. In the latter sense, saṁnyāsa appears comparatively late.[66] The Upaniṣads, while fully recognizing the value of this preparatory training, do not ordinarily dwell at length upon it. They rather take it for granted and address themselves to such as have already successfully undergone that training and have acquired vairāgya.[67] That is the implication, for example, of the efforts made to keep the Upaniṣadic truth as a secret which we have already mentioned. The preliminary discipline, however, should not be viewed as wholly implicit in the Upaniṣads, for occasionally direct references to it in one or other of its various aspects are found, as for instance in a very short but-most interesting section of the *Bṛhadāraṇyaka Upaniṣad.*[68] Here the in-

mates of the world ire classified as gods (deva), men (manuṣya) and demons (asura), and are all described as the children of Praja-pati. They approach their father seeking instruction from him as to how they should conduct themselves. The answer is brief, but it clearly indicates the necessity for grades in moral discipline according to the capacity and temperament of the persons in question. To the asuras, the commandment given is 'Have compassion on man' (dayadhvam); to the manuṣyas, 'Be generous' (datta); and to the devas, 'Learn self-control' (dāmyata). The first two of these prescribe regard for others as the chief principle of action. The third is unlike them and may appear to be purely individualistic; but, being addressed to the best, it should be taken to presuppose the training of the other two stages. The same Upaniṣad in another of its sections represents the gods as unwilling to allow man to withdraw from the sphere of social or relative morality, which is merely a rhetorical way of expressing that man ought not to break away from society (p. 21) until he has discharged his duty towards it and gained its goodwill, so to speak.[69]

(2) *Acquisition of knowledge (jñāna).*—Evil being due to a misconception of the nature of Reality, its removal can be only through right knowledge; and if the cultivation of detachment is also laid down as necessary, it is only to render the acquisition of such knowledge possible. Detachment is a pre-condition of right knowledge. 'Having become calm, subdued, quiet, patiently enduring and collected, one should see the self in the self' says the *Bṛhadāraṇyaka 'Upaniṣad.*[70] The training of this second stage is threefold: śravaṇa, manana and nididhyāsana.[71] The first stands for the study of the Upaniṣads under a proper guru: 'He that has a teacher knows.[72] It defines the place of precept and tradition in the training. It also means that the influence of an ideal is never so great on us as when we are brought into personal contact with one who is a living embodiment of that ideal. Though necessary, śravaṇa is not enough; so it is supplemented by manana or continued reflection upon what has thus been learnt with a view to get an intellectual conviction regarding it. This training is to be further supplemented by nididhyāsana or meditation, which assists directly in the realization within oneself of the unity underlying the multiplicity of the universe. The necessity for this part of the training arises as follows: Our belief in the reality of diversity as such is the result of perception and is therefore immediate. So nothing but an equally immediate apprehension of unity can effectively remove it. If variety, in the reality of which we almost instinctively believe, is not to delude us, we must *see* the unity underlying it, not merely know it. Seeing is believing. That is why the Upaniṣads speak of darśana or 'Spiritual perception' in respect of the Ātman or Brahman.[73] A mere reasoned conviction is not enough, though it is necessary to give us the mark, as it were, at which to shoot.[74] A successful pursuit of this course of train-

ing will result in right knowledge, which, according to the eschatological view, will lead to Mokṣa later, but which, according to the other, secures it at once.

Nididhyāsana in this sense is the highest form of meditation and is possible only after considerable practice in concentration of thought. Hence the Upaniṣads prescribe several meditative exercises of a preliminary character. They are usually called upāsanas, and the prominence given to them in the Upaniṣads is comparable to that given to rites in the Brāhmaṇas. We need notice only one or two points about them. In upāsanas, the thought may be directed wholly outwards and two selected objects, both external, may be mentally identified as in the meditation of the universe as a 'horse' alluded to above; or only one external object may be chosen and it may be thought of as identical with the contemplative's own self. There is an important difference between the two forms of meditation. While the former affords exercise only in concentration, the latter gives scope, in addition, to the cultivation of sympathetic imagination—the power to place oneself in the position of another. It accordingly serves as a more direct aid to Brahma-realization, wherein also what is contemplated, viz. Brahman, is to be identified with the contemplative's self. Again the objects of contemplation may be real objects or only symbols. Among real objects which the disciple is asked to think of as one with Brahman, we often find conceptions which were once taken for ultimate reality itself, but which in course of time, as philosophic thought progressed, were superseded by higher conceptions. Such for instance is the case with Prāṇa[75] which marked an actual stage in the evolution of the conception of the Absolute. Among the symbols used for Brahman may be mentioned the famous Om, the mystic syllable, which finds a very important place in the Upaniṣads.[76] Whatever form these meditations may take, they prepare the disciple for the final mode of contemplation as Aham Brahma asmi. When a person that has morally purified himself and has after formal study and reflection convinced himself intellectually of the truth of unity, succeeds through nididhyāsana in transforming what was heretofore known only mediately into an immediate certainty, he attains the spiritual goal.

It is, however, only a very few that can achieve this goal. The Upaniṣads themselves refer to a knower of Brahman as a rarity. 'What is hard for many even to hear, what many fail to understand even though they hear: a marvel is he that can teach it and lucky is its obtainer—a marvel is he that knows it, when taught by the wise.[77] The many fail, the one succeeds. The majority, according to the Upaniṣads, are born again after death.[78] The constant stream of births and deaths until Mokṣa is attained is what is known as saṁsāra or transmigration. It is the lot not only of those that are not virtuous, but also of those that restrict their activity to works of piety and lack right knowledge. The law which governs the kind of birth which such a jīva gets every time it dies, is known as the law of karma. It signifies that nothing can happen without a sufficient cause in the moral as in the physical world—that each life with all its pains and pleasures is the necessary result of the actions of past lives and becomes in its turn the cause, through its own activities, of future births. It traces all suffering eventually to ourselves and thus removes bitterness against God or our neighbour. What we have been makes us what we are. According to it the future, as we shall see in a later chapter, lies entirely in our own hands so that belief in this law serves as a perpetual incentive to right conduct. The principle underlying it is thus essentially different from the notion of good as a gift of the gods which we found prevailing in an earlier period.[79] It may appear to substitute fate for the gods of old, but it is a fate of which man himself is the master. The doctrine, however, cannot be regarded as embodying a demonstrable truth. Nevertheless, its value as a hypothesis for rationally explaining the observed iniquities of life is clear.

There is some difference of opinion as regards the origin of this doctrine. Some have stated that it was borrowed by the Aryans from the primitive people of their new home, among whom a belief in the passing of the soul after death into trees, etc., was found. But the view ignores that that belief was a superstition and therefore essentially irrational, while the doctrine of transmigration aims at satisfying man's logical as well as his moral consciousness. On account of this important difference, the doctrine should be regarded as not connected with any primitive belief, but as gradually evolved by the Indians themselves. It is true that it is not distinctly mentioned before the age of the Upaniṣads and, even among them, not all lay equal emphasis on it. All that can be said with certainty is that it had fully developed and belief in it had widely spread by the time of Buddha. But it is not difficult to trace its gradual development from earlier times.[80] The Mantras indicate a belief in the immortality of the soul; and there is also prevalent in them the idea of ṛta or moral order. But these notions, though underlying the doctrine of transmigration, do not constitute its distinctive features. The survival of the soul after death and the determination of its condition then by the moral worth of its deeds in this life are assumed by practically all religions. A true link with the doctrine is found in the notion of iṣṭāpūrta, which indeed has been described as a 'distant precursor' of karma[81]; and it already occurs in the Ṛgveda. Iṣṭa stands for the sacrifice offered to the gods and the word pūrta means the gifts given to the priests. The main point about it for us to note is that the merit resulting from these acts cannot strictly be termed ethical and that it was yet believed to precede the person to the other world and there to await his arrival like a guardian angel, to secure bliss for him. In a funeral hymn the dead man is asked to join his iṣṭāpūrta. If we dissociate this belief from its exclusively sacrificial reference and widen it so as to include all deeds—good and bad, religious and secular—we see its closeness to the belief in karma. Again a gradation of rewards and punishments corresponding to the good and evil deeds of this life appears in the Brāhmanas and among the serious punishments meted out to the sinful is 'repeated dying' (punar-mṛtyu), which is represented as taking place in another world. The notion of repeated birth is not mentioned; but it is clear that it is implicit in that of repeated death. What the Upaniṣads did was to render this idea explicit and transfer the whole circle of births and deaths to this world from a hypothetical region. The soul according to this belief passes at death into another body whose character is determined by its former deeds. In its initial form, as enunciated by Yājñavalkya.[82] there is no interval between the end of one life and the beginning of the next. The belief did not, however, long remain unmodified, because it got mixed up with the earlier belief in recompense in another world. In this modified form the doctrine teaches a two-fold reward or punishment, first in the world beyond and then in a life here.[83] But that is a detail of Hindu faith which need not be further dwelt upon here.

IV

We have described how the theism of the Mantras decayed in later times under the ritualistic preoccupation of the priests. So far as it survived, it was transformed by the general philosophic bias of Indian thinking and resulted in the monotheistic conception of Prajā-pati—a god who does not represent any of the old Vedic deities, but is one above and beyond them (p. 40). The old nature-gods do not regain their position in the Upaniṣads. They are not indeed abandoned, but find mention in one connection or another. Some of them even continue to be cosmic powers which is not different from their original character; but they pale before the single reality that has now been discovered and are invariably represented as subordinate to it. Asked how many gods there are, Yājñavalkya makes light of the number thirty-three fixed in an earlier period and replies that there is but one, viz. Brahman.[84] All the other gods, being only its manifestations, are necessarily dependent upon it. The *Kena Upaniṣad* speaks of Agni, vāyu and even Indra as worsted by the might of Brahman and represents them as unable to meddle even with a blade of grass without its aid. Elsewhere the sun and the other gods are described as discharging their functions through its fear.[85] This is the case not merely with the ancient gods of the Mantras; even Prajā-pati, the supreme god of the Brāhmaṇas, becomes thus subordinated.The *Kauṣītakī Upaniṣad* portrays him and Indra as the doorkeepers of the abode of the Highest[86]; and in the *Chāndogya Upaniṣad* he figures as but a preceptor.[87] The fact is that we cannot properly look for any theistic view in the Upaniṣads whose main concern is with the philosophic Absolute, except where that Absolute itself is personified and spoken of as God. Such a theistic rendering of the doctrine of the Absolute is sometimes found. Of the two forms of this doctrine, it is the cosmic that lends itself easily to such transformation. But a God so derived, being identical with the ātman, cannot ultimately be differentiated from the jīva. He can stand only for an inner principle and not for an object of adoration distinct from him that adores. The Upaniṣads explicitly repudiate such an objective conception of God 'Whoever worships a deity thinking that to be one and himself another—he does not know.[88] The idea of God in the Upaniṣads therefore differs fundamentally from the old Vedic view of deva—a luminous something presented as external to us—or even from that of the later Prajā-pati and can be described as theistic only by courtesy. The Upaniṣadic God is described as the 'inner ruler immortal' (antaryāmyamṛtaḥ) or the 'thread' (sūtra) that runs through all things and holds them together.[89] He is the central truth of both animate and inanimate existence and is accordingly not merely a transcendent but also an immanent principle. He is the creator of the universe, but he brings it into being out of himself as 'the spider does its web' and retracts it again into himself, so that creation really become another word for evolution here. In the terminology of the later Vedānta he is the efficient and at the same time, the material cause of the universe (abhinna-nimittopādāna).[90]

Though theism in the ordinary sense thus really is incompatible with the general spirit of the Upaniṣads, we occasionally come across it in them. In the *Kaṭha Upaniṣad*[91] references are made to a God who appears to be differentiated from the individual soul. A clearer indication of it is seen in the *śvetāśvatara Upaniṣad,* where we find all the requirements of theism—belief in God, soul and the world and the conviction that devotion to the Lord is the true means of salvation.[92] But even here the personal conception more than once gets assimilated to the impersonal or all-comprehensive Absolute, and it is difficult to believe that we have here anything more than monotheism in the making, though some scholars like Bhandarkar are of a different opinion and take it as distinctly personal.[93]

REFERENCE

1. SPU pp. 61-2, 396; Macdonell: *India's Past*, p. 46.

2. I. ii. 7.

3. interpretations are common in the Āraṇyakas or 'forest,' which in the several Vedas serve as a connecting link between Brāhmaṇas proper and the Upaniṣads. The Āranyakas were forest (araṇya). See PU. pp. 2 3.

4. and ii. See Deussen: *system of the vedānta*, p. 8.

5. ii. 6 and 7 See PU. pp. 64-5.

6. See PU. p. 396; Rel. V. pp. 220ff.

7. Cf. śaṁkara on *Kaṭha Up.* Introduction.

8. PU. pp, 10-15.

9. Schopenhauer used to have the Oupnekhat lie open upon his table, and was in the habit, before going to bed, of performing his devotions from its pages—Rel. V p. 55.

10. Cf. VS. I i. 4.

11. See e.g. VS I ii 38 31.

12. *Kaṭha Up.* II. ii. 15.

13. This derivation is what Max Müller gives, following Indian commentators. See SS. pp. 52-5. Others have seen in it other

14.SS. pp. 79-2.

15. RV. X. 16.

16. See e.g. *Aitareya Up.* i.

17. Cf. *Taittirīva Up* iii.

18. Cf. *Taittirīya Up.* ii. i.

19. See *Aitareya Āraṇayka*, II. iii. 2.

20. Even this synthesis is not quite unknow to literature anterior to theUpaniṣads (See AV. X viii. 44); but it appears there only faintly and may therefore be justifiably described as Upaniṣadic. Compare in this connection the remark of Deussen (*System of the Vedānta*, p. 18). that 'the sparks of philosophic light appearing in the Rigveda shine out brighter and brighter until at last in the Uanishads they burst out in that bright flame which is able to lightand warm us to-day.

21. *Ch. UP.* VI.

22. We have an example of this in *Ch. UP.* V. xi-xviii. See p. 45.

23. III. ii. 11. ff.

24. See e.g. *Praśna Up.* i. 1; v.

25. I. i. 6.

26. 'Brahma-pariṇāma-vāda' and 'Brahma-vivarta-vāda' are later Vedāntic terms. See Ch. XIII.

27. See *śvetāśvatara Up.* iv. 10.

28. Cf. *Kaṭha Up.* I. ii. 5.

29. *Br Up.* IV. v. 15.

30. PU. pp. 228 ff. See alos Macdonell: *India's Past.* p. 47.

31. Cf. BP. p. 101, where its association is referred to a primitive period when the name was treated as 'a possession and part of the individual.'

32. *Bṛ. Up.* I vi. 1.

33. *Taittirīya Up*. II. i.

34. Strictly the mode of deriving the gross from the subtle elements (tri-vṛtkaraṇa) is explained in the Upaniṣads only with reference to three elements (see *Ch. Up*. VI. ii. 3-4). The Vedānta extended it to the five elements (pañcī-karaṇa). See VS. II. iv. 22.

35. *Praśna Up*. iv. 8.

36. *Ch. Up*. VI. iii. 1.

37. *Aitrarey Up*. v. 3.

38. iii. 2; v. 3.

39. *Bṛ Up*. II. Iv. 14.

40. *Kaṭha UP*. II. ii. i, 3 and 5.

41. ii. 1-5.

42. The corresponding adjuncts constitute three of the five kośas or 'sheaths' regarded as enfolding the soul. The remaining two are termed annamaya and prāṇamaya—the first, whcih is the outermost of the kośas, being the body or materialcovering of the jīva and standing for the physical side of indiviudal existence; the second represening its vital or organic side.

43.cf Brahma puccham pratisthā.

44.Compare in this connection the term rasa, 'aesthetic Brahman' for Brahman Rasa vai eah (*Taittivāava* II ii. 2).

45. Cf *Prasna Up*.iv.9; *Kaṭha Up*.I.iii.4.

46. If we reckon manas as three-fold with its conscious, self-conscious and self-transcendent phases, we have here the five 'sheaths' of the doctrine of kośas. Se Note won the previous page.

47. PU. p.263.

48. I.I.4-5.

49. Cf.*Ch.Up*. VI.i. 3-4.

50. *Taittirīya* Up.ii.4.

51. Mantra 5.

52. III. ii. 17.

53. *Muṇḍaka Up* II, ii. 9.

54. PU. p. 298.

55. See e.g. PU. p. 306.

56. *Taittirīya Up*. i. 9.

57. According to the acosmic ideal, no doubt, both the unity and diversity are equally unreal. Yet even in that view evil disappears the moments unity is realized. In other words, there is no difference between the two teachings so far as the problem of ethics is concerned. Evil originates, according to both alike, in the consciousness that diversity *alone* is true and it is overcome by the knowledge that unity underlies it, whatever explanation may eventually be given of that unity-in-diversity itself.

58. *Īśa Up.7.*

59. *Bṛ.Up*. I. iv. Io

60. Deussen regards this as the mokṣa doctrine apperaing in an empirical form and therefore as derived from the other. See PU.pp.358-9.

61. Cf. Bṛ. UP. I. iv. 2: 'Fear springs from a second.'

62. These two views were described later as krama-mukti and jīvan

63.*Ch.Up*. VIII.iii.2.

64. *Katha Up.* I. ii. 1 and 2

65. See PU. p. 374

66. The failure to recognize this fact has been the source of some incorrect views regarding the place of morality in the Upaniṣadic scheme of life. Thus one of the common critisms livelled against it is that it cares little or nothing for social morality and concerns itself soley with pointing out the way for individuals perfection. Deussen e.g. has stated (PU. pp. 364-5) that among the ancient Indians 'the consciousness of human solidarity, of common needs was but slightly developed.'

67.

68. I. iv. 10. Cf. śaṁkara's commentary.

69. *Bṛ.Up.* IV. iv. 23

70. Id. II. iv.5.

71. Ācāryavān puruṣo veda: *Ch. Up. vi. xiv. 2.*

72. Cf. Ātma vā are draṣṭavyaḥ: *Bṛ. up. II. iv. 5.*

73. Cf. *Muṇḍaka Up.* ii. 2-4.

74. See e.g. *Bṛ. Up.* I. iii.

75. Cf. *Praśna Up.* v.

76. *Katha Up.* I. ii. 7.

77. See *Ch. Up.* V. x. 8.

78. It is more akin to the view that sacrifices properly per performed

79. See PU. pp. 313 ff.

80. Prof. Keith. *Religion and Philosophy of the Veda,* pp. 250. 478.

81. The word in classical Sanskrit means 'charitable deeds.'

82. *Bṛ. Up.* III. ii. 13.

83. See *Bṛ. Up.* VI. ii; *Ch. Up.* V. iii-x.

84. iii; iv. 1-3.

85. Cf. *Katha Up.* II. iii. 3.

86. i. 5.

87. VIII vii-xii.

88. *Bṛ Up.* I. iv. 10 Cf. *Kena Up.* i.4-8.

89. See Bṛ. Up. III. vii.

90. Such a conception, being the personalized from of Brahman, may have been desianaed Brahma. It does not however, seem to be the case anywhere inthe Upanisads or in the literature of the earlier period. Where the word Brahma occurs as inthe Muṇḍaka Upaniṣad (I. i. i), it is not the name ofhte Highest but represens Prāja-Pati regarded as a secondary deity or the 'first embodied' (prathama-ja). See SS. p. 281.

91. I.ii. 23.

92. i. 10 and 12.

93. *Vaiṣṇavism, śaivism,* etc. p. 110.

CHAPTER XX

BHAGAVADGĪTĀ

In point of popularity the Gītā is second to no work in the world of Indian thought. It has always commanded great admiration and its popularity now, if anything, is on the increase. This unique position it owes to a variety of causes. It forms a portion of an epic whose study has enraptured generations of men and women. The two characters that figure in it are most fascinating; and the occasion which call forth its teaching is one of extreme seriousness when the fate not only of the country but of righteousness (dharma) itself is at stake. The work is written in a simple and charming style, and is in the form of a dialogue which imparts to it a dramatic interest. But such formal excellences alone are not adequate to account for its great attractiveness. It has, as we shall see, a specific message to give. For the present, it will suffice to refer to one or two, other points in its teaching which invest it with special value. The work breathes throughout a spirit of toleration which is an outstanding characteristic of Hindu thought. 'Whoever with true devotion worships any deity, in him I deepen that devotion; and through it he fulfils his desire.' 'Those that devotedly worship other gods, they also worship me though only imperfectly.'[1] The thought here is not, as it sometimes unfortunately is, that 'one man's God is another's devil,' but that every conception of God, however crude or defective in itself, still has its own divine side and that it is not so much the nature of the object worshipped as the spirit in which the worshipper turns to it that counts. To this feature, which entitles the poem to the first place in Hindu scriptures as bringing out best their governing spirit, it adds another which explains why it has been reckoned as part of the world's literature ever since it came to be known outside India. Its author, as may be expected from one whom tradition reckons as the inspirer of practically all the Sanskrit poets, does not discuss here the subtle and recondite details of ethics or metaphysics, but deals only with the broad principles underlying them, relating them at the same time to the most fundamental aspirations of man. And this he does not by means of any abstract disquisition, but by selecting a specific situation involving a moral dilemma and pointing out how it is overcome. This concrete mode of treatment, with the suggestiveness natural to it, very much widens the scope of the teaching and makes its appeal almost universal.

All this, however, does not mean that the work is easy of understanding. Far from it. It is one of the hardest books to interpret, which accounts for the numerous commentaries on it—each differing from the rest in some essential point or other. Part of this diversity in interpretation is due to the assumption that the Gītā not only concerns itself with the problem of conduct whose solution is a pressing need for man if he is to live without that inner discord which arises from consciousness of the ideal unaccompanied by mastery over self, but also is a treatise on metaphysics. Dealing as it does with a moral problem, the work necessarily touches upon metaphysical questions now and again; but they form only the background to the ethical teaching. To regard a consideration of ultimate philosophical questions as falling within the main aim of the Gītā, appears to us to misjudge its character. Though the features characteristic of the background are only vaguely seen and explain the divergent accounts given of them by interpreters, what is in the focus of the picture, viz. its practical teaching, is quite distinct. Another cause of difference among the interpreters of the work is the forgetting of the occasion that evoked the teaching and expecting to find in it a complete theory of morals. The occasion is a particular one and Śrī Krśṇa, in enunciating a course of conduct suited to it, naturally draws attention only to *some* of the principles on which right living should be based. The theme of the work is not accordingly the whole of moral philosophy; and there are, as will become clear later, omissions of importance in it. Our aim will be to explain the nature of the central moral truth inculcated in the work and point out its importance in the history of Indian thought. We shall also try to indicate the general features of the theory which underlies that teaching, but we shall not attempt a complete exposition of the work, by taking into account all the other teachings that may be found interspersed here and there in it. The Gītā in that respect resembles the Mahābhārata, whose heterogeneous character has already been described. Since the *motif* of the poem is in its practical teaching, we shall take it up first. As regards the age to which the work belongs, there has been a great deal of controversy; but scholars are now mostly agreed that in its essential portions at least, it is not later than 200 B.C.—a date which falls within the period at present under consideration.

I

We have stated that so far as the practical teaching is concerned, there is no ambiguity. The reason for this is the setting of the poem. In the beginning, we find Arjuna despondent and declining to fight; but, as a result of Śrī Kṛṣṇa's persuasion, he makes up his mind to take part in the contest. This important element in the conception of the poem would lose its entire significance if we did not regard action as its essential lesson. We may accordingly conclude that the central point of the teaching is activism, or, to use the expression of the Gītā, karma-yoga. To understand what exactly is meant by this expression, it is necessary to consider separately the two terms constituting it. *Karma* literally means 'what is done,' 'a deed'; and the word of course appears with this general meaning sometimes in the work.[2] But by the time of the Gītā it had also come to signify that particular form of activity which is taught in the liturgical portion of Vedic literature, viz. sacrifice. Though we cannot say that the word does not at all bear this special sense in the poem,[3] it by no means represents its prevailing use. What it usually signifies here is duties that, in accordance with custom and tradition, were found associated at the time with particular sections or classes of the people,[4] the varṇa-dharmas as they are described.[5] The word is also sometimes used in a fourth sense in the work, viz. divine worship and devotional acts connected with it such as prayer.[6] Of these several meanings, we should, when thinking of karma-yoga as taught in the Gītā, ordinarily take third, viz. social obligations which in one form or another are acknowledged in all organized society. The word *yoga* means 'harnessing' or 'applying oneself to' so that karma-yoga may be rendered as 'devotion to the discharge of social obligations.' A characteristic of all voluntary deeds is that they are preceded by a desire for something, which is described as their motive or phala. Whenever we knowingly act, we aim at achieving some end or other. In the present case, for instance, Arjuna is actuated by a desire for sovereignty over his ancestral kingdom; and he has undertaken to fight for regaining, if possible, that sovereignty which through the force of circumstances has passed on to his wily cousins. Such an undertaking, however, would not be devotion to karma. It is devotion to its phala, because the karma here, viz. fighting, but serves as a means to bring about a preconceived end. For karma-yoga, the act should be viewed not as a means but as an end in itself. That is, the idea of the result, which is to ensue from the action, must be dismissed altogether from the mind before as well as during the act. The term signifies, as Śrī Kṛṣṇa is never tired of repeating, the doing of a deed without any the least thought of reaping its fruit. 'Your concern is solely with action—never with its fruit.[7] There follows, no doubt, a result from the deed that is done, but in the case of the karma-yogin ceases to be his *end* for this simple reason that it is not desired and that there can be no end conceivable apart from relation to desire. An important consequence of following this principle of action is that one can act with complete equanimity. Desire or self-interest when allowed to have its sway over us may blind us to what is right; and even when we succeed in choosing to do the right deed, undue eagerness to secure its fruit may induce us to swerve from the path of rectitude. The term yoga is in one place explained as signifying just such equanimity or 'balance of mind' (samatvam), This teaching that we ought to engage ourselves in our work as members of a social order in the usual way and yet banish from our mind all thought of deriving any personal benefit therefrom is the meaning of karma-yoga and constitutes the specific message of the Gītā.

The importance of this teaching will become clear if we refer to the two ideals of life that were prevalent at the time among the orthodox—the negative ideal of renunciation and the positive one of active life. The first deal of nivṛtti, as it is called, advocated the giving up of all karma and withdrawing from the work-a-day world entirely. The second one of pravṛtti, no doubt, recommended living in the midst of society undertaking all the obligations implied thereby; but it did not exclude the element of selfishness altogether. This is clear in the case of ritualistic activities. Those that engaged themselves in such activities, because they realized the enduring character of the self, did not, it is true, yield to the impulse of the moment, but strove for a good which was attainable in another life. Yet it was their own good they sought. Though their belief in a future life saved them from rating too high the value of worldly good, what they worked for was similar in character and their efforts cannot therefore escape being characterized as at bottom selfish. And in the case of activities which are not other worldly, they directed their thoughts as much towards rights .as towards duties. They regarded themselves as not only bound to discharge their indebtedness to others, but also as having a claim upon those others for what was due to themselves; and so far they fell short of a truly spiritual conception of life. The object of the Gītā is to discover the golden mean between the two ideals of pravṛtti and nivṛtti or of action and contemplation as we might term them, preserving the excellence of both. Karma-yoga is such a mean. While it does not abandon activity, it preserves the spirit of renunciation. It commends a strenuous life, and yet gives no room for the play of selfish impulses. Thus it discards neither ideal, but by combining them refines and ennobles both. That particular attitude of the soul which renunciation signifies still remains; only it ceases to look askance at action. In other words the Gītā teaching stands not for renunciation *of* action, but for renunciation *in* action.

Arjuna who at the outset undertook to fight under the influence of one of these old ideals has, as we see his portrayed at the beginning of the work, come to be influenced by the other. He has resolved on a sudden to renounce the world and withdraw from the contest. But he forgets that, the advocates of that ideal require, as a condition of adopting it, real detachment in the would-be disciple. Arjuna is but slenderly equipped for it, and yet he thinks of giving up the world. That he has not really risen above the common level in this respect is clear from the fact that his vairāgya does not spring from true enlightenment, but from narrow-mindedness, viz. the love of kith and kin.[8] He continues to make a distinction between his own people and others; and his excuse for inaction, as set forth in the beginning of the poem, leaves the impression that his interest even in his subjects, as distinguished from his kinsmen, is after all secondary.[9] His detachment, or rather his disinclination to fight, is in a large measure due to the uncommon situation in which he finds himself somewhat suddenly. It is not, therefore, his considered view of the universe or of the life-that he has to lead in it which prompts him to this indifference . It is the result of weakness—surrendering to the power of the moment. Arjuna's vairāgya is also in a subtle and unconscious manner due to the diffidence and fear that he might not after all win the battle, so that it is at bottom faint-heartedness (hrdaya-daurbalyam) as Śrī Kṛṣṇa characterizes it and eventually rāga, not viraga.[10] He is still worldly-minded; and it is on empirical, not on ultimate, grounds that he adopts an attitude of inaction. He fails to realise that he is not fighting for himself or for his family or clan (kula), but for king and country—that the interests of righteousness are in jeopardy and that, like every right-minded person, he is bound to do his best to set the situation right. The final test that Arjuna is not actuated by genuine detachment is the sadness and despondency (viṣāda) that pervade his speech. Not only is he sad, he is also in doubt.[11] Neither doubt nor sadness is a sign of true spirituality which would result in a feeling of triumphant freedom. Śrī Kṛṣṇa's teaching is that the narrow selfish impulses of which sadness and doubt are the sign should first be overcome; and the way to do it is not to resort to the loneliness of the forest, but to live in the midst of the storm and stress of social life, doing one's duty without any thought of recompense.

This teaching has been traced by some to earlier sources.[12] It is no doubt mentioned in the Īśa. *Upaniṣad*, but without any elaboration whatsoever. Even granting that the ideal of karma-yoga is not altogether new, there is no doubt that its general acceptance is due to its impressive enunciation in the Gītā. None- of the orthodox creeds or systems of thought that were evolved afterwards discarded it. Detached action became the starting-point of life's discipline according to all, superseding virtually the earlier view of activity pursued for its fruit. In this transformation of the ideal of pravṛtti consists one of the chief contributions of the Gītā to Hindu thought. We may add that though the particular circumstances that called forth the teaching have changed, it has not been rendered obsolete. For good or ill, the monastic ideal has all but disappeared now. Ours is an age of self-assertion, not of self-suppression. Men are not now likely to give up their duty to become recluses, as Arjuna wanted to do. The danger comes from the other side. In our eagerness to claim our rights and exercise them, we may ignore our duties. Hence the need for the teaching of the Gītā now is as great as ever. Its value has not lessened through lapse of time; and that is a mark of its greatness.

The propriety of selecting the battle-field for imparting the teaching is that nowhere else is the subordination of individual aim to the general good so complete. The soldier may know the cause for which he is fighting, but he can hardly say how that fight is going to end. Even supposing that it is to end favourably to his cause, he, for aught he knows, will not be there at the time to share its beneficial results. Yet this uncertainty does not in the least reduce his responsibility as a fighter. He has to do his best and should therefore realize to the utmost his value and importance as an agent, but at the same time forget altogether that he is to participate in whatever good may accrue from the discharge of his duty.[13] It is the cause of a wider entity than himself that he is serving; and his thought should not go beyond realizing that his individual responsibility as an actor in the scene remains at the maximum. That represents the highest form of self-sacrifice—to work for no profit to oneself, but yet to exert oneself to the utmost; and the finest exhibition of this spirit in the world is to be seen on a battle-field. We should, however, remember that Śrī Kṛṣṇa is really addressing all men through his devotee, Arjuna; and the teaching, as already observed, is not restricted in its application to the particular situation that gave rise to it. Its appeal is to all men that find themselves placed in a similar dilemma in life. In this wider sense, it takes as its essential basis the principle that activity is natural to man and that no view of life which overlooks that feature or minimizes its importance can be right. More than once is it stated in the course of the work that no man can abjure activity altogether,[14] but this natural activity needs to be properly directed, for otherwise it is apt to be utilized for selfish or material ends and thus become the means of obscuring from man the higher end for which he exists.

What is the direction in which the activity should be exercised? In answer to this question, the Gītā enjoins on all the performance of their respective duties. 'One should never abandon one's specific work, whether it be high or law.[15] It attaches little or no value to the intrinsic worth of the deed that is done by any person, so long is it is his own dharma (sva-dharma). The word sva-dharma may bear a wide significance but, as required by the particular context and as specified more than once in the course of the book, it means chiefly, though not solely, the duties incumbent upon the main classes into which society is divided. In other words, it is social obligations mainly that are asked here to be discharged—such as are calculated to secure and preserve the solidarity of society. It is a proof of the severely practical character of the teaching contained in the book that it does not attempt to describe these duties any further. It realizes the impossibility of detailing the acts appropriate to every station in life, and leaves their determination to the good sense or immediate judgment of the individual. There is an attempt made in one or two places[16] to indicate *what* these obligations are, but only in a general way. It may be thought that the mere injunction that one should do one's dharma leaves the matter vague. But we must remember that in the relatively simple organization of the society when the teaching was formulated, the duties of the several classes were known fairly clearly. In the present case at any rate, there is no doubt as to what the sva-dharma of Arjuna is. The prominence given to relative duties, such us depend upon the position in society of the individual, shows by the way that the treatment which the problem of conduct receives here is, as we remarked before, only partial. There is, for example, no allusion to what may be described as 'right in itself except incidentally, as in distinguishing the worthy from the wicked—the two broad classes into which the book in one of its sections divides the whole of mankind.[17] It emphasizes the social character of man, and, generally speaking, declines to look upon him apart from the community of which he is a member.

From what we have stated so far, it appears that a karma-yogin works without a purpose in view. No voluntary activity, however, seems conceivable without some motive or other. Will without desire, it has been said, is a fiction. What then is the motive for exertion here? There are two answers to this question furnished in the book: (1) ātma-śuddhi[18] which means 'purifying the self or 'cleansing the heart,' and (2) subserving the purposes of God (Īśvara[19]—a fact which, by the way, implies a mixture of teaching here. The spirit in which one engages oneself in activity is different according to the two aims. What is done is done in the one case for the sake of the social whole of which the doer is a member; but in the other it is done for the sake of God, resigning its fruit to him. What in the one appears as duty to others appears in the other as service to God. The former type of agent is directly conscious of his relation to his environment and realizes it as a factor demanding his fealty; the latter is conscious only of God conceived as a personality in constant touch with the world, and whatever he does he regards as God's work, which has therefore to be done. But whether we look upon the work done as duty or as divine service, it is not 'disinterested' in every sense of the term. The first keeps self-conquest or subjective purification as the aim; the second looks forward to the security that has been guaranteed by God—that no godly man will perish: Na me bhaktaḥ praṇaśyati[20]. But if karma-yoga is thus motived by desire, it may be asked, in what sense it has been described as detached. In replying to this question, we should recall what we have stated before—that the activity which is natural to man if not properly guided, will become the means of obscuring from him the higher end for which he exists. By such an end the Gītā understands something more than moral rectitude. It aims at the elimination of worldly desire—even of the type commonly regarded as legitimate. Or as we night otherwise put it, it does not rest satisfied with rationalizing our impulses; it means to spiritualize them. It teaches that an active life led without any thought of securing the worldly results it may yield, sets free the springs of that inner life whose development is the one aim of man. And karma-yoga is disinterested only so far as it turns our mind from these results and sets it on the path leading to the true goal—not that it has no end at all. It does not thus do away with motives altogether; only it furnishes *one and the same* motive for whatever we may do, viz.[21] the betterment of our spiritual nature. Thus though the teaching, by insisting upon the discharge of social obligations at all costs, seems to ignore the individual, it does not really do so since it provides at the same time for his advancement on a higher plane of life.

The goal to be reached on this plane is conceived in two ways, according to the double motive that is set before the karma-yogin. If the motive is 'cleansing the heart,' the goal is self-realization; if, on the other hand, it is subserving the purposes of God, the end is God-realization. Of these, the first is to be understood here much as in the Upaniṣads. It is becoming Brahman (brahma-bhūyam)[22] or absorption in the Absolute. The second is reaching the presence of God,[23] though it sometimes appears, evidently under the influence of the first, as merging in him: 'He who departs from here,, thinking of me alone, will enter my being.[24] The important point here is whether individuality persists in the final condition—whether the finite as. finite can attain perfection. The absolutist view decides against persistence; the purely theistic view, in favour of it. Even though the latter does not recognize the union of the individual with God, it admits the merging of the individual's will in the divine will. Whichever be the goal—becoming Brahman or attaining God's presence—samsāra or the realm of good and evil is transcended. Although there are statements in the work which indicate that the goal—particularly the second one—is to be reached after death[25] the prevalent idea 's that it is realizable within the limits of this life.[26] There is more than one beautiful description of the man[27] that has perfected himself; and in the eleventh chapter we find a thrilling account of a direct perception of God by the devotee.[28] The distinctive feature of the perfected state, which is variously termed as 'the life absolute' and 'dwelling in God[29] is peace. Only the attitude is predominantly one of jñāna in the case of a person that sets before himself the ideal of self-realization, and one of bhakti or passionate devotion to God in the case of the other. Karma-yoga in the former fulfils itself in enlightenment which enables one 'to see oneself in all beings and all beings in oneself[30]; in the latter, it finds its consummation when a loving communion is established with God. If we describe the one as the ideal of enlightenment, the other represents the ideal of love; only it is love of God, and through him, of his creatures. But whether we look upon the Gītā as the gospel of enlightenment or of love, it is equally the gospel of action.

The point to which it is necessary to draw special attention in this connection is that the Gītā requires man to continue to work even in this perfected state, there being nothing in outer activity which is incompatible with inner peace. Here we see the exalted position assigned to work by the

Gītā. It contemplates no period, when activity may be wholly renounced. Passivity, in its view, is almost as reprehensible as wrong activity. Janaka, king of Videha, renowned in the Upaniṣads, and Śrī Kṛṣṇa are our examples here. The one has become perfect and the other has always been so; and both[31] alike are active. Such a view totally transforms the notion of samnyāsa by dissociating it from all inaction; and in this transformation of the ideal of nivṛtti consists another important contribution of the Gītā to Hindu thought. Karma-yoga is accordingly to be understood in a double sense—one having reference to an earlier stage of strife when the disciple, with a steady resolve, is continually weaning himself from selfish activity; and the other, to a later stage when, at the dawn of truth, the strife is over and right conduct becomes quite spontaneous—the outward expression of an inner conviction that has been attained. It is karma-yoga in the first sense, which is ancillary[32] that forms the essential theme of the Gītā; the second appears now and then as but a characteristic of the goal to be kept in view by the spiritual aspirant.

Before leaving this topic we must refer to an important question discussed, though but briefly, in the work. The teaching so far set forth presupposes that man is free to choose the path he likes in the conduct of life. But it appears that he can only follow the bent of his nature (prakṛti); and when that is predominantly evil, it may be said, persuasion to adopt the right path will be of little avail. In meeting this objection the Gītā first points out how the disposition to act in an evil way operates. 'In respect of every object of sense, there is always love or hatred. One should not come under the sway of either, for they are one's foes.' That is, an evil disposition operates not automatically, but invariably by appealing to our lower or what, in the light of the description given in this connection, may be styled the sensuous self. 'The senses and the mind are its habitation; and through them it deludes man. Do thou subjugate them first in order that you may bring down the ruinous foe.' We are not accordingly driven to do evil against our desire, as Arjuna wrongly assumes (anicchan). No responsibility attaches to man for mere impulsive reaction, except in so far as he is accountable for that impulse itself. In the case of actions on the other hand, which evoke moral judgment, they are always 'willed' by the doer, so that the opportunity to have acted differently after appropriate reflection was presented to him. He should not let go the opportunity by thoughtlessly yielding to the promptings of the sensuous self. But the question still remains whether we can ignore that self. The reply is that we can, if we only will; for we are conscious of the presence in us of a self higher than it. It may remain half-concealed, 'as fire does when enveloped in smoke'; but it is still there giving rise to that inner conflict between wish and will with which we, as human beings, are necessarily familiar. It is in the consciousness of this conflict that the possibility of a right choice lies. For the nature of the higher self is such that it will not allow itself to be subordinated to the other unless we have once for all sunk back into the life of the mere animal. The Gītā takes its stand upon this fact, that man cannot ignore the still small voice within, when it asks us to 'steady the self by the self[33] and commends activity without any reference to the ends which the lower of the two selves may like to pursue. The replacement of the lower aim by the higher, we must remember, is not to be made when or as often as a selfish motive presents itself. That might prove impracticable. We are asked to be forearmed by accepting the true ideal once for all, and to see that our actions become the expression of a single coherent purpose as implied by its acceptance. That is the meaning of telling us to substitute a uniform aim, viz. the betterment of our spiritual nature, for the necessarily divergent ends of the many actions which we have to do in life. Progress in this course may be difficult and protracted, requiring continual self-training. But the Gītā heartens us to put forth our best effort by assuring us that nothing of what we do for self-development really runs to waste. 'No such effort is lost; nor is there any obstacle in the way of its coming to fruition. Even the little that we may do will help to take us nearer the goal[34]; and again, 'The doer of good, O dear one, never comes to grief.[35] It is here that precept is of service. It clarifies our notion of the true self and encourages us to persevere in our course. The question discussed here is the familiar one of freedom of will; only the Gītā, as in other matters, restricts the scope of the discussion to the point arising from the context, viz. whether a man can choose the path to the higher life.

As belief in the karma doctrine characterizes the teaching of the Gītā, we may also briefly refer here to the allied question: how freedom is consistent with the necessity implied in this doctrine. If everything we do is the inevitable consequence of what we have done in the past, all moral responsibility should cease and self-effort should become meaningless. In considering this point, it is necessary to remember that every deed that we do leads to a double result. It not only produces what may be termed its direct result—the pain or pleasure following from it according to the karma theory, but it also establishes in us a tendency to repeat the same deed in the future. This tendency is termed saṁskāra; and the direct fruit of the karma is known as its phala. Every deed is bound to yield its phala; even the gods cannot prevent it from doing so. But that is all the necessity involved in the karma theory. As regards the saṁskāras, on the other hand, we have within us the full power of control, so that we may regulate them as they tend to express themselves in action. There is thus nothing in the doctrine which either eliminates responsibility or invalidates self-effort. The necessity that governs the incidence of the direct fruit or phala and renders escape from it impossible, so far from unnerving us, should stimulate us to exertion. It must enable us to work for the future with confidence, unmindful of what may happen in the present as the result of our past actions over which we have no longer any control. The important point about the karma doctrine then is that, paradoxical though it may seem, it inspires us both with hope and resignation at once—hope for the future and resignation towards what may occur in the present. That is not fatalism, but the very reverse of it.

II

Coming now to the theoretical teaching we find that, as already stated, it occupies the background and as such its details are not clearly determinable. But it is manifest that there is a mixture of doctrines. All will recognize in the work a current of Upaniṣadic thought which stresses the cosmic conception of the Absolute rather than the acosmic. Expressions drawn from the Upaniṣads occur throughout the work, and even what may be regarded as quotations from them are sometimes found[36] These references to the Upaniṣads, both direct and indirect, may lead one to think that the work is entirely Vedāntic. That is indeed the traditional view as shown by the familiar verse which, evidently as suggested by Śrī Kṛṣṇa's cow-herd upbringing, pictures him as drawing the milk of the Gītā from the Upaniṣads, figured as a cow, for Arjuna, the calf. But, though the Gītā owes much to the Upaniṣads, it would be wrong to take them to be its only source; for there is, as we know, another stream of thought mingling with it, viz. theism of the Bhāgavata type.[37] The theoretical teaching of the Gītā, like its practical one, is a blend of these two distinct creeds whose chief features were set forth in the previous chapters. In fact the distinction on the practical side is the natural counterpart of that on the theoretical. Some have held that the Upaniṣadic doctrine is the older in the work, and that it was later modified in the interests of the Bhāgavata creed; others, that precisely the rever has taken place. Either way there is no intentional mixing of the doctrines here. In the words of Senart it is 'spontaneous syncretism.' A deliberate blending of them would have .eliminated the contradictions which now remain side by side in the poem.[38]

Some scholars have seen in the work the influence of a third current of thought, viz. the Śankhya, and it is maintained by them that that system is very old—in fact as old as the Upaniṣads—and that the Bhāgavata creed, quite early in its history, made use of it to furnish itself with an appropriate metaphysical basis. The creed, as it appears in the Gītā, is according to these authorities already thus 'philosophically equipped[39]; and that is the reason, they say, why Sāṇkhya elements find a place in the work. The third view as found here, it is admitted, is not fully identifiable with the Sāṇkhya, for there are some vital differences between the two. For instance, it recognizes a super-soul (uttama-puruṣa)[40] which is unknown to the Sāṇkhya. Again there is no reference whatever in the work to the well-known Sāṇkhya ideal of kaivalya or spiritual aloofness, the goal of life, as represented here, being different—'becoming Brahman' or 'reaching the presence of God.' The idea of severance from prakṛti may be implicit in the latter, for without wresting itself from the clutches of matter, the soul has no chance of being restored to its original abode. But what we should remember is that the separation from prakṛti is not conceived here as the ultimate ideal. It is only a means to an end, which is positive unlike the negative one of classical Sāṇkhya. Such differences are explained as due to the circumstance that the Sāṇkhya, as it appears here, has been adjusted to the requirements of the Bh'āgavata creed. There is, no doubt, some reason to speak of an additional current of thought in .The work, for the Upaniṣadic doctrine, as contained in the Gītā, does not throughout retain all its old features, but shows here and there an advance towards realism and dualism. In the Upaniṣads, the single Absolute is sometimes viewed under the triple aspect of Brahman, Ātman and the world, though no distinction in fact between them is intended. The Gītā exhibits a tendency to separate them and conceive ui them as coeval, although the two latter, viz. Ātman and the physical world, are still held to be dependent upon Brahman—the highest principle[41] The physical universe is no longer traced to Brahman as in the Upaniṣads, but to another source named prakṛti or matter; and it is represented as standing over against Ātman or the individual soul which is designated puruṣa. Attention has already been drawn to the prevalence of such a view in the epic taken as a whole, and to its partial resemblance to the Sāṇkhya. But, instead of taking it as the Sāṅkhya doctrine modified to suit the needs of a theistic creed, it seems preferable, for the reasons we shall mention when treating of the topic in the next Part, to regard it as a step in the movement of Upaniṣadic thought towards the Sāṇkhya in its classical form. What particular stage in the growth of the Sāṇkhya is represented in the Gītā it is difficult to say, for the history of that doctrine still remains obscure.

REFERENCE

1. vii. 21-22: ix. 23. See also iv. ii.
2. Cf. iii. 5: v. 8-9.
3. See iii. 14-15 xviii 2.
4. Cf. iv. 15 (pūrvaiḥ pūrva-taram kṛtam) and xviii. 41, where four castes are mentioned.
5. There is not much reference in the work to the āśrama-dharma twin companion of varṇa-dharma.
6. Cf. xii. 10.
7. ii. 47.
8. Cf. i. 31. ii.6
9. Cf. i. 33.
10. ii.
11. ii. 1 and 7.
12. See Bhandarka: *Vaiṣṇavism, śaivism*, etc., p. 27.
13. To use Sanskrit words, this means that while one should realize to the full that he is a kartā, he should altogether forget that he is a bholtā.
14. Cf. iii. 5; xviii. n.
15. xviii. 47-8.
16. ii. 31-8. xvii 41-4.
17. Ch xvi.
18. v. ii.
19. iii. 30: ix. 27.
20. ix. 31.
21. Cf. śaṁkara on *Bṛ Up*. (Ānandāśrama Edn.) pp. 57-58.
22. xviii. 53.
23. iv. 9; ix. 25.
24. viii. 5.
25. viii. 5.
26. Cf. v. 19 and 26.
27. ii. 55-58; xiv. 22-25.
28. Note the expression I give you the eye divine—divyam dadāmi te.
29. Cf. ii. 72; xii. 8.
30. vi. 29.
31. iii. 20-28.
32. Cf. v. 6; vi. 3.
33. iii. 54
34. 40.
35. vi. 40.
36. Cf. ii. 29 and vi. II with *Kaṭha Up.* ii. 7 and *śvetāśvatara Up. it.* 10 respectively.
37. Cf. references to 'Vāsudeva' in vii. 19 and xi. 50.
38. See e.g. ix. 29; xvi. 19.
39. See Garbe: *Indian Antiquary* (1918)
40. xv. 17-18.
41. Cf. ix. 10.

BOOK 2

CHAPTER XXI

VEDĀNTA AND ITS GREAT EXPONENTS

This last section will be devoted to a review of the lives and teachings of certain of the saints and thinkers of India, ancient and modern, who have been followers of Vedānta. These include not merely distinguished commentators upon the Indian scriptures, but others who have influenced philosophical thought and brought spiritual blessings to their fellow men.

GAUḌAPĀDA

To Gauḍapāda, the first historic philosopher of the system of Vedānta and the expounder of its nondualistic aspect, no definite date can be assigned. There is a tradition that Śaṁkara, who lived in the seventh century A.D.[1] met Gauḍapāda and received his blessing. Śaṁkara in his commentary on the Māndūkya Upaniṣad, makes obeisance to Gauḍapāda as his guru's guru. Thence arose the belief of many scholars that Gauḍapāda and Śaṁkara were contemporaries. Other scholars, on the contrary,, consider that Gauḍapāda lived many centuries before Śaṁkara, perhaps even before Buddha. And contention is that the tradition ofŚaṁkara's meeting with Gaudapāda is true, but that they met each other on the yogic plane, where, the spiritual eye of the aspirant being opened, a direct communion with the great souls of the past may be obtained. Śaṁkara is also said to have met Vyāsa, author of the Māhabhārata; if so, he must have met him too on the yogic plane, for undoubtedly Vyāsa lived many centuries before Śaṁkara. Gauḍapāda's being saluted by Śaṁkara as his guru's guru might be due to the fact he was one of the most important of the early teachers of the Vedāntic order. Scholars quote another tradition to the effect that Gauḍapda was a disciple of Suka and therefore a contemporary of the Māhabhārata.

Some Western scholars claim Gauḍapāda as a Buddhist saint main argument being that at the beginning of the fourth chapter of his philosophical treatise, the Kārikā. he adores the 'superman' whom they identify with Buddha. But the word superman had been used in the Māhābhārata and the Pūraṇas, even before the advent of Buddha, to denote one who has known Brahman, and also to denote God conceived in human form—Narayana: and according to tradition Gauḍapāda also used the word superman to denote Indian yaṇa. Ānandagiri, a disciple of Śaṁkara, mentions that Gauḍapāda practised austerities and meditation in Badarikasrama,[2] and that Nārāyaṇa, God in human form, appeared before him and revealed to him the highest truth of Vedānta.

Whatever may have been the period in which Gauḍapāda lived, he is regarded by Indian authorities as the first Vedantic philosopher and one of the greatest seers of all the ages.

The Kārikā

The advaita Vedānta (Vedānta in its nondualistic aspect) is as old as the Upaniṣads, for, however variously the ancient scriptures have been interpreted, and however much they have supplied the foundations for varying schools, it is the consensus of opinion that their final truth consists in the identification of the Self with Brahman and the absolute reality ot one and only one existence. Of the Upaniṣads, the Māndūkya most emphatically declares the turth of advaita. Gauḍapāda made himself famous by writing the Kārikā, a commentary Upon this single Upaniṣad. Saṁkara, who wrote commentaries on the Kārikā ot Gauḍapāda, very trulv remarked, 'The Māndūkya Upaniṣad, with the Kārikā, embodies in itself the quintessence of all the Upaniṣads or Vedānta.'

The Kārikā is divided into four chapters. The first, the āgama (scripture), glosses the verses of the Māndūkya Upaniṣad. The second, the vaitathya (the nature of sense experience), through an elaborate argument explains the relative and phenomenal nature of the objective universe. The third, the advaita (nondualism), establishes by means of logic and reason the truth of nondualism. The final chapter, the alātaśānti (the quenching of the firebrand), further establishes the sole reality of the Ātman and the relative nature of our experiences in the ordinary states of consciousness.

The Philosohy of Experience

To arrive at the ultimate truth, philosophy must consider not only our experiences in the waking state but those in other states of Consciousness, such as dream and dreamless sleep, and co-ordinate them all by extending its inquiry to the possible source of all consciousness. Gauḍapāda, as well as the Upaniṣadic rsis, meets this requirement. V. Subrahmanya Iyer rightly remarks of Gauḍapāda:

'His distinction lies in the emphasis he lays on the impossibility of reaching the highest truth unless the *totality of* human experience or knowledge be taken into consideration.[3] This totality Gauḍapāda himself investigates.

"Western philosophy, in contrast, seems to have run into a blind alley, not only because it fails to recognize transcendental consciousness, but also because it does not attempt to *co-ordinate* the three other states of consciousness. Says Mr lyer:

'Philosophy, according to Gauḍapāda and Śankara, is an interpretation of the totality of human experience or of the *whole* of life from the standpoint of truth. Philosophy, therefore, is the whole, of which Religion, Mysticism (Yoga), Theology, Scholasticism, Speculation, Art and Science are but parts. Such philosophy or Vedānta as ignoresany part or parts is no Vedānta... . And the object sought by philosophy, as these two pre-eminent Hindu philosophers say, is the happiness (*siikham*) and welfare (*hitam*) of all beings (*sarva sattwa*) in this world (*ihaiva*)[4]

In analysing the three states of consciousness, waking; dreaming, and dreamless sleep, Gauḍapāda discovers as the witness behind them an unchangeable reality. For in all these states there is the Self ever-present, though remaining unknown. It is the experiencer of all actions and thoughts in all the three states, but it is never affected by them. It forever remains pure, free, perfect.

Through our ignorance, however, the Self becomes identified with experience and appears to be changing, as when it appears first happy and then miserable, or to be born and then to die. But the appearance has no absolute reality. The Self remains unaltered, and when we rise above and beyond the three states to turīya, Pure Consciousness, its absolute oneness with all things, the absolute nonduality, is at last clearly revealed.

It is true that in deep sleep all experience seems to be annihilated. What then is the difference between deep sleep and turīya? In the words of Gauḍapāda, 'Deep sleep (prajfla) does not know anything either of the Self or of the non-Self, either of truth, or of untruth. But turīya is ever existent and ever all-seeing.[5] Again he says: 'Dream is the wrong apprehension of reality. Sleep is the state in which one does not know what reality is When the false experience in these two states disappears turiya is realized.[6] In the following verse he makes a clear distinction between a man who is asleep and a man who is in turīya: 'In deep sleep the mind is withdrawn. But it is disciplined, and not withdrawn, in turiya. One whose mind is disciplined becomes one with Brahman—who is fearless and the light of whose knowledge shines in every direction.[7]

The real Self, the ultimate reality, remains unknown in the three ordinary states of consciousness. 'When, however,' says Gauḍapāda, 'the individual soul, sleeping under the influence of māyā (ignorance), is awakened, it then realizes nonduality, beginningless and endless.?[8]

The Self (or Ātman), as we know, is immortal, in that it has neither birth nor death. It is nondual, though it appears to be many, just as the one sun, reflected in many lakes, appears manifold. Describing the nature of the Ātman, Gauḍapāda says, 'This Atman is beyond all expression by words, beyond all acts of the mind. It is peace, eternal effulgence, absence of activity; and it is attainable when the mind becomes pure and tranquil.[9]

Gauḍapāda, like all the other saintly philosophers of India, points out the way to illumination within one's own soul. With patience and perseverance, he tells us, we should seek to control the vagaries of the mind; then through the practice of discrimination we must learn to renounce the pleasures of the senses; and finally, by the practice of concentration and meditation, when we are quite absorbed in our devotions, we arrive at a kind of bliss, a lower stage of samādhi. We must also, Gauḍapāda insists, give up our attachment to this bliss if we would realize the supreme bliss. My master, Swami Brahmananda, also, used to tell us that we must not stop with the bliss we may find in deep contemplation but go deeper and deeper. In the words of Gauḍapāda:

'The mind should not be allowed to enjoy the bliss that arises out of the condition of absorption. It should be freed from attachment to such happiness through the exercise of discrimination. When the mind does not lose itself in inactivity and oblivion, or is not distracted by desires that is to say, when the mind achieves quietness and does not give rise to appearances it verily becomes Brahman. This, the highest bliss, is based upon the realization of Self; it is peace, identical with liberation, indescribable, and unborn. It is further described as the omniscient Brahman, because it is one with the unborn Self, which is the object sought by knowledge[10]

Gauḍapāda contends that the waking and the dreaming states are equally real and equally unreal. They are real only in a relative sense, and they are unreal as compared with the transcendental, turiya, which is identification with the ultimate reality, the unchangeable Self. The definition of Reality is that it is never contradicted at any time but persists forever. 'Anything which is nonexistent at the beginning, and also at the end, necessarily does not exist in the middle.[11] By this test, all experience of both dreaming and waking is unreal. And from the standpoint of the ultimate reality, experience of the waking state is but a prolonged dream. Shakespeare seems to have caught the dreamlike quality of this world of appearances in the famous lines:

> ... These our actors,
> As I foretold you, were all spirits, and
> Are melted into air, into thin air;
> And, like the baseless fabric of this vision,
> The cloud-capp'd towers, the gorgeous palaces,
> The solemn temples, the great globe itself,
> Yea, all which it inherit, shall dissolve,
> And, like this insubstantial pageant faded,
> Leave not a rack behind. We are such stuff
> As dreams are made on, and our little life
> Is rounded with a sleep.

Consistent with his philosophy of nondualism. Gauḍapāda did not believe in the absolute reality of creation. The one absolute, nondual Self, or God, neither created this universe nor did he become this universe. In reality there is no creation, for the one infinite Existence appears to be the manifold universe just as a rope may appear to be a snake. The universe is not a reality but something superimposed upon the Atman.

'There is no death,' says Gauḍapāda, 'no birth; there is no one in bondage, no one aspiring to knowledge; there is no seeker after liberation, no one liberated. This is the absolute truth,[12] In evident allusion to expressions such as these, S. Radhakrishnan observes: 'The general idea pervading Gauḍapāda's work, that bondage and liberation, the individual soul and the world, are all unreal, makes the caustic critic observe that the theory which has nothing better to say than that an unreal soul is trying to escape from an unreal bondage in unreal world to accomplish an unreal supreme good, may itself be an unreality[13]

Now if one fails to take into consideration the main contention of Gauḍapāda, the above criticism may apply. What is his main contention? That the highest good, that is, freedom, supreme bliss, is the very nature of the Ātman, an absolute reality which persists. The supreme good, therefore, is not, as Dr Radhakrishnan alleges, unreal, but something you already have. To seek to possess something that you already have is foolish fancy. To think that you do not have something, though you always have it, is delusion. The story is told of a man who had a towel on his shoulder but sought for it everywhere. He but needed to awake to the fact that the towel was where he had placed it. So it is with us. Thinking we are bound, we seek liberation, though the liberation we seek is already within us. We but need to awake from the sleep of ignorance to realize 'I am Brahman'. Either that we are bound or that we seek liberation is false.

Dr. Radhakrishnan further remarks: 'If we have to play the game of life, we cannot do so with the conviction that the play is a show and all the prizes in it mere blanks. No philosophy can consistently hold such a view and be at rest with itself. The greatest'condemnation of such a theory is that we are obliged to occupy ourselves with objects, the existence and value of which we are continually denying in theory[14]

To this one may reply with the question. Can we play the game of life if we take life itself as a reality? The game is then no longer a game but a burden. Only for a genuine yogi, who has seen life as mere play, is it possible to play with satisfaction the game of life. To him the prizes are not blanks but the bliss of a free soul. We can play the game of life well only when we recognize that it is not everlasting, that joys and sorrows are in their very nature impermanent. The genuine yogi enjoys the game, plays it better than does one who clings to the enjoyments of life and finds to his despair that they elude his grasp at every moment, howsoever he may 'bid the clouds to stay'. Howsoever one may try to fool oneself by asserting the reality of the world, there is no world when life ends in death. As one holds fast to life and its experiences, the prizes in the game become mere blanks. The fact is that Gauḍapāda does not in any way reveal a romantic desire to chase the shadows of life nor does he attempt lo hide his head in the .sand. Rather does he boldly seize upon naked reality and fearlessly face the facts of life by rising above them, above life and death, above joys and sorrows, into the realization 'I am Brahman'.

ŚAṀKARA

Introduction

As prophet and as thinker, Śaṁkara stands among the greatest figures in the history of the world. He is, primarily, the unrivalled propounder of advaita Vedānta, the nondualistic aspect of the Vedic teachings. By means of his remarkable clearness, his supreme wisdom, and his profound spirituality he has so stamped himself upon Vedanta that it has remained the paragon of Indian philosophy, and has given solace to the sorrowful heart of a large segment of mankind.

Life of Śaṁkara

Beautiful and fantastic clouds of legend surround the austere, charming, boyish figure of Śaṁkara—saint, philosopher, and poet. But, historically speaking, we know very little about the circumstances of his life.

He was born in or around the year AD 686 of brahmin parents Kālādi, a small village of western Malabar, in southern India.[15] By the age of ten, he was already an intellectual prodigy. Not only had he read and memorized all the scriptures, but he had written commentaries on many of them, and had held discussions with famous scholars who came to him from every part of the country. Yet the boy was dissatisfied. At a time when most children are only beginning to study, he was already disgusted by the emptiness of book-knowledge. He saw, moreover, that his teachers did not practise die lofty principles they preached. Indeed, the whole society in which he lived was materialistic and pleasure-seeking. India was passing 'through a period of spiritual decadence'. Śaṁkara, burning with youthful zeal, resolved to make his own life an example which would lead men back to the paths of truth.

The death of his father set him puzzling over the riddle of life and death, and he determined to solve it. He would renounce everything in his search for the meaning of existence. It was then that he wrote the poem called 'Moha Mudgaram'—'The Shattering of Illusion'. Of this the following is a more or less literal translation:

> Who is thy wife? Who is thy son?
> The ways of this world are strange indeed.
> Whose art thou? Whence art thou come?
> Vast is thy ignorance my beleonged
> Therefore ponder these things and worship the Lord

Behold the folly of Man:
In childhood busy with his toys.
In youth bew itched by love,
In age bowed down with cares—
And always unmindful of the Lord!
The hours fly, the seasons roll, life ebbs,
But the breeze of hope blows continually in his heart.

Birth brings death, death brings rebirth:
This evil needs no proof.
Where then, 0 Man, is thy happiness?
This life trembles in the balance.
Like water on a lotus-leaf—
And yet the sage can show us, in an instant,
How to bridge this sea of change.
When the body is wrinkled, when the hair turns
When the gums are toothless, and the old man's staff
Shakes like a reed beneath his weight,
The cup of his desire is still full.

Thy son may bring thee suffering,
Thy wealth is no assurance of heaven:
Therefore be not vain of thy wealth,
Or of thy family, or of thy youth—
All are fleeting, all must change.
Know this and be free.
Enter the joy of the Lord.
Seek neither peace nor strife
With kith or kin, with friend or foe.
O befoved, if thou woudst attain freedom,
Be equal unto all[16]

Śaṁkara now persuaded his mother to let him take the monastic'" vow, promising that he would return to visit her before she died. Then, having made arrangements for herneed, he set out in search of a teacher.

On the banks of the River Narmada he met Gauḍapāda[17] a famous philosopher and seer, who had attained knowledge of the Reality. Śaṁkara asked the old man for initiàtion, but Gauḍapāda refused. He had made a vow to remain absorbed in union with Brahman. However, he sent the boy to his foremost disciple, Govindapāda. Govinḍapāda initiated him and instructed him in meditation and in the whole process of yoga. Within a very short time, Śaṁkara achieved complete mystical realization, and himself went out to teach.

One morning, when he was on his way to bathe in the Ganges, he met a caṇḍāla, a member of the'lowest caste, the untouchables. The man had four dogs with him, and they were- blocking Śaṁkara's path. For a moment, inborn caste-prejudice asserted itself. Śaṁkara, the brahmin, ordered the candala out of his way. But the caṇḍāla answered: 'If there is only one God, how can there be many kinds of men? How can there be any distinctions of caste or creeds Śaṁkara was fillei' with shame and reverence. He prostrated himself before the caṇḍāla. This incident inspired one of Śaṁkara's finest poems, the ''Manīṣa Pancaka'. It consists of five stanzas, each one ending with the refrain:

> He who has learned to see the one Existence everywhere,
> He is my master—be he brāhmin or caṇḍāla.

Śaṁkara began his teaching among the scholars of the country, converting the teachers first, and then their pupils. One of the teachers was the famous philosopher Manḍan Miśra. Manḍan Miśra held that the life of the householder was far superior to that of the monk, and his opinion was respected and widely shared throughout India. Śaṁkara determined to argue with him, and journeyed to his home. When he arrived, he found thedoors locked. Miśra was holding a religious ceremony and did not wish to be disturbed. Śaṁkara, with the mischievous spirit of a boy in his teens, climbed a near-by tree and jumped down from it into the courtyard. Miśra noticed him among the crowd. He disapproved of monks—especially when they were so youthful—and asked sarcastically: 'Whence comes this shaven head?' 'You have eyes to see, sir,' Śaṁkara answered saucily: 'The shaven head comes up from the neck.' Miśra lost his temper, but Śaṁkara continued to tease him, and at length the two of them agreed to hold a debate on the relative merits of the life of the monk and the life of the householder. It was understood that Samkāra, if he lost, should become a householder, and that Miśra, if he lost, should become a monk. The debate lasted for several days. Bharati, the learned wife of Miśra, acted as umpire. Finally, Śaṁkara was able to convince Miśra of the superiority of the monastic life, and Miśra became his disciple. It was he who later annotated Śaṁkara's commentaries on the Brahma Sūtras.

Śaṁkara's life came to an end at Kedarnath in the Himalayas. He was only thirty-two years old. During this brief period, he had established many monasteries, and had founded ten monastic orders. This was the first time that Hindu monasticism had ever been organized in India, and Śaṁkara's system still exists. He was a reformer rather than an innovator. He preached no new doctrine or creed. But he gave a new impulse to the spiritual life of his time. Separated by intervals of a thousand years, Buddha, Śaṁkara, and Rāmakṛṣṇa dominate India's religious history.

Śaṁkara's literary output was enormous. He not only made i .commentaries on the Vedanta Sūtras, the principal Upaniṣads, and the Bhagavad-Gita, but produced two major philosophical, works, .'the *Upadeśāsaharī*and the *Vivekacūḍāmṇi* (*The Crest-Jewel of Discrimination*). He was also the author of many poems, hymns, prayers, and minor works on Vedānta.

Brahman—the absolute exister knowledge, and blisses real. The universe is not real. Brahman and Atman are on.[18]

In these words, Śamkara sums up his philosopli.. What are the implications of this statement? What does he mean by 'real' and by 'not real'?

Śamkara accepts as 'real' only that which neither changes nor ceases to exist. In making this definition, he follows the teachings of the Upaniṣads and of Gauḍapāda, his predecessor. No object, no kind of knowledge, can be absolutely real if its existence is only temporary. Absolute reality implies permanent existence. If we consider our various experiences during the states of waking and dreaming, we find that dream-experiences are contradicted by waking-experiences and vice versa—and that both kinds of experience cease in dreamless sleep. In other wurds, every object of knowledge, external or internal (for a thought or idea is as much an object of knowledge as is the external world), is subject to modification and therefore, by Śamkara's definition, 'not real'.

What, then, is the reality behind all our experiences? There is only one thing that never leaves us—pure consciousness. This alone is the constant feature of all experience. And this consciousness is the real, absolute Self. In dreamless sleep, even, the real Self persists (as we realize on waking, there being no break in essential continuity), while the ego-sense, which we call 'ourself, or individuality, has become temporarily merged in ignorance (avidya) and has disappeared.

Vedānta philosophy occupies a central position between realism and idealism. Western realism and idealism are both based on-a distinction between mind and matter; Indian philosophy puts mind and matter in the same category—both are objects of knowledge. Śamkara should not, however.'be regarded as a precursor of Berkeley: he does not say that the world is unreal simply because its existence depends upon our perception. The world, according to Śaṁkara, 'is and is not'. Its fundamental unreality can be understood only in 'relation to the ultimate mystical experience, this experience of an illumined soul. When the illumined soul passes into transcendental consciousness, he realizes the Self (the Atman) as pure bliss and pure intelligence, the one 'without a second. In this state of consciousness, all perception of multiplicity ceases, there is no longer any sense of 'mine' and 'thine', the world as we ordinarily know it has vanished. Then the Self shines forth as the One, the Truth, the Brahman, the basis of the apparent world. The apparent world, A it is experienced in the waking state, may be likened, says Śaṁkara, to an imagined snake which proves, on closer inspection, to be nothing but a coil of rope. When the truth is known, we are no longer deluded by the appearance—the snake-appearance vanishes into the reality of the rope, the world vanishes into Brahman.

Other systems of Hindu philosophy—Samkhya, Yoga, and Nyāya—maintain that the phenomenal world possesses objective reality, even though it may not be apparent to the eyes of an illumined soul. Advaita Vedānta denies this objective reality. The point is a vital one. . Mind and matter, finite objects and their relations, Śaṁkara holds, are a misreading of Brahman—and nothing more.

The Nature of the Apparent World

When Śarhkara says that the world of thought and matter is not real, he does not mean that it is nonexistent. The apparent world is and is not. In the state of ignorance (our everyday consciousness) it is experienced, and and it exists as it appears. In the state of illumination it is not experienced, and it ceases to exist. Śamkara does not regard any experience as nonexistent as long as it is experienced, but he very naturally draws a distinction between the private illusions of the individual and the universal, or world, illusion. The former he calls prātibhāsika (illusory) and the latter vyavahārika (phenomenal). For example, a man's dreams are his private illusions; when he wakes, they cease. But the universal illusion—the illusion of world-phenomena—continues throughout a man's whole waking life unless he becomes aware of the truth through knowledge of Brahman. Śarhkara makes, also, a further distinction between these two kinds of illusion and those ideas which are altogether unreal and imaginary, which represent a total impossibility or a flat contradiction in terms—Such as the idea of the son of a barren woman.

Here, then, we are confronted by a paradox—the world is and is not. It is neither real nor nonreal. And yet this paradox simply recognizes, the existence of what Śamkara calls māyā. Māyā, this apparent world, has its basis in Brahman, the eternal. According to Śamkara, it consists of names and forms. It is not nonexistent, yet it differs from the Reality, the Brahman, upon whom it depends for its existence. It is not real, since it disappears in the light of knowledge of its eternal basis. The apparent world is māyā; the Self, the Ātman, alone is real.

Superimposition or Māyā

The most difficult of all philosophical problems is that of the relation between the finite and the Infinite; the problem of how this finite world came into being. If we believe that the finite has an absolute reality of its own, and that it has emerged from the Infinite add is an actual transformation of the Infinite, or if we regard the Infinite as a transcendental first cause of the phenomenal world (a position held by most Christian theologians), then we must admit that the Infinite is infinite no longer. A God who transforms himself into the visible universe is himself subject to transformation and change—he cannot be regarded as the absolute reality. A God who creates a world limits himself by the very act of creation, and thus ceases to be infinite. The question 'Why should God create at all?' remains unanswered.

This difficulty is overcome, however, if we consider the world as .māyā; and this explanation of our universe is, moreover, in perfect accord with the findings of modern science.

'A soap-bubble with irregularities and corrugations on its surface is perhaps the best representation of this new universe revealed to us by the theory of relativity. The universe is not the interior of the soap-bubble but its surface—and the substance out of which this bubble is blown, the soap film, is empty space welded into empty time.[19]

Thus it is only when we analyse the nature of the universe and discover it to be māyā—neither absolutely real nor absolutely nonexistent—that we learn how the phenomenal surface of the soap-bubble safeguards the eternal presence of the Absolute.

The Upaniṣads, it is true, appear to consider Brahman the first cause of the universe, both material and efficient. They declare that the universe emanates from, subsists in, and finally merges in the absolute Brahman. Sarhkara never directly contradicts the Upaniṣads, although sometimes he appears to interpret them to suit his own views. The unherse, he says, is a superimposition upon Brahman. Brahman remains eternally infinite and unchanged. He is not transformed into this universe. He simply appears as this universe to us, in our ignorance. We superimpose the apparent world upon Brahman, just as we sometimes superimpose a snake upon a coil of rope.

This theory of superimposition (vivartavāda) is inseparably linked with the theory of causality. Causal relation exists in the world of multiplicity, which is māyā. Within māyā, the mind cannot function without causal relation. But to speak of cause and effect with reference to the Absolute is simply absurd. To seek to know what caused the world is to transcend the world. To seek to find the cause of māyā is to go beyond māyā—and, when we do that, māyā vanishes, the effect ceases to exist. How, then, can there be a cause of a nonexistent effect In other words, the relation between Brahman and māyā is, by its very nature, unknowable and indefinable by any process of the human intellect.

Māyā: A Statement of Fact as Well as a Principle

Thus, according to Śamkara, the world of thought and matter has a phenomenal or relative existence, and is super-imposed upon Brahman, the unique, absolute reality. As long as we remain in ignorance (that is, as long as we have not achieved transcendental consciousness), we shall continue to experience this apparent world, which is the effect of superimposition. When transcendental consciousness is achieved, superimposition ceases.

What is the nature of this superimposition? In the introduction to his commentary on the Brahma Sūtras, Śamkara tells us that 'Superimposition is the apparent presentation to consciousness, by the memory, of something previosuly observed elsewhere.[20] We see a snake. We remember it. Next day we see a coil of rope. We superimpose the remembered snake upon it, and thereby misunderstand its nautre.

Śamkāra foresees an objection to his theory and goes on to anticipate and answer it. We may challenie theory ofsuperimposition by pointing out that Brahman is not an object of perception. How can we superimpose a snake upon a rope which we do not perceive? How can we superimpose a world-appearance upon a reality which is not apparent to our senses? 'For every man superimposes objects only upon such other objects as are placed before him (that is, as come into contact with his sense organs.[21] To this, Śamkara answers:

'Brahman is not, we reply, non-objective in the absolute sense. For Brahman is the object of the ego-idea. We know quite well, by intuition, that the inner Self must exist, since the ego-idea is a presentation of the Self. Nor is it an absolute rule that objects can be superimposed only upon such other objects as are placed before us; for ignorant people superimpose a dark blue colour upon-the sky, which is not an object of sense perception.[22]

This statement needs some further explanation. Although Brahman is never apparent to our everyday sense perception, there is a manner in which we are aware of the Reality, the inner Self. Brahman, it has been said, is absolute existence, knowledge, and bliss. Only in transcendental consciousness can we know this fully. Yet Brahman is partly apparent, to our normal consciousness also. Brahman is Existence, and we all know that we exist. In this sense, every one of, us has an intuitive knowledge of the inner Self (the Ātman or Theinner Self, the Reality is never an object of sense perception, however—because, in our ignorance, we superimpose of a private individuality—of being Mr Smith or Mrs Jones—upon our awareness of Existence. We are unable to understand that Existence is not our private property, that it is universal and absolute. The inner Self is therefore present in our normal consciousness as 'the object of the ego-idea'—a literal translation ofSamkara's phrase. The superimposition of the ego-idea upon Existence is our first and most important act as human beings. The moment we have made this, central act of super-imposition—the -moment we have said 'I am I, I am private, I am separate, I am an individual'—we have made further super-imposition inevitable. The claim to individuality for ourselves implies individuality everywhere. It mtomatically superimposes a multiple world of creatures and objects upon the one, undivided reality, the Existence which is Brahman. Ego-idea and world-appearance depend upon each other. Lose the ego-idea in transcendental consciousness, and the world- appearance must necessarily vanish.

When and how did this act of superimposition occur? Was it at our latest individual birth, or in some previous life? Was there a historical moment—corresponding to that in which Adam is said to have fallen—in which the phenomenal world came into being as the result of the ego-idea? The futility of such questions should be self-evident. We merely go round in a circle. What is this world-appearance? Māyā. What causes it? Our ignorance. What is this ignorance? Māyā, also. If there always was, and is, and always will be one unchanging "reality, how can we possibly assume that māyā began at some definite historical moment in time? We cannot. Therefore we are forced to conclude, as Śamkara does, that māyā, like Brahman, is without-any beginning. Ignorance as the cause and the apparent world as the effect have existed always and will always exist. They are like seed and tree. The 'coupling of the real and the unreal', produced by our ignorance, is a process universally evident in our daily lives. Śamkara says: 'It is obvious and needs no proof that the object, which is the nonego, and the subject, which is the ego-idea (superimposed upon the Self), are opposed to each other, like light and darkness, and cannot be identified. Still less can their respective attributes be identified... Nevertheless, it is natural to man (because of his wrong ideas) not to be able to distinguish between these distinct entities and between their respective attributes. He superimposes upon each the nature and attributes of the other, uniting the real with the unreal and-making use, of such expressions as "I am that." "That is mine"[23]

Samkara is speaking here of two stages in the process of superimposition. First, the ego-idea is superimposed upon the inner Self, the existence-reality. Then the ego-idea, reaching outward, as it were, identifies itself with the body and the body's mental and physical attributes and actions. We say, as a matter of course, 'I am fat', 'I am tired', 'I am walking', 'I am sitting down'—without ever stopping to consider what this '1' really is. We go further. We claim purely external objects and names for our own. We say 'I am a Republican', or 'This house is mine'. As superimpositions multiply, extraordinary statements become possible, and normal—such as 'We sunk three submarines yesterday' or carry a good deal of insurance'. We identify our ego, more or less, with every object in the universe. And all the while, the inner Self looks on, utterly detached from these moods and antics, yet making them all possible by lending to the mind that light of consciousness without which māyā could not exist.

That māyā is beginning less can be shown if we return for a moment to the image of the rope and the snake. The superimposition of the snake upon the rope is possible only if we can remember what a snake looks like: a child who had never seen a snake could never superimpose it. How then is it possible for the newborn child to superimpose the world-appearance (the snake) upon Brahman (the rope)' We can answer this question only if we postulate a universal snake-memory that is common to all mankind and that has existed from a time without beginning. This snake-memory is māyā.

Māyā, says Śamkara, is not only universal but beginningless and endless. A distinction must be made, however, between māyā as a universal principle and ignorance (a', avidyā), which is individual. Individual ignorance is beginningless, but it can end at any moment; it is lost when a man achieves spiritual illumination. Thus the world may vanish from the consciousness of an individual and yet continue to exist for the rest of mankind. In saying this, Śamkara's philosophy differs essentially from the subjective idealism of the West.

Brahman and Iśwara

In a sense. Brahman is the ultimate cause of the universe, since, by the action of māyā, the world-appearance is superimposed upon him. Brahman is the cause, māyā the effect. Yet Brahman cannot be said to have transformed himself into the world or to have created it, since absolute Reality is, by definition, incapable of temporal action or change. Another word, Iśwara, must therefore be employed to describe the creative principle. Iśwara is Brahman united with māyā—the combination which creates, preserves, and dissolves the universe in an endless and beginningless process. Iśwara is God personified, God with attributes.

According to the Sāmkhya system of philosophy, the universe is an evolution of Prakṛti—undifferentiated matter, composed of three forces called the guṇas.' Creation is a disturbance in the balance of these forces. The guṇas enter into an enormous variety of combinations—somewhat like the atoms in Western physics—and these combinations are individual elements, objects, and creatures. This concept of Prakṛti corresponds, more or less, to Samkara's concept of māyā—but with this important difference: Prakṛti is said to be other than and independent of Puruṣa (the absolute Reality) while māyā is said to have no absolute reality but to be dependent on Brahma. Therefore, according to Samkara, it is Iśwara, rather than Prakṛti, who can be described as the ultimate cause of the universe.

Are there then two Gods—one the impersonal Brahman, the other the personal Iśwara? No—for Brahman appears as Iśwara only when viewed in the relative ignorance of māyā. Iśwara has the same degree of reality that māyā has. God the person is not 'Brahman in his ultimate nature. In the words of Swami Vivekananda, 'The personal God is the highest possible reading of the Absolute by the human mind.[24]

The idea is thus ingeniously illustrated by Sri Rāmakṛṣṇa:

'Brahman may be compared to an infinite ocean, without beginning or end. Just as, through intense cold, some portions of the ocean freeze into ice and the formless water appears to have form, so, through the intense love of the devotee, Brahman appears to take on form and personality.[25] But the form melts away again as the sun of knowledge rises. Then the universe also disappears, and there is seen to be nothing but Brahman, the infinite.[26]

Although Iśwara is, in a. sense, a person, we must beware of regarding him as similar to, or identical with, the jiva, the individual human soul. Iśwara, like the jiva, is Brahman united with māyā, bin with this fundamental difference—Iśwara is the ruler and controller of māyā, the jiva is māyā's servant and plaything. We can therefore say, without paradox, that we are, at the same time. God and the servants of God. In our absolute nature, we are one with Brahman; in our relative nature, we are other than the Iśwara, and subject to him.

Devotion to the Iśwara, the Personal God,may lead a man very far along the path of spirituality; it may even make him into a saint. But by itself it does not give the ultimate knowledge. To be completely enlightened is to go beyond Iśwara, to know the impersonal Reality behind the personal divine Appearance. We can become Brahman, since Brahman is present in us always. But we can never become Iśwara, because Iśwara is above and distant from our human personality. It follows, therefore, that we can never become rulers of the universe. To rule it is Iśwara's function, and the desire to usurp this function is the ultimate madness of the ego. It is symbolized in Christian literature by the legend of the fall of Lucifer.

Vyāsa, the author of the Brahma Sūtras, makes the same point when he says that no one will acquire the power of creating, ruling, or dissolving the universe, since that power belongs to Iśwara alone. And Samkara in his commentary discusses the problem as follows:

'If a man, *by* worshipping the qualified Brahman (Iśwara), achieves knowledge of the Supreme Ruler while still preserving his individual consciousness—is his power limited or unlimited? When this question arises, some will argue that his power is unlimited, and they will quote the scriptural texts (referring to those who achieve knowledge of Iśwara) "They attain their own kingdom", "To them all the gods offer worship", and "Their desires are fulfilled in all the worlds".'

'But Vyāsa answers this question when he adds: "Except for the power of creating the universe." The powers of Iśwara can be acquired by the liberated, but that power belongs to Iśwara alone. How do we know this? Because he is the subject of the scriptural texts concerning creation. These texts do not refer to the liberated souls, in any connection whatsoever. That is why he is called "the ever-perfect". The scriptures also say that the powers of the liberated are acquired by worshipping and searching after God; therefore the liberated have no place in the ruling of the universe. Again, because these liberated souls still preserve their individual consciousness, it is possible that their will may differ, and that, while one desires creation, another may desire destruction. The only way to avoid this conflict is to make all wills subordinate to some one will. Therefore we must conclude that the wills of the liberated are dependent on the will of the Supreme Ruler[27]

If there is only one consciousness, one Brahman, who is the seer and who is the seen? Who sees Brahman as Iśwara, and who is the jīva?

Are they different or one?

As long as man is within the limitations of māyā, the One is seen as many. Ignorance can do no better than to worship Appearance; and Iśwara is the rules of all appearances—the highest idea which the human mind can grasp and the human heart can love. The human mind can never grasp the absolute, Reality, it can only infer its presence and worship its projected image, in the process of this worship, the mind becomes purified, the ego-idea thins away like mist, superimposition, ceases, Iśwara, and world-appearance both vanish in the blaze of transcendental consciousness, wherein there is no seer, no seen—nothing but Brahman, the single, all-embracing,' timeless fact.

The Problem of Evil

Every religion or system of philosophy has to deal with the problem of evil—and unfortunately it is a problem which is usually explained away rather than explained. 'Why', it is asked, 'does God permit evil, when he himself is all goodness?'

One of two answers is usually given to this question by Western religious thought. Sometimes we are told that evil is educational and penal. God punishes us for our sins by visiting us with war, famine, earthquake, disaster, and disease. He employs temptation (either directly or through the agency of the Devil) to test and strengthen the virtue of the good. This is the answer given by the Old Testament. It repels many people today and has become unfashionable—although, according to Vedānta, as we shall see in a moment, it contains a certain amount of truth.

The other answer—now more generally accepted—is that evil does not exist at all. If we view life *sub specie aeternitatis,* we shall know that evil has no reality; that it is simply a misreading of good.

Vedānta philosophy disagrees with both these answers—with the second even more radically than with the first. How, it asks, can evil be changed into good, merely by viewing it in a special manner? Pain and misfortune may be borne more easily than would otherwise be possible, if we fix our minds upon God, but they are very real experiences nevertheless, even though their duration is limited. Vedānta agrees that evil, in the absolute sense, is unreal. But it reminds us that in this sense good is unreal also. The absolute Reality is beyond good and evil, pleasure and pain, success and disaster. Both good and evil are aspects of māyā. As long as māyā exists, they exist. Within māyā they are real enough.

The question 'Why does God permit evil?' is, in fact, most misleadingly phrased. It is as absurd as if one were to ask 'Why does God permit good?' Nobody today would ask why rain 'permitted' a catastrophic flood; nobody would blame or praise fire because it burns One man's house and cooks another man's dinner. Nor can it be properly said that Brahman is 'good' in any personal sense of the word. Brahman is not good in the sense that Christ was good—for Christ's goodness was within māyā. The Reality itself is beyond all phenomena; even the noblest. It is beyond purity, beauty, happiness glory, or success. It can be described as good only if we mean that absolute consciousness is absolute knowledge, and that absolute knowledge is absolute joy.

But perhaps the question does not refer to Brahman at all. Perhaps, in this connection, 'God' means Iśwara, the Ruler of māyā. If this is granted, can Vedānta philosophy agree with the Old Testament that God is a law-giver, a stern and somewhat unpredictable father, whose ways are not ours, whose punishments and rewards often seem unmerited, who permits us to fall into temptation? The answer is yes and no. The Vedānta doctrine of karma is a doctrine of absolute, automatic justice. The circumstances of our lives, our pains and our pleasures, are all the result of our past actions in this present existence, and in countless previous existences, from a beginningless time. Viewed from a relative standpoint, māyā is quite pitiless. We get exactly what we earn, no more, no less. If we cry out against some apparent injustice, it is only because the act that brought it upon us is buried deep in the past, out of reach of our memory. To be born a beggar, a king, an athlete, or a helpless cripple is simply the composite consequence of the deeds of our other lives. We have no one to thank but ourselves. It is no use trying to bargain with Iśwara, or propitiate him, or hold him responsible for our troubles. It is no use inventing a Devil as an excuse for our weakness. Māyā is what we make of it—and Iśwara simply represents that stern and solemn fact.

Viewed from a relative standpoint, this world of appearance is a bleak place, and as such it often drives us to despair. The seers, with their larger knowledge, tell us otherwise. Once we become conscious, even dimly, of the Atman, the Reality within us, the world shows itself in a very different aspect. It is no longer a court of justice but a kind of gymnasium. Good and evil, pain and pleasure, still exist, but they seem more like the ropes and vaulting-horses and parallel bars which can be used to make our bodies strong. Māyā is no longer an endlessly revolving wheel of pain and pleasure but a ladder which can be climbed to consciousness of the Reality. From this standpoint, fortune and misfortune are both mercies—that is to say, opportunities. Every experience offers us the chance of making a constructive reaction to it—a reaction which helps to break some chain of our bondage to māyā and bring us nearer to spiritual freedom. Śamkara therefore distinguishes between two kinds of māyā—avidyā (evil or ignorance) and vidvā (good or knowledge in a relative sense). Avidyā is that which causes us to move farther away from the Self and obscures our knowledge of the Truth. Vidyā is that which enables us to come nearer to the Self by removing the veil of ignorance. Both Vidyā and avidyā are transcended when we pass beyond māyā into consciousness of the absolute reality.

It has been said already that māyā is the superimposition of the ego-idea upon the Ātman, the real Self. The ego-idea represents a false claim to individuality, to being different from, or separate from, our neighbours. It follows, therefore, that any act which, contradicts this claim will bring us one step back towards right knowledge, towards consciousness of the inner reality. If we recognize our brotherhood with our fellow men; if we try to deal honestly, truthfully, charitably with them; if we work for equal rights and equal justice, politically and economically, and for abolition of barriers of race and class—then we are in fact giving the lie to the ego-idea and moving towards awareness of the universal, nonindividual Existence. All such actions belong to what is known as ethical goodness—just as all selfish actions belong to ethical evil. In one sense, and in one sense only, goodness may be said to be more 'real', or more valid, than evil: since evil actions and thoughts involve us more deeply in māyā, while good thoughts and actions lead us beyond māyā, to transcendental consciousness.

The words sin and virtue are somewhat alien to the spirit of Vedānt philosophy, because they necessarily foster a sense of possessiveness with regard to thought and action. If we say 'I am good' or 'I am bad', we are only talking the language of māyā. '1 am Brahman' is the only true statement regarding ourselves that any of us can make. St Francois de Sales wrote that 'even our repentance must be peaceful'—meaning that exaggerated remorse, just as much as excessive self-congratulation, simply binds us more firmly to the ego-idea, the lie of māyā. We must never forget that ethical conduct is a means, not an end in itself. Knowledge of the impersonal reality is the only valid knowledge. Apart from that, our deepest wisdom is black ignorance and our strictest righteousness is all in vain

The Supreme Goal

It may be objected that Vedānta philosophy, like every other system of religious thought, is based upon a central hypothesis. Certainly, the supreme goal of life is to know Brahman exists. But can we be sure of this? Isn't it possible that there is no underlying reality in the universe? Isn't it possible that life is just a meaningless flux, a dying and a becoming in eternal alternation?

What is so attractive about Vedanta is its undogmatic, experimental approach to truth. Śaṁkara does not tell us that we must accept the existence of Brahma as a dogma before we can enter upon the spiritual life. No-he invites us to find out for ourselves.

Nothing-no teacher, no scripture can do the work for us. Teachers and scriptures are merely encouragements to personal effort. But, as such, they can be very effective. Imagine that the, existence or nonexistence of God is the subject of a lawsuit and that you are the judge. Try to listen impartially to both sides. Consider the witnesses for Brahman—the seers and saints who claim to have known the eternal-' reality. Consider the circumstances of their lives, their personalities, their words. Ask yourself. Are all these witnesses liars or hypocrites or insane persons, or are they telling the truth? Compare the great scriptures of the world and ask. Do they contradict each other, or do they agree? Then give your verdict.

But mere assent, as Śaṁkara insists, is not enough. It is only a preliminary step toward active participation in the search for Brahman. Direct personal experience is the only satisfactory proof of his existence, and each of us must have it.

Modern science goes a long way towards confirming the Vedānta world-picture. It admits that consciousness, in varying degrees, may be present everywhere. Differences between objects and creatures are.

Only surface differences, varying arrangements of atomic pattern. Benients can be changed into other elements. Identity is only provisional. Science does not yet accept the concept of absolute reality, but it certainly does not exclude it. Sarhkara knew nothing of science, but his approach is fundamentally scientific. It is based upon the practice of discrimination—a discrimination to be apply d to ourselves and to every circumstance and object of our experience, at each 'instant of our lives. Again and again—thousands and thousands of times a day—we must ask ourselves. Is this real or unreal, is this fact or fancy, is this nature or only appearance? Thus we probe deeper *Had* deeper towards the truth. 'We all know that we exist. We are all aware of our own consciousness. But we hat is the nature of this consciousness, this existence? Discrimination will soon prove to us that the ego-idea is not the fundamental reality. There is something beyond it. We can call this something 'Brahman'—but 'Brahman' is only another word. It does not reveal the nature of the thing we are looking-for. *Can* Brahman be known as an existing substance or thing? Not in the ordinary meaning of the verb to know. To know something is to have objective knowledge of it, and such knowledge is relative, depending upon space, time, and causation. we cannot know absolute consciousness in this manner, because absolute consciousness is knowledge itself. Brahman is the source of all other knowledge; he comprises the knower, the knowledge, and that which is known. He is independent of space, time, and cause.

In this sense, the practice of discrimination differs from the method of scientific research. The scientist concentrates upon some object of knowledge, and pursues it beyond the range of physical sense perception, with the aid of mechanical apparatus, chemical analysis, mathematics, and so forth. His research extends like a journey, deeper and deeper into time and space. The religious philosopher; on the other hand, is trying to annihilate time and space, the dimensions of the ego-idea, and thus uncover the Reality which is nearer and more instant than the ego, the body, or the mind. He is trying to be aware of what he already and alw ays is, and this awareness is not an aspect of consciousness, but consciousness itself. The illumined seer does not merely know Brahman; he is Brahman, he is Existence, he is Knowledge. Absolute freedom is not something to be attained, absolute knowledge is not something to be won, Brahman is not something to be found anew. It is only māyā which has to be. pierced, ignorance which has to be overcome. The process of discrimination is a negative process. The positive fact, our real nature, eternally exists. We are Brahman—and only ignorance divides us from knowledge of the fact.

Transcendental consciousness, or union with Brahman, can never be investigated by the methods of scientific research, since such research 'depends ultimately upon sense perception, and Brahman is beyond the grasp of the senses. But this does not mean that we are doomed to doubt, or to blind trust in the experience of the seers, until we have reached the supreme goal for ourselves. Even a little effort in meditation and the spiritual life will reward us with the cuiction that this is really the way to truth and peace, that we are not simply deceiving or hypnotizing ourselves, that Reality is accessible. We shall '! have our ups and downs, of course, and our moments of uncertainty, but we shall always return to this conviction. No spiritual gain, however small, is ever lost or wasted.

By temperament, Śamkara inclined toward jñāna yoga, the way of pure discrimination, although he was capable of great devotion also.'

Renunciation, discrimination, self-control—these are his watchwords. Some may find his austerity too forbidding, but it is precisely this austerity which supplies a valuable corrective to the dangers of an easy sentimentality, an excess of carefree optimism, a confusion of real devotion with mere emotional self-indulgence. Śamkara was under no illusions about this world of māyā; he condemns its apparent pleasures and delights with brutal frankness. For this very reason he was able to describe so powerfully the complete transformation of the universe which takes place before the eyes of the illumined seer. When Brahman is experienced, when all creatures and objects are seen in their real relation to the Absolute, then this world is indeed a paradise; it is nothing but Brahman, nothing but utter consciousness, knowledge, and peace.

To quote Śamkara describing the experience of an illumined soul: 'The ego has disappeared. I have realized my identity with Brahman, and so all my desires have melted away. I have risen above my ignorance and my knowledge of this seeming universe. What is this joy that I feel? Who shall measure it? I know nothing but joy, limitless, unbounded!

'The ocean of Brahman is full of nectar- the joy of the Atman. The treasure I have found there cannot be described in words. The mind cannot conceive of it. My mind fell like a hailstone into that vast expanse of Brahman's ocean. Touching one drop of it, I melted away and became one with Brahman. And now, though I return to human consciousness. I abide in the joy of the Atman.

'Where is this universe? Who took it away? Has it merged in something else? A while ago, I beheld it—now it exists no longer. This is wonderful indeed!

'Here is the ocean of Brahman, full of endless joy,. How can I accept or reject anything? Is there anything apart or distinct from Brahman?

'Now, finally and clearly, I know that I am the Atman, whose nature is eternal joy. I see nothing, I hear nothing, I know nothing that is separate from me.[28]

SELECTED PASSAGES FROM SAMKARA'S VIVEKACUDAMANI

Crest-Jewel of Discrimination

The spiritual seeker who is possessed of tranquillity, self-control, mental poise and forbearance, devotes himself to the practice of contemplation, and meditates upon the Atman within himself as the Atman within all beings. Thus he completely destroys the sense of separateness which arises from the darkness of ignorance, and dwells in joy, identifying himself with Brahman, free from distracting thoughts and śelfish occupations.

Those who echo borrowed teachings are not free from the world. But those who have attained samadhi by merging the external universe, the sense organs, the mind and the ego in the pure consciousness of the Atman—they alone are free from the world, with its bonds and snares.[29]

Be devoted to Brahman and you will be able to control your senses. Control your senses and you will gain mastery over your mind. Master your mind, and the sense of ego will be dissolved. In this manner, the yogi achieves an unbroken realization of the joy of Brahman. Therefore let the seeker strive to give his heart to Brahman.[30]

The self-luminous Atman, the witness of all, is ever-present within your own heart. This Atman stands apart from all that is unreal. Know it to be yourself, and meditate upon it unceasingly.[31]

When the mind achieves perfect union with Brahman, the wise man realizes Brahman entirely within his own heart. Brahman is beyond speech or thought. It is the pure, eternal consciousness. It is absolute bliss. It is incomparable and immeasurable. It is ever-free, beyond all action, boundless as the sky, indivisible and absolute.[32]

To taste, within his own heart and in the external world, the endless bliss of the Atman—such is the reward obtained by the yogi who has reached perfection and liberation in this lifes.[33]

The fruit of dispassion is illumination; the fruit of illumination is the stilling of desire; the fruit of stilled desire is experience of the bliss of the Atman, whence follows peace.[34]

Teachers and scriptures can stimulate spiritual awareness. But the wise disciple crosses the ocean-of his ignorance by direct illumination, through the grace of God[35]

Our perception of the universe is a continuous perception of Brahman, though the ignorant man is not aware of this. Indeed, this universe is nothing but Brahman. See Brahman everywhere, under all circumstances, with the eye of the spirit and a tranquil heart. How can the physical eyes see anything but physical objects? How can the mind of the enlightened man think of anything other than the Reality [36]

BHĀSKARA

Still another aspect of Vedānta, known as Bhedābhedavāda, or doctrine of identity in difference, finds its exponent in Bhāskara. Oudulumi originated the system, but his writings are not now available, and we know of him only through mention of him in the Brahma Sūtras of Vyāsa. Bhāskara wrote commentaries upon the Sūtras and in so doing explained his own and Oudulumi's philosophy. In the main he attempted an attack upon Śaṁkara's doctrine of māyā. He therefore lived after Śaṁkara according to Indian authorities, in the early part of the ninth century.

The Philosophy of Identity in Difference

Brahman is one without a second, the unchangeable reality, endowed with blessed attributes, including the power to create, sustain, and dissolve the universe. He is the formless, personal God who in his causal state is transcendental—beyond time, space, and causation; in his aspect as effect, he has evolved or become transformed into the empirical universe. Since Brahman, the Infinite, has made himself finite, as finite ha is real, though he, the Infinite, is not necessarily conditioned by the finitude. Brahman as cause contains the whole universe potentially within himself, and the universe is the cause actualized, though in part only, since the cause has not exhausted itself in the effect.

Again, as effect, Brahman is both jīva, or the individual soul, and the world. He is endowed with power of two kinds: bhogya, the kind which evolves as the objective universe, and bhoktr, the kind which evolves as living souls. This power of Brahman is not māyā, but is real in the absolute sense.

Empirical existence therefore consists of (1) the subject, the experiencer, the jīva, and (2) the object of experience, the world of the senses. Though the empirical world of subject and object is not separate from Brahman, for it is Brahman that is evolved as the universe, yet again Brahman is not merely the universe of name and form—he is transcendental as well.[37]

Individual souls are many, and they are parts of Brahman. They are related to him as are the rays of the sun to the sun. They are neither absolutely different from God, nor are they absolutely identical with him. In the state of bondage—that is, ignorance—individual souls are different from God; and in the state of liberation—that is, knowledge—they become one with him. To the self, purified by spiritual discipline, is revealed the knowledge of Brahman, and as the self finally becomes one with Brahman, all consciousness of separation is dissolved. But this union is possible only after death, never at any time during life. In this respect the philosophy of Bhāskara differs from all the other systems we have studied.[38]

Union with Brahman is the supreme goal. As the means of achieving this, Bhāskara, like all other teachers of religion, offers the ideal of non attachment, the ideal of being in the world and yet not of it, and the worship of Brahman and meditation upon him

YĀMUNA

Viśiṣṭādvaita Vedānta, the Vedānta in its aspect of qualified non-dualism, traces its origin to the period of the Upaniṣads; at least it had gained followers at the time of the composition of the Mahābhārata, being identical with the doctrine of Pañcarātra mentioned in that poem. In the tenth century A.D. however, it received greater impetus and a brighter light from the teachings of the saint Yāmuna; and in the eleventh century the great teacher Rāmānuja, who had been influenced by Yāmuna, gave it a sound philosophical basis, and made it a popular religion, particularly in southern India. Yāmuna and Rāmānuja belong to the long line of Vaiṣṇava saints recognized in southern India and generally known as Ālvārs. Ālvār is a Tamil word which means lie who rules the world by his love of and devotion to God'. Many legends are to!d of these ancient Ālvārs, and all of them clearly express love of God and devotion and self-surrender to him.

One of the Alvārs was Nāṭhamuni, grandfather of Yāmuna. He was known to history as a great saint living in the early part of the tenth century. Born of a well-known brāhmin family, on the death of his son he gave up the life of the world and embraced a life of renunciation. He wrote two books which are regarded as authoritative by the Śrī Vaiṣṇava, the school of qualified nondualism.

Yāmuna, his grandson, was born in AD 953. At the age of twelve he became king of half the kingdom of Pāṇḍu. There is extant an interesting account, though obviously legendary, of how he ascended the throne.

The king of Pāṇḍu, it seems, had a court pundit who was very clever in debate; and it was the custom of the country that whoever challenged the scholarship of the pundit and defeated him in argument was appointed court pundit in turn; and whoever challenged the pundit and was defeated by him must pay him an annual sum as tax. Bhāśya, teacher of the boy Yāmuna, had been defeated by the pundit and had thus become subject to the penalty. Now it so happened that once the tax-collector appeared when Bhāśya was absent from home, and Yamuna, feeling the humiliation of his master, challenged the pundit to debate. Though the king and his pundit were amazed at the child's temerity, they were obliged to accept the challenge.

The boy was brought to court and accorded due honour and respect. The queen felt sure that he would be crowned victor, for she could see that he was no ordinary child. When she confided her thoughts to the king, he laughed and jokingly offered to lay a wager against him. The queen said, 'If the boy is defeated, I promise to be the slave of Your Majesty's slaves.' To this the king replied, 'If the boy wins, I will offer him half my kingdom.'

So the boy and the pundit entered into debate. To the surprise of all, the boy was victorious, and the pundit was obliged to acknowledge himself beaten at the hands of a child. The king, paying his bet, offered Yāmuna half his kingdom. The boy accepted the gift and ruled for many years at peace with all men.

The news of Yāmuna's elevation to the throne came to the ears of Nāthamuni, his grandfather, who was then living as a monk. Fearing lest his grandson should give himself over to worldliness, Muni charged Nambi, his favourite disciple, to watch over him and see that he did not lose himself in love of the world but that instead he sought the truth.

When Yāmuna was thirty-five years of age, and still reigning over his kingdom, Nambi appeared before him and said, 'Your grandfather has left a vast treasure with me. If it is your desire to find this treasure, you must follow me, and follow me alone.' So Yamuna left his kingdom and followed Nambi. As he associated closely with his grandfather's disciple, he came to admire his greatness, his love for God, his purity of conduct, and above all the peace and joy that shone in his countenance. And there arose, in the heart of King. Yāmuna a mighty longing to find God and attain peace. He lost all taste for the enjoyments of the world, even the desire to return to his kingdom. Both king and devotee retired to the temple of Śrī Raṅganātha. Thus Yāmuna became a monk and teacher.

In his later years Yāmuna wrote four famous books. He wished to write, in addition, a commentary on the Brahma Sūtras, but passed away before the fulfilment of this desire. As he lay dying, he expressed a wish that Rāmānura, whom he loved much, shuuld write the commentary. Hearing of this, Rāmānuja, who had already won fame for himself, hastened to him, but arrived too late. He promised, however, to carry out Yāmuna's wish, and succeeded in doing so.

Briefly—for we shall consider the doctrine of qualified nondualism in some detail in the chapter on Rāmānuja—the philosophy of Yāmuna consists of the following ideas.

God to the Supreme Being. He is the whole, of which individual souls are the parts. We are related to him as are the waves of the ocean to the ocean. The universe is a transformation of God. God is its soul; he visible world is his body.

The ideals of all-consuming love for God, and self-surrender to him, Yāmuna has expressed beautifully in a famous prayer:

'God is beyond the realm of speech and mind. He is the ground of speech and mind, and he is the ocean of mercy. How can we pray to him or praise him, who is worshipped and praised even by the great gods? In the ocean are drowned the high mountain and the small atom. No difference between them is felt by the ocean.

'My beloved, O thou Sweet One, "I" and "me" and "mine" all belong to thee. And if I am conscious of this truth that whatever I have—all—belongs to thee forever, then what can I offer thee?"

'I am Thine': this expresses the attitude of the devotees of. Visistadvaita. The Vaiṣṇava devotees of Bengal preach another beautiful truth.' 'Thou art mine.'

Elsewhere Yāmuna writes: 'Thou art father, thou art mother, thou,, art son, thou art daughter, thou art dear friend, thou art guru, thou art the supreme goal and refuge of the whole universe.' According to Yāmuna, the highest ideal is to take refuge in the Lord and surrender oneself completely to him. This ideal of surrendering oneself to God was developed by Rāmānuja, as we shall now see, into a complete philosophy.

RĀMĀNUJA

Since human beings possess widely differing temperaments, they conduct their lives upon different levels. For this reason, no one system of religion can equally well satisfy everyone, and there exist diverse forms of religious truth. And yet, however divergent they may be, they have an underlying unity, and all of them lead men by one path or another to a single goal. The varied scriptures of the world may be likened to a kind mother who cherishes her many children by granting their demands according to their needs.

After Śamkara, Rāmānuja ranks first among the greatest interpreters of Vedānta. Śamkara's philosophy, though it did afford spiritual comfort to many, yet did not meet the requirements of all aspirants. There are men in every age who hunger for a God whom they can love, whom they can worship. Now the Absolute of Śamkara becomes to such men entirely too much of an abstraction to be the object of love and worship. It is true that Samkara does reserve a place in his system for a God of love, and there is room in it for devotion to him; but to many his Iśwara not wholly satisfying, for they regard him as but a lower aspect of Brahman, the Absolute. The Śamkara philosophy touches indeed such dizzy heights of abstraction, and at the same time offers such a surpassing degree of spiritual illumination, that it becomes extremely difficult, if not impossible, for most men either to comprehend it or to accept it. They are therefore inclined to regard this Absolute of Śamkara as, in the words of Dr Radhakrishnan, 'a bloodless Absolute dark with the excess of light.[39]

So the kind mother, the scriptures, spoke once more, this time through the lips of Rāmānuja and led the people to the bosom of truth.[40] Rāmānuja argues that God and the souls of men are not the same, though they are not separate from each other, and that the highest ideal and the ultimate goal are to love and worship God and surrender ourselves utterly and completely to him. The material world and human beings, though different, have a real existence of their own as the body of Brahman, who is their soul and controlling power. Apart from Brahman they are literally nonentities. So Rāmānujas philosophy is known as Viśiṣṭādvaita—that is, advaita, nondualism, with viśeṣa, or qualifications—because it admits the plurality both of matter and of souls.

Life of Rāmānuja

Rāmānuja was born at Śrī-perum-budur in southern India in the year AD 1017. His mother was the granddaughter of Yāmuna, the saint and philosopher who we have already met. In his youth Rāmānuja journeyed to

Conjeevaram in order to study Vedānta with a teacher known as Yādava Prakāś.

Yādava Prakāś, a celebrated interpreter of Vedānta, wrote a commentary upon the Brahma Sūtras which has unfortunately been lost. We do know, however, that his interpretation closely followed that of Bhāskara, who, as we have already discovered, believed in the unity of the soul with Brahman in relation to transcendental knowledge, and acknowledged difference from him in relation to ignorance. In the view of Yādava, this difference is as real as is the unity. Like Bhāskara, Yādava interpreted the philosophy of Bhedābheda, or unity in difference.

For a time, the youthful Rāmānuja pursued his studies under the direction of Yādava, but their paths soon parted.'The fact was that the young man soon developed his own interpretation of the philosophy of Vedānta, and this seemed more reasonable to the other students gathered about the master than did that of the master himself. Yādava became furiously angry. He accordingly conceived a dislike and a consuming envy of his brilliant pupil.

Matters came to a head when Yādava was requested by the ruler of the country to heal his little daughter supposed to be possessed by demons. When the master failed, Rāmānuja was called upon. The story goes that at the young man's bidding the spirit left the girl, and she became quite well. Yādava now hated Rāmānuja, who was obliged to leave the master's school. But this was not enough, Yādava became so possessed by hate and jealousy that he even attempted to assassmate his young pupil, who was saved by warning given to him by a hunter and his wife. Many years later, however, Yādava recognized Rāmānuja's greatness, repented, and became his loyal follower.

Rāmānuja now returned to his mother's home, and at her request took upon himself the state of a householder by marrying a girl of her choice.

About this time, Yāmuna, head of the temple of Śrīraṅgam, being old and sick and hearing of Rāmānuja's learning and purity of character, desired to install him as his successor. When the aged saint was about to breathe his last, his disciples sent for Rāmānuja to come to his bedside, but he did not arrive till just às Yāmuna's body was being conveyed to the riever bank for cremation. As Rāmānuja viewed the corpse, he remarked that the three fingers of the right hand, remained closed. The disciples in explanation said that the closed fingers indicated the existence of an unfulfilled desire, which—as already mentioned—was a wish to compose a commentary upon the Brahma Sūtras. When Rāmānuja promised to take upon himself the fulfilment of this task, legend has it that the three fingers forthwith assumed their natural position.

After Rāmānuja's return to Conjeevaram, his spirit grew restless, for he could see no way to fulfil his promise. Accordingly, he sought advice of the head priest of the temple of Śrīraṅgam, who uttered a Sanskrit verse which seemed to be the word of God, and his will: 'I am the Supreme. The Truth is based upon distinction. Self-surrender is the surest way to the door of salvation. Whether man Struggles or not, salvation will come in the end. Accept the disciple ship of Periā Nambi.' So Rāmānuja set out to meet Nambi at the same time that Nambi was approaching Conjeevaram to meet him. They came together in a temple on the road, and Nambi initiated Rāmānuja into the mysteries of Vedānta.

Rāmānuja was not happy in his marriage, for in his heart he longed for the time when he might devote himself uninterruptedly to a life of worship and meditation. His wife, instead of aiding him to attain the spiritual ideal he desired, constantly irritated him by her thoughtless conduct. At last Rāmānuja, feeling the call of God from within, renounced all wordly ties, took monastic vows, and set out for Śriraṅgam, where the great saint Yāmuna had desired that he should live.

While he was a monk at Śriraṅgam, Rāmānuja became extremely popular, and man aspirants gathered round him. But still he remained unsatisfied. Now there was living at that time another saint, whose name was Gosṭhi-pūrna. Rāmānuja went to him and reverently begged to be initiated. Six times he went to him, and six times was refused.At last, however, seeing Rāmānuja's earnest 'devotion, Gosṭhi-pūrna initiated him with a holy mantra, a name of God, but warned him that he must never give that mantra to anyone, for if he did he would be damned, while whoever heard the sacred words would attain salvation. Upon hearing this, Rāmānuja went at once into he temple, gathered a crowd around him, and uttered the holy mantra 'Om namo Nārāyaṇāya', in the hearing of all. Gosṭhi-pūrna pretended to be very angry and rebuked him for his disobedience, but Rāmānuja replied, 'If by my damnation so many can be saved, damnation is my supreme desire.' Pleased, the saint answered, 'Because of your great love for humanity, the philosophy of Viśiṣṭādvaita shall henceforth be known as the Rāmānuja Philosophy.'

Rāmānuja now made Śrīraṅgam his headquarters, but travelled occasionally to various parts of the country, preaching and gathering many disciples. It was during this period that he wrote his commentary upon the Brahma Sūtras, as he had promised before the corpse of Yāmuna that he would do. This work is known as Sri Bhāsya, and is held in great respect by the followers of Śrī Vaiṣṇavism. He also wrote commentaries upon the Gitā and some original philosophical treatises propounding his doctrine. He passed away in the year AD 1137 after a fruitful life of one hundred and twenty years. He is worshipped today by thousands of his followers, and is regarded by all India as one of the greatest saints and philosophers in its history.

Viśiṣṭadvaita of Rāmānuja

At the beginning of our discussion of Rāmānuja's philosophy, we need to make quite clear the distinction between the definition of knowledge given by Śamkara and that given by Rāmānuja, for upon this distinction is based the entire difference between these two great philosophers. If properly understood, it will at once make clear in how many different lights the same truth may be viewed.

According to Śamkara, knowledge is self-luminous, light itself, It illumined objects of knowledge, and is therefore apart from and beyond the relation of subject and object. Relative knowledge is not true knowledge; it is not pure consciousness, though grounded upon it. Knowledge, by itself, is absolute. It is the Ātman, Light itself. Relative knowledge is infinite knowledge made finite.

Rāmānuja, on the other hand, does not take into consideration knowledge that is self-luminous and absolute. Knowledge, he declares is always relative, and in it there. is always a distinction between subject and object. In short, Rāmānuja does not admit nirvikalpa samādhi, the unitary consciousness, the experience of the Self as one with Brahman. He was at heart a bhakta, a devotee, who preserved his distinction from Brahman in order to enjoy the bliss of divine love. In consequence, his philosophy is one of devotion, although, being based on careful reasoning, it is not merely emotional in its nature.

One other point of difference between the two great philosophers should be noted. What Śamkara calls māyā, which is neither real nor unreal, and which, when joined to Brahman, the Absolute, attributeless and impersonal, becomes the personal Iśwara, or God, Rāmānuja calls Sakti, or power, which in its nature is real and eternally, co-existent with Brahman. Thus Rāmānuja does not accept the impersonal, attributeless Brahman of Śamkara, but rather aneternal personal Brahman, the repository of all blessed qualities.

Theory of knowledge

Perception, inference, and scripture are valid as sources of knowled ge and also, each on its own level, as an affirmation of reality. Unlike Śamkara, Rāmānuja does not admit a distinction between illusory perception and true perception, for he declares that even in illusory perception, so-called, there is some perception of reality. Thus all experience has its validity.

Rāmānuja's theory of dharma-bhuta-jñāna, or consciousness as an attribute and not the thing itself, explains his conception of the threefold function of knowledge: it gives reality; it has the power to reveal the truth: and it can reveal the truth of Brahman.

So long as man, owing to his imperfections imposed by karma, is crippled in knowledge. Brahman may not be revealed to him. But after he has been purified, he may have immediate intuition of God. This immediate intuition, as we have elsewhere remarked, is not the highest transcendental consciousness described in the Upaniṣads and by Śamkara as turīya, and as nirvikalpa samādhi by the yogis, but rather it is a transcendental experience of God in which there still remains the ego as distinct from him. The experience is described as savikalpa samādhi by\ the yogis, and it comes through absorption in meditation and devotion. This revelation of God in meditation possesses a self-certifying character, and, further, the fact that God is so revealed in the heart of man is borne witness to by the seers and saints of the Upaniṣads, as well as by the saints and seers of all ages and in all lands.

Brahman, or God

In the Upaniṣads we read, 'The knower of Brahman attains the highest'[41]. This text expresses the unity of the threefold nature of wisdom, namely: tattwa. or intellectual and philosophic understanding of Brahman: hita, or way to Brahman; and puruṣartha, direct perception of Brahman as the supreme goal.

Let us first try philosophically to comprehend the nature of Brahman. This is tattwa. Brahman is determinate and can therefore be defined by a statement of his essential attributes. In the words of the Upaniṣad, 'Brahman is satyam, or real, jñānam, or conscious, and anantam, or infinite.'[42] Śamkara does not consider these as attributes of Brahman. But Rāmānuja accepts them as essential.

Brahman is the basis of all existence, and since he is also the supreme good, he is also the supreme goal. The universe is composed of cit, the sentient, and acit, the nonsentient. Cit and acit have their source in Brahman, and he is the indwelling Self within all and the ruler of all.

Brahman is both the first cause and the final cause of the universe of the sentient and the nonsentient. 'Brahman .. wills to be many', we read in the Upaniṣads, and he divides himself into the manifold universe, of the living and of the nonliving. This fact does not mean, however, that the act of creation had an absolute beginning in time. The universe, as explained by all systems of Indian thought, alternates between the phases of involution and evolution. In the phase of involution it remains latent in Brahman, and creation or evolution is the actualization of the latent. The one becomes the many, not in the pantheistic sense of emanation, but in the sense that Brahman, by exercise of his will, evolves the twenty-four categories and the jīvas, or individual souls. Brahman is the material as well as the efficient cause of the universe. 'From him the universe has emerged, in him it exists, and unto him it returns.[43] As the web comes out of the spider and is withdrawn, as plants grow from the soil and hair from the body of man, so springs the universe from the eternal Brahman[44] God, as the source and support of the universe, has transformed himself into the cosmic manifold; and he is the indwelling Self in his creation, the ruler and director of the cosmic process. The evil that the universe contains is the result of the karma of individuals, for whom God is the dispenser of the law. He, himself, remains unaffected by evil, and is forever absolutely good.

God, though he has transformed himself into the universe of sentient and nonsentient forms, remains distinct from them. Matter is the object of experience, individual souls are the experiencing subjects, and God is the lord and ruler of all. He is defined in the Upaniṣads (as we have seen) as satyam, real: jñānam, conscious; and anantam, infinite. Rāmānuja, in commenting on this text, points out that because of these distinctive attributes God is above and beyond matter (which is changing phenomena) and distinct from individual souls caught in its meshes. Thus, though the universe is a transformation of Brahman, he remains by his nature beyond change, and though immanent, he is transcendent.

So does Rāmānuja define God as the repository of infinite, noble, and blessed qualities, and as one 'not only differentiating himself into the cosmos but remaining absolutely distinct from it'. Yet, again, 'he is its stuff and soul'.

Brahman, then, is related to the cosmos as the soul is related to the body. As a man has a soul and a body, and as the soul, though distinct from the body, yet controls and guides it, lives in it, and uses it as an instrument, similarly Brahman is the soul of the universe, the source and sustenance of all beings within it, and the ruler over all. In this body-and-soul connection between Brahman and the cosmos are included the three relations defined by Rāmānuja: 'ādhāra and ādheya—support and the supported; niyāmaya and niyamya—the controller and the controlled; sesin and śeṣa—the Lord and his servant'. Professor P. N. Srinivasachari, a deep student of Rāmānuja, speaks of this triune relationship thus:

'The relation of ādhāra and ādheya [support and the thing supported] is from the point of view of metaphysics which defines Brahman as real (satya), conscious (jñāna), and infinite (ananta). This relation emphasizes the inner unity of Reality. The relation of niyāmaka and niyamya [controller and the controlled] brings out the transcendental goodness of God and his redemptive impulse. The relation of śeshin and śesha [the Lord and his servant] satisfies the highest demands of ethics and aesthetics by defining God as the supreme Lord for whose satisfaction the world of chit [the sentient] and achit [the insentient] lives, moves and has its being. The relation of body and soul combines all the three together and serves as an analogical representation of a spiritual truth.[45]

God as the controller of the universe is absolutely good and the redeemer of all beings. Evil and suffering, be it repeated, are caused by the individual's karmas. Karmas—good or evil deeds—create happiness or misery; but by karmas alone man cannot redeem himself. Only the grace of God can save him; God is therefore the saviour. In his infinite love, his absolute goodness, he is forever merciful, for he even becomes flesh in human form in order to redeem the prodigal and to rejoice in the ecstasy of communion with his devotee. The Gitā, as we have seen, expounds the idea of avatār, or divine incarnation; Rāmānuja tells us that the central motive of God in descending to earth in human form is his love for humanity and his desire to save it.

The finite self is not a separate self-existent entity, but an organ, an element of Brahman. It is a part of Brahman, essentially different from him but inseparably bound to him. The finite self is anu, or atomic like the point of a goad, though it admits of no spatial division from the fact that it is spirit. The finite self, then, is an essential attribute (prākāra) of God; and as substance and attribute, though inseparably associated, are yet absolutely distinct from each other, so God as substance is absolutely distinct from the individual soul. As inseparably associated with God, the individual self is eternal; and at distinct from him, it has a personality of its own and a free will. Bus God, being also the inner ruler of the cosmos, which forms his body, 'makes the soul act'. Not that man's acts are good or evil as guided or forced by God—for God permits the individual to choose between good and evil. Eventually, however, by his grace God restores all souls to himself. Man's choice of good or evil, in short, is an exercise of his free will. That makes him responsible for his actions, while God remains unaffected by them.

Free will, furthermore, is given in order that man may eventually detach himself from the meshes of ignorance and grow into the 'personality of God'. Though Rāmānuja tries to refute the doctrine of māyā as expounded by Śarhkara, he is obliged to admit in the final analysis the existence of māyā, or ignorance, in man; for the self, he believes, has forgotten its divine origin and its divine destiny, and tends to identify itself with matter, until it becomes subject to the evils of sarhsara, or empirical existence. The true Self, which is an eternal mode of God, has degenerated into ego by becoming a mode of matter. We free ourselves from this ego when we surrender ourselves to God. Our free will, a gift of God, finds fulfilment of its purpose when we live in conformity with the will of God, who is our divine source and the Self of ourselves.

The poet Tennyson in two lines sums up the implications of free will and self-surrender:

Our wills are ours we know not how,
Our wills are ours to make them Thine.

The Supreme Goal

As we have already stated, God is the tattwa, the truth; he is the hita, the ways and means, and he is the puruṣartha, the supreme goal.[46]

Not only must we give intellectual assent to the truth that we live, move, and have our being in God, but we must have awareness or this truth. Like all true saints and philosophers, Rāmānuja held that God can be known and realized, that a vision of his being is possible for man, and that man must Strive to attain it. And he realized, like all saints, that the vision of God is vouchsafed to man by God himself out of his infinite love and grace.

Self-effort and divine grace are not opposed to each other; neither is divine grace conditional. In the words of Śrī Rāmakrṣṇa, the breeze of divine grace is blowing, but we must set sail to catch it. In the same way Rāmānuja explains how we must love God, serve him, and meditate on him: and then, as spiritual hunger grows within us, we experience love and divine grace flowing from him and flooding our whole being. The culmination of spiritual experience, he says, is then realizing God's unbounded love and finding complete refuge in him. To find complete refuge in him is the ideal of self-surrender, or prapatti, which is not extinction of self, but rather a union of our will with the will of God.

Rāmānuja did not believe in a complete identity of man with God. For him kaiṅkarya. or living in the service of God, was the supreme ideal. This ideal of service, however, must not be confused with a modern Christian ideal, that of helping God to realize his own fullness. In this Christian ideal there exists a strong element of egotistical pride. The truth is that God does not need our help; we realize our own fullness by loving and serving him.

Rāmānuja did not, however, believe in jīvanmukti, or liberation in this life, but rather in videha mukti, or liberation after death—death, for him, being a passing 'through the path of light' to our permanent home in God. In death the self realizes union with God as his body, his part, his attribute. Never is there a dissolution of jīvahood, or individual personality. Professor P. N. Srinivasachari has beautifully summarized this ideal of freedom in the following words:

'Release is not freedom in embodiment but freedom from embodiment; it refers to the return of the prākāra or mukta [released soul] to his home in the absolute. [Rāmānuja's absolute, however, is not the Absolute proper—but the Personal God.] Mukti [freedom] is beyond the range of materialism and mentalism and involves the intuition of the infinite as well as its attainment. The finite has its roots in the infinite and in mukti there is she coalescence of content without the abolition of existence. When the freed self sees God face to face, its logical outlook becomes a spiritual insight, and freed from the nescience of empirical life, it expands into omniscience. It has a sense of the infinite and sees everything with the eye of the all-self. When the self is Brahmanized, it is stripped of its self-hood and sense of separateness, shakes off the shackles of karma based on kāma [desire] and effaces itself in spiritual service and solidarity. The finite remains, but the fetters of finitude and individualism are removed.[47]

The Ways and Means of Attainment

In explaining hita, the practical aspect of his philosophy, Rāmānuja insists that God is the Lord of Love, and he prescribes bhakti yoga. 'Bhakti yoga', explains Swami Vivekananda, 'is a real, genuine search after the Lord, a search beginning, continuing, and ending in Love. . One single moment of the madness of extreme love of God brings us eternal freedom.[48]

Śamkara laid great stress upon jñāna yoga, the path of knowledge, but Rāmānuja laid stress upon bhakti yoga, the path of love. Both these saintly philosophers admit the need of love and devotion as well as the need of knowledge; only Śamkara preaches love as a means to knowledge and Rāmānuja preaches love as both means and end. Rāmānuja, on the other hand, admits knowledge as a means to love, whereas Śamkara insists that knowledge is both means and end. I do not believe that there exists, after all, any real difference between their explanations of the means. Swami Vivekananda declares, it is a distinction without much difference. When Rāmānuja speaks of knowledge as a means, he has in mind not transcendental knowledge but intellectual analysis; and when Samkara speaks of love as a means, he has reference to an inferior form of worship. 'Each seems', says Swami Vivekananda, 'to lay a great stress upon his own particular method of worship, forgetting that with perfect love true knowledge is bound to come, even unsought, and that from perfect knowledge true love is inseparable.[49]

As he explains what meditation is, Rāmānuja also explains what true love is, and how with love and devotion we necessarily must meditate upon God. In his commentary upon the first aphorism of the Vedānta Sūtras, he gives an illuminating explanation of this interlocking of love and meditation:

'Meditation is a constant remembering [of the thing meditated upon], which flows like oil poured from one vessel to another. When this kind of remembering has been attained [in relation to God] all bonds break. Thus the scriptures speak of constant recollectedness as a means to liberation. This remembering again is the same as seeing, because it has the same significance, as is evident from the passage, "When He who is far away and near is seen, the bonds of the heart are broken, all doubts vanish, and all effects of karma disappear." He who is near can be seen, but he who is far away can only be remembered. Nevertheless the scriptures say that we have to see Him who is near as well as far away, thereby indicating to us that the above kind of remembering is as good as seeing. This remembrance when exalted assumes the same form as seeing. . . . Worship is constant remembering, as may be seen from the principal texts of the scriptures. Knowing, which is the same as repeated worship, has been described as constant remembering ... Thus the memory, which has attained to the level of direct perception, is spoken of in the Sruti [scripture] as a means of liberation. "This Ātman is not to be reached through various sciences, nor by intellect, nor by much study of the Vedas. Whomsoever this Ātman desires, by him is the Ātman attained; unto him this Ātman reveals himself." Here, after saying that mere hearing, thinking, and meditating are not the means of attaining this Atman, the passage continues—Whomsoever this Atman desires, by him the Atman is attained. The extremely beloved is desired; he by whom this Atman is extremely beloved becomes the most beloved of the Atman. So that this beloved may attain the Atman, the Lord himself helps. For it has been said by the Lord: "Those who are constantly attached to Me and worship Me with love—I give that direction to their will by which the come to Me." Therefore it is said, to whomsoever this remembering, which is the same as direct perception, is very dear, because it is dear to the object of such memory-perception, he is desired by the Supreme Atman, by him the Supreme Atman is attained. This constant remembrance is denoted by the word bhakti (love).[50]

With respect to the method and means of attaining bhakti, Rāmānuja remarks: 'Its attainment comes through discrimination, control of the passions, habitual practice of religious disciplines, sacrificial work, purity, strength, and suppression of excessive)joy.'

By discrimination is meant the distinguishing, among other things, of good food from bad. Body and mind being interrelated, purity of food is important, especially for beginners, because it enables them to think pure thoughts.

Control of the passions is the strengthening of the will and its guidance toward meditation on the Lord. 'By practice and non-atttachment is it to be attained.'

Sacrificial work refers to the five great sacrifices mentioned in the Vedas.

Purity is both external and internal. In the list of qualities conducive to purity. Rāmānuja enumerates the following: satya, truthfullness; ārjava, sincerity; dayā, doing good to others; ahimsā, noninjury; abhidyā, noncovetousness, not thinking vain thoughts, not brooding over injuries received from others. Strength is vigour of mind.

Lastly is suppression of excessive joy. Excessive joy fritters away the energies of the mind, and yet we must be cheerful. Swami Vivekananda rightly says:

'The person who aspires to be a bhakta must be cheerful. In the Western world the idea of a religious man is that he never smiles, that . a dark cloud must always hang over his face, which, again, must be long-drawn with the jaws about collapsed. People with emaciated bodies, and long faces are fit subjects for the physician, they are not yogis. It is the cheerful mind that is persevering. It is the strong mind that hews its way through a thousand difficulties. And this, the hardest task of all, the cutting of our way out of the net of maya. is the work reserved only for giant wills.[51]

Rāmānuja makes some slight distinction between bhakti, or devotion, and prapatti, or self-surrender. When love for God arises in the heart, the highest attainment comes in the surrendering of our wills to God's will and in our living, literally, in the service of God. But, as we have seen, according to Rāmānuja there never comes complete union of man and God, of the lover and the beloved. And yet the greatest lovers and devotees tell of the ultimate consummation of love in mystic union—'I and my Father are one'—the union which knows neither separation nor distinction.

To the student of Western philosophy, Rāmānuja's ideas concerning God and the soul bear an astonishing resemblance to ideas on the same subjects with which Scholastic philosophy concerned itself during the Christian Middle Ages. The personality and the attributes of God the Heavenly Father, the relation of man to God. the question of free,will and divine grace, the submission of the will of man to a higher will than his, the union of human and divine, the relative positions of reason and love in the divine scheme, the vision of divine love and grace, and the release of the soul from bondage after death—It was principally on these topics that the Schoolmen speculated through many hundreds of years, from St Augustine until the final synthesis of faith and reason in St Thomas Aquinas. And Rāmānuja, living in the tenth century, might well have been the spiritual father of the Christian Dante. It is true that medieval Christianity placed far greater emphasis upon the sense of sin than is to be found anywhere in Hindu philosophy, but in the teachings of Rāmānuja all the other mysteries of Christian theology seem to find their counterpart. We may add in this connection that the greatest Christian mystics atained the height of realization by following bhakti yoga, or the path of love and devotion, the same method of attainment that was taught by Rāmānuja.

NIMBĀRKA

There are four chief schools of Vaiṣṇavism (Vedanta in its devotiona, aspect)'. Śrī, of which Rāmānuja is the principal exponent; Sanakal founded by Nimbārka in the eleventh century; Brahma, founded by Mādhwa in the twelfth century; and Rudra, founded by Vallabha in the sixteenth century. To these should be added the Bengal Vaiṣṇavist school, whose founder was Sri Caitanya, the prophet of Nadiā. We are here concerned with Nimbārka only.

Very little is known of Nimbārka's life, but he is held in reverence as one of the greatest saints of India, and the monastery he is said to have founded is still a celebrated place of pilgrimage.

Nimbārka's philosophy remains unique in that it never attacked other schools of philosophy. Nearly all of those who wrote commentaries on the Brahma Sūtras in the wake of Śamkara attempted to refute his doctrine of nondualism, but without much success. In my discussion of certain of these: philosophers I have avoided their endless disagreements with Śamkara and with one another in favour of points of agreement and harmony. Infinite is God and infinite are the ways to apprehend and comprehend him—and such was the opinion of Nimbārka also as he approached the fundamental problems of God, the universe, and the human soul.

According to Nimbārka's philosophy of Bhedābheda, or dualism in nondualism, Brahman has two aspects, the absolute and the relative, or, in other words, the impersonal and the personal. In his personal aspect, Brahman possesses attributes, and from him as person has issued the universe of name and form. But Brahman has not exhausted himself in the creation of the universe, for he is also transcendental and impersonal, without attributes, and as such he is greater than the universe.

The universe is, however, one with, as well as different from, Brahman, even as the wave is one with but different from the ocean, or a ray of the sun is one with but different from the sun. Such also is the relationship between individual souls and Brahman; they are at once one with him and different from him. It is not merely a distinction between part and the whole that we have in mind, for they are both a part of Brahman, and one with him.

Thus there exists almost an identity between the philosophy of Nimbārka and that of Bhāskara, but with the important difference that according to Bhāskara the individual soul is a part of Brahman only so long as it remains in ignorance—that in knowledge and emancipation it becomes one with him; whereas Nimbārka declares that the individual soul is a part of Brahman, and is also one with him, both in the state of ignorance and in that of knowledge and emancipation

In the state of ignorance—according to Nimbārka—the individual soul experiences the empirical world of phenomena, while in the State of liberation it attains the superconscious, transcendental vision of the noumenal. the absolute Brahman, at the same time that it realizes itself as living both in union with Brahman and separate from him

Nimbārka lays stress upon both knowlege and devotion as means of attaining freedom. Knowledge reveals the.' true nature of Brahman, and devotion culminates in all-absorbing love for him and in complete surrender of the finite will to the infinite will, although in both the love and the surrender the individual self remains.

For the followers of Nimbārka, Krṣṇa and his divine consort Rādhā embody both supreme will and supreme love.

MĀDHWA

Mādhwa, another celebrated commentator upon the Brahma Sūtras, founded the Vaiṣṇava sect known as Brāhma or Sad Vaiṣṇavism.

He was born in the year AD 1199, of brāhmin parents, in the village of Biligram, which is near the modern town of Udipi in the western part of what is now the Madras Presidency. He was sent to the village school but proved himself to be more an athlete than a scholar. Physically strong and swift, he defeated his playmates in running, in jumping, in swimming, and in other athletic feats. But he left school at an early age and continued his studies of the sacred scriptures at home alone. In later years, his learning was shown in his knowledge of these scriptures, especially the Purāṇas, and of the science of logic.

During the period of his study at home, he was seized with a burning desire for renunciation, and at the age of twenty-five he took monastic vows and devoted himself to the Vedānta philosophy under the guidance of a teacher who expounded its nondualistic aspect. Soon, however, Mādhwa began to differ from his guru in his interpretation of Vedanta. He wrote an independent commentary upon the Gītā, revealing scholarly ability and logical penetration. As a result of his studies, he soon developed a school of philosophy of his own.

In the course of, extensive travels in the peninsula of India, he encountered the exponents of many systems of thought, discussed ideas with them, and attempted with success to gain a hearing for his doctrines. He passed away at the agė of seventy-nine.

Mādhwa wrote commentaries upon the Upaniṣads, in addition to those on the Brahma Sūtras and the Gītā already mentioned, and also many treatises in which he expounded his own views and attacked others, particularly Śamkara's theory of māyā. In the following paragraphs are summed up main aspect, of his philosophy. The proposition on which Mādhwa bases his realism is that both the knower and the object of knowledge must be real, for otherwise no knowledge would be possible. Knowledge necessarily implies them. All knowledge is relative. Absolute knowledge, or the transcendental consciousness, in which all distinction between knowledge, knower, and known vanishes—as absolute knowledge is defined in Yoga and by Śamkara—cannot be admitted. 'No knowledge can be known', says Mādhwa, 'without the knower and the known.'

Pramāṇas. the means and instruments of knowledge, are perception, scriptural texts, and inference. Whatever is known through these is directly related to the object of knowledge, which has a reality of its own.

On this theory of knowledge, Mādhwa erects his theory of the objective reality of the world. The world is real because it is perceived as such. The objects presented to our perception may be either subject or not subject to change, and the fact that an object is fleeting and chagneable does not mean that it is not real.

Our experience is the experience of difference. We see things and things, people and people, and we perceive them to be different from one another. Different from all living beings and nonliving things is God, who exists in order that his law may be fulfilled in the universe, and in order that finite souls, less limited than nonliving things in power and intelligence, may find release from the sufferings and bondage of the world in loving him and surrendering themselves to him.

Mādhwa's whole philosophy is thus based upon the idea of difference or distinction. And distinctions are known to be five in number: (1) God is distinct from individual souls; (2) God is distinct from nonliving matter: (3) one individual soul is distinct from every other; (4) individual souls are distinct from matter; and (5) in matter, when it is divided. the parts are distinct from one another.

The universe is divided into two categories: Swatantra, independent being, and aswatantra, dependent beings. God is the only independent being. He is the one omnipotent, omniscient, and omnipresent being. How God, who is distinct from individual souls and nonliving things, can be omnipresent is explained by saying that he is not limited by time and space and that the dependent beings 'do not form a resisting medium to his presence'.

(1) Matter is distinct from God and human souls and in itself is only a dependent being. (2) God is the ruler of the universe, but the universe is real and eternally existent.

Each soul is distinct from every other, and all souls are distinct from God though they have dependent existence in him. By nature souls are intelligent. Each soul when born into this world and invested with body and senses is in a state of bondage, but by continued struggle through many lives release from this bondage may be obtained.

Moreover, although souls are distinct from one another, they fall into classes. Of these there are three, differing in their essential nature as well as in their destiny. One class, who are moral and devoted to God alone, will attain salvation and enjoy the eternal felicity of heaven—an abode called Vaikuṇṭha. The second class will never attain salvation but will remain subject to rebirth, experiencing in life after life both happiness and misery. The third class, who revile Viṣṇu and his devotees, will never attain salvation but will be subject to damnation.

This belief of Mādhwa, that only a few attain salvation while the rest cannot, and some even suffer damnation, is contrary to the teachings of all other Indian religious schools. Mādhwa may possibly have been influenced by certain Christian missionaries who during his time may have penetrated into India.

Only such souls as are devoted to Viṣṇu will attain salvation—that is, go to Vaikuṇṭha and enjoy the beloved company of God. But even in Vaikuṇṭha there are gradations of souls and therefore differences between them.

ŚRĪ CAITANYA

In Śrī Caitanya is to be found the culmination and fulfilment of the philosophy and the religion of love. Through him Vaiṣṇavism, which is the philosophical expression of the ideal of love for God, ushered in a new era in the higher life of Bengal. His ideas have found exquisite expression in a richly emotional collection of hymns which have been a peculiar contribution of Bengal to Indian culture. Every Bengal has in his blood liberal admixture of Śrī Caitanya's religion or love.

Even more than his philosophy it is as Śrī Caitanya's pure and gentle character—his loving-kindness and his ecstatic love of God—that has ruled, and still rules, the hearts of the people of Bengal. He knew no distinction of caste or creed in his immense love of God and man; all men whether they were sinners or saints, were to him but creatures of God and his heart overflowed with sympathy for the lowly, the suffering, and the destitute. So his very name excites genuine spiritual emotions in the hearts of those who know about him. His followers see in him Kṛṣṇa reborn in the flesh.

Śrī Caitanva was born in the year 1485 at Navadwip, at that time a large city in Bengal and the seat of Sanskrit learning, particularlv of grammar and logic. His parents lost their first eight children, all of them daughters, in infancy, and the ninth, a boy named Viswarūpa, at an early age entered a monastery in southern India. Śrī Caitanya was the youngest son. He was given the name of Viśwambhar and was nicknamed Nimai. He was also called Gour or Gourānga (fair complexioned) because of the exquisite beauty of his person. The name Śrī Kṛṣṇa Caitanya he received when he was admitted to the order of monks.

As a small baby he was afflicted with prolonged fits of weeping, the only remedy for wnich his mother found to be the chanting of the name of Hari (God). As a boy, he was full of mischief and took pleasure in teasing others and playing pranks. He lost his father when he was eleven years old. It was then that he seriously applied himself to studies in literature and grammar and other branches of knowledge. His master was Vāsudeva, the well-known teacher of Sanskrit and the famous founder, in conjunction with his brilliant pupil Raghunāth, of the Neo-logic (Nabya-Nyāya) of the Bengal school.

An interesting story is told of the relation between Raghunath and the young Caitanya. The former, a fellow-student, being at work upon his famous treatise on logic, learned that Caitanya was writing a book of the same character. He asked his friend to read a few pages to him, and when he heard them he grew dispirited. 'I cherished a hope', he said in answer to a question from Caitanya, 'of leaving a name behind me, but I realize that mv work will not be read if yours is given to the public.' To this Caitanya replied: 'This trivial matter must not disturb you. I will see that your w ork is recognized.' Thereupon Caitanya threw his own manuscript into the Ganges.

Though he had not yet completed his education, at sixteen he opened a school of his own at Navadwīp, and in that city he gained fame as one of the greatest teachers of grammar and logic of his time. Hundreds of students flocked to him. While he was teaching at Navadwīp, he wrote a book on Sanskrit grammar which was widely used.

At the age of twenty one or twenty two he embanced upon a pilgrimage to Gaya, the site of a famous temple dedicated to Viṣṇu. It was at Gaya that Buddha, centuries before, sat under the Bodhi tree, and here the young Śrī Caitanva, then known as Nimāi Pundit, while worshipping at the feet of visnu received a sudden illumination the transformed his being. Tears rolled down his cheeks, and he lost himself in ecstasy. Amongst the pilgrims was a monk, Iswar Purī sannyasin of the order of Sarhkara, who had met Caitanya before a and knew him as a great scholar. Now, as he witnessed his ecstatic condition, he recognized in, him a great devotee. Caitanya asked foe blessing from Iswar Puri, who then initiated him into the worshipr of Krsna.

Nimāi returned to Navadwīp a changed man. The unrivalled scholastic debater, the grammarian, the logician, now disappeared. Instead, there stood before men a serene, exalted person, continually chanting Krṣṇa, Krṣṇa'. His former students gathered about him as had been their custom, but he could no longer teach them. 'Brothers,' he cried, 'I can no longer give you lessons. Whenever I attempt to explain anything to you, I see before me the little boy Krṣṇa, playing upon his flute. You had better seek some other teacher.' Thereupon he sang a kirtan (chant), which has come down to this day and is sung by the Vaiṣṇavas of Bengal.[52]

Now there gathered round the master devotees who found joy in the contemplation of God. So did Śrī Caitanya become a great spiritual force in the city of Navadwīp, and the lives of many unbelievers were transformed by the touch of this God-intoxicated man. Some of his disciples in later years played an important part in the religious life of Bengal by preaching his message of love and giving peace and consolation to many a hungry soul.

At the age of twenty-five, but two years after his conversion at Gāyā, Śrī Caitanya was seized by a burning desire to forsake the world. Of his renunciation Swami Durga-Chaitanya Bharati, a follower of Śrī Caitanya, and his biographer, writes as follows:

'The story of Gouranga's renunciation has few parallels in history. The heart-rending story of his renunciation, when he left his aged mother, loving young wife, and all Navadwīp bewailing his separation from them, soon spread in all directions and moved the people a way that nothing else had done before in Bengal. This story has isince been carried to the furthest corners of the country through poetry, songs, ballads, dramas, and discourses, and yet even after these four hundred and forty-four years it has not lost in the least in its original pathos. There is no man or woman, young or old, who even to this day hearing of Gouranga's renunciation is not moved to tears.'

He took monastic vows at the hands of Keśava Bhārati. To him he related how in a dream he had received a mahāvākya—the sacred words Tat Tvam asi [53] That Thou art which were revealed to the seers of the Upaniṣads, and which the great saint and philosopher Śamkara accepted as containing the very essence of ultimate truth. Kesava Bharāti, in initiating Gouranga into the mysteries of the life of a monk, also initiated him into this same mahāvākya.

Whatever his disciples may have set forth in their systems of thought, Śrī Caitanya discovered an essential harmony between love and knowledge. His biographers tell us that he possessed a dual personality. On the one hand, while. he as in samādhi, having lost consciousness of the outer world and all sense of me and mine, he taught men that he was one with God; on the other, upon his return to normal consciousness, he remained a lover of God, and he could not bear the thought that he was one with him.

In the normal state of consciousness he desired 'to taste the sweetness of sugar, not to become sugar'. Śrī Rāmakrṣṇa has explained this attitude of the saint by remarking that like an elephant he had two sets of teeth, one with which to chew his food, the other with which to defend himself against attack. Śrī Caitanya moved in two states of consciousness. While in the normal state, he was a dualist: he was the lover of God, and God was the Beloved. In samādhi, however, he realized the truth of nondualism; the lover and the Beloved became one. To the outside world and for the masses of men, he preached the ideal of love and the philosophy of dualism; but to the chosen few he preached the highest truth, which he dared not reveal to all men since not all men are prepared to receive it—the supreme truth of nondualism. This aspect of his practice is corroborated in his famous conversation with Rāmānanda Roy, which we shall describe later.

Śrī Rāmakrṣṇa, who fully appreciated the spiritual greatness of Śrī Caitanya, remarked:

'Śrī Caitanya used to experience three moods. In the inmost mood he would be absorbed in samādhi, unconscious of the outer world. In the semi-conscious mood he would dance in ecstasy but could not talk. In the conscious mood he would sing the glories of God.[54]

It is interesting to note in this connection that Śrī Caitanya, though he did not accept Śamkara's doctrine of māyā, nowhere denounced Śamkara, as did most of the philosophers of the doctrine of love who preceded him. On the contrary, he very plainly stated, as is recorded by his disciples, that Śamkara wrote his commentary, and expounded his philosophy by direct command of God.[55]

But to return to the story of Caitanya.

After his initiation into the monastic order he set out for Puri, the well-known place by pilgrimage. There he resided for many years, with occasional departures for preaching or teaching. At one time he toured southern India, worshipping in many of the temples, but without prejudice against forms or aspects of the one Godhead other than those which they represented. He also visited Brindaban, the holy seat of the Vaiṣṇavas, where Kṛṣṇa had engaged in his divine play with the shepherds and shepherdesses. The present Brindaban owes much to Śrī Caitanya and his disciples for rescuing the holy place from oblivion.

During most of the last twelve years of his life, Caitanya lived in samādhi and in the state midway between samādhi and normal consciousness. In these states he was like mad in his love of Kṛṣṇa, sometimes enjoying the sweetness of union with him, and suffering the pangs of separation from him. The pangs, too, were sweet.

Śrī Caitanya's last days were spent in Puri. Here his overmastering, consuming love for God transformed the lives of thousands. In the Jagannath Temple of Puri his influence continues to be felt.

The passing of Śrī Caitanya is shrouded in mystery, his biographers giving no certain account of it. Most of them, however, do state that at the age of forty-eight he entered a temple and came out no more, simply disappearing. So there exists the belief that in the image of God in the temple Caitanya lives for eternity

Śrī Caitanya's Philosophy of Love

Śrī Caitanya gave little care or attention to a theoretical consideration of the problems of God, the human soul, and the universe. Above all things he was a God-intoxicated man. His spiritual experiences transcended the realm of time, space, and causation; his mind plunged into the domain where God is not an abstraction, but a reality in which dwell all joy all sweetness, all love—a reality situated deep in the loving hearts of his devotees.

God, it is said, is Sat-chid-ānanda—Existence, Knowledge, and Bliss—he is absolute, indefinable, inexpressible. He is the repository of infinite blessed attributes, the one Existence from whom the universe has issued forth, in whom the universe at last dissolves—the omnipresent, the omniscient, the omnipotent.

Such has been the account men have given of God, but to Śrī Caitanya these aspects of the Godhead meant little. For him God was Kṛṣṇa, the God of love—enchantingly beautiful, eternally youthful; and man was the eternal playmate, the eternal companion. For him, however, this Kṛṣṇa was not the Kṛṣṇa of history, who uttered the mighty spiritual discourses of the Gītā, the philosopher and the harmonizer and the avatar. For him he was the Kṛṣṇa of Brindaban, the great lover and the embodiment of love, divested of all the powers of the Godhead, the companion of shepherds and shepherdesses, playing upon his flute and drawing souls unto him by his compelling love; he is the Soul of souls eternally dwelling in Brindaban—not a land one can point to on a map but the heart of man, the Brindaban that is beyond time and space.

Love divine, which is Kṛṣṇa, is not to be acquired by man, for it is already existent in the soul, though covered by ignorance, by attachment to the world of the senses. When the clouds of ignorance have been swept away, this love, forever existing, becomes manifest. Then does man realize himself.

We may remind the reader in this connection of the philosophy of Śamkara. Śamkara declared that infinite knowledge is identical with the Self, but that this knowledge is covered over by ignorance. What Śamkara called infinite knowledge Śrī Caitanya called infinite love. In reality, there is no difference between the two.

To make manifest this infinite love—according to Śrī Caitanya—one must practise sadhan-bhakti, or disciplinary devotion, by chanting the name of God, hearing and singing his praises, meditating upon the divine play and deeds of Kṛṣṇa, and engaging in the rites and ceremonies of worship. He laid special stress on japa—repeating the name of God to the count of beads. Patañjali, also, the father of Yoga philosophy, approved the practice of japa as one of the methods of spiritual attainment, for the name of God and God, he said, are inseparable. In chanting God's name one necessarily meditates upon his presence.

Śrī Caitanya also emphasized the practice of ethical virtues, particularly humility and forbearance.

By the conduct recommended, one causes the divine love to be made manifest in the heart. Of this manifestation there are five stages, corresponding to various expressions of love on the plane of human life.

First there is śanta, the peaceful stage, in which, as he finds joy in the thought of God, the aspirant attains poise and tranquillity. He feels God near him, but still no definite relationship between the two has been established.

Then comes dāsya, the servant stage, in which the aspirant feels that God is the master, or that he is the father, the protector.

The third is sakhya, the stage of friendship. God is now realized as friend and playmate. He is felt to be nearer as the sense of awe vanishes and the God of power and grandeur is forgotten. He is now only the God of love—a cherished friend.

The fourth is vātsalya, the child stage. Now, Kṛṣṇa, God of love, is a child, and the devotee must take care of him. This stage we think of as higher than the preceding stages because in our human relation-ships a father or mother has a deeper affection for a child than a child has for its parents.

The fifth and last stage is madhura, the sweetest of relationships, the relationship between the lover and the beloved. The strongest of human ties, that between man and wife, finds its ultimate realization in the new tie between man and God, in which God is the beloved. and in which all the elements of love—admiration, service, comrade ship, communion—are presents.[56] The highest expression of this type of love is to be found in the shepherdesses of Brindaban, above all in Rādhā. When this kind of love possesses the heart, mystic union is attained.

The following famous conversation between Śrī Caitanya and Rāmānanda, one of his principal disciples, epitomizes the philosophy of the master as this is recorded by his biographers, and which I give here in my own words.

Śrī Caitanya what is the goal of life?
Disciple. A man must follow the rules and injunctions prescribed in the scriptures.
Śrī Caitanya. This is the external part of religion—only a means, not the goal Try *again*
Disciple. Surrendering the fruits of action to Kṛṣṇa.
Śrī Caitanya. This, too, is external. Try again.
Disciple . Realizing the devotion that arises from self-surrender. *Śrī Caitanya.* This, too, is external. Try again.

Disciple. Realizing demotion with knowledge.

Śrī Caitanya. This, too, is external. Try again. *Disciple.* Realizing pure devotion, which knows no reason.

Śrī Caitanya. That is good Go further. *Disciple.* Realizing lov ing devotion, which is the best goal.

Śrī Caitanya. That is good Go further. *Disciple.* Acquiring the spirit of service to Krṣṇa,

Śrī Caitanya. That is good. Go further. *Disciple.* To love Krṣṇa as a friend.

Śrī Caitanya. That is very good. Go further.

Disciple. To love Krṣṇa as a child.

Śrī Caitanya. That is also good. Go further.

Disciple. To love Krṣṇa as the beloved bridegroom.

Śrī Caitanya This is no doubt the ultimate goal. But tell me if there is any attainment further than this.

Disiple. My understanding does not reach beyond this. But there is another stage called Prem-Vilās-Vivarta.

The biographers of Sri Caitanya record that at this point Sri Caitanya stopped Rāmānanda from speaking, indicating thereby that the highest truth, the highest secret, must not be divulged. Prem-Vilās-Vivarta is the truth of mystic union, wherein there is no longer a distinction between the lover and the beloved. In this is realized the truth of nondualism Tat Tvam asi—Thou art That.

A Prayer.[57]

by

Śrī Caitanya

Chant the name of the Lord and His glory unceasingly
That the mirror of the heart may be wiped clean
And quenched that mighty forest fire,
Oh Name, stream down in moonlight on the lotus-heart,
Opening its cup to knowledge of Thyself.
On self, drown deep in the waves of His bliss,
Chanting His Name continually,
Tasting His nectar at every step,
Bathing in His Name, that bath for weary souls.

Various are Thy Names, Oh Lord,
In each and every Name Thy power resides.
No times are set, no rites are needful, for chanting of Thy Name
So vast is Thy mercy.
How huge, then, is my wrethedness
Who find, in this empty life and heart,
No devotion to Thy Name!

Oh, my mind,
Be humbler than a blade of grass,
Be patient and forbearing like the tree,
Take no honour to thyself,
Give honour to all.
Chant unceasingly theName of the Lord

Oh Lord and Soul of the Universe,
Mine is no prayer for wealth or retinue,
The playthings of lust or the toys of fame;
As many times as I may be reborn Grant me,

Oh Lord, a steadfast love for Thee.

A drowning man in this world's fearful ocean
Is Thy servant. Oh Sweet One.
In Thy mercy
Consider him as dust beneath Thy feet.

Ah, how I long for the day
When, in chanting Thy Name, the tears will spill down
From my eyes, and my throat wwill refuse to utter

Its prayers, choking and stammering with ecstasy,
When all the hairs of my body will stand erect with joy!

Ah, how I long for the day
When an instant's separation from Thee, Oh Govinda,[58]
Will be as a thousand years,
When my heart burns away with its desire
And the world, without Thee, is a heartless void

Prostrate at The feet let me be, in unwavering devotion
Neither imploring the embrace of Thine arms
Nor bewailing the withdrawal of Thy Presence
Though it tears my soul asunder,
Oh Thou, who stealest the hearts of Thy devotees,
Do with me when Thou wilt—
For Thou art my heart's Beloved, Thou and Thou alone.

ŚRĪ RAMAKṚŚṆA

Śrī Rāmakrṣṇa has appeared frequently in the preceding chapters, at points where he has been invoked to light up some obscure doctrine or to reconcile some apparently conflicting views. He now becomes, himself, the subject of a chapter.

He was born in 1836 in Kāmārpukur, a small village in West Bengal, to a brāhmin family. His parents were of humble means, but extremely pious and devout. When Śrī Rāmakrṣṇa was five years old, he was sent to the village primary school. Here he learned to read and write, but showed great. aversion to arithmetic. His speech was charming, and he was endowed with so wonderful a memory that if he but once heard a song or a play he could perfectly reproduce its text. He loved acting. Instead of attending school and minding his studies, he would run away with some of his school fellows to a mango-grove on the outskirts of the village, and there, with boyish exuberance, perform the pastoral drama of Śrī Krṣṇa's life.

When he was six or seven years old, he had a striking experience—one which he often related to his disciples in later years. 'I was walking alone in a paddy field,' he would say, 'carrying a small basket of puffed rice. Looking at the sky overhead while eating the rice, I saw that it was covered with rain clouds. Suddenly I noticed snow-white wild cranes flying in a row against that dark background. I was overwhelmed by the beautiful sight. An ecstatic feeling arose in my heart, and I lost all outward consciousness. I do not know how long I remained in that state. When I regained consciousness I was in my home, brought there by some friendly people.[59]

At the age of nine Śrī Rāmakrṣṇa was invested, according to brāhmin custom, with the sacred thread, and initiated into the Gāyatrī mantra, a Vedic prayer. He was thenceforward allowed to do the worship of the household deity, Rāma. He manifested religious moods. He would often remain for a long time absorbed in God, losing all outward consciousness. He used to go alone into the woods, find a solitary place, and there meditate for hours under the shade of a tree.

Many wandering monks would halt and rest at Kāmārpukur on their way to Puri, the well-known place of pilgrimage. A rich man of the village had built a guest house for the pilgrims and had also made it a practice to provide them with food. As a young boy, Śrī Rāmakrṣṇa was often in their company and would do small services for them, and they loved him.

During his early teens, the ideal of a monastic life attracted Śrī .Rāmakrṣṇa, but he soon gave up the idea, thinking to himself, 'To renounce the world just for one's own liberation is selfishness. I must do something that will be of benefit to all mankind.[60]

Within a short time after his investiture with the sacred thread, 'there occurred an incident which showed his keen spiritual understanding. An important gathering of pundits took place at the house of a rich man of the village on the occasion of a memorial service. At this meeting there arose a controversy regarding a complicated philosophical question, and the scholars could not arrive at any correct solution, Śrī Rāmakrṣṇa and other young boys were present to see the fun. While his friends were enjoying themselves mimicking the gestures of the pundits, Śrī Rāmakrṣṇa was seated silently by an f elderly scholar and was listening intently to the discussion. Suddenly he touched the pundit and whispered in his ear. The elderly man listened attentively to Śrī Rāmakrṣṇa's words, and seeing immediately that the boy had given a cogent solution, he stood up with him on his shoulder and repeated it to the company. All the pundits praised young Rāmakrsna and blessed him with all their heart. And the villagers marelled at his understanding.[61]

When he was seven years old, Śrī Rāmakrṣṇa's father died. Ramkumar, his eldest brother, who was a great Sanskrit scholar, went to Calcutta and opened a Sanskrit school to earn his living and; support the family. When, years later, he learned that young Ramakrṣṇa was neglecting his studies in the village, he sent for him, intending to have him study in his Sanskrit school. It is a shame, Ramkumār thought, that a brāhmin boy of his family should remain ignorant. So Ramakrṣṇa, now seventeen, went to Calcutta. But when Ramkumār asked him to attend his school, the young boy replied with great firmness, 'Brother, I do not wish to waste my life on a mere bread-winning education. want to acquire that knowledge which would awaken in me consciousness of the eternal Reality and thus make my life blessed forever.' He remained adamant*on* the Subject, and his brother was at a loss what to do with him.[62]

An unexpected event solved the problem. An enormously wealthy woman named Rānī Rāsamaṇi built a temple on the bank of the Ganges at Dakṣiṇeśwar, five miles north of Calcutta. It was dedicated to the Mother of the Universe. Ramkumar was asked to be the priest of this temple, and he took his young brother to help him. Śrī Ramakrṣṇa liked the calm, serene atmosphere of the place, and so it came about that here at Dakṣiṇeśwar, by the sacred river, he spent the rest of his life.

Rāmkumār died after serving only a year as temple priest. Rāmakrṣṇa was now appointed to his brother's place. He performed the daily duties of a priest, but his inquiring mind longed for something more, and he questioned within himself: 'What is all this for? Is the Divine Mother real? Does she listen to my prayers, or is this mere imagination conjured up by human brains?' He began to yearn increasingly for the direct realization of God the Mother. And soon life became unbearable without her. He would rub his face in the ground like one gripped by pain and cry: 'Oh, Mother, another day is gone and still I have not seen you!' Finally, one day, she revealed herself. Śrī Rāmakṛṣṇa later described his first vision of the Divine Mother to his disciples. To quote his words:

'House, walls, doors, the temple—all disappeared into nothingness. Then I saw an ocean of light, limitless, living, conscious, blissful. From all sides waves of light, with a roaring sound, rushed towards me and engulfed and drowned me, and I lost all awareness of outward things.'

When Śrī Rāmakṛṣṇa regained consciousness, he was uttering the words 'Mother, Mother'.'[63]

To his disciples he used to say:

'When true yearning for God comes, then follows the sight of him, then rises the sun of knowledge in the heart. Yearn for him, and love him intensely! .. .The mother loves her child, the chaste wife loves her husband, the miser loves his wealth; let your love for God be as intense as these three loves combined—then shall you see him.[64]

After the first vision of the Mother of the Universe, Śrī Rāmakṛṣṇa longed to see her continuously. A sort of divine madness seized him. And then, to use his own words he began to see the Mother 'peeping from every nook and corner'. After this he could no longer perform the ritualistic worship. Worldly people thought he had lost his sanity. One day, in the midst of the food offering to the Deity, he gave the offering to a cat which had walked into the temple, recognizing the presence of the Divine Mother in the cat. Naturally in the eyes of the world this was either madness or sacrilege.

Śrī Rāmakṛṣṇa's behaviour became stranger and stranger; but it must be noted that whenever persons of genuine spirituality met him they considered him to have attained a blessed state—as we shall see later.

At last rumours of his strange conduct reached the ears of his mother at Kāmārpukur, and she became anxious to see him. So he went to his village to visit her. He was now twenty-three years old. In Kāmārpukur he continued to live in a God-intoxicated state, Indifferent as ever to worldly concerns. Finally his mother and brother thought marriage would be just the thing by which to interest him in worldly' matters. Accordingly they began to look about for a suitable bride. Śrī Rāmakṛṣṇa did not object, and the search was enthusiastically continued, but with no success. In the end, finding his mother and brother depressed by their failure, Śrī Rāmakṛṣṇa said to them in a semiconscious state: 'It is useless to try here and then do lo javrambati a village three miles from Kāmārpukur and there God to ill find the bride, the daughter of Rāmacandra Mukhopadhyaya providentially reserved tor me.' The girl was found, but she wasonly fiveyears old. Her parents were agreeable to the marriage, but Chandra Devi, mother of Śrī R.amakrsna, was somewhat hesitant because of her tender age. However, considering the fact that the girl was the one selected by her son, she assented. So without delay Śrī Rāmakrṣṇa was married to Sāradā Devī. After the marriage ceremony was over—was more a sort of betrothal—Sāradā Devī as sent back to her parents' home. Śrī Rāmakṛṣṇa continued to stay at Kāmārpukur for about a year and a half.

When Śrī Ramakṛṣṇ returned to the temple garden at Dakṣiṇeśwar, he forgot his marriage and its responsibilities and plunged deeper and deeper into spiritual practices.

In 1861, about six months after his return from Kāmārpukur, Śrī Rāmakṛṣṇa one morning noticed a sannyasini (nun)) with long dishevelled hair alighting from a country boat and entering the courtyard of the temple. He sent for her. As soon as the sannvasini met Śrī Rāmakṛṣṇa. she burst into tears of joy and said, 'My son, you are here! I have been searching for you so long, and now I have found you at last.

'How could you know about me. Mother'? asked Śrī Rāmakṛṣṇa.

She replied, 'Through the grace of the Divine Mother I came to know that I was to meet three of you. Two I have already met, and today I have found you."[65]

This nun's name was Yogeswari, but she was known as the Brāhmanī. She was a woman of high spiritual attainments and was well versed in Vaiṣṇava and Tāntric literatirre. Śrī Rāmakṛṣṇa sat beside her like a little boy sitting by his mother, and told her of his spiritual struggles, visions, and attainments. He further mentioned to her that people thought he was mad. Full of motherly tenderness, she said, 'Who calls you mad, my son. This is divine madness. Your state is what is known as mahābhāva. Śrī Rādhā experienced it, and so did Śrī Caitanya. I shall show you in the scriptures that wiwever has earnestly yearned for God has experienced this state.[66]

So far, whatever spiritual advances Śrī Rāmakṛṣṇa had made were the result of his own independent struggles. Now he sought out the Mother of the Universe, and talked with her, and she commanded him to undergo spiritual disciplines under the direction of the Brāhmanī. Śrī Rāmakrṣṇa accepted her as his first guru. She also, as we have seen, had received the mandate from the Divine Mother to teach this young man.

The Brāhmaṇī, as already stated, was learned in Hindu religious literature. She began at once to teach Śrī Rāmakṛṣṇa the spiritual disciplines recommended in the Tantras. But of this we may hear from Śrī Rāmakṛṣṇa himself:

"After performing the worship of the Divine Mother, I used to meditate according to the Brāhmaṇī's directions. As soon as I" began to tell my beads, I would be overwhelmed with ecstatic fervour and enter into samādhi. I cannot describe the wonderful spiritual visions I used to have. They followed one another in quick succession. The Brāhmanī made me undergo all the sixty-four kinds of spiritual disciplines mentioned in the principal Tantras. Most of these were difficult practices, but the infinite grace of the Mother carried me through them with ease".[67]

After attaining the goal aimed at in the Tantric spiritual disciplines, Śrī Rāmakrṣṇa took to the practices of Vaiṣṇavism. The Vaiṣṇavas follow the path of devotion, which advocates worshipping God as a Personal Being in his aspect of Viṣṇu. It is Visnu who from time to time appears on earth in human form—an avatar. He once lived as Rama, the hero of the Rāmāyaṇa, and again as Krsna, the avatar of the Bhagavad-Gītā and the Bhagavata Purana. In following the path of devotion, the worshipper enters into a relation to God in his form of Rāma or Krṣṇa. There are five such relations, corresponding to those on the human plane (we have met them before): Sānta, the peaceful attitude, with only an indefinite relation; dasya, the relation of servant to master or of child to parent; sakhya, the relation of friend to friend; vātsalya, the relation of parent to child; and madhura, the sweet relationship- of lover to the beloved. Vaiṣṇavism is the philosophy propounded and lived by such saints and seers as Rāmānuja, Vallabha, Mādhwa and Śrī Caitanya.

Śrī Rāmakrṣṇa entered into the Vaiṣṇava path first by worshipping Rāma as his own child, the relation of vātsalya, for there had come to him a mystic saint, Jaṭādhāri, who had attained the highest spiritual state as a devotee of Rāma, and who initiated him into his own form of worship. Afterwards Śrī Rāmakrṣṇa took up various relations in his devotion to Krṣṇa. Through each of these he achieved union with God.

A few months later Totā Purī came to the temple garden at Dakṣiṇeśwar. Totā Puri was a Vedāntic monk of the order of Śamkara, and an illumined soul, a knower of Brahman. As soon as he met Śrī Rāmakrṣṇa, he recognized in him a highly advanced spirit. He asked him, 'Should you like to learn Vedānta from me?'

Śrī Rāmakrṣṇa answered, 'I don't know, but I shall ask Mother.'

'All right, go and ask Mother. I shall not be here long!' Śrī Rāmakrṣṇa went to the temple and received a command from the Divine Mother—'Yes, go and learn of him. It is for this purpose that he has come here.' In a state of semiconsciousness, and with a beaming countenance, Śrī Rāmakrṣṇa returned to Totā Purī and said that he had received the Mother's permission.[68]

Totā Purī now acquainted him with the Upaniṣadic teaching of the identity of the Ātman with Brahman, and initiated him into the monastic life.

After the initiation [says Śrī Rāmakrṣṇa] "the naked one"[69] asked me to withdraw mv mind from all objects and to become absorbed in contemplation of the Ātman. But as soon as, I withdrew my mind from the external world, the familiar form of the blissful Mother, radiant and of the essence of pure consciousness, appeared before me as a living reality and I could not pass beyond her. In despair I said to the naked one, "It is hopeless. I cannot raise my mind to the unconditioned state and reach the Ātman." He grew excited and sharply said, "what! You say you can't do it! No, you must!" So saying he looked about him, and finding a piece of broken glass picked it up. Pressing its point between my eyebrows, he said, "Concentrate the mind on this point." Then with great determination I began to meditate as directed, and when this time also the blessed form of the Mother appeared before me, I used my discrimination as a sword and severed her form in two. Then my mind soared immediately beyond all duality and entered into nirvikalpa, the nondual, unitary consciousness.[70]

Totā Purī sat for a long time silently watching his disciple. Then he left the room, locking the door behind him. Three days passed, and still he heard no sound. When Totā Puri finally opened the door, he found Śrī Rāmakrṣṇa seated in the same position in which he had left him. Totā Puri watched him, and wondered, 'Is it really true that this man has attained in the course of a single day what took me forty years of strenuous practice to achieved. He examined Śrī Rāmakrṣṇa closely and in joyous bewilderment exclaimed, 'Great God! It is nothing short of a miracle!' It was the nirvikalpa samādhi—the culmination of nondual Vedāntic practice. Totā Purī now took steps to bring his disciple's mind down to the normal plane. Slowly Śrī Rāmakrṣṇa regained concioir ness of the outer world, and seeing his guru before him the prostrated. And Totā Purī gave his disciple a warm embrace.[71]

After Totā Purī had left Dakṣiṇeśwar, Śrī Rāmakrṣṇa resolved to remain immersed in nirvikalpa samādhi, and he passed six months in this state without any consciousness of body or of external surroundings. In later years he referred to this period of his life as follows:

'For six months I remained continuously in the bliss of union with Brahman. I was not conscious of day or night. It would have been impossible for the body to survive except that a monk who was present at the time realized my state of mind and regularly brought me food; and whenever he found me a little conscious, he would press it into my mouth. Only a little of it reached my stomach. Six months passed in this way. ... At last I received the Mother's Command: "Remain in bhāvamukha for the good of mankind."'[72]

Henceforward, in general, Śrī Rāmakrṣṇa lived in bhavamukha, a state between samādhi and normal consciousness. It is very difficult to understand exactly what this state is. In later years, however, the Master described it. He said it was as if on the ocean of Brahman, that infinite ocean of existence, knowledge, and bliss, a stick was floating, dividing the ocean into two parts. On one side is God, and on the other side his devotee—in this case Śrī Rāmakrṣṇa. The stick which divides the ocean is the ripe ego'[73] never forgetful that it is a child of God. The ripe ego is not harmful. It is like a sword that has touched the philosopher's stone and turned into gold.

In later years while Śrī Rāmakrṣṇa would be teaching the word of God he often went into samādhi. This was a daily occurrence.

Now to resume our story. The practice of spiritual disciplines, however, did not stop with the Vedāntic experience in Śrī Rāmakrṣṇa's case. He had travelled the paths of devotion, yoga, and knowledge, and he had realized the truths taught in Tāntrikism, Vaiṣṇavism, and Vedānta. But his heart longed to enjoy the divine life of those outside the pale of Hinduism.

Buddha he regarded as, one of the incarnations of God. He remarked about him: 'People think Buddha was an atheist, but he was not. Only he could not express in words what he had experienced. When one's buddhi [intellect] merges in the absolute, pure consciousness, one attains the knowledge of Brahman, one realizes one's true nature, and that is to become Buddha—enlightened'.[74] So, according to Śrī Rāmakrṣṇa, Buddha was a Vedāntist—only misunderstood.

Islam and Christianity, however, belonged in a different category. These now attracted Śrī Rāmakrṣṇa. A Sufi mystic living at Daksineswar initiated him into the Islam faith. In Śrī Rāmakrṣṇa's own words:

'I began to repeat the holy name of Allah, and would recite the Namaz regularly. After three days I realized the goal of that form of devotion'.[75]

First, Śrī Rāmakrṣṇa had a vision of a radiant person with a long beard and a solemn countenance. Then he experienced Brahman with attributes, which finally merged into the Impersonal Existence, the attributeless Brahman.[76]

It was some years later that Śrī Rāmakrṣṇa wanted to explore Christianity. One devotee used to explain the Bible to him whenever he came to Dakṣiṇeśwar Thus Śrī Rāmakrṣṇa became drawn to Christ and Christianity Then one day while he was seated in the drawing-room Jadu Mallick's garden house, he saw a picture of the Madonna and Child. He fell into a deeply meditative mood, and the picture suddenly became living and effulgent. A deep love for Christ filled Śrī Rāmakrṣṇa's heart, and there opened before him a vision of a Christian church with devotees burning incense and lighting candles before Jesus. For three days Śrī Rāmakrṣṇa was under the spell of this experience, and on the fourth day, while he was pacing near the Pañcavati grove at Dakṣiṇeśwar, he saw an extraordinary-looking person of sence countenance approaching with his gaze intently fixed on him. From the inmost recesses of Śrī Rāmakrṣṇa's heart came the realization: 'This is Jesus, who poured out his heart's blood for the redemption of mankind. He is none other than the ṛṣi Christ, the embodiment of love.' The Son of Man then embraced Śrī Rāmakrṣṇa and became merged in him. At this the Master went into samādhi. Thus was Śrī Rāmakrṣṇa convinced that Jesus'was an incarnation of God.

Once Śrī Rāmakrṣṇa was asked why he had followed so many paths; was not one path enough by which to reach the supreme goal? His answer was: 'The Mother is infinite—infinite are her moods and aspects. I longed to realize her in all of them. And she revealed to me the truth of many religions.' Thus, though he did not practise varied spiritual disciplines with the specific purpose of bringing harmony among the many faiths, his life demonstrated that harmony. In this connection let us hear some of Śrī Rāmakrṣṇa's teachings on the essential identity of the great religions:

'So many religions, so many paths to reach the same goal[77] have practised Hinduism, Islam, Christianity, and in Hinduism again, the ways of the different sects. I have found that it is the same God towards whem all are directing their steps, though along different paths.[78]

'The tank has several ghāts.At one Hindus draw water and call it jal; at another Mohammedans draw water and call it pāni; at a third Christians draw the same liquid and call it water. The substance is one though the names differ, and everyone is seeking the same thing. Every religion of the world is one such ghāt. Go with a sincere and earnest heart by any of these ghāts and you will reach the water of eternal bliss. But do not say that your religion is better than that of another.[79]

To complete the story of Śrī Rāmakrṣṇa's life, we must now turn our attention to his relationship with his wife. We have already mentioned how when he was twenty-three years old he married Sāradā Devī, then a five-year old girl. Afterwards, for a time, he apparently forgot all about his marriage. But when he was about to take monastic vows, and Totā Pun was ready to initiate him into sannyas, Śrī Rāmakrṣṇa told him of his marriage[80] Totā Puri said merely, 'What does it matter? Have your wife near you. That will be the real test of your vows and the real proof that you have become a knower of Brahman.'

All these years Sāradā Devī had been living with her parents. From her earlier years she had shown an intensely spiritual temperament. Like her husband she had divine visions. When she grew to be a young woman she longed to be near Śrī Rāmakrṣṇa. But there was no call from him. Then during the period of the Master's practice of Islam, people again began to say that he had lost his mind. How could it be that a Hindu priest should worship Allah! The rumour spread and reached the ears of Sāradā Devī—now eighteen years old—and though she did not believe it, she felt it her duty to be by the side of her husband. Accordingly she expressed her wish to her father, who took her to Dakṣiṇeśwar. Śrī Rāmakrṣṇa welcomed his wife and made arrangements for her to stay near him.But he askedher, 'Tell me, have you come to drag me down toworldly ways?' Her prompt reply was, 'Oh no. I have come to help you in your chosen path.' Śrī Rāmakrṣṇa initiated her into the mysteries of spiritual life and supervisedher progess. She became his first disciple.

Within six months of his wife's arrival, on an auspicious night, Śrī Rāmakrṣṇa made special preparations for worshipping the Divine worship were read. There was, however, no image on the altar. Śrī Rāmakrṣṇa seated himself on the worshipper's seat and beckoned to Sārāda Devī to be seated on the altar. In an ecstatic mood she obeyed him. Śrī Rāmakrṣṇa invoked the presence of the Mother of the Universe in his wife and began to worship. Sāradā Devī, in the meanwhile, entered into samādhi, and Śrī Rāmakrṣṇa likewise became absorbed. Thus they remained for a long time. When partial outer consciousness came to Śrī Rāmakrṣṇa, he, laid, with appropriate mantra, the fruits of all his spiritual struggles, together with his rosary, at the feet of the Mother of the Universe in the form of his wife.

Sāradā Devī lived in her husband's company for fourteen years and served him and his disciples until Śrī Rāmakrṣṇa's death. In later years known as the Holy Mother, she became the guiding spirit of the Order founded in her husband's name.

Śrī Rāmakrṣṇa. speaking of his wife. used to say: 'After marriage I earnestly prayed to the Divine Mother to root out all consciousness of physical enjoyment from her mind. That my prayer had been granted, I knew from my long association with her.'

Among the sayings of Śrī Rāmakrṣṇa is this: 'When the lotus blossoms, the bees come of their own accord to seek the honey. So let the lotus of your heart bloom, realize God seated within it, and the bees, the spiritual aspirants, will seek you out'of the moment of Śrī Rāmakrṣṇa's readiness for aspirants, Swamī'Vivekananda, his chief disciple, speaks thus:

"All the struggles which we experience in our lives Śrī Rāmakrṣṇa had passed through. His hard-earned jewels of spirituality, for which he had given three-quarters of his life, were now ready to be offered to humanity, and then began his mission".[81]

Many noted intellectuals of the day soon began to visit Śrī Rāmakrṣṇa, among them Keshab Sen, who was the first man of Western education to recognize his spiritual genius. Keshab, one of the great religious leaders in India at the time, had a large following, and both in his sermons and in his magazines he spread the name and fame of the new saint. As a result, manv men and women were attracted to religion—including college protessors, actors, and scientists. Some of them became Śrī Rāmakrṣṇa's disciples.

But Śrī Rāmakrṣṇa's real work took root when there came to him a number of young men, mostly in their teens, untouched by worldly ways. Some of them began to live at Dakṣiṇeśwar, associating with him intimately. Among them was Rākhāl, who later became known as Swami Brahmananda, and who was regarded by Śrī Rāmakrṣṇa as his spiritual son.

During Śrī Rāmakrṣṇa's fatal illness, when he was removed to Cossipore garden house, most of these young men remained with him to serve and nurse him. Of these, Naren, later known as Swami Vivekananda, was chosen as the leader. It was Naren that Śrī Rāmakrṣṇa taught how to organize an order of monks to propagate his message.

Śrī Rāmakrṣṇa died in August, 1886. After his death his young disciples banded together and dedicated their lives 'to our own salvation and to the good of mankind'. This is the order known today as the 'Ramakrishna Math and Mission', whose headquarters is located at Belur, near Calcutta.

Since the founding of the Order., in 1886 participants in the Rāmakrṣṇa movement, or Vedāntic revival, have gradually increased in numbers, strength, and influence, both in India and in foreign countries. Vedānta societies, so called, founded in Śrī Rāmakrṣṇa's name and presided over by monks trained in the Math at Belur, have been established in many parts of the world, especially in Western Europe and in North and South America.

Easily the most characteristic aspect of Śrī Rāmakrṣṇa's doctrine can be summed up in the words tolerance, reconciliation, harmony.

The ideas the words stand for are not of course new to Indian religion, which, from its remote beginnings, as we have seen, has seldom been narrowly exclusive or dogmatic; but in Śrī Rāmakrṣṇa they found a comprehensive and seemingly definitive embodiment. He not only brought into agreement the diverse views of Hinduism, but also managed somehow to include in his native faith all the faiths of the outside world. The idea of the unity of the religious sentiment could hardly be carried further.

In the ultimate reaches of Hinduism, there were, to be sure, no diverse views to be reconciled. When the aspirant attained his ultimate goal, views, of whatever kind, ceased to exist. He was absorbed in turiya, the transcendental consciousness, he had become one with God. But at lower levels, where the mind tried to determine the nature of and God the universe, differences early arose. Some said that God was personal, some that he was impersonal; some said that he was with form, some that he was without form. Śrī Rāmakrṣṇa, bringing to bear his own mystic experiences, dissolved, in his simple way, all such oppositions:

'Infinite is God and infinite are his expressions. He who lives continuously in the consciousness of God, and in this alone, knows him in his true being. He knows his infinite expressions, his various aspects. He knows him as impersonal no less than as personal.[82]

'Brahman, absolute existence, knowledge, and bliss, may be compared to an infinite ocean, without beginning or end. As through intense cold some portions of the water of the ocean freeze into ice, and the formless water appears as having form, so through intense love of the devotee the formless, absolute, infinite Existence manifests himself before him as having form and personality. But forms and aspects disappear before the man who reaches the highest samādhi who attains the height of nondualistic philosophy, the Vedānta.[83]

'So long as there is yet a little ego left, the consciousness that "I am a devotee", God is comprehended as personal, and his form is realized. This consciousness of a separate ego is a barrier that keeps one at a. distance from the highest realization. The forms of Kali or of Krṣṇa are represented as of a dark-blue colour. Why? Because the devotee has not yet approached them. At a distance the water of a lake appears blue, but when you come nearer, you find it has no colour. In the same way, to him who attains to the highest truth and experience, Brahman is absolute and impersonal. His real nature cannot be defined in words.[84]

Following the teachings of Śrī Rāmakrṣṇa, the highest vision of God can be described in the following words: He indeed has attained the supreme illumination who not only realizes the presence of God, but knows him as both personal and impersonal, who loves him intensely, talks to him, partakes of his bliss. Such an illumined soul realizes the bliss of God while he is absorbed in meditation, attaining oneness with the indivisible, impersonal Being; and he realizes the same bliss as he comes back to normal consciousness and sees this universe as a manifestation of that Being and as a divine play.

What is the relation of God to the universe? In discussion of the Upaniṣads we have seen that in the nondual unitary consciousness the universe disappears and there remains only Brahman—the absolute existence, knowledge, and bliss. Again, the universe is seen as Brahman when the divine sight opens up. In the Bhagavad-Gītā we read about the illumined soul:

> His heart is with Brahman,
> His eye in all things
> Sees only Brahman
> Equally present,
> Knows his own Atman
> In every creature,
> And all creation
> Within that Atman.[85]

Śrī Rāmakrṣṇa reconciled the two views of the universe, the one in which it dissolves in illusion, and the other in which it is one with God, in the following words:

'In turīya, the universe of plurality becomes annihilated—there is attained oneness with Brahman.

'When, having attained the nondual Brahman in samādhi, one comes back to the plane of the ego, one realizes that it is Brahman who has become this universe of plurality. To get to the flesh of the fruit you discard its skin and seeds. But when you want to know the total weight of the fruit, you must weigh them all together. The skin, the seeds, the flesh—all belong to one and the same fruit. Similarly, having realized the unchangeable reality—the one absolute Existence—one finds that he who is the absolute, formless, impersonal, infinite God is again one with the relative universe. He who is absolute in one aspect is relative in another aspect, and both aspects belong to one and the same substnace. . .

'The sacred syllable Om is explained in the scriptures as a combination of the sounds A, U, M, representing creation, preservation, and dissolution respectively. I compare the sound of Om to the sound of a bell that dissolves in silence. The relative universe dissolves in the imperishable absolute—the great silence. The gross, the subtle, the causal—everything visible and invisible, dissolves in the Great Cause. Waking, dreaming, and dreamless sleep, the three states of consciousness, are dissolved in the turīya, the transcendental. Once more the bell rings. The sound Om is heard and as it were a heavy weight falls on the bosom of the calm, infinite ocean; immediately the ocean becomes agitated. From the bosom of the absolute rises the relative; from the Great Cause issues forth the causal, the subtle, the gross universe; from the transcendental come the three states of consciousness—waking, dreaming, and dreamless sleep. Again the waves dissolve in the ocean, and there is the great calm. From the absolute comes the relative, and into the absolute the relative dissolves. I have experienced this infinite ocean of bliss and consciousness; and Mother has shown me how innumerable worlds issue from the ocean and go back into it. I donot know, of course, what is written in books of philosophy.[86]

'I see the truth directly: what need have I to philosophize? I see how God has become all this—he has become the individual beings and the empirical world. There is nothing but he. But this truth cannot be experienced until the heart is illumined. It is not a matter of philosophy, but of experience. Through the grace of God the light must first shine in one's own soul. When that comes to pass, one attains samādhi. Then, though one comes back to the normal plane, one loses the material sense, one loses all attachment to lust and gold. One then loves only to hear and speak the word ofGod.[87]

To reason out the truth of God is one thing, and to meditate on God is another. But again, when illumination comes through the grace of God, then only is the truth of God known and experienced. Just as a dark room is lighted up when you strike a match, so is the heart lighted up the grace of God. Then alone are all doubts dissolved aways.[88]

The three main schools of thought in Vedānta—dualism, qualified—monism, and nondualism—Śrī Rāmakrṣṇa reconciled in the following manner. Quoting an ancient verse from the Hindu scriptures, he told how Rāma, who was worshipped as a divine incarnation, asked his faithful devotee Hanuman how he looked upon him. Hanuman replied: 'When I consider myself as a physical being, thou art the master, I am thy servant. When I consider myself as an individual being, thou art the whole, I am one of thy parts. And when I realize myself as the Ātman, I am one with thee.[89] Thus Śrī Rāmakrṣṇa pointed out that dualism, qualified monism, and nondualism are not mutually exclusive and contradictors concepts but successive steps in realization—the third and last being attained when the aspirant loses all consciousness of self in union with God.

Thus, in a way more or less peculiar to himself, through attention mainly to the mystic experience, Śrī Rāmakṛṣṇa harmonized conflicting notions of God and the universe and of their relations to each other. But this was not his only way. Another, still more peculiar to him, might 'be called, in current terms, pragmatic. Any idea of God, any mode of worshipping him, that *worked*—that led the aspirant to the ultimate goal—must be valid and true. But how could one be sure that an idea or a method is really thus effective? Clearly, by trying it oneself. And that, in all simplicity and sincerity, is what Śrī Rāmakṛṣṇa did. He practised the teachings of many divergent sects within Hinduism, and through each of them achieved the same supreme realization. But even this was not sufficient. What of the Mohammedanism that had long been alive in India? What of Christianity? The story of his experimental contacts with these religions we have already told. In the end he arrived at the grand conclusion with which the ancient ṛṣis began, and which we have more than once recalled: Ekam sat viprāh bahudha vadanti— in Śrī Rāmakṛṣṇa's words, 'So many religions, so many paths to reach one and the same goals.

In defining this goal Śrī Rāmakṛṣṇa was of course at one with all his spiritual ancestors. It was simply to realize God within one's own soul. Śamkara declared that 'Study of the scriptures is fruitless so long as Brahman has not been experienced'; and 'Hẹ is born to no purpose,' says Śrī Rāmakṛṣṇa, 'who, having the rare privilege of being born a man, is unable to realize God.'

Continuing, Śrī Rāmakṛṣṇa emphasized the importance of means:

'Adopt adequate means for the end you seek to attain. You cannot get butter by crying yourself hoarse, saying, "There is butter in the milk!" If you wish to make butter, you must turn the milk into curd, and churn it well. Then alone you can get butter So if you long to see God, practise spiritual disciplines. What is the use of merely crying "Lord!' Lord!'"[90]

To an aspirant who should ask about particular means to adopt we can easily anticipate Śrī-Rāmakṛṣṇa answer. Pursue sincerely and diligently any spiritual path, he would say, and you will ultimately achieve realization.

As to what the basic paths are he accepted the Hindu belief that for all religions they can be reduced to the four yogas: jñāna yoga, the path of discrimination between the Real and the unreal; bhakti yoga, the path of loving devotion; karma yoga, the parth of selfless work; and raja yoga, thepath of oncentrat in and meditation. In our study of theBhgavad-Gita we have seen that Śrī Kṛṣṇa advocated a harmonious combination of all the yogas. The spiritual aspriant should cultivate discrimination and devotion as well as concentration and meditation. Sir Rāmakṛṣṇa stressed this again and again in his teachings. He did not want anyone to be one-sided.

To be sure, special emphasis should be placed on one or another path according to the temperament of the devotee. Śrī Rāmakrṣṇa advocated emphasis on jñāna yoga, however, only for an exceptional few, pointing out that if this path is followed without the necessary unfoldment of certain virtues, such as dispassion, meditation on the unity of Ātman and Brahman will be misunderstood and misapplied. For most spiritual aspirants he recommended emphasis on bhakti yoga, because the path of devotion is a natural one leading to realization. Everyone has love in his heart—it merely needs to be directed towards God; and for a follower if bhakti yoga dis crimination, dispassion. and all the other virtues unfold easily and naturally. Srī Rāmakrṣṇa used to says: 'The more you move towards the light, the farther you will be from darkness.' He told his disciples how he himself prayed for devotion during a period of intense spiritual disciplines:

'O Mother, here is sin and here is virtue; take them both and grant me pure love for thee. Here is knowledge and here is ignorance; I lay them at thy feet. Grant me pure love for thee. Here is purity and here is impurity; take them both and grant me pure love for thee. Here are good works and here are evil works; I lay them at thy feet. Grant me pure love for thee.[91]

But whatever path the aspirant chiefly follows, according to Srī Rāmakrṣṇa. meditation is the most important aspect of his spiritual life. Somehow or other he must keep his mind fixed on God. Meditation is performed not merely with closed eyes but with eyes open as well.

There are many ways to mediate and many forms of meditation. For the jñāna yogi, for example, there is the meditation on the identity of Ātman and Brahman; he tries to live in that identity. There are many means to achieve this end, the one best for a particular aspirant depending on his temperament.

For the bhakti yogi there is meditation on a chosen ideal of God, which may be with or without form. To those who preferred to meditate on God with form, Srī Rāmakrṣṇa said:

'Wash away all the impurities of your mind; then let the Lord be seated within the lotus of your heart. Meditate on him as a living presence. Tie your mind to the feet of your Chosen Ideal with a silken thread, but remember not merely to think of him while you are formally meditating: keep recollectedness at other times. Don't you know that in the shrine of Mother Dūrgā a light burns continually before tne image, and the housewife sees to it that the light never goes out? Keep the light of awareness always burning within your heart. Keep your thoughts awake. While engaged in your daily activities, occasionally gaze inward and see if the light is burning[92]

To those who preferred to meditate on God in his formless aspect, he said:

'Think of him as an infinite, shoreless ocean. You are like a fish swimming in that ocean of existence, knowledge, and bliss absolute, or like a vesseldipoped in it with that Presence inside, outside, and everywhere[93]

'Some devotees approach God by going from the aspect without form to that with form; others by going from the aspect with form to that without form. To realtize that he is both with form and without form—that is best.[94]

Two watchwords Śrī Rāmakrṣṇa set before mankind were renunciation and service.

Spiritual aspirants can follow either the way of the monk or the way of the householder, but renunciation is an ideal which the two ways have in common. The monk's renunciation must be external, however, as well as mental. The householder renounces mentally.

But what, really, does renunciation mean? It is deification—which means seeing God everywhere and in everything, knowing for oneself the truth expressed in the Iśa Upaniṣad: 'In the heart of all things, of whatever there is in the universe, dwells the Lord. He alone is the reality. Wherefore, renouncing vain appearances, rejoice in him.'

Srī Rāmakrṣṇa used to tell his householder disciples to live in the world in spirit of detachment, keeping their minds on God. Gradually they would begin to realize that all objects and persons are parts of him. The aspirant, he said, must serve his parents, his wife, and his children as manifestations of God. He who lives in the world in this manner, renouncing all sense of possession, is the ideal householder. He overcomes all fear of death. But in order to reach this ideal the aspirant must occasionally go into solitude, practice contemplation, and yearn to realize God.

In connection with the ideal of service taught ṣrī Rāmakrṣṇa, I shall mention a very interesting incident from his life. One day, in a state of ecstasy, he was recalling the precepts of another great saint. One of these preached compassion for mankind. ṣrī Rāmakrṣṇa repeated several times the word compassion. Then he exclaimed: 'Compassion! Who am I to be compassionate! Isn't everyone God? How can I be compassionate towards God? Serve him, serve him, serve him!' In this way Srī Rāmakrṣṇa elevated the ideal of philanthropy to the worship of God in every being.

He considered the attainment liberation for oneself to be a low ideal. Swami Turiyananda, one of his disciples, used to say that nirvaṇa was the highest state of realization and was rebuked for what his master called a 'mean conception'. Naren, later known as Swami Vivekananda. one day was asked by Srī Rāmakrṣṇa what his ideal was. When Narrn answered that he wanti' to remain immersed in samadhi and return to normal consciousness only in order to keep his body alive.. Śrī Rāmakrṣṇa exclaimed: 'Shame on you! I thought you were greater than that!' And he taught him the twin ideal on which Vivekananda later founded the monastic Order of Rāmakrṣṇa: liberation for oneself and service to God in man'.

Concerning this same Swami Vivekananda a story is told which illustrates the extraordinary means to which Srī Rāmakrṣṇa sometimes resorted in order to advance the spiritual welfare of his disciples. When young Naren first came to Srī Rāmakrṣṇa, he was a member of the Brāhmo Samāj, an Indian reform movement which believed in the ideal of theism. Recognizing in his new disciple an aspirant with the capacity to follow the difficult path of jñaña'yoga, Srī Rāmakrṣṇa asked him to read treatises on advaita Vedānta and made him sing a song expressing the nondual conception. Naren complied with his master's wishes, bilt he could not accept the doctrine of nondualism, for to him it seemed blasphemous to look on man as one with his Creator. One day he laughingly remarked to a friend: 'How impossible! This vessel is God! This cup is God! Whatever we see is God! And we ourselves are God!' At this moment Srī Rāmakrṣṇa came out of his room, smiling, and touched Naren. The effect of this touch Naren described as follows:

'That strange touch immediately caused a complete revolution in my mind. Wherever I looked I saw Brahman and Brahman alone. I lived in that consciousness the whole day. I returned home, and that same experience continued. When I sat down to eat I saw that the food, the plate, the server, and I myself—all were Brahman. I took one of two morsels of food and again was absorbed in that consciousness. ... All the time, whether eating or lying down. or going to college, I had the same experience. While walking in the streets I noticed cabs plying but did not feel inclined to move out of the way. I felt that the cabs and myself were made of the same substance. . . . When this state changed a little, the world began to appear to me as a dream. While walking in Cornwallis Square I struck my head against the iron railings to see if they were real or only a dream. After several days, when I returned to the normal plane, I realized that I had had a glimpse of nondual consciousness. Since then I have never doubted the truth of nondualism.[95]

To sum up the message of Srī Rāmakrṣṇa, especially in its relation to practice, we perhaps could do no better than quote the following words of the distinguished swami to whom we have just listened:

'Do not depend on doctrines, do not depend on dogmas, or sects, or churches, or temples; they count for little compared with the essence of existence in man, which is divine; and the more this divinity is developed in a man, the more powerful is he for good. Earn that spirituality first, acquire that, and criticize no one, for all doctrines and creeds have some good in them. Show by your lives that religion does not mean words, or names, or sects, but that it means spiritual realization. Only those can understand who have perceived the Reality. Only those who have attained to spirituality can communicate it to others, can be great teachers of mankind. They alone are the powers of light.?[96]

Selected Precepts of Sri Ramakrsna

Know yourself and you will know God. .What is your ego? Is it your hand or foot or flesh or blood or any other part of your body? Reflect well and you will find that the ego has no real existence. Just as, if you peel off the skin of an onion layer after layer, in search of a kernel, for a while more and more skin appears, and then nothing at all, so it is if you go looking for the ego. There is no kernel within the onion; there is no ego within yourself. In the last analysis what is within you is only the Ātman—Pure Consciousness. When the illusion of the ego disappears, then appears the Reality—God.

There are two kinds of ego—one ripe, and the other unripe. The unripe ego thinks, 'This is my house, *my* son, *my* this, *my* that.' The ripe ego thinks. 'I am the servant of the Lord, I am his'child; I am the Ātman, immortal. free; 1 am Pure Consciousness.[97]

The light of the sun shines equally on all surfaces, but it reflects clearly only on bright surfaces like water, mirrors, and polished metals. In like manner, although God dwells in the.hearts of all, he is clearly manifest only in the hearts of the holy.[98]

How long does one argue about the meaning of the scriptures? Only until the Sat-chid-ānanda becomes revealed in one's own heart. The bee buzzes only so long as it does not sit on the flower. As soon as it sits on the flower and begins to drink of the honey, all noise stops—there is complete silence.[99]

Useless is the study of the scriptures if one has no discrimination and dispassion. One cannot find God unless one is endowed with these. Discrimination is knowledge of what is eternal and what is noneternal, and devotion to the eternal, which is God; it is knowledge that the Ātman is separate from the body. Dispassion is non attachment to the objects of sense.[100]

The true hero is he who can discipline his mind by devotional exercises while living in the world. A strong man can look in any direction while carrying a heavy burden on his head. Similarly, the perfect man can keep his gaze constantly fixed on God while carrying the burden of worldly duties.[101]

A boy holds on to a pillar and circles round it with headlong speed. While he is spinning, his attention is constantly fixed on the pillar. He knows that if he lets go his hold upon it he will fall and hurt himself. Similarly, the wise householder holds on to the pillar of God: keeps his mind fixed on him, and performs his worldly duties. Thus is he free from all dangers.[102]

Let the boat stay on the water: there is no harm. But let not water get into the boat, lest the boat sink. Similarly, there is no harm if the devotee lives in the world, provided he lets not worldliness enter into his mind.[103]

Clay in its natural state can be moulded into any form, but burnt clay cannot. Similarly, spiritual truths cannot be impressed upon hearts that have been burnt by the fire of lust.[104]

To bring one's heart and one's speech into accord is the goal of all spiritual discipline. If you say, 'O Lord, Thou art my all in all,' while in your heart you believe the objective world to be all in all, your devotional exercises are bound to be fruitless.[105]

Countless are the pearls lying hidden in the sea. If a single dive yields you none, do not conclude that the sea is without pearls. Similarly, if after practising spiritual disciplines for a little while you fail to have the vision of God, do not lose heart. Continue to practise the disciplines with patience, and at the proper time you are sure to obtain grace.[106]

Strike a match, and the light disperses all at once the darkness of a room, even though accumulated for centuries. Similarly, a single gracious glance of the Lord disperses the accumulated sins of innumerable births.[107]

The magnetic needle always points towards the north, whatever the direction in which the ship is sailing; that is why the ship does not lose her course. Similarly, if the mind of man isalways turned towards God, he will steer clear of every danger.[108]

There is only one God, but endless are his aspects and endless are his names. Call him by any name and worship him in any aspect that pleases you, you are sure to see him.[109]

1. See chap. 16, p.

2. Badarikasrama, in the Himalayas, is a well-known place of pilgrimage, where devotees from throughout India gather in great numbers every summer. At Other times of the year the roads to it are covered with heavy snow. The place has in it a famous temple, dedicated to the worship of Nārāyaṇa. I had the privilege of visiting this holy shrine in 1916.

3. Foreword to *Māṇḍūkyopaniṣhad with Gauḍapāda's Kārikā and Sankara's Commentary* (Swami Nikhilananda trans., Sri Ramakrishna Ashrama: Mysore, 1949), p. v.

4. *Ibid*.,. pp. vi-vii.

5. Kārikā. I 7. 12. This and the following passages from the Kārikā have been translated by the author.

6. Kārikā

7. *Ibid.*, III 35.

8. *Ibid.*, III 17, 16

9. *Ibid.*, III 37.

10. *Ibid.*, III 45, 46, 47.

11. Kārikā, IV. 31.

12. *Ibid.*, II 32.

13. *Indian Philosophy,* vol. II, p. 463.

14. *Indian Philosophy,* vol. II, p. 463.

15. The date is that given by Pandit Rajenda Nath Ghosh, a noted authority on—Samkara. S. Radhakrishnan writes (*Indian Philosophy*, vol. 11, p.447): "According to Telang. Samkara flourished about the middle or the end of the sixth century A.D (His argument is that Pūrṇavarman referred to in Samkara's commentary on the Brahma Sūtras was a Buddhist king of Magadha about that time.) Sir R.G Bhindarkar proposes AD 680 as the date of Samkara's's birth, and is even inclined to go a few years earlier. Max Müller and Professor Macdonell hola that he was born in AD 788 and died in AD 820. That he flourished in the first quarter of die ninth century is also the opinion of Professor Keith.supported by the investigations made by Prof. Max Mullerand Prof. Macdonell as well as by Prof. Keith and Dr Bhāndarkar. Prol Telang, on the *basis of* a reference to Pūma Varman, the Buddhist king of Magadha, in the *Sūtra Bhaṣya* of Sanrnra. pleads that he must have lived in the sixth century A.D. (*Prabuddha Bharata*, November. 1957)

To an Indian scholar, A. V. Sankaranarayana Rao, I owe the following recent statement:

The date of Saṅkara has not been definitely arrived at and is still a matter of controversy. It is the consensus of opinion that he lived after Bhagavān Buddha. The dates assigned to him vary from sixth century BC to eighth century AD. The traditional date is Kaliyuga 2593 or 509 bc. It has been generally accepted by many modern historians that he lived between 788 and 820 AD. This has been more or

16. Translated by Swami Prabhavananda and Christophe Isherwood.

17. There is difference of opinion regarding the meeting of Samkara with

Gauḍapāda. See chap. xv.

18. *Brahmajñānavalīmālā,* v. 21.

19. Sir James Jeans.

20. Commentary on I i. 1.

21. *Ibid.*

22. *Ibid.*

23. Commentary on I i. 1.

24. *Complete works of Vivekannda,* vol. III, p. 37.

25. *Kathāmṛta,* vol. v, p. 40

26. *Ibid.,* vol. IV, p. 255.

27. Commentary on the Brahma Sūtras, IV. iv. 17.

28. *Vivekacūḍāmaṇi,* vv. 481-5.

29. *Vivekacūḍāmaṇi,* vv. 481-5.

30. *Vivekacuḍāamaṇi,* vv. 355, 356.

31. v. 368.

32. v. 380.

33. v.108.

34. v.-118.

35. v.-119.

36. Vivekacūḍāmaṇi v. 321.

37. Na prapañcamātram Brahma.

38. Compare this philosophy of union with God after death with the Pauline—interpretation of the teachings of Christ.

39. The above remark reminds one, by way of contrast, of the bold,impersonal thinkers of the Vedic age who asked, 'Who has seen the first-born, when he taht had no bones bore him that has bones?' (Rg-Veda, i. 4. 164, quoted by S. Radhaḳrsihana, *Indina Philosophy,* vol. I. p. 93.)

40. Ramanuja did not originate the philosophy associated with his name, but he is its chief exponent.

41. Taittiriya, II. i.3.

42. Taittiriya, II. i. 3.

43. *Ibid.,* III. i.

44. Muṇḍamka, I. i.7.

45. *Cultural Heritage of India,* vol. I, p. 567.

46. Cf.: 'I am the way, the truth, and the life' (John xiv. 6).

47. *Rāmānuja's Idea of the Finite Self pp. 98-9.*

48. *Complete Worksof Vivekananda,* vol. III, p. 31.

49. *Ibid.,* vol. III, p. 34.

50. Vivekananda's translation; *Complete Work of Vivekananda,* vol. III, pp. 34-5.

51. *Complete Works of Vivekananda,*vol. III, p. 69.

52. This chant, which is composed of the many names of Kṛṣṇa, together with words describing his various attributes, is sung tothe accompaniment of certain musical instruments. The devotees join in the singing and dance in ecstatic joy The chant begins thus: 'Hari Haraye namah, Kṛṣṇa adavaya namah; Gopāla, Govinda, Rāma, Sri Madhusudana.

53. Chāndogya, VI. xii. 3.

54. *Kamāmrta*, vol. IV p. 223

55. Śrī Caitanya did not comment on the Brahma Sūtras as did his predecessors. Once he remarked that the Bhāgavata Purāṇa is the best commentary on the Brahma Sūtras. Valadeva Vidyābhuṣan, one of his followers, wrote a commentary called Govinda Bhāṣya, in which he expounded the Caitanya philosophy.

56. An analogy may be drawn between this attitude of madhura and the mystic marriage which are performed in certain Christian monastic orders between the nuns and Christ the Heavenly Bridegroom.

57. Translated from the Sanskrit by Swami Prabhavananda and Christopher Isherwood, *Vedanta for the Western World* (Christopher Isherwood, ed.. New York Viking Press, 1960), p. 225.

58. Govinda is another name of Śrī Krṣṇa.

59. See *Līlāprasaṅga*, Sādhak bhāv, p. 47.

60. See Lilaprasanga, Balya Jivan, p. 140

61. Ibid., Guur Bhav, Pt. 1, p. 137.

62. Ibid., Sadhak Bhav, P. 64.

63. See *Lipāprasaṅga,*, Sādhak bhāv, p. 124.

64. *Kathāmrta*, vol. I, p. 27.

65. *Līlāprasaṅga*, Sādhak bhāv, p. 204

66. *Līlāprasaṅga*, Sādhak bhāv, p. 205.

67. Ibid., PP- 220-1.

68. *Līlāprasaṅga*, pp. 311-12.

69. Śrī Rāmakrṣṇa used to refer to Totā Puri as nanta, the naked one.

70. *Līlāprasaṅga,*, Sādhak bhāv, pp. 319-20.

71. *Ibid.*, p. 321.

72. *Ibid.*, Guru bḥāv, Pt. I, pp. 61-2.

73. The unripe ego is the barrier that separates man from God and makes him forgetful of the divine.

74. *Kathāmtra*, vol. V, p. 109.

75. See *Līlāprasaṅga*, Sādhak bhāv, p. 335.

76. *Ibid.*

77. *Kathāmrta*, vol. ii, p. 166.

78. See Gospel *of Śrī Ramakrishna*, Swami Nikhilananda (trans.), p. 35.

79. *Kathmṛta*, vol. I, p. 49.

80. It was on his initiation into sannyas that he received the name Rāmakrṣṇa—combining the names of two of India's great avatar's; the 'Śrī'—a title of reverence—was added later when his high spiritual gifts became apparent. His original name was Gadadhar Chatterjee.

81. *Complete Work of Vivekananda*, vol. IV, pp. 172-3.

82. *Kathāmṛta*, vol I, p. 71.

83. *Ibid.*, vol. I; p. 69.

84. *Ibid.*, pp. 71-2.

85. VI. 29. To see God in the universe, to see Brahman in all, was considered *by* Śrī Rāmakṛṣṇa to be the highest spiritual attainment. Once when a young disciple came to him, the Master asked him what his goal of life was. When he received the reply 'To see God everywhere', Śrī Rāmakṛṣṇa remarked, 'Well, my

boy, that is the last word of religion.'

86. *Kathāmṛta,* vol. I, pp. 213, 214, 215.
87. *Ibid.*, vol. I, p. 239.
88. *Ibid.*, vol. I, p. 240.
89. *Ibid. Kathāmrta* vol. III, p. 13
90. *Kathāmrta,* vol. II, p. 185, Cf. Matt. vii. 21.
91. *Ibid.*, voll. I, p. 54
92. *Līlāprasaṅga,* Guru bhāv. Pt. I, pp. 89-90.
93. *Kathāmrta,* vol. III, p. 256.
94. *Līlāprasaṅga*, Guru bhāv, Pt. I, p. 90.
95. *Līlāprasaṅga,*, Divya bhāv. pp. l6l, 162, 163.
96. *Complete Works of Vivekananda*, vol. IV, pp. 182-3.
97. Swami Brahmananda, *Srī; Srī Rāmakrṣṅa Upadeśa*, pp. 1.ff
98. *Ibid.*, p. 24
99. *Ibid.*, p. 35.
100. *Ibid.*, p. 37f.
101. *Ibid.*, p. 46.
102. Swami Brahmananda, *Srī Srī Rāmakrsna Upadesa,* pp. 49f.
103. *Ibid.*, p. 50f.
104. *Ibid.*, p. 65.
105. *Ibid.*, p. 68.
106. *Ibid.*, p. 101.
107. *Ibid.*, p. 118.
108. *Ibid.*, p. 124f.
109. *Ibid.*, p. 132.

CHAPTER XXII

THE HINDU TRINITY[1]

To pave our way for a proper conception of the Trimoortis—Brahma, Vishnu and Rudra, we shall first deal with in consistency with our Hindu writers. The theory of God propounded by the Purānas is in no way in conflict with that of the Upanishads.

God

Now, the Upanishads postulate that this eternal principle is above all thought and speech. It is over this principle that the different religionists of the world super-impose many attributes. It is this principle that they fight about, which has produced manifold jarrings and disputes on this earth of ours. To put an end, as it were, to all these foolish wranglings, the Upanishads say it is Nirguna, Niranjana, Nirabhasa and so on, thus giving it only negative attributes. It is not even according to Herbert Spencer, "that universal and eternal energy from which all things proceed," for then the attributes of matter will have to be ascribed to that universal and non-dual principle. Energy is only Sakti in Sanscrit, and Sakti is but the phenomenal aspect of that principle in the primordial matter, Mulaprakriti. It is not the Absolute itself. But the Absolute of the Upanishads is that which is above all our present and future conceptions, in consistency with the epithets eternal, absolute and infinite, applied to it. This is the logical . conclusion which the highest philosophers of the West have come to about God as formulated long ago by the East.

Such being the theory of God propounded by the Upanishads, what do the Puranas say on the subject ? It is here that the moderns accuse our Purānas of the promulgation of personality about God, as also of the introduction of idolatry. It will be seen from several passages in the Puranas, (see the Vishnu Purana which is considered to be an authoritative work by the three sects in Southern India) that they inculcate the theory of non-personality and the non-anthropomorphic nature of God according to the Puranas.

If God were, according to the Puranas, impersonal and non-anthropomorphic, what is the meaning of the personal and other descriptions in the Puranas, attributed to God, such as for instance, Narayana moving on the waters, Vishnu bestriding the serpent Adisesha, again bestriding Garuda, and again wearing some weapons, and similarly with reference to Siva, Brahma, and others ? In the first place, as God *per se is* non-dual and impersonal,. Brahma, Vishnu, Rudra or others cannot be termed God; but they are only manifesting energies of God, just as the universe is said to be its manifestation, and hence are "perishable. In the second place, the weapons, ornaments, vehicles, and actions, these Devas manifest should not be construed literally. That the Puranic writers of old did not wish that these symbols should be construed literally by the wise, is clear from some passages in the Vishnu Purana.

The Trimoorti

The universe is composed of the two eternal verities or principles—Purusha (spirit) and Prakriti (matter.) These inseparable twins acting upon one another, constitute this phenomenal universe. The former can be termed the intelligent aspect or pole of the Absolute, while the latter represents the other pole, *viz.,* the inert. But Prakriti or matter has got its Three aspects *viz.*, Satva, Rajas and Tamas. Hence Purusha has also got its Three aspects, which are termed Brahma, Vishnu and Siva or Rudra, since Purusha, acting as it does on its inseparable consort Prakriti, should also have the three differentiations.

In the Puranas Brahma is stated to create the world through Rajas; through Satwa, Vishnu preserves the universe; Rudra destroys it through Tamas. What does this mean ? To quote the words of Madame Blavatsky—"The fact is, that all the three 'persons' of the Trimurti are simply the three qualificative gunas or attributes of the universe of differentiated Purusha-Prakriti (spirit-matter), selt-formative, self-preserving, and self-destroying, for purposes of regeneration and perfectibility. This is the correct meaning, and it is shown in Brahma being made the personified embodiment of Rajoguna, the attribute or quality of activity, of desire for procreation, that desire owing to which the universe and everything in it is called into being; Vishnu is the embodied Sat-vaguna, that property of preservation arising from quietude and restful enjoyment, which characterises the intermediate period between the full growth and the beginning of decay; while Siva being embodied Tamoguna—which is the attribute of stagnancy and final decay becomes of course the destroyer. This is as highly philosophical under its mask of anthropomorphism as it is unphilosophical and absurd to hold to and enforce on the world the dead letter of the original conception."

Thus we find that the Trinity—Brahma, Vishnu and Rudra, are no other than the creative, preservative and destroying forces or powers of nature—not the inert automatic forces of the present day orthodox official science, but the intelligent ones which are called Saktis among the Hindus, for, is it not irrational and illogical to suppose the existence of self-creating, self-preserving and self-destroying forces without intelligence at the bottom ? How can an inert object of itself move and create or do any other thing ?

Time is but the relation of sequence. In the homogeneous space the conception of time, *viz.*, the relation of sequence arises only when this rhythm of motion is caused. Hence rhythm of motion is but time itself. This rhythm being zigzag or annular according to Herbert Spencer, how can we best symbolise it ? Serpent alone is the most befitting symbol on this plane of our present perception to denote the spiral motion existing throughout the cosmos. There is one other fitting reason why the serpent should stand for time. When two forces are at right angles to one another, and have a certain ratio, then it is said that circular rhythms are caused. Hence time which is infinite in its true nature, revolves in a circle being subject to two forces, one tending towards the Absolute and the other towards Manifestation, acting as the centripetal and centrifugal forces in nature (which are called in Sanscrit Avarana and Ikshepa Saktis). Every year returns with its ever-recurring cycles of spring, summer, autumn and winter. Day is followed by night and *vice versa*, and so on. Hence the circular annular serpent depicted with its tail in its mouth to denote the ever recurrent cycles of time.

Narayana, though *per se*, above all time, has to be conditioned by it when he represents the transition stage from the unmanifested to the manifested state. Hence it is we find in the pictures, the serpent overshadowing Him with its hood over Him. So that, Narayana represents, when he brings out Brahma from his navel, the transition stage of the universe from Avyakta (the unmanifested state) to Vyakta (the manifested one).

Brahma

Coming to Brahma, we find that it comes from the root Brahm, to expand. At the period of creation, this power begins to expand for work. How does he evolve or rise from Narayana ? It is peculiar to find that he arises from the navel of Narayana.

Why not arise, as in ordinary processes, from the womb or from the mind or *vak:* (speech) of Rishis as stated in our books ? Why should the navel be pitched upon as the starting-point of the universe from its unmanifested to its manifested state ? At the outset, it may be stated that the universe issues from the subjective state to the objective, not through the ordinary process but in some mysterious manner. In the navel of man's body is located a mysteriou. Sakti or force called Kundalini, which has the power when mastered by a great spiritual personage, of creating or undoing things at will. Carrying this analogy to the universe, we find it has also this Sakti in its navel. This force in the navel projects a lotus-like form, world. Moreover it is the umbilical vesicle in the naval that forms the connecting link between the offspring within and the ether without, and imparts by osmosis the extraneous influence to the child within, in its initial stages in tha womb. Again as Narayana is then sexless this mode of evolution is given out to differentiate it from the ordinary one. Now the lotus represents the objective universe on matter, and Brahma is the .Rajopurusha of Narayana who fructifies it in order to bring the objective universe into order and form. Previously, the unmani-fested universe was represented by the all-expansive waters of infinite space, whereas here the objective universe, being conditioned, is represented by the lotus, a limited symbol. .Moreover the Sanscrit word for lotus is Kamala, which means also Akas or space. In the cosmogonies of different religions, the symbol of a lotus or an egg is given to the objective universe of forms. These two symbols play a great part in our Hindu cosmogony.

To have the nearest approach to the conception of an infinite universe the conditioned symbol of a spherical or an oval form is the best, for expand such a form mentally in all directions, and no mathematical point will be excluded from its sweep. The different layers of the lotus petals, higher and lower, represent the different worlds, gross and subtle and on the Karnika (pericarp) within the lotus, reigns the Rajo Purusha, Brahma creating the world through Rajas or red color to represent the Kamic (passionate) tendency through which all things are generated. This Brahma has faces.

It is stated that these four faces represent the four rounds, which humanity has undergone in this day of Brahma. Of course the four Vedas stand for the sounds or rhythmic vibrations which have been developed during these four Rounds.

It is here that Narayana or Brahma becomes sexual Brahma has a wife called Saraswati. In Yoga Vasishta she is styled Lila. It is this consort of his, that plays all the *lila* or sport in this universe and brings it to action. To prove that these characters ought not to be construed in their dead-letter sense, there is a chapter in the Vishnu Purana devoted to the actions of Vishnu and Lakshmi.' It is indubitably shown therein that Vishnu and Lakshmi are no other than the two aspects or pairs, positive and negative, or the abstract and the concrete, which go to produce action in this universe. If Vak (speech) is Lakshmi, then its meaning is Vishnu. If Dharma is Vishnu, then good deeds are Lakshmi, Vishnu is Siva and Lakshmi is Gouri. The Puranic writers are non-sectarian in their character. It is only in the manifested stage that differentiations of pairs set in.

The long lotus-stalk connecting the navel of Narayana with the lotus on which Brahma is seated is the line of medium through which the influence from the higher world is radiated to the lower. One higher world is connected at the time of evolution with another of a lower state through a thin golden line as it were. But in involution, the lower worlds merge into the higher through this line and then this line disappears, and "Pralaya (or deluge) ensues.

Thus we find that the one Narayana Principle through his Rajo-guna as Brahma brings into formation the lotus of the objective universe with its stalk issuing from the root of the navel in the mud of himself (Narayana, who issues subjectively in the one universal water of space, *viz.*, Mulaprakriti).

Vishnu

This second "person" of the Trinity should not be confounded with the'non-dual Maha-Vishnu or Narayana, who is also termed Vishnu.

After the one expansive power, *viz.*, Brahma was born or had brought all things to manifestation and done its work, the Vaish-navic power pervades everywhere to preserve created objects, the word Vishnu coming, as it does, from *vis,* to pervade. In other words, the Vaishnavic power which was commingled with the former began to predominate when the predominance of the former ceased and was no longer required for work. Similarly with reference to all objects in the world. While the Brahmic force is latent during the preservative stage so far as the whole universe in totality is concerned, it may be active so, far as a part of that universe is considered; for instance, a body may be created newly and then Brahmic force predominates in it.

In the invocation addressed to Vishnu in the very first chapter of the Vishnu Purana, no appendages are given him. It is stated merely that it is the one on whom is super-imposed creation, preservation and destruction through the three gunas, &c. But some epithets only are bestowed on him. In the second chapter where he is described as one with Brahma, Vishnu and Rudra, his rest on the couch of Adisesha comes in, to do his work as Brahma, Vishnu and Rudra. Here he is represented as both single and manifold. The fourth chapter invests him with the ornaments Sankha (conch), Chackra (discus), Mace and sword with Adisesha as bed. Then in other chapters he comes's on his vehicle Garuda &c. These differences are greatly significant and point to the different stages of evolution. In the first stage, it represents the world in its unmanifested stage of Pralaya. No vehicles or ornaments do exist in that state. The terms Vasudeva, Viswabhavana, Hrishikesa and others are applied to him. The first word simply means the effulgent one, abiding in all. The second word means the creator of the universe or the cause of the existence of all things. The third word signifies the lord of the senses. So we see these are merely epithets to describe the indescribable. That, Narayana moving on the waters on the couch of Adisesha represents the transition stage of the world from the unmanifested to the manifested, has been already explained.

Coming to the third, this is the Vishnu of the period called Pratisarga or secondary creation, This refers to our solar system 'after a day of Brahma. All life germs or primordial elements having been evolved by Brahma'during the primary period stated in the Puranas, form or Rupa creations have to go on on earth during this period. Here we find the symbols suited to the end in view. Referring the Vishnu Purana we find that Sanka or conch represents the lower or subtle Akas. The Tanmatra or the rudimentary property of Akas is sound which sound is given out by couch. Hence the applicability of the conception of lower Akas or that from which the five subtle elements arise, to the symbol conch. The discus or Chakra stands for the mind or reasoning faculty. This is called Antahkarana or the impure or lower mind. According to Hindus, this faculty evolved in man at a late stage in the scale of evolution. Originally there was intuition in him in full display, which guided him then and when he a Ivanced further and further into the, region of desires, his intuition became obscured by them, and then he had to depend upon the ratiocinative process for his guidance, which is now the case with the majority of mankind. Hence it is, we find that Vishnu appears: with the symbol of mind in a lower stage of evolution. Now mind, or as it is technically called Chitta flits through the laws of asso-elation of ideas and this can best be represented by a wheel or discus which rotates or flies faster than winds. The mace stands for Buddhi. The sword stands for Gnana (spiritual wisdom) sheathed in the scabbard of Agnana. As remarked above, Adiaesha represents time. The Strivatsa mark, which is a black point on the breast of Vishnu represents the original homogeneous atom or Mulaprakritil out of which the universe arises. The Koustubha gem, radiant as it is, stands for the Purushas or souls. The bow Saranga typifies the organs of sense and the shafts, the organs of action. Vishnu wears the necklace Vajayanti composed of the five precious gems of 5 colours, ruby, sapphire, emerald, &c., to denote the five Tanmatras, out of which the five elements arose. Thus much for the third stage.

The fourth stage is where Vishnu appears seated on a Garuda or eagle with all teh above symbols. The Vishnu Purana makes Garuda the father of Jatayu. In the Ramayana, Jatayu says "It is 60,000 years since I was born &c." Thus Jatayu stands for a cycle of 60,000 years. The derivative meaning of Jatayu is accumulated life. Hence Garuda should stand for a greater cycle of time. It may be a symbol for a Manvanteric period.

Besides these Vishnus, there are others who figure in the Puranas when a race or tribe of men do flourish. They may be called racial or tribal Vishnus. Next come the Avatars of Vishnu.

Siva

In this third "person" of the Trinity, we have more difficulties to encounter, for the word used to represent this third person is Siva, the derivation of which remains a mystery.

In the aspect of Siva, he is not only the destroying power of nature as well as of all objects in the world, but he is also represented as the great patron of the Yogis—the Maha Yogi, the great ascetic in whom is centred the highest perfection of austere penance and abstract meditation by which the most unlimited powers are obtained, marvels and miracles are worked, the highest spiritual knowledge is acquired and union with the great spirit of the Universe is eventually gained. Now the symbols with which Siva is represented in the Puranas can be applied to both these aspects of Siva and explained from both the stand points. In the former case the whole universe is destroyed in its present form to develop to a higher stage: and in the latter the lower mind or passions are destroyed and the real or higher ego in man reaches the Nirvanic seat through Yoga.

There are two kinds of symbols to represent Siva The first is the Linga with which Mahadeva is represented in the Sukla Yajur Veda; the second is the personal form he is invested with, with one face and four hands, or with five faces and ten hands wearing all the necessary implements of destruction. These are the two symbols with which he is represented in our Sivite temples. The Mula Vigraha or the immovable image of Siva is represented by a Linga unlike the Mula Vigraha in Vishnu temples which has human figure only. But, the Utsava Vigraha, or the idol carried about in procession, is of human form. In the temples he is represented with one face and four hands wearing all the above kinds of instruments. The first, *viz.,* Linga, is the most mysterious symbol of all. Only he can understand its true and many-sided significance, who is an occultist. He will then know that it is not a phallic symbol, bat that it is one containing all the principles in man with which the powers of nature can be wielded. The word Linga means a symbol only. The Linga Purana states that the primitive Linga is a pillar of radiance in which Maheswara is present. Incarnating first as a pillar of radiance, it takes by and by a distinct form of Linga in it with the increase of all the dross of earthly enjoyments. But with the gradual spiritual experience, all the rubbishes are disposed of in the Linga, and then the untarnished Jyotis is again resumed and that in a higher stage. Upon this Linga is inscribed the word Om, and the Vedas are said to proceed from it. When this Linga is fully permeated with the vibrations or utterances of Om it is able to shake off all its dross from it and appear as the full spotless light. In the same Purana is recorded. a contest between Vishnu and Brahma who, in the interval of a creation, fight for supremacy when the Linga suddenly springs np between them. Thereupon Brahma flies up as a Hamsa (Sivan) towards the head of the Linga to cross it, and Vishnu goes down as a (Varaha) boar to its bottom to wade through to the other side; but none succeeds to find out his termination. This means firstly, that while the Rudraic or any other power is in the ascendant, the other powers cannot gauge its depth or height; secondly, that inasmuch as Brahma is to succeed Siva for fresh creation, the former rises up to the head of the symbol while Vishnu goes down, since he had already finished his work..

In the above story when the Linga appeared as a pillar of radiance, a Rishi appears on the spot and explains to them that the sound which nrose in the pillar of radiance was no other than the sacred Om composed of A, U, and M standing for Beeji (seed frnctifier), Yoni (womb), and Beeja (seed) or Siva, Vishnu and Brahma respectively. Instead of understanding properly the significance of these words a phallic significance has been attached to them. Even supposing it can be, it can be attributed not to the Linga but to the Pranava (Om) in it. To say that Pranava is phallic in its significance is absurd, since it is only a word or Sabda.

As to the formation of this symbol, man is represented by five-pointed star and the universe by two triangles interlaced Revolve these two figures round, with the apex of the upper triangle and one of the apices of the lower triangle fixed, and then we have a perfect Linga in the former case; and in the latter, a Linga with its bottom pointed perhaps in the earth and thus invisible as in our Hindu Sivite temples. Moreover, if a person should sit with his legs crossed, then such a position, if photographed, will resemble a Linga.

Now coming to Siva in his personal representation, to begin with, it may be stated that Siva, wherever he is represented, is always connected with the destructive agency only. When he destroys the world, he dilates himself into seven suns and burns the whole universe. Vishnu is stated to assume the form of Rudra to effect this. In connection with man, he is said to hover over Crematoriums with his Ganas or hosts. Being a destructive agency, he is naturally associated with burning grounds, with skulls in his. hand and saturated with blood and other things. But when he destroys many Asuras as in the Puranas?, he plays the part of a yogi also. The Asuras represent here the passions which bar the progress of an individual and which have to be crucified in one, before he reaches the higher state.

With reference to Siva in his human delineations, with one face only, it represents his generic character of a destroyer. But when he is represented with five faces, then it is we find him shining with his ten hands, three eyes, and the Moon and the Ganga on his head. As regards the Ganga, the different books give versions which differ in their minor details. But on the whole, they agree; the difference in their minor details, is owing to the different periods during which they occurred. In some places, the incidents refer to the evolution of the universe; in others, to the evolution of earth and such like.

According to the ancient Hindus, the evolution of the cosmos, the earth, human body &c.—all proceed on parallel lines. If the evolution of the cosmos in all its details is known, then that of the earth, and others also can be inferred therefrom by applying the above principle to the earth, *mutatis mutandis.* Vishnu Purana gives a description of Ganga which is rather comprehensive enough. "From that third region of atmosphere (or Sivaloka) or the seat of Vishnu proceeds the stream that washes away all sin, the (celestial) river 'Ganga, embrowned with the unguents of the nymphs of heaven who have sported in her waters. Having her source in the nail of the great toe of Vishnu s left foot, Dhruva receives her and sustains her day and night devoutly on her head; and thence the seven Rishis practise Pranayama in her waters .wreathing their braided locks with her waves. The orb of the moon encompassed by her accumulated current, derives augmented lustre from her contact. Falling as she issues from the moon, she alights on the summit of Meru and thence flows to the four quarters of the earth for its purification. The Sita, Alakananda, Chakshu and Bhadra are four branches of but one river, divided according to the region towards which it proceeds. The southern branch that is known as Alakananda was borne affectionately by Mahadeva upon his head for more than 100 (divine) years and issuing from his matted locks raised to heaven the sinful sons of Sagara by washing their ashes." In another place in the same Purana, it is stated that the current Sita flows to the west of Meru and Bhadra to the north to it. The southern branch, Alakananda is said to divide itself into 7 rivers and flow into the southern ocean. Here is the division completely analogous to that given in the theosophical literature. The one becomes three and out of the fourth arises the seven. According to the Hindu Spiritual Astronomy, all the Solar systems rotate round Dhruva, the Polar star which in turn rotates round Vishnu, the spiritual sun of all. So that, he who is at the centre of all the formative worlds and preserves the same is the Vishnavic power in the seat or loka called Vaikunta. Of course this Vishnavic power has in itself the other powers, the Brahmic and Rudraic which manifest themselves at their allotted periods. Now just as water serves to cement the things of this world, so also the waters of Ganga or the subtle magnetic and watery currents serve the same purpose in the universe. The whole universe as well as earth are, according to the Hindus, of an oval form which is symbolized by an egg or lotus. The central axis of the earth or the universe they termed Meru, Meru passing from the higher spiritual centre of Vishnu down to

Dhruva, then to the sphere of the 7 Rishis or the Great Bear, to the lunar orb and lastly to the north pole of the earth, which is its northern Meru where it diverges into 4 currents. Thus it is given out that even the earth receives the benefit of this current in order that it may be preserved. Here it is that Mahadeva receives her in his tresses of hair in order that, after the preservative stage of earth is passed, and destruction ensues, Siva may draw her to his tresses and keep her latent with him in order that she may be handed on again to Vishnu in the next cycle as will appear from the Siva Purnas. As Siva is himself an embodiment of all suns, he being said to dilate himself into many suns at the period of deluge, he wears, after Pralaya, the moon also in his head, as it is but a reflection of the sun and is considered by the Hindus to be the opposite aspect of the sun. Ganga can be said to be the one Fohatic power which running through the core of all organisms links them all in one chain of existence. In man the spinal column is the Meru through which this current runs.

The five faces represent the five Races humanity has undergone. With every race of mankind, just as there is a Vishnu to preserve it, so there is a Siva to destroy it. In addition to the two eyes which men ordinarily have, there is yet another eye in him of which he is quite oblivious. Originally as mankind arose from a spiritual state, they had then this eye only which is situated in the Pineal gland or Sahasrara. But in the symbolic representations of Siva, we see in the middle of his forehead an opening made with red flames issuing out of it. This should not be thought of as the third eve itself which is the eye of omniscience, for it is only the opening through which the third eye acts and manifests itself in the external world. But gradually as mankind became more and more immersed in sexual pleasures, this eye became more atrophied and then the present two eyes opened. Thus man has now become quite oblivious of even the existence of this eye. This third eye and the genital organs being as it were the two scales in the body, one of the two has to "kick the beam" when the other grows heavy. One of the two has to become defunct in order that the other may play its full part. Now that the procreative organ in man has its full play in him, we are not able to witness the existence or the manifested action of the higher organ, *viz.*, the third eye in the generality of mankind. Therefore it is we find that in the transition period 'of Ravana, there existed in his ranks Rakshasas with one eye, two eyes and three eyes. As regards the weapons in his hands those on his right hands are Sula (the trident), Khadga (sword), Parasu (axe) and Vatavagni (the deluge fire). The fifth hand is the Abhaya hand (or the refuge-giving hand). The left hands wear Naga (serpents), Vajra (diamond), Pasa (Noose), Ghanta (spiritual sound or Nada), Ankusa (elephant-goad). That many of these are instruments of destruction is clear. But from the Yogic standpoint, all of them symbolize the different trials which a neophyte has to undergo. For instance, Pasa is like a cross on which all the human passions have to be crucified before the Yogi passes through the straight gate, the narrow circle that widens into an infinite one as soon as the inner man has passed the threshold. Ghanta or Nada is the spiritual sound which a Yogi has to hear in his progress. As regards the other weapons, the following explanations seem reasonable. Sula or the trident is represented as one long rod branching off into three separate elongations as its end like a fork with its three prongs. The original Satva, Rajas and Tamas of Prakriti have each their own infinite sub-divisions of a triune nature like themselves. Thus the original Tamas of Rudra has also its sub-divisions of Rajas, Satwa and Tamas. Hence it will be clear that even Siva who is the destroying power, has in itself the potency of creating, preserving and destroying things through its sub-divisions of Satwa, Rajas and Tamas in order that after Pralaya or the Universal Cataclysm is over, he may hand on the power of creation to Brahma through Narayana for the build-up of a fresh universe. Being thus a metaphysical concept of a universal nature, these three divisions are found prevalent in all departments of nature such as food and others. Thus the sword and axe are the instruments through which Agnana or our lower nature or passions are controlled; the former tending to the permanent eradication of all evils and the latter, to the temporary eradication of some only as can be inferred from the use of the above two instruments. Vatavagni is that ferocious fire which swallows up all things at the end of time. The fifth hand with its upraised palm evinces His readiness and willingness to offer an asylum to those who surrender themselves up to him and to him alone.

Then going to the left hand, we have first serpent and Vajra or the diamond weapon. The serpent, besides symbolising time as in the case of Adisesha, also stands for the poison ejected by it 'which is no other than' his Tamasic aspect. This poison has to be transmuted into a nectar by those who reach unto him. In the case of highly developed individuals, poison too if taken within by them does not hurt them and becomes one conducive to their progress. The fifth hand on the left side is the Varada or the boon-giving hand. In it, figures the elephant-goad. This perhaps stands for the pain and ordeals which a person has to undergo through performing Tapas for a long time; and when the ordeals are safely gone though, there He is ready to grant any boon which .the weary disciple has been long craving for.

The Nandi or bull, the vehicle of Siva, is the Om inscribed on the Linga as stated before. It is he or it that takes all Yogis to the divine seat of Siva. Hence it is he is posted in the front of the sanctuary of Siva. Without its aid, no Yogi will be able to attain the Nirvanic seat. Again, according to the Skandha Purana, Dharmadevata (or the Divine Law) also stands for the bull.

Siva's two sons are Ganesa and Kartikeya or Subrahmaniya. Both these seem to represent the Pravritti (worldly) and Nivritti (non-worldly or spiritual) aspects of man. The former is called Ganesa, since he is the Lord or commander of the Ganas, who are Siva's attendants. He represents wisdom. Therefore he relinquishes all idea of marriage and devotes himself solely to spiritual pursuits. He removes all the obstacles to those who invoke his aid in the spiritual path. He is always the commander of the heavenly hosts under his father to put down all the Asuras, *viz;* passions in man. His head is that .of an elephant or he is Gajamukha. Gaja is literally sound, and hence, it applies to the totality of Nivritti egos. All egos of the Nivritti state have to be absorbed in Nirvana or Pralaya through him unto Siva. All the appendages of this God, such as Pasa, &c., point to this same construction only. His vehicle is Mushika or mouse. Mushika is from a root meaning to steal. Hence he is the appropriator of all. Next coming to his brother Subrahmanya, he is said to be Kartikeya, the God of war. He is born out of the sweat of Siva and Earth. He is the foster son of Krithika or the six stars of the Pleiades. He is represented as of red color and going in for wedlock, which shows that he is identical with Mars and the generative principle of nature. He represents the Pravritti path or the totality of those *egos* who go in for the worldly path. His vehicle is the peacock, the color of which is dark-blue, which can be identified with the higher *manas.*

Going into the origin of these two brothers we find it very mystic. It is said in Skanda Purana, that Pranava took the dual forms of a he-elephant and a she-elephant, and mating together generated Ganesa. The other was born out of the sweat of Siva and preserved in Ganga.

Having given some of the aspects of Siva we shall now refer to the next term applied to him. Rudra is from a root meaning to weep. As he makes all creatures weep at the end of time by creating all sorts of terror, he is so called. In this sense Rudra is a synonym of Siva. But Rudra is applied in other senses in Vishnu Purana. When the first mention of him is made, Brahma becomes incensed with Munis, Sanaka and others for not creating any progeny. So he knits his eyebrows to a point, when from his forehead springs Rudra Ardhanari or half-male and half-female. Having been ordered by Brahma to separate his two natures he becomes twofold. His male being he divided into 11 forms, some agreeable and some hideous, and his female being he multiplied manifold of different complexions. These are called Maruts in some Puranas. Here Rudra represents that stage of humanity and universe which were originally a-sexual and then bi-sexual. They may also represent the races of men which had different complexions. In enumerating the Devas, 'we generally count 8 Vasus, 11 Rudras, &c. In Brihadaranya Upanishad, when a question is put as to who these 33 Devas or crores of Devas are, a reply is made, wherein the 11 Rudras are explained as meaning the ten Pranas with Manas as the eleventh. Clearly this can be applicable to *an* ego only. Besides, Rudras as Devas can also be applied to the developed entities of egos or elementlas in their nascent stage of evolution. In another chapter of Vishnu Purana, Rudra is used in quite a different sense. Here the Tamasic aspect of creation is dwelt upon. Brahma purposing to create at the beignning of a Kalpa a son, who will be like himself, a youth of a red-blue (Nila-lohita) complexion appeared running about with a low cry. Brahma when he beheld him thus afflicted, said to him, why dost thou weep ? Give me a name, replied the boy; Rudra be thy name, rejoined the grandfather of all creatures, be composed, desist from tears. But thus addressed, the boy still wept seven times and Brahma therefore gave him seven other denominations and to these 8 persons he gave regions, wives and children. The eight manifestations then are named Rudra, Bhava, Sarva, Isana, Pasupati, Bhima, Ugra and Mahadeva, which names were given to them by their great progenitor. He also assigned to them their respective stations, the sun, water, earth, Vayu, Agni, Akas, the Hota (Ministrant Brahman) and the moon, for these are their several forms. Then the text gives out his 8 wives and their issues, among whom figure Saturn, Mercury and other planets. It is evident from the elements to which the 8 Rudras are attached that the Rudras herein mentioned are no other than the vivifying powers of the elements, &c., and that the sources of the material composition of the planets is herein disclosed.

Conclusion

It will thus be seen that though we find seeming incongruities in our books, such as the Upanishads and the Puranas, yet, if we try to understand the key by which the fundamental canon of interpretation can be known, then we shall be able to travel on the path of Puranas and other Hindu books smoothly and without much misgiving. It is this invaluable aid that Madame Blavatsky has given us, in her monumental work, "The Secret Doctrine," which has unearthed the many truths underlying the grotesque and fantastic stories contained in our spiritual books. It is only by giving a better and a more rational interpretation of our sacred literature that the claims of our archaic religion can be vindicated and progress can be made in it. Our ancient writers having written our. books in a double language, so as to suit the higher and the lower minds, the latter will be pleased finding in them stories to their taste, and the former metaphysical truths underlying the same, and this seems to have been the policy of almost all the religious writers of the world.

---

1. From the Theosophic Thinker contributed by Mr. K. Narayanasami Aiyer.

CHAPTER XXIII

MAN AND UNIVERSE

Physics and Metaphysics[1]

The causes of existence are not only the physical causes known to science, but also the metaphysical causes. According to esoteric teaching, the real cause of all existence remains for ever hidden and its first emanations are the most complete abstractions mind can conceive. These abstractions must of necessity be postulated as the cause of the material universe which presents itself to the senses and intellect, and they underlie the secondary and subordinate powers of Nature, which, an thropomorphised, have been worshipped as god and gods by the common herd of every age. It is impossible to conceive anything without a cause; the attempt to do so makes the mind a blank. This is virtually the condition to which the mind must come at last when we try to trace back the chain of causes and effects, but both Science and Religion jump to this condition of blankness much more quickly than is necessary; for they ignore the metaphysical abstractions which are the only conceivable cause of physical concretions. These abstractions become more and more concrete as they approach our plane of existence until finally they phenome-nalize in the form of. the material universe, by a process of conversion of metaphysics into physics analogous to that by which steam can be condensed into water and the water frozen intoice.

Involution and Evolution[2]

We recognize the manifestation of matter and spirit, as the two poles of being, spirit being involved and matter evolved. These two meet and blend in all created forms. The one gives power and ideal form. the other structure.

The phenomenal existence in space and time is only one member of the equation of existence, the other lies in the subjective world, not in time and space. The pattern after which nature everywhere builds and the laws winch determine her mechanism though displayed in matter are derived from the subjective world. There is a coming forth and a receding back into the unseen world, so that manifestation on the phenomenal plane is synonymous with duality. The recognition of this dual law is the reconciliation of Science and Religion. If we call evolution materialistic, we may with equal propriety call involution spritualistic. And neither term can be construed into a reproach. The physical world is thus the embodiment and manifestation of the spiritual in terms of matter, space, time, and motion; for matter and force being regarded as ineparable and indestructible might nevertheless be resolved back into magnetic substance from whence they came, which would not destroy them, but merely cause them to disappear from the physical planes. They may pass from the active to the passive plaue and still exist as invisible, unparticled matter and potential force.

Origin of Man[3]

Tradition tells us that the human race has been procreated by a single pair (one man and one woman). This does not seem to be an idle theory. It is very easy for us, the Hindus of the present day (*viz;* the twice-born classes) to trace back our origin to Brahma, the first progenitor; because if not all, at least a majority of the different sections of the upper three classes have a gotra or a tribal name informing them of the first Man from whom the tribe has descended. These progenitors, ten in number, were the sons of Manu who was produced by Brahma. But even now if we trace any tribe or nation back to its origin, we may arrive at the same result, namely, that there was a single pair at its origin, though this enquiry may lead us to far remote times of which the accounts may appear ieredible at a first reading. We have shown that there is a time when the evolution of the world takes place, and as a consequence of the above argument, it necessarily follows that there must have been a common progenitor of the race at the beginning of human origin. The highest condition to which by the good quality a soul can be exalted is that of Brahma. As to how Brahma is born subjectively or potentially, one should study Manu on Creation, Brihad Aranyaka Upanishad and Mandukya Upanishad. It is difficult to give here all the information necessary on the subject.

Septenary Constitution of Man[4]

The following is the deep analysis of man, made by the Hindu philosophers:—(1) The Material body—*Stoolasariram.* (2) *The Linga-sarira.* (3) The Life Principle—*Jiva.* (4) The *Kamarupa* resulting as *Mayavirupa.* (5) The physical Intelligence or Animal Soul—*Manas.* (6) The Spiritual Intelligence—*Buddhi.* (7) The *Atma* or the divine and eternal principle. The Hindu Philosophy of man fits in with the lines of modern science much more snugly than that of either the supernaturalistic religions or the materialistic man of Science. As the successive forms of water run up into the invisible world, so Esoteric Hindu philosophy gives us a graduated series of molecular arrangements in the human economy at one end of which is the concrete mass of the *Stoolasarira,* at the other the last sublimation called *Atma* or spirit. Each of these several sets of atoms which compose the seven parts of man occupy the interstitial spaces between the next coarser set of atoms. The atoms of the *Buddhi* pervade the interstices of *Manas,* those of the Manas, those of the *Kamarupa,* those of the latter, those of *Jiva,* and those of the

Jiva those of the *Stoolasarira.* And as each coarser contains the particles of all the finer principles, therefore the Stoolasarira is the gross casket within which the several parts of the composite man are contained. Pervading and energising all is the Atma, or that incomprehensible final energy which cannot bo comprehended by the physical senses.

Spirit and Matter[5]

In the secret philosophy spirit and matter are viewed as graduated. Though *one and the same thing* in their origin, spirit and matter, when once they are on the plane of differentiation, begin each of them their evolutionary progress in contrary directions—Spirit falling gradually into matter and the latter according to its orignal condition, that of a pure spiritual substance. Both are inseparable, yet ever separated. In polarity, on the physical plane, two like poles will always repel each other, while the negative and positive are mutually attracted; so do spirit and matter stand to each other—the two poles of the same homogenous substance, the root-principle of the univers

Spirit and matter are the two states of the *One.* which is neither spirit nor matter, both being the absolute life, latent Spirit is the first differentiation of (and in) *space;* and Matter, the first differentiation of spirit. That, which is neither Spirit nor Matter—that is It—the Causeless Cause of spirit and matter, which are the cause of the cosmos. And That we call the One Life or the Intra-Cosmic Breath.

The following Extracts are also in point:—Says Annie Besant, F.T.S. in several places:—

From the Theosophical stand-point, Spirit and Matter are essntially one, and the universe one living whole from centre to circumference, not a molecule in it, that is not instinct with life. The physical plane may serve the student as a model from which by analogy he may gain an idea of the subdivisions of the spirit-matter of other planes. When a Theosophist speaks of a plane, he means a region throughout which spirit-matter exists, all whose combinations are derived from a particular set of atoms.

Again Mrs. Annie Besant in speaking of the several planes of existence (according to Theosophy, there are seven planes, Physical, Astral, Kamalokic, Mental, Devachanic, Buddhic and Nirvanic in order of succession, Nirvanic being the highest, beyond which Theosophy does not go) says:—

The phenomenal spirit and matter of any universe are finite in their extent and transitory in their duration, but the roots of spirit and matter are eternal. The energy of the Logos, or the, Supreme Lord as whirling motion of inconceivable rapidity "digs holes in space" in this root of matter, and this vortex of life encased in a film of the root of matter is the primary atom; these and their aggregations, spread throughout the universe, from all the subdivisions of spirit-matter of the highest or seventh plane. The sixth plane is formed by some of the countless myriads of these primary atoms setting up a vortex in the coarsest aggregations of their own plane, and this primary atom enwalled with sprial strands of the coarsest combinations of the seventh plane becomes the finest unit of spirit-matter, or atom, of the sixth plane. These sixth-plane atoms and their endless combinations from the sub-divisions of the spirit-matter of the sixth-plane. The sixth-plane atom in its turn, sets up a vortex in the coarsest aggregations of its own plane, and with these coarsest aggregation as a limiting wall, becomes the finest unit of spirit-matter, or atom, of the fifth-plane. Again, these fifth-plane atoms and their combinations form the subdivisions of the spirit-matter of the fifth-plane. The process is repeated to form successively the spirit -matter of the fourth, the third, the second, and the first planes. These are the seven great regions of the universe, so far as their material constituents are concerned.

Universe and Man[6]

The principal ideas, advanced by teachers of Theosophy are somewhat as follows-—briefly stated.:—

The Universe a spiritual instead of a material basis. The various things in Nature which appeal to our physical s senses are merely transitory forms assumed by this basic Akasic substance and can all be dissipated and. restored to their primary or invisible condition in harmony with certain law a, as readily as a lump of ice can be dissipated by heat and evaporation. The Universe is one vast unit, all its parts being closely and inseparably connected with the whole: Ultimate Spirit or Parabrahm, being the root of all, and Essential substance or Mulaprakriti, its negative aspect opposite pole, or first differentiation, from which, by gradual changes, the appearance which we call matter is formed. The Universe is also subject to cyclic law, resulting in immense periods of alternate rest and activity, which may be very faintly illustrated by our day and night.

Man also in his inmost nature is a spiritual being—a spark or offshoot from the great primal source of all, and this spark is destined for ultimate reunion with its source. He uses from time to time, for the unfoldment of his powers, a physical body,. the elements of which have been gradually built up, by slow precesses of evolution through the mineral, vegetable and animal kingdom, until they have become fitted to form parts of that temple designed for the indwelling spirit. Thus all mankind are, by necessity of their origin, when viewed spiritually, one great brotherhood whether the fact be recognized by them or not.

The human being, on this earth, may be said to consist of seven constituent parts, *viz,—1st, Spirit or Atma*—the illuminuting spark or ray from the Divine; *2nd, Spiritual soul* or *Buddhi*—the highest discriminating principle in man, one remove from pure spirit; *3rd, Human soul or Mind, called Manas*—a radiation from the Universal Mind. This in conjunction with the two higher principles previously named, constitutes the reincarnating ego—the Individuality of Man. But Manas is dual in its nature and in order to come into relation with matter, it casta its reflection upon the finer portion of the inner body and as a result we have, 4th, *The Animal Soul or Kama* illuminated by the Manasic reflection making what is called Kama Manas; Kama being the seat and totality of the purely animal instincts, passions and sensations to which the Manasic radiation adds *reason*, and a higher grade of memory than the lower animals possess, together with a consciousness of distinct personality.

Thus Mind or Manas in its upper aspect touches spirit, while its lower aspect touches refined mattar, so as to enable the body to become the vehicle of the soul's manifestation on earth; the higher Manas telegraphs messages of guidance to the Animal-Man, while the lower Manas, in its turn telegraphs the finer portions or essence of its earthly sensations, experience and knowledge, up to the re-incarnating ego, for registration and future use. Next we have *5th, Prana, the vitality or 'Life-principle and 6th, Astral 'body,* both of which are necessary as connecting links in the chain of communication with *7th, The outer body,* and through it with the material world around us; for Manas cannot touch the gross physical body. The astral body or Etheric Double is the model which attracts to itself the particles composing the material form or gross body, which are moulded through the agency of vitality, or the life-principle; and when this latter departs, the outer body becomes amere lump of earth, and the Astral body soon disintegrates along with the physical.

Atma, Buddhi and Manas are termed the higher triad, the other four—the body, its Ethereal double, Prana and Kama-Manas—the Lower quaternary.

Each individual atom which enters into the cells and tissues of the physical body has its separate life which it contributes to help from this body—the grand unit of the higher order. Though these little atoms which have been styled microbes, are continually changing, the human form remains permanent, for it existed before the physical structure was built. As Mrs. Besant says in *Death and* after:—

"The death of the physical body occurs when the withdrawal of the controlling life-energy leaves the microbes to go their own way and these many lives, no longer co-ordinated, scatter from each other and scatter the particles of the cells of the man of dust."

The Linga Sharira or Etheric Double is the contact body wherein are located the centres of sensation, through the agency of which we come in touch with material things. The bullet or the knife does not destroy this Etheric or Astral body, yet the intense action of the mind of a mother, caused, by some sudden shock, may be sufficient to wither some portion of this invisible model and as a result a child may be born minus an arm or a leg. Thought is the primal power which builds forms, and which can also mar them. Mrs. Besant, in speaking of the great ocean of life in which we and all living things are immersed, and of which we constantly partake compares each individual living organism to a sponge; and the infinite sea of Jiva or Life-force to the ocean in which the sponge is immersed, and by which its every pore is filled, and says "we may think of the ocean outside the sponge, or of the part of the ocean which is appropriated" by the sponge. Theosophy distinguishes this appropriated life under the name of Prana".

Kama may be defined as that principle in us which includes all our lower appetites, passions, emotions, desires and instincts Hatred, envy, pride and jealousy as well as the lower aspect of love or lust come under this head. It gives the desire for physical existence, for the experience of animal sensations and purely material pleasures. This is the principle which anchors us to earth-life. It is by no means the human body which is the growest factor in the constitution of man, but this middle principle or Kama, which is the real animal centre. The body is but the irresponsible channel through which the beast, the human animal in us, acts out its life. Our consciousness may function on separate planes of our being. It may for a time be limited to physical sensations which have their centres in the Astral body, again it may be wholly occupied on the Kamic plane, as in the heat of passion or the excitement of battle, when slight wounds pass entirely unnoticed. To give free action to the purely Manasic or intuitive plane of consciousness, the entire animal nature must be completely stilled.

The quarternary constitutes the personality of the man, Kama Manas being its leading principle, the one that makes us recognize our own selfhood as distinct from that of others. This lower Manas when swayed by material sensations and emotions, fails to recognise the unity underlying the great whole, and turns a deaf ear to that inner voice which speaks for harmony.

It is well to regard Manas as the Thinker, the re-incarnating ego, the real individual, now reaping its harvest of earthly experiences in a temporary physical body. When we can thoroughly realise that the body is in no sense this Thinker, bat only its useful machine; and that we can enjoy full individual consciousness and power of thought when entirely out of this body, and that many now living in earth-life do enjoy this privilege, we are in a condition to control the body better. We can then view it as a garment which we usually wear for protection, but which we can also lay aside and view as being entirely separate from our real self.

The animal man differs from its purely animal relatives, the beasts, according "to the influence exerted over it by the Thinker, who has come to train and ennoble it." Take away the Thinker and you have the animal—whether its form be human or otherwise.

The Thinker imparts to the animal-man such of its own capacities as this lower man by virtue of his organisation, is able to manifest and these capacities working in and through the human brain, are recognized by us as the brain-mind, lower mind or lower Manas.

"In the West, the development of this brain mind is regarded as tnarking the distinction in ordinary parlance between the brute and the human being. That which the Theosophist looks on as merely the lower or brain-mind is considered by the average Westerner to be the mind itself; hence there is often much confusion of thought between the Theosophist and the non Theosophist. We are taught that the Thinker, striving to reach and influence the animal-man, sends out a ray that plays on and in the brain, and that through the brain are manifested so much of the mental powers as that brain, by its configuration, by the extent of 'its convolutions and other physical qualities, is able to appropriate or translate. This ray sets the molecules of the brain nerve-cells vibrating as a ray of light sets in motion the molecules of the retinal nerve-cells, and so gives rise to consciousness on the physical plane. Reason, memory, will, ideation, as these faculties are known to us, are manifested when the brain is in full activity. All these are the outcome of the ray sent forth by the Thinker, modified by the material condition through which it must work." "These conditions," so plainly stated by Mrs. Besant, "include healthy nerve-cells with a properly balanced development of their respective groups, and a full supply of blood containing nutritive matter that can be assimilated by the cells, so as to supply their waste. If these conditions or any of them are absent, the brain cannot function, and thought processes can no more be carried out through such a brain than a melody can be produced from a violin without strings or an organ with a broken bellows. The brain no more originates the thought than the organ originates the melody; in both cases there is a player working through the instrument. But the power of the player to manifest himself in thought or in melody is limited by the capacities of the instrument."

Let this difference between the Thinker and the animal-man be clearly viewed.

"The Thinker re-incarnates, the animal-man does not." The animal-man is born and the true man or the Thinker is gradually linked to him. Through the brain of the animal-man the true man works; at one time in one body, again in another.

"The question 'why do I not remember my past lives is based on a misconception. 'I'—as the true 'I'—do remember; but the animal-man not yet in full responsive union with his true higher self, cannot remember a past in which his functioning in his present personality had no share. Brain-memory can contain only a record of the events in .which that special brain has been concerned, but as the true self becomes increasingly able to affect its bodily habitation, glimpses of past incarnations will flash on the lower consciousness and these will at length become less like flashes and more like permanent visions, until finally the past is recognised as 'mine 'by the continuous thread of memory that gives the feeling of individuality. Then the present incarnation is recognised as being merely the last garment in which the self has clothed itself."

"Death consists indeed in a repeated process of unsheathing. The immortal part of man shakes off from itself one after another its outer casings and emerging therefrom as the butterfly from its chrysalis, it passes into a higher state of consciousness. When the fact that this escape from the body and this dwelling of the conscious entity either in the Astral Double or in a yet more ethereal Mind-body can be effected during birth-life, is thoroughly realised, man may become familiar with the excarnated condition and if the life has been a noble one, death will finally be shorn of the last vestige of terror. One cannot travel far from his body in his Astral Double, but if he learns to use his Thought-body, he is no longer chained to the neighbourhood of his material body and realizes in full consciousness the independence of the spiritual intelligence. Why should a man who has thus repeatedly shed his body and his Astral Double and has found the processes result not in unconsciousness bill in a vastly extended freedom and vividness of life,why, I say, should he fear the final casting away of his fetters and the freeing of his immortal self?"

Mother Lotus[7]

The Lotus or Padma is a very ancient and favorite simile for the cosmos itself and also for man. The Lotus seed contains within itself a perfect miniature of the future plant, which typifies the fact that the spiritual prototypes of all things exist in the immaterial world before those things become materialized on Earth. Further the Lotus plant grows up through the water, having its root in the mud and spreading its flower in the air above. The Lotus thus typifies the life of man and also that of the cosmos; for the Secret Doctrine teaches that the elements of both are the same, and that both are devoloping in the same direction. The root of the Lotus sunk in the mud represents material life, the stalk passing up through the water typifies existence in the Astral world, and the flower floating on the water and opening to the sky is emblematical of spiritual being.

Planes[8]

The phenomenal spirit and matter of any universe are finite in their extent and transitory in their duration, but the roots of spirit and matter are eternal. The energy of the Logos or the Supreme Lord as whirling motion of inconceivable rapidity "digs holes in space" in this root of matter, and this vortex of life encased in a film of the root of matter is the primary atom; these and their aggregations spread throughout the universe, form all the subdivisions of spirit-matter of the highest or seventh-plane. The sixth-plane is farmed by some of the countless myriads of these primary atoms setting up a vortex in the coarsest aggregations of their own plane, and this primary atom enwalled with spiral strands of the coarsest combinations of the seventh-plane becomes the finest unit of spirit-matter or atom of the sixth-plane. These sixth-plane atoms and their endless combinations form the subdivisions of the spirit-matter of the sixth-plane. The sixth plane atom in its turn, sets up a vortex in the coarsest aggregations of its own plane, and with these coarsest aggregations as a limiting wall, becomes the finest unit of spirit-matter or atom of the fifth-plane. Again these fifth-plane atoms and their combinations form the subdivisions of the spirit-matter of the fifth-plane. The process is repeated to form successively the spirit-matter of the fourth, the third, the second, and the first-planes. These are the seven great regions of the universe, so far as their material constituents are concerned.

NOTE—The word *spirit-matter* is used designedly. The word impliesthe fact that there is no such thing as dead-matter. All matter is living; the tiniest particles are lives. Science speaks truly in affirming 'no force without matter, no matter without force. They are wedded together in an indissoluble marriage throughout the ages of the life of a universe and none can wrench them apart. Matter is form, and there is no form which does not express a life; spirit is life and there is no life that is not limited. by a form.

Universe.[9]

The Universe is two-fold, since it is composed of the two principles Purusha and Prakriti or Spirit and Matter. These two principles are variously denominated in different religions and sub religions. They are called Chit and Achit by some, motion and nam-motion by some others, Atma and non-atma by some and so on. But all of them convey the same idea. Purusha is so-called, since, according to the Aitreya Upanishad, it (from Puri-Sayanam) resides in the (Puri) City of Prakriti or Matter; and Prakriti is that which is acted upon, *viz.,* by Purusha. Hence these two represent the male and female principles of the Universe.

Parabrahm (God) has two aspects, the imperishable and the perishable. The imperishable is its true nature; but the perishable in this Universe. On this perishable aspect of Parabrahm, the Visnu Purana says:—

"Brahm, in its totality, has essentially the aspect of Prakriti' both manifested and unmanifested (Mulaprakriti) and also the aspect of Spirit (Purusha) and the aspect of Kala (time). Purusha is the leading aspect of the Supreme Brahm. The next is a two fold aspect—Prakriti, both manifested and unmanifested, and (Kala) time is the last."

From these passages it is clear that the Universe has its two stages of Avyakta and Vyakta, *viz.,* its noumenal condition, when it is in an unmanifested state and the phenomenal condition when it manifests itself. The Ancient Hindu writers maintained that the Universe is ever oscillating alternately between manifestation and non-manifestation. The manifested stage they termed Maha Manvantara or Kalpa, while the unmanifested was dubbed with the title of Pralaya, when all nature goes to repose for a fresh struggle and work. But the Vishnu Purana terms this unmanifest ed stage Mahavishnu or Narayana and the manifested, Brahma. H. P. Blavatsky states that the former is the unmanifested Logos and the latter is the manifested Logos. The former may be termed Purusha Prakriti stage. When these two are in their Laya state (or state of absorption), while the latter may be styled the stage of Purusha and Prakriti, differentiated. Narayana is represented prior to creation to be merely resting in a natatory position in the waters of space and it is only at the commencement of a period creation that Brahma rises from his navel and begins to create So that we clearly understand from this allegory that Narayans stands for the sleeping aspect of the universe in its unmanifested stage, while Brahma stands for the active period of creation.

It is only when we enter into the question whether Purusha and Prakriti are principles like Brahm or the ephemeral aspects of the non-dual Principle that there arises "the apple of discord between the different religious sects of Southern India. When Pralaya sets in, are these two merged into the bosom of Par-brahm, as one or do they yet preserve a distinct individnality their own ? The Advaitins contend that there is a Sayiljya- Laya state when nought else is but the one principle. They say that this universe of dualities is merged as one into its noumers of Parabrahm and that it is not real, since it ever changes name and form. Dwaitins contend that the two Principles, Pnrusha and Prakriti are as real as Parabrahm and are co-eternal with it. But Vishishtadwaitins take a middling course. According to the illustration given by H. P. Blavatsky, shall we take Oxygen and Hydrogen, when they combine together as water, to be yet existing as two in the state of solution or as one ? Water can be said to beone in its liquid condition or in ease, but to be two in posse, since it can again be decomposed into two. This is merely a metaphysical difficulty which it is not worth our while to be ever fighting about as the three sects in Southern India are always doing. Even these difficulties can be set at rest by holding that they are only different standpoints from which each observer looks at the question, while they tend towards the same end. They present but the three aspects of the one troth, wherein the universe is first in its latent state, secondly in that transition stage when the latent becomes patent, and thirdly, in its patent tate.

Space.[10]

(OR LOKAS OR TALAS.)

The seven Lokas, such as Bhu, Bhuvar, *&c.*, and the seven Talas—Atala, Vitala, *&c.*, are not the visible worlds of oar present vision; but are different states, whether of consciousness or of matter; for Hindu philosophy asserts that the one consciousness or cosmic ideation maniftests itself in different states of consciouness trough different states of matter. These different states of matter are not the same as the solid, liquid and gaseous states of modern science, since these latter pertain to our physical earth only; but idnde in it, as one, the physical with all its sab-divisions.

Hindu philosophy postulates the existence of one primordial matter, called Mulaprakriti. It is the one homogeneons matter, at of which all other states of matter producing differentiations arisen. It is not even the protyle posited by Professor Crookes, since according to him, it is the homogeneous substance underlying the physical world only. But as the Hindu philosophy holds to the existence of higher and higher states of matter, than the physical, Mulaprakriti can be called the primordial protyle When in our progress we ascend to higher heights of matter we find that what was considered Protyle in a certain stage and of the physical world, becomes differentiated; for then only is progress possible. The fact is that even Mulaprakriti, which the Hindus consider as the primordial protyle, becomes differentiated in a still higher evolution; therefore Mulaprakriti is primordial in a relative sense only and is protyle for all the evolution to come in this Maha-Kalpa.

Turning to the differentiation of the original matter, we find it evolves to seven stages or planes of manifestation, each grosser than the preceding one, till the last stage of density, *viz.*, our present stage is reached. Again this septenary division has in itself endless septenary sub-divisions which are too difficult to be mentioned. It should not be supposed that this septenary division is the only possible division existing in the cosmos. Both the septenary and the triune divisions are only different ways of dividing the universe; the triune being included in the septenary which alone is the occult and comprehensive division of the cosmos.

Now about the nature of these universes. As already stated the whole universe is nothing but a compound of Purusha and Prakriti or Spirit and Matter. It should not be supposed that spirit and matter are two entirely different principles. They are according to Vishnu Purana, but two aspects of one and the same principle.

Even this physical universe, when looked at from the plane of the mind, is one vast mass of intelligence, but is in itself inert. So carrying this conception still higher to the several subtle universes, a person finds when he ascends to the higher plane that the whole space is nothing but one intelligence of the highest order. So that what we find is that the intelligence exhibited on the highest or the seventh-plane, is far superior to them on lower planes. And why? Because of the differentiation of matter in each of the seven planes. Thus therefore we find that intelligence and inertness are the two poles of the universe, whether we take into consideration one alone or the seven, all together. Therefore all the seven worlds can be treated of either in the light of matter or in the light of spirit. It is only when both the views are had, that we can understand the phenomena completely.

Now to the view of the worlds or space from the standpoint of matter, all the Lokas or worlds are coexistent in space. The matter of one world is so attenuated as to pass through the matter of its next lower world since the former is so subtle as to pass through the molecules of the latter. Amongst these seven Lokas, the higher three, *viz.*, Jano, Tapo, and Satya are said to be Arupa or without form. The first three are Rupa or with form. The middle one serves as their connecting link being Rupa-Arupa. With every Kalpa all the creations of form are destroyed in the three worlds; when they do reside in the fourth world, untrammelled by the matter of the three lower Lokas, to reanimate again in the next Kalpa for fresh progress.

Bhu or the physical world extends as far as it is illuminated by the rays of the sun and moon. Wherever earthy substance exists, which may be traversed by the feet, that constitutes the sphere of the earth. Bhuvarloka is that region which extends from the earth to the sun. If a sphere be described with a line joining the sun and the earth as the radius, then in this space move the atoms of Bhuvar space. Suvarloka is that region comprised by a sphere made with its radius extending from the sun to Druva, the polar star. Then beyond Suvarloka are Mahar, Jano, fact, and Satya

Lokas, which are said to be formless. From the Tapu that Bhu, Bhuvar and Suvar are described to include a space which recur in all the three, it is clear that they should refer merely to planes of matter, one within another, in space. The books merely describe the extreme limits to which matter of one state can pervade and act in space. It is these worlds that from the region of the consequences of Karmas, they being enacted on the land of Bharata. Then as to the denizens of these Lokas. In Bhuvar Loka are said to live Yakshas, Rakshasas and other elemen-tals, which are of a lower order. In that Loka are also stated to live Siddhas and other Munis since it is the seat also of developed men who have thrown off the trammels of matter. The third in the region of pure elementals such as Vasus, Rudras, Adityas as well as still highly developed human beings. In the fourth Loka, such Rishis, as Bhrigu and others live, giving astral forms to all creation, humanity included. Janoloka is said to be tenanted by such saints as Sanaka and others who contain in themselves the egos of all humanity which incarnate in the bodies prepared for them. They are also the perfected saints. Vairajas do live in the sixth world. They are said to be the sons of Viraj or Brahma They are the same as Manus. They are those who have reached the Atma-Buddhi state or Dharmakaya state. Beyond these is the seventh state or the Loka of Brahma, that Loka which contains in itself all the other Lokas.

The matter that we know of in our present state obeys certain laws. It is perceived by our sense and has form or dimensions color, &c. Its dimensions are length, breadth and height. The matter of Bhuvar Loka has fourth dimension called "Throughth." It means permeability. Our organs of sight are able to responsible light vibrations which lie between two means. Beyond a certain maximum and minimum vibrations, our visual organs do not pass Likewise with sound and others. Our tympanum is not able to pass beyond certain limits when the vibrations of sound get too weak or too strong, our powers of audition are too feeble to synchronism to and hence sense them. Not that the sound vibrations are destroyed; but they are in the ether, and our ears are not so delicate as to sense them. All these mean that if there exist in man subtle organs of perception, they will render men susceptible to the higher and subtle impressions. And this is exactly what the Hindu philosophy says. It says that there is a subtle or Lings Sarira in man which increases man's powers of perception and makes him perceive objects which no microscope or other physical instruments will reveal.

Then as to the Talas. They are also to be stated as seven They are generally given as Atala, Vitala, Sutala. Talatala, Mahatala Rasatala and Patala.

All the universes have got their two aspects of positive and negative. And the Talas do merely represent one of these aspects. This can be better understood only when they are explained from the standpoint of consciousness. It should not be supposed that the states are fourteen, but only seven; each of the different states of matter having its dual aspect. When our Puranas state that there are seven higher and seven lower worlds, they refer merely to states and not to locality. Each world has its higher and lower aspects.

Corresponding to these seven Lokas are the seven elements. Though in each Loka there are seven elements, one element preponderates in one plane in order to give its distinct impress to that plane. Prithvi (earth), Ap (watery Agni, Vayu, Akas, Bhutadi (or Ahankara) and Mahat-these are the seven elements corresponding to the seven Lokas beginning with Bhu. This world consisting of the seven Lokas and Talas is said to be the Mundane Egg; and above and below it are said to be the seven Avaranas or envelopes which together constitute the whole universe. Of course, these seven envelopes are not the seven elements that we see now, but are the subtler ones.

The Lokas and Talas may also be interpreted metaphysically as septenary states of consciousness.

Unless this main conception of the Hindus that space, as we know it, is but a compound of different states of consciousness or density of matter which constitute the different planes or Lokas of the world, one permeating another, and that Lokas and Talas are but aspects of the same space, is properly grasped, all our Hindu writings containing references to the same will be nothing but fairy tales to them.

Hindu Chronology[11]

The four ages of the Hindu Chronology contain a far more philosophical idea than appears on the surface. It defines them according to both the psychological or mental and the physical states of man during their period. Crita-Yug, the golden age, the age of joy, or spiritual innocence of man Treta-Yug, the age of silver, or that of fire—the period of supremacy of man and of giants and of the sons of God; Dwapara-Yug, the age of bronze—a mixture already of purity and impurity (spirit and matter) the age of doubt; and at last our own, the Kali-yug or age of iron, of darkness, misery and sorrow. In this age, Vishnu had to incarnate himself in Krishna, in order to save humanity from *the* goddess Kali, consort of Siva, the all-annihilating—the goddess of death, destruction and human misery. Kali is the best emblem to represent the fall of man; the falling of spirit into the degradation of matter, with all its terrific results. We have to rid *our*-selves of Kali before we can ever reach Moksha or Nirvana, the abode of blessed Peace and Spirit.

Sea-Girt Continent[12]

The ancient Hindus knew more of this earth than what is known at present. The Shastras say that the known earth (including Asia, Europe. Africa and America) is but a small fraction the actual extent of this globe and that the four continents known to us comprise an insignificant portion of what is known as Bharatavarsha. The Earth according to the Hindus occupies a circle in space whose diameter is 50 crores of Yojans (1 Yojan 8 miles). The Earth is divided into seven large tracts of land each of which is surrounded by an ocean. The names of these tracts are Jumbu. Plakha, Shalmali, Kusha, Krouncha, Shak, and Pushkara. The first piece of land is surrounded by Lavan some dra (salt ocean); the second by Ikshu Samudra, the third by Sun the fourth by Sarpi, the fifth by Dadhi, the Sixth by Dugdha and the seventh by Jala. The central tract or globe is subdivided into nine parts by the Varsha mountains; for this reason each of the nine parts is called a Varsha. The Southernmost tract of the Jambu Dwipa is termed Bharatavarsha. All these Varshas are divided from oee another by mountains and seas. Bharatavarsha is again divided into nine Dwipas (tracts of land) and one of these tracts of land is called Sagara Samvrita Dwipa, the sea-girt continent. This latter ontinent is 1000 Yojans, *i.e.*, about 9000 miles in diameter. The dameter of the known earth as calculated by the Europeans is about the same. The nine tracts of land into which Bharatavarsha. is divided is separated from one another by mountains and oceans. The divisions of Bharatavarsha are:—(a) Indra Dwipa, (b) Kase-raman (c) Tamra barna, (d) Gavasthiman, (e) Nag Dwipa, (f) Soumma, (g) Gandharva, (h) Baruna and (i) Sagara Sam-vrita Dwipa.

It is very curious to note that the extent of the Sagara Sam-vrita Dwipa almost exactly coincides with the extent of the world as known to the moderns. It has been mentioned before that the sea-girt continent is one thousand yojans in diameter, which is equivalent to 9091 miles. The distance between the extreme north of Greenland and Cape Horn is only 131 degrees, *i.e.*, 9104 miles.

According to the Hindus the eastern part of the sea-girt continent was inhabited by the Kiratas; the western part by the Jaranas, and the middle portion by the Hindus. The Matsa Puran definitely says that all the extremities of the sea-girt 'continent were inhabited by the Mlechas and only the middle portion by the Brahmans, Kshatriyas, Vaisyas and Sudras. From this it would appear that the habitation of the ancient Hindus far exceeded in extent the area inhabited by the modern Hindus. The word bharanas frequently occurs in the Puranas and it seems that this word includes every other nation except the ancient Hindus. Further point that should be remembered in this connection is that the vast stretch of the Atlantic Ocean which flows between the old world and the new was formerly a continent which joined both of them, and such is the opinion of many modern geologists. The geography of the Puranas cannot be properly understood without taking into consideration one or two submerged Continents. That the Atlantic continent, is one of them, there is not the least shadow of doubt. The wide view which the Shastras take of the earth is not so improbable as may appear at first sight. Who can vouchsafe that there do not exist oilier continents on this earth than the four well-known continents ? The geography of the earth at the time of Mahabharata is likely to bear very little resemblance with the geography of the present time. According to the statements in the Puranas, the world to us is an insignificant part of the great world, which lies beyond the pale of our knowledge. There are seven such earths as we have shown before, each surrounded by an ocean belt. Whether the materials by which all these earths are composed are the same or whether they are subject to the same law;, of gravitation is not known to us. A little difference in the degree of gravitation will produce quite a different race varying from us in essential characteristics. The changes in the physical body of animals will be immense by a mere change in the degree of gravitation.

The earth according to the ancient Hindus is therefore a vast stretch of land and water extending far beyond the limits of the four continents. Its diameter is about 400 crores of miles and it stretches far beyond the north and the south poles. Even now we know very little of this earth though we have discovered another continent. America. The human intellect is trying to extend its knowledge beyond the starry spheres but there are many things under our feet of which it is quite ignorant. The future will reveal what is closed at present and humanity will at last smile at its own ignorance.

Sun Drawn by Horses[13]

The sun is depicted as drawn by seven horses, and by one horse with seven heads:—the former referring to his seven planets, the latter to their one common origin from the One Cosmic Elements. This One Element is called figuratively *Fire.*

Dwipas.[14]

Dwipas can be examined either geographically or metaphysically. Metaphysically, the division of Dwipas in the Swayambhu period is but a general formula for the understanding of the different divisions of the Dwipas in the different rounds or periods. If we know the general division of Dwipas in the First Round, it will make us understand the divisions of Dwipas obtaining in the other Round, also, as they are simply analogous. Looking at the Geographical aspect of this division of Swayambhu Manu period, the seven Dwipas refer to several localities, first of all to our planetary chain,

Jambu Dwipa alone representing our globe, the six others are (to us) invisible companion globes of this earth. This is shown by the very nature of the allegorical and symbolic descriptions. Jumbu Dwipa is in the centre of all these (the so-called insular) continents, and is surrounded by a sea of salt water whereas Plaksha, &c., are surrounded severally by great seas of sugar-cane juice, &c., and such like metaphorical names. These seas represent nothing but the Milky Way and the various congeries of Nebuloe.

Now, therefore, when the geographical description of these Dwipas is taken into consideration as obtaining in the first Round, what do these Dwipas signify ? They stand for this earth of ours remaining in different states of matter. All the Dwipas except Jambu Dwipa, do stand for those earths which were or are in existence in a very subtle state unperceived by our present vision. Hence it is said that they are stated to be the invisible companions of our present earth—invisible to our present eyes, but visible to our subtle ones when developed. All these subtle invisible companions of our earth are even now co-existent with it, do inter-penetrate it. When the seas are stated to surround these Dwipas in higher states of matter, all that we mean is that some kinds of gaseous subtle particles of watery matter surround them in their subtle states just as physical water surrounds this physical earth.

Then, turning to the second description of Dwipas in this Round of ours, what does it refer to? Each of these is not strictly a continent in the modern sense of the word, but each name from Jambu down to Pushkara, refers to the geographical. names given (firstly) to the dry lands covering the face of the whole earth during the period of a Root-race in general: and (secondly) to what remained of these after a geological (Race) Pralaya as Jambu for instance, and (thirdly) to those localities which will enter after the future cataclysms into the formation of new universal continent, peninsulas or Dwipas—each continent being, in one sense, a greater or smaller region of dry land surrounded with water. Dwipas here mean that they are the beds of dry earth surrounded by water upon which each Root-Race humanity incarnates and fulfils its allotted mission, parts of which beds surviving after a Pralaya, or the destruction of a Root-Race, and when another Root-Race or bed of the earth springs up afresh—four Root-Races have passed away, and hence four Dwipas or beds of earth welled up from the ocean depths and returned whence they came. We are now in the 5th Root-Race tenanting the regions of Jambu Dwipa. Two more Root-Races have to spring up on this earth of ours, and hence require two more beds of earth to bubble up from the earth's surface underneath the waters. Excluding the Dwipas. Jambu, Saka and Pushkara which constitute the regions for the 5th, 6th and 7th Races of humanity, we have to identify the other Dwipas which flourished in past times and have passed away. In these Dwipas, there are seven rivers and seven moun-tains in them. All these refer to the seven Sub-Races which humanity has to undergo.

If these Dwipas are meant to apply to the different portions of the earth that build out of the ocean to form the bed on which each Root-Race humanity nourished, then we can identify them with the different portions of the gross earth. In the Secret Dectrine it is stated that the First Race flourished near the North Pole; the Second Race on the beds of the Antarctic Ocean, *the* relics of which are found in the Islands of Nova Zembia; the Third Race or Linurious flourishing on the beds of the Pacific Ocean, the remnants being Australia Ac.; the Fourth Race on the bads of the Atlantic Ocean. Jambu Dwipa, that portion of the earth in which present Race flourished is mainly in the centre of the earth and nearabouts is clear. Round Jambu Dwipa is stated to be Plaksha Dwipa where the Fourth Race men lived. The Atlantic Ocean encircling mainly this earth of ours, Pushkar is said to be round this our Junibu Dwipa. Then comes the pacifie Ocean, on the beds of which stood Salmali Dwipa, where the Third Race humanity lived. Round this is Kusa Dwipa where the Second Race abode. Krauncha Dwipa, which comes next, encircling Kusa, was tenanted by the first Race men. The Sixth Race humanity will incarnate North of where the First Race men were. Beyond these at the North Pole will incarante the Seventh Race humanity in seat, called by our Puranic writers, Pushkara.

The names of these Dwipas are supposed to have been given from some objects in them. These Dwipas are named after some trees or others growing in them since probably they possess some mysterious properties which give the tinge to the humanity that incarnats in them.

The different kinds of oceans which are sevenin number are metaphorical names representing nothing but the Milky Way and the various congeries of Neubloe. Prior to the earth becoming fit for the First Race, Astral men to tenant it, it should have been at first like Jala, or fresh water. Then, though the process of churning, it should have become Milky and then condensed itself into the appearance of curds, or the icy state of water which we see in the North. Then, the butter stage is reached. As heated butter becomes red in the ghee state, it reaches the state of the redness of wine. Then, water reaches the color of sugar-cane Juice, till it becomes the saltish water of the color we now see it to be.

---

1. From the Secret Doctrine.
2. From the Theosophist, Vol. X.
3. From Har Narayan's "Vedic Philosophy".
4. From Ocott.
5. From the Secret Doctrine.
6. From the Theosophist Vol.. XIX. "This article consists mainly of glemings—condensed and modified—from Mrs. Besant's Manuals; so but little orginality is claimed far it. It is now published by request, with the hope that it may be useful as an elementary treatise—ED."
7. From the Secret Doctrine.
8. From Annie Besant's Ancient Wisdom.
9. From the Theosophic Thinker.
10. From the Thinker, Vol. II.
11. From Isis Unveiled, Vol. II.
12. From the Light of the East, Vol. V.
13. From the Secret Doctrine.
14. From the Theosophic Thinker, Vols. II and III.

CHAPTER XXIV

METAPHYSICS OF HINDUIM [1]

All the manifestations of the Cosmos can be universally generalised and interpreted in terms of matter and motion (or Force).

What warrant, it may be asked, have we to go beyond Matter and Force in quest of a Final Cause? And why must we invoke the aid of Metaphysics, *i.e.*, the ultra-experimental philosophy in interpreting the ultimate truths of Physics? Why? Because the axiomatic truths of Natural Philosophy could never be explained by Positive Science *per se,* unless in synthesis with Metaphysics. As Herbert Spencer says, "Every physical question, probed to the bottom opens into a metaphyscial one." Metaphysical conceptions are by far the most powerful solvent in the solution of question concerning the fundamental laws and principles of physics. And the methods of our arguments must be physico-metaphysical.

The doctrine of the Homogeneity or unity of matter is the goal towards which chemistry, physics, and astronomy are drifting. The spectroscope reveals to us that the various celestial' bodies are all composed of the very same elements; and chemistry, whose special province lies at the root or base of matter, proposes and propounds the theory of equivalents, which substantiates the Monistic hypothesis of matter, the essential oneness of things. The multiplicity of the properties of material things is owing to the multiplicity of the modes of atomic combinations, as well as to the multiplicity of the forms of atomic motion

Is Matter a dead or inert substance, and is Force generally a thing or a mode of motion ? or is Force an inherent power us Matter ?

Has Science succeeded in unravelling the mystery connected with the universal co-existence of Force in Matter ? No. Let us see what the leaders of Western Science say about the achievements of modern European science and philosophy. "The explanation of that which is explicable," says Herbert Spencer "doth but bring out into greater clearness the inexplicableness of that which remains behind. The sincere man of science, content to follow wherever the evidence leads him. becomes by each new enquiry more profoundly convinced that the universe is an in soluble problem. If, tracing back the evolution of things, he allows himself to entertain the hypothesis that all matter once existed in a different form. he finds it utterly impossible to conceive how this came to be so. Though he may succeed in resolving all properties of objects into manifestations of force, he is not thereby enabled to realise what force is, but finds, on the contrary, that the more he thinks about it, the more he is baffled. Inward and outward things he thus discovers to be alike inscrutable in their ultimate genesis and nature."

"Our notions of the origin of matter are," say Professors Balfour Stewart and Tait, "at best but hazy. As to what it is we know no more than Democritus or Lucretius."

And "the greater the circle of light, the greater the-circumference of darkness: and the mystery, which has been driven before us, looms in the darkness that surrounds this circle, growing more mysterious and more tremendous, as the circumference is increased."

Professor Tyndall remarks, "Science knows nothing of the origin and destiny of Nature. Who or what made the sun, and gave his rays their alleged power, who or what made and bestowed upon the ultimate particles of matter their wondrous power of varied interaction ? Science does not know."

"Carlyle says," This world after all our science and sciences, is still a miracle, wonderfully inscrutable, magical, and more to who soever will think of it."

Let us now discuss the problem of Force and Matter. Force may be related to matter in any of these four ways:—*Istly,* it may be an extraneous power to matter, acting upon it from without; *2ndly.* it may be an inherent power in matter, influencing it from within, but yet distinct from the substance of matter; *3rdly,* it may be an innate power in matter, influencing it from within, and not distinct from the substance of matter; or *4thly,* it may be a function of the substance of matter.

Firstly.—Is Force a power extraneous to matter, impelling it from without ? We have first to consider whether such a power is an unextended, i.e., abstract principle or a physical, *i.e.*, space-occupying entity. Were it an unextended principle, we cannot conceive how a certain influence that does not occupy space can exert any power upon a thing that occupies spaces. For that which occupies no space can have no existence; that which has no existence can possess no power; that which possesses no power can display no activity; and that which displays no activity can exercise no influence (upon any *thing*). The hypothesis that Force is an unextended principle is therefore quite inconceivable. Therefore Force must be a physical existence, and this physical existence does, according to the present hypothesis, influence matter from without. Now, if there be in nature one kind of physical existence *viz..* Force, that can move by itself and influence another body, there can be no absurdity in recognizing that another kind of physical existence, *viz.*, Matter, can also move by itself. It must not be forgotten that we first arbitrarily assumed that Matter is inert, and cannot move, unless when acted upon; and to account for its motion, which is inseparably associated with its existence (for Matter is never seen or known to be without motion, which fact itself is a strong refutation of the theory of the Inertness of Matter), we again arbitrarily assumed some power as existing outside matter, and causing its motions. But this Force or Power is, we are forced to recognise, as much a physical entity as Matter. We have thus come round the circumference of the circle; and in the end find ourselves precisely whence we took our first start—we have simply begged the whole question. To prevent unnecessary circumlocution, it may fairly be asked, what data have we for supposing that Matter is dead and passive, unless it be said that it is an extended body, and must therefore be moved by some foreign power ? If, on the ground of being extended or physical, the power of motion be denied, or more correctly, be withdrawn from Matter, how can it be argued consistently with logic that Force, which is also, as shown above, as much substantial in constitution as Matter, has motivity in it ? It is very clearly deducible from these considerations that motivity need not be sought outside Matter, that is to say, Force is inside or inherent in matter. Strangely enough, the hypothesis which says that Force is an external power to Matter, is thus logically resolved into the hypothesis which says that Force is an innate power of matter.

Secondly.—Is Force an inherent power, impelling Matter from within, but distinct from the substance of Matter? If so, then,. in other words, Force and Matter are two separate entities. Each of these must be a substantial existence. According to this theory Matter is equal to substance or extension, plus Force. Matter having substance or extension merely is inert or dead. Therefore, whatsoever engenders motion in it, is other than its substance or body. And that principle other than its substance is the Inhereat Force. Call this principle an impulse, Force, influence, only that principle is not a non-existence. If non-existent, it cannot exert any influence; because it cannot do so, while it itself does not exist. Therefore that principle must exist; if it exists, it must occupy space; if it occupies space, it must have dimensions; and, if it has dimensions, it must be a substantial existence. Where fore, Force is a substantial existence, as much as Matter. Force and Matter, are, according to the present hypothesis interlacing each other. If Force and Matter be space-filling entities, and if Force be inherent in Matter, then these two must have intermixed at some time in the past. When did this intermixture take place ? Why, and bow ? Science says to us that Force and Matter cannot *per se* present any phenomena of motion, unless in association with each other. Accordingly, during the period prior to their. conjunction, Matter *per se* must have been remaining inactive with no power to impel it; and Force *per se* most have also been remaining inactive with no vehicle for its conveyance. But to produce motion, they must have previously united; and to unite they must have previously moved towards each other. But they could not have moved, being each of them, unable to do so, *per se.* What then induced their subsequent amalgamation ? It may be replied here that they never once existed separately, but unitedly from. all eternity. If so, why then distinguish between them, and assert they are two different existences ? Unless we see two bodies existing independently of each other, or have valid reasons for inferring that at some previous period, they so existed, or unless we can disengage them now by some means mechanical or chemical or can conceive that they can ever in the future part company, we have no grounds for conceiving them distinct; and none, therefore, for maintaining the dualism of Matter and Force. Clearly things that have existed as a unity from all time, and cannot be separated, have no claim to be considered and classified as more than one existences, "Force and Matter" is then but a useless periphrase to denote one and the same thing (namely, Force). Therefore they are not a duality, but only unity and Identity. Thus we see the hypothesis, which postulates that Force is inherent in, but different from, the substance of Matter, is reduced to the next hypothesis. Which says.

Thirdly.—Is Force an inherent power of matter, but not distinct from the substance of Matter ? If Force is not distinct from. the substance of Matter, it is the substance of Matter; but the same substance of Matter is matter itself because Matter minus its substance or existence, is naught, is a nonentity. We see then that the substance of Matter is Force; and the same substance is Matter also. Therefore Matter is *Force*.

Fourthly.—Is Force a function of the substance of Matter? This is the conception of Cosmos of the (usual) Monistic philosophy. Hackel, Bain, Tyndall, Spencer, and a host of other scientific celebrities regard Matter and Force as the two faces of one and the same thing. Among others, Professor Hackel says. According to the materialistic conception of the Universe, matter or substance precedes motion or active force. According to the spiritualistic conception of the universe on the contrary, active Force or Motion precedes Matter. Both views are dualistic; and we hold them both to be equally false. A contrast to both views is presented in the *Monistic* philosophy, which can as little believe in Force without Matter, as in Matter without Force," As Goethe says, "Matter can never exist and act without spirit neither can spirit without Matter."

The above Monistic exposition clearly means, that Matter and Force are co-eval and co-existent, and the latter is not a distinct entity from the substance of the former, but is its function merely. Now, the very conception of the function of the material substance presupposes the dynamic activity or motion of the substance presupposes the dynamic activity or motion of the substance the constituents of tlv substance of matter; for without from vious motion, how can any function be performed ? then, dynamic activity or motion of the substance of matter pres Each some potential motive energy in it, for without any poetry motivity how can there be produced actual motion? Inver there must be some latent motor energy in the substance of matter for the genesis of motion in and of it, and there must be motion the substance of matter for the performance of its function.

Therefore function is simply the phenomenal effect of the latent cause, namely, Force; but never force itself. To say them that force is the function of the substance of matter is tantamount to saying that the cause is the effect, which is absurd. This potential energy, which is in matter is a physical existence. If not it cannot produce any impression whatsoever upon and in the substance of matter. According tothe hypothesis, there is nothing in the boyd of matter,but its substance. Therefore the potential energy of the substance of matter is the substance ofmatter. But the same substance of matter is itself matter. Therefore matter is its own potential pwoer of motion that is Matter is Force.

Now we have solved the problem of Force and Matter in four differnt ways, which are the only possible ones; but all these differnt ways, which are the only possible ones; but all these differnt solutions give out but one and the same result namely., Matter is Force. It would be well not to confound the proposition Matter is Force with its converse proposition Force is Matter (merely) because Matter is only a form or mode of force, wheras force has various forms, such, for instance, as electricity, magnetism, light, matter, etc.

Now that it has been shown that Matter is Force, we have next to consider what Force is.

Force is the intellignet primordial principle, which pervades all the Infinity of Space—nay, to speak more correctly and philosophically, which is Space itself.

Is Infinite Space then something? Yes, Infinite Space is Infinite something. When we say space, our Idea is a comprehensive one, including all affirmation and excluding all negation. Our idea of space is the product of the endless continuity, of conversions, beginning from a centre and circling away from around the center towards a circumference having infinity for the radius. The definite Space is a positive Infinite Existence. Again, if Infinite space is not something, then it is a vaccum, a nothing, a non-existence. If space is a non-existence, that is if it does not exist, where then does force work and matter move? Space is something. Infinte Space is neither a nothing nor a vacuum, but, an infinite Plenum; and this Infinte Plenum is the Infinite Intellignet Principle.

It having been shown that Infinite Space is an Infinite Intelligent Principle, it may be asked, what is this principle? Is it the phenomena of cosmos? No. Because the cosmic phenomena are merely the products of the dynamic energies of nature. Is it, then, these dynamic energies ? No Because they are merely the vibratory motions of the medium that pervades space. Here is the most critical point in the spiritual philosophy'. The fraternity of scientific religionists march, hand in hand, as far as the cosmic forces, in quest of the ultimate cause of the Universe, but here they break company and divide into two branches, one drifting in the direction of an hypothetical Deity, and the other, in the direction of a Universal Impersonal Principle or Being.

The doctrine of Anthropomorphism is alike untenable and unphilosophical. For, if a personal God exists, creating and governing the physical universe, he must, of necessity, be Omnipresent. This Omnipresent Deity having a person or body, be it ethereal or any other, his body must of necessity be ubiquitous too, that is, present in all space; in fine it must be an Infinity. We know a body consists of the head, the trunk and the limbs. Accordingly the body of God must have also the same members. Now, are the members of his body, each of them, finite or infinite in extension? If each of them be finite, can any number of finite things make an Infinity ? No, never. Again, if each of them be infinite a extension, his head or trunk, or any of the limbs alone would occupy infinite space. Where will there be room in space for the other members ? Is there any trans-infinite space ? Nonsense! The Theist's God cannot therefore be ubiquitous, whether we regard each of the members of His body as finite or infinite in extension. The Theist will now reply it is not His body, but His mind, whose presence is everywhere in space. But there is then this difficulty to surmount. How can a mind, whose phenomenal expression is through the medium of the head of a finite body, pervade and comprehend Infinity. Again, the Anthropomorphic God is and can be neither Time, nor Space, nor Force, nor Matter. For He, as a person, has personal attributes, whereas these latter are each of them impersonal in their manners of existence and a qualities. Now, if Time, Space, Force and Matter are not, each of them God, then they must have either been created by God, or have existed from all time. Creation is an event of time, implying, as it does, the pre-existence of a creator. Let us suppose they were creations of time. They must then have come into being at some epoch or other before which they had had no existence. Was there, then, a time when there was no space (in—where?)? Was there, then, a period (of—what ?) when there was no time ? Surely, we cannot conceive a period when Time and Space were not. And, as respects the others, namely, Force and Matter, it may be asked, were they created out of something or nothing? If out of something, then that something must have existed from all eternity, unless indeed the same explanation of its existence be given; and thus though we extend the creation out of creation backwards in an infinite series, we still arrive at the something, the ultimate root of Force and Matter, as existing from all eternity. But if it be said that Force and Matter were created out of nothing, how could something have been ushered into being out of nothing? Space, Time, Matter and Force must therefore have existed throughout the past eternity. Whatsoever exists from eternity are infinites and eternals. Therefore Space and Co. are eternals and infinites. The personal God of the Theist, is also eternal and infinite. There are thus five co-eternals and co-infinites, to wit, Time, Space, Force, Matter and God! These Infinites, existing from eternity, do not each of them owe their existences and specific, characteristics to the agency or the medium of either of the others. Space, Time, Force and Matter are not therefore dependent upon the personal Deity, either for their being or for their individual functions, or the products of taeir functions. These three things, namely. Space, Force and Matter given, and we have our objective universe. For what else is our objective nature than Space and the products of the actions and re-actions of Matter and force existing and moving in Space ? We have, therefore, no reason nor necessity whatever to step outside of nature or beyond the realm of Space and Matter; and Force in quest of a supernatural Deity to account for the existence of Nature, and the proceedings of her laws and forces.

The Theist will naturally urge that there is design in Cosmos, and that design implies a designer and that Designer must possess personality. In reply it may be said, you speak of an artificer in Nature. Pray, what design is there in the existence of rudimentary organs in vegetable and animal organisms that are useless to their owners, and are undergoing the processes of elimination; in a large planet, that requires much light having fewer (and sometimes no) moons than a small one; in a plant growing on a rock, but withering before it attains maturity fur want of sufficient roil, and in other similar innumerable instances ? But even .ranting that design is evident in nature (and no one can deny this, despite its apparent lapses and failures in so many cases), still this design can be explained without a perional God, such as the ordinary Theist conceives. Out of the impersonal "One and Only," the Infinite and the Absolute that we think of as Space. Time, Force and Matter, develop conscious Intelligences, finite and conditioned, it is true, compelled to work with the forces at their command (and hence the apparent failures in design), but still able to supply all that skill and design which is apparent in the universe, as well as the supposed personal God. Nay, in one ease, they explain the universe far better than any Omnipotent-personal Deity could. For, if we accept the latter, we must hold him answerable for all the evil and misery that is in this world, all the sickness.? suffering and sin, as if Omnipotent, he could have prevented all this and indeed, if beneficent, as well as Omnipotent, would and must have prevented it. Whereas if the designers however elevated and glorious, are merely conditioned Intelligences, having to make the best they can of the circumstances which condition them, the origin of evil ceases to be a stumbling block, and while we cannot believe an Omnipotent Intelligence who permits all the evil and misery which we see in the world to be really good, and cannot, therefore, though we might fear him, love him as a father, we can believe in the entire goodness of conditioned Intelligence, we can understand that, despite all that is wrong here, they may have done their very best for all and we can love them as divine though not Omnipotent fathers or guardians. Therefore, evidence of design in Cosmos cannot prove the existence of an Infinite and Omnipotent anthropomorphic God. We see thus that the ordinary Theist is on the horns of a dilemma. Either he must endow this God with personality, and thereby restrict his knowledge and power to relativity and finity or he must rid his God of his anthropomorphic attributes and there by tublimate Him into Absoluteness and Infinity. Both are equally detrimental to the doctrine of the ordinary Theist.

The foregoing arguments indisputably prove that there neither does nor can exist, any such being as an Infinite, Omnipotent, Omniscient Personal God, acting upon the Universe from any suppositious ultra-universe region.[2]

The other alternative of this doctrine which is really Pantheism or *Monism* asserts that the nearest representative of the Theist's supposed God is the Infinite Impersonal Excito-Motor principle of cosmos—some Imponderable Essence is imminent in the infinity of Space. This Essence being the originator and propagator of the diverse undulatory movements or dynamic energies of Nature, is the source and seat of all Cosmic Laws, Forces and Phenomena. Waves are produced in this absolute Substance in virture of its innate impulsive tendency. Hence Motion, the necessary attribute and condition of its existence. And this Infinite Substance is the Potentiality of al' Cosmic Motion, i.e., the Latent Force of the Universe. This Cosmic; Force is an Absolute Intelligence. Therefore the Infinite Substance is the Intelligent Potentio-Motive Force of the Universe. Is not the Supreme Substance or Essence often spoken of as an incognizant, unconscious, unintelligent Principle ? Yes, this Essence, this Impersonal God (?) is both cognizant and incognizant, conscious and unconscious; intelligent and unintelligent—cognizant, conscious, and intelligent in the absolute sense and incognizant, unconscious and unintelligent in the relative sense. As an Infinite One, it is a perfect Eternal Substance. This Perfect Substance is the Intelligent Potentio-Kinetic Energy of Nature. It has an infinity of attributes, each of which is of consummate perfection in its own way. And being itself the Cosmic Motor, it agitates its own Self; which action, stirring into play all its attributes produces in its substance a multiplicity of modes of rhythmical motion. These modes of motion are the various energies that constitute the harmony and preserve the integrity of the Cosmos. Only a few of these energies of Nature are sensible from the plane of human perception, from the grandest and most durable down to a few of the successively smaller and more easily transmutable forms of motion—from Matter to Electricity. There are countless other forms of motion, that is, forces, which are too subtle for our dull, matter-blinded perceptive power, but these will, one after another become cognizable to us as we progress in the evolution of our souls.

Now to the theory of the Evolution of Matter from the Infinite Primordial Substance, this Primordial Existence being itself the Potentio-Kinetic Energy of Nature, transforms its protentiality of motion into actuality of motion by excito-motive capacity. Hence all manner of waves are incessantly generated and popagated by and in the substance of the Infinite. These waves of force flow in and through this Infinite Substance and are subject to innumerable modifying impacts from all directions, and are turned and twisted here and there, now intensified, now enfeebled, now neutralised, now regenerated, by other vibrations upon all planes from all sides. Amidst the tumultuous and wild scene of incessant flows, impingements, intersections upheavals and subsidence of waves, it is quite natural and possible that some waves should be synchroniously impinged upon and augmented in bulk and power by the waves upon several planes on one side of them. And these waves, consequent upon the increased size and strength taken on from the impact of those other waves, bend upon themselves on that side when they are less subject for the time being to undulatory impacts, and begin to revolve and rotate. Hence there will be vortices formed wherever larger waves develop and bend upon themselves. It is these rotations or eddies or vortices of the Infinite Substance which are the beginnings or units of Matter. These units of Matter are the particles of Ether.

We see thus that the ultimate units of Matter are the primary manifestations of the Essence of the Absolute Existence-in other words of the Infinite Potential Force.

The ether particles, being emanations of the Absolute intelligent Force, have a remnant of their Parent-Force, Inherent in them. Hence the mechanical forces of Matter, namely, attraction and repulsion. Besides these forces, there are also others in the shape of the undulations of the Primal Substance, dashing and acting upon these particles. Some of these forces are known to Physical Science as the Chemical Forces, Magnetism, Electricity, Heat. &c. As Motion is incessant, in the Absolute Essence, these mechanical and physical forces are incessantly active also. Impelled by their native powers, and propelled by the foreign forces the units of Matter start upon the grand procession of the evolution of Cosmos. We see thus that Matter is evolved from and in and by this perfect Substance or Force of which it is one mode. This geneology of Matter from. let us say, the substance of Force (for it comes to that) is true and reliable and Modern Science countenances this doctrine evolution of Matter.'

The ordinary theist will of course deny this theory of the evolution of Matter from the perfect substance, or if partially accepting it, will still hold the genesis of Matter to have been in some way the result of a miracle, or in other words, of a special creation. And the so-called scientist will dispute the truth of this doctrine, on the ground that rotations could not be produced bv and in a frictionless perfect substance. Both can. For what grounds have they for assuming that space is filled with dead particles, with blank interstices; and that these dead particles have to cross these intervals and collide and join with each other before they can rotate intervals, and collide and join with' each other before they can rotate. Infinite space is One Infinite Monad and this Monad is the Absolute Intelligent Potentiality of motion. Take any point in space you please, and you will find it full of Life, and Mind and Motion.. While every point of space is Intelligent Motion, the divine interposition of the theist and the internal friction of the scientist are unnecessary for the originstion of rotatory motions in the Absolute Perfect Essence.

From the above considerations, we understand that Matter is a form of wave in the same manner that forces are forms of waves The only distinction between them is that the waves of Matter which are the largest and most complex of waves, and which can-not therefore be easily and quickly affected by their collisions with other waves, have attained the consistency of a distinct permanent type, whereas those of forces, which are too small and simple to organise into and maintain distinct individualities against incessant attacks of other waves, are easily affected and translated into one another. However these waves of force which we know as Matter (though not as readily affected by external circumstances as those other waves which we recognize as forces) will under the constant action of those other less stable waves, gradually but insensibly, diminish in bulk and power, until after cycles of ages they become as small as any of the ultra-material waves, and consequently being no longer able to preserve their individual existences, they get lost among them With this absorption of Matter into Force the objective universe will vanish. Thus the grand cycle of objectivity will be run; but the waves of forces, amongst which those of Matter were disintegrated and lost will still continue to dash upon each other, and some of them will, under favourable circumstances, coalesce and swell into complex, stable, and rotating waves. Here in these waves we again have vortex-rings or matter. There will thus be another Cosmos; but this will also vanish after countless ages with the resolution of Matter into Force. Thus another cycle of objectivity will be run, and so on, and thus the cosmic cycles will continue wheeling round the axle of the Infinite Force or Beving from everlasting to everlasting, now blazing in the splendour of manifestation, and now shrouded in the gloom of latency. The decays and the revivals are the Inter-cycles or epicycles of Cosmos; and the final total absorption of the Visible Universe into the Invisible Universe is the cycle of Cosmos. What are these inter-cycles or epicycles of Cosmos but the Pralayas and the cycles of Cosmos but the Kalpas of our Cosmogony. What are these Eternal Potential Energy and Kinetic Energy and Matter but the Trinity of Brahma and Iswara and Maya or Bhraman, Sakti and Prakriti of our Cosmological Science.

When we examine and compare the European and the Hindu theories of Cosmic Evolution and Involution, we find that the former are narrow and incomplete, and the latter broad and comprehensive. Let a circle represent the cycle of Cosmos; let any two of its consecutive quadrants, 1 and 2 represent the Evolution—1 from the Primordial Substance or Brahma up to Atoms and—2 from the Atoms up to the perfect Adept, or whatever is higher than this; and let the other two, 3 and 4 indidicate the Involution—3 from the Adept down into the Atom, and 4 from the Atom back again into the Primodial Substance. The European philosophers whose cosmic knowledge ranges from Atoms to Atoms, leave out of account the quadrants of 1 and 4. Hence his knowledge of Nature is only one-sided—a Half Truth. But the Hindu Philosopher, who recognizes that Material Universe issued forth from the bosom of Parabrahman and will ultimately become re-absorbed into it comprehends the whole circumference of the circle. Hence his knowledge is a whole Truth.

Man is not created of any ultra-mundane materials by an Ultra-Cosmic God, but is evolved out of the Cosmic Substance by the immutable and intelligent laws and forces which pervade and are part of the Infinite and Absolute. Hence it is that whatever factors constitute the universe, also constitute man. There are matter, motion, formative principle and soul in Cosmos, and these very same factors are also in Man. Man is thus the child of Cosmos. The child of Cosmos is a Minor or Little Cosmos, just. in the same manner that the child of man is a Minor or Little Man. Minor or Little Cosmos in Microcosmos or Microcosm. And it is because of this kinship between the Macrocosm and Microcosm that there exist is much sympathy and reciprocity between Nature and Man. In the broadest sense of the term, a molecule or any other natural object is as much a microcosm itself as man. Because it is as much a product of Cosmic laws and forces as man, the only difference between them being that it is a rudimentary microcosm, and man a developed one.

From the above it is plain that everything in Nature has, like Nature, a noumenon that is, soul, that persists and continues; and an outer co-phenomenon, that is body, that changes and dissolves away. The soul, being constituted of ethereal particles which, on account of their excessive minuteness, strong affinities, close proximity, and the resultant coherence and strength, have' confederated into a league against all dismembering influences is endurable for cycles of ages. Bat the physical body is just the reverse as regards the nature of its constituents and constitution, and is consequently liable to be easily disorganized by chemical or mechanical forces. It is on account of these differences, elementary and constitutional, that the soul is a continuous, progressive existence, carrying with it its past experiences, its latent capabilities to be developed into more and more perfection as it ascends the scale of progression; and the Body is but a short-lived entity, dissolving into its component elements after its severance from the soul. The difference between the Body and the Soul is not such as is held by dualists who say they are essentially and eternally distinct. According to our definitions of Matter, Body and Soul, Body must be convertible into Soul, if only we could decompose its constituents into such subtle particles as those of Ether and re-arrange and compose them after the fashion of the structure of the soul, and vice versa. To the question, how is it known that Body is a loose collection of discrete lives, and that there is within it such a separate entity as soul, which is the collective life of its components, we reply that the fact is such, is amply and irrefutably demonstrated by the phenomena of Mediumism, Clairvoyance as above all Occultism.

The finite soul begins its march of development in the purest and most elementary form. After passing through certain subjective kingdoms, of which nothing can be said here, it comes in contact with the gross matter of the surrounding world by the processes of attraction, absorption and assimilation in the lower grades of development in the Mineral Kingdom; and by attraction, absorption, nutrition and assimilation in its higher phases of development as in the Vegetable and Animal Kingdoms. The particles of this gross matter do, owing to the actions and reactions between themselves, and the particles of the soul, inter-blend with those of the latter, and settle and organize themselves in to the physical body of the soul. The soul and body are disturbed in their mutual relations and unbalanced in their relative equilibrium, when either of them imposes too much strain on the other, as in the cases of extreme fear, anger, joy, &c., or extreme physical labour; or when any internal or external causes or accidents, such as severe diseases, or injuries, &c., work upon them so violently that they are forced to repel each other—and separation is the result. When body is thus divorced from soul, the latter does not continue to remain bodiless, but is in obedience to the ever vigilant law of infinity attracted to some reproducing individual pair or couple according to the stage that it has reached with whom it is in sympathy; taken up in the female reproductive system it gathers gross matter from without through the processes of nutrition and absorption which, as it accumulates, is organized into a new physical body, by the cosmic formative principle. In its ascension on the ladder of evolution, the soul is upon every rung, alternately jetting on and throwing off body after body without number. But it is not left unaffected by its almost incessant contacts with gross matter because each time it is interblended and clothed with a body, a small quantity of the more ethereal mather which gross matter of the corporeal body carries with it in its graviation to and contacts with the soul, is on account of its comparative rarity retained in permanent cohesion by the soul partly assimilated in and partly held loosely around it in and partly held loosely around it. This attenuate ethereal coating is the psychic body. Once the soul become thus affected or corrupted by matter, it is no longer that simple pure entity it once was, but becomes forth with a materio-spiritual existence; and its further evolution is a co-ordination of physicallity; and psychicality.

The phenomena of dual evolution simultaneously progresses and finally culminates in man. So far progress is inevitable. After reaching this stage, that is, the man—stage of progression, either the physical development stagnates or retrogrades according to the modes of life led by worldly-minded or wicked people; or the physical frame owing to the disuse of bodily functions and the abstention from material desires, becomes more and more attenuated till at length the process of elimination is complete; its dissolution or death has been gradually and almost in sensibly achieved; the soul as in the case of perfect adepts or yogis, is for the time left unfettered in its upward march

In all these phases of evolution we see that the soul is the Only real permanent factor of existence; and the numberless series of bodies which it has donned and doffed during its past career of development, are but its consecutive and varied moulds for greater and greater perfection. And it is these grades or phases of evolution which constitute the progression or the Transmigrations of the soul. Is the Doctrine of the Progression of souls true and scientific? Why not? If these three things, namely (*1*) the existence in man of some sentient entity other than the body (*2*) the necessity of the previous existence of that entity and (3) the necessity of the future existence of that entity—if these three things are proved, then we have the whole truth of the history of the Progression of Souls.

First, that there is in man some sentient principle which is distinct from the body of the man may be proved inferentially and phenomenally.

Next as regard the necessity of the previous existences of the human soul; man is a product of evolution. Evolution implies a series of changes; for unless a thing undergoes a series of changes, it cannot be evolved; and a series of changes implies a succession of causation and sequence. Therefore, every phase of the development of a living being is the inevitable result or effect as well of the conditions of life under which it has lived, as edits its individual experiences, during its next antecedent stage of being. It logically follows from this that every creature that exists must have had a previous existence. Accordingly the man must have has a previous existence. New man is essentially a creature that lives, feels, thinks, reasons, &c. These are what make him a man, and if he does not live. feel, think and reason he is no more man. but only a lump of clay, &c. We have already said there is in man a soul which is not his material frame. Man is thus a duality, composed of a body and a soul. Which of the two great divisions of man's nature does really live. feel think, reason &c.—his body or his soul. His body may live and feel, thought it is through his soul only that the sensations of his body become known, but it is his soul and not his body that thinks, reasons, &c; as is indubitably established by the facts of spiritualism, clairvoyance, somnambulism. psychometry and occultism. Therefore the soul of man is the true man (and not his physical body, which is merely the soul's casket or shell, and it is this which must have had a prior existence

There remains the question of the future of man, but this becomes a simpler matter nor that his previous existence has been demonstrated to be a natural necessity. Why has the man entered on this present life ? Because this was the unavoidable outcome of the experiences, &c., of his previous birth. He underwent certain influences, acquired certain experiences and thought, spoke and did certain things. Those influences, experiences, thoughts, words and deeds were so many material causes, and out of the combined action of these causes, these necessarily had to be, and was evolved an effect. And what was that effect. It was the present birt'.. Man does, in his present life, live under certain conditions of life, is affected and modified by those conditions, acquires in his struggle for life new experiences and knowledge.; thinks, speaks and acts. All this engenders an entire series of material causes. Shall these causes disappear resultless ? Can so many causes be, as it were, annihilated without developing the necessary correspondential effects ? Never. They must have their effects.. What must these effects be clearly such as can only be resumed in future existence. Hence re-birth in the future is also a natural necessity.

It has therefore been scientifically demonstrated that the past, present and future births of man are a natural necessity; being simply a beachless continuity of evolution, an unbroken chain of causes and effects.

The Awful wheel of Re-births and Re-deaths will revolve for the soul so long as its lives continue to be characterized by attach ment to material and worldly objects, the good results of ill karma being experienced in that subjective world or state in which it exists between death and re-birth, and the evil in a re-birth and the conditions attaching to that new life. All earthly lives are inevitably attended with much of care, sorrow and suffering. To escape all this, our only resource is to put a stop to the recurrence of births. But re-births or re-incarnations are the unavoidable results of Psychic Attraction, and Psycho-Physical Evolution, this Attraction and this Evolution are the unavoidable result of psycho-physical existence; this existence is the unavoidable result of the attraction, accumulation and assimilation of Cosmic-Matter; this attraction, &c., *&c.*, are the unavoidable results of the dynamic energies of the soul; and these dynamic energies are the unavoidable exercises or activities of the Will or Desire for life. Thus we see that the will of man is the cause of his re-births and re-deaths. Is not, then, the birth of man the product of mere circumstances ? Is it reality his Will that determines his birth ? Insentient beings as well as sentient beings, from the lowest order up to man, are merely the creatures of circumstances; but when they evolve into mature, rational, responsible men they need no longer remain simple toys or puppets of the surrounding influences and elements; for they become, to some extent, able to influence and modify circumstance, and command and control the elements, by their intellectual powers (which are other and more intensified forms of the Will), exercised and utilized in the occult or mechanical way. With the cessation of the Will, re-incarnation will also cease. But how to stop the Will ? Will is the concomitant of the Desire for Existence; and this Desire is the concomitant of Ignorance or Aridya of the real origin, and nature and destiny of being.

Though the world teems with evil and misery, though its weary ways, fanned only by sighs, watered only with tears, lead alike over the burning sands of suffering, and the fated swamps of in yet by far the majority of humanity, so far from growing disgusted with, mundane life, cling to it with an irrespressible desire to live on. They are wallowing in the mire of casuality, a rarice and what not, are born again and again in consequence of their earth-tending karmas; and are fated to taste and retaste the better fruits of life. On the other hand there are also some few, who, regarding this world as a prison and all worldly enjoyments titles, honours and riches as mere vanities (tinsel-decked toys seen against a mirage), hunger and thirst after spiritual emancipation and felicity. They are no longer deceived and satisfied by the shadow, but crave and seek for the substance. These or did material life of the world does not suit or please them, and they quit it sooner or later, when their duties in it have been rightly discharged and be take themselves to solitary recesses in the bosom of nature, there to meditate, secure perfect control over their minds spiritualize their natures, and attain deliverance from Matter, ie from the Relativity and Finity of Existence. The above spiritually inclined who fly this world of evil and sin take refuge in solitude and practice Yoga or Psychism. That is the science and the Art of the Evolution and culture of the soul and its final involution or Absorption into the absolute Being. Darkness, silence, and the concentration of the mind, or contemplation are the conditions required for the evolution of the powers of Abstraction and Introspection, and for the inducement of Tranquillization or quietism of the mind. When the mind or willis thus tamed down into concentration, abstraction, &c. it does not disturb the relative equilibrium of the psychic constituents; and thereby ceases to attract gross matter from the surrounding spaces and to hold in cohesion the gross partricles already in contact with it in the shape of the molecules of the corporeal body. These latter molecules are consequently drawn or pulled away and despaired by the attractive forces exercised by the molecules or atoms floating in space. So the whole corporeal body will become disintegrated or eliminated in the course of time. The soul will not now be psychophysical entity, but a purely ethereal or psychic one. Not only does the adept escape many rebirths, but he has to a great extent, secured his safety (while reducing its length) throughout the rest of that weary journey, which every man and every adept, yea even a Buddha, must travel after quitting this world before he is ultimately resolved into the substance of the external spirit and life: then the Finite existence is absorbed into the Infinite Existence; the Personal Soul merges into the Universal Impersonal Soul; Relative Knowledge is sublimated into Absolute Knowledge; the Relative Happiness into the Abselute Happiness or Brahmanandam. This is Beatitude—Final Beatitude—Nirvana—Moksha. It may be asked why is it necessary that man should strine to attain Mukti, if it be true that the whole Material Universe, and all the things (including Man of course) therein shall be resolved and absorbed into the Eternal Principle or Parabrahman on the day of Kalpa. The answer is:—Man should strive to attain Mukti. If he does not do so, he will, before the time of the Kalpa, be born and re-born again and again innumerable times, in inevitable consequence of his Karmas; and ceaselessly continue to experience all the miseries, which are the indissoluble concomitants of finite sentient existence during those births. It is simply to escape, as soon as possible, the unemitting rotations of the crushing wheel of births and deaths that man should and if wise does, endeavour heart and soul to obtain exemption from reincarnation, and attain Moksha before the Kalpa arrives and relieves him.

A materialist may ask:—"you say that the Soul and the Body are material in constitution; and that the soul loses its personality and individuality

CHAPTER XXV

PSYCHOLOGY AND COSMOLOGY OF VEDANTA.[1]

The two words macrocosm and microcosm, represent the external and the internal worlds. Truths flow to us from both of them through the channel of experiences; and we have internal experience and external experience. The truths gathered from internal experience contitutes psychology, metaphysics, and religion, while those from external experience make up the physical sciences. All perfect truths cannot but be in harmony with each other. The microcosm must bear witness to the macrocosm and the macrocosm to the microcosm; physical truth must have its corresponding psychical truth in the internal world, and the truths of the internal world must find their verification in the world outside. Yet it so happens, that many of the truths known to man are often seen to be constantly conflicting with one another; at one period of the world's history the internals become supreme, and they begin to fight the externals; or as at the present time, the externals become supreme, and the physicists try to crush down the claims of the psychologists and metaphysicians for the possession of truth. The really essential truths of psychology cannot but be in perfect accord with the essential truths of modern physical science. The European nations are very strong in their knowledge of the external physical world and we, orientals, have never been verv strong in our knowledge of the external physical world, but all along our strength has been in our psychology, metaphysics and religion. It is therefore that oriental physics inferior to occidental physics; and that occidental psychology and metaphysics are not in harmony with the highly advanced oriental psychology and metaphysics.

We know how the modern theories of the cosmos according to modem astronomers and physicists and biologists have been wo fully hurting many of the theologians of Europe and how every new bit of scientific discovery has been taken to be a bomb thrown into the house of religion, and how offended religion attempted long in Europe the put down all scientific researches. The study of the psychological ideas of the Hindus, and of their cosmology and all that pertains to it, will bring out most beautifully how wonderfully their knowledge of the inner essence of man is in accordance with all the latest discoveries and conclusions of modern science. Our old Sanskrit philosophers called nature by two different names, Prakriti, which means very much the same as the word nature, and avyakta, the undifferentiated from which everything that differentiated proceeds. It is startling to find that some of the philosophers and metaphysicians of India stated ages ago that mind is but the product of nature, and that thought and intelligence also come from the avyakta, un differentiated. The old yogins define this avyakta as the equilibrium of the three forces Satwa, Rajas and Tamas. Tamas, the lowest of these forces, may be looked upon as attraction, the higher Rajas *as* repulsion, and the highest Satwa as the controller of these two; so that when the two forces of attraction and repulsion are held in perfect control by the Satwa, there is no creation, no movement going on in the world; and so that as soon as this equilibrium, is lost, the balance is disturbed, and one of these two opposing forces gets stronger than the other, movement and creation begin, and all this wonder of the world goes on. This alternation in the state of nature goes on cyclically; that is to say, there is a period of the disturbance of the balance, when all the forces in nature begin to combine and re-combine, and form man, anil all the things in the world which are as it were, projected outwards from the real being, and because at the same time, everything has a tendency to go back to the primal state of equilibrium, another period comes when the total annihilation of all the mainfestations of being is reached. Again, after a time, the equilibrium is disturbed and being is projected outwards; again it slowly quiets down Some of our philosophers hold that the whole of the universe quiets down in this fashion for a period; others hold that this quieting down goes on always partially and applies only to particular systems of stars and planets at particular intervals of time. According to this latter view, our solar system may quiet down and go back into the undifferentiated state, and there may be at the same time millions of other systems going the other way, *i.e.,* growing in differentiation. That the quieting down of nature or her growing in differentiation is not simultaneous over the whole universe seems, indeed, to be the true position to hold in this matter. The principle, however, is the same whatever view we may hold, that all that we see, that nature herself, is progressing in successive rises and falls. There is a falling down, a going back to the condition of balance of perfect equilibrium; and there is a rising up to the state of differentiated manifestation. The Kalpa is such a cycle; and creation has been compared by theistic writers in India to the inbreathing and out breathing of God; God, as it were, breathes out the universe, and it goes back unto Him again. When it quiets down, what, indeed, becomes of the universe. It is then only in the finer form; or as they call it in Sanskrit, in the form of the cause. At the end of a cycle the universe does not get beyond causation, time and space; even then it will and must be subejct to them. If the whole universe begins to shrink simultaneously, and goes on doing so till every one of us becomes just as small as a little molecule, then surely we shall not feel the change at all; because everything relating to us has gone on shrinking in the same proportion and at the same time. In this way the whole thing goes down, and again projects out; and thus the cause brings out the effect, and the chain of causation continues unending.

Really the most extraordinary thing in the universe is what we call gross matter. Our ancient psychologists called it Bhutu, the external element. They mention five bhutas, and there is one element, which according to them is eternal, every other element being produced out of this one; and this one is called Akasa. It is in conception somewhat similar to the modern idea of ether. The akasa is the primal element out of which everything material has proceeded, and along with this element there has been in operation something called the prana. This prana and this akasa exist in nature; they combine and recombine, and give rise to the elements and all other things. At the end of the Kalpa everything subsides, and is resolved back into the akasa and prana. There is in the Rig Veda, the oldest human literary record in existence, a beautiful hymn describing creation and it is most poetical. "When there was neither aught nor naught, when darkness was rolling over darkness, what existed then ?" is the question asked; and the answer is given—"It then existed without motion". This prana existed then, but there was no motion in it. Avyakta really means that which is without vibration. Vibration stops when the Kalpa is finished; after an immense interval this Avyakta, (the mass of unvibrating atoms) begins to vibrate, and blow after blow is given by the prana to the Akasa, the atoms became congregated, and the different elements are formed. The live bhutas or the external elements of perception are often wrongly translated, as air, fire and so on. We do not mean air or anything of the sort by the word Vayu, in our psychological Cosmology. The akasa, made to vibrateby the repeated blows of the prana, produces the Vayu, or the vibrating thing. This vayu vibrates, and the vibrations result in light and heat, tejas. Then the diffusion of this heat ends in the production of liquid matter, apas. Then the liquid becomes, through the further diffusion and diminution of heat converted into solid, prithivi. To start with, there is the ether, then comes motion among material molecules, then light and heat, then we get liquid matter, and finally we get the still more condensed solid matter of the universe. After a certain period of evolutionary changes going on in this fashion, the reverse process of dissolution sets in. The solid melts down into a mass of liquid under the influence of heat, and slowly becomes a mass of discrete and separats molecules in motion; and when that motion stops, the kalpa comes to an end. All is again dissolved back into ether; and this is the way in which creation .and dissolution are going on. We know from modern astronomy that our earth and our sun have been undergoing similar changes. It is expected that even the solid earth will melt down and become liquid, and will eventually go back to the akasa state from which it has been evolued. Prana cannot work alone without the akasa to act upon. Indian philosophy kuows that motion, vibration thought, and every kind of movement that exists in the universe, is a modification of the prana; and every thing that we know in the form of matter, all form and resistance, result from the akasa. The prana cannot live alone, nor act without a medium; and when it is pure prana, it has the pure akasa to live in; but when it gets changed into forces and forms of energy in nature, like gravitation, or magnetism, it must have envolved matter for its home We can never see force absolute apart from matter, nor matter free from all force; what we call force and matter are simply the gross manifestations of the Prana and the akasa. Some may be called life, as it is the living force of the universe; it need not be restricted to the life of man, at the same time care must be taken not to identify it with the spirit, the one universal Atman.

Another position of our old psychologists is that the Bhutas are themselves the results of five materials. Everything that is gross is composed of a combination of finer things; so, the Bhutas are composed of finer materials, the tanmatras, the fine particles Everything gross is composed of things that an more and more fine. So we first have the Bhutas and then the tanmatras within which our organs of sense come in contract. What is the cause of these tanmatras? Our psychologists say it is self-consciousness. That is the cause of the fine materials and the cause of the organs of sense What are these organs ? We have the eye, but the eye does not see. Something really sees, of which the eye is the instrument: is really the organ of sense Modern physiology tells you that it is one or more nerve centres in the brain which, form these organs. The senses are simply the external instruments The different organs or the indriyas are the real seats of perception.

One organ cannot serve the purpose of all the senses. If there were only on organ common to all the senses, the mind would see and hear and smell at the same time; but it is impossible for it to do all these things at the same time. Attention is one-pointed. Therefore it is necessary that there must be separate organs corresponding to the separate senses. This has been borne out by modern physiology and psychology also. The senses or the instruments of these organs are really made up of gross materials, just as our body is composed of gross material, so as to give room for the play of prana to appear as the finer force of perception and other kindred psychological phenomena. All these organs together with the mind form the finer body of man; the Linga or Sukshma Sarira. This Linga-sarira has a real form, because every thing material must have a form. In association with the Indriya we have what is called the "Manas, the Chitta in Vritta, that is the mind in the active state. When any impression strikes on the Chitta it vibrates a little. Tins vibrating Chitta is the Manas. Then comes the reaction, the will. It is really not the same thing, for there is another thing behind the will which accompanies all the acts of the mind, and that is Egoism, Ahamkaram. Behind the Ahamkara the self-consciousness, which says I am I is what is called Buddhi the intellect which is indeed the highest form of existence in nature. Behind the intellect is the self of man, the Purusha, the Atman, who is alone the pure and the perfect Seer and for whom is all this change and all the magic of nature is phenomena. Man is really standing as a witness looking on at all the wonders and changes in the phenomenal Universe. He himself is neither impure nor changeable but by implication by what the Vedantists call Adhyasa or superimposition.

Let us take it for granted, as the Sankhyas said, that there are many selves; that each self is pure and perfect, bat that all the various kinds and conditions of gross matter and fine matter are imposing on the self, and making it variously colored. Why is nature doing all this.

Nature is undergoing all these chances and changes for the evolution of the freedom of the soul. All this creation is for the benefit of the soul, to enable it to become and be free. This immense book, which we call the Universe, is stretched before man so that he may read it and come out, in the end, as an omniscient and omnipotent being. Indeed some of our best psychologists do not believe in God in the sense in which common men ordinarily believe in Him. The original father of our and of all psychologists, Kapila, almost denies the existence of God. According to him, a God is not wanted for the complete explanation of things, nor can this existence be positively proved. His idea is that a personal God is quite unnecessary, nature itself is sufficient to work out all that is. What is called the Design theory, tending to make of God a carpenter or something like it he knocked on the head, and. held that a more childish conception of creation could never be advanced. Bat even he admits peculiar kind of God: he says that men are all struggling to get free, and that when they become free, they, as it were, melt away into nature for the time being, only to come out at the beginning of the next cycle as its ruler; thus every free soul comes out as an omniscient and omnipotent being. In that sense Kapila grants a God; the humblest of beings may thus become Gods in different cycles Such a God is necessarily temporal; but an eternal God, eternally omnipotent, and eternally ruler of the Universe, there cannot be. If there were such a God, there would be this difficulty—he must be either bound or free. A God who is perfectly free will not create; there is no necessity for it. If He be bound, even then He will not create, because He cannot, being weak Himself. So the very existence of creation proves that there cannot be an omnipotent or omniscient eternal ruler of the Universe. Whenever the word God is mentioned in our Scriptures, it means according to Kapila, only those perfected human beings who have become free. And all such human beings may also melt away into one great Being eventually; but the Sankhya does not believe in the unity of all souls. The Vedanta believes that the sun and the substratum of the whole Universe is God; the Sankhya is dualistic. Kapila's analysis, so far as it goes, is simply marvellous. He is the father of Indian thinkers; even Buddhism and other heterodox systems of Indian thought are simply outcomes of his thought. His theory has been taken up by the Buddhists and they too hold that it is only the souls that become perfect and that the question of God need not be taken up at all for consideration.

According to this psychology all souls may regain their freedom and their purity and omnipotence and omniscience and the question naturally arises, whence is this bondage ? The Sankhya says that it is without beginning. But if it be without beginning, it must have no end either, and then one can never be free. It is however said that everything in nature is constantly changing like the water in a flowing river, while the soul never changes. Since nature is always changing, it must be possible for the soul to come out of its bondage. Moreover, the psychology of the Sankhya believes that the whole of the Universe is built upon the same plan as a single man, or any little living being, and just as man has a mind, the Universe must have a cosmic mind. The evolution of the cosmos is accordingly along the same line as the evolution of the individual. The whole universe is therefore one body, so to say; and all that we see and perceive in it are really the grosser things; behind these are their finer bodies, and behind them there is the Chitta, and behind that the universal egoism, and behind that the universal intelligence. But all this is *in* nature, all this is simply the manifestation of the evolving processes of nature; not one of these entities is outside of nature. "Every one of us is indeed a part of that cosmic consciousness. When, somehow, the cosmic consciousness becomes broken, as it were, into parts, we are the results in the same way in which we get our gross body from our parents, our consciousness also comes to us from our parents, subdivisions after subdivisions going on, strict heredity rules both physiology and psychology; a man's body is a part of his parent's bodies, and the material of his consciousness and egoism is similarly a part of that of his parents. After receiving our small subdivision of consciousness from our parents we may again and again draw upon the universal consciousness for our inner psychic growth and nourishment. There is a sum-total of universal intelligence out of which we draw what we require, there is a sum-total of mental force in the universe, out of which we get all our mental strength and energy, the seed which grows into a tree must itself come from another tree. But our theory is heredity and reincarnation too. In accordance with the law of heredity, appropriate material is put into the hands of the liberty-losing soul to manipulate and manufacture man, so that generation after generation liberation becomes easier and easier of accomplishment.

In the process of creation there is an involution and an evolution. All is volved out of indiscriminate nature: and then comes back again the avyakta. It is impossible, according to the Sankhya, for any material thing to exist without having on its basis some portion of universal consciousness. Consciousness is, as it were, the substance out of which all our material manifestations come into existence. We do not and cannot know anything as it is; but the impression of the thing comes to the *indriyas* and then to the mind, and the mind reacts, and that reaction is for us the thing as it appears. There is something outside of us which forms only the occasion or the suggestion for the consciousness to be alive and upon that suggestion we project our mind, and it takes the form of the things we perceive. How then do we all see the same things? Because we all have a part of the cosmic mind in us. Those who have that mind will see the thing and those who have it not will not see it.